TRADER CONSTRUCTION KIT

Second Edition

Joel Rubano

Cephalopod Publishing
Needham

Copyright © 2020 Joel Rubano

All rights reserved. No part of this book may be reproduced in any form or by any electronic or mechanical means, including information storage and retrieval systems, without permission in writing from the publisher, except by reviewers, who may quote brief passages in a review.

ISBN 978-0-9976295-1-4

Library of Congress Control Number: 2019920260

Excerpt from *The Pricing of Options and Corporate Liabilities* by Fischer Black and Myron Scholes reprinted by permission of the University of Chicago Press.
Excerpt from *Measuring Market Risk* by Kevin Dowd reprinted by permission.
Excerpts from *Technical Analysis of the Financial Markets: A Comprehensive Guide to Trading Methods and Applications* by John J. Murphy reprinted by permission.
Excerpt from *Elliott Wave Principle: Key to Market Behavior* by Robert R. Prechter, Jr. and A.J. Frost reprinted by permission.

June 2016:   First Edition
January 2020:   Second Edition

Published by Cephalopod Publishing
P.O. Box 920179
Needham, MA 02492

Visit www.traderconstructionkit.com

Common-sense Disclaimer

Trader Construction Kit describes strategies and techniques employed by professional traders in the financial markets, which involve the intentional, proactive assumption of risk and the very real possibility of loss. Neither the author or publisher shall be liable for any loss of profit or other commercial damages, including but not limited to special, incidental, consequential or other damages. Every reader must evaluate their own particular personal circumstances before attempting to employ any information contained in this book. Use of the information and instructions contained in this work is at your own risk.

Neither the author or publisher is a registered investment advisor and neither the author nor the publisher offers the content as investment, accounting, business or legal advice.

Trader Construction Kit is intended to be the best first book for aspiring risk takers, but cannot and does not represent the totality of the available information on any of the covered topics. While best efforts have been made in preparing the content, the author and publisher make no representations or warranties of any kind and assume no liabilities of any kind with respect to the accuracy or completeness of the content and specifically disclaim any implied warranties of merchantability or fitness of use for a particular purpose. Readers must be prepared to continue their study to achieve a professional level of competency.

The author strongly believes that every trader has a responsibility to comply with all of the laws, rules, and regulations of their particular market, and to operate in an ethical fashion at all times. *Trader Construction Kit* is a product of the laws, rules, regulations and operational environment at the time of its initial publication in 2016. Future changes to the laws, rules, regulations and operational environment could conceivably render any or all of the information in this book obsolete, and readers must educate themselves on the current state of play. Nothing in *Trader Construction Kit* is intended to provide an aspiring trader with any type of training or instruction regarding their legal or ethical obligations to clients, employees, co-workers, or any other person or entity they might encounter or interact with during their work as a trader. *Trader Construction Kit* does contain several examples of non-conforming activities intended to illustrate clearly inappropriate behavior that compliant market participants may observe, or that could potentially impact their activities.

Acknowledgements

Trader Construction Kit would not have been possible without:

Harte Weiner and the staff at CambridgeEditors.
Rachel Siegel's multiple rounds of manuscript editing.
William Braff, A.J. Camelio, Julian Gibson, and Mike McDonald's review and critique of countless working drafts.
Glenna Collett's book design and publishing process advice.
Daniel McMurtry's book design, layout and assembly.
Lars Astrom's cover design.
Paula Huston's design advice.
Christopher Bernard's legal and compliance advice.
Sailesh Ramamurtie's risk and quantitative advice.

The redesigned & expanded second edition would not have been possible without the additional contributions of:

A.J. Camelio, Sergey Crane, Erica Engle, Mike McDonald and Chris Peters' review and critique of the manuscript and Appendix B.
Tom Sullivan's book design, layout and assembly.

Joel Rubano - 2020

Contents

0	Introduction	1
1	Know Yourself	9
2	Know the Enemy	25
3	Fundamental Analysis	63
4	Technical Analysis	101
5	Understanding Volatility	145
6	Understanding Risk	175
7	Developing a Cohesive Market View	213
8	Directional Trading Strategies	253
9	Spread Trading Strategies	295
10	Option Trading Strategies	333
11	Quantitative Trading Strategies	399
12	Evaluating Trades & Creating a Trading Plan	433
13	Trading Mechanics	463
14	Managing Positions & Portfolios	483
15	Pricing & Hedging Structured Transactions	505
16	Navigating the Corporate Culture	531
00	Conclusion	551

Appendix A - Resources 553

Appendix B – Data Science & Programming 555

Index 579

0

Introduction

Working on a trading desk is one of the most coveted careers in the world. The competition is fierce and the lure of money and everything it brings attracts all kinds, from high school dropouts to elite over-achievers who would otherwise make fine mathematicians, brain surgeons, or fighter pilots. In stark contrast to the years of preparation at a university, medical school, or military academy, a novice trader is generally expected to do battle with the best (and worst) that the market can offer, in a zero-sum game, with little or no practical training. No matter how beautiful the mind, steady the hand, or steely the nerves, each newly minted trader is initially operating at a significant disadvantage. When it is every trader for himself, few are inclined to help their coworkers grow into competitors. In the rare cases when a well-meaning trader does want to offer assistance, there has traditionally been a scarcity of relevant, practical resource material. It is that informational void that I am attempting to fill.

This book was written for the aspiring trader, risk manager, or analyst struggling to come to grips with the sound and fury of a trading floor. The goal is to explain simply, methodically, and with maximum clarity how to be a professional trader.

I draw from the books considered to be benchmarks in the field (as they have formed the foundation of my technique) and will refer the reader to more specialized texts for deeper study. I present as non-technical a treatment of the subject as possible and leave the underlying mathematics, for those interested, to the original authors.

Traders develop conceptual frameworks to help them understand the markets they inhabit. There were not a lot of practical resources for understanding how to deal with financial tumult when I was educating myself, so I sought lessons from other high-risk, high-reward endeavors like gambling, sports, and war. A combative, conflict-oriented model allowed me to contextualize and operate within the extreme volatility of the markets I inhabited and, as a result, my pedagogy is frequently expressed in metaphors of force, pressure, and stress.

I do not claim to be the World's Greatest Trader. I am a fairly workaday, blue-collar risk taker. I have been profitable across my career and never broken the law or blown up my firm. I have traded my way across the United States from a Houston oil producer to a Boston hedge fund with stops at utility companies and energy merchants along the way. Between jobs, I gambled on precious metals and agricultural futures from a Michigan apartment and speculated on currencies from a seedy motel room in the California desert. I have bought and sold power, coal, oil, and natural gas on an institutional scale and dealt in financial swaps, over-the-counter forwards, exchange-traded futures, and physically delivered options. The trading techniques I employ have been refined by years of practical experimentation across variegated markets with real money on the line. Being more Salieri than Mozart, I have had to try harder to work out how markets operate, and as a result, perhaps understand the plumbing and wiring of the financial system better than most.

Trading Is a Process
Being a professional trader is about having a stable, robust methodology for examining the market, developing trading ideas, selecting the best possible implementation, efficiently executing the trade, and monitoring and optimizing the resultant position. The market will be different every day, but a trader's approach, once developed, should be consistent.

In flowchart form, the idealized process would look like this:

Introduction

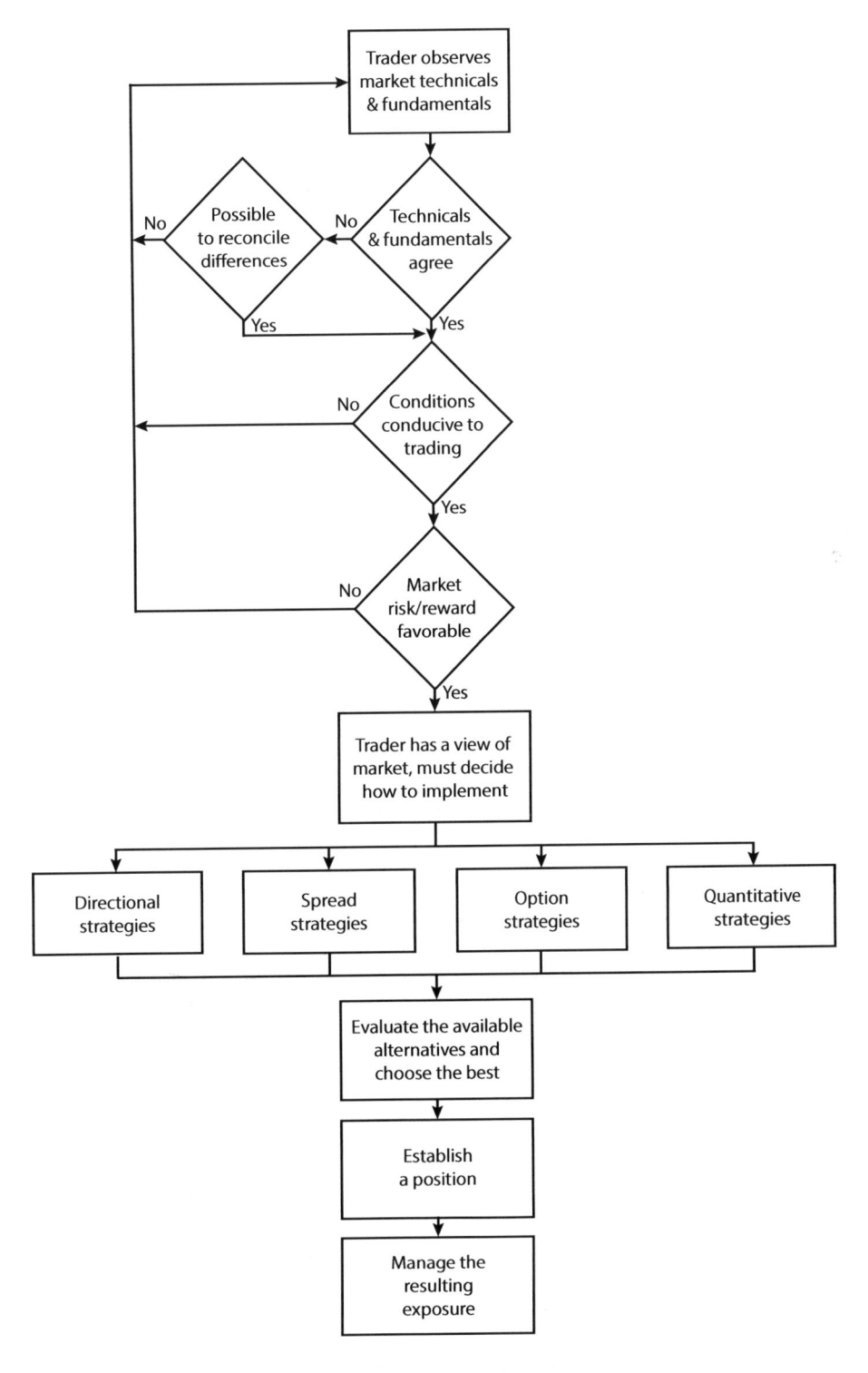

Figure 0.1 Flowchart of an idealized trading process.

This text discusses the process with each chapter addressing a specific aspect of the whole. The chapters are also broadly grouped into five sections:

1. Introduction to the Industry
2. Developing a View on the Market
3. Evaluating Trading Strategies
4. Managing Positions and Portfolios
5. Being a Professional Trader

Introduction to the Industry, Chapters 1-2

Chapter 1 – Know Yourself
What does it mean to be a professional trader? What sorts of character traits are markers for success, and what behaviors inevitably lead to ruin? Not all traders do the same thing, and there are a variety of different decision-making styles and approaches to the market that can be productively deployed.

Chapter 2 – Know the Enemy
We explore the transactional ecology, where some entities are seeking to acquire risk for a profit while others seek to shed risk for a fee. How to identify and categorize the various types of firms present in the market, understand their motivations and know the types of business activities they typically undertake.

Developing a View on the Market: Chapters 3-7

Chapter 3 – Fundamental Analysis
Explores how analysts collect data, process it, and turn it into actionable information. How traders work with subject matter experts to develop a consensus of market opinion which, when contrasted with internal projections, leads to a perception that current prices are relatively too cheap or too expensive.

Chapter 4 – Technical Analysis
Studying charts of price fluctuations as a window into market sentiment and as a means of understanding the probability and magnitude of potential price responses to market events and new information.

Chapter 5 – Understanding Volatility
Learn how to observe and categorize the fluctuations in market prices, and how its characteristics affect liquidity and trader participation.

Chapter 6 – Understanding Risk
Explore how the market volatility combined with the trader's positions translates into risk. How to measure risk and understand the potential P&L impacts of normal and extreme market fluctuations.

Chapter 7 – Developing a Cohesive Market View
Learn to combine fundamental information, a technical analysis, an assessment of market volatility, and risk implications into a view of the market. Having a view of the market is the primary task of any trader, and the remainder of the book will cover implementing the view and managing the resulting position.

Evaluating Trading Strategies: Chapters 8-12

Chapter 8 – Directional Trading Strategies
Directional trading strategies are the simplest, most immediate means of gaining exposure to the market. The chapter explores how to evaluate pure long/short directional implementations of the trader's view.

Chapter 9 – Spread Trading Strategies
Spread trading strategies involve offsetting long and short positions that are designed to profit from the convergence or divergence of the initial price relationship. Explore different types of spread position implementations of the trading view.

Chapter 10 – Option Trading Strategies
Option trading strategies involve using instruments with complex, non-linear risk characteristics that can be used to take leveraged directional views, create structures that profit under specific, predetermined conditions, or take positions that profit from changes in market volatility. Understanding the basics of this complex topic and evaluating various types of option implementation.

Chapter 11 – Quantitative Trading Strategies
In some data-intensive markets it is possible—or necessary—to utilize a quantitative, machine-based approach to understanding the market and implementing trading strategies. How to consider different types of machine-based trading strategies as potential means of implementing the market view.

Chapter 12 – Evaluating Trades & Creating a Trading Plan
How to take the candidate directional, spread, option, and quantitative trading strategies and determine the best means of implementing the trader's market view of the market. Once the trader has decided on their preferred strategy, she will create a trading plan that describes its implementation.

Managing Positions & Portfolios: Chapters 13-14

Chapter 13 – Trading Mechanics
After arriving at the optimal strategy for the current conditions and drafting a trading plan, the trader must accumulate the desired position. The trader must develop and maintain solid trading mechanics to efficiently operate in the market.

Chapter 14 – Managing Positions & Portfolios
Securing a position is not the end. A trader must continue to assess both the market and the viability of his thesis, and stand ready to take any necessary action to optimize the profitability of the trade.

Being a Professional Trader Chapters 15-16

Chapter 15 – Pricing and Hedging Structured Transactions
Traders exposed to deal flow at financial institutions will frequently be called on to assist with complex structured transactions, which can originate anywhere from the organic hedging needs of a producer or consumer to a sophisticated player looking to opportunistically shed or assume an esoteric exposure. The trader's involvement can range from performing routine price discovery and hedging, to risk decomposition, extracting value from embedded optionality, and warehousing significant volumes of non-standard products. The chapter concludes with a practical example of pricing and hedging a common structured transaction.

Chapter 16 – Navigating the Corporate Culture
Trading firms are complicated organizations, with a host of written and unwritten rules. A look at how things actually work, and how to avoid common pitfalls that derail trading careers. Just as markets evolve, traders progress through an evolutionary trajectory during their careers. How to avoid stagnation, diagnose technique flaws, and continue making progress.

Prerequisites and Requirements for Usage
This book was designed for undergraduate, MBA, and Masters of Finance students interested in a career in trading, recent graduates seeking to gain practical insight, neophyte traders looking for an edge, and support staff seeking a greater understanding of the industry or eyeing a jump to the commercial side of the desk. To successfully navigate this text, the reader should have:

1. An undergraduate-level familiarity with math, statistics, and economics; more is obviously better.
2. Access to the Internet and knowledge of how to search for information.
3. Access to financial information, including stock, bond, and commodity prices and the basic tools used to do fundamental research and create rudimentary historical price charts.

Introducing Product X

My goal is to explain the common strategic building blocks that are applicable to all markets. In the interests of being useful to the maximum number of readers I have attempted to present the material in a product-neutral fashion. This would be challenging (if not impossible) if I were to draw the preponderance of the examples from my personal experiences in the energy market. Conversely, using a broad range of examples from currencies, equities, and fixed income would ensure that I was frequently pontificating on subjects of which I had no practical knowledge.

I have attempted to resolve this dilemma by creating a highly detailed case study describing the market for a fictional commodity called Product X, complete with underlying market fundamentals, historical prices, and a global balance of trade. The Product X case runs through the entire book, and will be incrementally examined and interpreted with the tools developed in each successive chapter. The reader will get to see, start to finish, how to analyze a market, develop actionable information, evaluate trading strategies, and select the optimal means of implementation.

Working through the process as a trader would when approaching a new market will provide a depth of understanding of the material impossible to achieve with dozens of individual stand-alone examples. There will be occasional real examples, most commonly to illustrate historic market events that have a bearing on the topic at hand. Many will be from the energy commodity space, as it is my area of greatest personal experience.[1]

This book covers a lot of ground and must occasionally, out of necessity, present concentrated overviews of complicated subjects. Each chapter will conclude with suggestions for further exploration of the topic(s) and continued self-education.

Trader Construction Kit contains a large number of graphics, the majority of which are price charts. Unless otherwise specified, all price charts will be line graphs of end-of-day close data for a standard 252 business day year.

---

[1] I was an employee of an energy-trading firm during the majority of the time the first edition of this book was in development, and will not discuss any information that would be deemed proprietary to my former firm and its core business. All energy-based examples are drawn from either publicly available information or presented as generic, hypothetical situations.

1

Know Yourself

The TV Question
A person has a television (TV) to sell. The seller thinks for a while, pondering its value, and decides that the TV is worth $20.00. He makes a sign that says "TV For Sale - $20.00," tapes it to the television, and wheels it down to the curb to sell. As he does, he sees a neighbor pushing the exact same television down to the driveway with a sign taped to it that says "TV For Sale - $10.00."

What should he do?

Everyone wants to know what it takes to be a trader, what intangible characteristics separate the winners from the losers. For the vast majority of successful traders, there is no single thing that steers them down the path toward either the penthouse or the outhouse. If there were a perfect trader, her approach might look like this:

Vitruvian Trader

- The ideal trader has a clear sense of what she is trying to achieve at all times.
- The trader expects a particular market response when a base set of fundamental and technical conditions are disturbed by incremental change or the influence of external stimuli. This informed perspective on the future of price is called a view.
- The trader considers a variety of strategies to implement her view, selecting the one with the closest response to the underlying driver with the best potential reward, the lowest probable risk, and the best performance characteristics.
- The trader sets the position with a defined profit target and a stop-loss.

- The trader monitors the position for changes to the underlying thesis while maintaining an alert, intellectually engaged but emotionally detached state.
- If action is required, the trader executes with the maximum possible efficiency.
- The trader evaluates the results and adjusts the operational parameters (trade selection criteria, stops, targets, etc.) of the methodology as necessary.
- Repeat.

Being a professional trader is a two-part problem, how to evolve to be the best possible risk-taker and how to develop, refine, and deploy the most efficient process.

For most people, success as a trader is less a matter of deus ex machina brilliance and more a result of a steady progression, an ongoing evolutionary process wherein every student starts with innate skills and attempts to out-learn and out-develop peers. This chapter will explore the attributes common to successful traders and the common mistakes that keep neophytes from reaching their potential. Not all traders approach the job in the same way, and not all trading jobs are the same. Understanding the subtle distinctions will shed light on the development necessary, in terms of both the steepness and duration of the learning curve. All roads may lead to Rome, but not all paths end at the job of one's dreams. In this case, they all start with another question:

Do You Play Poker?
Poker is the only game in the casino that does not, by definition, have the player's odds mathematically fixed and permanently stacked against them. While random chance can play a part in any particular hand, the long-run odds of a player prevailing depend primarily on her proficiency relative to that of opponents. Poker is a game of strategy, tactics, probability, and calculation and is a serviceable, albeit simplified, simulacrum of trading. Playing No-Limit Texas Hold 'Em[2] for a meaningful amount of money involves the same kind of decision calculus and personal involvement as managing a trading position. It is by far the best and most accessible means of learning to take risk, short of actually sitting on a trading desk.

Poker as a Whetstone
Good poker players are extremely analytical, as success depends both on an advanced understanding of the underlying probabilities of the game and a feeling for the nuances of human nature. Professionals spend a great deal of time studying their opponents, and characterizing their playing style based on two attributes: the degree to which they are conservative or adventurous with their money, called being "tight" or "loose," and their

---

[2] Frequently called "The Cadillac of Poker," No-Limit Texas Hold 'Em is by far the most popular variant of the game and is the preferred form of competition at every level, from major tournaments to penny-ante home games. I was once wasting time playing with a friend in an airport using M&Ms instead of chips when a disheveled guy came shambling in off the concourse and said "Hey man, ummm, can I get in on the action?" I looked up at him and said, "That depends. Got any M&Ms?"

Chapter 1 - Know Yourself

general inclination toward passivity or aggression. Mapped on intersecting axes, they yield the quadrants Loose/Passive, Loose/Aggressive, Tight/Passive, and Tight/Aggressive:[3]

Maniac:
Plays every hand to feel the rush, consequences be damned

Professional:
Disciplined enough to wait for good hands, then extracts maximum profit

Calling station:
Wants to be involved, but lacks conviction and is easily pushed around

Rock:
Risk-averse player that waits for the perfect, can't-lose cards that never arrive

(Y-axis: Inclination toward aggression — Aggressive / Passive)
(X-axis: Inclination toward participation — More involved / Less involved)

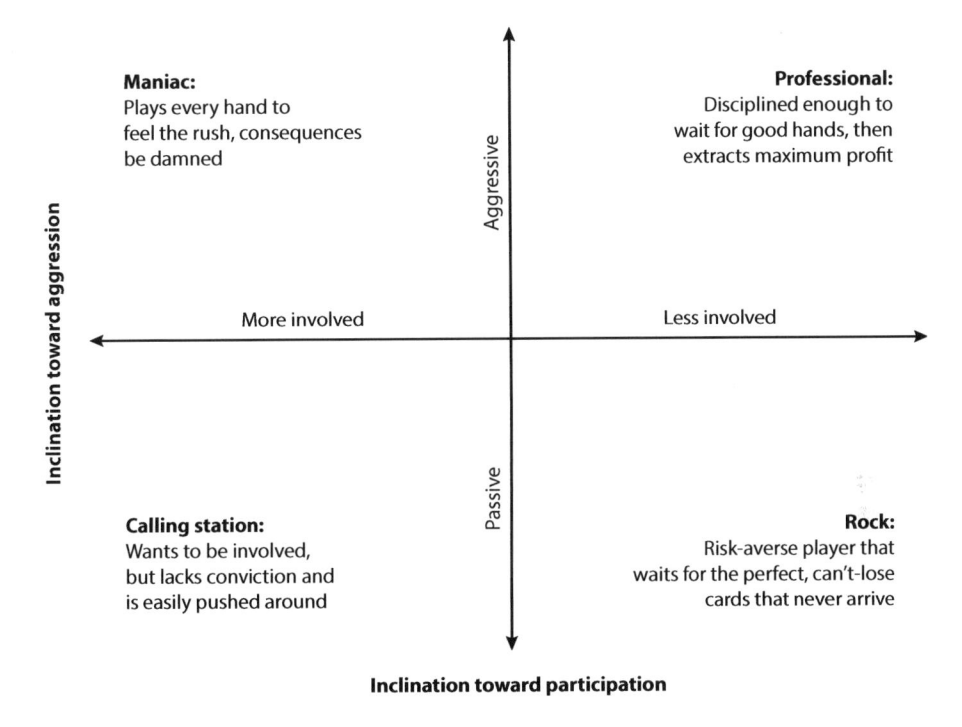

Figure 1.1   Characterization of various poker styles.

A Loose/Aggressive player, sometimes called a maniac, gambles wildly and without control. This player is a thrill-seeker, who plays to feel the rush and takes huge swings up and down, rarely having enough money to withstand the self-induced volatility and usually going broke as a result.

A Loose/Passive player gets involved indiscriminately but gives up easily, squandering small amounts of money over and over as the game goes on. This person, derisively labeled a calling station, wants to be involved but lacks commitment, making him an easy mark for aggressive players.

A Tight/Passive player will sit at the table forever waiting for the perfect situation that never, ever materializes. She is frequently referred to as a rock, is not inclined to get involved, and doesn't like to take any risk when she does.

---

[3] This common model for categorizing player behavior may have originated from Alan N. Schoonmaker's grid-based system seen in *The Psychology of Poker* (Henderson: Two Plus Two Publishing LLC, 2000), 71-79.

A Tight/Aggressive player will wait patiently until the odds are decisively in his favor, then act with maximum aggression to extract as much money as possible from opponents at the table.

Tight/Aggressive for the Win!
Most top poker professionals believe that Tight/Aggressive is the only winning behavior over the long run. More interestingly, elite players feel that a Tight/Aggressive approach to the game is not a naturally occurring set of traits. Very few people are intuitively disciplined enough to limit their participation to situations when they have a real statistical advantage and also willing to exert maximum pressure on their opponents. It is a learned behavior. A winning poker player has consciously, intentionally modified her decision making and approach to the game to be both more calculating *and* more aggressive in order to maximize the chances of success. This is exactly the right mindset for a professional trader, and the behavioral model maps perfectly.

A Loose/Aggressive trader is a thrill-seeking adrenaline junkie, swinging around in the market to satisfy a need for action, consequences be damned.

A Loose/Passive trader will always have some sort of a position, but never anything significant, and will tend to give up at the first sign of a loss.

A Tight/Passive trader is waiting, always waiting, for the perfect opportunity that just never quite seems to appear.

The Tight/Aggressive trader waits for the conditions to be favorable, and then commits to a strategy with a meaningful position managed in a tactical, controlled fashion.

The first thing strong poker players do when sitting down at a table full of opponents is, surprisingly, nothing at all. They will sit and watch the ebb and flow of the game for a half hour, an hour, or as long as it takes to preliminarily classify their opponents and to see how the game is playing at the moment. They will study the betting, the aggression level of the participants, and the quality of cards being played. They will listen to the players talk about how they played previous hands to gain insight into their thought processes, style, and skill level. They will see how much money is in play, and by whom, as an indicator of how much profit there is to be made. Finally, they will make a candid assessment of themselves relative to what they have learned about the game, its participants, requirements, and profit potentials relative to the risks involved. As the saying goes, "if you can't spot a sucker at the poker table, then you are the sucker." Smart players know when to stand up and walk away from a game that is too tough or that does not suit their style, even without playing a single hand. They also know when to settle in for the long haul if they find a situation that seems profitable.

Here is the previous paragraph again, with replacements in italics.

The first thing strong *traders* do when *entering a market* full of *counterparties* is, surprisingly, nothing at all. They sit and watch the ebb and flow of the *market* for a half hour, an hour, or as long as it takes to preliminarily classify their *counterparties* and to see how the *market is*

Chapter 1 - Know Yourself

trading at the moment. They will study the *prices*, the aggression level of the *traders*, and the *fundamental information*. They will listen to the *traders* talk about how they *put on* previous *positions* to gain insight into their thought processes, style, and skill level. They will see how much money is in play, and by whom, as an indicator of how much profit there is to be made. Finally, they will make a candid assessment of themselves relative to what they have learned about the *market*, its participants, requirements, and profit potential relative to the risks involved. As the saying goes, *if you can't spot the sucker in the market, then you* are *the sucker*. Smart *traders* know when to stand up and walk away from a *market* that is too tough or that does not suit their style, even without *doing a single trade*. They also know when to settle in for the long haul if they find a situation that seems profitable.

How can novices develop a trading style analogous to the tight/aggressive poker style? By understanding what attributes contribute to success and emphasizing them, and by recognizing destructive tendencies and seeking to avoid them.

Traits of Successful Traders:

1. Disciplined.
2. Self-analytical.
3. Intellectually honest.
4. Rationally accepting of failure.
5. Have an ability to suffer.
6. Learn from their mistakes.
7. Hyper-competitive, driven.
8. Have a strong work ethic.
9. Positive.
10. Prepared.
11. Ethical.

Good Traders Are Disciplined
It is very easy for anyone to say what they are going to do; it is much more rare to find someone who consistently does what they say, particularly when the course of action may be unpopular, unpleasant, or involve personal or professional costs. The other ten traits are important; discipline is mandatory. Discipline enables all of the other traits to be expressed, and allows a strong analytical process to be translated into thorough trade selection, rock-solid execution, and effective position management. This is one major reason why former athletes and ex-military are so highly prized by trading firms, often above more highly intellectually pedigreed individuals. If an ex-Marine or Navy SEAL says they're buying here and selling there, you had better believe things are getting bought here and sold there.

Good Traders Are Self-Analytical
All machines break down from time to time, and every motor needs the occasional tune up. Flaws can creep into any (or all) aspects of a trader's methodology, and if left undiscovered or unchecked will destroy even the most robust process. While honest, objective feedback should

always be welcomed, a trader cannot rely on others to diagnose the flaws in his technique. A trader's peers may be unwilling or unable to offer productive critique, and even if they are, the trader may not be able to process and use the information. A professional trader must be both willing and able to forensically examine the decision-making process and all aspects of the methodology to determine if there are flaws that need to be addressed. Debugging a trader's methodology will be discussed in greater detail in Chapter 16 – Navigating the Corporate Culture.

Good Traders Are Intellectually Honest
Most people find it extremely easy to lie to themselves about the underlying motivation for their actions. This prevents personal growth by denying them opportunity to learn from their mistakes.

Taking a significant amount of risk is a very committing exercise, requiring a great deal of forethought and no small amount of emotional stress. Once invested (in both senses of the word), it can be difficult to hear counter-arguments or process incremental new information, regardless of how critical, timely, or obvious. In extreme cases, traders will go to elaborate lengths to convince themselves the market is acting "irrationally" or "stupidly," that the shift in fundamentals was "bad data," and that devastating information is "just noise." It is difficult to believe how fully intelligent, perceptive individuals can deceive themselves under stress.

Intellectual honesty allows traders to self-police their actions. Traders must be able to step back and ask themselves "why am I doing this?" If they don't have an answer, (or it isn't a good one) they need to check themselves before they wreck themselves.

Good Traders Are Rationally Accepting of Failure
Poker players sometimes say, "A real gambler doesn't need anything." It does not take any self-actualizing philosophy to imagine that desires can, and do, influence the decision-making process. Wanting to win too badly can muddy up what needs to be a clinical assessment of the risks and rewards inherent in any proposition. Needing a particular result makes it paradoxically more difficult to achieve.

This behavior is on display every weekend on television as highly compensated professional athletes miss short putts, drop easy catches, and brick free-throws that they could make with their eyes closed with nothing at stake. The sudden pressure of having to do something completely ordinary (and the associated consequences of failure) can transform any task from routine to impossible. Losing traders who approach their maximum allowable loss for the year almost inevitably explode violently shortly thereafter. The combined pressure of wanting desperately to succeed but being unable to fail is too much, leading to poor decisions and, ultimately, the exact circumstances the trader was seeking to avoid.

A trader must put himself in a space where, given what is at risk and what he hopes to gain, he is completely comfortable with either outcome. The potential profit is worth the probable risks involved. A trader needs to learn to think that a particular trade could work, given the probabilities, not that it should work or that it will work. It must never need to work. Trading ideas that don't work are an unpleasant yet inevitable byproduct of the process. A trader must accept that losing is part of the game and move on with the minimum of psychological damage, because there will be a lot of losing over a career. Traders are not in the perfection business. The name of the game is batting for average and controlling the risk, so that the trader can afford to play again tomorrow. Traders need to learn to trust in themselves and trust in their process. Poker, with its reduced probability set and defined outcomes, is a perfect laboratory for developing this kind of self-confidence.

Poker also teaches the difficult-to-grasp concept of divorcing the short-run outcomes from the quality of the decision-making process that created them. This may seem counterintuitive, particularly when applied to a results-centric endeavor. "Isn't the point to win, to make money? Isn't it a good decision if it makes money, and a bad decision if it does not?" Sometimes good decisions lose, and poor decisions win. If offered a chance to bet $1.00 to win $1.00 on the flip a coin that comes up heads 99% of the time and tails 1% of the time, any trader would be insane not to bet on heads. If, when flipped one time, the coin comes up tails, it was not a bad bet, just a bad probabilistic outcome. There will always be exogenous events and instances of random chance. Bad luck happens.

For many high achievers, not succeeding immediately as a trader may be the first significant failure in life. Athletes with experience losing have more likely developed productive coping/compensation behaviors. When I studied karate as a boy the first thing I was taught was how to fall so that I did not injure myself. Every trader must learn how to fail so that he does not hurt himself.

Good Traders Have an Ability to Suffer, or to Displace Suffering
One key survival mechanism involves having or developing a larger than normal ability to tolerate suffering or the intellectual capability to compartmentalize it. The trader must find ways of dealing with the pressure and discomfort such that it does not degrade the decision-making process. If the trader has structured and sized trades correctly and adopted a good gambler's mindset, it is possible to not care *too* much about any one particular outcome, trusting that in the long run there will be more gains than losses. Sooner or later, however, every trader will misjudge the market and find out what he is made of under the worst possible circumstances.

Good Traders Learn From Their Mistakes
In any given day, month, or year, a trader's approach to the market will be a success or a failure. It is easier to learn from failure where it is possible to start from the logical premise that the method may be flawed and forensically examine it for defects. Adapting to a changing environment while still generating productive results is vastly more difficult, and will require a visionary sense that the underlying conditions are either eroding or are vulnerable to a seismic shift. Observant traders will look for clues like a decreasing winning percentage, greater difficulty finding good trades, greater execution slippage, and thinner margins. Profitable traders are like snakes, shedding their strategies like so much dead skin when they are no longer productive.

Making mistakes is part of the evolution of a trader, but there is no excuse for making the same mistake twice (let alone multiple times). Whenever possible, it is far better to learn from other people's mistakes by studying other markets and trading styles and observing what does (and more importantly) does not work.

Good Traders Are Hypercompetitive, Driven
Traders must first be profitable (or they will not be traders for long), and then distinguish themselves relative to their peers. Traders will be compared to their desks, to traders in other products at the firm, and to standardized industry benchmarks. They will be graded on total dollars earned relative to the cost of the resources utilized, and on the amount of risk taken. At most firms, management will start to look askance at the minimally productive trader, and will usually manufacture some reason to shuffle an underperformer into a different role (or out the door) to make room for a shiny new up-and-comer with potential.

Good Traders Work Very Hard
Good traders work much harder than average traders, and do so throughout their careers. A strong work ethic helps a trainee outlearn peers and get a shot at the desk. Junior traders must claw their way up to competency as fast as possible to keep their seats. Traders must continually out-work their peers in the market to remain profitable and be compensated for their production. Senior traders must remain current while at the same time always pushing to find the next product, market, or strategy that will expand or extend their career.

Good Traders Are Positive
Good traders believe that they can accomplish what they set out to do, that through hard work and skill that they can find profitable opportunities, design and execute a trading plan, and make money for their firm and themselves over time. Part of this is having rational expectations, but most of it is fairly straightforward psychology. A baseball player who thinks he can't hit the ball will never step up to the plate. There is no point adding artificial barriers, there will be plenty of real ones there already.

Good Traders Prepare
Good traders do vast amounts of research to minimize the chances of being surprised by a data item, research report, or economic indicator that they should have factored into their decisions. Traders are in the anticipation and reaction business. The more time spent pre-planning for contingencies, the faster and the more precise the reactions. Doing the homework allows the trader to spend the critical time period after any market event executing a plan, not pondering the possible ramifications as the market moves.

Good Traders Are Ethical
Most traders are ethical because they acknowledge and accept the carrot and stick implicit in their job description. A good trader at an aggressive firm can make so much money that there is no justifiable, logical reason for them to break the law or do anything else that could jeopardize their extremely lucrative career. Being ethical is also is good for their business. Once established, a trader's reputation becomes well known and difficult to shake. Behaving unethically eventually becomes extremely counterproductive, and failure to honor a

transaction or live up to the terms of a deal will lead to an immediate cessation of business with the offending party. A trader cannot expect to get better treatment in the market than she is willing to give, and in a fast-paced environment the shoe will be on the other foot very quickly. Within the rules rough play is allowed, however, and should be expected.

For those that, for some unknown reason, do not value the tremendous privilege their position implies, there are substantial penalties for transgression, including severely punitive fines and the very real threat of significant jail time.

Traits of Bad Traders

1. Not admitting that they are wrong.
2. Not taking responsibility for poor decisions.
3. Making the same mistakes over and over.
4. Trading too much.
5. Engaging in thrill-seeking behavior.
6. Making simple things complicated.
7. Ignoring their limitations.

Bad Traders Do Not Admit They Are Wrong
A trader holding a losing position faces a painful decision: suffer the losses in the short term in the hopes that things get better and not worse, or exit the position and move on to other opportunities. Some traders allow their ego to become part of the decision making process, refusing to remove negative positions because they cannot accept booking a loss. In other cases, particularly with an inexperienced trader, they may fear that the losing position will be a referendum on their capabilities as a risk taker. Regardless of the underlying reason, if the trader is unable to admit that a position is not working and proactively rectify the situation, then he has stopped managing risk and has become a passive spectator, riding the exposure wherever it may go.

Bad Traders Do Not Take Responsibility for Poor Decisions
This is a classic symptom of a weak, undisciplined trader. Every good trade is a product of her unique and singular genius, planned with the calculating tactical brilliance of Sun Tzu and executed with the effortless virtuosity of Paganini. Any losing trades are obviously the fault of the stupid analyst, the stupider weatherman, the insipidly stupid salesman, the buffoonishly stupid quant group, or the toxically stupid management, all of whom are conspiring to bring down the One True Hero of the markets. This distancing from any sort of negative outcome prevents productive self-critique and impedes refinement of a trader's technique and methodology.

Bad Traders Make the Same Mistakes Over and Over
Poker players refer to any persistent problem in their life or their game that causes them to lose money as a leak. Visualize water leaking out of a hole in a bucket. Whenever a trader says "I always lose money when I do this type of trade," the obvious question is, "Why do you keep

doing it?" There are allowances for suboptimal performance when learning a new market, instrument, affecting a stylistic change or implementing a new methodology. Beyond some point, however, consistently unprofitable behavior cannot be tolerated and the trader will have to revise his approach or cease activity. This can be tremendously difficult, particularly for historically high achievers unaccustomed to failure.

Bad Traders Trade Too Much
It can be very frustrating for a trader to not be able to find any positions that seem worth taking, particularly early in the year when all of her colleagues are off and running or late in the year when they are desperately trying to meet a goal. If a trader cannot find anything that meets the normally exacting criteria, the easiest remedy is to simply lower the standards a bit and start re-considering previously discarded ideas. Eventually, with a low enough hurdle to clear, something has to seem worth doing, even if it is a 50/50 coin flip or worse. "At least I've got a position! I'm in the game!"

Having tasted the sweet nectar of bad decision making, professional over-traders rarely stop there. With newly lenient standards they become transactional dervishes, executing every trade not patently awful, buying and selling and buying again with reckless abandon.

Bad Traders Engage in Thrill-Seeking Trading
Overtrading is a good impulse warped by desperation and desire. Thrill-seeking trading is a manifestation of boredom and an unhealthy, destructive attitude toward risk taking. Thrill seekers trade to feel the rush, to be in the action, and are generally poor stewards of the firm's capital as a result.

Bad Traders Make Simple Things Complicated
A close cousin to both the desire to overtrade and a desire to not take responsibility for losing positions is the tendency to take a bad position and, instead of cleanly exiting and taking the pain, attempting to fix things by putting on some sort of semi-equivalent off-setting trade to hedge the exposure. When the new trade inevitably exhibits some unwelcome performance characteristics, the trader tacks on a third deal to correct that, and a fourth to compensate for flaws in the third. The end result is a giant knot of positions that wobbles inexplicably back and forth with every tremor in the market, but that allows the trader to brag on any particular day that he has something that is working.

Bad Traders Ignore Their Limitations
There is a saying: "a good trader can trade anything." Given time to learn the structure of a market, assimilate the applicable fundamentals, and discover the unique nuances, any trader with a disciplined, rigorous methodology should have a better-than-even chance of finding a way to be profitable. Many traders take the success they have worked so hard to achieve in one market and simply assume that the underlying methodology is universally applicable, without bothering to understand how the unique characteristics of a different market will influence their approach. This is particularly common in young traders who, caught up in the excitement of mastering a market assume that they have mastered all markets. This can be a particularly expensive delusion.

There is a delicate balance. Traders must not unnecessarily limit themselves, but once an area of poor relative performance is identified, it must be respected.

The Middle Path

Every trader has strengths and weaknesses. Perversely, since it will take a while to work through the manifold possible permutations of market events and trader responses, it is possible to discover new and exciting inefficiencies well into one's career. Technique flaws break down into: easily correctable mistakes that can be remedied with critique and advice (or more commonly, self-critique); persistent flaws that require analysis and some re-programming; and deeply ingrained behavioral defects that will have to be slowly massaged out in the long term (if that is even possible) and managed around in the interim. Worse, new problems will crop up and old problems will re-emerge in moments of weakness or inattention.

Every successful trader I have known has changed materially as he has progressed through his career. Part of it is the obvious reactions to living a life under constant pressure and the various tolls it takes, but part is the intentional and continual re-programming that successful traders do to themselves in the name of surviving and prospering. As soon as traders stop learning and evolving, they have started to decline relative to their peers.

Traders can, and do, minutely dissect decision making and the personality factors that influence it, which can be exceedingly creepy for the non-initiated. Weirder still are the methods for "self-improvement." When I became dissatisfied with what I felt was an unacceptable latency in my decision-to-action timespan, I took up speed chess and spent the next 18 months waging Internet death matches with fast-fingered teen-aged prodigies until my reaction time to a cognitive input was whittled down to nil. Some self-programming will involve a change of approach that, once validated, becomes permanent. Other cases (like my speed chess example) are more akin to athletic training, where the results will fade without continued practice. Becoming a better trader is both a matter of heuristic and physical programming.

Stylistic Species of Traders

A trader's personality will manifest itself as a variety of positive and negative traits, some will need to be encouraged, and others repressed or eliminated. This balance of behaviors will determine whether or not the individual will have any prolonged success as a trader. Those same personality traits will also influence the methodology a trader deploys and the style of trading she is naturally drawn to. There are some immutable constants in any successful trading methodology: risk management, position control, and stop-loss discipline. Around that rigid skeleton are areas where personality will define the approach to the market and manifest as a natural preference for a fundamental, technical, or quantitative style of market analysis.

Adherence to a particular style is the initial differentiator between traders. An individual's style and choice of market view forms the foundation of the methodological framework that shapes how he gathers data, distills it into actionable information via an analytical process and evaluates and implements trading ideas.

Choosing a style is arguably the most critical part of any trader's evolution. It cannot be forced, because it has to suit the trader's personality and strengths. There are three principal styles of trading, fundamentally based, technically based, and quantitatively based. Fundamental traders are facts people. Technical traders are sentiment people. Quantitative traders are numbers people.

Fundamental traders examine the variables that affect supply and demand to attempt to understand the market's current price equilibrium, and then look for drivers that could meaningfully alter that balance. Some markets require a heavily data-intensive approach, which necessitates sophisticated collection, processing, and analytical functions. The ability to render data into actionable information will be the limiting factor in a firm's ability to grow, as each new market will require an almost parallel build out of capacity. Fundamental Analysis will be covered in detail in Chapter 3.

Technical traders believe that all fundamental information is instantly reflected in the current price and attempt to analyze the short and long-term fluctuations as a window into market psychology. Technical analysis is less about volume of data and unique interpretation methodologies, and more about recognizing recurring patterns in the market and making probabilistic trading judgments. One significant advantage of technical analysis is the ability to survey many products at the same time, and translate profitable methodologies from market to market. The principal weakness is a lack of understanding of the underlying motivational factors. The trader sees what is happening, but does not know why. Technical Analysis will be discussed in Chapter 4.

Quantitative traders build data-intensive models to derive an estimate of a product's "value" then seek to transact on any material divergences from that level, believing the market will eventually arrive at the "correct" price. Systematic traders construct elaborate computer models to derive transactional ideas from market data, in some cases allowing the software agent to execute and manage positions in real time without human involvement. Numerical methods of analyzing a market will be touched on in Chapter 3, with quantitative trading methodologies explored in Chapter 11.

Hybrid Theory
There is a sort of person who prefers the intellectual purity of a methodology based entirely on one style. This can be a valid, productive approach as long as the trader fully understands the strengths and limitations inherent in the chosen methodology and has a personality well matched to its requirements. I believe that there are tremendous benefits to adopting a hybrid approach built around the simultaneous use of multiple styles. Fusing disparate elements into an intellectually cohesive whole provides checks and balances and adds reinforcing or clarifying analysis to ambiguous situations. The challenge lies in weighing the informational

inputs in a consistent fashion. It is all too easy to overemphasize analysis that suits the trader's current view or position while ignoring dissenting warning signs.

Types of Trading Strategies

The trader may derive informational inputs from a fundamental, technical, or quantitative source, or a combination thereof. The second major differentiator between traders is the type(s) of strategies they choose to deploy, how they implement their view in the market. There are a number of main thematic styles of trading, the most common are directional trading, spread trading, option trading, and the utilization of quantitative tools.

Directional Trading

Directional traders seek to profit by correctly forecasting the future price trajectory of an instrument, then positioning themselves to capture the anticipated movement. Directional trading is conceptually straightforward, but requires the greatest level of discipline from the practitioner. Unlike other forms of risk taking, the directional trader is tasked with controlling all of the operational parameters of the strategy. The main advantage of a purely directional position is also its greatest drawback, the linear, unmitigated exposure to the totality of market fluctuations and the myriad underlying drivers. Sometimes called flat price or macro trading, directional trading is covered in Chapter 8.

Spread Trading

Spread trading is a strategy that involves the purchase of one instrument and the sale of another, a position designed to profit from either the convergence or divergence of the initial price relationship over time. The trader is either betting on a correlation breakdown, or the resumption of a traditional price relationship. Spread trades are very popular as the long/short structure is, to an extent, self-hedging, protecting the trader from overall directional market risk. Spread trading will be discussed in Chapter 9.

Option Strategies

Options are part of a larger family of products called derivatives because they derive their price from another product, called the underlying security. As the price of the underlying moves, the price of the derivative will change by a contractually specified (but not necessarily equal) amount, and the rate of change can have either linear or non-linear attributes. This subtlety adds significant complexity to the valuation of options and other derivative securities, but also exponentially increases their utility as financial engineering products. Strategies for pricing and trading options will be discussed in Chapter 10.

Quantitative Strategies

The requirements for productive participation in some extremely high-speed or massively complex markets can exceed the capabilities of human traders, leading them to develop machine-based tools and systems to compensate. There is a tremendous range of applications, from simple data acquisition and manipulation tools to sophisticated autonomous algorithmic agents designed to replace the human trader entirely. Quantitative strategies will be explored in Chapter 11.

Structured Transactions

Structured transactions are the ne plus ultra of complexity in the trading business. They are most commonly seen when an entity is trying to off-load a complex risk package in one fell swoop, or when a financial intermediary is pitching a novel structure to a client. Complex transactions are like risk onions, with many different layers that need to be carefully peeled away, and if not handled properly will most surely lead to tears. Pricing and hedging structured transactions will be covered in greater depth in Chapter 15.

Trading strategies are the wrenches, hammers, and screwdrivers in a trader's transactional toolkit. There is a right tool for each job, and there is a best strategy for the trader's position and market. The best traders are technically proficient with all of the strategies, and will simultaneously evaluate flat price, spread, option, quantitative, and structured solutions for every potential position they are considering.

Unfortunately, there is no pre-packaged personality test to determine what trading style and approach to the market will best suit a neophyte trader. Inferences can, and should, be made to try to narrow down the field of exploration, but at the end of the day the student is going to have to expose herself to as many styles and types of trading as possible in order to see what is interesting and what her rudimentary aptitudes are.

The TV Question Revisited

Recall the question at the start of the chapter:

A person has a television (TV) to sell. The seller thinks for a while, pondering its value, and decides that the TV is worth $20.00. He makes a sign that says "TV For Sale - $20.00," tapes it to the television, and wheels it down to the curb to sell. As he does, he sees a neighbor pushing the exact same television down to the driveway with a sign taped to it that says "TV For Sale - $10.00."

What should he do?

The Answer
He should buy the neighbor's TV for $10.00, and then try to sell both for $20.00 each.

The Reason
The neighbor has underpriced her TV relative to its theoretical value, $20.00. To a natural trader, this represents a potential $10.00 profit opportunity. Most people do not intuitively differentiate the value proposition (the neighbor's TV is too cheap, relative to its value) from their goal of the moment (selling their own TV set). The most common response is to remain fixated on the initial goal and either match the neighbor's price or attempt to undercut them.

I have asked The TV Question to a broad cross-section of my colleagues in the industry, from fresh-faced trainees to the biggest swingers on the floor. The vast majority did not get the answer. Without exception, however, all of the truly elite traders answered correctly. Most responded instantly, reflexively, and with virtually no contemplation. It was obvious to them. Many traders who got the question wrong were well-respected risk takers in the midst of extremely productive careers, so it is not a predictor of absolute success or failure. The TV Question seems to distinguish the naturals from the (relatively) more pedestrian masses that are going to have to work harder to survive and thrive.

Chapter One Summary

Very few people naturally possess the combination of traits necessary to be a successful trader. Evolving into a productive risk-taker is a process analogous to the cognitive re-programming practiced by tight/aggressive poker players. A trader must be disciplined, self-analytical, intellectually honest, rationally accept failure, have an ability to suffer and to learn from mistakes, be driven, have a strong work ethic, and be positive, prepared and ethical. Characteristics of weak traders and impediments to progress are an inability to admit error and take responsibility for poor decisions, and a tendency to repeat the same mistakes, over-trade, engage in thrill-seeking behavior, make simple things complicated, and ignore limitations.

Traders must identify and play to their strengths, minimize their weaknesses, and choose an analytical framework and trading strategies that complement them. A trader may gravitate toward fundamental, technical, or quantitative methods or analyzing a market, or choose to employ a combination of all three. They may elect to express their view of the market with directional trades, spread positions, option structures, or quantitative strategies.

Before they can begin to evaluate a market, traders must understand the entities that make up the transactional ecosystem, which will be explored in Chapter 2.

Review Questions

1. Describe the idealized trading process.
2. Which poker style is the most productive for a trader to adopt, and why?
3. Which is the most important trait for a trader to have, and why?
4. What are the three primary styles of trading, and how are they practiced?
5. What are the four primary types of trading strategies? What does each involve?

Resources

- *Reminiscences of a Stock Operator* by Edwin Lefèvre
- *Every Hand Revealed* by Gus Hansen
- *Doyle Brunson's Super System: A Course in Power Poker* by Doyle Brunson and Chip Reese
- *The Biggest Game in Town* by Al Alvarez
- *The Psychology of Poker* by Alan N. Schoonmaker
- *The Theory of Poker: A Professional Poker Player Teaches You How To Think Like One* by David Sklansky

2

Know the Enemy

The Abridged Modern History of Trading
Even on a short timescale, what it means to be a trader is a moving target. The current state of the industry will impact the business a trader does, the type of firm she does it at, and her overall approach to risk taking. Industry participants need to understand this and evolve in order to remain relevant, which can be seen from the recent history of trading.

Pre-1960
The Speculator era, which is almost akin to saying the alchemist era. Fortunes were made, lost, and made again in obscure proto-markets like real estate, mineral holdings, and, presumably, top hats and monocles. Regulation was largely nonexistent, risk was poorly understood, and everybody was always trying to corner the market in everything, usually with little to no success. In this era a trader would probably be a millionaire by age 26, swindled and broke by 27, and would have re-swindled his way back by age 30.

1960-70s
The Partnership era. Trading was an unglamorous business predominantly practiced at clubby Wall Street banks or by individuals on an exchange floor. Capital was either tied up in a partnership interest or the trader's personal funds, which fostered a very methodical, conservative approach designed to yield long-term prosperity with a minimum of volatility and drawdowns. There were few products to trade, implied leverage was low, and there was no structural optionality. In this era a very good trader would have a long career with a stable firm and make a good living.

1980s

Money culture emerges front and center. Oliver Stone's 1987 movie *Wall Street* forever changes attitudes toward banking, capitalism, and pink dress shirts with white cuffs and collars. Activity is heavily bank-centric. A decade-long boom in equities and a crash in bonds made a lot of money for a lot of people very rapidly. All of that new money needed to be invested, and the asset management industry exploded to accommodate that need. Computing power allowed the industry to expand as new products like mortgage bonds, junk bonds, and exotic derivatives could be modeled, priced, and traded. In this era a very good trader would get paid enough for a Porsche 911 Turbo and a sweet penthouse apartment in Manhattan.

1990s

Hedge funds exploded onto the scene, then almost immediately started literally exploding. The 1990s proved to be by far the most financially innovative and adventurous decade as, in the newly popular derivative markets, bank and hedge fund traders dueled to out-math each other to eight-figure bonuses. Unbridled creativity met unsupervised risk, which ultimately resulted in untested products, unmanageable exposures, and unemployed traders. In this era a very good trader would get paid enough to buy a reasonably nice jet.

2000s

Hedge fund world goes completely insane, as every underpaid trader, underappreciated trader, or underage trader with a four-monitor setup in his parents' basement incorporates in the British Virgin Islands and immediately gets $100M of funding. Banks build out gigantic proprietary trading groups, as gambling with the firm's capital is the only thing making money anywhere in the industry. The transactions are less creative, structurally, but leverage explodes and huge risks are taken. In this era, a very good trader could get paid a billion dollars in one year.

The Crash of 2007-8

Everything falls apart. All that was uncorrelated correlates in a massive flight away from risky instruments. Lehman Brothers disappears and Bear Stearns is devoured by JP Morgan at a fire-sale price. Everybody is poor. Some guy nobody has ever heard of named John Paulson makes about $15B shorting subprime mortgages. People hear about *that*.

The Recovery & Present Day (2009-2019)

Accommodative monetary policy and a strengthening economy lead to a decade-long rally in equities that occurs against a backdrop of increasing regulation and anti-speculative fervor. Paradoxically, the two most popular investing trends are passive equity indexing and its complete opposite, aggressively deploying highly quantitative methodologies built on machine learning, artificial intelligence and data science. Political risk is at an all-time high, with the 2016 and upcoming 2020 Presidential elections serving as hard inflection points between higher tax & increasing regulation and lower tax & business-friendly regimes.

Regardless of the political and regulatory landscape, there is still a tremendous amount of risk organically present in the global financial system. This chapter will explore where it resides and how it ebbs and flows between institutions.

Chapter 2 - Know the Enemy

The Continuum of Risk

There is a continuum of risk present in the market. Firms are distributed across the continuum based on their awareness of risk, sensitivity to risk, and ability and inclination to act. At one extreme are entities that have exposures to market-based risk as a byproduct of their day-to-day business activities, called hedgers or naturals. The natural's goal is to understand exposures and modify them to suit the risk appetite of the firm, which in practice generally means reducing the total amount of risk to be in line with peers.[4] At the other end of the spectrum are speculators, entities that deploy capital according to their expertise and operational mandates to attempt to earn the maximum possible return and are, by definition, consumers of risk. Between the extremes lie market participants that are in some senses risk seeking, in others risk averse. Financial intermediaries like banks and insurance firms act as professional middlemen, charging a fee for omnivorously consuming any risks that their clients wish to lay off and trusting in their diversified business and transactional acumen to maintain booked margins. Merchants are opportunistic firms that are frequently first on the scene of any new market, entering into complex structured transactions with hedgers and attempting to squeeze out value through superior market knowledge and optimization skills. Banks take any risk for a fee as long as there is margin in the deal, while merchants seek out specific kinds of risks and previously identified profitable transaction types.

Hedgers or Naturals

A hedger is an entity that, in the normal course of its day-to-day activities, has or will accumulate an identifiable risk exposure that materially impacts the potential profitability of the core business. Hedgers frequently lie at the ends of the value chain, either consumers or raw material producers with a "natural" need to buy or sell a particular product, service, or commodity. Risk exposures can be manifest as a significant raw materials cost, an expensive input to the manufacturing process, or an end product with uncertain future value.

As an example, consider a metal refinery that buys raw material, uses an electrically intensive process to separate and melt down the ore, and then casts it into ingots for sale into the global market. The refiner's margin is dependent on the price for raw ore, the cost of the electricity, and the price the product will bring when taken to market. In times of constant prices and low volatility, the refinery may not even be aware that it is taking any risk.

However, if the price of ore, the price of electricity or the price of metal ingots were to change, the refinery could be impacted in either a positive or negative fashion. If ore prices drop, power prices drop, and metals prices rise, the owners will likely become very rich and wear themselves out patting each other on the back for being savvy businessmen. Conversely, if ore prices rise, power prices skyrocket but the metals market becomes depressed, they may very quickly be out of business. More likely, the prices will fluctuate in some sort of semi-stable day-to-day relationship punctuated by occasional periods of panic and violent dislocation.

---

[4] Though occasionally a firm will choose to adopt a risk position clearly outside of industry norms, either to differentiate itself or to achieve some hoped-for advantage.

In the past it was possible for a natural to ignore the fluctuations in the costs of doing business, so long as they were not destructive. The world has become more sophisticated, and it is becoming harder and harder for management to keep their heads safely buried in the sand. As the financial markets have become deeper, more liquid, and more transparent, it has become increasingly difficult to avoid both the logical case for proactively mitigating risk and the siren call of peer pressure to compete with (or at least match) competitors that are already playing the game. The rise of volatility and, in particular, non-traditional correlation disruptions, have highlighted the necessity for managing complex risk to shareholders, analysts, and bankers, all of whom will bring pressure to bear.

Maintaining a wide-open risk profile can also make securing financing more difficult, as hedges make cash flows more predictable and will give lenders a surer sense of what the business is worth. Analysts will compare hedge sophistication, strategy, and execution with the firm's peers and issue favorable or unfavorable research based on their conclusions. Finally, shareholders will take management's hedge/no hedge decisions into consideration when deciding to buy, sell, or hold equity, which influences every aspect of a firm's business, including the ability to borrow and the ability to attract and retain talent.

Hedgers are therefore generally incentivized to at least partially mitigate the risks surrounding their core business, or have a compelling reason for not doing so. This presents a variety of challenges, first among them their ability to recognize, measure, and generate actionable strategies around their core risks.

Assuming the firm has achieved an understanding of the organic risks in its operations, there is the question of motivation and a desire to act to modify what, up until now, has been a business that "was running just fine." Modifying risk is a proactive decision, which can be culturally challenging for some managers, firms, and indeed entire industries. Even among sophisticated players with a full understanding of the risks there is sometimes a tendency toward complacency, as bad results from an unhedged portfolio can be blamed on "poor business conditions" but hedging losses will be quite visibly management-directed mistakes. Having a "story" about the overall hedging program is key for long-run success. Conversely, some visionary managers will realize that being the first in their market segment to proactively manage risk can differentiate them from their peer group and be a genuine competitive advantage. Getting approval from senior management and the board of directors can be challenging, particularly given the actual implementation details.

Having realized that it faces certain risks and made the proactive decision to manage them, the aspiring hedger must determine what can be done to modify the exposures. Mitigating risk comes with both implicit and explicit costs. The ability to hedge is largely proportional to the degree of financial sophistication present at the firm, the size and strength of its balance sheet, the amount of cash on hand, and the overall complexity of the business. For a firm with a simple business model operating under short-term supply and delivery contracts, with a small amount of working capital and a bank line of credit for emergency use only, it may be all but impossible. The easiest method would be leveraging existing business relationships to contract for future supply or forward sales of product at mutually agreeable prices under industry-

Chapter 2 - Know the Enemy

standard legal terms. This has the advantage of being conceptually palatable and probably credit-friendly, but leaves the firm with performance risk and forces it to locate a willing counterparty to the transaction from among its peers, which can be particularly difficult for early adopters.

An alternate method would involve setting up the ability to trade directly in the financial markets, allowing the firm to modify its risks with a variety of financial instruments. This removes the counterparty performance risk, but adds additional transaction fees and forces a large amount of cash to be placed in a clearing account to be held as collateral against the hedge positions.

A third option is to seek out a financial intermediary. There are a variety of institutions that exist primarily to "help" the unsophisticated natural players learn about markets and what they can do for them. Naturals tend to give away value to get business done. Just as professional gamblers rely on a succession of well-funded amateurs at the table, markets that thrive need a steady presence of natural interest that is willing to give up value in exchange for access to the market.

Generic Hedger Structure

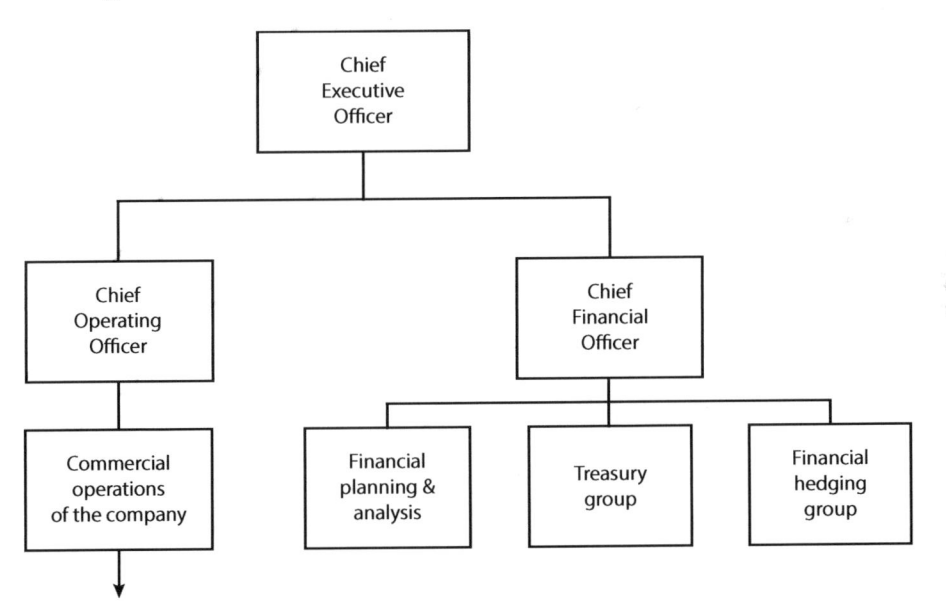

```
                      ┌──────────────────┐
                      │ Chief Executive  │
                      │     Officer      │
                      └────────┬─────────┘
              ┌────────────────┴──────────────────┐
       ┌──────┴──────┐                    ┌───────┴───────┐
       │    Chief    │                    │     Chief     │
       │  Operating  │                    │   Financial   │
       │   Officer   │                    │    Officer    │
       └──────┬──────┘                    └───────┬───────┘
              │                    ┌──────────────┼──────────────┐
       ┌──────┴──────┐      ┌──────┴─────┐ ┌──────┴──────┐ ┌─────┴──────┐
       │ Commercial  │      │  Financial │ │  Treasury   │ │ Financial  │
       │ operations  │      │ planning & │ │   group     │ │  hedging   │
       │of the company│     │  analysis  │ │             │ │   group    │
       └─────────────┘      └────────────┘ └─────────────┘ └────────────┘
```

Figure 2.1   Generic organizational structure of a hedger.

Organization Description
Unlike a bank or hedge fund, a natural is in the market because it feels it has to be, not because it wants to be. Naturals do not want to be seen as gamblers and will generally avoid even the slightest perception of speculative activity, frequently to the extent of refusing to refer to the

market-facing individuals as "traders," preferring the less risky-sounding "hedgers," "risk managers," or "portfolio managers." There are typically multiple layers of management at the firm, who may or may not choose to participate in the decision-making process at any point, but who will require constant updates, status reports, and after-the-fact forensic analysis.

Hedging Programs

Hedgers start with an organic exposure that they seek to transform, either by partially or wholly mitigating it or modifying it into a position designed to profit from anticipated market fluctuations. When seeking to mitigate risk, it is generally a good idea to have an idea of what constitutes risk, how much of it there is, and how much should be mitigated away or kept.

The natural's choice of risk-measurement techniques and its relative sophistication are directly related to the complexity of the underlying business, and the number, observability, and measurability of primary risk factors. The degree to which a hedger has limits that govern its trading is proportional to the degree that the firm has any sort of extant risk metrics in place surrounding its core business.

Naturals will frequently adopt a structured or programmatic hedging approach, where the trader follows a pre-defined, management-approved plan and executes on a chronological schedule with given volume targets. A programmatic approach yields results that should reasonably approximate the weighted average price for the period, with some expected variability for transaction costs and trader execution skill. The much more rare discretionary hedging methodology either entirely delegates hedging responsibility to the trader or employs management-approved volume and price targets that act as standing orders to be executed if reached. Depending on the latitude given to the trader and his skill, a discretionary methodology will result in highly variable results. The primary risk is that the trajectory or price potential of the market is misjudged and hedges are sub-optimally placed or not executed at all.

The following chart compares a structured hedging program that sells 5% of the desired volume per month up to a maximum of 60% (gray line) and a discretionary program where the trader attempts to place the maximum volume at or near market peaks with a similar year-end target (black line):

Chapter 2 - Know the Enemy

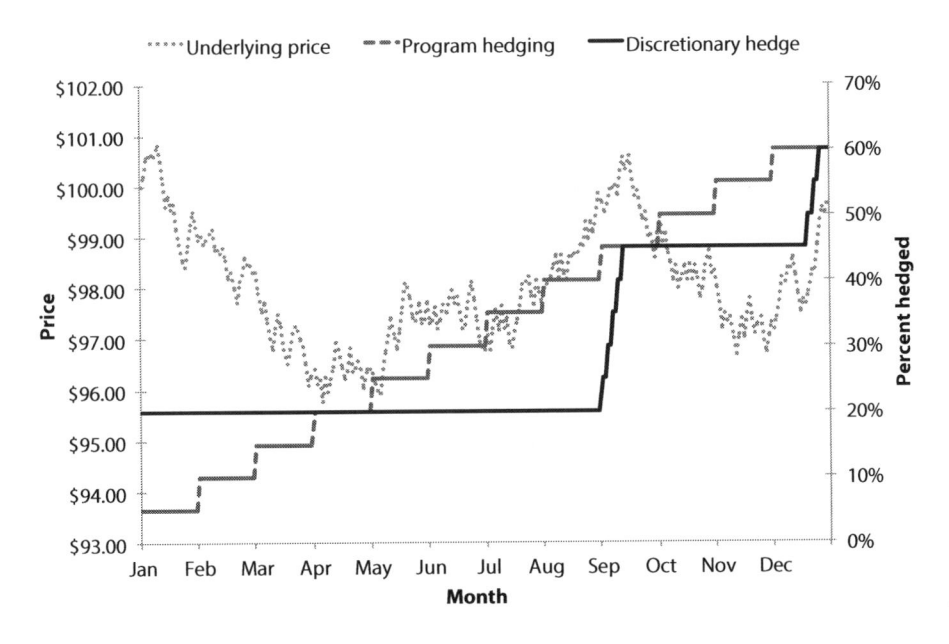

Figure 2.2 Systematic hedging program vs. discretionary hedging.

The average price of the hedges accumulated under the structured program is $98.05. The trader exercising discretion was able to time the market with good skill, selling when the market was at a local maximum and yielding an average price of $99.60, outperforming the systematic approach by $1.55 over the period.

Trading at a Natural

Trading at a natural tends to be a collaborative endeavor involving consensus building, team decisions, and a formal approval process. With multiple layers of management participating, the loci of actual decision making will likely not be the market-facing trader, and may be difficult to ascertain at times. The best-case scenario will be a delegation of some portion of the total risk inherent in the business to the trader and the latitude to transact autonomously within that defined box. The need to seek approval beyond the allocated limits invites the totality of the management structure back into the decision-making process, which can prove devastating when dealing with fast markets or rapidly evolving situations.

Financial Intermediaries

Banks are the ultimate financial intermediaries. The large so-called "bulge bracket" firms do business in every country of the world, borrow and lend in every currency, buy and sell every product, and stand ready to modify any risk at any time for any client as long as they can weigh it, measure it, and (most importantly) charge a fee for it. A well-run bank will enjoy several advantages over other market participants, most notably access to plentiful low-cost capital, a desire and an ability to warehouse risk, and a tremendous analytical and experiential resource base.

The ability to borrow cheaply is a tremendous tactical advantage in an environment where almost every transaction is financed. The cost of capital is, after all, a cost. The higher the interest rate charged on the funds necessary to hold a position, the higher the required profit margin and the more favorable the risk-reward ratio needed to justify the transaction. The entity that can borrow at the cheapest rate can be more aggressive with its pricing while still maintaining a similar (or larger) profit margin. A bank's competition for a deal may ultimately intend to borrow money from the bank to finance the proposed transaction, the added fees for which will, by definition, make those funds comparatively expensive.

Banks service customers, though a particular firm's interpretation of serving customers can range from sincere attempts to provide a value-added service to, in some cases, predatory behavior. The very best traders at banks have an ability to be both trader and salesman, and understand that they have a significant personal interest in fostering the growth of their market by providing good but lucrative service and aggressively acting to expand their client base. Perhaps the best example is Mike Milken at Drexel Burnham Lambert, who first pointed out that high-yield bonds were systematically, fundamentally cheap relative to their default potential, then created a reason to use junk bonds as low-cost financing for the wave of leveraged buyouts and corporate takeovers that characterized the 1980s. Other notable examples are Lewis Ranieri, who almost single-handedly created the market for mortgage-backed securities at Salomon Brothers, and Marc Rich, the driving force behind the development of the spot oil market.[5]

Banks do face some notable challenges, particularly in the current environment of increased oversight and regulation following the 2008-9 bailouts.[6] Complying with new regulations will have both real and implied costs in terms of time, effort, and additional procedures around disclosure, reporting, and compliance. This uncertainty has led to a substantial talent drain as

---

[5] It would be irresponsible to not point out that self-inflicted legal trouble ultimately toppled Milken from his perch atop the bond market and drove Rich to seek asylum in Switzerland under indictment for tax evasion and trading with the enemy after allegedly dealing with Iran during the hostage crisis. In recognizing their contributions to the development of their respective markets, I am not endorsing the totality of their subsequent actions.

[6] While some of the regulatory challenges have abated in the past four years, the rise of technology has had transformative effects on most large financial institutions. The bank model is shifting away from human flow traders and market makers and toward platform-based algorithmic execution systems. While there is still substantial room for human intermediation in "high-touch" and non-standard products, the current business model is to replace a floor full of expensive traders with a room full of expensive servers on a floor full of expensive quantitative strategists and programmers. The ultimate success or failure of this strategic shift will not be known for years, but regardless of where the human/machine balance lands, the markets have become significantly more quantitative and current and future traders will have to adapt to the newly required skill set. For an introduction to the basics of data science and programming, please see Appendix B.

Chapter 2 - Know the Enemy

top producers move to merchants and hedge funds for a freer operational environment and, in most cases, more lucrative compensation structures.

The banking business is almost incomprehensibly interconnected, as hundreds of large global institutions execute millions of trades daily, forming a complex web of payments that must be exchanged at the close of business. One large firm unable to settle their accounts could tip several others into default, each in turn would damage others, and so on throughout the system. This phenomenon, called Herstatt Risk[7] or cascading default risk, is one of the real underlying dangers in the financial system, and is the reason why bank regulators are so quick to step in and stabilize a failing institution. Unless the exchange of payments is secured, a sizable bank simply cannot be allowed to shut down operations.

Banks are not the only financial intermediaries, though they are by far the largest and the most prominent in the market. Insurance companies (and their shadowy brethren re-insurance companies) operate along the same principles, but with a much more specific, actuarial mindset. Actuarial firms will write a policy[8] on anything that they can contractually define and statistically model. In exchange for providing coverage, the insurer will be paid an up-front premium. The skill lies in pricing the premium high enough to cover the probability of the contract being triggered and paid out, with some margin built in for safety. The more unusual the product requested and the more complicated the modeling and valuation necessary, the larger the premium.

What insurers covet is large, un-serviced demand for products or services that either complement their current business mix, or that can be offered to a large cross-section of clients to achieve a level of risk-mitigating diversification. It is very dangerous to sell a $1B notional policy to a single entity, to which literally anything can happen. It is very good business to sell a thousand $1M policies to people scattered all over the globe. The total diversified portfolio will inevitably have some defaults or incidents where the contract is paid out, but if the product is priced correctly the premium taken in should cover those costs, and more.

---

[7] Named for a German bank that, in 1974, failed to make the standard exchange of payments to counterparties at the market close.
[8] **Writing an insurance policy is conceptually very similar to selling a derivative contract called an option, which we will explore in depth in Chapter 10.**

Financial Institution Structure

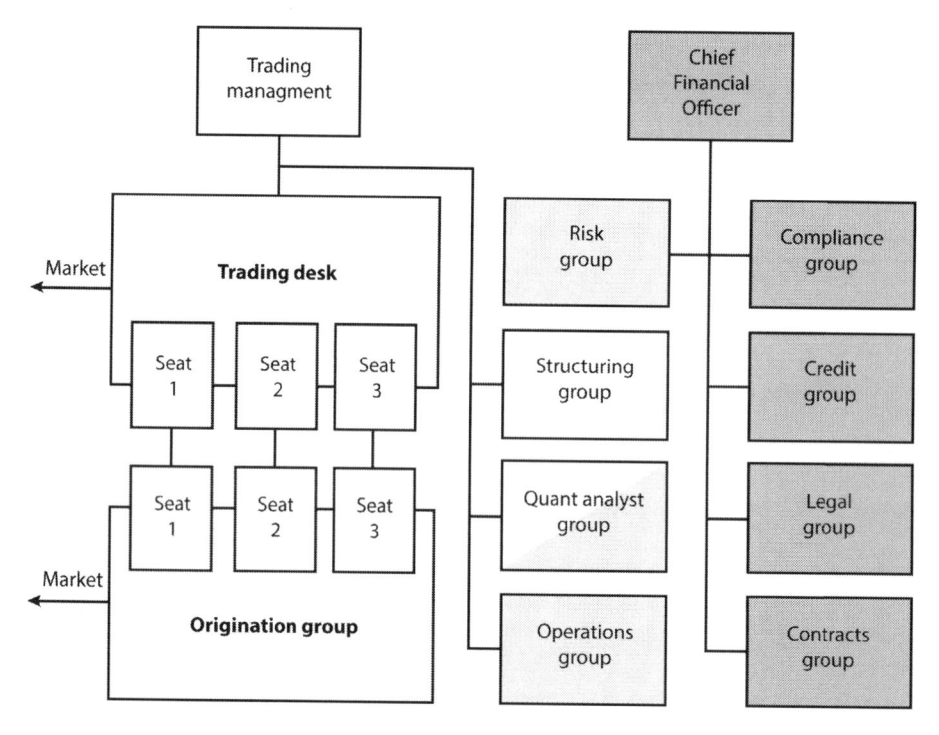

Figure 2.3   Financial institution organizational chart.

Organization Description

Banks generally have the largest and most evolved trading infrastructure of any market participant. Supporting the wide variety of products and services that their clients demand requires a degree of subject matter expertise and specialization and a resource depth impossible for a leaner merchant or hedge fund to support. The trading group will commonly be subdivided into the front office (white), middle office (light gray), and back office (dark gray).[9]

The front office is the commercial function of the firm, and will encompass the entire trading and origination desks and personnel that work closely with them, including dedicated on-desk analysts, members of the structuring group, and senior fundamental and quantitative analysts.

The middle office is engaged in the primary business of the firm, but may not have much direct contact with the trading desk and its management. Middle office functions include the risk group (though it is technically outside of the trading reporting chain), the portion of the

---

[9] The distinctions between front, middle, and back office are not set in stone, and are often interpreted differently across the industry.

analytics groups that does not report directly to trading, and the operations group that handles the scheduling and delivery of physical transactions.

The back office handles purely administrative functions, and is composed of the credit group, the legal group, the contract administrators, and the compliance group.

The support for the front-line traders and originators does not come without a significant cost. A well-supported revenue producer can be responsible for the costs of 5 to 10 support staff that are covered directly by his profit-and-loss (P&L). Taking into consideration the cost-per-unit of labor in New York, London, or Tokyo, it is not surprising that bank traders have some of the largest performance goals in the industry.

Customer-Facing/Deal-Flow Traders
A customer-facing or deal-flow trader is responsible for servicing a group of external counterparties, either directly or via an internal middleman called an originator. The process of showing pricing to external entities is called market making, and is the core responsibility of most traders at financial institutions. The product, term, and volume are determined by the customer's request for a quote, but the ultimate transaction price depends on the negotiation process, which starts with the bid to buy and/or offer to sell (also called the bid-offer spread) the trader feels comfortable showing. If a transaction is consummated, the trader will either attempt to back-fill the equivalent product from the market at a better price and realize a small profit, or take the other side of the transaction and keep the exposure, buying when the customer wants to sell and selling when the customer needs to buy. One of the primary businesses of any large bank is warehousing risk, taking the other side of a never-ending stream of customer transactions and aggregating and managing the risk inherent in the resulting position.

The Origination Process

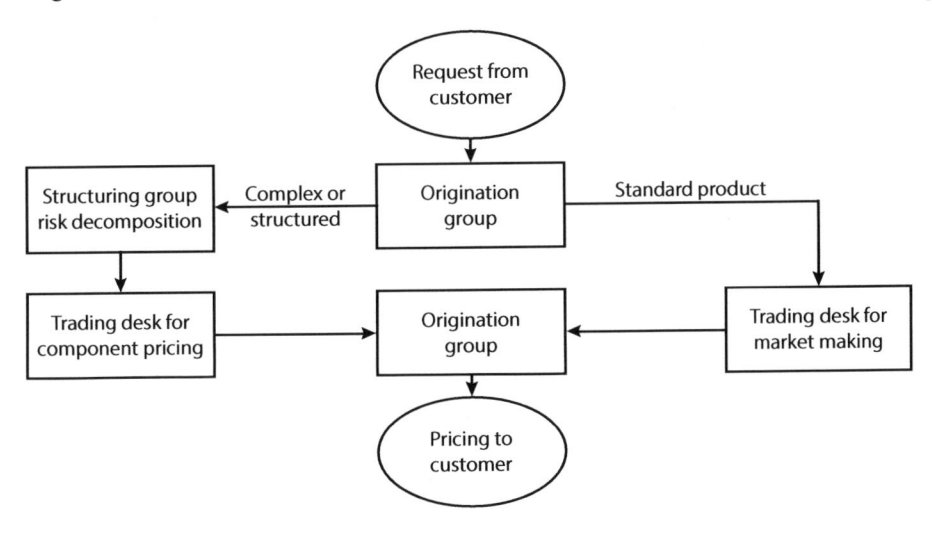

Figure 2.4   Flowchart of the origination process.

Originators speak with their clients frequently, exchanging market information, inquiring about the clients' current needs and inevitably proposing bank-provided solutions. If the client has business to do, the originator will approach the trading desk with the client's bid to buy or offer to sell. Clients can also ask for the market on a product, requesting the bank's bid to buy or offer to sell without giving away their transactional intent. If the client's interest is complicated, like a Request for Proposal (RFP) on a long-term deal or a transaction with significant optionality, it will first be routed through the structuring group for analysis and risk decomposition before being sent to the trading desk for pricing of the component products. Complex transactions will be covered in greater depth in Chapter 15.

When asked for a market by an originator, the trader will first ask the details of the transaction and the requesting client. The originator will brief the trader about the client's level of interest ("just shopping around," "looking to transact now," etc.), previous behavior ("this is the third time they've called looking for this, and they've always been looking to buy"), and any other errata that the trader might find useful ("They want to get this done this morning. I think they're talking to two other people, max. We're close but need to be more aggressive to get this done."). Just as the trader is responsible for knowing the market, the originator is expected to be aware of what is going on in the deal space at all times.

Once the trader understands the client's needs, she will consult the market and examine her current inventory. If the client's order compliments the trader's current interests (the client wants to sell and the trader is already buying, or vice versa), it is said to "fit the book," and the trader will execute the transaction and keep the position. This eliminates the need to go to the market and saves execution costs for the trader, as she is buying on the bid or selling on the offer. If the client and the trader both want to buy or sell, they are said to be going the same way in the product, the trader will have to fill the order and attempt to back-fill out of the market at a profit. It is rarely acceptable for a trader at a bank to say she has no interest, or lacks the capacity to execute the business or the sophistication to price the component risks.

Location of the Pricing, Location of the Risk
The trader or originator will need to capture a margin as compensation for facilitating the customer transaction and (possibly) warehousing the resulting risk. Some firms will have the trader add margin into the price they show the client/originator and keep it in their book to pay them for the execution risk, leaving the originator as a salaried service provider. Other firms will expect the trader to price the product with no margin (or a very small one) built in, allowing the originator to set the final price and giving them P&L responsibility. It is critically important to coordinate this activity, because if both the trader and originator add margin to the transaction it will quickly become prohibitively expensive relative to any competing offers.

Once the trade has been booked the P&L responsibility can reside with the trader, be owned by the originator, or be shared in a strategic portfolio. There is no inherently better or worse structure; each has strengths and weaknesses. The trader-owned deal P&L tends to lead to fewer, higher quality transactions (as traders will only take what they feel they can handle), more proactive hedging, and better controls on the resultant positions. Originators with transactional authority tend to close more deals and do a wider range of business, but are often less precise stewards of the resulting portfolio. Shared ownership can be productive, as long as the roles and responsibilities are clearly defined.

How Traders Make the Market
Making a market involves quoting both a bid to buy and an offer to sell. Traders make markets for two reasons: proactively to provide liquidity and facilitate transactions, or reactively in response to a specific customer or originator request. Merchants and hedge funds tend to be liquidity providers and transaction facilitators, with most of the customer-related business gravitating toward bank traders.[10]

For an extremely illiquid product, the bid-offer spread the trader quotes may be the only visible indication of value to other participants, and if sufficiently "tight" and reliable may be used as an established source for the industry's mark-to-market accounting. The willingness to both buy and sell provides liquidity, irrespective of the market maker's view of the overall trend. A market maker generates profits by buying on the bid and selling on the offer as many times as possible with as little elapsed time between transactions as possible. Market makers prosper with a large base of frequently transacting clients and a low volatility, liquid market that is not yet completely efficient.

Traders will generally take their current inventory into account when making markets. If a trader owns a large volume of a particular company's stock, for example, he might prefer to be a less aggressive buyer and a more aggressive seller. Sophisticated customers will survey the market, contacting numerous firms in the hope of finding a trader who is motivated by inclination or inventory to show a good price.

In a perfect world, a market maker would face an infinitely long line of alternate buyers and sellers, each transacting in similar sizes at the quoted bid or offer, paying away the spread in return for the convenience and liquidity provided. More commonly, the market maker is buffeted back and forth as waves of sellers and buyers alternately besiege its product, forcing rapid adjustments in price to try to balance the market. Much like an odds-maker, a dedicated market maker's goal is to find the equilibrium level where the selling and buying interests are approximately equal, minimizing short-term volatility and allowing it to get back to collecting tolls in peace and quiet.

The disaster scenarios for market makers are serious crashes or price explosions, where there can be no balance, only stampeding buyers or sellers. Market makers with access to more than one product or the latitude to trade in other instruments will become adept at hedging an unbalanced book with whatever semi-correlated products they can get their hands on in an emergency. Non-bank market making firms are not deeply capitalized, as a rule, and are certainly not in the business of maintaining large long or short speculative positions. When

---

[10] One of the many results of the evolving regulatory environment for banks has been a transition away from the traditional practice of showing two-sided markets in favor of producing a customer-requested bid or offer and the firm's estimate of the current mid-point of the market, allowing the customer to have a sense of the firm's potential margin on the transaction.

the whole world runs for the exits at the same time leaving the market maker holding the position, its losses can be violent and career ending. The less scrupulous will widen the bid-offer spread to untradeable levels, or in some cases refuse to make a price at all. Traders refer to earning money in tiny increments day in and day out only to go broke in a flash as "picking up pennies in front of a bulldozer."

In the trading pits and on exchange floors, a single individual or firm might be responsible for making markets in one security or a small handful of interrelated products, either by pride of place or official exchange designation. This made sense when the market maker was expected to physically process, analyze, and execute on the real-time order flow from within a screaming mob of traders in an open-outcry pit. With the transition to electronic trading platforms, traders can now sit in front of a half-dozen screens calmly clicking away at hundreds of bid-offer pairs without breaking a sweat. Customized software allows traders to formulaically adjust prices, linking their posted bid-offer spreads to a benchmark, moving them up or down or widening them out on autopilot as the referent price changes.

Depending on the characteristics of the product, making the market can be a more or less complex proposition. An equity specialist on the floor of the exchange will buy and sell the same shares all day long, adjusting the price to balance the order flow on his books and hopefully emerging at the end of the day with a small profit. A pit trader on a commodity exchange has a slightly more complicated job, showing different prices for different discrete delivery months which will lead to a net position composed of longs and shorts scattered across the curve, which will require constant balancing. A bank trader will be expected to transact across the curve in a variety of products in a multitude of sizes, leading to a complex aggregation of positions with directional risk and several varieties of spread risk. This misshapen risk will, at times, have a mind of its own, and its care and feeding is called running the book.

Running the Book
Running the book at a bank is less about high-volume toll taking and turnover, more about absorbing large and/or non-standard pieces of business on request. The name of the game is warehousing risk, and the result is a large, misshapen mass of positions aggregated from a stream of buys and sells of various products, sizes, and maturities. The skill lies in buying at or near the bid and selling at or near the offer to capture margin whenever possible and managing the net position to ensure that the book is set up for the overall up or down trend of the market. Running a large book is like steering a supertanker. It is impossible to make quick adjustments to the course, so it is critical for the trader to know where the current is heading and be tolerant of a certain amount of drift. A big book trader with a steady stream of flow business will never be flat and will always be attempting to reconfigure the net position to match its view of the market and its anticipated direction.

Chapter 2 - Know the Enemy

Some risk-seeking firms elevate market making to an art form, particularly those that believe they have a clear edge in their marketplace. Banks and large merchants[11] occupy the market-making role in developing over-the-counter markets with no organized specialist system to provide structure, trading pit to gather in, or screen-based exchange to monitor. If a firm can successfully price the deals, aggregate the risk, and manage the resultant position, not only will it have hopefully booked profit on each transaction, but will also have collected an incredibly valuable data set of the interests of a cross-section of market participants. Clients tend to move in herds, either through groupthink or common fundamental impulses, and a bank or merchant that understands the migratory pattern can profit tremendously.

At a bank the trader is a team player. The originator is paid to bring in deals and close business, and the trader exists to facilitate the transactions, book the margin, and maintain the inherent value in the deals. Depending on the balance of power within the firm and the relative levels of swagger, either the trader will work for the originator or vice versa, regardless of how the boxes line up on the organization chart. If working in an environment where the trader has pricing power—and therefore veto power—over the originator's deals, there will be a great deal of pressure brought to bear if the trader's conservatism impedes business.

Proprietary Traders
The rise of the hedge funds in the late 1990s did not go unnoticed by the banks. As the margins on their core businesses began to dwindle in the 1990s bank management looked on with envy at the fat profits and gigantic bonuses earned by their avant garde alumni and thought, "We can do that, too." Banks have a lot of capital, and lending it to some dull agricultural concern for a 4% return seems awfully boring compared to giving it to a hot-shot prop trader who can maybe double or triple it before lunch.

And so a change swept through the financial markets in the early 1990s, a shift away from this stable revenue source in favor of the high-risk, high reward world of proprietary trading. By the early 2000s, a number of large firms only did client business to inform the large speculative bets made by their proprietary trading group.

Stand-alone proprietary trading groups carved out within in a large institutions benefitted by being able to leverage the significant information and resource base already carrying out the core business of the firm. Bank prop traders saw deal flow and pricing, knew customer behavior, could borrow freely and cheaply, and had a near limitless research capacity at their disposal. At times, the informational advantage went from being figuratively to being literally unfair. There were potentially massive conflicts of interest for any firm with both a proprietary group and client-facing group, and great care had to be taken not to advantage the prop traders to the detriment of the firm's customer base.

Proprietary traders were the rock stars of the industry, so skilled at extracting value from their market segment that they were weaponized and turned loose to hunt down profitable

---

[11] A sub-class of the speculators will participate, but most hedge funds and asset managers are too focused on the exposures they want to entertain the possibility of any that they do not.

strategies wherever and whenever they found them. Proprietary traders gambled with their firm's capital and were generally pushed to take outsized risks, leading to profoundly large P&L impacts.

Proprietary trading has moved abruptly in and out of fashion, and has intermittently been a business that every major financial firm simply had to be in, and then shortly thereafter couldn't be seen to be involved with. Recent regulatory changes and a hard turn back toward customer business have been an extinction-level event for bank proprietary desks, leading to a wagon train of Bentleys departing Manhattan for the well-manicured suburbs of Connecticut, where the Merchants and Speculators roam.

Merchants

Where banks are the ultimate generalists, merchants are typically sophisticated niche players with medium capitalization and an appetite for risk that ranges from medium to psychotic. Banks have customers, and view their job as assuming risks that the customer needs to shed, for a fee. Merchants do not have customers; they have counterparties and trading relationships, with strong caveat emptor overtones. Banks tend to want to shear a sheep many times; merchants want to skin it right now.

Merchants earn their living by being first to a new market and by being willing to embrace risks and capitalize on ambiguous circumstances that more stolid entities would shy far, far away from. Merchants thrive on acquiring assets, usually through contractual control as opposed to an outright purchase. The name of the game is leverage, and merchants will seek to control as much productive risk capacity for as little actual cash as possible. They will frequently promise a share of the potential profits realized above and beyond a threshold level in exchange for a lower up-front acquisition cost or rental fee. The ideal time to buy control of assets is when they are "cheap," or valued at levels significantly below their future—or in exceptional cases, current potential—productive capacity. There tends to be a brief window early in the development of a market when this is possible. Merchants are expert at identifying sleepy markets that, through imminent structural or regulatory change are about to experience a seismic shift in volatility.[12] Their counterparties in the transactions, the naturals, are frequently pleased at the up-front payment for the use of an asset that they were unwilling or unable to fully monetize.

There are a number of ways to extract value from a controlled asset, many of which are tied to the physical operational characteristics. Consider a power plant, which is in the abstract nothing more than a machine used to monetize the relative price levels of electricity and the

---

[12] Asset-based transactions are also in the abstract (and frequently in actuality) forensically decomposable into smaller component instruments called options, which we will study in much greater depth in Chapter 10. One characteristic of options is that they tend to become more valuable as the general level of volatility increases in the market. All things being equal, an asset will become more valuable in a volatile market because there exists a greater chance that profitable circumstances could occur.

fuel burned to generate it. The larger the differential between the cost of fuel and the price of power, the more profitable the plant will be. The merchant can play that relative spread, buying control of the asset when it is narrow and margins are low, then waiting for an expansion of the price differential to lock in profits by hedging or re-selling the entire deal outright. If it thinks the market as a whole is heading up, it can buy the fuel and leave the power unsold until after the rally. Alternatively, if it feels the market is headed lower, it can sell the power and wait to lock in the fuel until after prices decline. In many cases, these are things that the original owner conceivably *could* do, but very likely never would do. Power plant owners, for example, generally use them to make power, and would never contemplate taking the risk of being short fuel or having no power sold against inventory. As a pure risk-taking entity, a merchant is intellectually freer to pursue profit without the burden of institutional dogma and entrenched historical precedent.

Merchant firms that survive and thrive tend to have a lean and predatory mindset. They understand their strengths and weaknesses, have a sense of how their core skill set is applicable to a nascent market, and are willing to trust that their business acumen and risk management skills will keep them alive long enough to learn the rules and find a profitable niche. At its core, the merchant business model hinges on identification of an underpriced asset or proposition that may, through a paradigm shift (by the market) or superior optimization (by the merchant), either produce significant profits, undergo a material change in value, or both. Some are geniuses at spotting cheap assets, while others are masters at squeezing every bit of juice out of a transaction.

The obvious question is, if merchants are as awful as all that, why would anyone in the market ever do business with them? The easy answer is, there is frequently no one else around, at the time. The naturals in an undeveloped market tend to have relatively similar operations and constraints, and it is difficult to unload excess risk if everyone else is also looking to be a seller of the same thing. Someone new has to step in and be a buyer of risk (or risky assets), at some price, and this is the void merchants fill. In this environment, not only will transacting with a merchant allow a firm to do something it may already want to do (sell risk), but in doing so it can differentiate itself from its peers (now less risky) and potentially derive a competitive advantage (surety of results, cash flow from merchant).

The other advantage of dealing with a larger, more sophisticated merchant is its ability to offer products and structures not currently present in the undeveloped market space. A merchant is not just attempting to do a better job with the asset within the same operational loci it has always inhabited (although they generally believe they can), but to co-optimize that asset as part of a portfolio of business across a geographic area. Merchants tend to find a good asset and then expand up or down the value chain, seeking to extract more value and ultimately control the process from end to end. Returning to the power plant example, perhaps the merchant has a large fuel portfolio, and having an outlet for supply helps diversify its total risk, or it is using the plant as a risk transformation instrument to diversify into a higher-margin end-use commodity. It may have a deal where it is short electricity to an industrial user and is seeking ways to lock in a secure source. The merchant may be an expert at fuel logistics and transportation, and realize that that competitive advantage would allow it to generate power more cheaply and earn larger relative margins. The ability to translate profitable structures from market to market and physically optimize a large portfolio of risky elements is one of the real, tangible value additions that merchants can offer their counterparties.

Merchant Structure

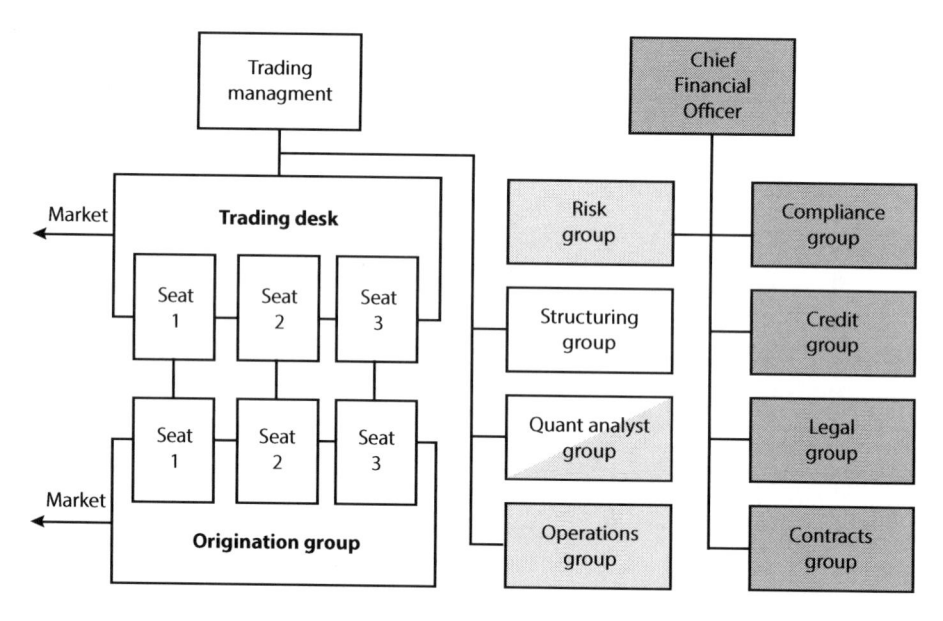

Figure 2.5   Merchant organizational chart.

The merchant organizational structure is very similar to that of a bank, but with fewer frills, less formal definition of roles, increased multiple roles to save on headcount, and much less bureaucracy.

Trading at a Merchant

Trading at a merchant is about the recognition, acquisition, and extraction of value. As an early-stage market participant, the trader must be comfortable in ambiguous circumstances and operating under partially-defined regulatory frameworks. Merchants initially take physical positions as opposed to financially settled transactions, and must possess an operational and logistical expertise. Significant incremental value is realized from optimizing the movement of material and understanding the nuances of the performance and delivery clauses of contracts. Merchants aspire to wring profits out of the entire value chain, and seek to optimize across their global portfolios, leveraging superior operational skills and relationships to facilitate transactions. Merchants live and die by their ability to deliver material in a crisis, and the word of a trader at a traditional, old-line firm is truly their bond.

Chapter 2 - Know the Enemy

Speculators

Naturals have risk that they are trying to shed, and they are willing to pay a fee for the service. Banks and merchants act as intermediaries and risk-modifying entities, seeking profit by extracting unrealized value and leveraging their superior risk management and transactional skills. At the far end of the risk spectrum lie the speculators, entities that have a pool of capital on which they must earn a return on an annual, quarterly, and sometimes monthly basis, to justify their existence and satisfy their investors.

Asset Managers – Mutual, Pension, and Retirement Funds.
Asset managers are firms charged with earning a prudent return on pools of capital formed by the aggregation of retirement funds, pensions, 401ks, and individual investment accounts. The amount of money under management can be truly staggering, with individual funds controlling in excess of $100B. Asset managers seek to get rich slowly by identifying profitable opportunities and deploying patient capital to earn a return designed to eclipse a pre-defined industry benchmark.

Asset managers will typically offer investors a variety of "products," thematically cohesive investable sub-portfolios within the fund that are grouped by performance characteristics and frequently designed to mimic a market sector or category of securities. Funds are typically required to have a prospectus, offer sheet, or other marketing document that summarizes the philosophy, the types of investments, the products, and a description of the authorized risk profile. An equity-focused manager might have portfolios that specialize in small-cap domestic equities, high-dividend utility stocks, and European growth companies. A bond fund could offer products divided into short-term low-yield notes, medium-term bills and longer-dated bonds with relatively higher interest rates. Large firms that court sophisticated investors will offer hundreds of different permutations of domestic and international stock, bond, currency, and commodity products designed to be mixed and matched to suit whatever risk tolerance and diversification that clients may desire. Nearly limitless creativity is possible, as long as the prospective investor is clearly able to identify how capital is to be deployed and the fund manager is careful to stay within the mandate and maintain a performance profile that meets or exceeds the target.

Asset managers have a tremendous fiduciary responsibility to their investors, as they are (in some cases) custodians of the net worth and/or retirement funds of millions of individual households. To do their job, and do it well, they must straddle the uncomfortable line between taking enough risk to earn a benchmark-beating return while never, ever losing money. Capital preservation is absolutely paramount, but so is outperformance. There are contradictory elements of groupthink and innovation, each of which plays an important role. Asset managers are typically serviced by the same banks, read the same research, attend same conferences, and therefore, unsurprisingly, tend to see the world the same way. Barring any unique perspective or brilliant strategy, the default asset manager behavior is to do whatever everyone else is doing. How, then, to differentiate oneself? By making small, highly targeted bets on securities that pay an anomalously high percentage returns or that offer a very favorable risk-to-reward ratio. If they fail, these small bets will shave a few non-fatal basis points off the total performance for the year, but if they succeed can possibly allow the firm to differentiate itself from its peers by a percent or two.

One of the main problems large asset managers face is finding ways to effectively implement their trading strategies, particularly when their capital under management climbs into the stratosphere. Institutional-sized money can have profoundly distorting effects on small or undeveloped markets. When in 2006-2008 the large pension funds became concerned about the potential of inflation eroding the value of their fixed income investments, they allowed themselves to be sold on the idea that purchasing commodities would be a reasonable hedge. Some of the larger, more aggressive players announced an intention to allocate between 5-10% of their total assets under management to the strategy. The only commodities that could remotely handle that amount of money are gold and oil. The total notional dollar value of the over-the-counter crude market is estimated at around $50B. As an investment thesis, it was a valid idea, but apparently no one bothered to consider what would happen when a couple of hundred billion dollars attempted to cram its way into a natural $50B market space. What actually happened is that the price of oil exploded from $60.00 in early 2007 to $145.00 by mid-2008. Ironically, in trying to hedge against inflation in their core asset class they created hyperinflation in their risk-mitigating instrument, completely destroying its utility in the process. Predictably, when the exact same firms went running for the door following the economic collapse in 2008-9, the price of crude crashed back down to $60.00.

Asset managers charge very low fees, less than a percent of funds under management, as a rule, and the ability to accumulate highly targeted exposures with minimal initial and ongoing transaction costs is a significant selling point to their customers. Asset management is a very low margin business, but nonetheless staggeringly profitable in notional terms when those small incremental fees are applied to tens or hundreds of billions of dollars. Trading at an asset manager is less about engineering a world-beating strategy and more about controlling positions, impeccable entry/exit execution, and finding liquidity when needed to preserve capital.

Hedge Funds
A hedge fund is a private investment vehicle restricted to only accepting capital from large institutions, pension funds, and wealthy "sophisticated" individual investors. While the goal was to keep the arbitrarily defined unsophisticated investors away from a product that they ostensibly could not understand, in practice it was like advertising that the coolest party in the world was going on, but that the average guy wasn't invited. Unsurprisingly, every dentist, veterinarian, and landscaper with a subscription to the Wall Street Journal immediately had to be invested in a hedge fund, leading to an explosion in the number of new, untested firms during the 1990s and 2000s to cater to the pent-up demand.

Within the hedge fund space, every possible investing and trading philosophy is represented, and the entire spectrum of risk appetites from "averse" to "foaming at the mouth" are on display. Though superficially similar, there are several key differences between hedge funds and the more commonplace asset managers.

Chapter 2 - Know the Enemy

Successful hedge funds believe that they have an edge in the market they occupy: some demonstrable skill, technology, or informational advantage over their competition. Everyone in the market says this (in some rare cases it is actually true), and it is the main reason for the secrecy of the business model. Profitable trading technology is worth far, far more than its weight in gold, as any number of billionaire fund managers can attest. Fund managers generally do not want anyone to know how they make money, and will go to elaborate lengths to protect any hard-won advantages.

Hedge funds need an edge because their primary product is outperformance, returns above and beyond those capable of being generated by plain-vanilla mutual funds, asset managers, and the market itself. Hedge fund investors will demand a return proportional to their perceived risk of being in the fund and tend to be extremely intolerant of laggards. At a hedge fund the mantra is make money today, now. There is no sense of loyalty to a particular market, strategy, or employee, and anything not immediately, continuously, and massively profitable will be instantly discarded. Near real-time benchmarking to competitor firms and comparable strategies, detailed performance metrics that grade the manager on return per unit of risk deployed, and month-to-month asset allocation decisions can, and do, lead to utterly insane levels of performance-related stress. As hedge fund traders say, pressure makes diamonds.

The obvious question is, "Why would anyone work in an environment that closely resembles a knife fight at a chess club meeting held in a meth lab?" The equally obvious answer is money. Compensation for a trader at a successful hedge fund can eclipse anything available in any other industry, with the possible exception of taking a technology startup public. It is strictly eat what you kill, but with payouts linearly linked to a trader's profits and an ability to re-invest in the firm for long-term (frequently tax-free) compounding, hedge funds are the premier wealth creation vehicle in the industry.

All of those lavish bonuses are paid for out of the fee structure that the fund manager charges investors. Hedge funds charge a management fee to cover their operating expenses and a performance incentive fee, most typically a percentage of the profits earned during the year. The fees are negotiable, and will vary from fund to fund as a function of the manager's track record, relative performance, and an ability find productive investments for incremental money. The standard deal is called a two and twenty, in which 2% of the assets in the fund are taken as a management fee and 20% of the profits as a performance incentive. A startup fund might do well to attract its first skittish capital at a rate of 1% and 10%, respectively, whereas rock star managers are purportedly able to charge management fees up to 8% and incentive fees as high as 50%.[13]

Given the secrecy, the high fees and the potential volatility, why do investors covet hedge funds? Again, the answer is money. In every market sector, there are a few fund managers that do not just outperform their benchmark, they demolish it. An investor prescient enough to

---

[13] The "2&20" fee structure has been under pressure in recent years (as have fees in general across the industry), with investors reluctant to pay up for anything other than a sterling track record of industry-beating performance.

identify a future prodigy and place funds with her early in her career can earn truly outsized returns. The superstar managers are the rising tide that lifts all boats, as money floods into the rest of the hedge fund universe. There even exists a sort of intermediary portfolio-aggregator called a fund-of-funds that collects a pool of capital and invests it with other managers, taking a small fee for passing through a theoretically diversified basket of performance. Fund-of-funds love to place tiny amounts of startup money with new firms with the understanding that, if the firm is a success, they will have the option to substantially increase the size of the investment. If they stumble on the next Peter Lynch or Warren Buffett, they will effectively re-sell that capacity for investment for a huge mark-up to people that desperately want access to the new genius.

Investors will frequently place money with narrowly focused hedge funds to gain exposure to market segments where they lack experience or are, for one reason or another, unable to participate. While some funds pride themselves on being globe-spanning masters of all markets, many firms realize that there is significant value in being focused on a particular niche and attracting money from investors seeking well-defined risk not correlated with their other exposures. Returning to the earlier example of pension funds wanting energy and metals commodity positions as an inflation hedge, most would prefer a solution that did not involve setting up a physical oil trading desk with all of the attendant headaches. Being able to market a fund as a turnkey solution to a specific investment problem is a fantastic way to increase total assets under management. The opposite is also true. Funds that wander away from their core focus are said to engage in style drift, which tends to agitate investors that expected X, but got Y or Z. Investors that end up with Z tend not to be investors for very long.

Well-Capitalized Individuals and Very Small Firms
The role of individual traders varies from market to market, largely depending on the level of sophistication required and other barriers to entry. The equity markets have far and away the highest level of individual participation, with a large percentage of the US population owning shares as long-term investments. In general, individuals approach the market as investors rather than traders. Even sophisticated, well-funded individuals face significant disadvantages relative to professional traders. A gap exists between transaction costs at the retail and institutional level, and the punitively wider bid-offer spreads and odd-lot size discounts or premiums can significantly erode any profits inherent in a strategy. Finding a unique advantage that will offset the individual's inevitable information differential to institutional traders is crucial for long-term success. The odds of success for an individual are materially increased if there is a community of other small traders present in the market. It is far easier to compete with near-peers than a trader at a bank, his analyst, risk manager, external data vendors, consultants, and giant line of low-cost credit.

Chapter 2 - Know the Enemy

Hedge Fund Structure

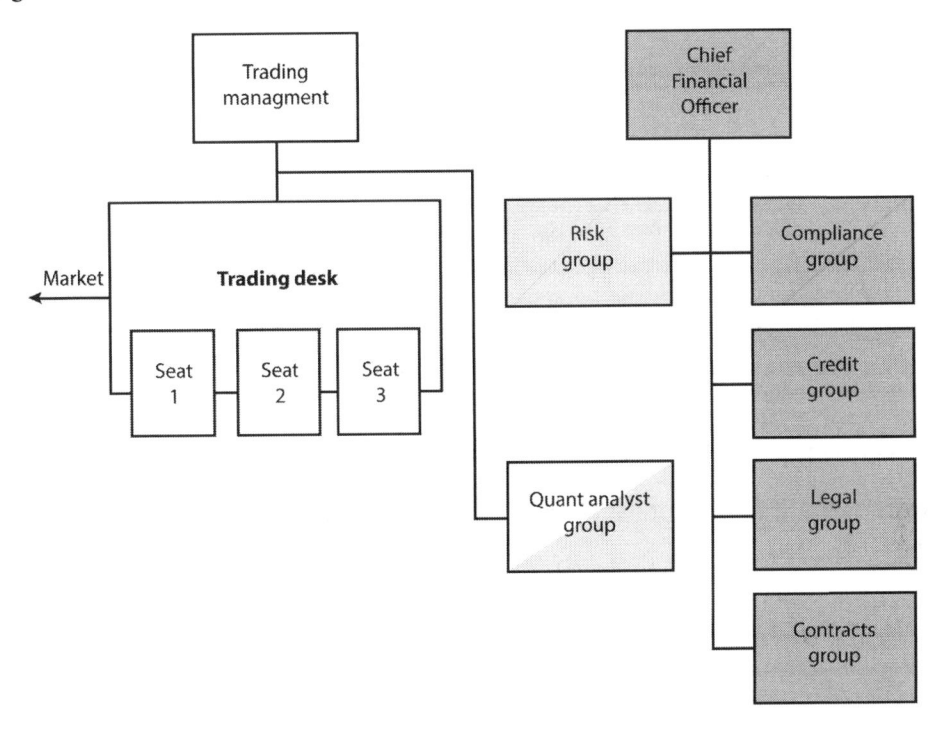

Figure 2.6   Hedge fund organizational chart

Organization Description
At a hedge fund, the whole world revolves around the producers. At a natural, the traders aren't really part of the machine that produces the firm's profits. They are like a seatbelt on a tractor. They may make things safer, but have nothing to do with plowing fields or harvesting grain. As a market maker/flow trader at a bank, the trader is part of the machine that is the business, maybe a big wheel, maybe a little cog; essential to the current operation, yes, but ultimately replaceable. A proprietary trader at a hedge fund is the business, and the entire firm exists to feed the trader capital and facilitate efficient implementation of his strategy.

Trading at a Hedge Fund
In the other entities, trading ranges from a necessary evil to an integral skill. At a hedge fund, trading is the business. Hedge fund traders need to be much more conscious of implementing their strategies within the performance needs and expectations of the fund. At a merchant or a bank, January 31st is just another day. At a hedge fund, however, it is the end of the month, and losing money at the end of the month can depress the monthly performance figures, which could cause the fund to underperform relative to its peer group, which could cause immediate withdrawals from the fund, which could change the trader's ability to execute, force closing of positions due to the need to raise cash to fund redemptions, and impact the viability of the fund going forward.

The Physics of Trading 101

Risk is not created or destroyed by the actions of individual firms, only modified and re-assigned from entity to entity within the ecosystem. Hedgers need banks, merchants, and speculators to allow them to shed exposures they do not want, or to reduce their overall level of riskiness. Banks and merchants need the fees and margins that hedgers and speculators will pay or give up to shed or assume risks. Speculators must have the ability to take on risk in order to earn a return for their investors, and require willing buyers and sellers to create transactable markets.

The Evolution of Markets

All markets have a life cycle and an evolutionary process. The market will be born out of some intersection of supply and demand, and grow through a slow accretion of interest and participation or, in some cases, a single catalyzing event. Once a critical mass of transactional activity and open interest is reached a market will tend to draw in more and more participants, particularly if there are intrinsically useful characteristics that appeal to a wider audience than just the naturals.

As each iteration of financial conquistadors traverses the new found land, the terrain is better understood, the maps are more precise, and the spoils more likely to have been discovered and claimed. There is a delicate balance between being a first or early participant and waiting for things to settle out. Early movers can get rich, or shipped back home in a box. Waiting is more prudent, but generally less lucrative. There is a developmental arc to every new market, and though the specific details are always different, the broad outline is the same:

Early – The initial activity in any new market is primarily deal based, mostly involving control of physical assets and monetizing hidden or fallow optionality. The deals tend to be fairly hairy, with much of the risk un-modeled due to a lack of information. The market may be marginally regulated, if at all, and the standard practices will be works in progress. Protecting the firm's interests will be critical. Merchants excel in this environment due to their knowledge of previous early-stage market events and a strong risk-seeking culture.

Early-Medium – The merchants need to modify their new-found risk exposures and create an over-the counter-market built around tradable forward contracts. Counterparty credit exposure rises. Options and other derivatives begin to emerge, and volatility increases as participants become more aware of, and quick to respond to, risks that were previously invisible.

Medium – The market becomes stable enough to reliably transact, but still offers attractive value propositions for origination and wide enough bid-offer spreads to entice banks and other financial players. Traded volume explodes, margins start to shrink, and early, unsophisticated players start to get squeezed to the periphery. Counterparty credit becomes a differentiator and barrier to entry, so financially cleared products emerge. This is generally seen to be the golden age of a market, in retrospect.

Chapter 2 - Know the Enemy

Medium-Late – Volatility begins to decrease, margins continue to erode, and the smart money is no longer able to earn excess returns and begins to scale back activity. Now that the market has grown large enough to entice the big global banks and hedge funds, there is not enough natural player money to sustain all of the financial players, who start to prey on each other. To compensate for the lack of margins, position sizes increase dramatically, leading to huge blow-ups and ominous black swan mutterings.

Late – The market becomes very transparent. Returns become tougher to achieve as bid-offer spreads shrink to near zero. Volatility becomes dampened. Flow-based customer business and origination deals drop off precipitously as now-sophisticated naturals are unwilling to give up edge to modify their exposure.

Defining Steps Up the Evolutionary Ladder

As any market matures there will be inflection points, paradigm shifts, and sudden reversals. They can be brought about by regulatory changes, changes in participant behavior, or innovations that remove impediments or streamline inefficient processes. For example, consider the impact of the development of a financial clearing system in a predominantly physical market.

The advent of a robust financial clearing and settlement process will lead to gains in efficiency and reductions in cost. It can also have a profound effect on the type of trading strategies that dominate a market. In the early and medium evolutionary stages of a market, counterparties are primarily dealing OTC physical products that have bilateral exposure, defined expiration points, and a deadline before which the position must be unwound prior to physical delivery, nomination, or scheduling. Failing to deliver at the agreed-upon time is considered a contractual default, potentially allowing the counterparty to take any steps necessary to keep themselves whole, including charging the defaulting party punitive fees to cover any expenses incurred in replacing the position. If it becomes widely suspected that a particular trading shop is holding a sizable position that they must exit before the close of business to fulfill their contractual obligations, things could get extremely unpleasant for them. By contrast, a firm in the same position in a market with cleared, financially settled products would always have the option to let the exposure settle against the index price if they do not like the terms the OTC market is offering. The removal of the gun-to-the-head dealing tactics of the physical markets can significantly dampen the volatility around product delivery periods.

The Entry of New Participants With Fresh Money

Elite poker players hate to play at a table full of other professionals, understanding that with their evenly matched skills no player has an advantage and the money will end up eddying aimlessly around the table. Eventually everyone will go home bored and with more or less the amount that they started with. The same can be said of a very homogenized, static market with similar, familiar entities circulating in well-established behavioral ruts. The entrance or departure of new classes of players, particularly if they are well funded, can have paradigm-shifting effects on a market.

On a macro level, the slow rotation of global money flows from asset class to asset class and country to country have huge impacts on both the absolute level of prices and the relative number of people paid to trade and analyze them. Any hot or up-and-coming market will see massive inflows of capital to the detriment of established mid- and late-stage products. From bonds (1970s-80s) to equities (1980s) to derivatives (1990s) to technology stocks (1990s-00s) to commodities (2000s) to cash (2008-2009) and riskless assets (2009-10) back to equities (2010 to present), one market will capture the collective imagination of institutional investors. Firms with an established presence in the hot market will assume a leadership position and see an influx of customer business, which will lead to investor interest, which will inevitably lead to growth and expansion. Those not participating will feel left out of the market, the profits, and all of the cool cocktail party conversation. They will panic, and try to buy their way in at any cost, raising the price of talent and, usually, the product itself. The inflationary effects of new capital are particularly intense for any ownership-based product, like equities or real estate. Contractually backed markets like derivatives can expand much more easily, which is one of the reasons why jumbo-sized institutions prefer financial products. It is significantly easier to buy a billion dollars worth of mortgage bonds than a billion dollars worth of houses.

Weapon of Choice – Commonly Traded Instruments

The developmental state of the market and the organic exposures, relative sophistication, and transactional needs of the participants will have a tremendous impact on the variety and creativity of the types of trading instruments that are developed and utilized.

Physical Products

A physical trade involves the purchase and sale of an actual tangible thing. Physical trades are very specification-intense, requiring the traders to agree on price, an exact description of the product, contracted volume, the delivery date and time, a delivery location, tolerances for variation, and a host of other contractual provisions. As a result, physical trades require high levels of support, including large numbers of operations staff skilled at scheduling, logistics and/or freight movement. Deep, local knowledge is critical, and successful physical traders tend to be dealing from an informational advantage built on hard-earned practical experience.

Most physical markets will trade both spot products intended for immediate or near immediate delivery and forward contracts for products yet to be produced to meet future supply and demand. Traders use the spot market to adjust their positions for unexpected short-term supply or demand changes. The physical spot market is typically the first thing to start trading in a new market. The forward market allows participants to take advantage of attractive prices in future periods.

Forward Contracts

A forward contract is a negotiated agreement to exchange a volume of material or a quantity of exposure at a predetermined time for an agreed-upon price. There is a degree of ad hoc flexibility in bilateral forward contracts negotiated between counterparties. Depending on the market, forward contracts can be physically delivered or financially settled. Many physically

Chapter 2 - Know the Enemy

delivered products are converted into a pure exchange of payments by counterparties that end up doing business together on both the buy and sell side of a transaction. Cancelling out physical delivery and converting it into a purely financial exchange of payments as a convenience to all parties is called "booking out" the exposure.

By being contractually linked to a time period, forward contracts allow the market to attribute different values (sometimes widely so) to products delivered in different months and years. The mid-market of the bids and offers for delivery in future periods will form the forward curve, a plot of month-to-month prices. There are two common forward curve shapes, backwardation and contango.

Backwardation vs. Contango
A forward curve where prices are decreasing month-to-month is backwardated, in backwardation, or has normal backwardation. A curve where prices are generally increasing month-to-month is said to be in contango.

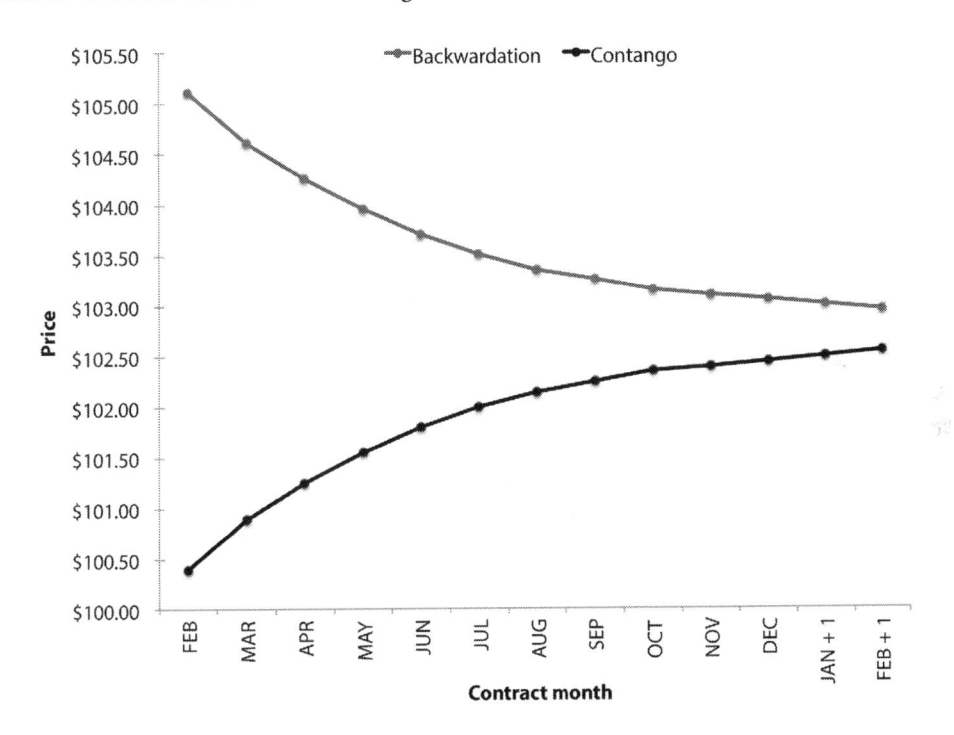

Figure 2.7 Forward curves in backwardation and contango.

A forward curve in contango is common with products that are physically stored or have some linkage to a storage- or delivery-based market, as the price in the future should reflect the current price of the product plus any costs or fees associated with maintaining the position until the delivery period. If the future prices do not allow for the cost of carry, then there is no incentive for market participants to store the product until the delivery period. Markets can transition between contango and backwardation, most commonly in times of extreme shortage or surplus. An agricultural commodity that is traditionally produced and stored that suddenly faces an extreme short-term supply disruption can see prices in the near term explode higher, tilting the curve from contango to backwardation until the crisis passes.

Some forward curves will exhibit persistent seasonality; this is a condition where, due to long-standing fundamental differences, some months are extremely highly valued and others are discounted on a relative basis.

The ability to accumulate a targeted exposure for delivery in a specific period is a tremendous risk-management tool. Forward contracts in most markets are semi-standardized, with commonly traded benchmark products sharing the space with more customized, one-off structures that are frequently of nonconforming size or unusual duration.

Forward contracts will usually involve direct exposure to the transacting counterparty, and are therefore credit and contract intensive. Trading firms will typically allocate a maximum volume of exposure to each counterparty they do business with, which will be a function of the firm's expected stability and ability to repay their debts. This fragmentation and allocation of the total transactional capability can be extremely inefficient and leads to problematic situations where a trader may be unable to modify an exposure because the only ready counterparty has a maxed-out credit limit and cannot be used for any additional business. Counterparty credit risk will be explored in greater depth in Chapter 6.

Futures Contracts
A futures contract is a highly standardized, exchanged-traded product that specifies the term, volume, product specifications, minimum tick size, maximum daily fluctuation, and the settlement and delivery procedures. While there is a degree of flexibility in many bilateral forward contracts negotiated between counterparties, a futures contract is precisely defined by the exchange.

The compensation for the diminished flexibility is greatly reduced collateral requirements due to the intermediation of a financial clearinghouse between otherwise contractually exposed counterparties. The firm's transactions will be held by a clearing broker, and a trader establishing a futures position will be required to post initial margin from the clearing account. There will be exchange-mandated minimum amounts that the clearing broker is required to hold per contract, the amount of which will be a function of the volatility of the product. The exchange minimum amounts will be modified (increased) to account for the relative creditworthiness of the trading firm. For even small, uncreditworthy firms, the initial margin required by the clearing broker will be a fraction of the notional value of the transaction, giving futures contracts tremendous inherent leverage.

As the trader's position fluctuates in value, the firm's account will show positive or negative deviations relative to the entry price. Positive changes will be credited back to the firm's account, reducing the amount of margin held by the clearing firm. Negative deviations will require the trading firm to deposit additional variance margin to support the minimum holding collateral required to maintain the position.

Futures contracts can settle into a physical product or against a financial index. Taking physical delivery, or "going off the board," is a somewhat involved process that involves exchanging full payment for the unleveraged value of the material and potentially arranging delivery, storage, and transportation.

Swaps
A swap is a negotiated contract that describes an exchange of payments between counterparties. Unlike forwards or futures, swaps are purely financial instruments with no capability for physical delivery.

The swap market was formally created in 1981[14] and is overseen by the International Swap Dealers Association, or ISDA. The initial rationale for swap transactions was to allow large, multinational entities with comparative borrowing advantages in one market but a need to borrow in another to match up with a firm with offsetting needs to their mutual economic advantage. It was necessary for a firm to establish a legal and credit relationship with an intended counterparty before consummating a trade, which led to the large, multinational banks initially becoming centralized swap dealers for the marketplace. Though it would be theoretically possible to negotiate a stand-alone contract from scratch for each transaction, the standardized ISDA transaction template and master agreement has become the industry-standard boilerplate language and greatly facilitated the explosive expansion of the swaps market. Swaps are now used to modify all categories of risk in all markets, and with the advent of financial clearing, became one of the most efficient instruments for all types of market participants.

There are two main types of swaps, fixed-for-floating and floating-for-floating.

Fixed-for-floating swaps involve paying an established, predetermined price and in return receiving a price that "floats" according to a specified index or other calculated value. The exchange is typically visualized in a flowchart-like diagram:

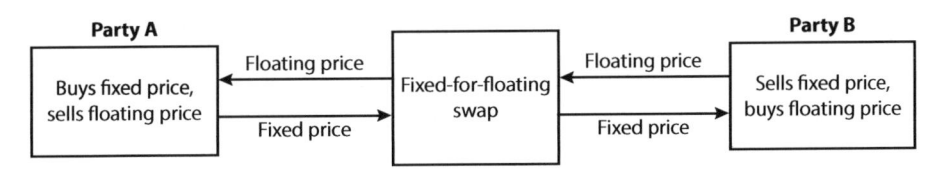

Figure 2.8   Generic fixed-for-floating swap diagram.

---

[14] While there were proto-swap transactions executed in the 1970s and before, the first transaction that bears the hallmarks of the current structure was an August 1981 currency swap between the World Bank and IBM arranged by Salomon Brothers.

For example, consider the following:

- Party A would like to bet that the settlement of a floating price index will average higher than $100.00 for the month.
- Party B would like to bet that the settlement of a floating price index will average lower than $100.00 for the month.

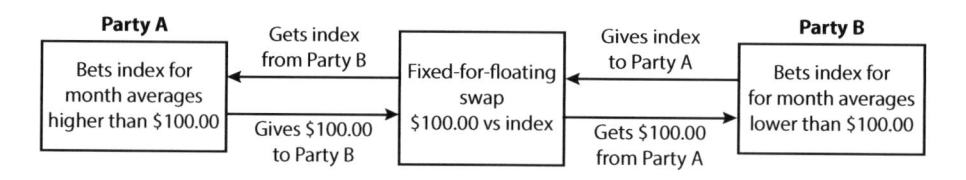

Figure 2.9   Fixed-for-floating swap diagram.

A floating-for-floating swap involves the exchange of two floating payments, each of which can float relative to a specified index, price, or other calculated value. The exchange is typically visualized:

Figure 2.10   Generic floating-for-floating swap diagram.

For example, consider the following:

- Party A would like to bet that the settlement of floating price index 1 will average higher than floating price index 2 for the month.
- Party B would like to bet that the settlement of floating price index 1 will average lower than floating price index 2 for the month.

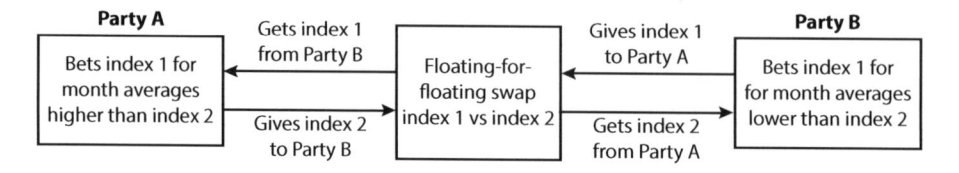

Figure 2.11   Floating-for-floating swap diagram.

A differential swap (also called a diff-swap, or contract for differences) is a contract by which counterparties exchange payments based on the disparity between two defined products, indexes, or other observed values. While similar to a floating-for-floating swap, differential swaps are frequently much more customized. Some diff-swap structures involve only the exchange of the net payment between the counterparties, making them extremely capital efficient.

Swaps immediately became an incredibly useful tool for traders to gamble on the price of a product or the value of an economic indicator without actually getting involved in the market for the underlying security. By creating a financial overlay on top of a pre-existing physical market, swaps allowed players constrained by regulatory, contractual, or credit issues to participate, bringing increased depth and liquidity. Without the operational constraint of actual physical production or consumption the so-called paper or financial markets typically grow to be several times the size of the underlying physical market. Though the underlying serves as a pricing referent for the swap, in time the tail can start to wag the dog and the swap market can become the pricing benchmark with physical deals will be priced off the more liquid, visible instrument.

The instrument of choice will vary from market to market, but the majority of swaps traded as directional instruments are simple fixed-for-floating swaps designed to financially replicate the performance characteristics of a physical product.

Instruments Evolve With Markets
The evolutionary and regulatory state of a market will greatly impact the participant's choice of instrument. The OTC energy markets in the US offer an interesting example:

- The initial product was electricity physically delivered to a specific utility interface or taken from a specific generating unit.
- The industry then developed standardized trading hubs that were used as trading posts and proxy hedging locations, which allowed the development of a "paper" forward market for transactions that, ideally, would be "traded out" prior to delivery and "booked out," resulting in no physical flow of power.
- In 1996 the NYMEX launched two electricity futures contracts for delivery in the West Coast market, followed shortly by products located in the Midwest and South at the CBOT and Minneapolis Grain Exchanges and additional NYMEX futures. The futures contracts were marginally successful, but never remotely challenged the OTC forwards in terms of liquidity and traded volume.
- Starting in the early 2000s the market transitioned to trading financial swaps that cleared against the prevailing locational marginal price of the local power pool. The swap products were massively successful due to the simultaneous growth and acceptance of financial clearing, yielding a deep, liquid, stable market.
- Impending Dodd-Frank regulation, which might require a firm to register as a swap dealer and potentially be bound by additional position limits and disclosure

requirements, prompted a migration back toward futures contracts circa 2012-13.

This makes the complete historical cycle physical to forwards to futures to swaps and then back to the futures.

End of Line
Different instruments have different performance characteristics, both during their existence and at the end of their lifespan. Some securities are evergreen and will exist in perpetuity, while others have defined expiration or delivery conditions built into their specifications. A share of common stock will exist as long as the firm that issued it remains solvent and a ton of coal will be a ton of coal forever, unless it is burned. The same share or ton can sit in inventory or change hands many times as needed. Other products like financially settled forwards, swaps, and futures contracts have a pre-defined termination date as part of their elemental makeup. It is critical for traders to understand the nuances of the expiration characteristics and the delivery process of the products they trade, even if they never intend to hold a position to its termination.

The settlement of the prompt or first contract can have pricing implications that can spread across the forward curve, and in some markets settlement volatility can account for a non-trivial percent of the total market fluctuations. Products where one counterparty has an obligation to secure and deliver supply to another at a predetermined date and time are ripe for all manner of squeezes. As a traded contract nears the end of its life, most players will close their positions and, if they desire to retain an exposure, re-establish them in a future period. The process of moving a trade from one term to another is called "rolling the position," and is very common in most established markets. As the total interest in the dying contract decreases, a small number of players with offsetting positions will wage a fierce staring match to see who will break first as the deadline approaches. Will the seller capitulate and give away value to get out, or will the buyer be forced to pay up to close their position? At the limit, in the last minutes and seconds, the stalemate often devolves into a bare-knuckle brawl, with prices lurching dramatically up or down as someone wins and someone loses, badly.

This used to be fairly normal behavior until the advent of financial contracts with pre-specified settlement criteria. Instead of meeting the opposing exposure in a metaphorical dark alley, traders could rely on the relative civility of settlement against a pre-specified index based on the average of traded prices in the closing minutes of the session.[15] This inevitably led to the stare down moving indoors to an exchange-provided ring, with desperate traders buying and selling with structured broker intermediation. Muscling the settlement into an advantageous price level became so commonplace that it got its own name, "banging the close." A spate of allegations of market manipulation, lawsuits, and convictions have led exchanges to attempt to ensure smoother, more reasonable trading activity around contract expiry and a host of traders to roll their positions even earlier in the month to avoid any perception of last-minute predatory misconduct and the potential for extreme P&L fluctuations.

---

[15] The exact mechanics of which would be spelled out in detail in the exchange and product rules.

Chapter 2 - Know the Enemy

Physical Settlement & Delivery

Futures contracts can be physically or financially settled. A financially settled futures contract will expire in an exchange of payments relative to the last posted price for the product. With a physically settled futures contract some percentage of the physical market for corn, cattle, or pork bellies will meet the contract specifications and will be said to be deliverable against the expiration. A physical future taken to expiration will result in an actual long or short position in the product, which will have to be picked up or delivered to a predetermined facility within a predetermined timeframe.[16]

Time to Pay the Piper

Post-expiry, the trader must actually exchange payments in the case of a financially settled contract or take or make physical delivery. In either case, the formerly margined instrument must be settled up at full price, which can be a huge potential problem for a thinly capitalized market participant that cannot suddenly come up with something like 5-10x the amount of cash that was needed to hold the financial position.

Options

Options are derivative contracts that grant the purchaser the right but not the obligation to buy or sell a particular product for a predetermined price at or before a specified point in time. The seller has an obligation to accept or deliver the product at the agreed-to price and time. To compensate the seller, the buyer pays an up-front fee called a premium. As the price of the underlying moves, the price of the option will change by a relative but not necessarily equal amount, the rate of which changes due to a variety of variables. This variable rate of response is called non-linear risk, which adds significant complexity to the valuation of options and, when understood and productively applied, exponentially increases their utility as financial engineering products.

Options are actually one of the earliest financial instruments. The first contracts are thought to have been be traded by the Greek mathematician and philosopher Thales of Miletus who was searching for ways to profit from what he felt would be a good olive crop. Thales eschewed the obvious plays of buying the ripening fruit or building the presses to convert it into oil and instead contracted with his neighbors for the right to use their presses for the coming season. He purportedly acquired controlling interest of the entire productive capacity of his region, while owning none of it. When the crop came in and Thales was the only one with the ability to process olives and deliver oil to the market, he likely became Thales of Millionaireus overnight.

---

[16] One of my greatest fears when trading futures for my own account was losing track of a position in corn or wheat, having the contract expire and go to delivery, then receiving a call from the manager of a warehouse inquiring when the trucks were coming to drop off the 15,000 lbs of feed I owed him: an inconvenient problem for an institutional trader, an unmitigated disaster for a thinly capitalized individual.

Basic Building Blocks – Calls and Puts

The basic building blocks of all option strategies are two instruments, calls and puts.

- A call grants the owner the right, but not the obligation, to buy a specified product at a predetermined time and price.
- A put grants the owner the right, but not the obligation, to sell a specified product at a predetermined time and price.

The owner of a put or a call has the choice to exercise the option or take no action and allow the contract to expire worthless. The seller has an obligation to perform, regardless of market conditions. This asymmetry of commitment is one of the key characteristics of the option market.

- The maximum amount that the buyer of an option has at risk is the dollar amount of the premium it has paid for the contract. The amount that it can gain is theoretically uncapped. The owner of the put or call is said to be long the option.
- The maximum amount that a seller of an option can make is the dollar amount of the premium it was paid for the contract. The amount it can lose is theoretically uncapped. The seller of the put or call is said to be short the option.

Both calls and puts share common terminology:

- The expiry date and expiration time on that day define the cut-off before which the owner of the option must elect to take action or forfeit his right.
- The strike price (or simply, strike) of an option is the predetermined level at which the owner buys (for a call) or sells (for a put).
- The premium is the price the trader must pay as an up-front fee to the counterparty for purchasing the option.
- The notional volume is the amount of the product the buyer of the option has the right to transact with the seller.
- The trader exercises the option by informing the counterparty of his intent to buy the product from it (for a call) or sell the product to it (for a put).
- European options may be exercised only on the expiry date at any time prior to the expiration time. American options may be exercised "early," at any time prior to the expiration time on the expiry date.

Options can be customized, highly negotiated bilateral contracts or standardized, rigidly defined exchange traded products. The level of creativity and variety present will vary heavily with the current evolutionary state of the market and the needs and interests of the participants. Options will be covered in much greater depth in Chapter 10.

Exercise and Delivery

Depending on the standards of the market and the contractual specifications of the product, the exercise of the option can trigger either physical delivery or financial settlement. Physical delivery at exercise triggers the receipt or delivery of an actual product in exchange for a contractually agreed payment. A financially settled option can, again depending on the market and product, exercise into a lump-sum cash payment for any in-the-money value or trigger the creation of a financially settled fixed-for-floating or floating-for-floating swap.[17]

Different Players Do Different Things In Different Time Periods At The Same Time
Every market will have different operational characteristics and a unique mix of players operating within the space, but there are some general tendencies common to all markets, particularly around the interests of the various players and the area of the curve they tend to focus their attentions.

Hedgers will typically place hedges opportunistically on a far-forward basis, typically 1-3 years out. They will seek to use inside-the-year liquidity to reshape the hedge positions to meet their short-term needs, and then close out any necessary transactions just prior to delivery.

Speculators will tend to focus on the near-term, inside-the-year markets to benefit from the greater liquidity while seeking to profit from the higher volatility.

Merchants and other deal-focused individuals will tend to seek to control attractive assets for extremely long periods of time, frequently 5- to 20-year terms. Merchant developers looking to construct physical infrastructure will seek off-take agreements or super-long-term hedges to bring cash flow certainty to enable them to secure financing for the project.

The banks that facilitate client business will need to be active across the entire curve to service their client's needs. This will mean warehousing some extremely illiquid, long-dated risk, which will necessitate some material fees for the service rendered.

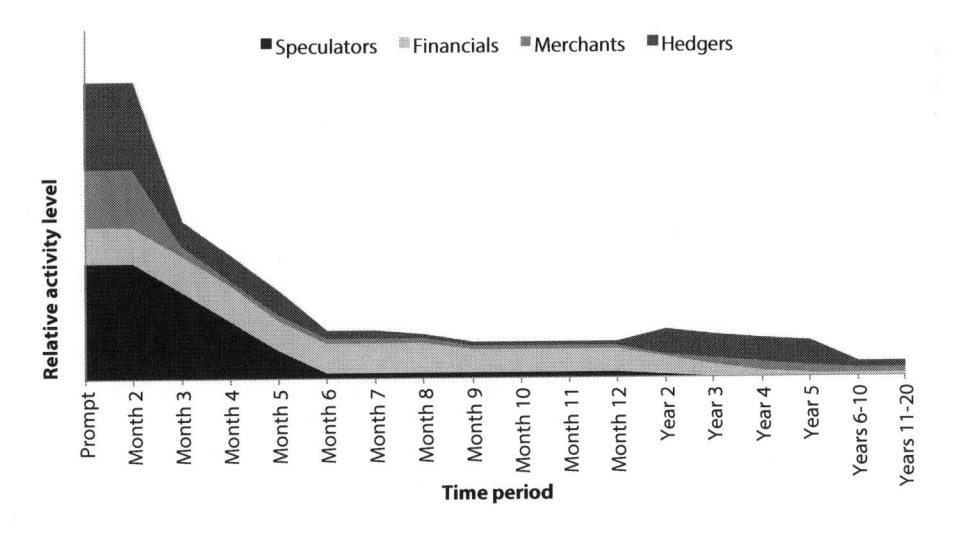

Figure 2.12 Operational timeframes of different industry participants.

---

[17] Financially settled options should be more correctly called swaptions, or options on a swap, but are frequently just called financial options.

Chapter Two Summary

There are four broad classes of market participants: naturals with organic risk that they are trying to shed, financial players that modify and warehouse risk for a fee, merchants that seek to acquire contractual control of assets, and speculators that seek risk to earn a rate of return on their capital. As a market transitions from early- to medium- to late-stage development the relative mix of participants will change, as will the business they will transact and the types of traders they will employ. The sophistication of the traded products will evolve in parallel, starting with physically-delivered contracts with direct counterparty exposure, transitioning to financially-settled and cleared options, futures and swaps, and ultimately complex custom-built derivative instruments.

Regardless of the current evolutionary state of a market, the first step in deriving an actionable perspective on the future of prices is a thorough analysis of the available fundamental information, which will be covered in detail in Chapter 3.

Review Questions

1. List the four primary types of market participants described in the continuum of risk and their main goals/objectives for transacting in the market.
2. How is a bank different from a merchant?
3. Why is the entry/exit of market participants important?
4. What are the advantages and disadvantages of expressing a view with forwards, futures, swaps and options?
5. Give an example of a real-world market currently in each evolutionary state (early, early-middle, middle, middle-late, late) and explain why.

Resources

- *Liar's Poker: Rising Through the Wreckage on Wall Street* by Michael Lewis
- *Bombardiers* by Po Bronson
- *Merchants of Grain: The Power and Profits of the Five Giant Companies at the Center of the World's Food Supply* by Dan Morgan
- *Metal Men: How Marc Rich Defrauded the Country, Evaded the Law, and Became the World's Most Sought-After Corporate Criminal* by A. Craig Copetas
- *The Vandal's Crown: How Rebel Currency Traders Overthrew The World's Central Banks* by Gregory J. Millman

Chapter 2 - Know the Enemy

Case Study: The Market for Product X

Product X is an ore-based mineral commonly found in most countries, with the largest, most concentrated deposits typically located in arid or mountainous regions. Product X is used as an input to numerous industrial processes, both in heavy manufacturing and, increasingly, high-tech applications. Product X requires labor-intensive mining and infrastructure intensive multi-stage processing to refine the raw ore into end-user-ready material for delivery. Depending on the country of origin, the significant contributors to the production cost of Product X are:

1. The cost of exploration, and leasing or purchasing productive acreage.
2. Labor costs for countries that do not utilize a technology-heavy extraction and processing model.
3. Capital costs and consumable materials for miners using a mechanized process.
4. The availability and chartering costs of bulk dry shipping vessels.

The largest producing nations are the United States, Russia, and several countries in South America. The largest consumers of Product X are the United States, Europe, and China.

Participants in the Product X Market

The physical market is composed of national mining companies, large global natural resources firms (both merchant and publically owned), processing firms and industrial consumers of all shapes and sizes. The largest production facilities are operated by national interests and multinational mining companies, with mid-tier players and smaller merchants operating higher cost facilities that generally suffer from poor economies of scale and utilize less productive acreage, and are consequently able to produce only when prices reach an elevated threshold level.

The Product X market is currently in the early-medium evolutionary state, with the majority of the transactional interest driven by the needs of hedgers and end users. Large multinational financial firms are active in the space, with a small group of US and European banks making a prescient early resource commitment and securing a significant first-mover advantage in securing counterparty confidence, gaining transactional acumen, and building up a book of business to leverage. Most bank business is based around medium- to long-term structured transactions with short to medium-term market making and liquidity providing services necessitating the build-out of dedicated trading desks. The bulk of purely speculative activity is driven by the merchant players, who are utilizing the recently developed futures contracts to both mitigate risk in their existing physical asset-based and paper swaps business and gamble on directional price movements. Large, secretive hedge funds are rumored to operate at the periphery of the space, occasionally surfacing to poach top trading talent or disclose breathtaking profits or losses only to disappear back into the ether.

The Evolutionary State of the Product X Market

Product X has both a physical market that revolves around the ability of the producers and the demands of the consumers, and a financial market that serves the needs of hedgers, speculators, and other financial intermediaries.

Most over-the-counter physical transactions are long-term, fixed-price supply contracts done at the mine mouth, production facility, or free-on-board (FOB) vessels at one of the main ports of loading or receipt terminals. The market for Product X is based on the prevailing price at the United States' Eastern Import Terminal (US EIT). The US benchmark serves as a pricing referent for a global market that features substantial volumes traded at the primary receipt or delivery point of every major consuming country. Substantial price differentials exist between the US and international markets based on regional supply and demand considerations, with a loose, semi-efficient transport arbitrage acting to keep prices in relative balance during periods of excess shipping capacity. If there are no incremental vessels available to move spot material during a particular period a section of the market can easily become islanded, creating the potential for violent price responses to unexpected local shortages and surpluses.

The financial market for Product X is based on a futures contract (ProdX) with a notional volume of 100 tons that settles based on the prevailing daily index price at the US EIT. A recently introduced, similarly sized European financial contract (EurX) has seen enthusiastic adoption by industry participants. Prior to the creation of the futures contracts, the vast majority of non-physical transactions were structured as direct medium- and long-dated financial swaps, most of which remain on the books, necessitate significant credit support, and involve material counterparty risk. The banks are very actively "helping" hedgers out of the relatively more onerous direct positions and into more efficient futures positions, for a fee. At present, there is no standardized financial contract for Product X based on the Japanese or Chinese markets, forcing hedgers and speculators to rely on negotiated bilateral contracts.

The US EIT futures market for Product X is relatively new, and was created during the recent low-volatility period. Prior fluctuations in price, though occasionally severe, were localized and invisible to the market as a whole, leading to both poor institutional memory and a generalized lack of comprehension of Product X's potential volatility characteristics under stress. The low volatility has been conducive to the development of a nascent options market, the principal demand driven by financial players and speculators seeking loss-limited and non-linear exposures. Banks are expending considerable effort "educating" hedgers and end users on the utility of option-based hedging programs, both to build out a high-margin market-making operation and source the products demanded by financial speculators.

There are a handful of recently launched electronic exchanges where market participants post bids and offers for forward physical volumes and Product X futures. Though the volumes transacted are currently small relative to the magnitude of a standard long-term supply contract, the exchanges provide a great deal of price discovery and provide a stable, efficient platform for traders to execute small incremental position optimization trades. It is anticipated that transaction volume will migrate to the exchanges at an increasing rate as players embrace the technology.

3

Fundamental Analysis

No matter how narrowly defined an operational interest, it is unlikely that even the most talented trader or analyst can come remotely close to collecting, processing, and assimilating all of the data, news, statistics, figures, and other assorted miscellany that go into understanding price movements.

Therefore, everyone in the market is operating from a subset of the total informational ecology at all times. The omnipresent factual deficit is meaningful for several reasons. First, and most obvious, traders must be aware that they are operating with less than perfect information, the degree being proportional to their resources and analytical capabilities. Second, they must be comfortable making decisions under uncertainty. Third, due to differences in access and differences in prioritization, processing, and interpretation, it is possible to arrive at any number of possible fundamental views starting from the same set of facts. A trader must be comfortable having a unique view, even to the extent that he may not agree with the people sitting around him.

Though there are firm-to-firm and market-to-market differences in approach, the basic template for developing a fundamental view on a market involves:

1. Assembling the available data about the demand for a particular product and the available supply, which can be examined on a short-, medium-, and long-term basis.
2. Conducting a detailed analysis of the equilibrium state where supply and demand intersect.
3. Exploring how the equilibrium state is influenced by new information and exogenous shocks, assessing the probable price impacts of shifts in the supply/demand balance.

As the world has become more complex, generating a serviceable fundamental analysis of even a small market space has become increasingly difficult. Information density rises as the volume and sophistication of transactions increase, adding to the analytical burden. At the same time, newly forged intermarket causality chains can disturb what, in a vacuum, would seem to be stable and persistent equilibrium states. Analysts (and their traders) must evolve to become more efficient at both processing core market data and responding to secondary and tertiary stimuli from tangentially related products.

The emphasis in the chapter is more on using analysis than on creating analysis, mostly because this book is called *Trader Construction Kit*, not *Analyst Construction Kit*. Actual market-based analysis involves a tremendous depth of subject matter expertise. A trader will tend to be more of a consumer of analysis than a producer[18], and as such the necessary skills are more analogous to those of a food critic than those of a chef. It is not essential to be able to produce the dishes, but to be familiar with the concept, ingredients, and process. The process starts with the ingredients (data) that are prepared (processing and post-processing manipulation) into a finished dish (information) for the trader's consumption. And as with all cooking, it is impossible to end up with a good dish without starting with the best possible ingredients.

It All Starts With Data

First and foremost, an analyst or trader must have access to a reliable stream of price data. The challenges inherent in obtaining and processing price data are different depending on the evolutionary state of the market.

Disorganized Observational Price Data

In the early days of a new or developing market, having data of any sort is a significant advantage. In a bilateral over-the-counter market, two counterparties will call each other to privately negotiate a transaction, frequently with little knowledge of where similar structures have previously traded. If neither feels like informing the market or the industry media about the trade (and given confidentiality restrictions, they may not be allowed to) there is no guarantee anyone else will ever hear of its consummation, let alone be privy to the transaction details.

In this environment a strong market-making firm that transacts frequently with a wide cross section of active participants will develop a comprehensive informational advantage. Where there are no standardized numbers, valuation of any proposed position or booked transaction is, by definition, proprietary. A reasonably tight two-sided market or an indication of value may be the only mark-to-market tools available for esoteric products or super-long dated strips of common instruments. In a market where numbers are only sporadically visible,

---

[18] While this is still generally true, the increase in information intensity in the financial markets is no longer exempting the trader from the analytical burden. For more information, see Appendix B – Data Science & Programming.

traders and analysts must note any unusual observations and log them for future consideration. The trader should record the price level, the bid-offer spread, and most critically, the relationship to as many other benchmark prices as possible. The spread differential between Illiquid Product A and Benchmark Instrument B will likely not remain constant over time, but can be used as a base case from which to add or subtract as necessary to take into consideration macro market movements or shifts in the underlying fundamentals. This will not yield an exact price, but rather a range of possible values within which Illiquid Product A should reside.

This can be frustrating for risk and senior management, who are used to seeing point estimates for prices derived from the mid-market of the bid-ask spread. It can also be challenging when new information, like a current high quality observation or even a verified trade forces a material shift in the on-the-books valuation of Illiquid Product A. Frequently, the price has either been drifting in that direction for some time but the movement was unobserved, or a shift in the fundamentals caused a step-function change in valuation. A database of illiquid prices for unusual products can be invaluable for traders and originators seeking to price customer-facing transactions, as end-user needs are rarely expressed at the liquid trading hubs and resident in the front of the curve.

Structured Observational Price Data

Eventually, the market will evolve to the point where a significant percentage of the total volume is transacted via third-party over-the-counter brokers. In addition to theoretically offering pre-trade anonymity and an ability to negotiate at arms length, brokers perform a valuable information aggregation and dissemination service. A brokerage will regularly canvass the traders it speaks to, asking about their interest in a variety of products. It will take the bid price of the best buyer and the offer price of the best seller and show it to each of their clients in turn. On hearing the market, the trader may transact at the quoted levels or counter with a better bid or offer, tightening the market. A broker-intermediated transaction will typically be printed to the market both as an advertisement of the broker's deal closing prowess and an informational service for clients.

The resultant stream of price quotations and deal reports give traders a sense of where value is throughout the course of the day. If a firm does not to speak with the brokerage doing the business, it will be left in the dark. Some brokerage firms publish end-of-day price sheets which, while extensively labeled "For informational use only" frequently become the de facto mark-to-market resource for the industry. It is still possible for a firm to have an informational advantage, which is typically gained by superior data collection and aggregation through more contact with brokers and other traders.

Systematic Price Data

As the market grows larger and more efficient, trading will migrate toward lower-cost organized exchanges with robust electronic trading platforms. Any firm that meets standardized collateral and contractual requirements will be able to log onto a 24-hour screen and see real-time bids, offers, and a continuous stream of verified, factual transaction history. Some platforms will also integrate basic analytical tools, position management utilities, and email and messaging functions. What was once a priceless resource becomes universally available as everyone enjoys access to the same information and the same ability to transact. The financial clearinghouses that support each exchange will require a set of robust, auditable end-of-day marks from which to calculate exposures and exchange margin payments. This data will immediately supersede all other sources (as long as sufficient coverage exists), due to the impartiality of the source and the by-definition robust and transactable nature of the bids and offers. Exchange data can be erratic if participants choose not to post numbers on a particular day for a particular product, so many markets will employ a monitor or settlement committee to vet the proposed end of day marks for completeness and reasonableness before publication. By this point it is difficult (or impossible) to have a meaningful data advantage over the competition and the material value addition lies in analysis and interpretation.

Close Data Does Not Tell The Whole Story
Most analysis is based on end-of-day price data, which is the mathematical mid-point of the best available bid-offer spread at exchange closing (or other market-standard sampling time).

- If the market for a product is quoted at $24.95 bid, $25.05 offered, then the closing mark will be $25.00, which is both a reasonable point estimate of value and an acceptable proxy for what a trader can expect to pay or receive for transacting.
- If the next day a market event leads to a great deal of uncertainty, the best numbers available at the close might be $23.00 bid, $27.00 offered, which also yields a $25.00 mid-market, though under completely different conditions.
- If on the third day a buyer emerges at the $25.00 mark level but no good sellers return, the end of day mark would be determined by a $25.00 bid and a $27.00 offer, yielding a $26.00 mid-market.
- If on the fourth day the unfulfilled buyer quits trying but a motivated seller emerges looking for their bid, then the end of day $24.00 mark would be derived from a $23.00 bid and a $25.00 offer.

Though nothing has traded and value has arguably never significantly diverged from the initial $25.00 level, it appears from the mid-market closing data that the market has rallied $1.00 then suddenly crashed down $2.00. This problem is very common in new markets and may require a tedious "cleaning" of the data set to remove obviously bad prices.

Non-Price Fundamental Data
The universe of price data is only the beginning, representing the past and present of the market. To begin to make productive inferences about the future, a firm must acquire or internally develop a vast array of non-price fundamental data. Price, correlation, and volatility are concepts common to all markets. Non-price fundamental data are highly market specific, and can vary in criticality as a function of time and prevalent conditions.

The most common non-price data are statistics, in all their various permutations. There are the pre-release estimates of key upcoming data, the aggregated industry consensus, and the actual reported value. Not all statistics are created equal. While some are rock-solid facts produced under rigorous controls, in many cases what is being reported is an approximated

Chapter 3 - Fundamental Analysis

value, a number derived from a survey methodology, or a more robust estimate subject to further revision. A statistic is said to be market moving if any material deviation from consensus expectations is capable of causing a violent, instantaneous price reaction.

Third-party information is produced by independent analysts on a retainer or subscription-fee basis. Third-party vendors are typically either niche specialists (weather forecasting firms, cargo vessel tracking services, etc.) or subject matter experts in their own right who compile a cross-section of disparate industry sources and dispense detailed forecasts on market conditions. It is definitely possible to gain an edge by out-spending the competition on research, as some high-level vendor data/analysis is prohibitively expensive for smaller players. Some large, resource-intensive firms make a practice of buying all of the available research in the market space just to know what other firms could be using to inform their decisions.

Proprietary data or analysis is the rarest and most valuable resource. It is difficult and/or expensive to achieve a material advantage from commonly available statistics and fee-based services. It is difficult to out-read or out-assimilate the market, but it is possible to out-interpret counterparties with the same set of starting data. A firm will need different, proprietary information built on a unique means of processing, analyzing, or interpreting the commonly available data.

Analysis

Observing the supply of a commodity produced and imported relative to the volume demanded for consumption and export, it is possible to characterize the market as oversupplied, balanced, or undersupplied. Over- and undersupplied are also sometimes called loose or tight. A market can be structurally over- or undersupplied, experience a limited duration change of state, or weather a short-term exogenous supply or demand shock. Structural imbalances give birth to the elongated macro trends that persist over weeks, months, or, in rare cases, years. Examples would include the demand for oil in 2006-2008, tech stocks in 1998-2001, and the desire to be out of all risk instruments in 2007-08. Limited duration changes of state can act to accelerate or retard the progress of the structurally driven market, leading to retracements against the dominant trend or accentuations of the move already in progress. Limited duration events can be planned, like routine maintenance at a nuclear generating station or unexpected, like hurricane-induced shutdowns on Gulf of Mexico drilling rigs. Super short-term or exogenous events can wreak havoc with any established market environment, leading to dramatic spikes and crashes that may or may not have longer-term consequences.

All things being equal, an oversupplied market will tend to move lower over time, an undersupplied market will tend to rally. The problematic aspect for all traders is that the market is never static. The myriad underlying factors that combine to produce the balance are constantly in flux, many in ways not easily observable or accurately quantifiable. Profound asymmetries of information can exist, and a factor that was once deemed unimportant can, given the right confluence of events, prove critical.

Common Analytical Methodologies

There are four broad categories of tools that analysts use to understand markets: balance sheets, supply curves, valuation models, and analogs. Balance sheets are used to build a basic understanding of the factors that affect the supply of a product and influence its demand, and are a great tool for framing a discussion of the factors that motivate a market. Supply curves chart the amount of a product that will be offered to the market at various price points, and are useful for understanding how incremental changes in demand translate into price responses. Valuation models can range from simple spreadsheets designed to return a point estimate from a handful of inputs to massive computational systems that solve mathematically complex multi-variable problems. An analog methodology involves searching a large number of historical periods for instances of a similar set of precursor conditions, then making inferences about the range of outcomes caused by a small handful of variable factors.

Balance Sheets

A balance sheet is a commodity-centric solution to understanding the interaction of the component sub-forces of supply and demand. Balance sheets are designed to accommodate a physically produced product with discrete period-to-period (typically month-over-month) changes in multiple fundamental variables. The analyst will typically compile historical data for a number of trailing periods (usually at least 12 months, to facilitate year-over-year comparisons) and generate going-forward estimates for as far out as is reasonably practical.

The key to utilizing a balance sheet is to understand:

1. The variables that combine to produce the balance.
2. The drivers currently influencing the balance.
3. What could potentially impact the balance.

Consider the following sample balance sheet divided by month into historical data spanning January to May (in shaded columns) and future projections for June through December:

Chapter 3 - Fundamental Analysis

	Supply											
	Jan	Feb	Mar	Apr	May	Jun	Jul	Aug	Sep	Oct	Nov	Dec
Domestic production	135	135	135	135	135	135	135	135	135	135	135	135
Large importer	35	35	35	35	35	35	35	35	35	35	35	35
Medium importer	25	25	25	25	25	25	25	25	25	25	25	25
Small importer	15	15	15	15	15	15	15	15	15	15	15	15
Total supply	210	210	210	210	210	210	210	210	210	210	210	210

	Demand											
	Jan	Feb	Mar	Apr	May	Jun	Jul	Aug	Sep	Oct	Nov	Dec
Industrial demand	95	95	95	95	95	100	110	110	110	120	120	120
Consumer demand	75	75	75	75	75	75	75	75	75	75	75	75
All other demand	35	35	35	35	35	35	35	35	35	35	35	35
Total demand	205	205	205	205	205	210	220	220	220	230	230	230
Net balance	5	5	5	5	5	0	(10)	(10)	(10)	(20)	(20)	(20)
Storage	505	510	515	520	525	525	515	505	495	475	455	435

Table 3.1 Sample balance sheet showing supply, demand, net balance, and storage.

A balance sheet will contain the following elements:

Supply
The supply section measures quantity of the product produced, generally subdivided by geographic regions or grouped into similar productive classes.

Demand
The demand section lists the consumers of the product, again generally subdivided into similar productive classes.

Net Balance
The net balance is the difference between the total quantity demanded and the total amount of supply available. This deceptively simple positive or negative figure is both the raison d'etre of the balance sheet and the primary driver of long-term macro price trends. While on any particular day unexpected events and intransigent short-term drivers will combine to introduce a stochastic element to price fluctuations, in the long term too much supply chasing too little demand will equal lower prices, and too many buyers will eventually rally prices to the point where sellers emerge to balance the market. The net balance indicates a market that is currently loose or tight, and provides a perspective on a future that may prove to be looser or tighter.

Over- and undersupplied markets are the result of over or under-producing relative to the forecasted demand. Even marginally efficient markets have a sophisticated method for bringing supply and demand back into balance: the price changes. At a high enough price production that was previously uneconomic will clear the market and be brought online. If that is insufficient to satisfy demand, new production facilities will be constructed and new sources of supply will be developed. Conversely, if lack of buying interest reduces the market price below the incremental costs of the most expensive tranche of producers, eventually they will be forced out of the market, reducing the oversupplied conditions. Price will eventually restore equilibrium to the market, and the net balance indicates the path that price will ultimately have to take.

Storage
For products that can be warehoused, the storage section will measure the quantity of material in storage, plus any additions or subtractions due to the net balance. The storage line is critically important to assessing the future direction of the market. For some products storage exists only to buffer unplanned short-term variations from the expected supply or demand. For other products, most commonly physical commodities with pronounced seasonal production or consumption characteristics, storage serves a crucial role in allowing the market to overproduce when possible in slack times to accommodate peak levels of demand. Every market will have a level of storage that is comfortable, with excess beyond that acting to dampen short-term volatility and any shortage below that level leading to immediate fears of scarcity and a corresponding increase in price and volatility.

Data Quality
The components of any balance sheet can, and do, vary in quality. At one end of the spectrum are rigorously defined, meticulously audited estimates with precisely measured actuals released on a predefined schedule by a government entity or research organization of unimpeachable integrity. At the other end are completely inaccurate best-guess estimates produced by third-party analysts that will never be fact checked or validated in any meaningful fashion. In some cases, for quantities that can be precisely measured there will be actual actuals. For variables where there will never be any concrete final number, the analyst will have to make do with increasingly refined estimates.

The level of clarity will vary with the relative sophistication and development of the production and consumption regions. Developed nations with a corporate industrial base will have the best data, as publicly traded producers, consumers, and financials will be required to disclose massive amounts of internal data to their shareholders as a normal part of their regulatory reporting. The quality will vary from country to country based on the prevailing disclosure requirements and the penalties for non-compliance. Government-backed producers and consumers tend to be more opaque, generally providing statistics of questionable quality and projections based more on politics than reality. Large merchants, particularly privately held mining and commodity concerns, will be absolutely silent on all non-transactional matters unless it suits their current needs to be temporarily forthcoming.

The Balancing Item as Panacea
Balance sheets are either cobbled together or carefully curated (depending on who you ask) from disparate sources of information, some of which will inevitably vary in quality and

timeliness. It is very common for large, complex balance sheets with a significant number of estimated parameters to simply not add up. It may be possible to have a balance sheet with rock solid storage figures, relatively good demand numbers via corporate reporting, but poor or inconsistent production figures that claims an estimated 50 tons of material produced and a relatively certain 40 tons consumed for a theoretical net balance of +10, but have only a verified 5 incremental tons appearing in the storage figures. The storage figure is beyond reproach, so the problem could be reasonably assumed to be producers' overstating production or poorly timing deliveries, consumers overconsuming or poorly timing deliveries, or some unknown factor. To bring balance analysts will often employ a balancing item or an error term to catch the unaccounted for slop. The analyst will insert a balancing item line into the balance sheet to remove 5 tons from the equation and rebalance the system.

Traders should closely scrutinize the disposition of the error line in a balance sheet, if it exists. A small term that fluctuates around a zero midpoint is generally not cause for concern, particularly for products with physical delivery characteristics or low-observable fundamentals. A balancing item that persists is bad; one that continually grows larger is extremely problematic. An increasing balancing item is a silent, tacit acknowledgement that the balance sheet is not capturing the totality of the market fundamentals, and that the analysts are missing production, demand, storage, or some combination of all three.

All Balance Sheets Are Local Balance Sheets
A global balance sheet is, by definition, an aggregation of the supply and demand characteristics of smaller, regional markets, each with their own fundamentals. In a perfect world, each component market would be considered in isolation, and firms with greater resources will tend to drill deeper into the problem, moving beyond a global balance sheet to a number of regional balance sheets to increase precision.

Balance sheets, as the name implies, are about the levels of supply and demand that create equilibrium in the market, and at what price that equilibrium can be expected to occur. The primary job of analysts is to forecast structural imbalances that will generate trends, and then understand how limited duration and exogenous events will impact that balance. The value of the balance sheet approach for a trader lies not in delivering a specific answer, but in envisioning the factors that could meaningfully alter the balance and translating the resulting change case into a potential market impact. These factors are called market drivers.

The trader must always ask: "what is the prime mover, and what can change that prime mover?" Sometimes markets are driven by a combination of small to medium factors that, in aggregate, produce a net impetus. Frequently, a single large driver moves the market. Where this is the case, every effort must be made to understand that variable, what could shift it from its current state, and the timeframe and conditions where change could occur.

Fair Warning
Some analysts and traders seek to further refine the oversupplied, balanced, or undersupplied perspective on the market by attempting to derive the fair value, or true worth of a product or instrument. This is a much, much finer analysis, usually undertaken in data-rich markets with

well-established analytical paradigms like equities and fixed income securities. Fair value calculations will almost invariably rely on analyst estimations or projections about the future in addition to hard data, making it very possible for different analysts to arrive at wildly different fair values for the same product. The fair value is an internal metric, and the market as a whole is both unaware and unconcerned when it trades dramatically to the upside or the downside of that level.

Fair value calculus typically relies on a relatively complicated model, and as with all models, the utility of the outputs is directly proportional to the quality of the inputs. The conclusions will never be better than the data.

A trader will constantly hold three values in mind: what something is worth (fair value), what are people prepared to pay for it (market value), and what does the analyst believe they will be willing to pay in the future (price forecast)

Fair Value – Supply Stacks and Demand Curves

For markets where the supply is provided and demand created in discrete, quantifiable and (in a perfect world) observable units, it is possible to create curves that plot the amount provided or required per unit of an underlying fundamental driver. It is a coarse tool, as it is difficult to precisely define the shape of the curve and establish a market's current position, but even given that limitation it can still be incredibly useful.

Supply Stack Fundamentals

A supply curve or stack is constructed by sorting the cost of each incremental unit of production and graphing the resultant points, most commonly with price on the vertical axis and volume on the horizontal axis. Consider a hypothetical market comprised of four producers, each capable of delivering different volumes of material at a range of different prices:

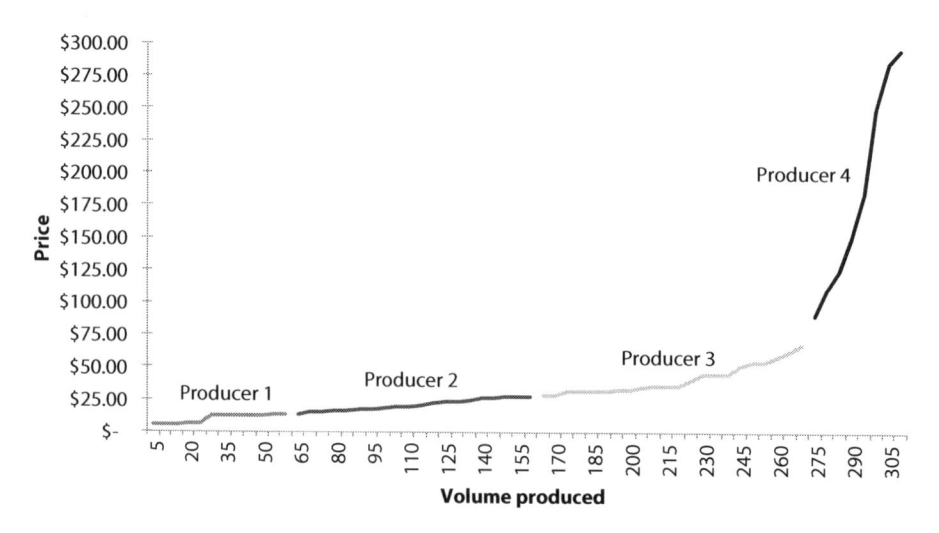

Figure 3.1   Sample supply stack with four producers.

Chapter 3 - Fundamental Analysis

The supply curve is a function of the underlying economic reality, and can describe a simple, near-linear arc or have a complex shape with multiple inflection points, flat spots, steep sections, and price gaps. Flat spots on the curve indicate loci of relative price insensitivity to incremental changes in supply or demand. Steep sections represent the exact opposite, areas where small changes in environmental variables can manifest themselves as large price fluctuations.

Of particular interest are inflection points, sharp transitions between steep and flat portions of the curve, implying an extreme price response to a localized increase or decrease in demand. Inflection points are massively interesting for traders, as legitimate opportunities for large profits with limited downsides are few and far between. Gaps frequently occur at the transition from one supplier to another (as can be seen here between Producers 3 and 4), but can also appear within a single producer's supply curve. Productive entities plotted on the curve are typically differentiated by color code and/or marker shape, which becomes critical when graphing a large number of suppliers with granular, non-continuous price points.

Supply curves change with the changing economics of production. They can shift up and down on the vertical price axis with increases or decreases in costs, move to the right or to the left on the volume axis as producers add or reduce their delivery estimates, and steepen or flatten due to changes that affect some but not all suppliers. The following chart shows the impacts of shifting costs higher, reducing production, and a case where both supply decreases and production costs increase:

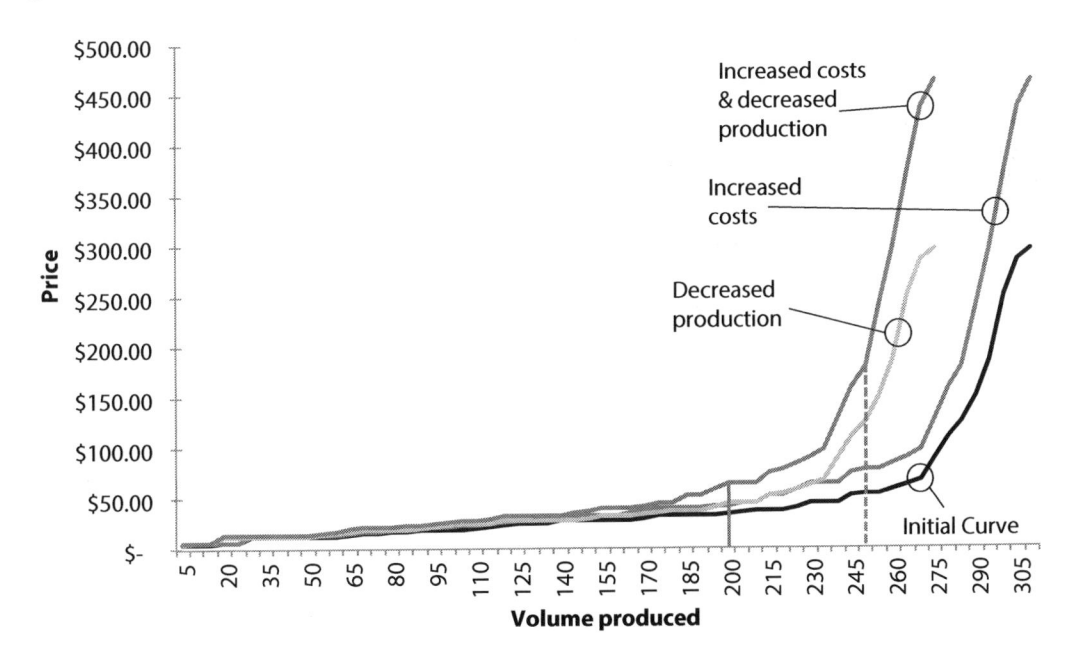

Figure 3.2   Shifts in the sample supply stack due to cost and production changes.

In a scenario where the market demands 200 units of production, the initial price would be $33.30, which would increase to $41.63 with higher costs, $45.00 with lower production, and $64.35 with both forces at work. The real difference is felt when demand increases from 200 to 250 under the same conditions. Where in the initial case this would only raise price from $33.30 to $54.00, with increased costs the price is $77.22, with lower production it skyrockets to $125.00 and with both lower production and higher costs the market reaches equilibrium at a robust $178.75.

Supply stacks and demand curves are useful for studying the potential price impacts of changes to the underlying market fundamental, which can manifest as modifications to the curvature, steepness, and location of inflection points. Supply stacks can also be used to do scenario analysis or generate comparative change cases relative to a base analysis. A trader anticipating a shift can run parallel scenarios and study the change in price per unit of demand.

The Problems With Supply Stacks
The notion of a global supply stack is something of a canard, as not all of the supply available in the world can serve the demand at a single market-clearing price without friction. There will be transportation, logistical, and contractual considerations that create friction and inefficiency. For smaller, more tightly connected markets a supply curve may yield more accurate results, for larger, more complex, more physical systems it may serve as a starting point for more detailed analysis. Firms will typically increase the precision of a supply curve (and a balance sheet) by breaking it down into regional or segmented markets and attempting to create more precise sub-curves and sub-sheets to locally balance supply and demand, then attempt to re-aggregate back up into a global solution.

Supply stacks are useful but relatively static tools, describing an arc of forecasted prices and volumes that can be shifted to examine case studies and interrogated with respect to the plausibility of the underlying assumptions. The economic forces a supply stack describes are fluid, sometimes extremely so, and any material shift in production cost or forecast volume would first change price, then through a recursive feedback process ultimately change production costs and/or forecasts of volumes to be produced. The changes in the economic realities would, in turn, impact price.

Scenario Analysis Using Analogs
Analogs are the study of past cause and effect relationships that traders and analysts study to gain insight into potential future outcomes. The method is most commonly used to examine extremely complex systems, such as weather forecasts, largely free of human interference, but also beyond precise numerical quantification. The analyst selects from a large pool of observations the instances with precursor conditions or environmental variables similar to the current or anticipated market conditions. The curated data subset is examined to see if the trajectories from the observation point forward form any coherent pattern(s). If the present conditions were matched by a sample set of ten prior data streams, of which three evolved randomly and seven converged to a similar end state, it is reasonable to entertain the possibility that the current environment could also end up in the same statistical cluster or evolve in a similar fashion. Much more interesting is when the sample set contains a sharp

bimodal distribution, forcing the trader or analyst to investigate the market force that created the division. Completely random outcomes do not provide any specific forward insight, but can be used to provide some context for the range of potential outcomes under uncertainty.

An analog approach is predicated on having a volume of historical data to examine, which in new or developing markets may not be possible. Analogs are most useful in evaluating fundamental scenarios that do not involve the randomizing effects of human decision making. An analog study is an extremely well thought out, principled way of saying, "The last time A, B, and C happened, it ended up like X, Y percent of the time (or Y out of Z times)." This will always be somewhat less intellectually satisfying than a detailed analysis of the underlying fundamentals, which is why analogs are traditionally used to buttress a pre-existing thesis or to provide additional perspective on an unresolved situation. The ability to quickly check or cross out a line of inquiry can be extremely useful, and analogs are frequently used to frame a question for further, more in-depth study. "The last time A, B, and C happened, it ended up like this X percent of the time." Why? What was driving that relationship and to what degree is that driver present in the current market?

Fair Value – Complex Valuation Models
The trader's interrogation of the facts and, most critically, the forward-looking assumptions underlying the supply/demand balance leads to a perspective on the relative tightness or looseness of the market. The over- or undersupplied condition, when combined with a supply curve, gives some sense of the potential future price of the market relative to current levels. Analogs provide historical context for the current market conditions and provide case studies that can help the trader or analyst estimate the change in a given variable or the magnitude of a potential move. Balance sheets, demand curves, and analog studies, while tremendously useful, are all relatively static tools. To examine more complex systems or to arrive at a more precise point estimate of value, analysts will deploy complex models that are capable of recursive or iterative solving on a variable set to allow supply and demand to converge on a market-clearing price.

There are, broadly speaking, two types of valuation models:

1. Heuristic pricing methodologies that structuring and origination groups deploy to price deals or evaluate opportunities. These financial engineering constructs disaggregate the risks inherent in a transaction and seek to derive a value (or a cost) for each sub-component, all of which are ultimately re-assembled to derive a total price for the structure. Such quantitative mechanics will be covered in depth in Chapter 15 – Pricing & Hedging Structured Transactions.
2. Large, extremely complex computational models that seek to replicate real environments to simulate either long-term evolutionary problems or short-term data-intensive scenarios. In the energy sector, this type of computational horsepower is often deployed to evaluate the future economic viability of a power plant at a particular point on the grid based on the probability of its production cost clearing the market across the next twenty years.

Valuation models are beasts. Anything more than a rudimentary spreadsheet-based construct will require a complex development or installation process, lengthy operator training, a period of optimization, and constant future tinkering with data inputs and operational parameters to fine tune the model outputs. Most models are third-party proprietary products that may or may not be fully transparent about their decision algorithms and may lack customization features that traders and analysts will inevitably demand. It is very common to have one or more analysts permanently tethered to a particularly critical model, adapting to its idiosyncrasies and heuristically compensating for its shortcomings.

There is an eternal build-or-buy debate with complex models. Building a proprietary model allows complete control of the product and infinite customization, but is expensive in terms of money and manpower, and may not yield better results than an off-the-shelf solution. An effective homebrew that outperforms the industry benchmark *can* yield significant competitive advantages, but a poor one that produces subpar results will be all but worthless. Buying a model will save time, initially, but it will likely be very expensive and the traders and analysts will have to adapt it to any unique considerations of their business or adapt themselves to its particular quirks.

Top-Down vs. Bottom-Up Perspective
For extremely complicated analysis it is common for the analyst to select either a top-down or bottom-up approach. The distinction between the two is somewhat akin to choosing to see the forest or the trees. A top-down view starts with an overall macro forecast of market conditions and attempts to intuit how this will filter down through myriad cause and effect linkages to the most granular level of consideration. A bottom-up approach starts with the individual building blocks and attempts to rationally fit them together and see what type of structure ultimately ensues.

Top-down analysis is experientially and paradigm based, and heavily contingent on the analyst's ability to understand the causal chains that link the macro market forces to the microelements. Bottom-up analysis is, by definition, much more computationally intensive, as it requires some methodology or algorithm for modeling the interactions of a potentially massive number of individual microelements.

An analyst attempting to determine how often and under what conditions a geographically co-located set of coal plants in the United States will run, and therefore impact prices, could approach the problem from a top-down and bottom-up approach.

The top-down approach would start with the global economy, as the general level of prosperity influences how much energy is needed, which would impact the overall level of price and impact the import/export balance to/from the United States. The United States has significant reserves, but the domestic market can be heavily influenced by demand for export, particularly of high thermal content coals for metal production. The analyst would look at the domestic price of the coal (or coals, as there are many varieties) that the plants burn, the expected forward production. She would obtain data on the current level of stockpiles and estimate how much will be demanded going forward. From that supply/demand intersection, the analyst will determine if prices are likely to decline, remain constant, or increase. She will take that price forecast and plug it into a model that simulates the basic characteristics of the plant, as well as other competing coal, gas, and oil plants. From that, she will have a sense of how the plants under study compare to their geographic peer group, and can make inferences as to how often they will clear the market based on demand scenarios.

A bottom-up approach would begin by collecting data on a unit-by-unit basis. The analyst would research the physical characteristics of the plants, their recent maintenance and outage history, their proximity to any constraints in the transmission grid that would impact their ability to produce energy, their contracted coal costs and delivery schedule, their emissions control technology and its costs, the variable operating and maintenance (O&M) costs, their start-up time, and their minimum run time. They would also compile the same information for other fuel units in proximity to the coal plants under study. They would then create a highly detailed unit-by-unit model. By feeding that model a set of market-based forward fuel prices, they will have a sense of how the plants under study compare to their geographic peer group, and can make inferences as to how often they will clear the market based on demand scenarios.

Neither top-down nor bottom-up analysis is intellectually superior, as both are approximations. A top-down analysis may feel more like an opinion and a bottom-up analysis can appear overly case-specific and feel too much like a mathematically rigorous answer. The ability of a firm to adopt either perspective is contingent on the characteristics of the particular market and problem under consideration, the skills and predilections of the analytics team, the computational horsepower available, and the preferences of the ultimate decision makers. Ideally, a trader would be presented with both analyses and allowed to evaluate and incorporate either or both, as deemed appropriate.

Price and Value – There is a Difference
There will always be a difference between what something is "worth" or what its "fair value" is and where it will be trading in the market. Products fall in and out of favor, fear premiums are added in and gradually eroded away, and irrational exuberance can persist far longer than common sense would seem to allow. The analyst's job is to determine value; the trader's job is to understand the gap (if any) between value and price.

Information
The primary job of an analyst is to transform data into information, actionable insights into the current and future state of the market. Working with fundamental data is a messy business, and it pays to be able to really root around in the numbers. Mixing data from different internal or external sources can result in potentially significant apples-to-oranges issues that need to be reconciled. The analyst must either find a way to normalize to one standard or fully understand and be able to reconcile the differentiating factors.

There are three ways that an analyst can produce better information than his peers at other firms:

- Running a different, hopefully superior, process relative to the rest of the market on a standard data set to get an internal, proprietary answer to the value question.
- Running an industry-standard process with better data or more refined assumptions about the future state of the dominant price drivers to get a different answer to the value question.
- Running a better proprietary process on a superior data set with more refined assumptions.

Experienced traders learn to aggregate external analysis to build a consensus picture of the world as the market sees it, then interrogate that consensus view with information generated by their internal resources.

Incorporating External Information – Shifts in Analytical Consensus

Markets are moved by perception, and that perception is (at least partially) shaped by the aggregated points of view of external analysts. The evolution of analytical consensus is a very tradable phenomenon. The key consideration lies in understanding the topography of the industry consensus and having a sense of how it could potentially evolve, over what time frame, and how that evolution will impact the market price. Knowing the key drivers that underpin the conventional analysis and the habitual differences in interpretation by the various forecasting entities allows the trader to have a sense of how forecasts will, and will not, change in response to new information.

The Solo Breakaway
A market-moving analyst abruptly changing their forecast away from a narrowly-clustered consensus can have a dramatic impact on the stability of the market, pressuring other players to re-evaluate their analysis and adjust their forecast or have a valid reason for standing pat.

Consensus Evolving Toward Proprietary View
To the extent that an internal analyst's view is on the ultimately correct side of the ledger and the rest of the world evolves in that direction, the trader is ahead of the information curve. All else being equal, the consensus will gradually evolve toward the proprietary view, which should result in the market moving in favor of the trader's position. This gradual shift in market sentiment frequently produces the highly structured trend channels that technical analysts get misty-eyed about. It is critical that the house view leads, however, as evolving the internal view to catch up with the prevailing consensus means the trader is lagging the information curve, and nothing good can come of that.

Capitulation of Stubborn Resistance
It is common for analysts that specialize in far-forward looking, long-lead-time forecasts to stake out an intellectual high ground and refuse to re-evaluate their position, even in the face of a steadily mounting stream of evidence to the contrary. This behavior is driven by a huge

Chapter 3 - Fundamental Analysis

reputational asymmetry: being the first to correctly identify an extreme event is worth much, much more to an analyst's career than the consequences of being wrong. Being wrong does have consequences, though, and finally, the holdout analyst dramatically recants. His analysis moves into alignment with the rest of the industry, seeking safety in the herd. Sometimes, he will even seek to atone by becoming even more extreme than the consensus.

This last-ditch conversion is quite common, as analysts tend to score themselves on their final forecast prior to the fundamentals becoming known, not the duration and magnitude of any deviations beforehand. Depending on the influence of the newly converted, this shift in view can have significant market impacts on the consensus. If the capitulator is an influential voice in the industry, it is possible that the radical shift in expectation will incite a mass exodus of wounded traders who had been clinging to that one dissenting viewpoint as justification for holding a position. As long as there exists a variety of intellectual stances, there can be a variety of potential justifications for a trade. A sudden uniformity of opinion that disagrees with her view can leave a trader little cover for a bad position.

Is That All You've Got?

Traders eternally debate whether the observed and anticipated future market fundamentals have been fully "baked in" to the current price. If all of the analyst forecasts are near the top of the theoretical boundary, where is the incremental piece of news going to come from that sustains the rally and pushes prices higher? Conversely, if the consensus is already completely and totally bearish, what must happen to drop prices lower? Markets like new information to process, and if there is nothing to inspire a repricing of potential risks it can be difficult for an in-progress move to avoid settling into an equilibrium, temporary or otherwise. A single large fundamental factor can sometimes fuel a rally or a sell-off, but in most cases it is a gradual stream of information or an evolving perception of the fundamentals that drives a trend.

When contemplating boundary conditions, care must be taken to consider a large enough probability space such that the trader or analyst does not create his own black swans by arbitrarily eliminating some of the possible as impossible or excessively improbable. Near-boundary conditions are trickier to work with, where values are extreme, but there is still possible progression toward the theoretical maximum/minimum. Near-boundary conditions with an asymmetric response for each incremental unit of deviation higher or lower are extremely dangerous. This is the case with the demand impacts of temperature on energy consumption, where during the high-load peak summer season each incremental degree hotter can be exponentially (sometimes devastatingly) more significant than a corresponding cooler change.

Who Forecasts the Forecasters?

A good in-house analyst should be able to clearly articulate the differences between his forecast and the opinions of other market participants, allowing the trader to compare and contrast the underlying intellectual arguments. A great one will be able to "forecast the forecasters," deconstructing the logic of external vendors and parsing how incremental changes in the fundamental landscape affect third-party analysis. This is massively useful information, which many external analysts freely provide to careful readers when describing the rationale for their view. Understanding the theoretical underpinnings of any market-moving forecaster's thesis and knowing under what conditions she will revise that projection is critical, particularly if her current opinion is extreme or has outsized influence on market perception. The periodicity of the underlying data relative to the frequency of analyst reports can offer opportunities for in-house analysts to get a jump on an imminent forecast revision. If Analyst A's forecast is principally based on the change in Indicator X (published daily) and he plans to issue a regular update in two weeks, then every trader in the market has 10 opportunities to observe the changes in X and ponder the implications for A's future forecast.

Game Theory and Forecasts

Analysts, particularly fee-based, third-party forecasters, are incredibly aware of the game theory aspects of agreeing with, or differentiating themselves from, the consensus. The herd is a very comforting place to be. In some fields there is a practitioner preference for being around the average, in others more aggressive firms will actively seek to distance themselves. There is some logic to this, as traders rarely remember poor calls after the fact, but an analyst can easily build a career on one well-timed market call. This asymmetry of result can lead to forecasts that seem to be more the product of wishful thinking or glory-hunting rather than sound analysis.

Spheres of Influence and Limited Resources

Third-party vendors and analytical services with a strong track record of results (and a flair for self-promotion) can become extremely influential. More commonly, however, a firm's influence will be limited to a core constituency of retained clients that have worked with and trust the forecasters and their methodology. There can be room for multiple successful vendors in large market spaces. Large firms often buy every product and service and retain any analytical firm worth talking to, as they will see significant value in being aware of all potentially market-moving information. Small- to medium-sized players frequently cannot afford access to the totality of the information ecology, and will have to pick and choose cost-effective alternatives as their budgets allow. That means that at any point in time a non-trivial portion of any market will be deriving inputs to their decision-making process from a single source (or a small handful of resources). Having a sense of who's hot and who's not, of who is being read by who, can be extremely useful. If a trader knows that a particular firm is very big with large, aggressive players and that firm calls crude oil higher, the trader should expect that money will flood into the space. If the top-rated analyst in the industry at a big bank hints that they have concerns about a high-flying technology company, two thousand brokers will immediately hit the phones to tell twenty thousand clients to start selling.

The Event Path of Future Fundamental Drivers

During the course of any given day, month, or year there will typically be a number of key events or inflection points that have the ability to materially change the value perceptions of the market participants and alter the future trajectory of prices. The common denominator is that events on the path are high-visibility, industry-wide data points that force a re-evaluation of the factors underlying the current market price.

Chapter 3 - Fundamental Analysis

For a trader holding a short-term natural gas position that is sensitive to every incremental piece of information, the event path for a typical day might look like:

5:00AM	Overnight weather models
6:00AM	Morning weather models
8:00AM	Production statistics
10:30AM	Prior week storage estimates
11:15AM	Intraday weather model #1
11:45AM	Intraday weather model #2
12:15PM	Intraday weather model #3
2:30PM	Futures market close
3:30PM	Intraday weather model #4

A trader with a longer-term, more investment-like natural gas position might need to take into consideration an event path that spans multiple weeks:

Monday	Forecast update for next month from weather vendor #1
Tuesday	No events
Wednesday	Production update from 3rd party analyst A
Thursday	10:30AM Weekly natural gas storage report
Friday	No events.
Monday	2:00PM Seasonal forecast from weather vendor #2
Tuesday	Energy Conference Day 1
Wednesday	Energy Conference Day 2
Thursday	10:30AM Weekly natural gas storage report
Friday	Medium and long-term demand report from 3rd party analyst B

The longer-term trader is concerned chiefly with events that will impact the intermediate or macro trend, where the short-term trader is dealing with micro trend phenomena. Every trader, regardless of product or market, will closely monitor the news of the day for any regulatory actions, geopolitical events or other unexpected, unscheduled factors with the potential to move markets.

Events come in all shapes and sizes. In the previous two-week example the trader must be on the alert for firm-reported statistics, model runs that will be compared to prior iterations of the same model and third-party pre-run forecasts, updates to analyst or vendor forecasts, and data items, news stories, and filtered and aggregated attendee chatter from an industry conference. The trader must be cognizant of and have a healthy respect for all of the data items, not just the ones that they have, in their judgment, predetermined to be significant. What may seem irrelevant to one trader can be interpreted as a critical, paradigm-shifting data point for another.

Not All Inflection Points Are Created Equal

The degree to which the ambiguity present in the market is resolved by an incremental event depends on the clarity of the pre-event supply and demand fundamentals and the ease of interpretation of the results. Consider the following two scenarios:

1. Waiting for an April 1st court decision that will contain a yes/no ruling on permits that will allow an idled mine to quickly ramp from zero to full production.
2. Attempting to divine when a similar facility hampered with persistent maintenance issues will return to service, estimating the ramp up in production, and attempting to guess the output level it will be able to maintain.

It is clearly easier to derive actionable information from a binary case with well-defined, immediate implications. It is rarely that straightforward. Traders must expect to expend a great deal of effort parsing out ambiguous circumstances and attempting to both clarify their own thinking and simultaneously developing a perspective on how the new information will play to a wider audience.

Understanding the key drivers arrayed along the event path is critical. Traders must be cognizant of how the events on the path are arrayed for the proposed holding period and know the probabilities of each event helping or hurting their position.

Chapter Three Summary

Fundamental information is the cornerstone on which a trader will build a view of the market. Fundamental drivers ultimately trump all other market-moving factors, and every trader must understand how they combine to create and influence the supply/demand balance. An oversupplied market will eventually lead to lower prices, and an undersupplied one should presage higher prices, ceteris paribus. Once he understands the basic supply/demand relationship, the trader must construct case studies where the key fundamental drivers are perturbed and study the potential impact on the balance. The trader must also be aware of the potential impacts of shifts in external analytical consensus and the potential for incremental inflection points on the event path to prove market moving.

The next chapter explores how it is possible to interpret the underlying market psychology via a technical analysis of fluctuations in price, adding tactical insight to the strategic perspective provided by the fundamental information.

Review Questions

1. What are the primary categories of information contained in a balance sheet and how do they combine to form the balance? Why is the balance of the market important to traders?
2. How can traders incorporate external analytical consensus into their decision making?
3. What is the event path, and why is it important?

Chapter 3 - Fundamental Analysis

4. What is the difference between price and value?
5. How does the developmental state of the market impact the observation of price data?

Resources

- *Market Wizards: Interviews with Top Traders* by Jack D. Schwager
- *The New Market Wizards: Conversations with America's Top Traders* by Jack Schwager

Case Study: Product X Fundamentals and Balance Sheet

The global economy is in the process of emerging from a shallow, multi-year recession marked less by an outright contraction of industrial activity and more by a reluctance to commit resources without clear signs of an improving future outlook. This uncertainty has caused end users of Product X to defer sourcing of material, and both large and small producers and shippers to avoid booking business and committing resources without clearer demand signals. The following chart shows the historical output and forward projections for the major Product X producing nations:

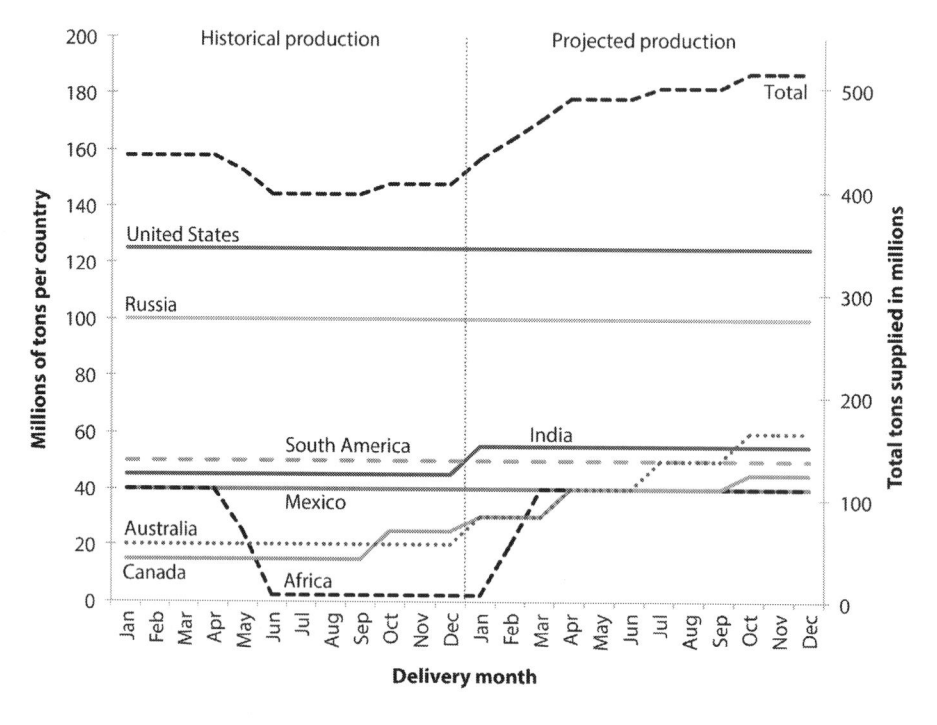

Figure 3.3   Historical and projected Product X production by country.

The United States is the largest single producer of Product X, with a steady-state 125M ton output, large, verified natural reserves held on government land, and substantial productive acreage owned by corporate participants, including large natural resources companies, global merchant entities, and small-to-medium sized speculative entities. Production figures are robust, published in a timely fashion by a centralized industry group, and cross-checked against the quarterly filings and annual reports of the publicly traded market participants. The majority of US supply is dedicated to serving domestic demand.

The Russian market is dominated by the state-controlled mining concern. The current and near-term 100M-ton production figures are reasonably accurate, but forward projections are less concrete and reserve estimates are closely guarded state secrets. A willingness to use supply

Chapter 3 - Fundamental Analysis

as a political weapon and an ability to shift deliveries from the traditional European customers to emerging Chinese demand makes understanding the current and evolving Russian dynamic critical.

Mexico is the lowest cost major producer, with reserves of high quality, relatively easily mined ore located close to processing and shipping facilities and major population centers with abundant, low-cost skilled labor. The land is held by the state, which sub-contracts all production and shipping operations to a small coterie of large North American mining concerns. Almost all of Mexico's 40M tons of production is purchased under long-term contract for delivery to the United States, with any available spot tonnage quickly snapped up by the highest bidder (which recently has been China).

India is a significant mid-cost producer of Product X, compensating for an inhospitable operating environment characterized by small, hard-to-mine deposits with a large, skilled low-cost workforce that overwhelms production and transportation challenges with brute force. It is not uncommon for a mining or processing facility to have an employee-to-ton-of-yield ratio that is a multiple to that of a more expensive, technology-driven mining country like the United States or Australia. The nature of the distributed operations with a heavier reliance on human power somewhat counterintuitively lends stability to the projected 55M tons of Indian production, as it is the opposite of the African centralized model where one large outage can significantly degrade the output from an entire country.

South America's 50M tons of low-cost production is sourced from a variety of medium to large entities, ranging from state-owned mining concerns to global commodity players and North American and European merchant companies. The majority of South American production is sold into the US and European markets.

The majority of African production is sourced from acreage owned by state-controlled entities but mined, processed, and delivered by large merchant commodity players via one enormous centralized handling facility that accounts for the majority of the tonnage shipped. The operating environment is harsh and unstable, and the reliance on one centralized processing super-facility for material introduces significant performance risk into all contracts. An April explosion at the handling facility curtailed Africa's monthly exports from 40M tons down to the current 2M tons. Though the owner/operator mining conglomerate has repeatedly assured customers that the facility will be online in Q1 and meeting contractual commitments in Q2, the lack of clarity around the cause (industrial accident, act of terror or protest) and the unwillingness of the owner-operator to provide status updates renders forward projections highly speculative, at present.

Canada is unique among producers, in that it has small deposits of relatively easy to mine Product X and vast reserves of inaccessible, hard-to-lift, and difficult-to-process ore. High labor costs and strict environmental regulations combine to make incremental Canadian production the most expensive tonnage on the market. Production from Canada is generally the last recourse for consuming nations desperate for spot tonnage or high-growth players like

China who are price insensitive when short of material. Canada expects to substantially increase exports, beginning at 30M tons and ramping to 45M by year-end.

Australia is one of the lowest cost producers in the market, with large proven reserves on relatively easy-to-access, easy-to-mine acreage in good proximity to processing facilities and export ports. Profits from selling long-term deals into the expensive China market have fuelled and funded aggressive infrastructure expansion, allowing the large global mining concerns that dominate the market to increase planned exports from 30M to 60M by year end. Australia is one of the few export nations that can realistically claim to have extra tonnage available to be brought online in the short to medium term to meet spot demand.

The historical and future projections for Product X demand can be seen in the following graph:

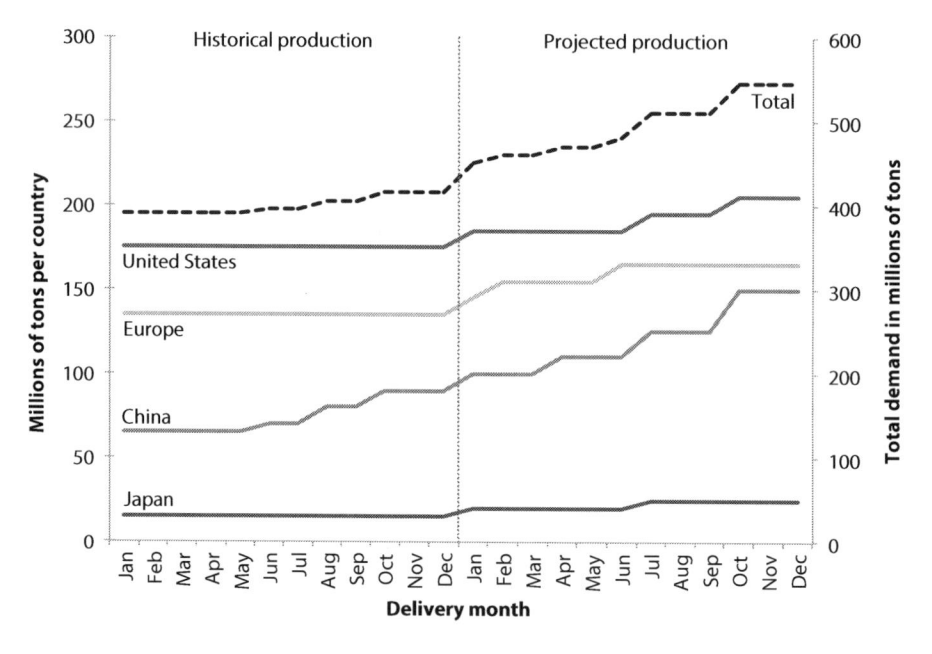

Figure 3.4   Historical and projected Product X demand by country.

The United States is the only major country that is both a significant producer and consumer of Product X, though based on current projections the growth in demand is expected to handily outstrip forecast near-zero production increases. Demand for use in technology-related applications is expected to remain constant and very strong, with future industrial demand highly sensitive to economic growth projections. Current consensus estimates for modest economic expansion have demand rising sequentially and year-over-year, peaking at 205M tons per month in Q4.

Europe is a large consumer of Product X for both technology-related applications and for use in industrial processes, with total imports expected to climb from 145M to 165M tons per

Chapter 3 - Fundamental Analysis

month during the year. The largest consuming nations are Germany (industrial and technology), Spain (industrial), England (industrial and technology) and Ireland (technology). Germany currently enjoys the strongest, most vibrant economy in Europe, and its demand is expected to increase slightly in most growth cases. Irish technology demand and English industrial demand are expected to remain flat, with the largest wildcard being Spanish industrial demand. Spain is coming out of a recession and the key to its resumption of growth will be increased industrial production. Prior uncertainty has forced customers to avoid long-term contractual obligations for supply, pushing a significant percentage of its total demand into the spot market, where it will be forced to compete against aggressive bidding from China.

China is the only major consuming nation with a centrally planned, command-driven economy and an aggressive growth agenda and unwavering mandate to achieve its goals. With an economy that is being force-fed growth and a productive engine second to none, China is expected to materially increase industrial usage of Product X, ramping imports from 100M to 150M tons per month during the year. Demand from China is heavily linked to both the domestic economy and the progress of the European nations and the United States, who are customer-states for their industrial outputs. China's centralized, command-driven economy renders it shockingly insensitive to the incremental costs of production inputs and allows it to source supply on an as-needed basis from the spot market, regardless of price. Chinese spot purchasing in Q4 caused the first global uptick in Product X prices. Estimates of future Chinese demand are heavily economy-driven and seem overly optimistic, at present, and are probably not priced into the market. This creates two-way risk, with the potential for a disappointment driven sell-off or a rally if demand comes in as expected.

Demand from Japan is almost entirely driven by the domestic production of high-margin, high-tech products, and is expected to increase by small absolute terms (though large percentage terms) in the current year. Japan has layered in medium-term contracts for supply increasing from a long-term base of 15M tons per month to 20M tons by the Q1, rising to 25M tons by the start of Q3. Japan's base contracts are sourced from Australia, with the incremental volume coming from the spot market.

The current balance of trade in the Product X market can be seen in the following diagram:

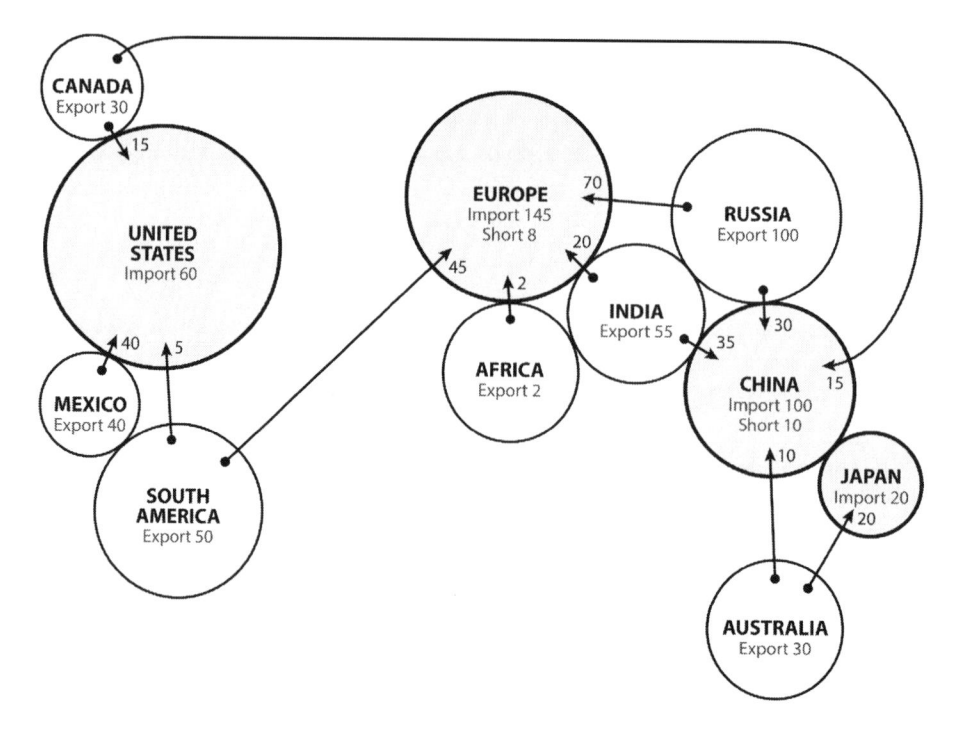

Figure 3.5   Current Product X imports and exports by country.

The Product X Balance Sheet
The Initial balance sheet for Product X for the prior year and the next twelve months:

Chapter 3 - Fundamental Analysis

	Prior year supply												Current year supply											
	Jan	Feb	Mar	Apr	May	Jun	Jul	Aug	Sep	Oct	Nov	Dec	Jan	Feb	Mar	Apr	May	Jun	Jul	Aug	Sep	Oct	Nov	Dec
United States	125	125	125	125	125	125	125	125	125	125	125	125	125	125	125	125	125	125	125	125	125	125	125	125
Russia	100	100	100	100	100	100	100	100	100	100	100	100	100	100	100	100	100	100	100	100	100	100	100	100
Mexico	40	40	40	40	40	40	40	40	40	40	40	40	40	40	40	40	40	40	40	40	40	40	40	40
India	45	45	45	45	45	45	45	45	45	45	45	45	55	55	55	55	55	55	55	55	55	55	55	55
South America	50	50	50	50	50	50	50	50	50	50	50	50	50	50	50	50	50	50	50	50	50	50	50	50
Africa	40	40	40	40	25	2	2	2	2	2	2	2	2	20	40	40	40	40	40	40	40	40	40	40
Canada	15	15	15	15	15	15	15	15	15	25	25	25	30	30	30	40	40	40	40	40	40	45	45	45
Australia	20	20	20	20	20	20	20	20	20	20	20	20	30	30	30	40	40	40	50	50	50	60	60	60
Total supply	435	435	435	435	420	397	397	397	397	407	407	407	432	450	470	490	490	490	500	500	500	515	515	515

	Prior year demand												Currrent year demand											
	Jan	Feb	Mar	Apr	May	Jun	Jul	Aug	Sep	Oct	Nov	Dec	Jan	Feb	Mar	Apr	May	Jun	Jul	Aug	Sep	Oct	Nov	Dec
United States	175	175	175	175	175	175	175	175	175	175	175	175	185	185	185	185	185	185	195	195	195	205	205	205
Europe	135	135	135	135	135	135	135	135	135	135	135	135	145	155	155	155	155	165	165	165	165	165	165	165
China	65	65	65	65	65	70	70	80	80	90	90	90	100	100	100	110	110	110	125	125	125	150	150	150
Japan	15	15	15	15	15	15	15	15	15	15	15	15	20	20	20	20	20	20	25	25	25	25	25	25
Total demand	390	390	390	390	390	395	395	405	405	415	415	415	450	460	460	470	470	480	510	510	510	545	545	545
Net balance	45	45	45	45	30	2	2	(8)	(8)	(8)	(8)	(8)	(18)	(10)	10	20	20	10	(10)	(10)	(10)	(30)	(30)	(30)
Storage	1045	1090	1135	1180	1210	1212	1214	1206	1198	1190	1182	1174	1156	1146	1156	1176	1196	1206	1196	1186	1176	1146	1116	1086

Table 3.2 Initial Product X balance sheet with prior year historical data (shaded) and current year projections.

The initial balance sheet represents the best information currently present in the market.

Net Balance

There is no balancing item for Product X (which could reasonably be expected to be present in a sheet of this complexity) because all of the figures are estimates, with no hard statistics to anchor the analysis (though some of the figures out of the United States and Europe are close). The net balance and storage figures are derived by the difference and cumulative difference between supply and demand.

Storage

Though some volume of Product X reserves exist in most producing regions, the realities of adjusting production schedules, processing requirements, and scheduling transportation mean that market-area storage plays the dominant role in buffering the inevitable fluctuations in short-term supply and demand. End users will strongly prefer to have a volume of material on the ground at their facilities at all times, which may not be reported and quantified in the balance sheet, depending on the inclination to transparency of the owner/operator. This observational challenge forces market participants to focus on interpreting the general trend of increasing or decreasing stocks rather than obsessing about the level of a particular monthly statistic, particularly when it is ultimately just an estimate.

Understanding the Product X Supply/Demand Balance Drivers

Global Risk Factors
1. The primary driver for the future price trajectory of Product X is the anticipated future growth of the global economy, particularly that of the United States, Europe, and China. Economic growth has direct impact on industrial production therefore the need for Product X as a process input for both basic and high-tech manufacturing. The current estimate is for robust, post-recessionary growth across the Product X consumers, with the US experiencing moderate year-over-year (YOY) growth (from a higher recessionary trough), Europe having much stronger sequential demand, and China anticipated to resume an extremely aggressive growth plan.
2. Based on current estimates for robust, post-recessionary growth across the Product X consuming region production is ramping up to accommodate anticipated demand in both current and future years. If economic demand slows (or fails to achieve what are, in some cases, aggressive targets), the market is in danger of becoming severely oversupplied.

The current state and future trajectory of the global economy are the largest drivers of potential bullish and bearish outcomes.

Secondary Economic Factors
1. Increased economic activity will also, all things being equal, increase labor costs, material costs, and add additional competition for ship and rail chartering (from other economically sensitive industries like energy and agriculture) to bring product to market, increasing competition for the materials crucial for production and transport of the product.
2. Cost of labor is a key factor in production. Countries with labor-intensive production are more sensitive to the cost of labor, those with more industrial processes having greater sensitivities to the price of materials and machinery. Canada is uniquely vulnerable to incremental production costs, faced with both high labor costs and the need for costly incremental production resources to bring on additional supply. This is largely why Canadian tons remain the highest-cost incremental supply.

Country Risk Factors
1. Africa – An April explosion at the main handling and loading facility knocked the majority of production off-line and, though the resident mining conglomerate has repeatedly assured customers that the facility will be on-line in Q1 and meeting contractual commitments in Q2, the lack of clarity around the cause (industrial accident, act of terror/protest, etc.) and the unwillingness of the owner-operator to provide status updates renders all forward projections highly speculative.
2. United States – Current consensus estimates for modest economic expansion have demand rising sequentially and year-over-year, peaking at 205M tons per month in Q4.
3. Europe – Spain is coming out of a severe recession and the key to its resumption of growth will be increased industrial production. Prior uncertainty has forced

Chapter 3 - Fundamental Analysis

customers to avoid long-term contractual obligations for supply, pushing a significant percentage of its total demand into the spot market, where it will be forced to compete against aggressive bidding out of China.

4. China – Estimates of future Chinese demand are heavily economy-driven and range from optimistic to absurdly aggressive. Given the dispersion of opinion, the extreme cases are almost certainly not priced into the market. This creates significant potential for both bullish and bearish price risks.

Understanding the Product X Supply Stack

The initial market supply/demand conditions overlaid onto a supply curve show the following:

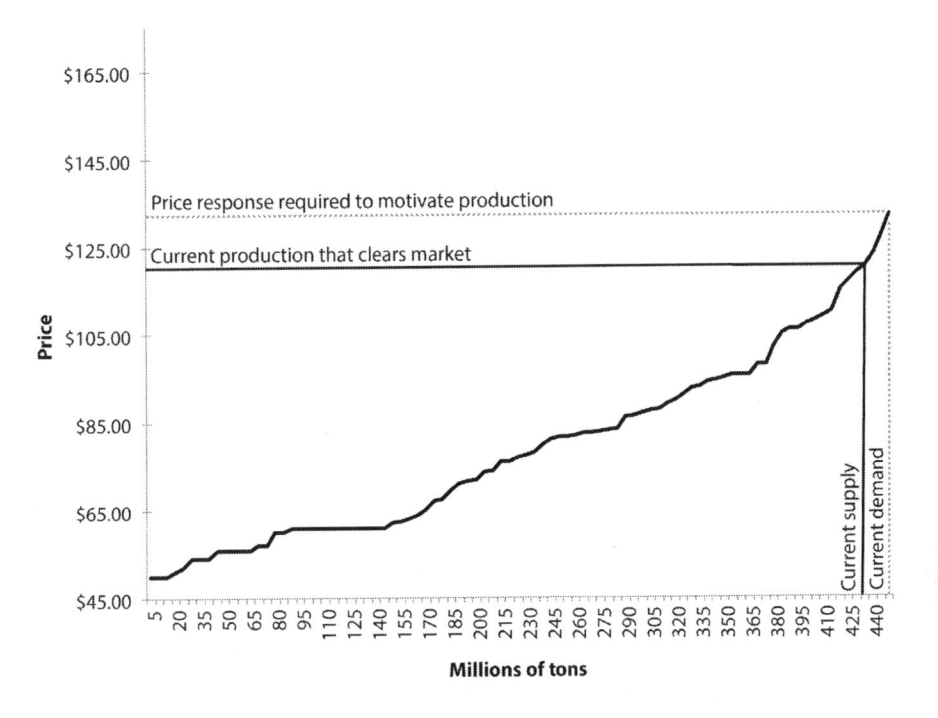

Figure 3.6   The initial Product X supply stack showing a supply shortfall.

The market is currently forecast to consume 450M tons of Product X in January, but only produce 432M tons, forcing end users to draw down stockpiles and pay a premium for spot tonnage, all of which has combined to push prices up to $105.29 for the prompt FEB contract.

By the end of the year, the supply-demand balance is forecast to look like:

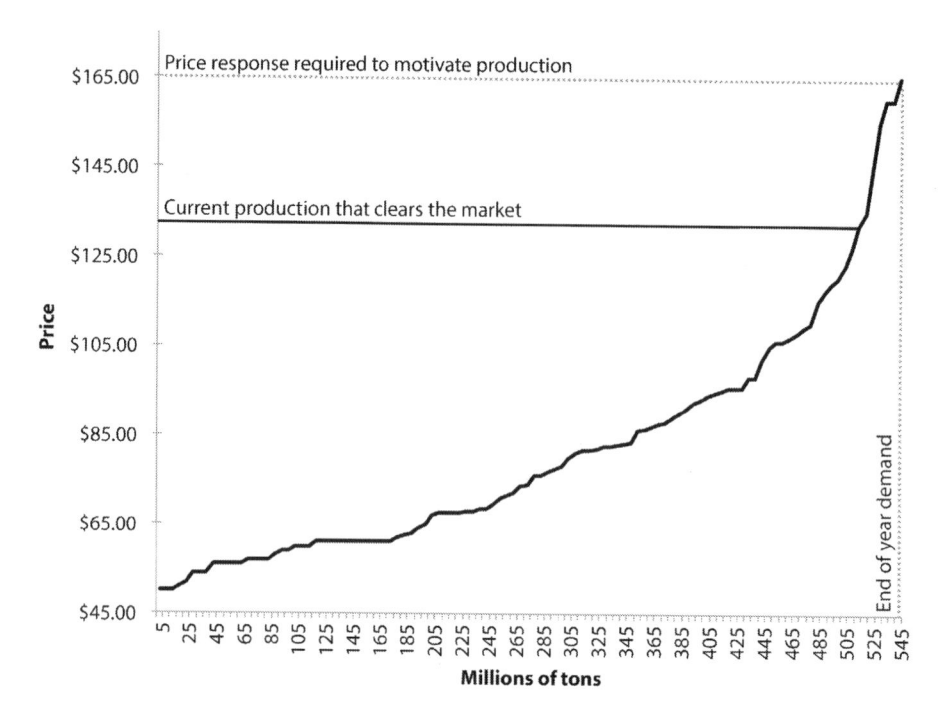

Figure 3.7 The year-end Product X supply stack, based on initial projections.

If the fundamentals evolve in this fashion, the Product X market will move from an 18M ton monthly shortage to a much more severe 30M ton monthly shortage, an extremely problematic situation given the shortfall-to-storage ratio. When markets have problems, they fix them with price.

Understanding the Product X Fundamentals

While it is possible to create an almost infinite number of possible outcomes based on a combinatorial array of the underlying event-path variables, practicality dictates that traders construct a small number of cases that represent expected classes of outcomes (bearish, neutral, bullish) which are studied in an attempt to deduce probable price implications.

Product X Cases

The Base Case for Product X

The base case is a series of reasonable compromises and probabilistic safe bets that, in aggregate, should reflect the best information available at the time.

Chapter 3 - Fundamental Analysis

The base case for Product X implies the following:

1. The global economy performs at target levels, leaving most estimates unchanged.
2. China demand is somewhat overstated and is reduced to a max of 130M tons per month.
3. Production from Africa is partially restored to 20M tons per month by April.

The base case balance sheet (modifications from initial conditions are shaded):

Supply

	Jan	Feb	Mar	Apr	May	Jun	Jul	Aug	Sep	Oct	Nov	Dec
United States	125	125	125	125	125	125	125	125	125	125	125	125
Russia	100	100	100	100	100	100	100	100	100	100	100	100
Mexico	40	40	40	40	40	40	40	40	40	40	40	40
India	55	55	55	55	55	55	55	55	55	55	55	55
South America	50	50	50	50	50	50	50	50	50	50	50	50
Africa	2	10	15	20	20	20	20	20	20	20	20	20
Canada	30	30	30	40	40	40	40	40	40	45	45	45
Australia	30	30	30	40	40	40	50	50	50	60	60	60
Total supply	432	440	445	470	470	470	480	480	480	495	495	495

Demand

	Jan	Feb	Mar	Apr	May	Jun	Jul	Aug	Sep	Oct	Nov	Dec
United States	185	185	185	185	185	185	195	195	195	205	205	205
Europe	145	155	155	155	155	165	165	165	165	165	165	165
China	100	100	100	105	105	105	115	115	115	130	130	130
Japan	20	20	20	20	20	20	25	25	25	25	25	25
Total demand	450	460	460	465	465	475	500	500	500	525	525	525
Net balance	(18)	(20)	(15)	5	5	(5)	(20)	(20)	(20)	(30)	(30)	(30)
Storage	1156	1136	1121	1126	1131	1126	1106	1086	1066	1036	1006	976

Table 3.3 Product X base case balance sheet for the current year.

If the changes in supply are re-graphed and the intersection with anticipated demand plotted, the resulting chart for the base case looks like:

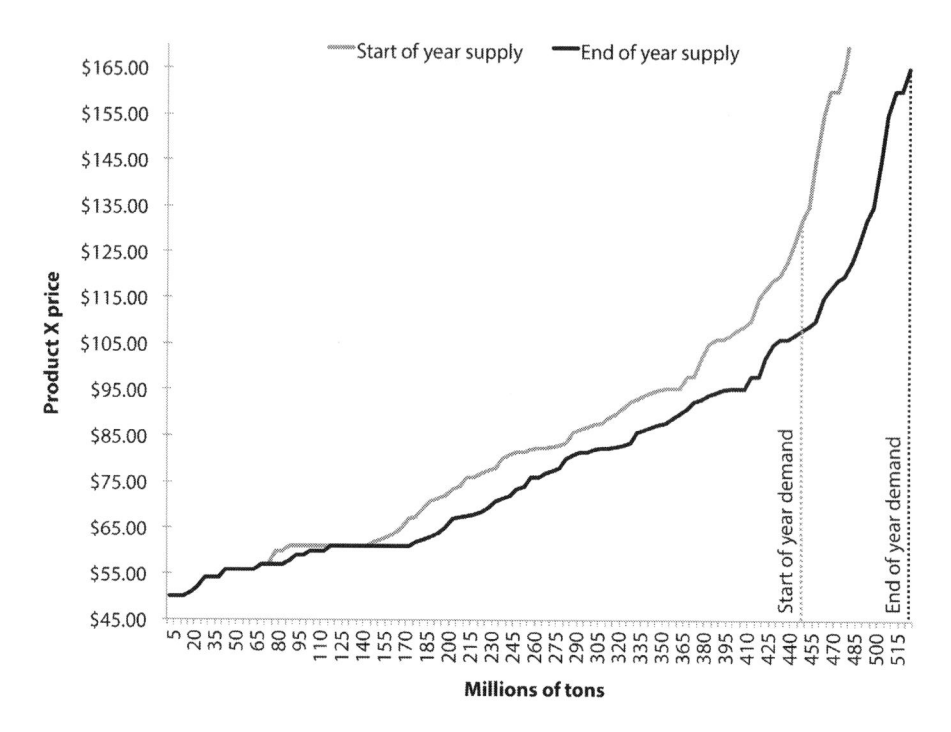

Figure 3.8 The base case year-end Product X supply stack, featuring supply growth and increasing demand.

The base case implies an anticipated fair value of $165.00 at year's end.

The Bear Case for Product X
The bear case reflects events that could reasonably be expected to occur and would increase supply or decrease demand, and is intended to put a relatively reasonable lower bound on expectations.

The bear case for Product X implies the following:

1. The global economy underperforms and fails to expand, dropping year-end demand estimates for the United States 185M tons per month, dramatically reducing growth targets for China to 100M tons per month, and actually decreasing economically sensitive manufacturing demand in Europe and Japan by 5M tons, to 135M and 15M per month, respectively.
2. Labor costs decrease and shipping is both cheaper and more plentiful, making the market as a whole more efficient globally and reducing the spread between markets.
3. African production returns to full 40M tons output on schedule.
4. Higher-priced Canadian production is forced out of market, yielding max output of 35M tons per month.

Chapter 3 - Fundamental Analysis

5. An additional 30M tons of low-priced Australian production comes onto market to service what was supposed to be robust Chinese demand.

The bear case balance sheet (modifications from initial conditions are shaded):

Supply

	Jan	Feb	Mar	Apr	May	Jun	Jul	Aug	Sep	Oct	Nov	Dec
United States	125	125	125	125	125	125	125	125	125	125	125	125
Russia	100	100	100	100	100	100	100	100	100	100	100	100
Mexico	40	40	40	40	40	40	40	40	40	40	40	40
India	55	55	55	55	55	55	55	55	55	55	55	55
South America	50	50	50	50	50	50	50	50	50	50	50	50
Africa	2	20	40	40	40	40	40	40	40	40	40	40
Canada	25	25	25	35	35	35	35	35	35	35	35	35
Australia	30	30	30	40	40	40	50	50	50	60	60	60
Total supply	427	445	465	485	485	485	495	495	495	505	505	505

Demand

	Jan	Feb	Mar	Apr	May	Jun	Jul	Aug	Sep	Oct	Nov	Dec
United States	180	180	180	180	180	180	185	185	185	185	185	185
Europe	140	140	140	140	140	140	135	135	135	135	135	135
China	95	95	95	95	95	95	100	100	100	100	100	100
Japan	20	20	20	20	20	20	15	15	15	15	15	15
Total demand	435	435	435	435	435	435	435	435	435	435	435	435

	Jan	Feb	Mar	Apr	May	Jun	Jul	Aug	Sep	Oct	Nov	Dec
Net balance	(8)	10	30	50	50	50	60	60	60	70	70	70
Storage	1166	1176	1206	1256	1306	1356	1416	1476	1536	1606	1676	1746

Table 3.4   Product X bear case balance sheet for the current year.

If the changes in supply are re-graphed and the intersection with anticipated demand plotted, the resulting chart for the bear case looks like:

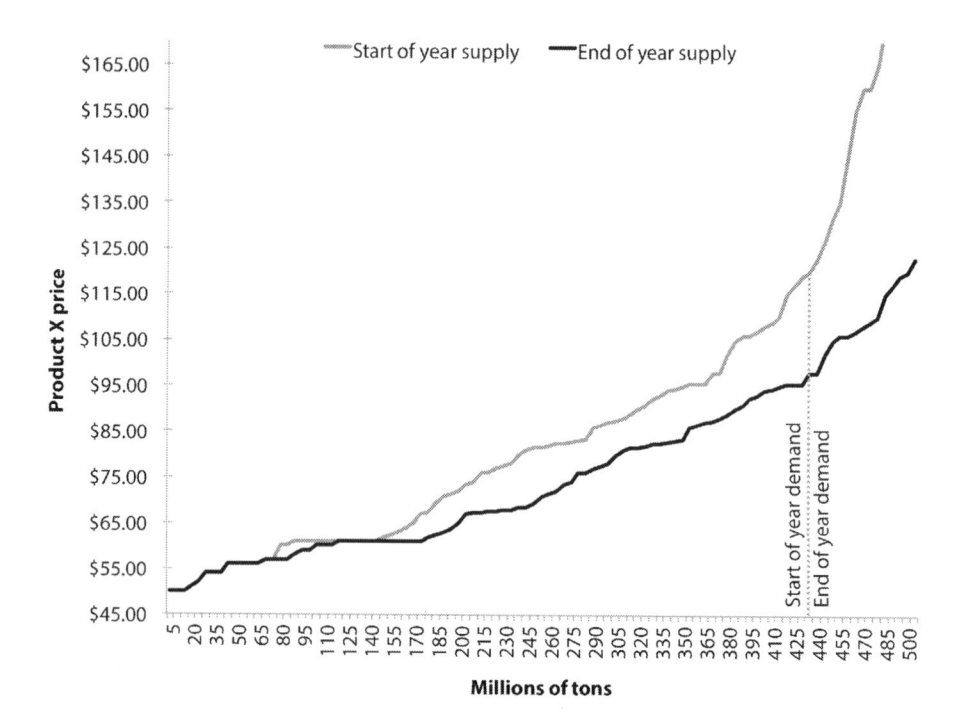

Figure 3.9 The bear case year-end Product X supply stack, featuring higher supply and constant demand.

The bear case implies an anticipated fair value of $98.00 at year end.

The Bull Case for Product X
The bull case reflects events that could be expected to occur and would decrease supply or increase demand, and is intended to put a relatively reasonable upper bound on expectations.

The bull case for Product X implies the following:

1. The global economy grows as expected during the period.
2. China achieves its aggressive growth and consumption target.
3. African production does not return to service during year.
4. Labor costs rise, and shipping becomes both more expensive and scarcer, widening market differentials.

The bull case balance sheet (modifications from initial conditions are shaded):

Chapter 3 - Fundamental Analysis

Supply

	Jan	Feb	Mar	Apr	May	Jun	Jul	Aug	Sep	Oct	Nov	Dec
United States	125	125	125	125	125	125	125	125	125	125	125	125
Russia	100	100	100	100	100	100	100	100	100	100	100	100
Mexico	40	40	40	40	40	40	40	40	40	40	40	40
India	55	55	55	55	55	55	55	55	55	55	55	55
South America	50	50	50	50	50	50	50	50	50	50	50	50
Africa	2	2	2	2	2	2	2	2	2	2	2	2
Canada	30	30	30	40	40	40	40	40	40	45	45	45
Australia	30	30	30	40	40	40	50	50	50	60	60	60
Total supply	432	432	432	452	452	452	462	462	462	477	477	477

Demand

	Jan	Feb	Mar	Apr	May	Jun	Jul	Aug	Sep	Oct	Nov	Dec
United States	185	185	185	185	185	185	195	195	195	205	205	205
Europe	145	155	155	155	155	165	165	165	165	165	165	165
China	100	100	100	110	110	110	125	125	125	150	150	150
Japan	20	20	20	20	20	20	25	25	25	25	25	25
Total demand	450	460	460	470	470	480	510	510	510	545	545	545
Net balance	(18)	(28)	(28)	(18)	(18)	(28)	(48)	(48)	(48)	(68)	(68)	(68)
Storage	1156	1128	1100	1082	1064	1036	988	940	892	824	756	688

Table 3.5   Product X bull case balance sheet for the current year, featuring lower supply at a higher price and constant demand.

If the changes in supply are re-graphed and the intersection with anticipated demand plotted, the resulting chart for the bull case looks like:

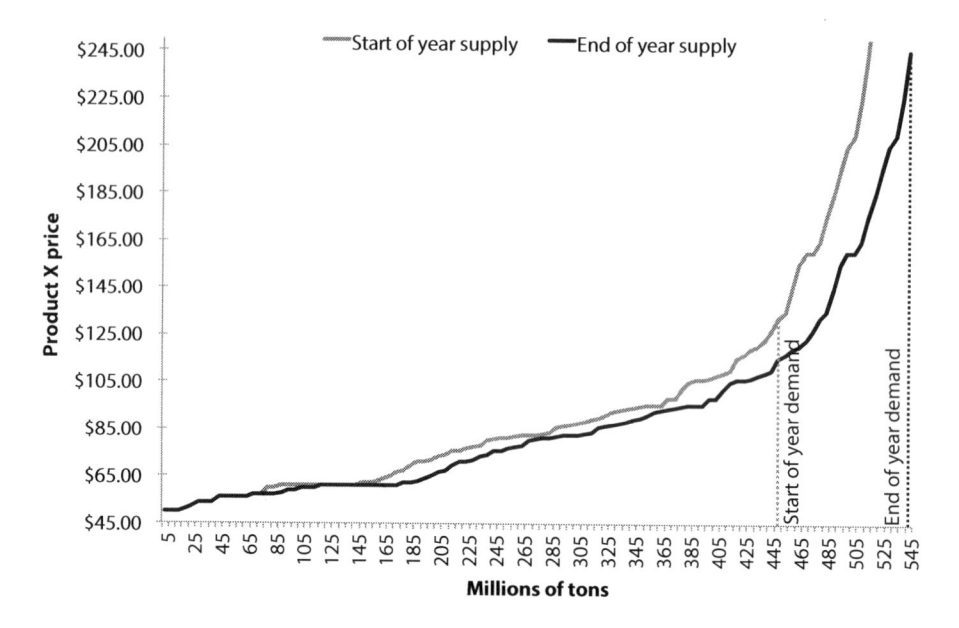

Figure 3.10 The bull case year-end Product X supply stack, featuring moderate supply growth and significantly higher demand.

The bull case implies an anticipated fair value of $245.00 at year end.

Combining the base, bull, and bear case supply curves yields the following chart:

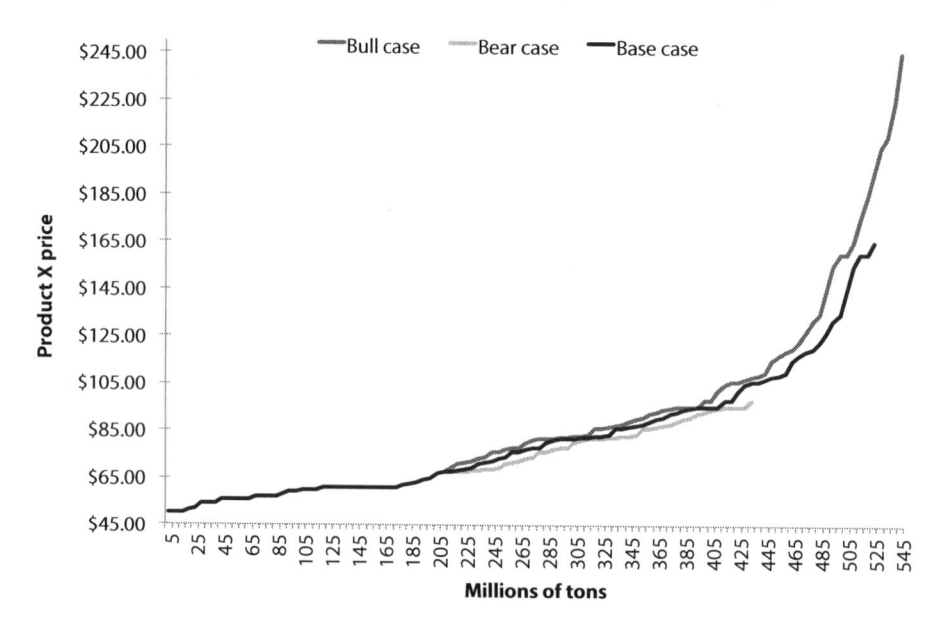

Figure 3.11 Year-end supply stacks for Product X base, bear, and bull cases.

Chapter 3 - Fundamental Analysis

It is clear that price of Product X is a function of both the available supply and the anticipated level of demand. The relative influence of either side of the balance depends heavily on the local shape of the curve and the market's current positioning on the curve.

The Product X Event Path and Fundamental Drivers
Viewed as a month-by-month list, the primary factors that will influence the price of Product X are:

January	The first inflection point will be the January statistics on total demand. A reading below 350M tons/month would support the bear case, anything above 450M tons/month leans toward either the base case or bull case.
February	The second data item will be the February scheduled return to service of the African processing plant, which will provide the first significant indication of which case is most likely. If production remaining unchanged at 2M tons/month supports the bull case, an increase to around 10M tons/month would suggest the base and a ramp up to 20M tons/month or more would argue strongly for the bear. If production is greater than 2M tons/month at this early stage the bull case loses some credibility.
March	The key event in March is the ramp up of African production, which will provide additional clarity. To validate the bull case, production will have to have remained unchanged from its initial 2M tons/month; any material increase would be problematic. The base case calls for production to reach 20M tons/month, while the bear case would require a nearly full return to service of 40M tons/month. Production levels above 20M tons/month challenge the base case and severely damage the bull case.
April	April provides the first meaningful demand-based inflection point, with consumption from China expected to ramp from a starting 95 in the bear case or 100 in the base case and bull case. If April demand comes in at 95M tons/month the base and bull cases are challenged. An increase to 105M tons/month is in line with the base case, anything past 110M tons/month strongly argues for the bull case. Readings in the 110M+ range cast doubt on the bear case. A secondary, yet critical, checkpoint in April is the net balance. A positive net balance argues for the bear case, where a negative net balance increases the probability of the bull.
July	American and European demands are expected to increase during the summer, providing a second demand-based inflection point.

The early portion of an event path is spent eliminating possible alternative evolutionary trajectories; during the middle, market opinion coalesces around the most likely path. The later stages are spent refining the thesis and interpreting every incremental data point with respect to its ability to modify the apparent case.

The first quarter of the year is dominated by supply considerations, with actual vs. projected demand taking center stage during the second quarter. By July or August it should be relatively clear by the evolution of the fundamental developments (and, very likely, the price action) which of the three initial cases is playing out in the market. The remainder of the year will be driven by successive refinements of that case.

Product X Fundamental Summary
The global Product X market seems destined for a period of higher prices and increased volatility, the main question being how severe and of what duration. The base case implies a partial return to service of the African production facility that will partially offset the effects of increased global demand, but by the end of the year the market will be facing a persistent structural deficit and probable pockets of very high prices as market participants compete for incremental production.

4

Technical Analysis

Technical analysis is one of most misunderstood disciplines in the financial markets, even among sophisticated industry veterans. It is frequently presented as a science, but in practical application edges too uncomfortably close to being an art for many.

Technicians, or chartists, analyze patterns of price movement in isolation as a window into market psychology. This tends to work best in relatively liquid markets with high transaction volumes, and as a result technical analysis is more commonly deployed in the mature financial markets. Technical analysis is the study of stress, of force, of pressure. This is a crucial aspect that is frequently unmentioned. The analyst is interpreting the war between buyers and sellers through the ever-evolving battle lines of a price chart.

Detractors will tend to focus on the trees, the chart pattern, and wholly ignore the forest, the market dynamics that created the pattern. A market does not go up because the squiggle of prices looks like this and not like that. A market goes up because the active buyers are overpowering the available sellers around a particular price level during a specific time frame, forcing them into a retreat and a flurry of short-covering. Conversely, a sudden paucity of buyers in a market full of willing sellers will often lead to a break lower. These interactions, and others like them, create recognizable patterns in the price data.

Fundamentals, We Don't Need No Stinking Fundamentals!

There is a common perception that technical traders do not concern themselves with fundamental information. This arises from the belief among the most intellectually pure technical traders that all fundamental information is instantly disseminated across the market and immediately factored into the prevailing price. The more nihilistic chartists believe that, since it is impossible know all of the fundamentals that affect prices (which is true), instead of making decisions on a partial fact set, they will choose to ignore it altogether.

Ignoring fundamental factors that drive the market does not mean that they will extend a trader the same courtesy. Many beautiful chart patterns with high predictive value and strong measurement potential have been destroyed by exogenous events, regularly scheduled economic announcements or game-changing regulatory reforms. While it is true that any robust technical trading methodology should be able to handle large price fluctuations, the potential for an intraday or overnight gap or high-velocity, low-liquidity move can prove very destructive. If the trader is operating in a persistently volatile or gap-prone market, this will need to be factored into the methodology and risk-reward assessment.

Advantages of Technical Analysis

One main advantage of a technically based methodology is the ability to screen a large number of candidate markets and select for further study only the interesting chart patterns. Before the personal computer revolution, being a technical analyst was an altogether more laborious, involved process. Data had to be manually compiled and painstakingly plotted by hand. Later, subscription services mailed out thick chart books on a monthly or weekly basis, but only on the major markets. Today, almost any data provider will offer a front-end tool capable of generating rudimentary graphics and analysis. Software developers stand ready to sell traders as much customization and sophistication as they care to pay for. Computing horsepower has made it possible to compare a nearly infinite number of charts against a central pattern repository in real-time, either executing autonomously or passing promising scenarios along for human interpretation.

This type of product-agnostic pattern trading is most commonly found at the more specialized hedge funds, among the Commodity Trading Advisors (CTAs) and with large individual traders. This makes sense, as all are facing an informational disadvantage relative to naturals, merchants, and banks that possess superior fundamental knowledge of the markets they inhabit. If a firm cannot compete with a hedger's firsthand business experience, a merchant's transactional acumen, or a bank's near-boundless research resources, it will learn to use whatever unique edge is available—in this case, technical analysis.

Technical analysis is also unique in that the basic precepts are very easy to learn and put into practice. This near-zero ramp up time leads to a large number of newly minted experts, which is both good and bad for the industry. It is bad for traders that happen to be listening to them, but potentially very good for those trading against them.

Chapter 4 - Technical Analysis

Disadvantages of Technical Analysis
The principal disadvantage of a chart-based methodology is that an analysis that does not incorporate or chooses not to acknowledge fundamental information is dangerously vulnerable to large price movements around economic information, regulatory announcements, or other data-based inflection points. Even in an environment where the trader deliberately chooses not to factor in fundamental inputs, they should at least be aware of their existence and the timetable to better brace for any impacts on the market.

Pragmatic Technical Analysis
Technical analysis is a very large discipline, with an enormous library of patterns to learn and measurement tools to deploy. I find that the simplest patterns and measurement techniques have the highest predictive value, and that the differentiating factor between unemployed chart oracle and profitable trader is more a function of a consistent, deliberate approach than pen-and-ruler virtuosity. There is a worthwhile discussion to be had about the utility of the more esoteric methodologies, but the ability of the stable core of technical analysis to add significant value in the near term is, to my mind—and in my market—indisputable.

Chart Types – Visualizing Information

Technicians employ a variety of chart types, depending on the aspect of the market they are trying to understand and the degree of focus and granularity they choose to bring to bear. The most common types are, in order of increasing information density: line, bar, and candlestick charts, which can be configured to display information from micro-granular ticks to macro-focused monthly aggregations. Each type of chart yields a slightly different perspective on the market and can be used for different types of analysis.

Line Charts
Line charts are the simplest graphical representation of a time series of prices. A line chart gives a good sketch of the market, but by only examining one of the four primary variables—the open, high of the day, low of the day, and the closing price—the chart ignores a significant amount of information. Line charts are most commonly used for super-short term trade-by-trade tick charts, long-term graphs where the need to condense a large amount of information into a small space is critical, or multi-price charts where it is desirable to restrict the amount of information to manage the visual clutter.

Bar Charts
Bar charts incorporate all four primary variables and as a result are often referred to as OHLC charts. The high and low prices for the period are connected by a thin vertical bar, with the open, first price occurring during the period, denoted by a tick mark on the left side of the line and the close, the last price, as a tick mark on the right. The addition of the entire period's trading range as defined by the high and low adds significant information to the chart, and technicians infer a great deal of meaning from the relationship between one day's close and the next day's open.

Candlestick Charts

A candlestick chart is a refinement of the standard OHLC bar graph. While not actually conveying any additional information, candlestick charts achieve a more visceral psychological impact by using different color-coding for up and down periods. As with a standard bar chart, the high and low of the period are connected with a thin vertical line. Instead of using a pair of alternating tick marks, the open-to-close range for the period is described by a rectangle superimposed over the line connecting the high and low prices. The solid rectangle will be filled in with one color if the close is higher than the open, another if the close is lower than the open. If the open and close for the period are the same, the box will be replaced with a horizontal tick mark. Most chartists will default to either a green for up, red for down or white for up, black for down color scheme (as seen here):

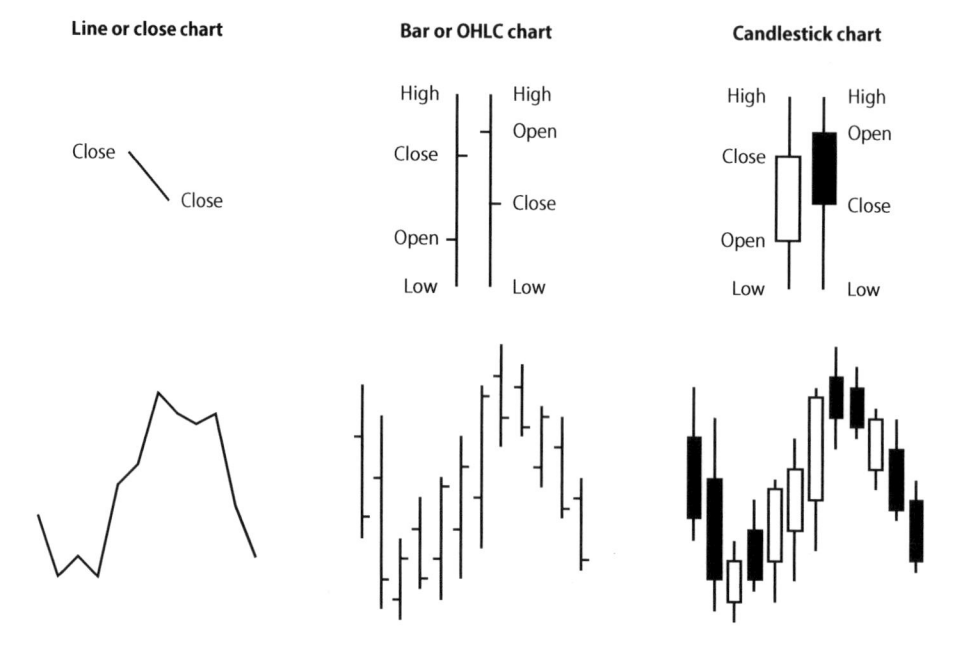

Figure 4.1   Information density of different chart types.

Time Frames

Technicians will examine both short- and long-term graphs of various types for a particular product; zooming out to evaluate what the market is doing on a strategic, long-term basis before zooming in to examine the shorter-term fluctuations that inform their tactical execution decisions. What is happening in the one-minute chart will inform the rest of the hour, which impacts the remainder of the day, which, if near a particular threshold, might make or break an entire chart pattern. Chartists also watch the different time horizons because not every trade has the same projected holding period.

The Trend Is Your Friend

Technical traders spend most of their time determining if a market is trending, and looking for patterns that would signal a continuation of that movement, a pause to consolidate gains or losses, or a reversal. For a technical trader, "trending" is a precise statement that implies more than a haphazard movement from A to B. The industry standard definition is derived from pioneering technician Charles Dow's theory:

> Dow defined an uptrend as a situation in which each successive rally closes higher than the previous rally high, and each successive rally low also closes higher than the previous rally low. In other words, an uptrend has a pattern of rising peaks and troughs. The opposite situation, with successively lower peaks and troughs, defines a downtrend.[19]

Dow was also the first to conceptualize a market trend being constructed from three overlapping, interacting forces of diminishing influence, comparing them to the tide, waves, and ripples of the ocean.

> The primary trend represents the tide, the secondary or intermediate trend represents the waves that make up the tide, and the minor trends behave like ripples on the waves.[20]

Though the terminology has evolved since Dow's time (macro, intermediate, micro), the underlying concept remains the same.

---

[19] John J. Murphy, *Technical Analysis of the Financial Markets*. (Paramus: New York Institute of Finance, 1999), 25.
[20] John J. Murphy, *Technical Analysis of the Financial Markets*, 25.

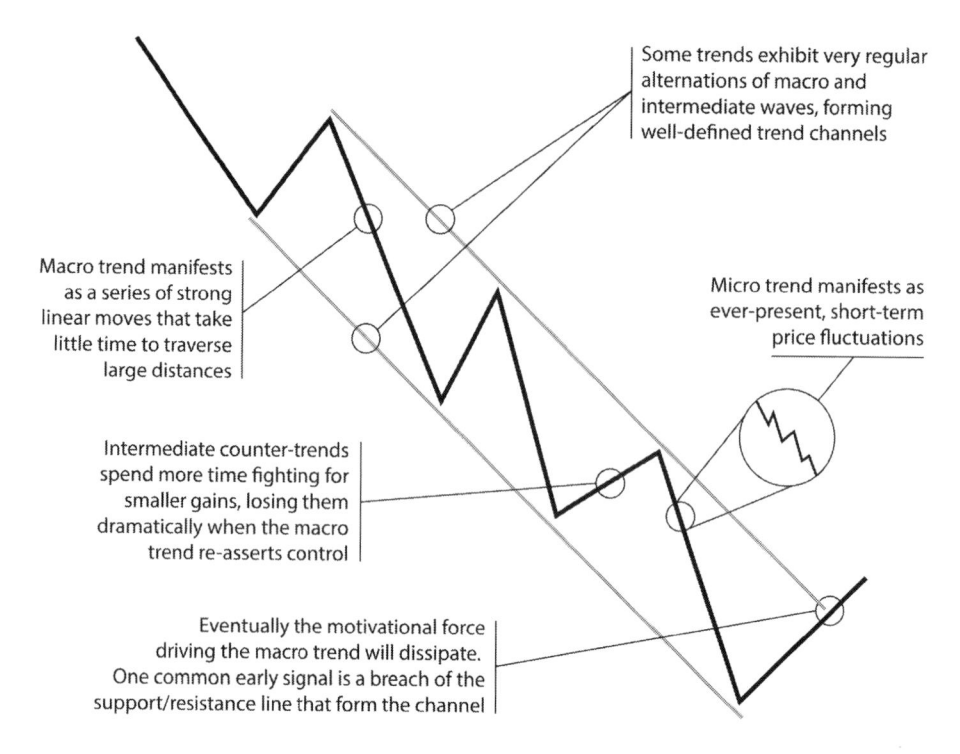

Figure 4.2   Elements of a market trend.

The Macro Trend
Macro trends are created by large, persistent fundamental structural imbalances in the market. Recent examples include:

- The great oil investment boom of 2006-8, when several hundred billion dollars of hot money tried to cram its way into an organic $50B market space, causing prices to ramp from $60.00 to $145.00 before all was said and done.
- The gold market of 2007-2012, when, as the dollar and equities collapsed, traders saw gold as both a store of value and an inflation hedge.
- The domestic natural gas market, in which a radical shift in onshore drilling and hydraulic fracturing technology turned a severe deficit into an epic supply glut within a decade.

It is critical that the trader correctly identify the macro trend, if one is present. The macro trend is the price response to the major underlying drivers of the market, and its overwhelming force will only be temporarily interrupted by periodic counter-trend movements. The macro trend is literally the path of least resistance, and establishing a well-timed position early represents the trader's best chance of achieving a favorable risk/reward ratio.

The Intermediate Trend

The intermediate trend is created by secondary factors that intermittently act on prices that are dominated by the macro trend. When they are in phase with the macro trend secondary factors can cause abrupt accelerations, when they are out of phase they create retracements of the macro trend called intermediate trends or "countertrend" moves. Trading the countertrend can be very dangerous, as the temporary influence of the intermediate trend can suddenly abate and allow the full force of the macro trend to reassert itself. Trading in the direction of the intermediate trend is signing up to both literally and figuratively take the short end of the stick, seeking to make money by betting against the main direction of the market. For those that dare, the key considerations are understanding how long the intermediate trend is likely to last and the potential distance it is likely to traverse.

The intermediate trend *can* be very constructively used to set positions designed to profit from the macro trend. The intermediate retracement is effectively offering the trader a cheaper cost of entry, a discount for the disciplined and patient. Again, the key is to understand how far it can go and how long it can last.

The Micro Trend

The micro trend is created by small, short-lived influences that contribute minor fluctuations in price. In volatile, low-liquidity products the normal real-time imbalances between buyers and sellers can be sufficient to create small fluctuations around the intermediate trend or countertrend. Seeking deep significance in the micro chop is usually a mug's game. The micro trend is best used to facilitate execution, to take in incremental market-making profits for larger players, or for short-term intraday trading.

Drawing Trend Lines and Creating Trend Channels

Some trends will exhibit very regular oscillations, making linear, evenly spaced highs and lows over a prolonged period of time. Once the trend has defined itself by making alternating higher or lower highs and lows, traders will attempt to extrapolate similar levels of oscillation into the future by drawing trend lines and trend channels.

Trend lines are drawn by connecting two successive highs or lows on a chart:

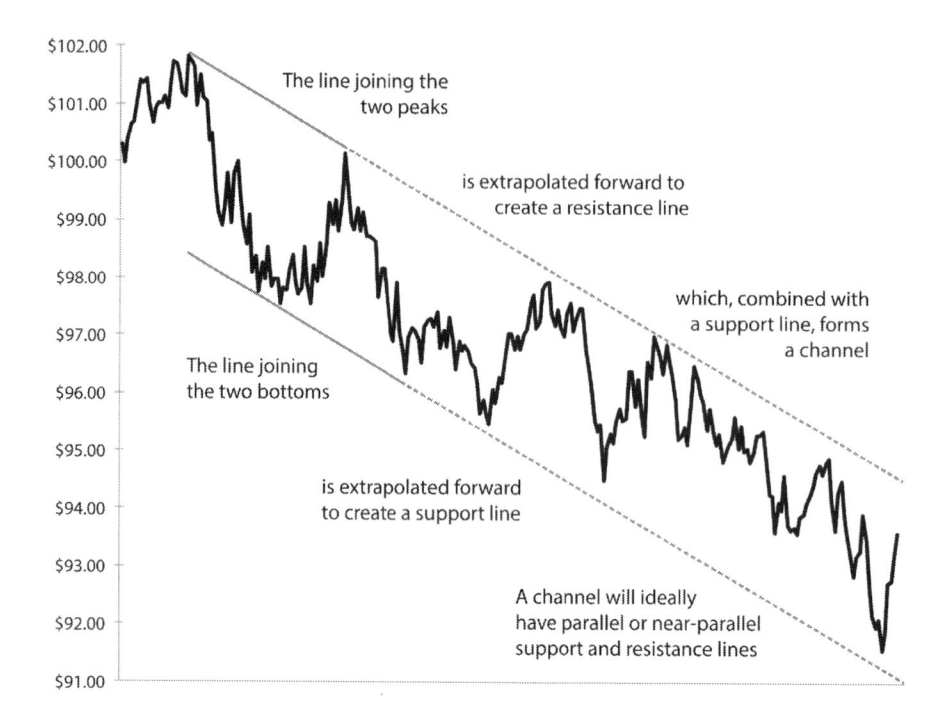

Figure 4.3 Using consecutive highs and lows to draw trend lines.

A trend channel is formed when the price action is bounded by parallel support and resistance lines. Trend channels, once established, have a tendency to become self-fulfilling prophecies for as long as the impetus driving the macro trend persists. The more times a support or resistance line is tested and retains its integrity, the more seriously technical traders will take it. One thing all trends have in common: eventually they must come to an end.

The End of the Trend

Markets do not have to be trending, nor does an extant trend have to stay in motion for a particularly significant distance or a long period of time. Trends are caused by a motivating force, and all forces eventually exhaust themselves and dissipate. An uptrend is defined as a series of higher highs and higher lows, which is ended by a break below the prior low. A downtrend is defined as a series of lower highs and lower lows, which is decisively ended by a move above the previous high. Some traders will consider a material intraday breach sufficient, others will require a close above or below the critical level.

When a trend ends, the market can respond in a variety of ways. Most commonly, it will enter into a consolidation period, where it either forms a somewhat regularly shaped mass or oscillates unpredictably within a range. If the prior trend was particularly strong and pushed the market significantly higher or lower than what could reasonably be considered "fair" on a fundamental basis, the market may immediately snap back in a violent reversal of the prior trend.

Chapter 4 - Technical Analysis

No Trend

Markets do not *have* to do anything. In a situation where there is no clear motivational factor(s) the price can be buffeted back and forth randomly by small incremental pieces of information or the normal interactions of buyers and sellers modifying their positions.

Support and Resistance

All trends have an underlying motive force, usually caused by an imbalance of fundamental variables that governs the price action and creates an overall upward or downward trajectory. It is very common for the inexorable march lower or higher to be halted dead in its tracks by what appears to be a collision with an invisible brick wall. With no new news or fundamental information to influence it, the market somehow just *stops*, and either trades sideways or reverses dramatically in a countertrend move. What has happened is that the ongoing movement has run into a large area of interested buyers or sellers who have congregated around a particular price point and collectively have enough order volume to temporarily counteract the fundamental imbalance fuelling the trend. Areas of significant vested interest are called "support" and "resistance" levels, and they are tremendously important technical indicators. A support level prevents a market from moving lower, and a resistance level impedes upward progress.

Support and resistance levels have a number of interesting properties. It is difficult (or impossible) to know exactly how much interest is lying in wait at a price point and therefore extremely challenging to determine if it will cause a temporary halt in progress or form an immovable barrier that ends the trend and forces prices sideways or higher.

More interesting is the tendency for a level that was previously support, if decisively breached, to act as a resistance level in the future (and vice versa). The phenomenon is caused by traders taking positions against the trend and immediately suffering losses, then seeking to get out of the position with minimal damage. The buying interest that temporarily paused a downtrend and created a support level (who are now holding losing positions) will seek to cut their losses if prices re-rally to near their entry point. Likewise, sellers shorting into a rising market that continues higher will seize on an opportunity to get out at breakeven, preventing the market from going lower.

Patterns

The market is not always in the grip of the irresistible force of a trend or battering against the immovable object of support or resistance. It is much more common for the price action to be buffeted back and forth by alternating waves of buying and selling pressure, each temporarily holding sway before running out of steam or being overwhelmed. These oscillations can form patterns within the price data. Patterns can form at the start of a trend and describe its trajectory and potential, at the end of a trend to signal consolidation or reversal, or anywhere along the price path in between.

Common Technical Patterns

Each market movement, like a snowflake or fingerprint, will be unique in character and appearance. A strong trend interrupted by a weaker force will tend to create a "continuation pattern" as the market works through the temporary blockage. The most common continuation patterns are bull or bear flags, wedges, triangles, and boxes. A trend that encounters a superior counterforce may be stopped in its tracks or, in some cases, turned back in what is called a "reversal pattern." Head and shoulders and rounding top or bottom are two of the most common reversal indicators or patterns. Frequently, the market will become trapped and move sideways as it stores up potential energy, creating a "sideways" or "range trading" formation, the most common of which are box and congestion patterns. Technical chart patterns all come with a probability attached. There are no sure things. Even the most robust, well-formed patterns are susceptible to an exogenous shock caused by an unexpected fundamental event.

It is crucial to remember that a pattern needs to form completely before it has any predictive value. A partial pattern is not a pattern. A pattern of price fluctuations is not predictive because it happens to describe a particular shape; it is predictive because the price trajectory compels traders to action. Traders with losing positions will be forced to capitulate, stop out of positions, and generate the accelerated move that follows a particular pattern. There must be damage, and the recognition by the losing trader that the damage is unsustainable in magnitude, duration, or the potential to worsen.

The following charts have the explanatory text placed directly on the graph to more clearly illustrate the nuances of each technical pattern.

Continuation Patterns

A continuation pattern is formed when a market under the influence of a strong motive force encounters a locus of opposing interest that temporarily halts its progress, creating a series of oscillations caused by medium and short-term imbalances of buying or selling pressure.

Chapter 4 - Technical Analysis

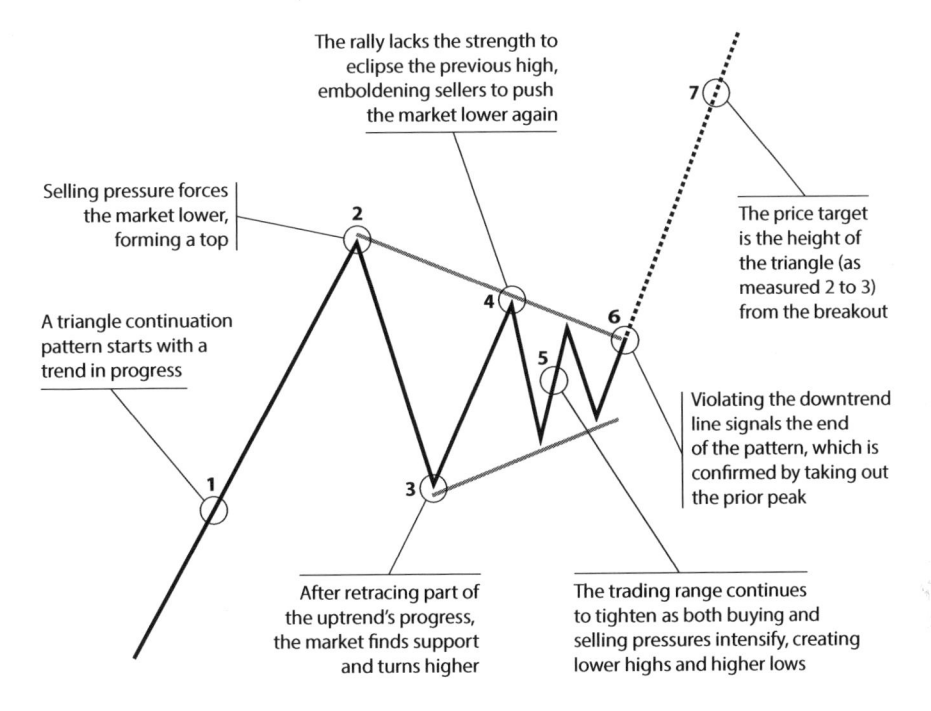

Figure 4.4   The triangle continuation pattern.

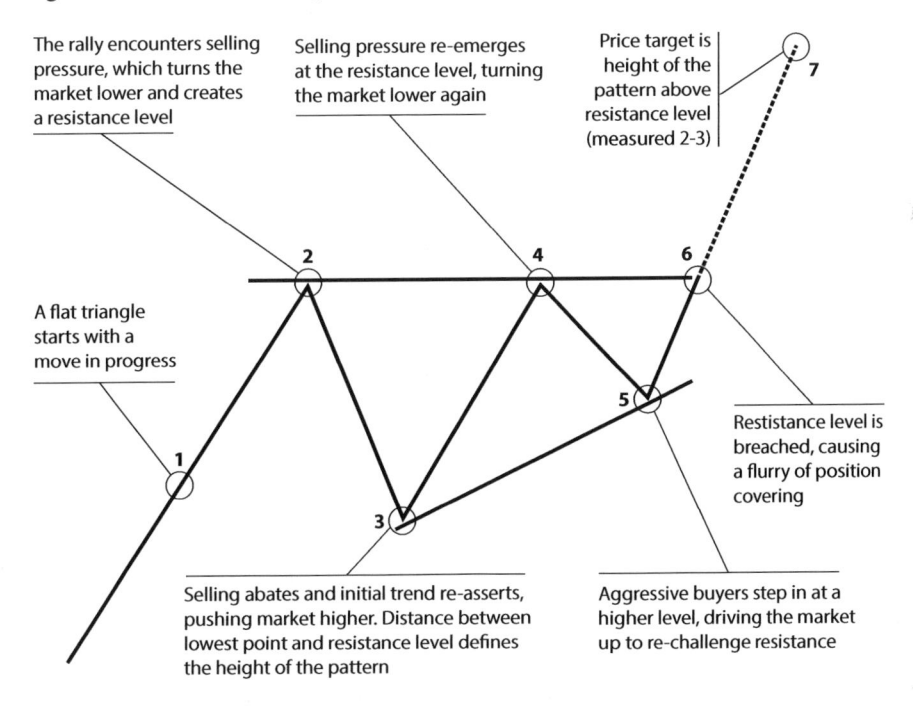

Figure 4.5   A flat ascending triangle continuation pattern.

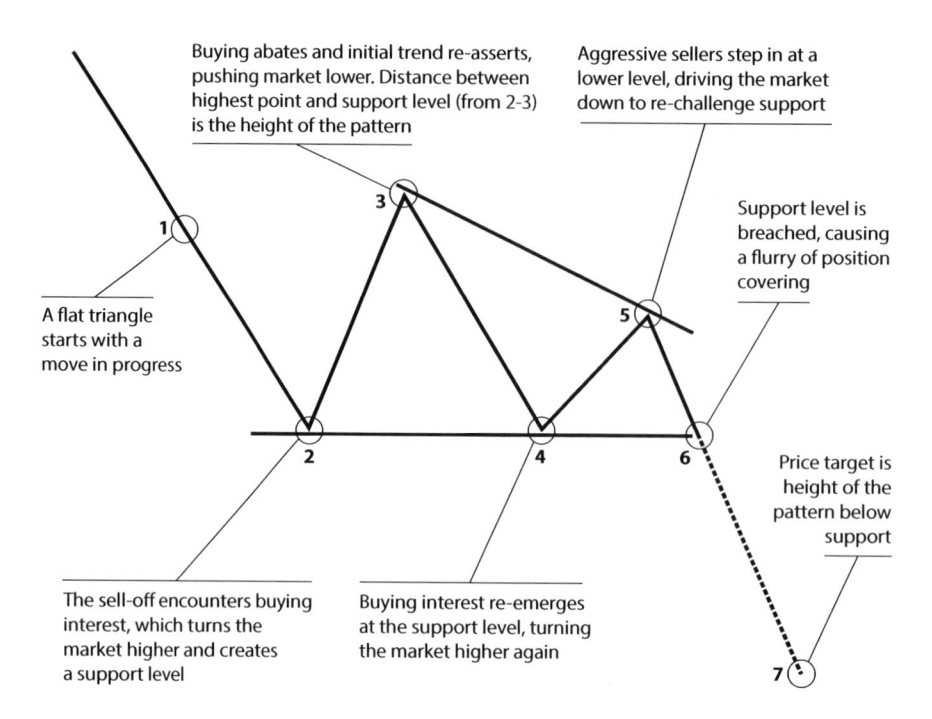

Figure 4.6 A flat descending triangle continuation pattern.

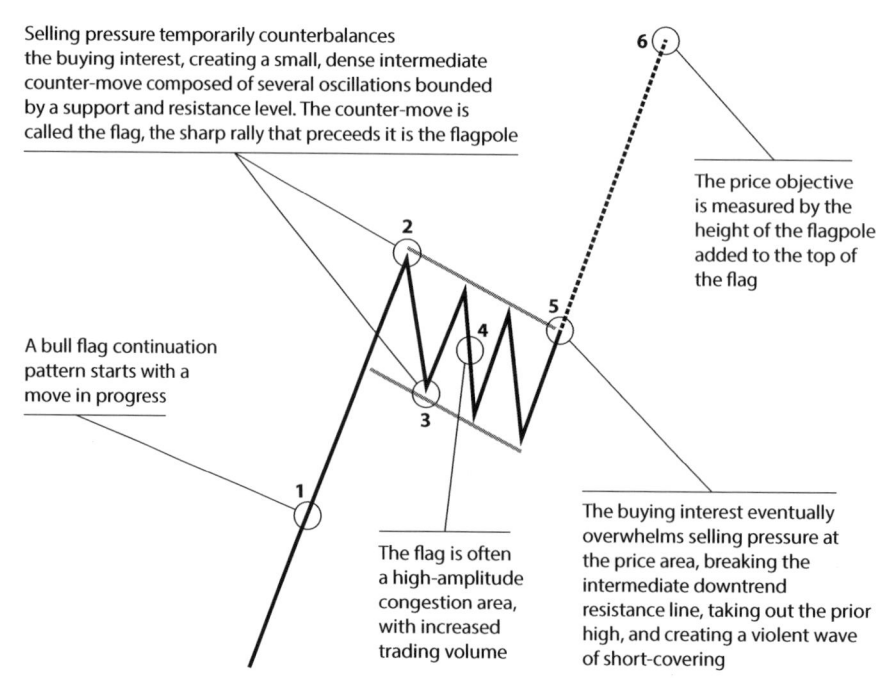

Figure 4.7 The bull flag continuation pattern.

Chapter 4 - Technical Analysis

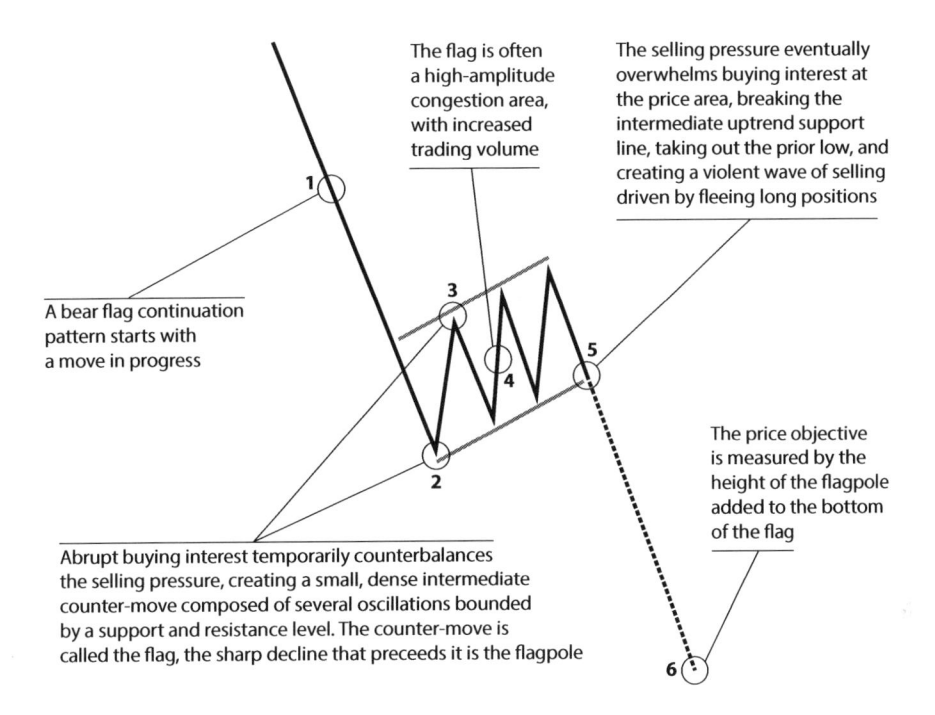

Figure 4.8 The bear flag continuation pattern.

Labels in figure:
- A bear flag continuation pattern starts with a move in progress
- The flag is often a high-amplitude congestion area, with increased trading volume
- The selling pressure eventually overwhelms buying interest at the price area, breaking the intermediate uptrend support line, taking out the prior low, and creating a violent wave of selling driven by fleeing long positions
- Abrupt buying interest temporarily counterbalances the selling pressure, creating a small, dense intermediate counter-move composed of several oscillations bounded by a support and resistance level. The counter-move is called the flag, the sharp decline that preceeds it is the flagpole
- The price objective is measured by the height of the flagpole added to the bottom of the flag

The Significance of Taking Out a Prior High/Low

One common characteristic of continuation patterns is breaking above or below a recently established peak(s) or valley(s). A large part of technical analysis is studying the actions of traders who are suffering with losing positions, and one of the clearest signals of an increase in suffering—and therefore compulsion to act—is a market that has rallied above a previous high or traded below a previous low. Most chart patterns consist of alternating feints back and forth between buyers and sellers, which will ultimately be resolved by one side overpowering the other and creating a breakout. This is usually signaled decisively by eclipsing a prior high or low point in the recent chart history.

Taking out prior highs and lows can also provide actionable information in the absence of a well-defined chart pattern. A breakout is one of the few truly incontrovertible indicators in technical analysis. If the market is making new lifetime highs then everyone who has ever sold it is wrong. A chart that has just blown through the low print means that everyone who has ever bought it is wrong. Breakouts higher or lower will leave a lot of traders with painful positions that are suddenly difficult if not impossible to justify. This rapid mass exodus will frequently lead to an acceleration of the rally or sell off and create sharp, spiky chart patterns that are called "capitulation" or "blow-off" moves.

Reversal Patterns

Reversal patterns form when a trending market exhausts its primary motive impetus or encounters a stronger opposing force that turns the market against its initial trajectory.

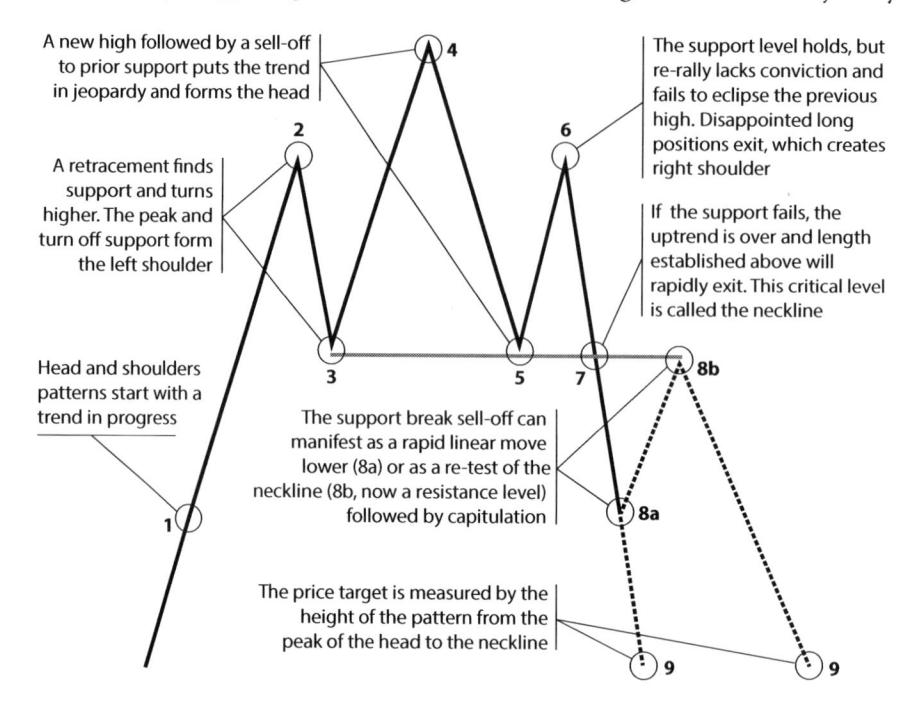

Figure 4.9   The head and shoulders reversal pattern.

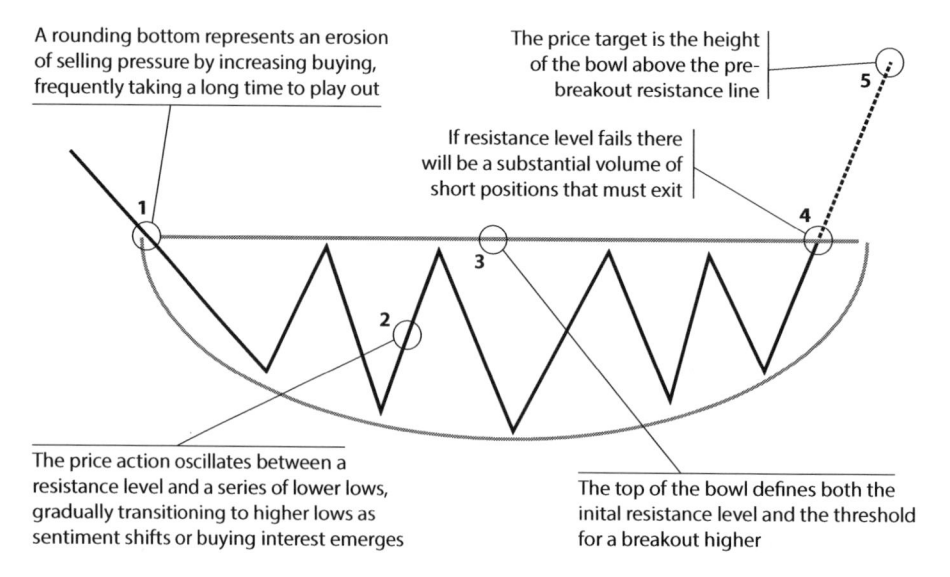

Figure 4.10   A rounding bottom reversal pattern.

Chapter 4 - Technical Analysis

Markets rarely transition abruptly from downtrend to uptrend, and vice versa. Those that do tend to be the result of the sudden and/or unexpected impact of an extremely powerful fundamental driver. For this reason, continuation and consolidation formations are generally much more prevalent patterns.

Consolidation Patterns

Consolidation patterns occur when a market becomes trapped between two approximately equal forces. A consolidation pattern is conceptually similar to a continuation pattern, but is not predicated on the pre-existence of a trend. A market will frequently form a consolidation pattern after exhausting its initial motive force and breaking out of the trend, chopping sideways and marking time until fresh information emerges to impact the price. Consolidation patterns can form anywhere on the chart, but are somewhat more likely to form at market bottoms as prices languish in a low-motivation trough. It is much harder for prices to stall at an elevated level, as continuous buying pressure is required to maintain high prices, which can easily fall of their own weight.

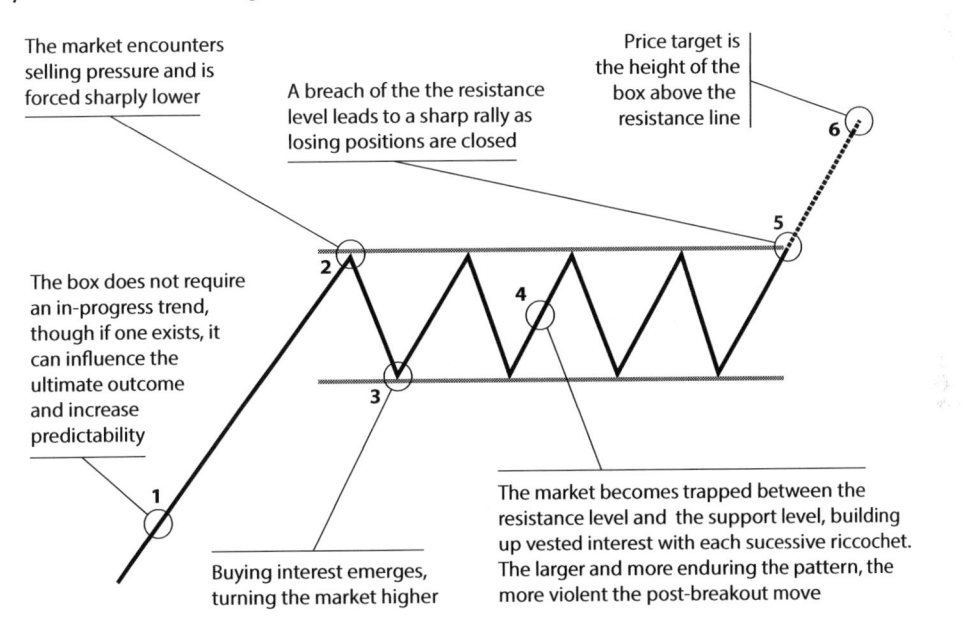

Figure 4.11 A rectangle or box consolidation pattern.

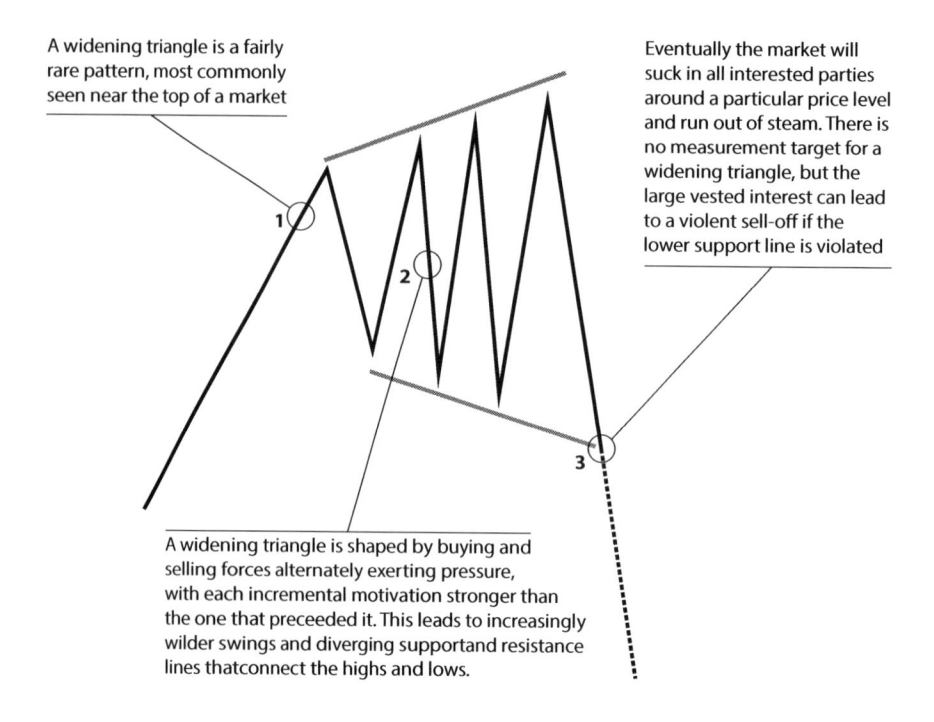

A widening triangle is a fairly rare pattern, most commonly seen near the top of a market

Eventually the market will suck in all interested parties around a particular price level and run out of steam. There is no measurement target for a widening triangle, but the large vested interest can lead to a violent sell-off if the lower support line is violated

A widening triangle is shaped by buying and selling forces alternately exerting pressure, with each incremental motivation stronger than the one that preceeded it. This leads to increasingly wilder swings and diverging support and resistance lines that connect the highs and lows.

Figure 4.12   A widening triangle consolidation pattern.

A Chart Does Not Necessarily Have a Pattern

Charts can also form congestion areas, pattern-less clusters of accumulated trader interest caused by large volumes of transactions clustered around a particular price point. This will be covered in greater detail later in the chapter.

Sometimes, there is no deeper meaning to the fluctuations on a chart; it is all just random noise. This can frustrate technicians to no end, and is frequently the downfall of novice technical traders, who assume that just because there is a chart, there *must* be a pattern, and therefore a trade to be made.

A Chart Does Not Necessarily Have a Prediction

Not all charts, even those possessing a reasonably well-formed pattern, have a predictive value. The key lies in asking what the pattern is indicating, and then asking if that makes sense given the chart as a whole. A head and shoulders pattern at the bottom of a well-defined downtrend would not signal a reversal, where an inverted one would. It is impossible to reverse a market that isn't trending, and impossible to break out of a market that isn't congested or reversing. Sometimes the price action on a chart indicates a sort of probabilistic no-man's land, where the market is equally likely to go up or down, and by a potentially similar amount.

Chapter 4 - Technical Analysis

Horses for Courses

Every market will form patterns that will recur with more frequency than others. The energy space tends to feature stable, elongated trend channels, frequent bear and bull flags, and well-defined triangles and wedges. In a different market (or in the same market at a different time) other patterns could dominate the price action. A chartist learning a new market would do well to peruse as much historical data as possible to get a feel for what types of patterns to expect, what is normal, and what is abnormal.

The Fractal Nature of Technical Analysis

A fractal is a geometric pattern whose general form is constructed out of smaller iterations of itself that repeat under increased magnification with infinite complexity.[21] Financial markets have a fractal element to their price fluctuations, as the same types of patterns form on monthly charts, daily charts, and 1-minute and tick charts, and the larger patterns and trends are built out of the aggregation of compounded smaller patterns and trends. The micro scale influences the intermediate scale, which impacts the macro scale. If a trader can figure out what a market is doing right now, it may inform what happens for the rest of the day. If a trader understands today, that will give greater clarity to their view of next month.

Most technicians will ultimately spend the majority of their time on a chart resolution and study timeframe that works well in their market and for their methodology. It is important to look at the same product through a different lens from time to time, dropping down to a faster chart for intraday patterns or zooming out to a multi-year perspective to look for long-term trends.

Tipping Points

The tendency of technical patterns to appear at all resolution levels of the data can lead to a circumstance where a small intraday pattern can have an outsized influence on the longer-term trend. Imagine a long-term downtrend experiencing a normal countertrend retracement to near the top of the downtrend channel, where on an intraday chart the market forms a bull flag. If the bull flag breaks out to the upside it may provide enough impetus to extend the countertrend and push the market outside of the downtrend channel, a neutral signal if not outright bullish. Conversely, if the bull flag fails then the countertrend movement is likely at an end and the long-term downtrend is intact.

---

[21] The best-known example is the Mandelbrot Set, named after renowned mathematician (and sometime financial theorist) Benoit Mandelbrot.

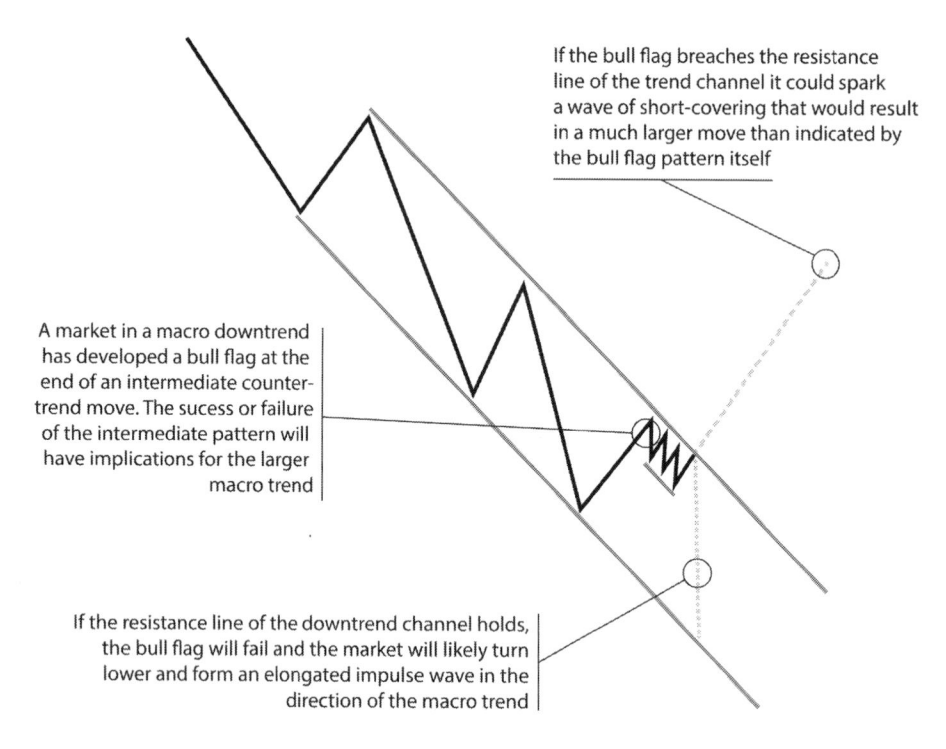

Figure 4.13 Micro-level patterns that impact intermediate patterns that impact macro patterns.

Technical Tools & Measuring Techniques
Technical analysis provides a variety of tools that allow the trader to make inferences into the magnitude of a potential move indicated by a trend, reversal, or pattern.

Pattern-Implied Price Objectives
Many chart patterns have an implied measurement component. Head and shoulders will typically generate a move back against the trend of approximately the height of the pattern. The same is true of boxes for retracements and continuations. Wedges and triangles will tend to exhibit a move in the direction of the prior trend of approximately the height of the widest part of the triangle. Bull and bear flags often have symmetrical movements immediately before and after the flag in the direction of the trend.

Numerical Methods
Technical analysts will also utilize a variety of numerical metrics to assist in interpretation of chart patterns. Most are methods for contrasting and contextualizing recent market fluctuations against the backdrop of longer-term trends. The most commonly used tools are moving average studies, Bollinger Bands, and Fibonacci retracements.

Moving Averages

Moving average studies are used to compare current market fluctuations against the recent price history and the totality of the macro move. A common study involves comparing short-term "fast" and longer-duration "slow" lines. The position of the fast line relative to the slow line indicates a market that is moving higher or lower, with any intersection of the fast and slow lines very closely watched as a momentum indicator. If the market is trending lower, the fast line should always be leading the way and be below the slow line. If the distance between the two lines contracts, or if the fast line crosses over the slow line, it is a signal that the long-term downtrend is certainly weakening, possibly ending altogether. A moving average cross can be a very convenient, logical exit signal and a useful entry signal. Moving average crosses make problematic reversal signals unless the trader incorporates some sort of minimum breach or duration criteria to screen out periods where the averages intersect multiple times within a short timespan. Markets that are prone to shallow up/downtrends or long periods of non-trending dithering will produce a lot of crossing but no real subsequent movement. Crosses in strongly trending markets, however, are significant, as seen in the following chart.

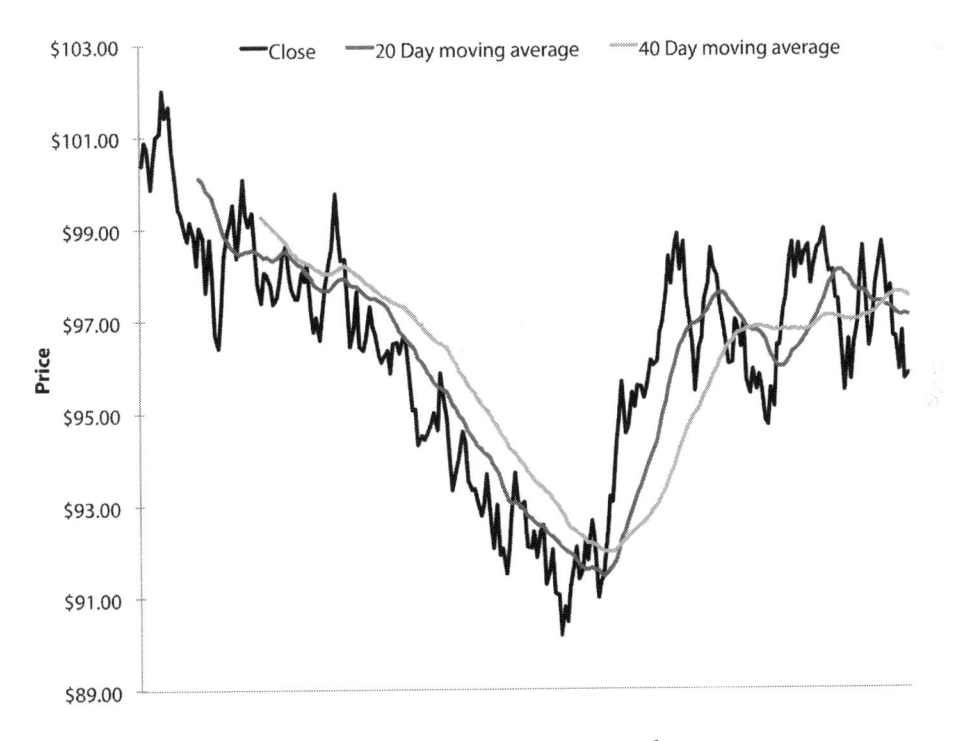

Figure 4.14 20-day and 40-day moving average studies.

Some technicians develop complex studies utilizing three, four, or more moving averages to generate trading signals. Extremely creative traders will sometimes utilize moving averages that lag or lead the price, where for example a 20-day moving average for days 31-50 would be calculated on day 50 but plotted against the close of an earlier or later date. The principal danger for traders attempting to deploy more esoteric combination moving average studies is misattributing predictive value to a set of quasi-random squiggles that happen to match well with the recent price history.

Bollinger Bands
Bollinger Bands are the creation of noted technical analyst John Bollinger. They are constructed around a multi-period moving average, with an upper and lower boundary around the current price based on the recent standard deviation. The upper and lower bands expand and contract around the moving average with the ongoing volatility. The most common Bollinger Bands are calculated at two standard deviations above and below a 20-day moving average and serve as an indicator that a market has, in the short term, become overbought or oversold. Prices have a tendency to become temporarily cheap or expensive (within the context of recent fluctuations), trade up or down to a Bollinger Band level, then quickly mean-revert back to a more normal value. If this sounds like a great recipe for a short-term trading strategy, it almost is. Bollinger Bands are extremely useful for contextualizing the micro-trend chop and finding good entry and exit points for short-term trades or constructive levels to add to larger, medium or longer-term positions. The main danger to a pure mean-reverting, short-term strategy is the tendency for prices to "ride" the top or bottom Bollinger Band for an extended number of periods instead of moving back to center, which can prove costly when the market is accelerating rapidly away from the moving average.

The following chart shows a standard 20-day moving average with the Bollinger Bands calculated based on two standard deviations of the 20-day moving average. Note both the tendency to touch and react away from the upper and lower bounds, as well as the propensity to ride the line for multiple periods of time.

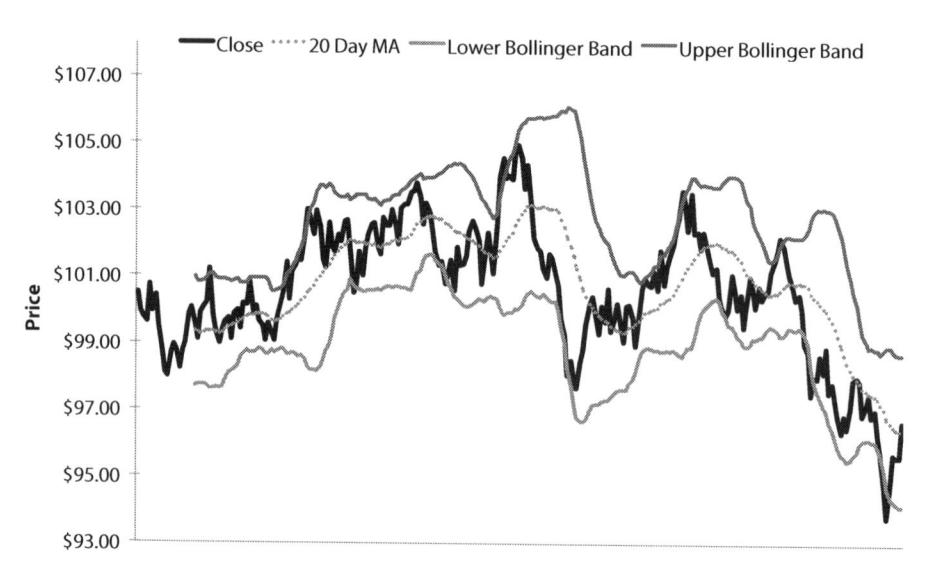

Figure 4.15   Bollinger Band study.

Chapter 4 - Technical Analysis

Fibonacci Retracements

Leonardo Fibonacci was a prominent 13th century mathematician who, when not otherwise occupied bringing the decimal system to Europe or writing the *Liber Abaci*[22] liked to research the big-picture problems of the day, like the growth rate over time of a colony of rabbits. Fibonacci discovered that the size of the colony of rabbits was best modeled as a series of numbers with each successive observation being the arithmetic sum of the two previous numbers. This results in an ever-accelerating trajectory beginning with one:

1, 1, 2, 3, 5, 8, 13, 21, 34, 55, 89, 144, 233, 377, 610, 987, 1597, 2584, 4181, 6765…

Technicians use the Fibonacci numbers to calculate the potential magnitude of an anticipated (or ongoing) reversal of a trend. The distance traversed by the trend is measured and six potential retracement target levels are calculated and plotted on the chart. The standard retracement levels are 0%, 23.6%, 38.2%, 50%, 61.8%, and 100%.

Consider the following chart, where a large trend that has taken prices from $100.00 down to $85.00 encounters buying interest and rallies higher:

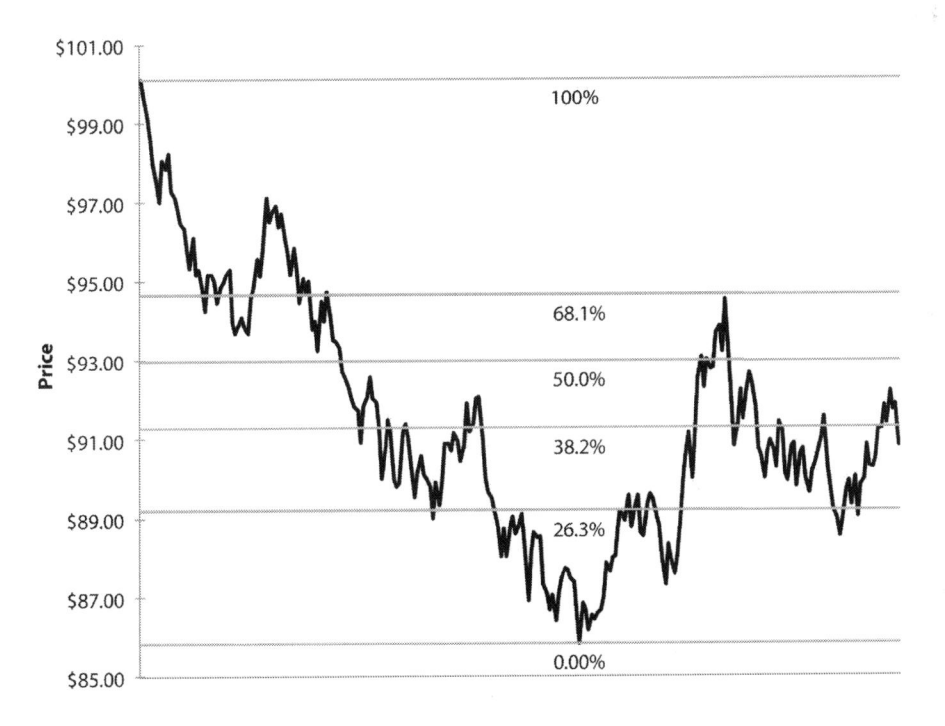

Figure 4.16   Fibonacci retracement levels for a macro market move.

---

[22] The "Book of Calculation"

Technicians measure the total distance traversed by the trend, then plot a set of lines corresponding to the Fibonacci retracement percentages of that range over the price chart. It is difficult to say exactly why Fibonacci retracement levels are such useful indicators. The accepted logic is that it is a combination of self-fulfilling prophecy made real by believing market practitioners and the somewhat obvious fact that the three most commonly targeted levels (38.2%, 50%, 61.8%) roughly correspond to a retracement of about half of the initial trend.

The fractal nature of technical analysis means that retracements can also have retracements, as seen in the following chart where the move from the bottom at $85.00 up to $95.00 turns lower and corrects:

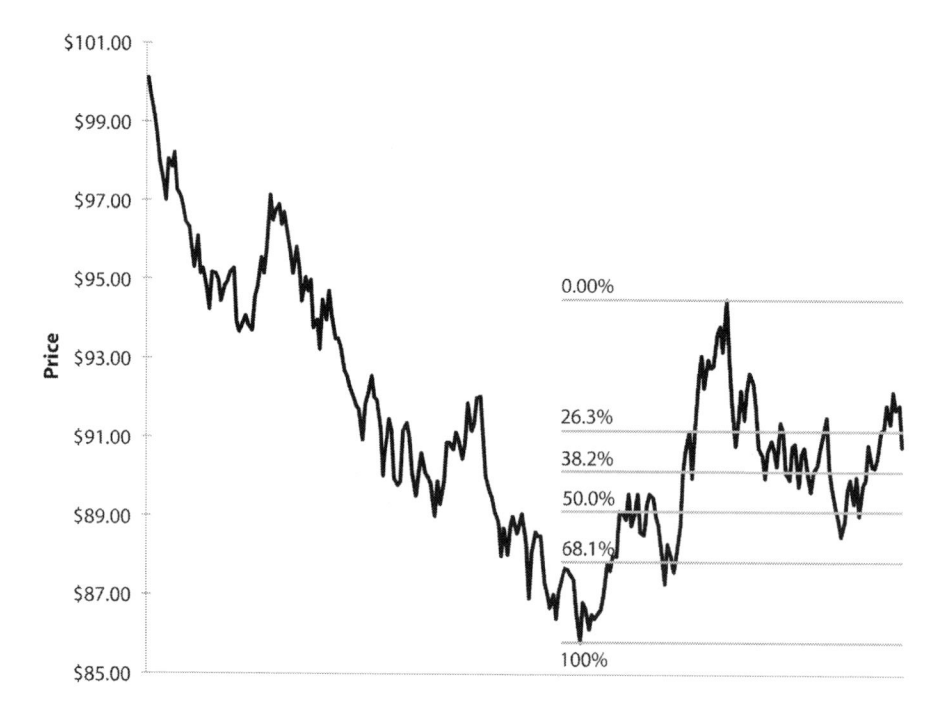

Figure 4.17   Fibonacci retracement levels for an intermediate countertrend move.

Fibonacci retracement levels are particularly useful when examining relatively large, long-term trends that have broken down or made a defined reversal pattern. They provide context for the potential magnitude of the reversal or retracement and provide an answer to the question "How far could it go?"

Fibonacci retracement levels take on increased importance, and have additional predictive value, when combined with pre-existing support and resistance levels or technical measurements derived from a reversal or continuation pattern. In the following chart a trend from $88.00 to $103.00 has reversed and is approaching the 38.2% retracement level, which

Chapter 4 - Technical Analysis

coincides with a support level just below $98.00 as defined by the two previous, pre-breakout peaks.

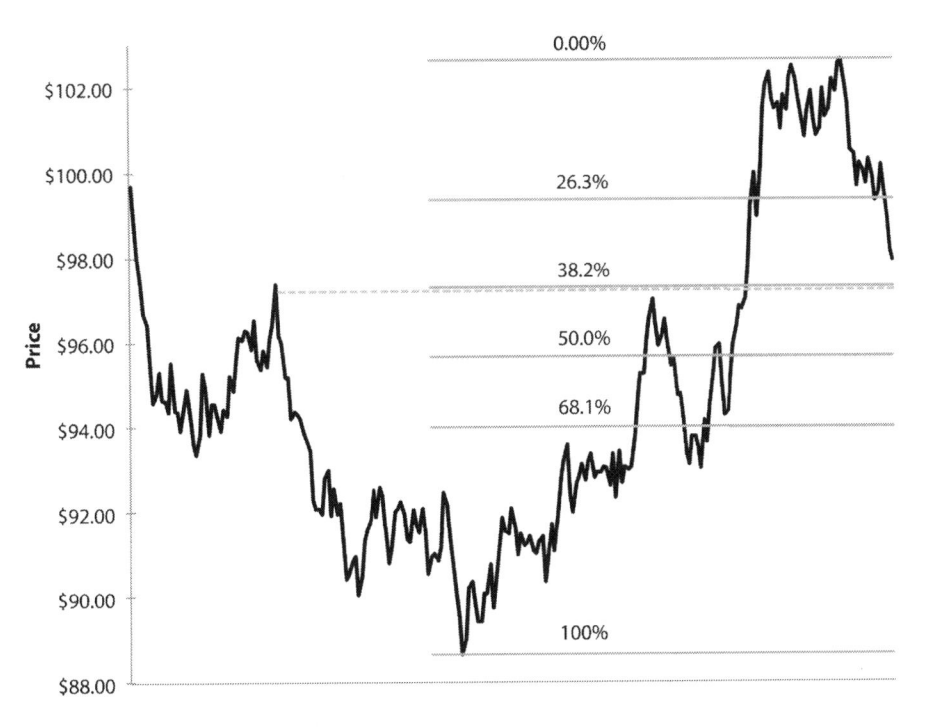

Figure 4.18   Combining Fibonacci retracement levels with support levels.

The 38.2% Fibonacci line represents a level where the market could conceivably pause, but the same could also be said of the 50.0% and 61.8% levels, in isolation. The fact that the 38.2% line lies very close to the two prior tops, which should serve as relatively robust support, adds additional credence to the assertion that the market will pause and possibly consolidate at that level.

Volume as an Indicator
Technical analysts pay close attention to the relative volume of transactions that accompany chart pattern creation and significant breaches of support and resistance. A breakout on increased volume is more interesting than one with minimal participation. A move made with fewer than normal transactions along the way will be easier to re-traverse than a robust, well-traded rally or sell off. The more trades at or around a particular level, and the greater the open interest, the higher the likelihood that it will function as a valid support or resistance level.

Congestion Levels
A congestion level is an area on a chart where the market trades a substantial amount of volume within a compressed area. While not a defined pattern with implicit predictive implications, congestion levels are interesting for technical traders as they represent the

creation of vested interest at or around a price level. Any rapid move away from that level will create winning and losing positions, which the winners will want to keep and the losers will be desperate to unwind. Congestion levels are particularly interesting in markets with low intraday liquidity, where a temporary surge of participant enthusiasm can create a volume of new positions that cannot easily be unwound without moving prices sharply higher or lower.

Consider the following tick chart, which depicts 500 individual trades:

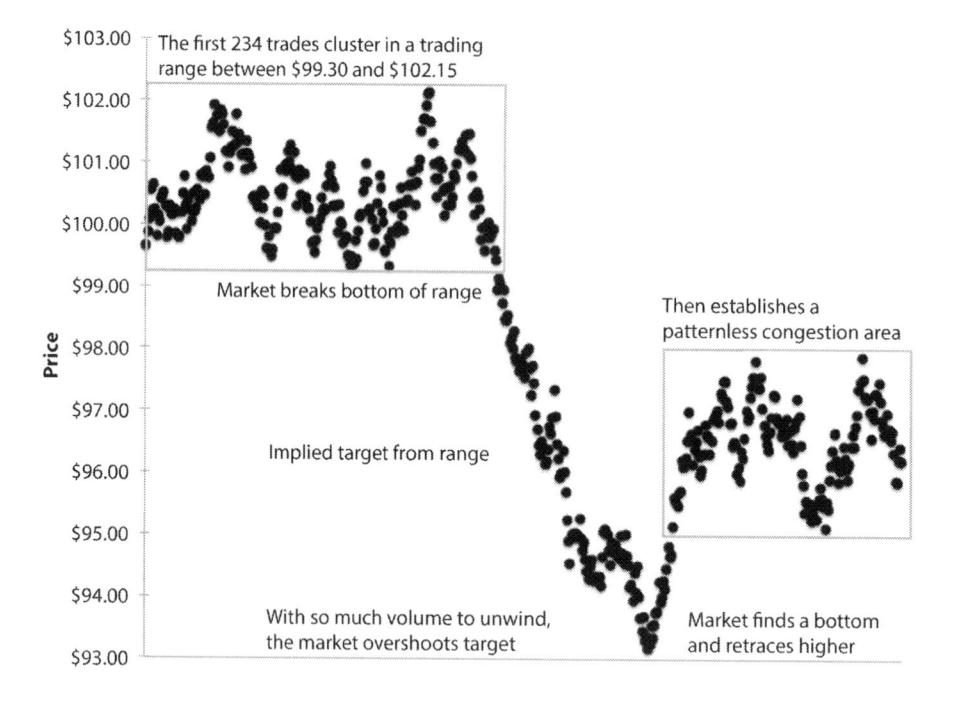

Figure 4.19   Congestion levels in tick data.

The first 234 trades on the chart are clustered between $99.30 and $102.15. As soon as the market breaks below $99.30 there are 234 winning short trades and 234 losing long positions. While not all losing traders will immediately seek to exit their position, many certainly will. If the market makes a low volume move away from the congestion level it may be difficult for the losing traders to exit, which will continue to drive the market lower. This type of self-perpetuating market move is sometimes called a "rolling stop-loss," where the actions of traders closing out positions push other traders past their point of comfort, motivating additional buying or selling. It can be very beneficial for traders to monitor the volume accumulated during a congestion formation, as even a rough estimate can provide a sense of the losing positions that will need to be unwound and give some perspective on the potential magnitude and duration of any buying/selling motivation.

Chapter 4 - Technical Analysis

Elliott Wave Theory

Trend channels and patterns are relatively straightforward concepts that tend to resonate with even hardcore, fundamental traders. Elliott Wave Theory is a bit of an inflection point, a dividing line beyond which many technicians feel that the complexity of the interpretation required starts to degrade the quality of the analysis. The definitive book on the subject is *Elliott Wave Principle: Key to Market Behavior* by A.J. Frost and Robert R. Prechter, and the foundations of the theory are constructed on the same rational bedrock as the best technical analysis:

> Under the Wave Principle, every market decision is both *produced by* meaningful information and *produces* meaningful information. Each transaction, while at once an *effect*, enters the fabric of the market and, by communicating transactional data to investors, joins the chain of *causes* of others' behavior.[23]

Elliott Wave Theory is built around a pattern of five waves, arranged in defined pattern.

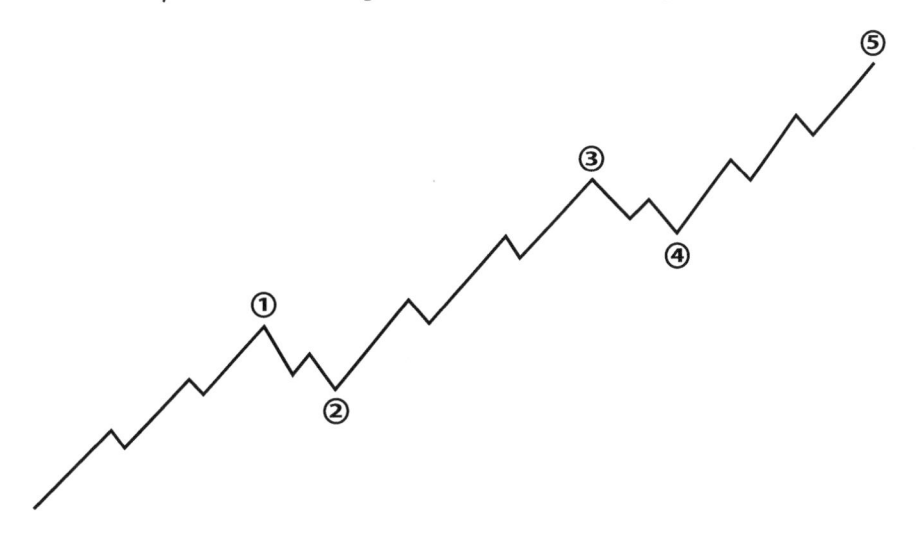

Figure 4.20   The basic Elliott Wave shape with five alternating waves.

Each of the five legs is numbered, with the impulses in the direction of the trend labeled 1, 3, 5 and the retracements 2 and 4. Each of the legs of the trend can be further divided into subwaves, five for each of the trend legs (1, 2, 3, 4, 5) and three for the retracements (a, b, c).[24]

---

[23] Robert R. Prechter, Jr. and A.J. Frost, *Elliott Wave Principle: Key To Market Behavior* (West Sussex: John Wiley & Sons Ltd, 1999), 20. Copyright © 1978-1998 Robert R. Prechter, Jr.
[24] There are a significant number of specific criteria that must be present in a proper five-wave pattern, i.e., the retracements must be proportional to the motive waves, the waves must not overlap, etc. Each wave will also have a unique set of performance characteristics.

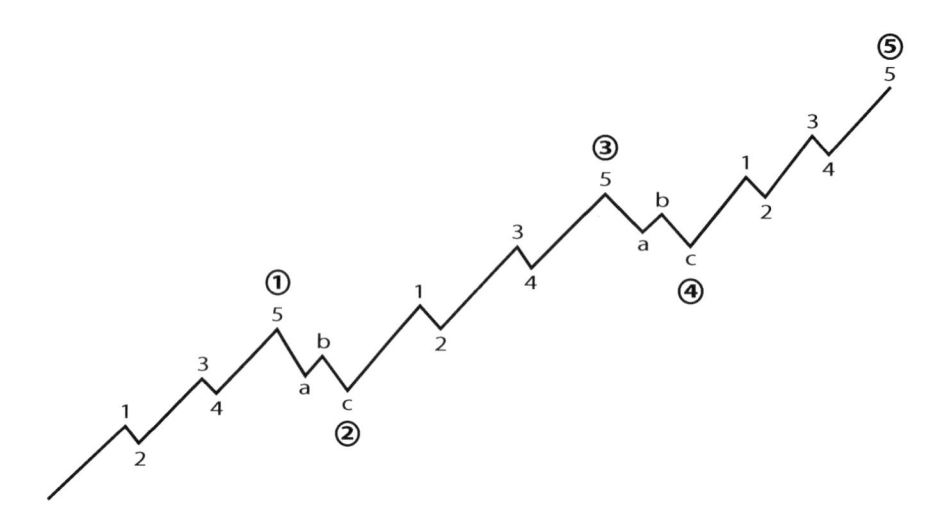

Figure 4.21 The Elliott five-wave pattern, with impulse subwaves numbered and retracement waves lettered.

Elliott disciples love to identify, classify, and count waves which, coupled with the fractal nature of technical analysis, allows the chartist to break down any portion of the pattern into smaller subwaves for a microscopic analysis. A trend or a retracement can also be recontextualized as minor portion of a larger wave pattern for long-term trend forecasting.

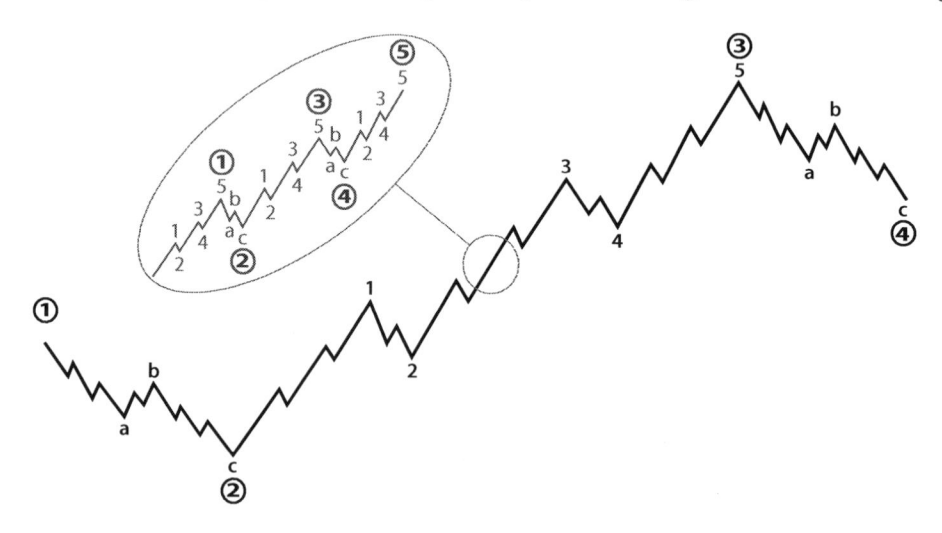

Figure 4.22 The fractal nature of wave counting.

Elliott Wave Theory more formally codifies the three interacting forces of Dow Theory, where the trend-producing motive force alternates with countertrend retracements in the presence of short-term volatility. One of the main benefits of Elliott Wave Theory is that it inculcates in the trader an understanding that markets rarely move in straight lines, and that mid-trend retracements and larger countertrend moves are both to be expected and, to the extent possible, anticipated.

Elliott Wave Theory is a favorite tool of long-term forecasters and buy-and-hold investors. The ability to place a market move within a larger macro context gives the trader both a sense of direction and a feeling for the scale and anticipated timeframe of the potential movement.

For a short- to medium-term trader, most of the value of Elliott Wave Theory should be obtainable via a much more straightforward trend and pattern analysis. My belief that *a partially formed pattern is not a pattern* conflicts with many hard-core Elliotticians' desires to identify a partial wave form early in its development and impute the remainder of the trajectory.

Understand What the Chart Is Saying as a Whole

Many traders cannot see the forest for the trees with technical patterns, obsessing over the smallest details and ignoring the totality of the chart and the picture it is painting. Others use the chart as a convenient rationalization for an action they had already planned to take.

Seeing What They Want to See

Any scientist worth her lab coat knows that constructing an experiment with a particular result in mind will, unsurprisingly, tend to produce that result. This is also true of technical analysis. Traders with a fundamental bias are particularly susceptible to this methodological flaw. They take a well-reasoned, sound fundamental view and attempt to use technical analysis to buttress the argument. "The market must be near a fundamental bottom, see if the chart says that." Worse yet, others will develop some hunch, pet theory, or "feeling," then pore over charts looking for some sort of significant squiggle or sketchy line they can draw to justify whatever they were planning on doing all along.

Connecting the Dots in a Thin Market

In extremely thin or choppy markets it is particularly important to look at the whole picture, as a lack of trades—and therefore observations—can make spotting breakouts and measuring responses challenging. The overall picture will be less crisp, so the trader must forget about micrometer-level precision and instead focus on the major theme, if there is one to be found.

How the Market Gets From Point A to B Matters

A trader must examine the texture of the chart, as a whole. If it is making lower highs and lower lows, the market is in a downtrend. But *how* is the market making the highs and lows? Is it grinding higher in small increments over many days, only to give it up in sudden, massive sell-offs? Does it drift lower only to be blown skyward by intermittent stimuli? Is the pattern regular and predictable, bouncing back and forth between channel lines, or does it surf the top then crash to the bottom before re-establishing somewhere in the middle? These are critical distinctions if the trader intends to utilize the intermediate trend to get positioned (generally a good idea) or to trade against the macro trend (possible, but risky). If the trader intends to ride the macro trend, understanding the "normal" intra-pattern characteristics is crucial for risk to reward assessment and execution strategy. A seemingly obvious trend may, on closer examination, not be tradable at all. Assessing the tradability of a market move will be covered in much more detail in Chapters 7 and 12.

Anyone Who Can't Spot the Technician at the Poker Table *Is* the Technician
People generally assume that elite poker players dream of sitting down to a game full of rich novices who can barely hold their cards. In actuality, nothing could be further from the truth. Beginning poker players have no idea of what they are supposed to do, no idea of the odds that govern the game, no paradigm for understanding when a player is strong or weak, and no concept of when to bet or fold. High-stakes poker is about applying pressure, forcing the other players at the table to evaluate the circumstances and arrive at the conclusion that the only logical course of action is folding and surrendering the chips already committed to the pot. Pros are much more interested in the certainty of making their opponents quit than they are in taking their chances by letting a challenger play to the end of the hand where the best cards prevail.

The same dynamic is at play in a market where a technical trader is faced with less aware, less responsive counterparties. A trader holding a winning long position is not going to get the hoped-for wave of short covering to push prices higher unless the other market participants 1) recognize that there has been a market event that they need to be aware of; 2) interpret that event in the "correct" way; 3) proceed to take the logical reactive steps and buy back their losing short positions.

When a chartist says:

> We had been trading in a range from $48.00 to $53.00 with a significant amount of volume accumulating between those levels. This break higher to $53.50 should cause a short-covering rally to approximately $58.00, if it plays itself out completely.

What he really means is:

> All the people who have sold this thing are wrong, and I'm fairly certain that if prices go a little higher, they won't be able to stand the pain and will have to start closing out their positions. That wave of buying will cause prices to rise significantly because there are a lot of people hurting and a lot of bad positions to close out.

This analysis works best in a market where the players are sophisticated enough to know that they have bad positions that they need to do something about. There is a certain amount of trader savvy required to incent action. In a market entirely populated by hedge-and-forget naturals or buy-and-hold investors, technical responses to events will not be as crisp or consistent as might otherwise be expected.

Conversely, in a market dominated by technicians, there will tend to be a higher than expected number of false breakouts, abrupt moves, and incomplete patterns as participants race to pile

Chapter 4 - Technical Analysis

into and back out of the same trades at the same time. Clearly defined technical patterns can become instantly self-fulfilling propositions. If a chart pattern has indicated a highly probable move from $45.00 to $50.00, there may be an explosive jump from $45.00 to $47.00-48.00 as every chartist rushes in to buy at the same time. If the market manages to rally a little more, it may get stuck as a wave of traders clamor to sell in advance of the $50.00 target. Ironically, in markets where technical analysis should work best, it can sometimes fail because the entire market is trying to do the same thing at the same time.

The most productive environment for a technical trader is a market with a diverse mix of technical and nontechnical participants with varying levels of sophistication, such that the trader's skills are a useful advantage but are neither so unique as to be useless or so prevalent as to make every move a matter of instantaneous manifest destiny.

Dealing With Imperfect Patterns
Once in a very great while a perfect chart pattern will appear. The structure will be pristine, the objective clear, the predictability high, and the measurement precise. The charts traders see on a day-to-day basis are never so well constructed or so easy to interpret. Learning to extract meaning from imperfect data and misshapen patterns is a critical part of a technician's job. The most common problems are that the pattern is too short, too narrow, or too small.

As a general rule, the larger the pattern the easier it is to observe and interpret and the higher the predictive value. The more visible the pattern is the more likely that people see it and attempt to trade it, making it more of a self-fulfilling prophecy. The larger the pattern, the longer it takes to play out, and the greater the vested interest accumulated during its creation. It is much more psychologically impactful to say, "everyone who has sold this year is now losing money," rather than "everyone who has sold in the last four minutes is losing money." It speaks to interested volume and pressure, which translates into potential energy for a price movement. If the pattern is so small that it is generating impractical trading suggestions, given the prevailing market characteristics, it is not worth considering. A vaguely head-and-shoulders-esque wiggle that seems to indicate a break $0.50 lower is not terribly useful if the market is quoted $0.25 wide. A target two ticks down would necessitate a less than one tick stop, which is effectively untradeable.

When a trader is confronted by a particularly ugly scribble of a chart that perhaps might contain some semblance of a pattern it is important to remember that though there may not be an obvious, well-defined trigger or an easily measured target, there can still be a significant amount of information available. If a fine detail analysis is not possible, what gross observations can be made that can at least help the trader sharpen a fundamental thesis? The trader should start with the basics then continue to layer on analysis until the chart no longer yields incremental information. Is it trending, making higher highs and higher lows, or vice versa? Is the trend in progress, or has it been halted by a pattern or reversal?

Markets with high levels of volatility (or highly variable levels of volatility) can present challenges for a technical trader. Most trading methodologies place significance on closing through key technical levels, with intraday violations seen as notable, but less meaningful, indicators. A market with large intraday ranges but relatively small open-to-close differentials can force an analyst to make some highly subjective decisions as to where to draw trend lines or pattern boundaries. Extreme outlier days are also problematic. A market used to $0.05-0.10 ranges that experiences an anomalous $0.50 intraday swing up and down and then closes almost unchanged will likely violate every trend line and pattern boundary in the vicinity, but to what actual effect? As always, a consistent interpretational methodology and knowledge of the product are critical. If the market still yields predictable results from patterns with false breakouts or wide intraday ranges, great. If not, the trader will have move to the sidelines and wait for tighter, more cohesive patterns to emerge.

The opposite problem occurs with markets that trade infrequently or have small intraday ranges coupled with large overnight gaps. Instead of a robust price formation the trader will be faced with what looks like a connect-the-dots puzzle. The shape will be present, but there will be no substance. A low-volume trace of what appears to be a pattern will not tend to have as much predictive utility, as the lack of vested interest accumulated during its creation will lead to less motivation to unwind losing positions and a correspondingly muted price response.

While it is possible to derive useful information from imperfect charts, the trader must be aware that the possibility for interpretational error increases. Beyond a certain point it may be necessary to concede that, even though it appears to be some sort of a pattern, there is no usable informational content.

Drawing Inexact Trend Lines
In theory, drawing a trend line on a chart should not be an interpretive event. A series of tops or bottoms is connected with a straight line, be it with a ruler and pencil or mouse click and a monitor. In practice, it is often necessary to take a more forgiving approach, particularly with markets prone to making sharp, low-liquidity intraday spikes. A simple price chart will not make any distinction between a low hammered out on massive volume and a couple of sketchy prints caused by market sell orders hitting garbage bids in a temporary buyer's strike. Consider the following daily bar chart:

Chapter 4 - Technical Analysis

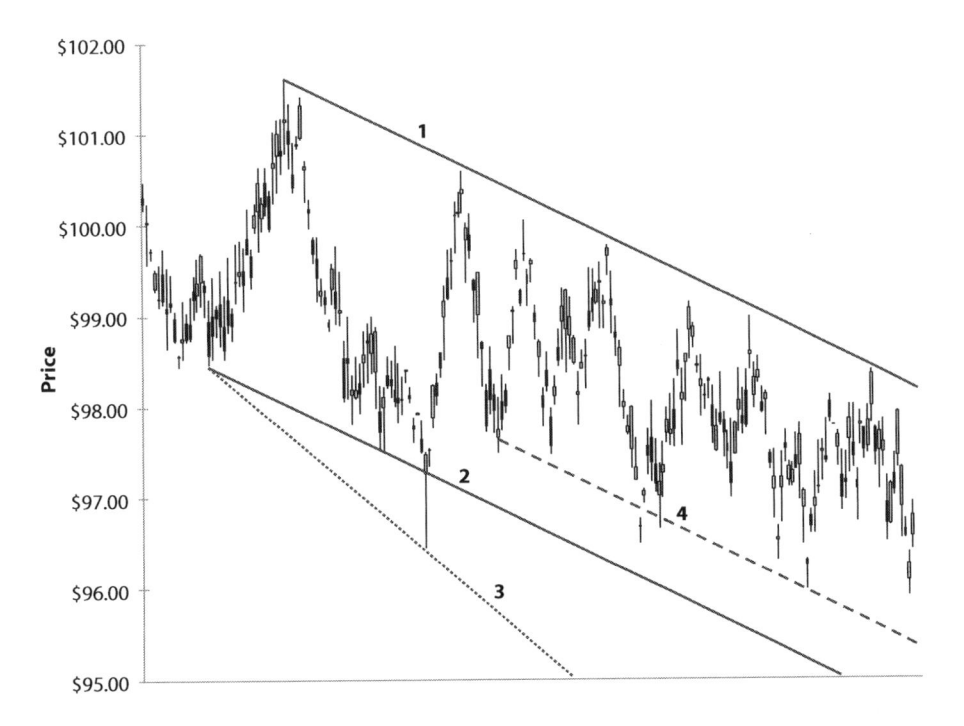

Figure 4.23   Drawing inexact trend lines.

Starting approximately 1/3 of the way through the price history, the market begins to form a series of successively lower highs and lower lows, the textbook definition of a downtrend. The situation becomes somewhat more challenging when the trader attempts to bound the downtrend with a channel. The upper line (1) created by connecting the peaks on Day 88 and 134 neatly bounds the next six peaks. Defining the bottom of the channel is significantly more problematic. Simply copying the trajectory of the topline and attaching it to the Day 68 low (2) works well for the Day 112 and 113 lows, but fails to account for the large intraday spike lower on Day 124. Attempting to incorporate the lows of Day 124 leads to a diverging line (3) that does not add any incremental information.

When the range begins to constrict in the second half of the chart, the trader is left with a channel that is too wide to be of predictive value. I feel that there is value to be had in copying the trajectory of the very well-defined, top downtrend line and imposing it on the relatively regular bottoms that form starting on Day 143. This fuzzy trend line (4) could arguably be placed higher or lower, or offset slightly to the left or the right. It is not as precise a tool as a well-defined top line, and no inferences should be drawn about intraday breaches or failure to exactly reach it before turning higher. The utility of a less-specific, fuzzily-defined trend line lies in reminding the trader that the market is still making lower lows and is still in a downtrend.

Given the increasing prevalence of low-liquidity, potentially HFT-driven price volatility, it is highly probable that technical traders will need to develop a tolerance for extracting information from less than perfect, fuzzy trend lines in the future.

An Analysis Without Probabilities Is a Guarantee
Technical analysis, with its highly visible charts and black-and-white interpretive tools, is frequently unfairly criticized after the fact when a breakout fails or a post-pattern move does not materialize as promised. When explaining a chart study, analysts and traders must avoid making overly definitive statements. Instead of saying, "It took out the top of the range, it's going up," it can be much more productive to say, "This is a clear breakout from an established trading range with good open interest. There are a sizable amount of trades (and traders) who are now losing money, so there should be a wave of short covering. There is probably a 70% chance we establish outside of the prior range and move higher. If the breakout fails, there is a 30% chance the market turns lower and continues to fluctuate within the range."

Believe It or Not
Paradoxically, technical analysis can also be useful to non-practitioners as long as they understand that in any given market there can be a very large number of clearly misguided people (from their perspective) who do believe in technical analysis with a burning, zealous intensity. If, by understanding the basic principles, an agnostic trader understands that a price breach will be interpreted by every technician in the galaxy as a bullish development that is a useful piece of information. Ironically, a disbelief in chart patterns can have traders watching them just as closely as any moon-phase tracking, point-and-figure junkie.

Chapter Four Summary
Technical analysis gives traders a set of tools that allow them to study a historical price chart and make inferences about future price fluctuations created by the ongoing battle between buyers and sellers. The trader will begin by determining if the market is or is not trending. From there, he will look for patterns that could indicate a temporary pause in a market's ongoing movement, signal its end, or presage a reversal. The trader will deploy a variety of numerical tools, including moving averages to assess the short-term vs. long-term momentum, Bollinger Bands to determine if the market is locally overbought or oversold, and Fibonacci levels that demarcate potential retracement levels. Elliott Wave analysis can be utilized to provide context for a market's near-term fluctuations relative to a larger, longer-term movements.

The next chapter will delve quantitatively and qualitatively deeper into the short-term fluctuations of the market by observing, characterizing, and calculating the volatility.

Review Questions

1. Describe the three primary forces that combine to create a market movement and how can each be used by traders.
2. What is the definition of a trend?

Chapter 4 - Technical Analysis

3. Give one example of a reversal, continuation and consolidation pattern.
4. Describe two numeric indicators used to assess the market and how they are used by traders.
5. What is the role of probability when expressing a technical perspective on the market?

Resources

- *Technical Analysis of the Financial Markets: A Comprehensive Guide to Trading Methods and Applications* by John J. Murphy
- *Elliott Wave Principle: Key to Market Behavior* by Robert R. Prechter, Jr. and A.J. Frost
- *The Psychology of Technical Analysis: Profiting from Crowd Behavior and the Dynamics of Price* by Tony Plummer
- *Bollinger on Bollinger Bands* by John Bollinger

Case Study: Technical Analysis of the Product X Market

Consider a graph of the ProdX futures end-of-day closing prices for the prior year for the prompt FEB contract:

Figure 4.24 FEB ProdX contract with prices of local highs and lows.

The first step is to determine if the market is, or is not, trending.

Chapter 4 - Technical Analysis

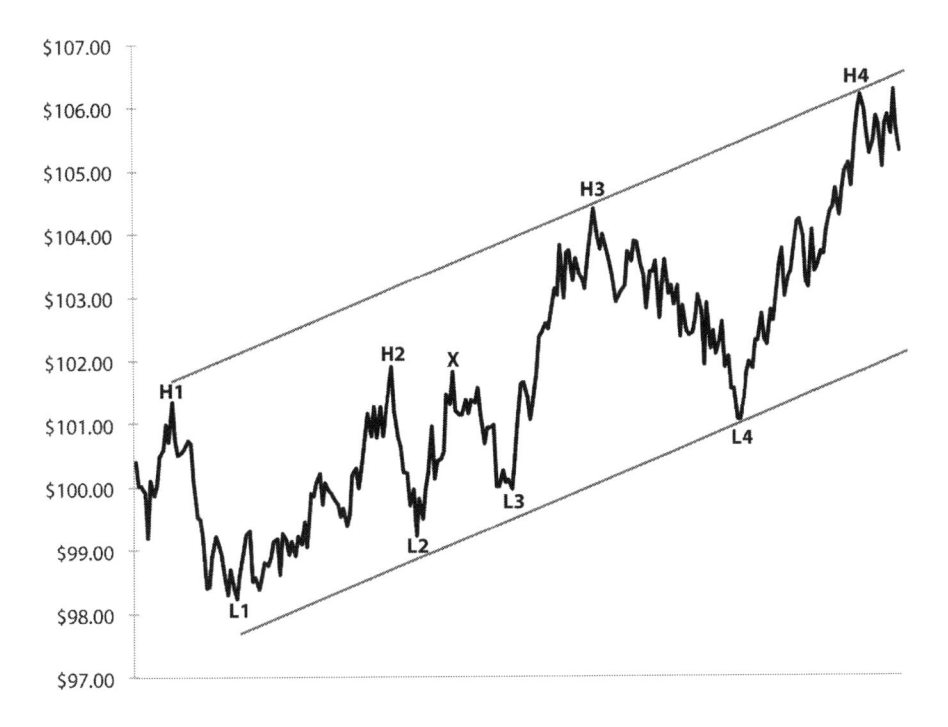

Figure 4.25   Is the FEB ProdX chart trending?

Beginning with the local low at $98.23 (L1), Product X makes an alternating series of higher highs and higher lows. There is a problematic consolidation area between the high at $101.89 (H2) and the low at $100.00 (L3), where the local peak at $101.80 (X) just barely fails to eclipse the previous high and, in so doing, casts some temporary doubt on the future of the overall uptrend. The fact that Product X immediately makes a constructive higher low (L3) and promptly rallies to new highs (H3) is sufficient to revitalize the macro trend and define the wide trend channel that encompasses Product X's price action.

Product X is clearly in an uptrend, and a trend in motion will tend to stay in motion until the underlying fundamental impetus dissipates, or it encounters an overwhelming opposing force. The trader must bring to bear all of the available technical tools to:

1. Understand the market's current position within the trend.
2. Assess the probability that the trend continues.
3. Understand the possible ramifications if it does not.

The first step is to examine the structure of the trend in progress, which can be done by attempting to map the standard Elliott 5-Wave pattern onto the closing price chart.

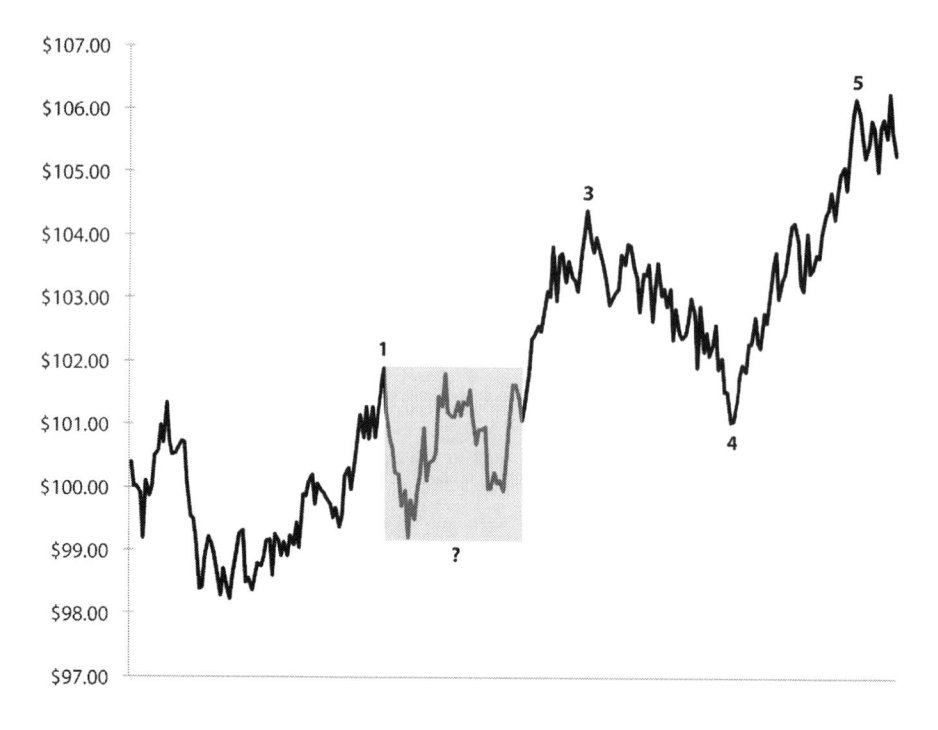

Figure 4.26   Consolidation pattern in the FEB ProdX chart.

Product X seems to have a generalized wave shape within the macro trend that has Elliott-like characteristics, with long, well-constructed primary waves interspersed with orderly retracements. The principal problem occurs within the shaded area (?), where following a macro-trend 1-wave, an Elliottician would expect to see a 2-wave making a three-step counter move. Instead, there is a medium-sized congestion pattern where the price action consolidates briefly before resuming a steep upward trajectory that peaks at $104.39 (3). The lack of well-defined sub-waves within the larger structure makes a precise count impossible. While it is possible (with some squinting and wishful thinking) to force the standard five count onto what would be the 1, 3, and 5 impulse waves, the 4th lacks clear definition in its choppy countertrend move, and the consolidation pattern obviously does not conform to the expected pattern.

Not hewing to the letter of the law does not mean that the chart does not contain useful information. Though the form may be somewhat irregular, the Product X chart clearly exhibits a well-defined upward-sloping macro trend featuring periodic intermediate countertrend moves with a moderate amount of micro chop present at all times. Since the chart does lack a clear Elliott wave pattern, it will be necessary to deploy additional metrics to gain insight into Product X's current trend.

A moving average study can give some sense of Product X's current momentum. Consider a chart of the 20-day and 40-day moving averages:

Chapter 4 - Technical Analysis

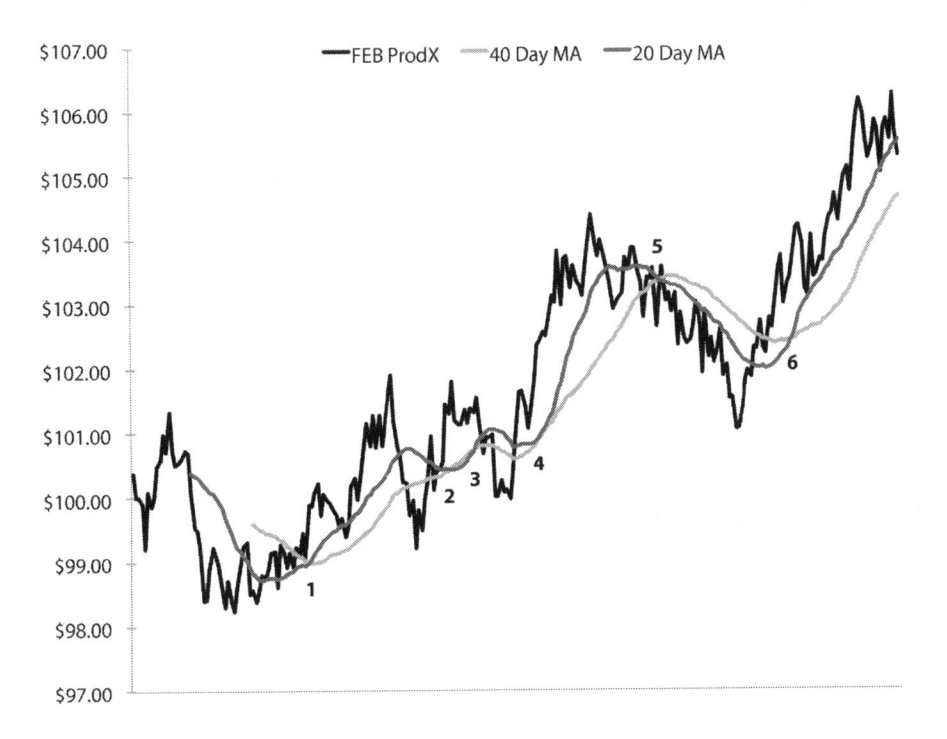

Figure 4.27 20-day and 40-day moving average studies for the FEB ProdX contract.

At the beginning of the chart Product X is in a short, steep downward trend with the faster 20-day moving average leading the slower 40-day lower. Product X makes a bottom at $98.23 and constructs a shallow consolidation pattern, during which the fast line crosses the slow line (1) and signals a bullish momentum shift and the start of the move to $101.89. During the consolidation pattern, the 20-day crosses below the 40-day (2), then almost immediately re-crosses back above (3), a common occurrence and a neutral signal as the market chops back and forth while trapped in a relatively narrow range. The fast line remains above the slow line during the conclusion of the consolidation and subsequent breakout higher, at one point getting as close as $0.02 (4) but remaining an overall bullish signal. The move concludes with a peak at $104.39, shortly after which the fast line decisively crosses below the slow line (5), generating a bearish signal that persists through the market bottom at $101.05. Product X makes a sharp bottom and rallies to new highs, with a confirming cross of the 20-day over the 40-day (6) generating a strong bullish signal that continues through the end of the chart.

The Product X chart illustrates how moving averages can do different things at different points on a chart. They are useful for signaling momentum shifts and potential future breakouts (1), indicating indecision and a lack of direction (2,3), or providing confirmation of a move already underway (5, 6).

Near-term overbought or oversold conditions can be examined by looking at a Bollinger Band chart for Product X. The following chart shows the end-of-day close data for Product X overlaid with a standard Bollinger Band analysis: a 20-day moving average and an upper and lower Bollinger Band calculated at two standard deviations.

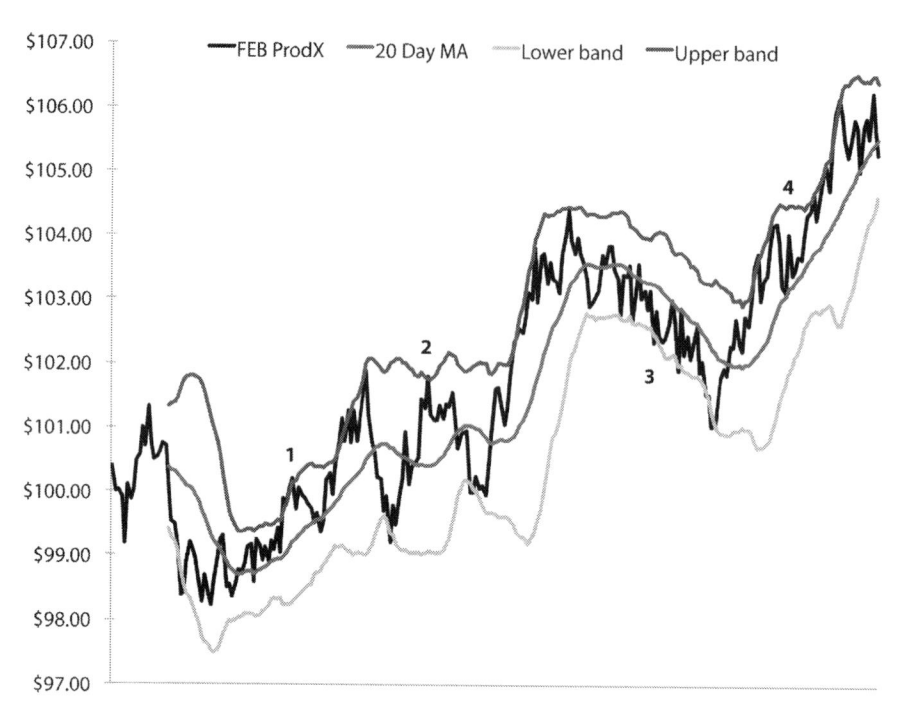

Figure 4.28   Bollinger Band study for the FEB ProdX contract.

The Product X chart seems to exist in one of two states, either riding the upper or lower Bollinger band during a well-defined trend move (1, 3, 4) or alternately bouncing off the top and bottom lines while constructing a choppy consolidation pattern (2). This diminishes the utility of the Bollinger Band as a short-term trading indicator, as it becomes difficult to interpret in real-time whether a brief initial contact is the start of a reversal, or the beginning of a prolonged period of being overbought or oversold. The Product X Bollinger Bands are of relatively constant width, with the exception of an expansion around the chop of the consolidation pattern (2), providing a non-quantitative visual indication that Product X has a relatively constant level of volatility (to be more formally computed in Chapter 5). In all three of the trend sections (1, 3, 4) the price has become trapped between the upper/lower band and the central 20-day moving average, indicating that Product X is capable of being relatively "cheap" or "expensive" for a protracted period of time. At the conclusion of the chart, Product X has recently been riding the top Bollinger Band in a bullish manner and has reverted back to the central 20-day moving average, indicating that it is currently at a locally "fair" price. Given Product X's tendency to confine its fluctuations to the top or bottom half of the Bollinger Band study, this could be interpreted as being somewhat undervalued if other

Chapter 4 - Technical Analysis

indicators suggest that both the current move and that particular behavior are likely to continue.

The next step is to examine the Product X chart for patterns that could presage the continuation of the current trend, signal a pause for consolidation, or warn of a potential reversal against the macro trend.

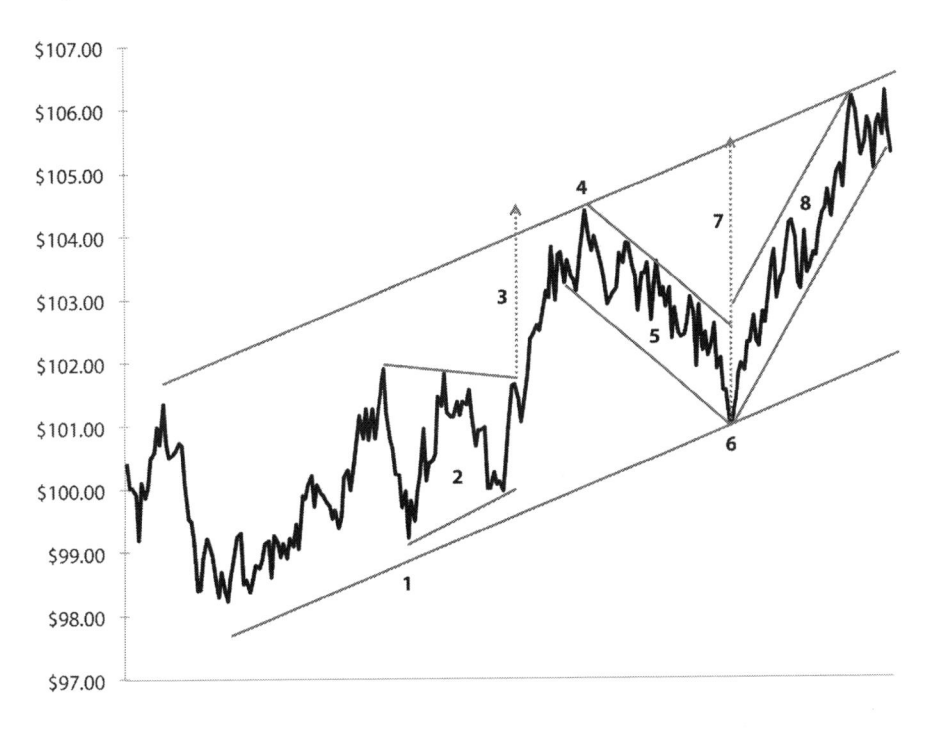

Figure 4.29   Pattern analysis of the FEB ProdX chart.

As noted before, Product X is in a macro uptrend bounded by a relatively well-defined trend channel. After making a low at $98.23 Product X rallies to $101.89 before falling to $99.21 (1) and bouncing off of what ultimately proves to be the support line that defines the bottom of the trend channel. The rally fails just below the prior peak, which sets up a series of decreasing-amplitude oscillations (2) with slightly lower highs and slightly higher lows, forming a symmetrical triangle. Symmetrical triangles are consolidation patterns, which have a higher probability of breaking out in the direction of the market's trajectory prior to the formation of the pattern (which proves true for Product X). The break of the top of the triangle implies a price target equal to the height of the widest part of the pattern (3), an objective that is achieved when Product X rallies to $104.39 (4).

Having used up the short-covering momentum, Product X encounters willing sellers and forms a well-constructed intermediate countertrend retracement that, combined with the prior sharp rally, forms a bull flag formation (5) that concludes with a sharp dive toward the support line (6) that forms the bottom of the macro up trend. The bull flag formation would imply a price target of approximately $105.50 based on the height of the pre-formation "flagpole" (7). The strong rally from $101.05 creates a V-shaped bottom that serves to clearly delineate the line that forms the bottom of the trend channel and leads to a strong rally to new highs (8). The peak at $106.25 further defines the trend channel. The last point at $105.29 sits on the bottom of the narrow channel that defines the most recent upward impulse wave, implying that prices are locally cheap but that constructive price action is necessary in the short term to maintain upward momentum and keep the rally alive.

To understand the magnitude of a potential countertrend move it can be constructive to examine the Fibonacci retracement levels. Consider the following chart superimposing the standard 0%, 23.6%, 38.2%, 50%, 61.8%, and 100% retracements over the totality of the move from the low at $98.23 to the peak at $106.25:

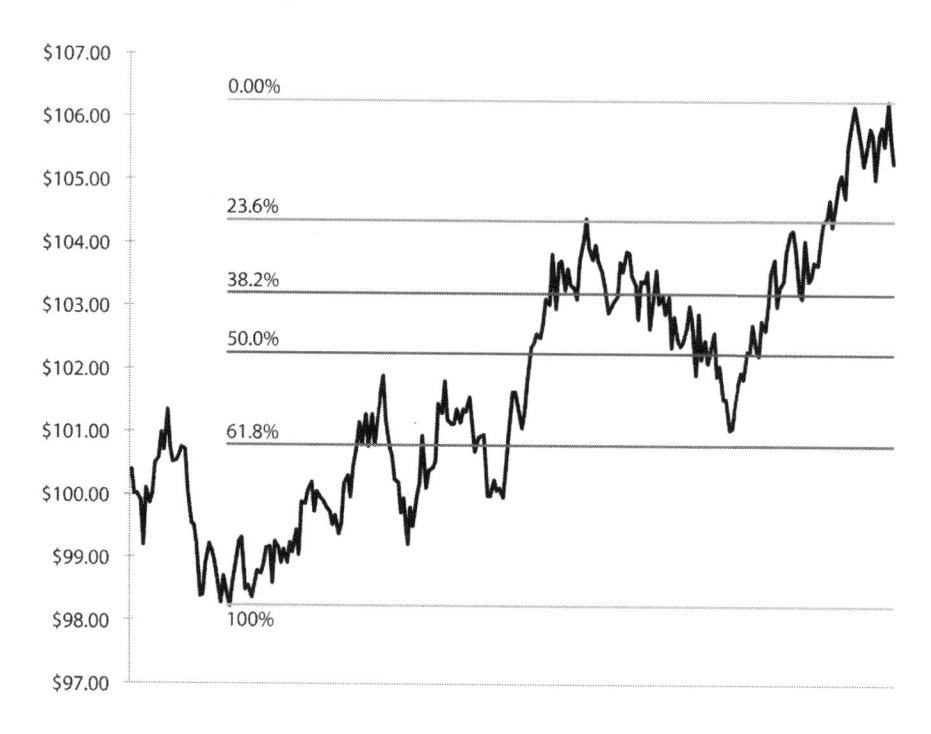

Figure 4.30   Applying Fibonacci retracement levels to the FEB ProdX chart.

Product X has a history of making wide, well-defined trend and countertrend movements, so it is entirely reasonable to expect that any sell-off from the current $106.25 level could bring the 23.6%, 38.2%, and possibly even the 50.0% lines into play without damaging the overall macro uptrend. For additional insight, it is frequently useful to examine a set of Fibonacci lines for just the most recent trend or countertrend move:

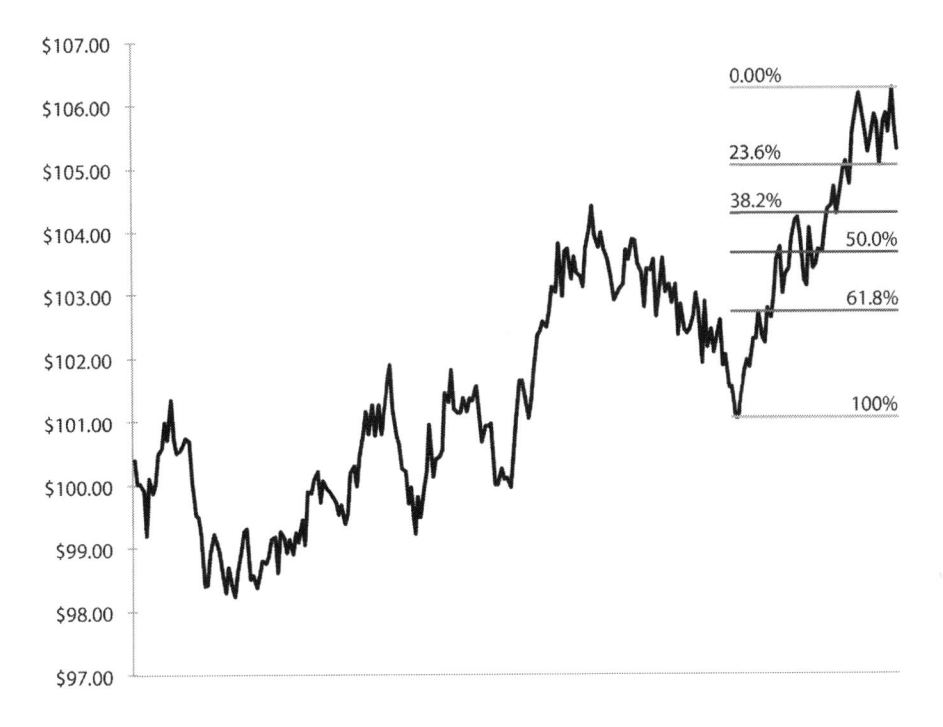

Figure 4.31 Applying Fibonacci retracement levels to the most recent impulse wave of the FEB ProdX chart.

It is particularly interesting to note that in the macro chart the 23.6% level falls at almost the same level as the 38.2% line in the short-term chart, which should indicate a higher probability of the level providing meaningful support.

There is also value in studying the extant chart features for additional clues to how far the market is capable of retracing if the macro motivational impulse wanes or encounters an immovable object. Reconsider the pattern chart:

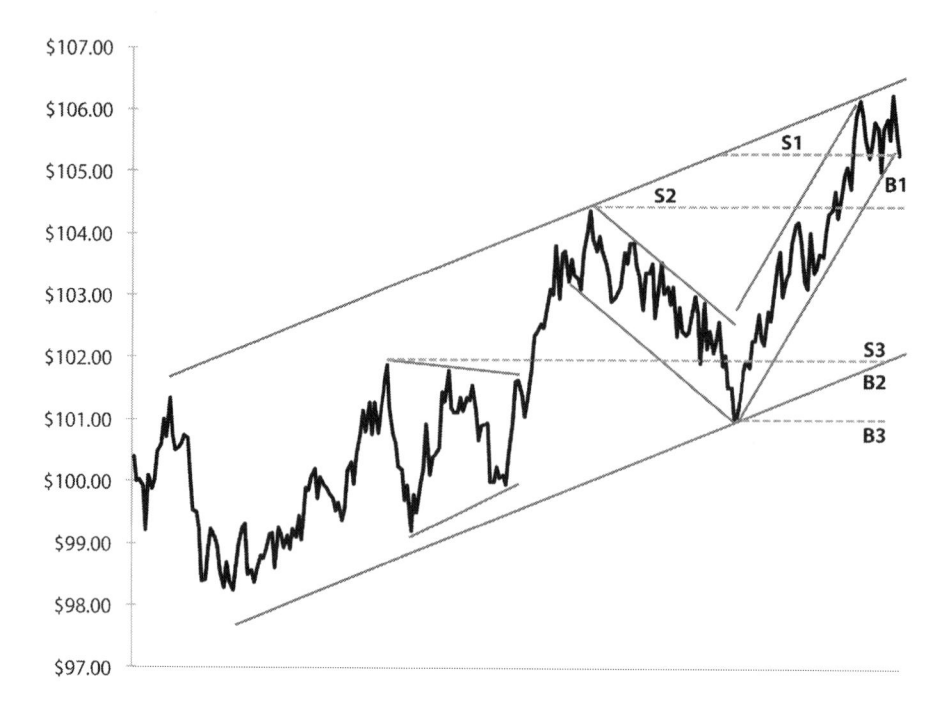

Figure 4.32 Analyzing the pattern study of the FEB ProdX chart for insight into possible retracement and support levels.

There are a number of features in the Product X chart that could reasonably be expected to serve as support in the event of a sell-off. The first would occur in the vicinity of Product X's current price of $105.29 (S1), where the compact channel that bounds the in-progress impulse wave comes into play. The first confirmation of trouble would involve violating the prior low (B1) that helped define the trend channel, a close below that point would invalidate the necessary premise that an uptrend makes a series of higher lows. Breaking the uptrend would likely incite a wave of selling that could easily push prices the short distance down to the prior high at $104.39 (S2).

Prior highs and lows, once defined, typically serve as support or resistance for future price action. Product X has a significant amount of trading interest between the prior high (S2) and the bottom of the trend channel, so while there is nothing to provide support between the two levels, a sell-off would most likely take the form of an elongated countertrend and not a sharp collapse. If prices do manage to work their way toward the bottom of the macro uptrend channel there are two supports that come into play in close proximity to each other (S3). The uptrend line that forms the bottom of the trend channel would come into play in the vicinity of $102, depending on the slope of the line and the time it takes to approach it, which should provide stout support. The top of the prior symmetrical triangle would also offer a large amount of vested interest that should act to blunt selling momentum. If concerted action by the sellers does manage to overpower the available buying interest and push below the uptrend

Chapter 4 - Technical Analysis

line (B2), the entire macro uptrend is in jeopardy. A decisive close below the prior low (B3) at $101.05 would end the macro uptrend by creating a lower low, and would almost certainly incite a wave of liquidation by long-side technical traders.

The only resistance level impeding the upward progress of Product X is the top of the macro uptrend channel, which would likely come into play somewhere between $106.00-$107.00, depending on the time taken to rally.

It is important to remember that a support or resistance level is neither a price target nor a justification for a market move for/against the trend. Saying that the price should "have a difficult time breaching" a particular level does not imply that the market "wants" or "needs" to go to that level. A retracement level is a point on the price chart where, due to vested interest from prior trading activity or sentiment-driven psychological factors, or both, the market could reasonably be expected to at least temporarily find balance and pause.

It is also critical to distinguish between retracements that are normal parts of a trend in motion and those that prove destructive to the trend. Countertrend moves that test support or resistance are normal and should be expected. Violating trend lines, taking out prior highs and lows and forming reversal patterns are cause for more serious concern.

I have found that pattern and trend retracement levels are more robust and provide more actionable trading information than those derived from Fibonacci numbers, due to the fact that they more accurately reflect the battle between buyers and sellers wherever it happens to occur, not just at particular, predetermined levels. Both types of retracement levels merit consideration in isolation, but take on increased importance—and have additional predictive value—when Fibonacci levels are combined with pre-existing support and resistance levels or technical measurements derived from a reversal or continuation pattern, as is the case with the $104.39 support level in the Product X chart, which sits at the relatively robust 23.6% macro- and 38.2% micro-move Fibonacci levels.

Understand What the Product X Charts Are Saying as a Whole
After deploying a suite of technical studies and analyzing each in isolation, the summary interpretation of the Product X market is:

1. The Product X market is in a reasonably well-defined uptrend marked by periods of consolidation, bounded by a wide trend channel.
2. There is no clearly defined Elliott Wave count, but the Product X chart does exhibit structure characterized by a macro uptrend with intermediate retracements and constant micro-level fluctuations.
3. Product X is currently in a bullish state based on the moving averages, with a clearly defined cross of the 20-day above the 40-day that has maintained a constant gap width through the end of the chart.
4. The Bollinger Band study shows Product X to be locally at or near "fair" value at the 20-day moving average.

5. Product X is currently in a well-defined impulse wave that has recently made new highs, and then pulled back to the bottom of the trend channel. There are no obvious measurement objectives motivating the market higher, and the current position at the top of the macro trend channel leaves Product X vulnerable to a countertrend move.
6. The Fibonacci analysis indicates that there is significant room for Product X to move lower, with the first stop on a study of the impulse wave being the 23.6% retracement and secondary support at the nearly overlapping 38.2% impulse and 23.6% macro levels.
7. The Pattern & Trend support analysis shows that the impulse uptrend channel should provide the first support at or near the current price of $105.29 (S1). A close below the prior low of $105.03 would signal the end of the impulse wave and likely signal a more significant sell-off that would first find support at the prior peak at $104.39 (S2), then the bottom of the trend channel/triangle consolidation pattern around $102.00 (S3). A close below the prior low of $101.05 decisively ends the macro uptrend.

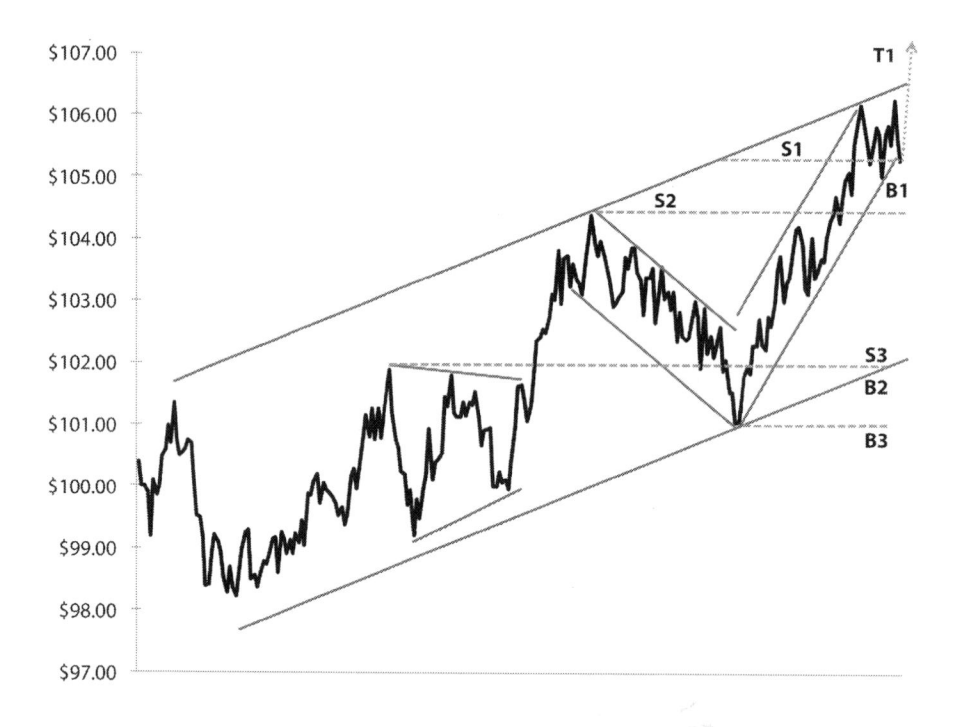

Figure 4.33 Combining the pattern and trend analysis of the FEB ProdX chart.

The Product X market is clearly in a macro uptrend bounded by a wide, relatively well-defined channel. The recent price action has taken the FEB ProdX contract to new highs, from which it is very possible that it sells off down to $104.39 in the near term, a price that combines relatively robust support (S2) and the overlap of the 38.2% impulse and 23.6% macro Fibonacci levels. Any retracement to the bottom of the trend channel at $102.00 should represent a compelling buying opportunity, given the fundamental backdrop.

5

Understanding Volatility

Visualizing Volatility
To a trader, volatility is the financial market equivalent of weather, and it is complained about with similar frequency and colorful language. Like the weather, volatility is difficult to forecast and prone to changing abruptly with little or no notice. A trader must know how the prevailing volatility will impact his current and proposed positions. Are the conditions amicable or treacherous? Are they an aid or an impediment to a trade? Understanding volatility is about developing a keen sense of when it is, and much more importantly isn't, a good idea to be a market participant.

The Eye of the Beholder
There exists a substantial difference in paradigm between how traders and risk managers perceive and respond to volatility. Risk managers primarily observe the world on a close-to-close basis, noting the day-to-day price differentials and using that delta as the basis of their calculus. Risk managers measure at the end of the day, but traders operate in real-time. While obviously interested in the day-over-day relationships, traders are much more focused on the intraday range, the speed with which the market moved throughout its oscillations, the volume traded throughout the day, and the tick-to-tick differentials in price. Speed, volume, range, and tick size define the market and impact what participants refer to as "tradability," a subjective assessment of the ability to easily conduct business without undue risk or penalty.

Consider the following price chart that contains ten days' worth of simulated data, with trades expressed as square dots and the closing level denoted by a larger gray circle.

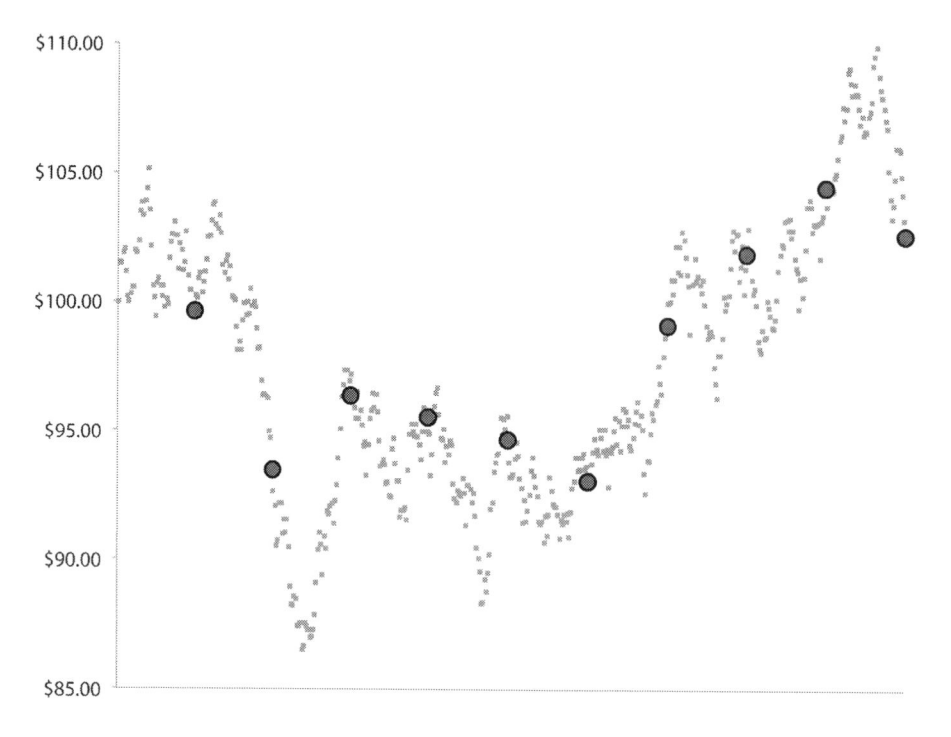

Figure 5.1   10 days of simulated data with individual trades as gray squares; end of day closes as larger gray circles.

It is clear from even a superficial examination that the closing data do not describe the totalilty of the price action. The range of the closing data is $15.00, but the tick data spans almost $25.00. The close-to-close differentials on Days 3, 4, 5, and 6 are minimal, but the intraday swings are substantial.

	Day-over-day change	Intraday trading range	D-O-D as % of intraday
Day 1	($0.37)	$5.91	6%
Day 2	($6.14)	$10.38	59%
Day 3	$2.88	$11.93	24%
Day 4	($0.82)	$5.66	15%
Day 5	($0.89)	$8.93	10%
Day 6	($1.57)	$3.87	41%
Day 7	$6.01	$6.65	90%
Day 8	$2.80	$6.52	43%
Day 9	$2.55	$7.33	35%
Day 10	($1.83)	$7.39	25%

Table 5.1   Comparing day-over-day change to intraday range for 10 days of simulated data.

Chapter 5 - Understanding Volatility

Day-over-day volatilty can approach that of the intraday market (as it does on Day 7), but it can never exceed it. Unless a firm uses a methodology that incorporates real-time information, a trader will always live in a more dangerous world than the risk management group can weigh, measure, and report on. This is significant, as the reporting from the risk group will frequently be management's only window into trader positions, their exposures, and day-to-day price fluctuations.

Simulating a reduction in liquidity by removing 75% of the observations yields a similarly shaped price path, but one with radically different tradability.

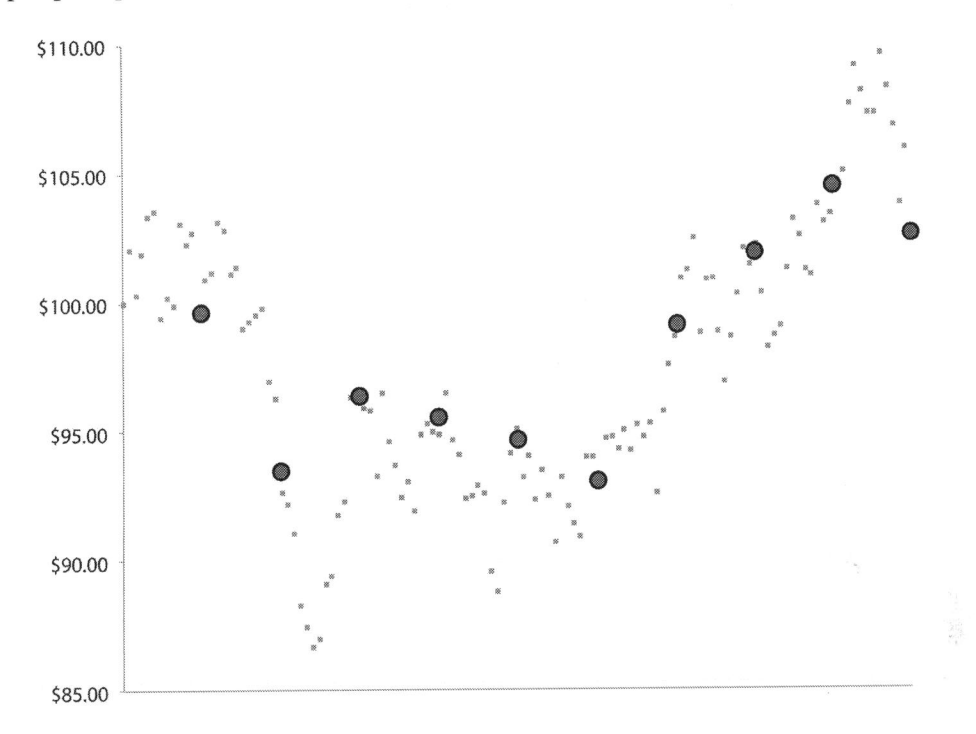

Figure 5.2   10 days of low-liquidity simulated data with individual trades as gray squares; end of day closes as larger gray circles.

Relative to the previous chart:

- The trade-to-trade gaps are bigger, making it more difficult to control exposure to risk.
- The movements are less defined, more random seeming.
- The end-of-day numbers, however, are exactly the same.

To the risk group, both days are equivalent. They are clearly very different to a trader.

What Causes Volatility?

Everything causes volatility. Large-scale, trend creating or market dislocating macro volatility is a price response to a significant, usually fundamental, event. Common major influences include but are certainly not limited to:

- Major changes to primary market-moving fundamental variables, most commonly through supply/demand/storage statistics or revisions to forecasts.
- The rapid entry, exit, or strategic shifts of major industry participants that add or subtract from the total pool of capital.
- Changes to market regulations, legislation, impactful lawsuits, or policy changes.
- Acts of war, terrorism, or geopolitical upheaval; extreme weather and natural disasters.

The common denominator in every case is how the market participants process new information. Just like Soylent Green, volatility is people.

Small, transitory market drivers and the constant interaction of buyers and sellers cause micro volatility, particularly when firms execute large trades (relative to the typical market volume) quickly, or without regard to price. With an "at-the-market" or "market" order, the broker or trader attempts to execute a specified volume at whatever price level is required to absorb the size, frequently resulting in sharp, temporary spikes or drops if the available liquidity proves to be less than anticipated. To understand why, it is important to know how buying and selling interest is cobbled together to form both the best bid-offer spread and the supporting prices above and below.[25]

A market is defined by the best bid to buy and the best offer to sell, as well as the volumes associated with each order. At any give time there can also be a number of bids and offers behind the best prices, which in aggregate make up the "stack" or depth of the market. The amount of size that habitually congregates at the best bid and offer varies from market to market as a function of trader preference and participant dynamics. Consider a high-volume product, which will typically have large amounts of participation both at and around the best bid and offer. The market stack might look like this:

---

[25] The interaction of buyers and sellers in markets and on exchanges has become its own field of academic research called Market Microstructure.

Chapter 5 - Understanding Volatility

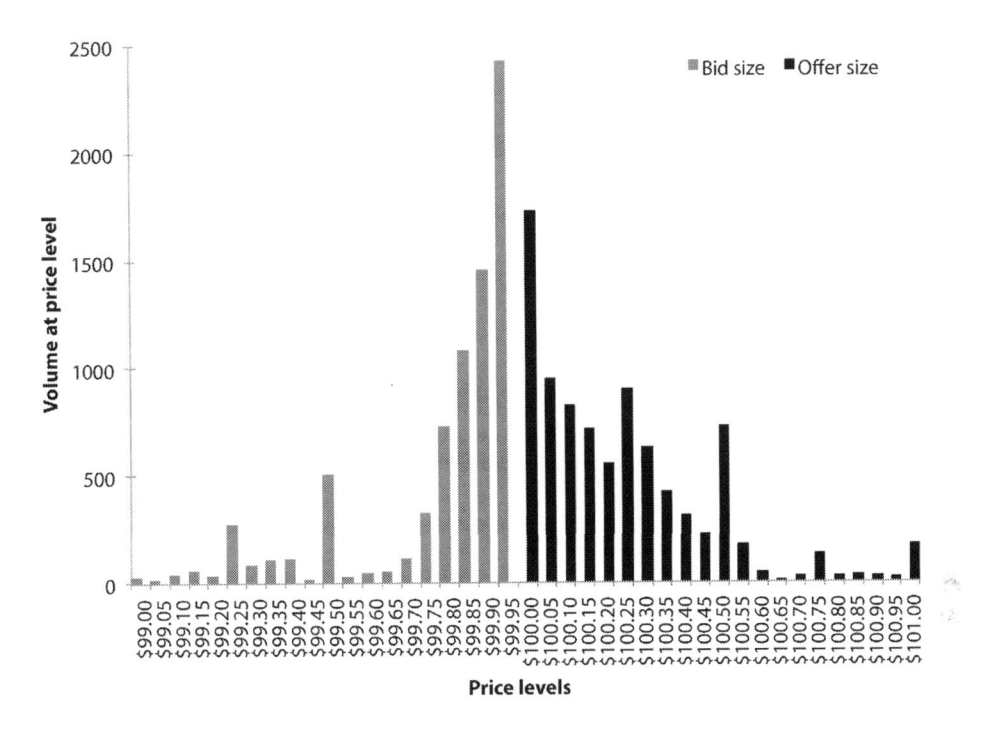

Figure 5.3 Bid/offer stack for a high-volume commodity.

For a firm that trades in increments of 50 or 100 per transaction there is ample liquidity available, with 2,425 lots available on the $99.95 bid and 1,725 offered at $100.00. A larger trader who may need to execute a 4,000-lot buy order is forced to be concerned with not just size available on the best offer (which is insufficient), but also the orders immediately behind at $100.05, $100.10, and $100.15. Purchasing 4,000 lots would involve buying everything at $100.00, everything at $100.05, everything at $100.10, and most of the available volume at $100.15.

Consider a market for a much lower-volume commodity:

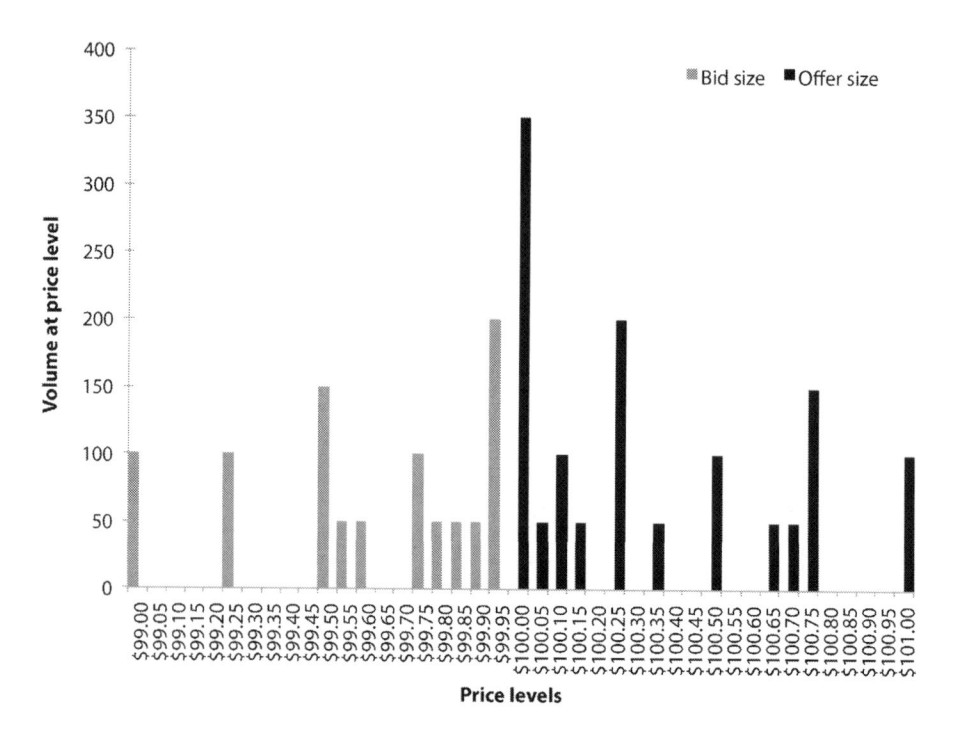

Figure 5.4   Bid/offer stack for a low-volume commodity.

With only 200 lots on the bid and 350 on the offer, there is not enough size to accommodate multiple 100-lot players or a single larger entity without getting deeper into the deck. Lower volume commodities may also have less robust grouping around the prevailing market price, with more instances of gaps within the bid and offer stacks.

Traders wanting to execute size in a low-volume instrument face a much more daunting challenge. They will have to weigh the need to fill the order against the anticipated slippage above or beyond the market price they will be expected to have to pay. They may also have to consider the distinct possibility that there is not enough current volume at any price to complete their trade, and that they may have to break it into smaller pieces and execute at intervals to allow market participants time to digest the trade information and put fresh orders back into the market.

This is the calculus of the institutional trader, for whom the first bid and offer is rarely adequate for their execution needs.

The markets as a whole have become enamored with trading volume as a meaningful metric. For the brokerage houses and exchanges that take nearly riskless pieces out of every transaction, this makes sense. For a trader, volume is a graven idol. Volume is not liquidity, and volume is not depth. This distinction is subtle, but critical. As a ridiculous extreme, consider two tiny high-frequency trading systems that can each take a one-share position,

Chapter 5 - Understanding Volatility

trading that one share back and forth every millisecond. The market as a whole will see 1,000 shares traded in a second, 60,000 per minute, 3,600,000 per hour and a staggering 28,800,000 in an eight-hour trading session. In a market without the ability to trade two shares at the same time, 28.8M shares will have changed hands. This is the hell that large institutional investors fear, a world of infinite transactionality with no substantial position modification possible.

Micro volatility resulting from purely transactional considerations is generally thought to be increasing in the financial markets. Faster trading and more interconnected markets have led to a reluctance to leave standing bids and offers that can help absorb buying and selling interest and provide stability to the market. As we will see in Chapter 11, the increasingly algorithm-driven trading is having a substantial impact on market microstructure and short-term volatility.

How Markets React to Information
Markets jump from states of equilibrium to states of disequilibrium and back again. The transitions between states, and the relative smoothness or violence thereof, are caused by the assimilation and interpretation of new information. The way a particular market reacts to new information will be highly contextual, depending on the players currently inhabiting the space and the fundamental factors that inform the balance of the market. Reactions will be dependent both on the quality and magnitude of the new information, but also the recent price action and fundamental history. A material piece of information may perturb a static market, cause a move to accelerate, or violently stop a trend and reverse it in its tracks. Or, perplexingly, it may have no impact at all.

Markets are moved by traders who are wrong. There are many varieties of wrong. Wrong by misjudging the direction, magnitude, or speed of a market move. Wrong for thinking that they had appropriately sized their position, only to find that their losses were more than they can stand, (or worse than they had considered possible). Uninvolved firms that rush in once a trend is under way will add fuel to the fire, and winners may add to their positions and provide continued momentum, but the primary impetus of any move will always be the people suffering the most, the traders and firms that need to exit, regardless of price.

No two markets are the same, and no two react in the same way to new information. The characteristics that will shape and influence the magnitude and ferocity of a market move are:

- Total volume or open interest of positions in the market. If there are no participants with a vested interest, there is no one to react violently to new information.
- The percentage of that volume that trades on a day-to-day basis.
- The number of players present, and the presence of one or more extremely large positions relative to the market as a whole.
- The mix of short-term speculators, hedgers, and long-term investors, and the disposition of the larger players on that spectrum.
- The extent to which the major players' positions are currently deep in the money, at the money, or far out of the money. Are the large winning/losing positions in "strong hands," or with easily rattled individuals?

- The extent to which the information ecology is currently very evenly distributed, well understood, and subject to a uniform interpretation, or the existence of a variety of simultaneous fundamental interpretations.

Traders spend a great deal of time pondering not just if, but how the market will go from A to B. Generally, there are two responses.

A Violent Reaction to New Information

Dramatic market movements are common when there is an established valuation paradigm under which each data item is homogenously interpreted, leading to an instant, consistent global revaluation of the market and a step-function price response. During equity earnings reporting season, public companies disclose their recent profitability, providing analysts and traders with data that will be instantly plugged into a proprietary valuation spreadsheet to yield a new fair value for the corporation. Within seconds, the share price will leap upward or downward to within cents of the "correct" fair value. The same behavior can occur for different reasons in thinly traded products with few information sources and a small number of highly visible data points.

A Gradual Migration of Consensus

In a large, liquid market with significant participant diversity, it is possible for even game-changing exogenous events to result in a gradual evolution in consensus that creates a structured, highly tradable price response. For every newly converted buyer or seller, there is a skeptical counterparty willing to take the other side of the trade and provide liquidity. These are the market conditions every trader wants to be in. High total volume, high turnover, low tick-to-tick differentials and small day-over-day open/close gaps allow traders to focus on the underlying risk thesis, as opposed to expending energy worrying about execution and risk management considerations. The ability to modify the position in a near-frictionless environment allows addition or subtraction from a core position to catch intraday fluctuations or to risk-on/risk-off to avoid potential market gaps around non-trading hours, etc. Slippage establishing and exiting the position is reduced, cost of modification is minimal, and the risk of getting stuck with the position is minimized with good volume all along the move.

Transitions From Tradable to Untradeable

For every market there is some range of volatility that yields a productive trading environment, given the standard products and their inherent characteristics. Too much volatility, and the trader risks severe potential damage. Too little, and the market will stagnate as traders realize there is no money to be made and turn their attention elsewhere. Traders must first observe and categorize the volatility present in the market, then learn to measure and contextualize recent fluctuations within the product's history.

Observing and Categorizing Volatility

The intraday fluctuations of the market are not typically captured by conventional risk metrics and are therefore effectively invisible to non-participants. Market-facing traders observe and experience volatility on a tick-by-tick basis and will tend to categorize and describe the

Chapter 5 - Understanding Volatility

intraday and day-over-day volatility in subjective, non-quantitative terms. Among the common characteristics and descriptors are:

"Gappy" markets have non-continuous price patterns, which can manifest as an on-going series of small interval-to-interval jumps, or as large price spans with no trading activity. Day-over-day price gaps are common as the market step-functions to incorporate new information, particularly for products with a 24-hour news stream but an 8-hour (or less) trading day. Intraday gaps are more rare, and are most common in markets with thin volume or discontinuous buying or selling interest. Intraday gaps can also be caused by reactions to significant new fundamental information or unexpected exogenous events that cause one side of the market to abruptly evaporate or shift their orders back, forcing desperate traders to cross a much wider bid-offer spread and, in so doing, create a void in the price chart.

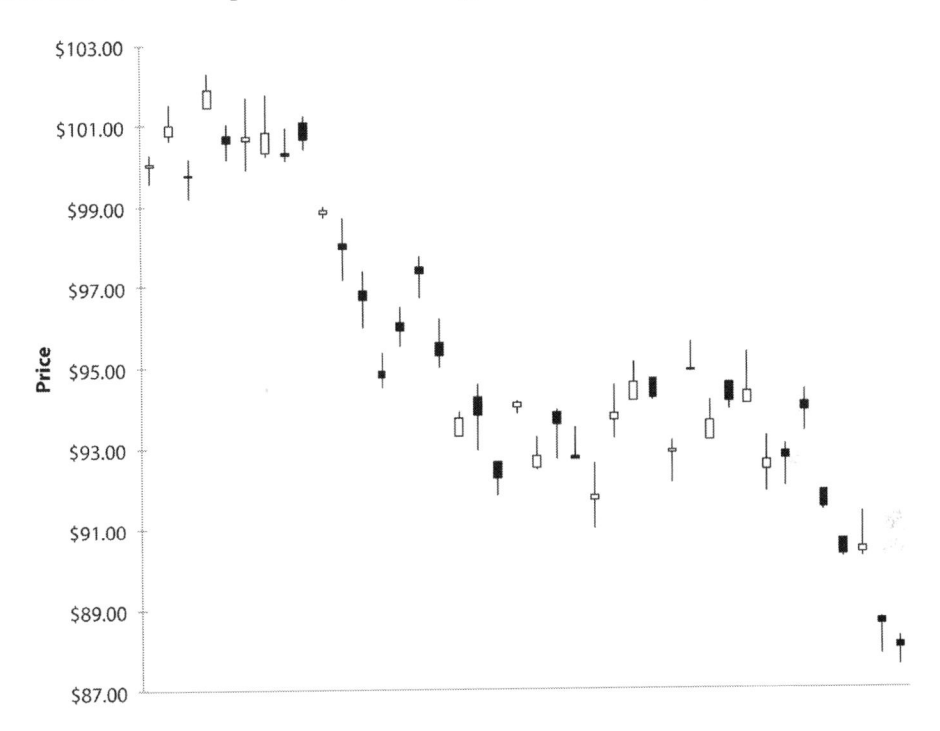

Figure 5.5 Candlestick chart of a market with pronounced overnight gaps.

Gaps in a time series generally irritate traders, as they represent an interval in which market participants were unable to act to modify their position, either due to an instantaneous transit from point to point or a lack of participation as prices drifted higher or lower. Neither is good. Isolated gaps within an otherwise continuous chart can have significance as indicators in their own right, particularly what are called "runaway gaps," where the price action accelerates so abruptly that it skips a few price levels before re-establishing a trajectory.

A "choppy" market exhibits a great deal of movement, but no real progress. The price action hacks back and forth, often with wide ranges and violent lurches higher and lower that are quickly undone by the next market-moving impetus. A choppy market can also be extremely gappy, as is the case with this example, which is the worst of both worlds. The propensity to jump from price to price with no motive trend can make risk assessment and position management extremely difficult and render a market all but untradeable. The exception is for market-making firms who can camp out in a sideways choppy market and extract fees for providing liquidity and execution facilitation while other traders fritter away money paying the bid-offer spread to enter and exit trades that never really seem to go anywhere.

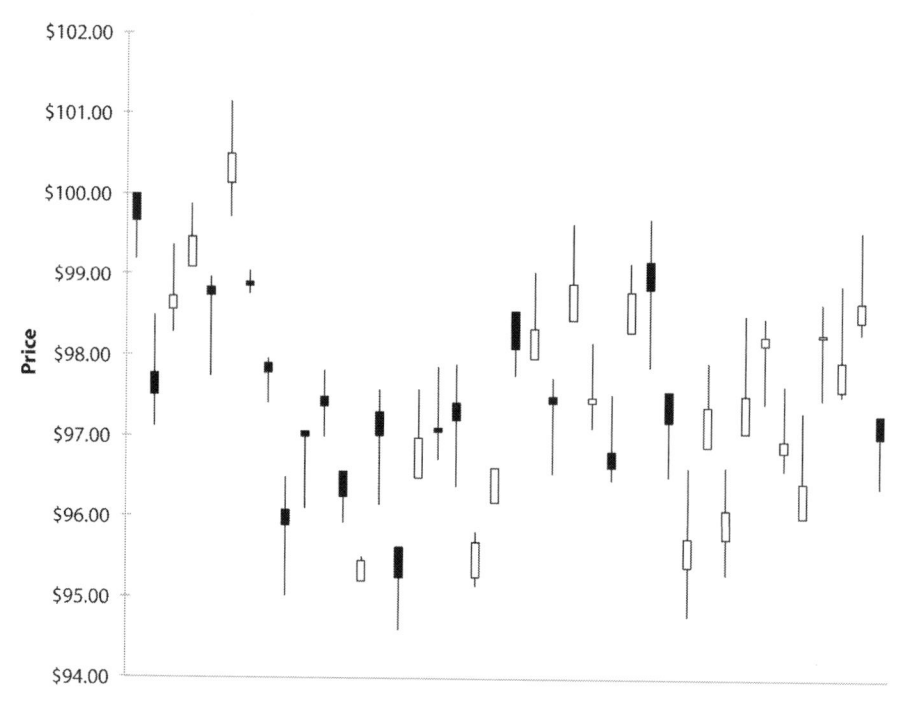

Figure 5.6   Candlestick chart of a choppy market with lots of movement but no progress.

Some markets feature very concentrated volatility, where prices drift or trend shallowly for long stretches only to be disrupted by violent one-period moves, after which the price quickly re-settles into a range. This type of market is very challenging. With a large percentage of total movement resident in one or a small number of periods the trader will either need to understand the conditions that precede potential volatility events, be able to operate within them, and ensure that her position is set up to profit from them, or avoid the market entirely. If the trader does choose to participate and gets the one volatility spike of the holding period wrong, there is little chance that she will be able to salvage her P&L with the comparatively minor fluctuations that occur before and after.

Chapter 5 - Understanding Volatility

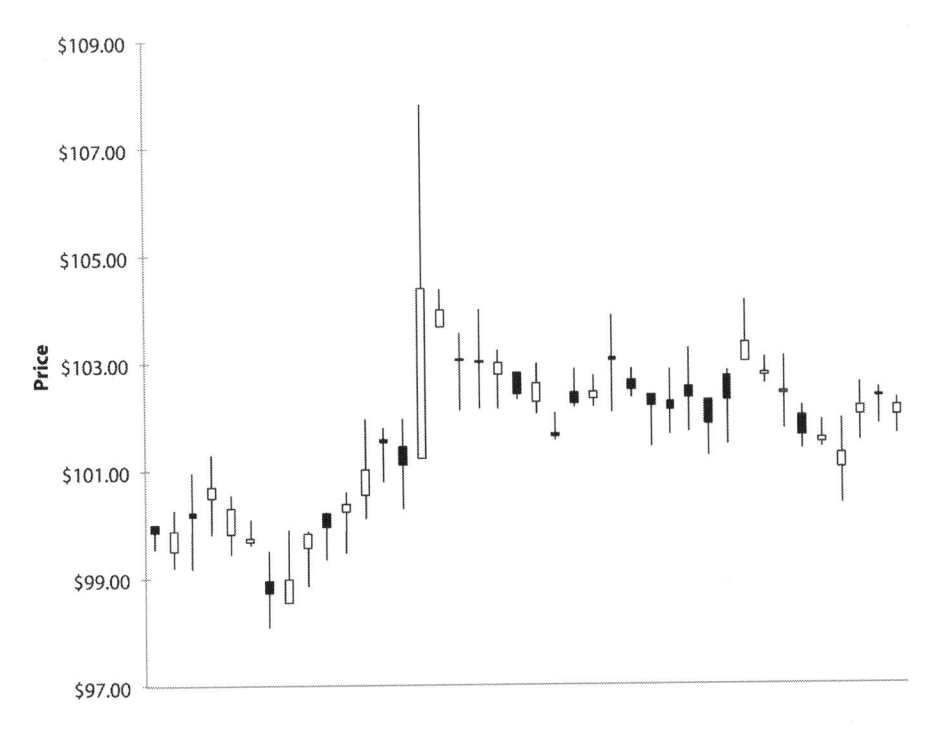

Figure 5.7 Candlestick chart of a market with one abnormally high-volatility period.

A tradable market features continuous price action with minimal overnight and intraday gaps, intraday swings that are wide enough to offer opportunity to short-term traders but a fraction of the overall distance traversed to not mask any underlying trend or patterns.

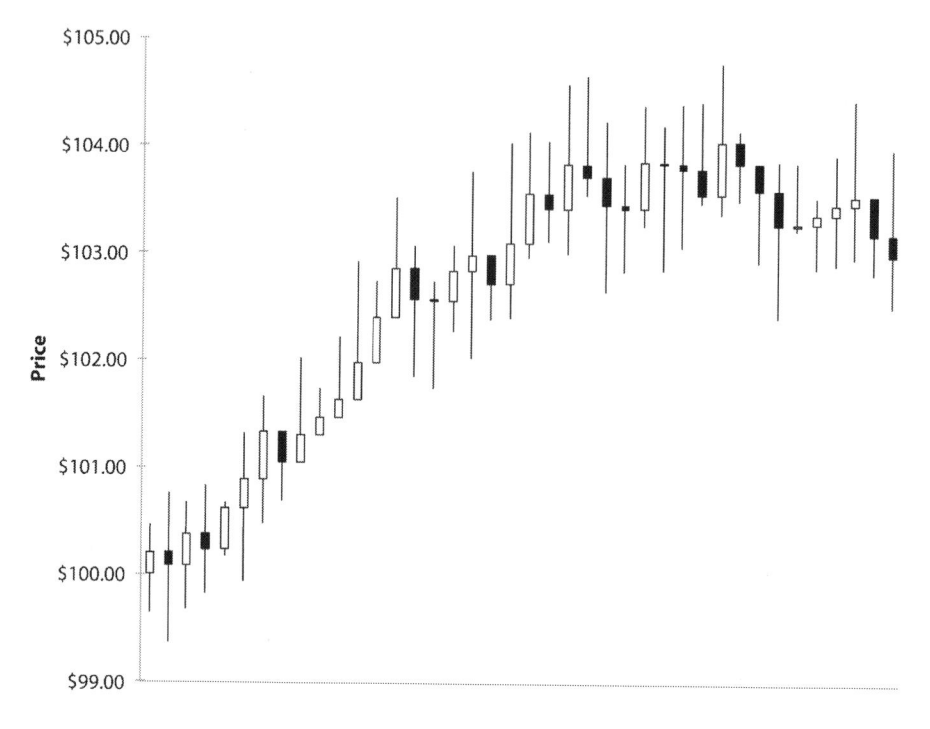

Figure 5.8 Candlestick chart of a tradable market.

Anything that materially impacts a trader's ability to efficiently enter and exit a position must be factored into the decision making process, and the ratio of total distance traversed during gaps or single-period volatility events relative to the total traded range is an important component of a trader's risk/reward calculus.

The relative impact of volatility is also highly dependent on strategy and context. Traders deploying a medium-term strategy with a 4-6 week holding horizon might be willing to live with choppy, gappy intraday price action in exchange for a smooth, tradable day-over-day trend. In doing so, they sacrifice execution efficiency and slippage costs for larger strategic profits. Market-makers or short-term traders could not make the same accommodation, as their long term may be measured in minutes, and if the microstructure is not conducive to low-friction transactions they may have to move to a different market or sit out altogether.

Measuring Volatility

There are two metrics used to describe and quantify the volatility of a product across time: the historical volatility and the implied volatility.

Historical volatility is calculated from a time series of end-of-day data. Consider a graph of the daily closing data from the gappy, normal, and choppy markets from the previous examples:

Chapter 5 - Understanding Volatility

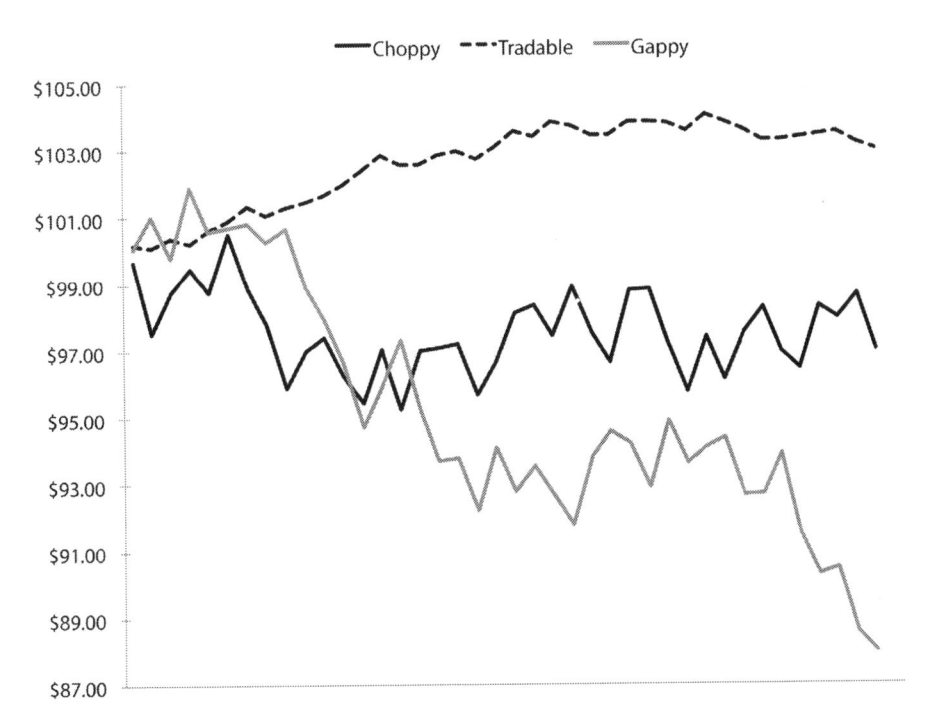

Figure 5.9   A comparison of the closing prices of the choppy, gappy, and tradable markets.

It appears that both the choppy and gappy markets are qualitatively more volatile than the tradable market, but it is difficult to make any more definitive quantitative statements. Traders and risk managers calculate the historical volatility of a product to allow for a precise measurement of the day-to-day fluctuations.

To calculate the 20-day trailing historical volatility measured on the 252nd and last business day of the year the trader would start with a column of end-of-day closing price data, then:

1. Calculate a series of daily returns by taking the natural log of Day X's price divided by the prior day's observation:

$$\ln(Day_X/Day_{X-1})$$

2. From that list, calculate the one-day standard deviation of a 20-day sample period of trailing daily returns, in this case from Day 233 to Day 252:

$$STDEV(Day_{233}:Day_{252})$$

3. Annualize the one-day standard deviation by multiplying it by the square root of the number of trading days in the year, in this case 252:

(Day 252 one-day standard deviation with 20-day sample period) × SQRT (252)

Many risk managers will simplify the calculation and multiply the Day 252 one-day standard deviation by 16, which yields approximately the same results.

In spreadsheet form this would look like:

Day	Closing price	Daily return	Standard dev	Historical volatility
233	$95.43	(0.0145)	0.0094	14.98%
234	$94.32	(0.0117)	0.0096	15.31%
235	$94.80	0.0051	0.0095	15.02%
236	$94.70	(0.0011)	0.0095	15.02%
237	$94.79	0.0009	0.0093	14.80%
238	$93.50	(0.0136)	0.0095	15.00%
239	$93.23	(0.0029)	0.0092	14.56%
240	$93.24	0.0001	0.0089	14.10%
241	$93.14	(0.0011)	0.0086	13.71%
242	$93.95	0.0086	0.0086	13.64%
243	$94.61	0.0071	0.0086	13.73%
244	$95.99	0.0144	0.0092	14.66%
245	$95.66	(0.0035)	0.0090	14.26%
246	$95.78	0.0013	0.0089	14.16%
247	$96.74	0.0100	0.0093	14.73%
248	$95.45	(0.0135)	0.0093	14.69%
249	$95.27	(0.0019)	0.0092	14.58%
250	$95.02	(0.0026)	0.0085	13.43%
251	$93.77	(0.0133)	0.0085	13.55%
252	$93.83	0.0006	0.0084	13.30%

Table 5.2 Rolling annualized historical volatility derived from 1-day standard deviation based on a 20-day sample period.

The historical volatility calculations starting with Day 20 for the tradable, choppy, and gappy markets are:

Chapter 5 - Understanding Volatility

Day	Tradable market	Historical volatility	Choppy market	Historical volatility	Gappy market	Historical volatility
20	$103.57	4.06%	$98.10	22.08%	$92.77	21.74%
21	$103.42	4.09%	$98.35	20.63%	$93.55	21.66%
22	$103.84	4.16%	$97.43	20.40%	$92.70	21.53%
23	$103.72	4.13%	$98.90	20.98%	$91.79	19.54%
24	$103.46	4.31%	$97.49	21.43%	$93.81	21.50%
25	$103.43	4.32%	$96.63	20.48%	$94.58	21.85%
26	$103.86	4.30%	$98.80	21.42%	$94.19	21.80%
27	$103.84	4.07%	$98.84	21.03%	$92.90	22.10%
28	$103.79	4.09%	$97.19	20.69%	$94.87	23.66%
29	$103.56	4.27%	$95.75	20.98%	$93.62	23.36%
30	$104.05	4.46%	$97.38	21.85%	$94.11	23.37%
31	$103.84	4.52%	$96.10	21.97%	$94.35	23.03%
32	$103.59	4.49%	$97.52	22.34%	$92.64	22.85%
33	$103.27	4.42%	$98.27	21.76%	$92.68	22.31%
34	$103.29	4.28%	$96.97	21.24%	$93.88	22.14%
35	$103.37	4.28%	$96.45	20.34%	$91.48	22.70%
36	$103.46	4.19%	$98.29	21.45%	$90.28	22.46%
37	$103.54	4.17%	$97.95	21.50%	$90.47	22.49%
38	$103.19	4.26%	$98.69	20.76%	$88.57	22.95%
39	$102.99	4.11%	$97.01	21.54%	$87.97	21.45%

Table 5.3 Historical volatilities for the tradable, choppy and gappy markets.

Which results in the following graph:

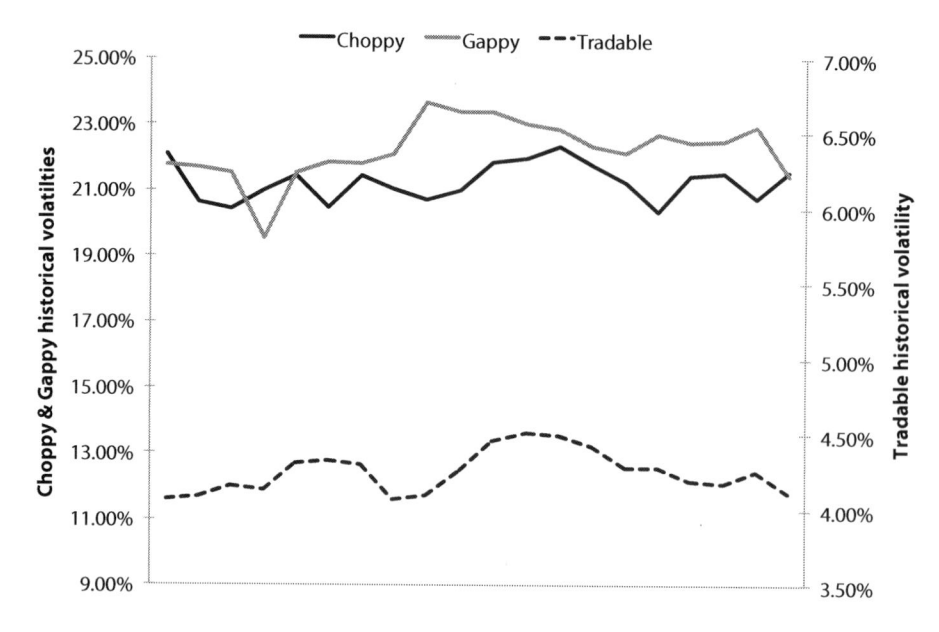

Figure 5.10 A comparison of the historical volatilities of the choppy, gappy, and tradable markets.

The tradable market has exhibited a relatively constant volatility that has generally ranged between 4.06% and 4.52%, with both the choppy and gappy markets fluctuating in a wider range between 19.54% and 23.66%. Though at similar levels at both the beginning and end of the study period, the gappy market was clearly more volatile for the majority of the observations. The historical volatility of a product is an interesting metric, but as the name implies, only offers perspective on how a product has fluctuated in the past.

Implied volatility represents the current estimate of future anticipated volatility of a product, and is calculated by examining the prices of options (or other derivative securities) in the market and reverse engineering an estimated number with a mathematical model. Historical volatilities are computable at any time from a standard data set. Implied volatilities depend on the current market price of a derivative security in relation to the underlying at a specific point in time, and must therefore be harvested, processed, and retained for future use. Implied volatility will be covered in greater depth in Chapter 10 – Option Strategies.

Distributions of Volatility

Homogenous securities like equities will have a single volatility that will vary over time, sometimes dramatically and with little prior notice. Markets that feature products with discrete delivery/settlement periods or classes of similar but non-fungible instruments, can display period-to-period differences in volatility which can either remain static or change over time and in response to market conditions.

Chapter 5 - Understanding Volatility

Stable Term Structure of Volatility
Some products have an established term structure of volatility, where a portion(s) of the forward curve exhibit(s) consistently high or low relative levels of response to stimuli. This behavior is common with products that have physical storage properties or pronounced seasonal production or demand characteristics.

Static Volatility Patterns
A number of non-evergreen physical products exhibit a persistent irregular, lumpy volatility pattern that is typically seasonally distributed. Most commonly seen in the products with established, well-defined production seasons (corn, wheat, soybeans) or established peak-consumption periods (summer driving season for gasoline, winter for heating oil, or summer for electricity). Traders must take static volatility patterns into account when planning trades or budgeting resources. A volumetrically equivalent spread trade will not be as self-hedging as intuitively expected if one of the legs is placed in a pocket of localized high or low volatility. The movement of the more volatile leg will dwarf the P&L contribution of the more tractable product, yielding a position that looks like a spread but acts like a directional exposure in the riskier of the two products. This will covered in greater depth in Chapter 9 – Spread Trading.

Non-Static Volatility Distributions
Established patterns of volatility can be disturbed by a variety of factors, some having short-term effects, others with enduring consequences. Changes in the cost of capital and margin requirements can make positions expensive to hold as long-term investments, increasing the amount of short-term churn and forcing the totality of the market volume to migrate to the front of the curve, increasing position size and volatility. Regulatory changes or other long-lead fundamental shifts can create sudden imbalances that cause inflection points in the forward implied volatilities. Supply and demand considerations can have both near-term consequences and impacts that linger far into the future, changing perceptions about previously expected periods of plenty or scarcity and driving forward trading activity.

Most markets will have some form of stable volatility structure or static volatility pattern that is intermittently perturbed by non-static volatility modifiers.

Liquidity Holes
Liquidity holes are gaps in the market caused by a lack of participants willing to bid or offer at a particular price point. Most liquidity holes are unexpected by market participants—though they really should not be—and the collective discovery of one can feel very much like running off the edge of the cliff. There can be logical, rational reasons for a lack of interest at a given level, though the causes may seem somewhat capricious, in hindsight. Perhaps the biggest buyer in the market pulled its bids and stepped into a meeting just as a huge sell order hit the market. Normally buyer and seller would have matched up somewhere near the prevailing price, but with the sudden lack of bid-side interest the seller's large order may temporarily crush prices. When the buyer returns and finds prices lower than it left them, it may step in and, in so doing, cause prices to rally right back up again.

While liquidity holes can be difficult to predict and anticipate, they are more likely to be found around fundamentally and technically significant levels. If the supply or demand curve is not smooth and continuous, if it changes slope abruptly or goes vertical at a particular inflection point, it is reasonable to assume that if the market arrives at that level it may not be sticking around for very long. The completion of a well-defined technical reversal pattern or the breach of a key support or resistance level can also trigger a massive wave of position liquidation into a market that has suddenly thinned out appreciably. This is another argument for a comingled fundamental/technical approach, as one discipline may provide the trader warning of potential danger while the other shows no cause for alarm.

Manifestations of Volatility

Why Volatility Matters to Physical Traders

Many hedgers utilize complex models to forecast future business conditions, generate production estimates, and budget resource needs. Fluctuations in the relative level of volatility exert an influence on the underlying mechanics of option-based valuation models, and will typically result in changes to the forecasts for the operational parameters of a physical asset. Accurately modeling physical assets, or "real options," is one of the most challenging applications of financial engineering. The problematic aspect is that, unlike contractual financial instruments, physical products have inherent idiosyncrasies that distort volumes, sub-optimize processes, and render exact valuation impossible.

Using a generic power plant as an example, the factors most likely to be affected by a shift in volatility are:

- The anticipated number of hours the plant will clear the market across a given period and the frequency of process startup and shutdown signals.
- The volume of fuel and other productive resources the facility will be projected to consume.
- The quantity of hedges necessary to protect the forward gross margin, and how much of the total risk in the portfolio has or has not actually hedged.
- The forward gross margin of the facility itself, which will directly contribute to corporate earnings.
- The ultimate value of the asset in a purchase or sale.

Changes in volatility will almost certainly impact a physical asset's net position and the anticipated forward gross margin.

Why Volatility Matters to Financial Traders

- Volatility will impact the risk metrics that govern a trader's activity, which impacts their capacity to do business.
- Too much volatility and a trader will exceed risk limits and have to shut down or potentially be destroyed by the chop.

Chapter 5 - Understanding Volatility

- Excessive volatility will lead to large P&L swings, which may not be acceptable to management.
- An extreme lack of volatility has the opposite effect, depriving traders of potentially profitable opportunities.

How Volatility Impacts Trading

Volatility is sometimes seen as the "noise" that surrounds the trend of the underlying market movement. As a practitioner, volatility has to be considered relative to the prevalent tendencies and historical norms for the particular market. 25% implied volatility might horrify an equity trader, but could bore a natural gas trader. The relative level of volatility present in the market impacts the following:

Execution

Trade-to-trade price fluctuations greatly impact a trader's ability to efficiently implement a strategy. The lower the volatility, the easier it will be to execute at the trader's preferred price and at the time of their choosing. This will be covered in greater depth in Chapter 13 – Trading Mechanics.

Decision Making

Excess volatility can impact the trader's ability to assess the situation and make productive decisions. At a certain point, the noise will start to overwhelm the signal and the price movement will cease to resemble a cohesive trajectory and start to look like a cloud of random data points.

Volatility vs. Liquidity

In the short term, liquidity is very much driven by changes in volatility. As a market becomes more volatile and traders pull bids and offers to assess the situation, the tick-to-tick trade differentials will start to expand. The bid-offer spreads quoted in the market will widen as market makers seek to protect themselves from adverse price movements and extract compensation for the risk of quoting prices. As the implied costs of doing business rise, the small players and short-term speculators will be priced out of the market. In some markets, small players generate a significant amount of the ultra short-term, churn-type trading volume. A bank, for example, isn't going to buy something and then look to sell it a tick higher. Locals and small speculators do those types of trades all day long, hoping to pile up a stack of nickels and eventually turn them into real money. Subtract all of the incremental $0.05 prints and the market can look a lot less inhabited. This behavior will feed on itself, as an increase in volatility will wash out some of the smaller and more conservative players, which increases the volatility, which washes out the slightly larger players, etc.

Volatility Is Not a Constant

Consider the following chart of three simulated market trajectories, all with the same general shape but having an incrementally increasing level of volatility and a reduced amount of liquidity.

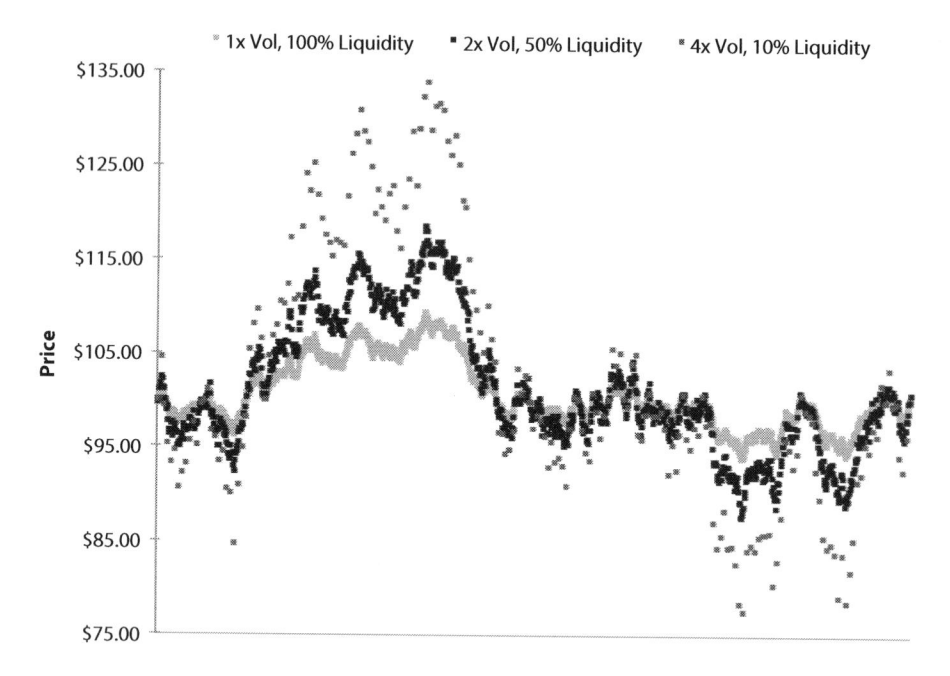

Figure 5.11 Comparison of three markets with increasing volatility and decreasing liquidity.

Graphing the historical volatility of each market yields:

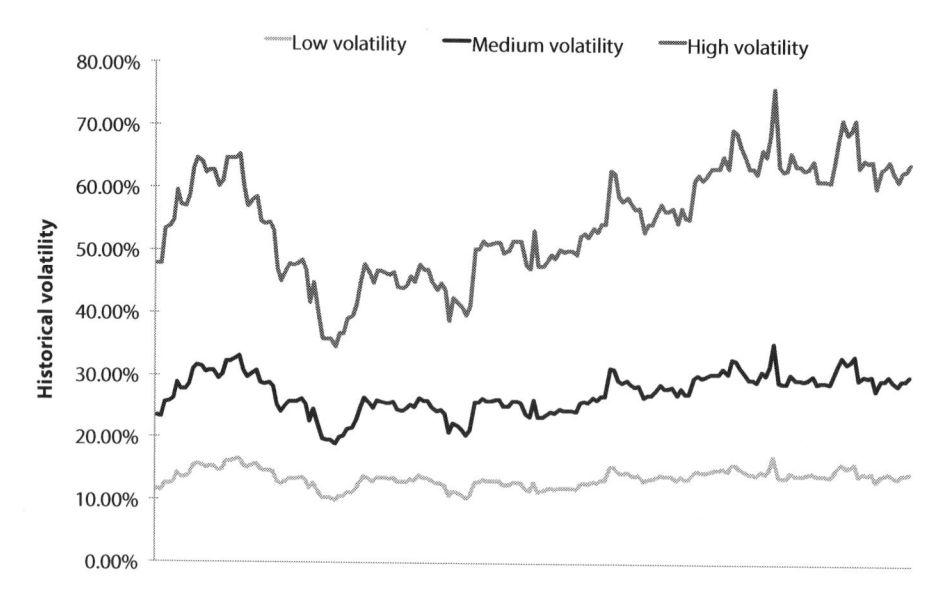

Figure 5.12 Comparison of the historical volatilities of the low, medium, and high volatility markets.

Chapter 5 - Understanding Volatility

Not only does the high volatility market exhibit greater potential for price fluctuations, but also the level of volatility itself fluctuates over a much larger range.

Given a choice, most traders would generally prefer to participate in the low-volatility, high-volume market, with some brave souls tolerating the medium-volatility market if they feel they can manage the swings. The significantly wilder fluctuations and the reduced ability to modify exposures would keep most traders on the sidelines in the high-volatility, low-liquidity market.

The decision to participate in or avoid a particular market is straightforward when the conditions are relatively static. The challenge lies in dealing with markets that abruptly shift from one volatility and liquidity state to another, as seen in this chart:

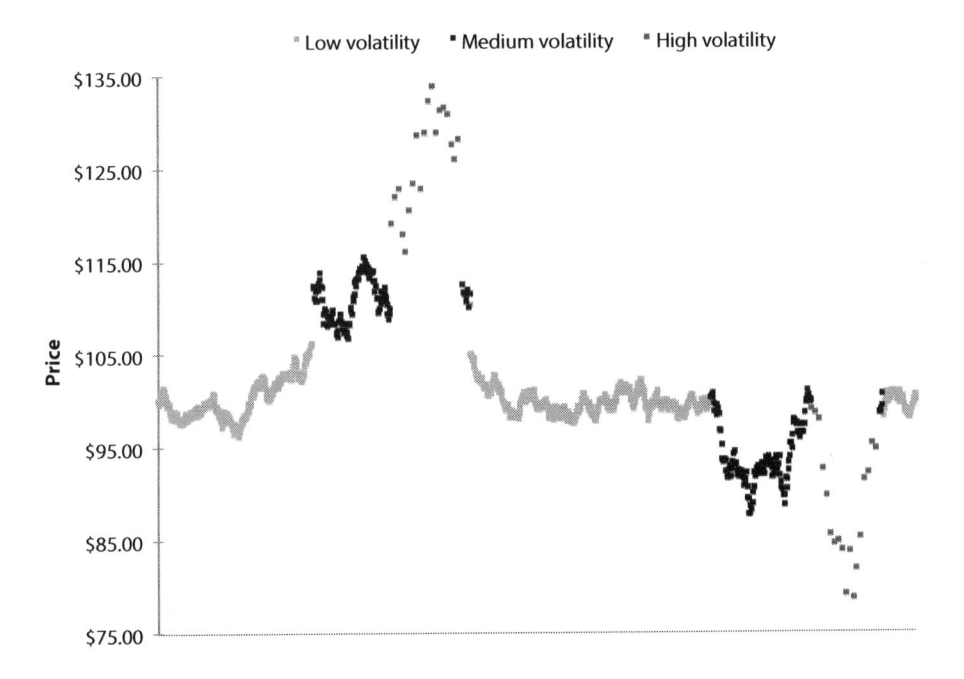

Figure 5.13 A market transitioning back and forth between low-volatility/high-liquidity and high-volatility/low-liquidity states.

Risk-Reward Assessment
Risk-Reward assessment can also be significantly degraded by increased volatility. Noise impacts the trader's ability to establish credible measurements on the risk and reward components, as well as creating an invisible tax via increased slippage costs on position entry and exit.

Volatility My Enemy, Volatility My Friend

As seen in Chapter 4, a macro trend in progress will be subject to countertrend impulses that cause price to zigzag back and forth across the central directional vector. Skillful traders will learn to gauge the level of volatility present in the market and use that information to enhance their execution when entering and exiting positions. Instead of immediately buying or selling, the trader may choose to set a resting bid slightly below the prevailing price or an offer above, counting on the intraday chop to bring the market to them. Longer-term traders will use intermediate retracements to add to positions or trade around a core exposure, which will be discussed in greater detail in Chapter 14 – Managing Positions & Portfolios.

Volatility Informs Price

Markets with a fear of scarcity as a part of their supply/demand calculus will often have a risk premium added to the product's price by nervous traders. The risk premium, frequently measured as the difference between the fair fundamental value and the current market price, will expand and contract depending on traders' perception of the relative level of danger present in the market. The risk premium is something akin to insurance, an extra fee that the trader is willing to pay now to avoid a scenario where they may not be able to secure a product that they may very badly want or critically need. A firm that has been badly burned before will frequently be willing to pay significantly more than fair value to ensure that it does not happen again.

The presence (or absence) of a risk premium in any market as well as its magnitude is, to a large extent, a result of the losers of the last battle overcompensating and assuming that the path to victory will be the same in the next war. Risk premiums traditionally inflate after a disaster then, when prices inevitably disappoint, are systematically undervalued until the next catastrophe.

Invisible Volatility

The rise of high-speed machine-based trading technology has reduced transaction times to a point where a human trader observing an exchange-based data feed may not be able to detect and respond to significant intra-second price fluctuations. In a world where institutional risk calculus is based on close-to-close granularity and traders look at 1-minute charts it is difficult to know how to intellectually contextualize a 5% price fluctuation that occurs and is reversed in milliseconds. Traders immerse themselves in a market to participate in events as they are happening, but are increasingly having to deal with events that have already happened.

Chapter Five Summary

Monitoring the volatility of the market is an immersive process, and is the first point in a trader's methodology where he observes the market in real-time, not as a theoretical fundamental abstraction or end-of-day chart pattern. Volatility is caused by traders' interpretation of, and reaction to, market events. Markets express volatility in a variety of ways: through intraday and overnight gaps in the chart, choppy price action, or large one-period moves. Traders will measure the volatility in two ways, by calculating the historical volatility of a series of price data or by observing the implied forward volatility, which will be covered

Chapter 5 - Understanding Volatility

at length in Chapter 10 – Option Trading Strategies. A trader must understand that the volatility of the market is not a constant, and that he must be prepared to operate in a rapidly evolving, ever-changing environment.

Once the trader has developed a feel for the market's oscillations she must consider how to translate observations of volatility into a quantification of risk, which will be the topic of Chapter 6.

Review Questions

1. What is the primary fundamental difference between how traders and risk managers view volatility?
2. How are historical and implied volatility defined and calculated?
3. Describe three types of experientially observed market volatility.
4. How does volatility impact a trader's activity?
5. Choose an equity and a commodity and calculate the rolling 10 period historical volatility of each for a trailing year. How do they compare over the observation period?

Resources
- *Measuring Market Risk* by Kevin Dowd

Case Study: Observing and Categorizing Product X's Volatility

Most of the Product X charts and technical studies have been constructed using end-of-day close data. To categorize the volatility, the trader must examine the magnitude of the intraday trading ranges and the overnight gaps between them, which is best represented on an OHLC bar or candlestick chart:

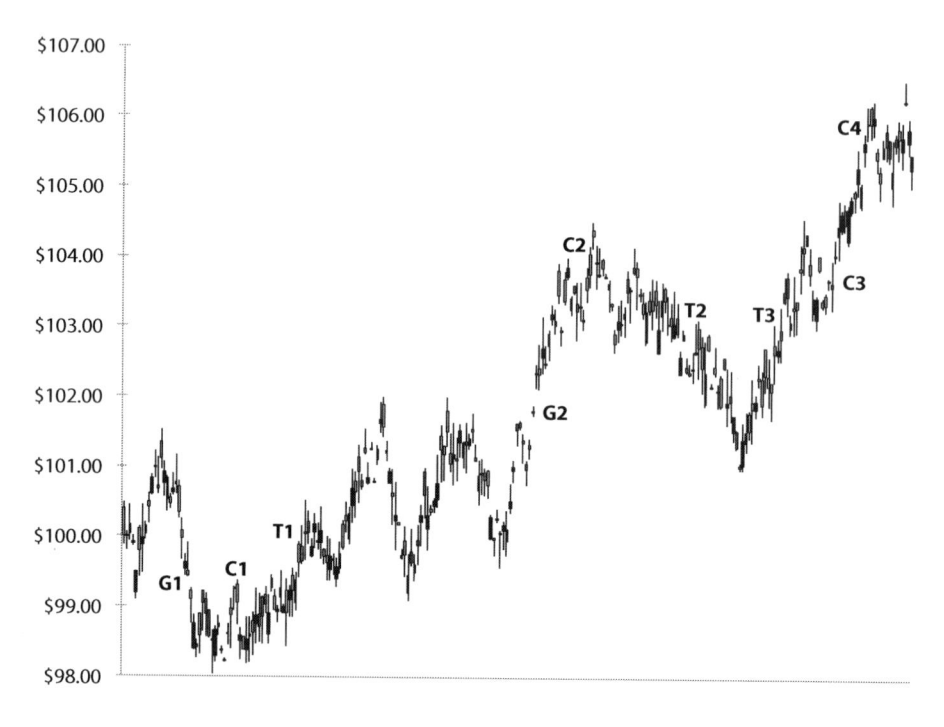

Figure 5.14   Volatility study of FEB ProdX candlestick chart with gaps, consolidation, and trends.

For traders that are contemplating short-term strategies, Product X exhibits elements of all of the volatility patterns. Most of the chart (T1, T2, T3) is eminently tradable, with consistently sized daily ranges and only moderate day-over-day gaps. Product X has some tendency toward gappy price action when traversing ground rapidly (G1, G2), and seems to signal market turns (C1, C2) or intramove consolidation areas (C3) with periods of choppy trading activity. Note that Product X has also started to chop toward the end of the price chart, which based on its recent behavior could indicate either an imminent reversal or the consolidation of an in-progress move, both of which are consistent with a market at highs and at the top of a technical macro trend channel.

Traders deploying longer-term strategies designed to capture the macro or intermediate movements would zoom out and take a wider perspective on the same price action:

Chapter 5 - Understanding Volatility 169

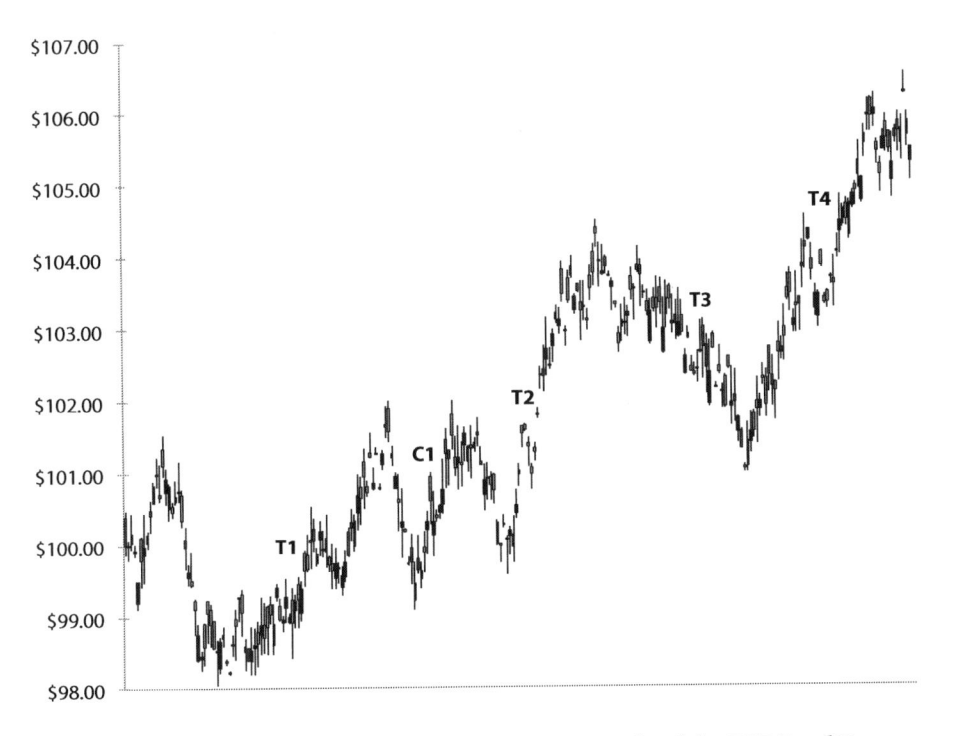

Figure 5.15 Long-term trend and consolidation study of the FEB ProdX candlestick chart.

With the exception of the sideways consolidation pattern (C1), the majority of the Product X chart (T1, T2, T3) exhibits long, linear moves with day-to-day price fluctuations of similar size and overnight gaps that are not consequential relative to the overall distance traversed. Product X appears eminently macro tradable, with only occasional instances where shorter-term strategies would encounter problematic chop or the potential for a gap move.

Measuring Product X's Volatility
In Chapter 4 – Technical Analysis, a Bollinger Band study provided a visual, non-quantitative representation of the volatility of the Product X market, with the varying differential between the top and bottom bands serving a proxy for a calculated value:

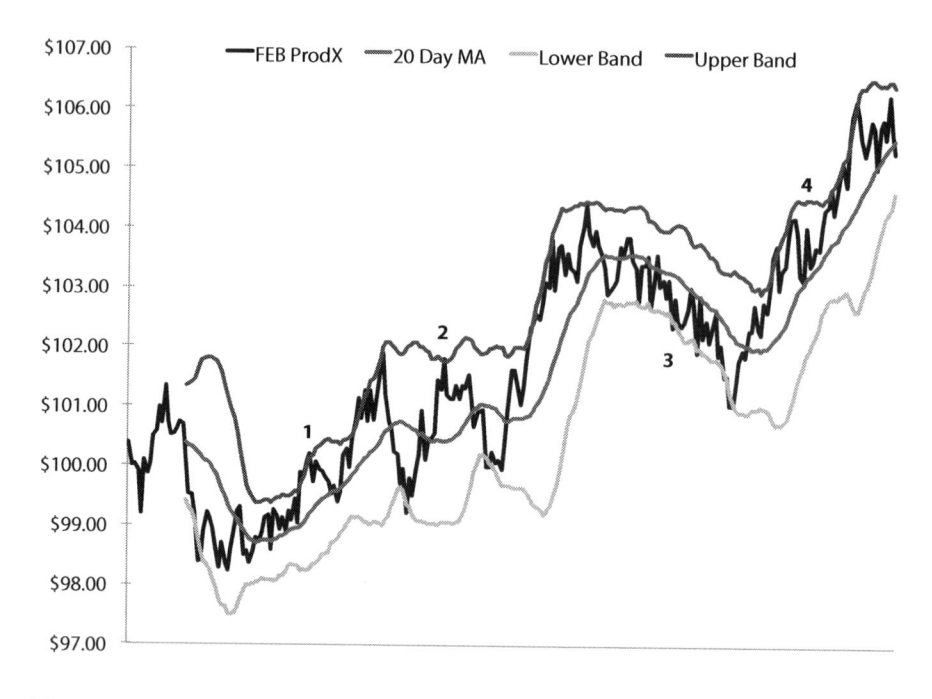

Figure 5.16 FEB ProdX Bollinger Band study.

While the Bollinger Bands provide a quick and dirty assessment of the relative level of volatility, calculating the actual value allows for more informed decisions and comparisons to other products and time periods.

Product X Historical Volatility Calculation Example
The volatility of Product X will be calculated using the historical data via the method described earlier in the chapter, yielding the following table of historical volatilities:

Chapter 5 - Understanding Volatility

Day	FEB ProdX price	Daily return	Standard dev	Historical volatility
233	$104.67	0.0039	0.0041	6.53%
234	$104.96	0.0028	0.0037	5.93%
235	$105.10	0.0013	0.0037	5.88%
236	$104.74	(0.0034)	0.0038	6.07%
237	$105.54	0.0076	0.0040	6.42%
238	$105.93	0.0036	0.0041	6.46%
239	$106.17	0.0023	0.0041	6.47%
240	$105.93	(0.0023)	0.0041	6.45%
241	$105.55	(0.0036)	0.0038	6.03%
242	$105.25	(0.0028)	0.0039	6.15%
243	$105.46	0.0020	0.0034	5.44%
244	$105.83	0.0035	0.0031	4.88%
245	$105.71	(0.0012)	0.0031	4.95%
246	$105.03	(0.0064)	0.0035	5.60%
247	$105.73	0.0067	0.0038	5.97%
248	$105.86	0.0012	0.0037	5.87%
249	$105.55	(0.0029)	0.0038	5.98%
250	$106.25	0.0066	0.0040	6.35%
251	$105.66	(0.0056)	0.0042	6.71%
252	$105.29	(0.0035)	0.0042	6.65%

Table 5.4 Rolling annualized historical volatility of the FEB ProdX contract derived from 1-day standard deviation based on a 20-day sample period.

Graphing the results for the FEB contract:

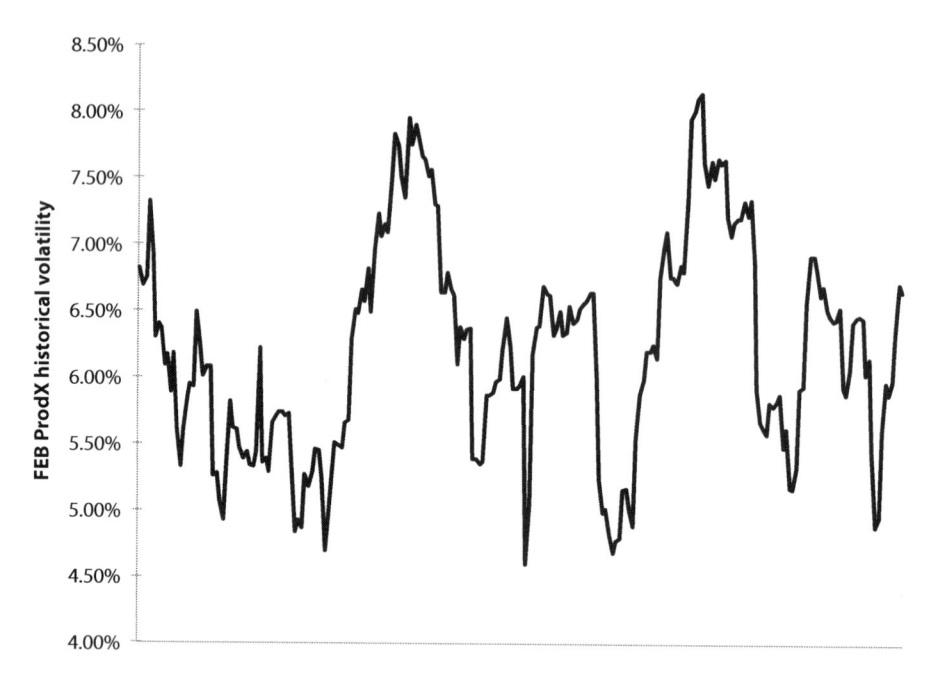

Figure 5.17 Chart of the rolling annualized historical volatility of the FEB ProdX contract derived from 1-day standard deviation based on a 20-day sample period.

PRODX Historical Volatility – All Months

While the main analysis of Product X has generally been concerned with the fluctuations of the prompt contract, examining the volatility characteristics of the entire curve can yield productive insights. Consider the chart of the end-of-day historical volatility of all currently quoted contracts:

Chapter 5 - Understanding Volatility

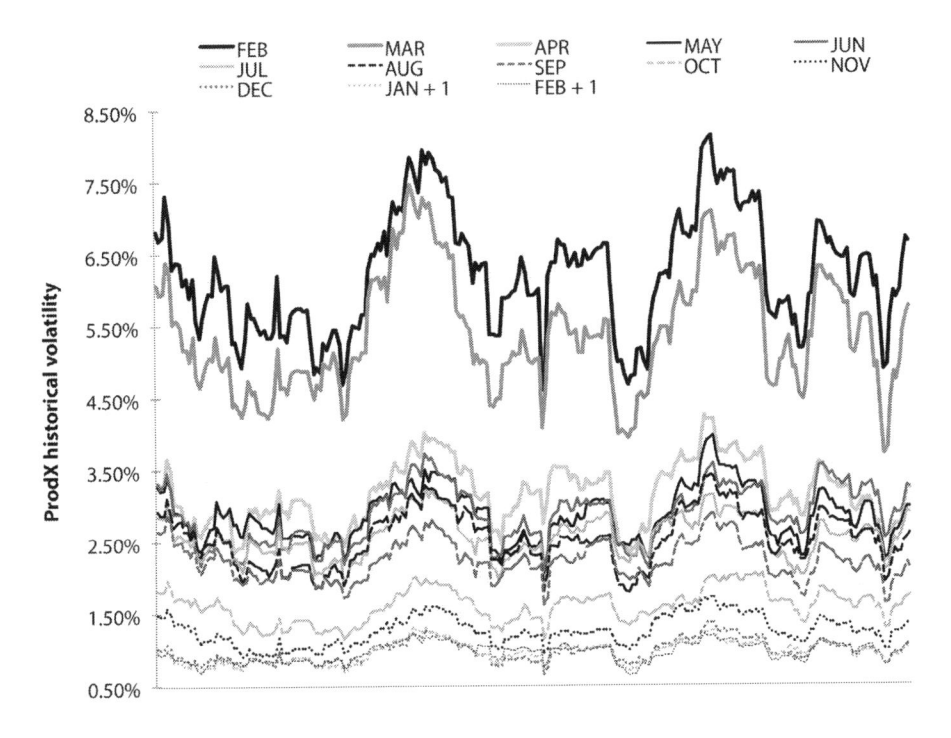

Figure 5.18 Rolling annualized historical volatility of all ProdX contracts.

There is a significant step-down in volatility across the curve from the prompt contract's average 6.22% (with a 4.60% to 8.14% range) to the third month's average 3.16% (with a 2.19% to 4.24% range). The drop off is even more severe when contrasted with the year-over-year JAN+1 contract's almost imperceptible 0.96% historical volatility, with a range of 0.63% to 1.21%.

Understand What the Volatility of Product X Is Saying as a Whole
Given numbers of potential fundamental drivers that could impact the market price of Product X in the short, medium, and long-term, it seems entirely rational to expect that the measured historical volatility should increase over time. Low baseline levels of volatility are a common phenomenon in early and early-medium stage markets that have yet to experience a significant supply or demand shock that translated into a price response. As a result, all Product X volatility "feels" low, with long-dated volatility almost non-existent at 0.96%. It is highly unlikely that volatility can remain this depressed through Product X's anticipated event path.

6

Understanding Risk

The Relationship Between Volatility and Risk
Volatility is like weather, an environmental variable common to all market participants. Risk is specific to the individual or firm and is predicated on its particular positions or exposures. The relationship is akin to:

$$\text{Market Volatility} \times \text{Exposure} = \text{Risk}$$

If a trader has no exposure to the market it does not matter to him how volatile it is, he has no risk. This is called being flat. If the trader has one or more exposures, the risk is proportional to the size and correlations of the exposures and the volatility of the market. If there is no volatility, a trader may have no current risk, but may still have significant potential risk.

Institutional Risk Management
Looming over every trader at all times, like the slide-rule of Damocles, is the risk management group. Risk management makes sure that the inmates are not running the asylum, and traditionally operates as a stand-alone function reporting directly to senior management outside of the established trading chain of command. This structure ensures unbiased, independent operation and avoids any potential conflicts that would arise if the group tasked with policing the traders was linked directly to the their performance and compensation. Risk management groups have three primary duties: collecting and aggregating price and position data, reporting on the firm's exposures, and, if necessary, proactively enforcing the risk policy.

Collecting and Aggregating Price and Position Data

Every trading firm will have a deal capture and risk management system, which can range from simplistic in-house constructed databases to an extravagantly expensive, all-conquering system that requires a small army of acolytes to maintain. The risk management database is the system of record, and its contents will be deemed to be to absolute truth with regard to price, position, and P&L. The care and feeding of the system is, therefore, of paramount importance. Every executed trade must, one way or another, make its way into the firm's deal capture and risk system in a timely fashion.[26] Deal tickets can be automatically loaded via a direct link from an electronic trading platform or manually entered by the trader, clerk, or other back-office functionary. Transactions and position balances will be checked against executing and clearing broker statements and exchange records to ensure that the volumes and prices entered are correct. All trades will be tagged by trader, portfolio, date, time, product, and price, allowing the information to be queried in any permutation to produce reports for internal clients.

Collecting and Aggregating End-of-Day Price Data

The risk management group is also responsible for collecting, processing, validating, and storing a vast amount of end-of-day price data. This carefully maintained and verified database is used to mark the books, which is done by assigning a price to every open position at the end of the day and then calculating a mark-to-market profit or loss based on the change from the previous day's closing level. The risk group will seek to independently source price data from unbiased exchanges and clearinghouses, relying on trader data and broker-provided, end-of-day sheets only if there is no other viable source of information. It is common for traders to provide marks in illiquid, low-visibility markets, usually in the form of a spreadsheet of "fair" values with supporting emails and instant messages from their brokers as evidence. Trader data cannot, by definition, be trusted in a vacuum. There is an obvious conflict of interest, as the marks determine the P&L, which directly impacts the trader's year-end compensation. A significant number of rogue trader incidents have been the result of unsound risk processes that relied on trader input to a high degree, sometimes with little to no auditing or management supervision.

The most glaring example occurred in the 1990s, when a trader named Nick Leeson was mistakenly allowed to be both the head trader and supervisor of the back office functions that governed wire transfers, position accounting, and risk controls for a small Singapore branch office of Barings Bank. By exercising near-total control over the entire trading and settlements apparatus he was able to conceal and obtain funding for trading losses that, though initially small, ultimately reached approximately $1.5B and caused the collapse of Barings Bank, which became instantly insolvent and effectively ceased to exist.

---

[26] Some horrifically non-standard deals or completely novel transactions simply may not be able to be entered into the firm's risk system, or will not model and mark correctly given the nuances of the internal pricing engine. These mutant products will generally be kept track of off-system, which will involve a lot of email exchange between trading, management, and risk about how it will be marked, tracked, and accounted for.

Chapter 6 - Understanding Risk

Nothing ever really dies in the risk system. When a trader executes a trade, a record is created. When she closes the position, an offsetting trade record is created. As the trader buys and sells, the number of deal entries in the risk system always increases, even if the trader maintains no net position. The trader's open position is derived by netting out every buy and sell transaction entered into the deal capture system for a particular product and maturity, leaving only unmatched longs and shorts for consideration. The resulting "live" position is what generates profits and losses based on the fluctuations of the market. The completed set of scrubbed end-of-day marks will be loaded into the risk management system, and the day-over-day change applied to the net open position on a product-by-product, term-by-term basis, then aggregated by trader and portfolio as necessary. By applying price deltas at the most granular level possible, the risk group and management can query the profitability of any individual trade, or by trader, portfolio, product, or tenor.

Correlation Basics

The correlation between two data series measures the degree to which fluctuations in one are explained by/related to changes in the other. Most trading firms will track dozens (if not hundreds) of price streams, which will involve calculating a large correlation matrix, a grid of the correlations of each price stream compared to every other. This correlation matrix is of critical importance in the mechanics of the risk management of the firm.

To calculate the 20-day trailing correlation measured on the 252nd and last business day of the year the trader would start with a column of end-of-day price data, then:

1. Calculate the daily return by taking the natural log of Day X's price divided by the prior day's observation:

    $\ln(Day_X/Day_{X-1})$.

2. From that list the trader will use the CORREL function (in Excel, or its equivalent) to calculate a one-day correlation for a pre-specified sample of trailing periods. As an example, to calculate the one-day correlation between the FEB and MAR futures contracts for a sample of the previous 20 periods:

    $CORREL(FEB_{233}:FEB_{252}, MAR_{233}:MAR_{252})$

3. This process is repeated for each pair of daily return columns.

Calculating the correlations of the 13 ProdX futures contracts results in 169 product-to-product relationship pairs arranged on a grid to form a matrix. The transitive property applies, so the correlation between A and B will equal the correlation between B and A. The correlation of any product to itself is 100%. To save processing time, many matrices will only calculate the A-to-B correlations for each possible pair, leaving the opposite but equivalent B-to-A and the diagonal A-to-A 100% correlations blank.

	FEB	MAR	APR	MAY	JUN	JUL	AUG	SEP	OCT	NOV	DEC	JAN+1	FEB+1
FEB	1.0000	0.9760	0.9750	0.9899	0.9747	0.9851	0.9746	0.9861	0.9823	0.9678	0.9711	0.9858	0.9873
MAR	0.9760	1.0000	0.9637	0.9640	0.9457	0.9570	0.9584	0.9638	0.9690	0.9232	0.9412	0.9631	0.9533
APR	0.9750	0.9637	1.0000	0.9573	0.9484	0.9599	0.9694	0.9678	0.9610	0.9182	0.9386	0.9560	0.9619
MAY	0.9899	0.9640	0.9573	1.0000	0.9578	0.9830	0.9572	0.9764	0.9672	0.9468	0.9637	0.9781	0.9787
JUN	0.9747	0.9457	0.9484	0.9578	1.0000	0.9560	0.9417	0.9598	0.9452	0.9574	0.9383	0.9584	0.9532
JUL	0.9851	0.9570	0.9599	0.9830	0.9560	1.0000	0.9433	0.9624	0.9493	0.9442	0.9723	0.9694	0.9703
AUG	0.9746	0.9584	0.9694	0.9572	0.9417	0.9433	1.0000	0.9698	0.9797	0.9257	0.9342	0.9693	0.9641
SEP	0.9861	0.9638	0.9678	0.9764	0.9598	0.9624	0.9698	1.0000	0.9719	0.9472	0.9478	0.9717	0.9706
OCT	0.9823	0.9690	0.9610	0.9672	0.9452	0.9493	0.9797	0.9719	1.0000	0.9539	0.9382	0.9686	0.9789
NOV	0.9678	0.9232	0.9182	0.9468	0.9574	0.9442	0.9257	0.9472	0.9539	1.0000	0.9363	0.9536	0.9539
DEC	0.9711	0.9412	0.9386	0.9637	0.9383	0.9723	0.9342	0.9478	0.9382	0.9363	1.0000	0.9621	0.9580
JAN+1	0.9858	0.9631	0.9560	0.9781	0.9584	0.9694	0.9693	0.9717	0.9686	0.9536	0.9621	1.0000	0.9560
FEB+1	0.9873	0.9533	0.9619	0.9787	0.9532	0.9703	0.9641	0.9706	0.9789	0.9539	0.9580	0.9560	1.0000

Table 6.1 Correlation matrix for ProdX futures contracts.

The correlation matrix sits at the heart of the risk management system and has a significant but generally underappreciated impact on the calculation of most of the risk limits that govern the activities of a trading firm.

Modern risk management theory has as one of its central tenets that portfolio diversification reduces risk. The financial crisis of 2007-09 showed that traditional correlation relationships were not as stable under duress as was commonly believed. As panicked investors fled the market en masse, closing every position at the same time in an attempt to have zero exposure, previously uncorrelated assets began to move in tandem. This type of previously unknown system-wide correlation breakdown can be massively destructive for firms that carry large, warehoused risk positions. All risk groups do studies of price shifts and correlation perturbations to see how they impact the overall levels of risk given the firm's positions but, strangely enough, nobody stress tests for the end of the world. Even in less dramatic circumstances, if the correlations between products, markets, or terms are unstable, unreliable, or unbelievable, the firm-wide risks may not be properly quantified.

For firms that maintain more than one trading position (which will be the vast majority), the correlation matrix is used in the calculation of the portfolio parameters that will determine and control the exposure: among them, the net position size for spread or offsetting positions and the credit and collateral requirements demanded by counterparties and clearinghouses.

For naturals seeking to mitigate risk, generally accepted accounting practices require at least an 80% correlation between instruments for a product to be deemed an economic hedge for an exposure or pre-existing position. Economic hedges are useful risk tools, as they receive a favorable accounting treatment, which can involve excluding them from some financial statements and exempting them from mark-to-market accounting. For purely speculative trades constructed as spreads or multi-instrument structures, the degree to which the products

Chapter 6 - Understanding Risk

are correlated will determine the net exposure that will be charged against the trader's limits. If the correlation materially changes during the holding period, the size of the calculated risk of the net position will increase or decrease accordingly.

There are costs associated with holding a position. For exchange-traded or cleared products the trader's firm will be required to post some quantity of initial margin at the inception of the position, followed by variation margin to cover any subsequent losses. The amount of margin demanded is proportional to the volatility of the product and the net notional volume of exposure. Though the exact treatment varies from market to market, holding offsetting, highly correlated positions can significantly reduce the calculated net exposure, and therefore the amount of margin demanded by the clearing broker.

For this reason, spread positions are often said to be credit or collateral efficient exposures. As is the case with the firm's internal risk metrics, material shifts in correlation can cause large changes to the net position calculated by the firm's clearing brokers, which translates directly into demands for extra collateral. Abrupt increases in collateral demands can be devastating for thinly capitalized firms or companies holding large volumes of very highly correlated instruments vulnerable to any breakdown in the traditional pricing relationship.

One Metric to Rule Them All – Value at Risk
Value at Risk (VAR or VaR or V@R) has split the risk management and trading ranks into a perpetual, irreconcilable feud. The divide lies between those that believe V@R is a functional tool with well-known, well-understood limitations and those who feel it is a siren song that calls the foolish and unwary onto the rocks. I personally feel that the flaws inherent in the metric are less dangerous than an uneducated or disingenuous trader or manager who misinterprets what is, for all intents and purposes, a conditional estimate as an ironclad guarantee and acts accordingly.

Value at Risk is a process for transforming positional exposure and market volatility into a single metric that was popularized by Philippe Jorion in his book *Value at Risk: The New Benchmark for Measuring Financial Risk*. Though Jorion is the standard bearer (and frequently the punching bag) for V@R, this approach to distilling risk into easily consumed metrics had its roots in management reporting developed at Bankers Trust in the mid-1970s. The basic premise is simple:

> "VAR summarizes the worst loss over a target horizon that will not be exceeded with a given level of confidence."[27]

V@R can be derived at any confidence level and across any time span, which allows the risk manager to be very precise about being imprecise. The gold standard is a calculation done at a 95% confidence interval with a 1-day holding period, implying that the day-to-day fluctuations should be less than the V@R amount for 19 out of 20 observations.

---

[27] Philippe Jorion, *Value at Risk: The New Benchmark for Managing Financial Risk*, 3rd ed., (New York: The McGraw-Hill Companies, Inc., 2007), viii.

V@R calculation methodologies can be either simulation-based using historical data or rely on simplifying assumptions that allow the use of readily observed and measured statistical values. Parametric V@R is easier to implement for most instruments.

Parametric Calculation:
To calculate the 1-Day 95% parametric V@R the trader will need:

1. The size of the position in dollar terms.
2. The daily volatility in percentage terms, derivable from the annual volatility by the following relationship:

$$\text{Daily Volatility} \times \sqrt{252} = \text{Annual Volatility}$$
$$\text{or}$$
$$\text{Daily Volatility} = \text{Annual Volatility} / \sqrt{252}$$

So for a $100M position that has a 64% annual volatility, the calculation is as follows:

$$\text{Daily Volatility} = 64\% / \sqrt{252} = 4.03\%$$

The standard deviation of the daily changes is the Daily Volatility multiplied by the Notional Value:

$$\$100M \times 0.0403 = \$4.03M \text{ standard deviation}$$

Assuming a normal distribution, the trader can look up the N value in a standard statistical table, in this case finding that:

$$N(-1.65) = 0.05$$

The N value of 1.65 (in this example) is multiplied by the standard deviation:

$$1.650 \times \$4.03M = \$6.65M$$

The 1-Day, 95% confidence interval Value at Risk is calculated at $6.65M.

Simulation-Based V@R
The primary reason firms use simulation-based V@R is flexibility.

> They are particularly good at dealing with complicating factors—such as path-dependency, fat tails, non-linearity, optionality, and multidimensionality—that often defeat analytical approaches.[28]

---

[28] Kevin Dowd, *Measuring Market Risk*, (West Sussex: John Wiley & Sons Ltd., 2002), 123.

Chapter 6 - Understanding Risk

V@R is most commonly simulated by two methods: constructing a branching series of up/down probability events arranged in a lattice or a tree, or generating a randomized set of potential price paths and end states which are statistically examined. Consider a chart of a simple Monte Carlo simulation involving one variable that is perturbed with a simple RAND function to a +1/−1 range, with one increment of time between the original and terminal observations, iterated 100 times.

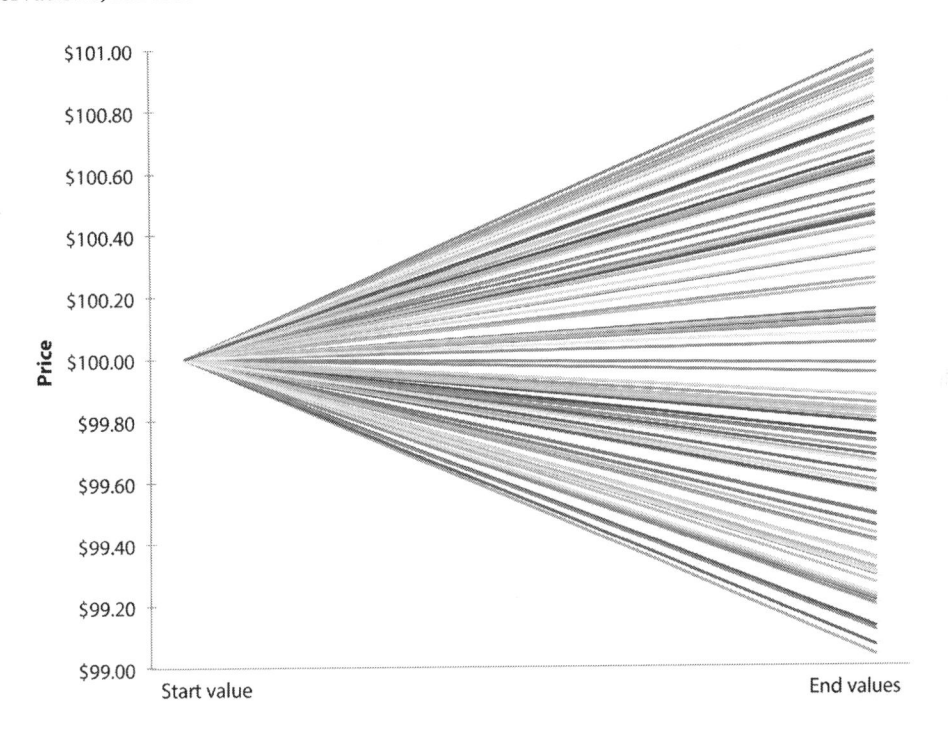

Figure 6.1 Monte Carlo simulation of 100 price paths.

The simplistic simulation yields 100 randomly generated price paths with 100 end-state prices. The V@R for a particular confidence interval is estimated by taking the bottom or top observations, averaging the results, applying the net price change to the notional value of the exposure under study and calculating the resulting P&L impact. For a 95% V@R, the bottom five observations would be used. For 99% V@R, the single worst observation would be used. In this manner, V@R can be calculated to any desired confidence level (though more precision would necessitate a larger number of iterations (1,000 at minimum for 99.9% V@R, and 10,000 at minimum for the rarely calculated 99.99% V@R). In reality, prudent risk management practice would demand that the number of iterations always be significantly larger than the minimum required to yield an answer to allow for more diversity of results and reduce the chance that one extremely anomalous observation skews the calculation.

There are a number of advantages and drawbacks with any user-defined methodology.

1. The ability to relatively precisely control the variables and operational parameters of the simulation allows for as realistic a simulation as the trader or risk manager cares to manufacture.
2. The ability to proactively test for conditions that do not currently exist, or have never existed, allows for greater flexibility to explore less-probable outcomes.
3. Highly detailed models that require prohibitively large numbers of iterations (10,000 or 100,000 passes are not uncommon for large, massively complex V@R models with a large number of component variables) can be highly resource intensive to build, maintain, and operate in a timely fashion. The quality of the inputs, both data and assumptions, must be assiduously tended and carefully curated, with any incurable flaws documented and understood, and their propagation effects through the model acknowledged.

The obvious problem with any simulation-based measurement of uncertain future events is that the conditions of the test or simulation will, to a very great extent, act to influence or (in extreme cases) determine the results. Testing to a 95% or 99% or 99.9% level is all well and good, until a 99.9999% event inevitably rears its ugly head. At the same time, the risk management group cannot grossly overstate the possible risks or the modeled exposures will be so grievously exaggerated that the firm will be paralyzed into inactivity for fear that the world is absolutely going to end every day.

Portfolio V@R

Most traders, and certainly most trading firms, will maintain more than one position at a time and will therefore need to calculate the total aggregated risk on the books. The relatively intuitive one-position calculus rapidly becomes a very complex proposition as additional exposures are added to the mix, since the V@R of the portfolio does not equal the sum of the component V@Rs, barring the improbable case of perfectly correlated positions. The portfolio V@R will depend on the relative volatilities and correlations of each position and, as a result, is typically only able to be accurately produced by the central risk engine in the deal capture system.

For most traders, portfolio V@R is a metric that they will be expected to monitor in an attempt to prevent their incremental position accumulation or distribution from becoming problematic at a book or firm-wide level.

Varieties of V@R

The V@R of a position or portfolio is calculated relative to the intended holding period or anticipated execution timeframe. The standard is to calculate 1-day V@R for liquid instruments, as it is expected that a trader should be able to modify the position quickly and with minimal slippage, so the risk of loss is only what would occur during the initial problematic day. Lower volume/lower liquidity markets will typically use 3-day or 5-day V@R in an attempt to make allowances for greater uncertainty and exposure to unfavorable conditions during position accumulation and distribution. For instruments with a realistic chance of being held to settlement, risk managers will calculate V@R to an assumed maturity date.

Chapter 6 - Understanding Risk

Due to the increased time under uncertainty, for any given position the 5-day V@R would be larger than the 3-day V@R, which will be greater than the 1-day V@R, etc. A back of the envelope method of converting between measurements is to divide longer-term V@Rs by the square root of the number of days under consideration. To convert 3-day V@R to 1-day V@R:

$$\$100{,}000 \text{ 3-day V@R} = \$100{,}000 / \sqrt{3} = \$100{,}000 / 1.732 = \$57{,}735 \text{ 1-day V@R}$$

Managers tend to cling to the security of V@R, feeling that even if they lose the full amount in a given day, things should be better tomorrow. It doesn't work like that. Not only can the position lose more than the V@R (and likely will, 1 day out of 20 when calculated at 95% confidence), it can keep losing day after day after day until the market calms down or the trader's firm runs out of money, whichever comes first. One of the most well-worn trader chestnuts is that "The market can remain irrational longer than you can remain solvent," which is usually uttered with significant sangfroid and schadenfreude by some wizened old head as they watch another young gun being walked off the floor.

Expected Shortfall (ES), Son of V@R
Expected shortfall is a more recently developed metric that, in a literal sense, attempts to pick up where V@R leaves off. Also called Conditional Value at Risk (CV@R) or Expected Tail Loss (ETL), Expected Shortfall is mechanically V@R calculated for larger standard deviation moves, frequently out to 5 or 6 sigma. This more inclusive probability space logically yields significantly higher potential P&L fluctuations.

Methodological Shortcomings
V@R has a number of well-documented shortcomings that should be understood by any practitioner. First, and most obvious, V@R pre-supposes a normal distribution of returns.

The Normal Distribution and Its Failings
Most basic, entry-level risk math is built on the assumption of a (log)normal distribution of prices. This is a necessary contrivance to get the models to solve, but when applied to the return characteristics of actual markets can be an assumption that ranges from somewhat unrealistic to borderline insanity.

Abnormal Distributions
Kurtosis is a measure of the relative volume of the tails of a statistical distribution to the middle. Effectively, kurtosis is how much more or less likely an extreme event is relative to expectations of lesser fluctuations. Leptokurtosis is the condition where the tails are fatter, meaning that extremely unlikely events are more probable than they "normally" ought to be.

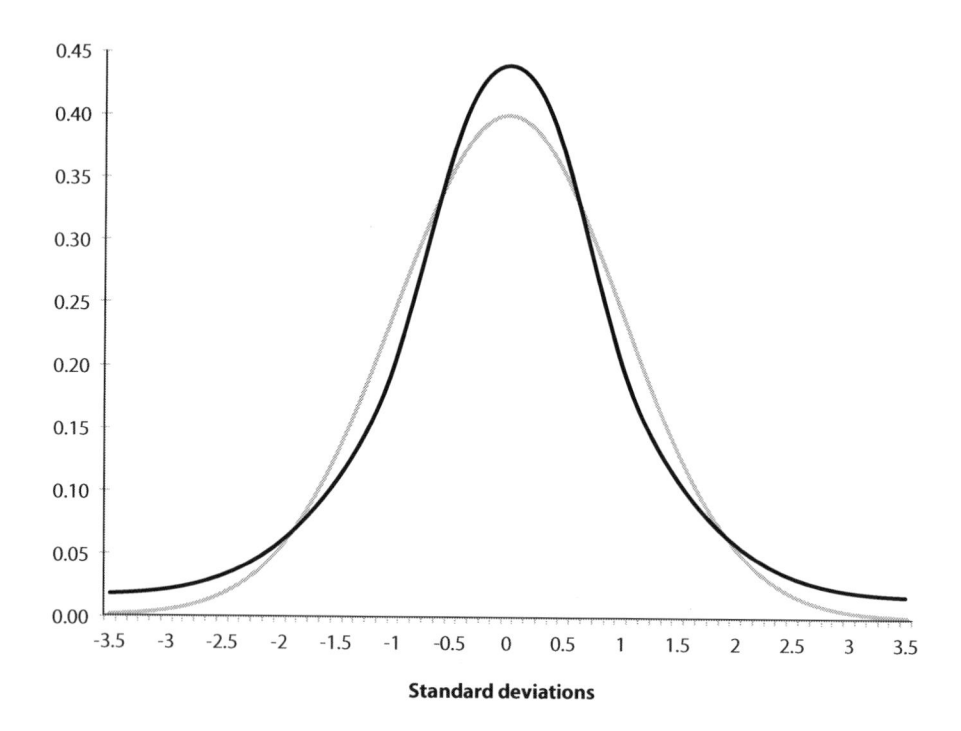

Figure 6.2 Normal distribution (gray) overlaid with a generalized Leptokurtic probability distribution (black) with more observations clustered around the mean and extreme tails.

The financial markets are profoundly leptokurtic in ways difficult for many, especially non-practitioners, to truly comprehend. Impossible things seem to happen fairly frequently. Even relatively non-volatile financial products are sufficiently leptokurtic to invalidate this assumption.

A second major problem with V@R is that it makes a probabilistic statement that losses will not exceed a pre-defined level with some level of confidence, but is completely silent on the magnitude of potential losses for "improbable" events. For leptokurtic, fat-tailed financial products this means that V@R will underestimate the chances of a negative outcome without providing guidance as to how bad that outcome could ultimately be. V@R is a measurement that gives the best results when the market is docile.

Relying on V@R is analogous having a worn-out, ratty old seatbelt in a car. The owner can buckle up and go for a drive, secure in obeying the law (staying within trading limits) and visibly protecting himself. Every seatbelt is designed to protect the wearer from collisions within certain speed parameters, from particular angles, and under a set of operational considerations. Much like a seatbelt, V@R will only protect the trader under a defined set of circumstances, which management and traders alike tend to forget. If the drive is uneventful (minimal market activity), the seatbelt will probably perform admirably as it sits there doing nothing. Even in a minor accident (some volatility) it is probable that the seatbelt will hold together and protect the driver. It is the large crashes where the seatbelt (or chosen risk metric) may fail. Moreover, no seatbelt in the world will do much if the car is hit by a meteor, crushed by a dinosaur, or vaporized by an alien death ray. Nobody could have seen *that* coming.

It is reasonable to ask why the industry clings to a marginally useful risk metric. For the same reason that people buckle up every day with seatbelts that they know might not save their lives. Without the veneer of confidence that V@R or seatbelts provide, no one would ever drive. While not perfect, V@R allows traders and the managers that supervise their activities to have some sense of, if not total confidence in, the risks that they are taking.

User Errors
There is an inherent asymmetry in the interpretation of P&L fluctuations relative to a trader's allocated or utilized V@R. There is a tendency on the part of trading management to overlook any positive P&L fluctuation in excess of V@R. While losing more than V@R is a sign of dangerously uncontrolled risk, making more than V@R is clearly due to trader genius and management prescience. While it is possible to construct a trading strategy, usually involving options, that has an extremely favorable risk-reward relationship and/or fixed downside to uncapped upside such that it is possible to out-earn the V@R, in practice, it is much more likely that the measured V@R will not capture the totality of the risks on the trader's book.

Risk Limits and Metrics

All trading firms have limits that bound their activities, both self-imposed parameters to govern the business and constraints due to an actual restriction, impediment, or prohibition from action. A firm's ability to take risk will be bounded by its ability to amass market-sensitive exposures and its capacity to borrow money to finance the positions. All firms that have any expectation of operating as a going concern will self-restrict their activities to a level far below this threshold. Trading firms have a number of controllable parameters at their disposal, which function as both levers for management to steer the business and constraints under which their traders must operate.

Capital Constraints
A firm will have access to capital, which it may choose to leverage with additional borrowing. This capital will be used to finance the firm's positions via a combination of margin payments to exchanges, collateral posted with counterparties and, in rare cases, cash used to pre-pay for positions where the firm does not meet the counterparty's standards for extending credit. Other creative financing options also exist, most of them bank-facilitated, that can allow a firm to pay with a letter of credit or back transactions with assets already on the books.

With the exception of highly focused hedge funds, most firms will have other uses for capital beyond financing the trading position. Most firms will dedicate some quantity of the total available capital to the trading function, with any amount beyond that threshold requiring special approval and allocation. The severity of this limit can vary significantly, ranging from a soft boundary for well-funded firms to an absolute, inviolable ceiling for thinly capitalized firms.

The trading desk will be allocated a maximum capital utilization, which will be sub-allocated to individual traders and portfolios.[29] At capital-constrained firms there will be continual competition for the ability to do business, with resources flowing toward the successful and away from underperformers.

V@R Constraints
As the relative volatility of the market fluctuates across time, the calculated V@R attributed to a position will shift higher or lower. Traders must take great care to be aware of the current V@R consumed by their positions and their utilization relative to allocated limits. Extreme market conditions that cause abrupt V@R spikes that can potentially force a trader out of a position (or never allow it to be put on in the first place) because the implied potential for P&L carnage has become unacceptably high.

V@R is taken very, very seriously at all trading firms. Exceeding a V@R limit is universally considered to be a severe infraction by the risk group and the management of the firm. A trader blowing through his V@R limit will generally receive a formal reprimand, at the minimum, and may face discipline or dismissal for repeat offenses.

Notional Constraints
The third way firms control exposure is through a notional limit, an upper boundary on the volumetric exposure allowed a trader or allocated to a portfolio. The V@R control will force traders to restrict themselves to proportionally smaller amounts of incrementally more volatile products, protecting the firm against currently observed risk. The notional limit helps protect the firm from dormant or unmeasured risk. A particular product may currently be extremely docile (low volatility and therefore low V@R), but there is no guarantee that it will continue to exhibit only minor fluctuations going forward. If the market experiences a sudden transition from low to high volatility the firm could be exposed to more risk than it ever intended. The notional limit also helps prevent the trader from amassing a position that would be excessively difficult to liquidate, given normal market conditions.

For directional vanilla positions, the notional volume is equal to the aggregated size of all of the trades and is a relatively straightforward calculation. More complex positions require both a slightly more complicated calculus and an established methodology.

Calculating the notional burden of a complex portfolio will involve using the correlations between positions to establish a net delta position, an approximation of how the position would act if distilled down to only the non-offsetting exposures that are actually impacting the P&L.

---

[29] The firm will typically charge the desk or the individual trader for allocated and/or utilized capital, the rates of which will greatly impact the types of trading strategies pursued.

Chapter 6 - Understanding Risk

The mechanical considerations must conform to the firm's methodological approach to the particular market and its traded products. While the calculated net delta position is the truest measure of the exposure, most trading firms will artificially modify the calculus to engineer in or out certain types of exposures by making them prohibitively expensive or irresistibly cheap when billed against the trader's limits.

Consider a simple long-short position, where an "undervalued" security is purchased and hedged with the sale of another "expensive" product. If the correlations are very high, the net delta exposure might be very small, on the order of a few percent of the size of each leg of the trade. This could, in theory, allow the trader to amass extremely large exposures if the firm is only monitoring the V@R or the net delta exposure. To control this behavior, and to protect against degradations in a high correlation, many firms will bill the trader for the notional value of one leg of the trade, radically increasing the limit burden and limiting the trader's activity. Extremely risk-averse firms will count both legs of the spread against the trader, creating a severe constraint on the volume of positions that can be accumulated.

Loss Limits

In addition to limits on allowable risk (V@R) and (notional) position size, traders will be controlled by the amount of losses they are allowed to sustain. There will typically be a number of loss limits that constrain the trader's activity. An annual limit will determine the total amount that a trader will be allowed to lose before ceasing activity and, not uncommonly, being terminated. Within the larger annual limit, the trader may be governed by a monthly limit that will typically be a fraction of the annual limit. The relative proportion between annual and monthly limits will vary widely depending on the market, the product, and management preferences. Sophisticated firms operating in developed markets will typically allow their traders relatively smaller monthly limits, where traders operating in less liquid, more volatile products will require more latitude to hold positions.

Within the allocated limits, the trader will budget resources according to his style and the opportunities present the market.

Aggregating Trader Limits Under a Firm-Wide Limit

Most trading firms will grant limits that, in sum, would exceed the firm-wide limit, relying on diversification across the portfolio to stay in compliance. This will require a degree of coordination by trading management to ensure that coincident maximum (or near-maximum) allowable exposures by a number of traders do not, in aggregate, create a problem with portfolio, desk, or firm-wide limits.

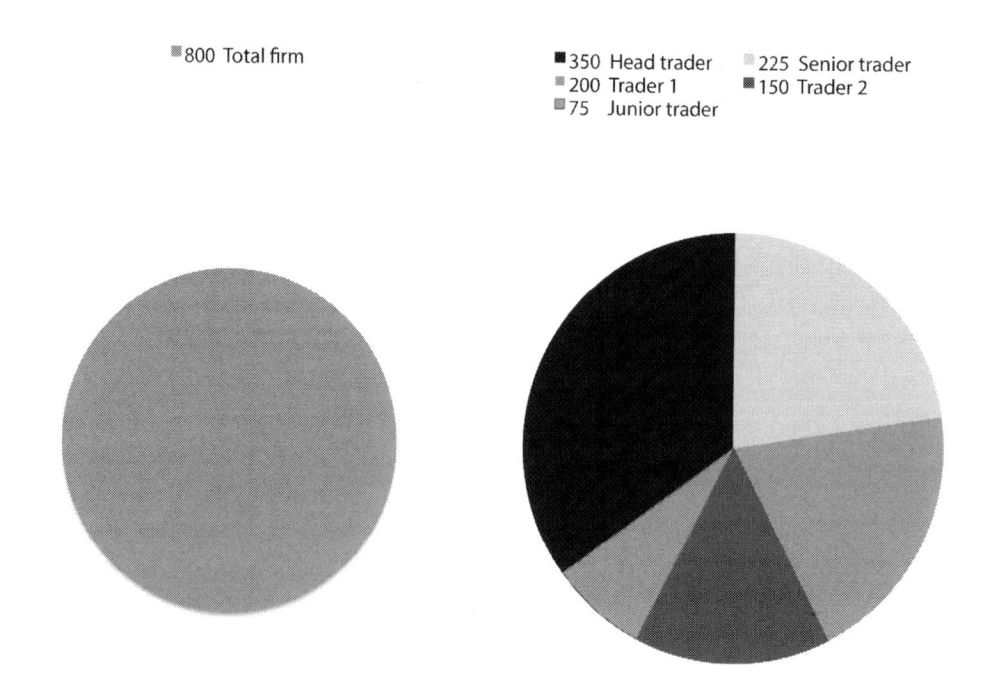

■ 800 Total firm   ■ 350 Head trader   ■ 225 Senior trader
                    ■ 200 Trader 1   ■ 150 Trader 2
                    ■ 75 Junior trader

Figure 6.3 The sum of the individual trader limits can be larger than the firm-wide limit.

Trading firms over-allocate resources to individual traders assuming that some percentage of the total positions will be negatively or minimally correlated, leading to a small net limit impact. For firms with diverse business interests and traders with well-defined, product-specific roles this is a reasonable assumption to make. For firms with a greater degree of trader latitude or a less-diverse product mix the aggregate exposure must be monitored much more closely. Over-allocating limits becomes problematic when all of the traders in a firm decide to max out their limits in the same product in the same direction and disastrous when a radical shift in traditional correlation relationships transforms a diversified portfolio into a swarm of temporarily aligned, similarly performing trades.

Traders and trading management will require accurate, detailed, and timely reporting on their positions and their consumption of the total available capacity to do business. Generating the necessary reporting is the responsibility of the risk group, with a likely assist from IT support.

Reporting on the Firm's Exposures
Once data has been collected and loaded into the risk system, the end of day process has been run, and any necessary post-processing completed, the risk group will generate a variety of reports for distribution to the group's clients throughout the firm.

Senior management will typically want only a gross overview of the net firm-wide position, a brief executive summary that depicts the total risk on the books, and the day-to-day, month-to-date, and year-to-date P&L figures. Detail-oriented managers may want a section highlighting material changes in credit exposure and a written explanation for any large changes in P&L. They will also be shipped a giant spreadsheet attachment containing every number the firm calculates which they will not open unless there is an epic disaster, at which point they will suddenly need to review every number.

The head of trading will need to see significantly more detail to effectively function as the interface between the traders and the rest of the firm. She will need to see the total risk on the books, as well as a breakdown of the positions by portfolio and/or by trader to see what strategies are working, and which traders are performing. She will want to see current and day-over-day changes in collateral and the percentage utilization of available limits by book. Finally, day-over-day, month-to-date, and year-to-date P&L changes are useful for preparing for the inevitable management questions on strategy and profitability.

Firmwide position by product and term

	FEB	MAR	APR	MAY	JUN	JUL	AUG	SEP	OCT	NOV	DEC	JAN+1	FEB+1
ProdX	326,236	(226,938)	255,603	5,578	5,893	6,203	6,478	7,129	32,999	7,593	8,239	0	0
EurX	273,781	666,283	150,000	150,000	150,000	50,000	50,000	50,000	50,000	50,000	50,000	0	0
CanX	50,000	50,000	50,000	50,000	50,000	50,000	50,000	50,000	50,000	50,000	50,000	125,000	125,000
AfrX	(100,000)	(100,000)	(100,000)	(100,000)	(100,000)	0	0	0	0	0	0	0	0
ChiX	(100,000)	(100,000)	(100,000)	(100,000)	(100,000)	(125,000)	(125,000)	(125,000)	(125,000)	(125,000)	(125,000)	(125,000)	(125,000)
AusX	75,000	75,000	75,000	75,000	75,000	75,000	75,000	75,000	75,000	75,000	75,000	0	0

Spread book

	FEB	MAR	APR	MAY	JUN	JUL	AUG	SEP	OCT	NOV	DEC	JAN+1	FEB+1
ProdX		(500,000)											
EurX	100,000	600,000	100,000	100,000	100,000								
CanX	50,000	50,000	50,000	50,000	50,000	50,000	50,000	50,000	50,000	50,000	50,000	125,000	125,000
AfrX	(100,000)	(100,000)	(100,000)	(100,000)	(100,000)								
ChiX	(125,000)	(125,000)	(125,000)	(125,000)	(125,000)	(125,000)	(125,000)	(125,000)	(125,000)	(125,000)	(125,000)	(125,000)	(125,000)
AusX	75,000	75,000	75,000	75,000	75,000	75,000	75,000	75,000	75,000	75,000	75,000	0	0

Directional book

	FEB	MAR	APR	MAY	JUN	JUL	AUG	SEP	OCT	NOV	DEC	JAN+1	FEB+1
ProdX	250,000	250,000	250,000										
EurX	50,000	50,000	50,000	50,000	50,000	50,000	50,000	50,000	50,000	50,000	50,000		
ChiX	25,000	25,000	25,000	25,000	25,000								

Option book (net delta position)

	FEB	MAR	APR	MAY	JUN	JUL	AUG	SEP	OCT	NOV	DEC	JAN+1	FEB+1
ProdX	76,236	23,062	5,603	5,578	5,893	6,203	6,478	7,129	32,999	7,593	8,239		
EurX	123,781	16,283											

Table 6.2   Firm-wide position with spread, directional, and option subportfolios.

	Firmwide notional limits		
	Exposure	**Limit**	**Utilization**
ProdX	435,013	4,000,000	11%
EurX	1,690,064	4,000,000	42%
CanX	800,000	4,000,000	20%
AfrX	(500,000)	4,000,000	13%
ChiX	(1,500,000)	4,000,000	38%
AusX	825,000	4,000,000	21%

	Firmwide value-at-risk		
	95% 1-day V@R	**Limit**	**Utilization**
Spread book	$643,200	$1,000,000	64%
Directional book	$865,748	$1,000,000	87%
Option book	$231,857	$1,000,000	23%
All books	$1,597,274	$2,500,000	64%

	Firmwide stop limits	
	Exposure	**Limit**
Daily P&L	($949,439)	($2,500,000)
Month-to-date	$6,754,224	($5,000,000)
Year-to-date	$35,093,929	($10,000,000)

Table 6.3   Firm-wide risk metrics, including notional, V@R, and P&L.

Traders will primarily be concerned with their specific exposures and the variables that impact their ability to transact in the market. They will want to see their net positions broken down by product type or grouped into strategic or thematic portfolios. They will want a set of the official marks to understand why the positions did or did not make money. They will want to see the amount of margin consumed by their positions and the total collateral outstanding with counterparties and clearinghouses. Most critically, they will need the control metrics that govern their business, including the notional volume of exposures, the day-to-day and month-to-date P&L, and the utilized V@R of the portfolio relative to allocated limits.

Chapter 6 - Understanding Risk

Position by product and term

	FEB	MAR	APR	MAY	JUN	JUL	AUG	SEP	OCT	NOV	DEC	JAN+1	FEB+1
ProdX		(500,000)											
EurX	100,000	600,000	100,000	100,000	100,000								
CanX	50,000	50,000	50,000	50,000	50,000	50,000	50,000	50,000	50,000	50,000	50,000	125,000	125,000
AfrX	(100,000)	(100,000)	(100,000)	(100,000)	(100,000)								
ChiX	(125,000)	(125,000)	(125,000)	(125,000)	(125,000)	(125,000)	(125,000)	(125,000)	(125,000)	(125,000)	(125,000)	(125,000)	(125,000)
AusX	75,000	75,000	75,000	75,000	75,000	75,000	75,000	75,000	75,000	75,000			

Day-over-day P&L by product and term

	FEB	MAR	APR	MAY	JUN	JUL	AUG	SEP	OCT	NOV	DEC	JAN+1	FEB+1
ProdX		209,733											
EurX	(53,313)	(365,952)	(34,265)	(24,490)	(28,173)								
CanX	(46,017)	(52,645)	(29,576)	(21,138)	(24,317)	(19,623)	(23,432)	(14,178)	(16,665)	(5,924)	(4,265)	(23,333)	(9,472)
AfrX	10,362	11,854	6,660	4,760	5,476								
ChiX	60,799	69,557	39,077	27,929	32,129	25,926	30,959	18,733	22,019	7,827	5,636	12,331	5,006
AusX	(35,573)	(40,697)	(22,863)	(16,341)	(18,798)	(15,169)	(18,114)	(10,960)	(12,883)	(4,580)	(3,297)		
Total	(63,742)	(168,150)	(40,968)	(29,280)	(33,684)	(8,866)	(10,587)	(6,406)	(7,529)	(2,677)	(1,927)		

P&L (373,815)

Table 6.4 Individual trader position report, including P&L by product and term.

Notional limits

	Exposure	Limit	Utilization
ProdX	(500,000)	2,000,000	25%
EurX	1,000,000	2,000,000	50%
CanX	800,000	2,000,000	40%
AfrX	(500,000)	2,000,000	25%
ChiX	(1,625,000)	2,000,000	81%
AusX	825,000	2,000,000	41%

Value-at-risk

	95% 1-day V@R	Limit	Utilization
Spread book	$643,200	$1,000,000	64%

Stop-loss limits

	Exposure	Limit
Daily P&L	($389,283)	($1,000,000)
Month-to-date	$1,654,356	($2,000,000)
Year-to-date	$12,986,392	($5,000,000)

Table 6.5 Individual trader risk metrics, including notional, V@R, and P&L.

The trader will also want to monitor the firm's relative utilization of limits to ensure that there is available capacity to do business for any future strategies they intend to deploy.

A conscientious risk group may try to provide forward-looking tools to help the traders assess potential exposures and proactively manage their positions. This can be as simple as precalculating and distributing a V@R utilization matrix by product and maturity to allows traders to make faster, more efficient resource allocation decisions.

Enforcing the Risk Policy
In the event of a breach of a limit or other unauthorized activity, the risk group will be required to take action. Small, obviously unintentional errors can often be resolved with an exchange of administrative emails. If there are legitimate concerns, there may be a formal investigation into the trader's activity. Disciplinary measures can range from a procedural email to a superior, a more formal disciplinary communication to several levels of upper management, temporary suspension of trading authority, and, ultimately, termination for severe infractions. In extreme cases of fraud, gross negligence, or dereliction of duty the risk group may be forced into direct market action to mitigate uncontrolled exposures.

Possible breaches of the risk policy:

- Compliance breach: unauthorized activity of any kind.
- Notional breach: too large of a position relative to allocated limits.
- Loss-limit breach: too large of a loss within a given time period.
- Credit threshold/margin breach: exceeding allocated capital utilization.
- V@R breach: exceeding the allowable amount of risk.

There are two schools of thought on the proper boundary of the risk management function, to act only in a reporting capacity with the ultimate decision authority residing higher in the management hierarchy, or as a proactive enforcement entity. Firms with a partnership structure (or their roots in one) tend to have more aggressive, proactive risk managers, as they share in the ownership of the firm and participate in its continued success. Reporting risk management is more common at large corporations with many layers of approval and control.

Trading Risk Management
Traders worry about all of the same things that keep risk managers up at night, plus a host of other considerations. Risk managers are concerned primarily with making an accurate measurement, generating timely reporting, and speedily resolving any issues. A trader has to understand and experience risk on a much more tangible, visceral level. Where a risk manager aggregates all risk into a single metric, traders prefer to examine the component risks in isolation.

Black Swan Risk
Nassim Nicholas Taleb's 1997 book *Dynamic Hedging – Managing Vanilla and Exotic Options* was the clarion call of the financial engineering revolution and should be considered mandatory reading for any aspiring trader. In it, Taleb espoused a more intellectually rational approach to measuring and managing risk, emphasizing realistic assessment of the actual and potential risks and denouncing dogmatic allegiance to pure model-based quantitative methodologies.

Chapter 6 - Understanding Risk

Dynamic Hedging is a challenging, relatively esoteric text that appealed primarily to a small coterie of hard-core derivative practitioners. Taleb's 2007 book *The Black Swan* debuted to widespread popular and critical acceptance and elevated him to the Mount Rushmore of Risk. *Dynamic Hedging* changed how traders thought about risk; *The Black Swan* changed how everyone thought about risk.

The eponymous "black swan" is Taleb's all-conquering übermeme for the unknown risk that cannot, by definition, be anticipated. Both the name and the philosophical underpinnings originate from empiricist David Hume:

> No amount of observations of white swans can allow the inference that all swans are white, but the observation of a single black swan is sufficient to refute that conclusion.[30]

Taleb's identification and categorization of black swan risk, distilled into risk-management terms, cautions the unwary that however hard they may try, it is impossible to account for all of the possible dangers. There will always exist some non-zero probability of a random, violent, impossible-to-predict occurrence. A legitimately brilliant insight, and one that has allowed a generation of inept traders, poor risk managers, and clueless executives to lazily utilize it as a crutch to explain away whatever horrific disaster they have created and don't know how to fix. Anticipating the unanticipatable, while an obvious impossibility, has still managed to occupy the best efforts of countless high-dollar mathematicians, financial engineers, and quantitative analysts. As Taleb himself succinctly notes in his most recent book, *Antifragile*:

> An annoying aspect of the black swan problem—in fact the central, and largely missed, point—is that the odds of rare events are simply not computable. We know a lot less about hundred-year floods than five-year floods—model error swells when it comes to small probabilities. *The rarer the event, the less tractable, and the less we know about how frequent its occurrence.*[31]

The obvious transitive implication for risk management is that V@R is, by definition, a flawed measurement and is being systematically relied on for a job that it is incapable of performing. Even expected shortfall, with its wider allowance for low probability, high standard deviation events, will not properly capture the unmeasurable chance that something truly unexpected may be about to happen.

Feeding Invisible Swans

If it is a given that black swans are fundamentally unpredictable, and that traditional risk metrics will provide little in the way of predictive utility, then how can any trader begin to understand the potential impacts of a high-sigma event, much less go about protecting

---

[30] Nassim Nicholas Taleb, Fooled by Randomness: The Hidden Role of Chance in the Markets and in Life, (New York: Texere, 2001), 100.
[31] Nassim Nicholas Taleb, Antifragile: Things That Gain From Disorder, (New York: Random House, 2012), 7.

positions? The answer lies in common sense, which as the saying goes, is not all that common. Many analysts and traders manufacture their own black swans by artificially limiting the data sets or probabilistic outcomes they consider. By relying on recent history, "analog conditions" or "historical norms," they weed out the troubling tail events that couldn't possibly happen again. Knowing where the volatility sensitivities or vulnerabilities lie within a position or portfolio is critical for avoiding blowups. Traders should also indulge in productive flights of fancy or disaster, playing theoretical what-if games to at least consider the potential impacts of absurdly unlikely events, which, though they cannot be measured, can at least be factored into the decision-making process.

Separating Swans From Other Foul Birds
Many so-called black swan events are actually the aggregated effect of a number of smaller, individually sub-critical events that coincide to produce a single, epic market response. As such, practitioners may be looking at the risk calculus incorrectly, attributing conditional probability hyperbole to a simple probability event. Instead of waxing eloquent about how wonderfully implausible it was to have A and B and C and D occur at the same time, it might be more productive to examine how probable D was, since by that time the market should have already seen and, in theory, may have priced in A, B, and C.

A true black swan, like a true force majeure event, is an extremely rare thing. If the weather forecast changes, a production statistic comes in unexpectedly large or small, or a lawsuit expected to fail somehow inexplicably succeeds, that is an outcome that could have and should have anticipated and been assigned a probability. Fortunately, there are a large number of "known knowns" for traders to obsess about when not fretting about unforeseen ice ages and imminent asteroid impacts, among them market risk, liquidity risk, product risk, volatility risk, correlation risk, counterparty/credit risk, contract risk, and clearing/margin risk.

Market Risk
Market risk is the potential for a trader's position to be advantaged or damaged by "normal" day-to-day price fluctuations. Proactively managing market risk and finding ways to turn it into profitable transactions is what traders do.

Liquidity Risk
Liquidity risk is something of a catch-all term that combines all of the anticipated costs that will have to be paid by the trader to enter or exit a transaction, including the bid-offer spread and the costs of possibly penetrating through multiple levels of the order book, weighed against the opportunity cost of waiting for more liquidity to emerge over time. Liquidity risk is highly market and product dependent, and can remain fairly constant—as is the case in most highly developed markets—or fluctuate wildly with the whims and transactional requirements of the market participants. Normal liquidity risk present in day-to-day transacting is mostly a matter of bid-offer spread and incremental costs from eroding the order deck with large buy/sell orders. In times of stress incremental participants will flee to the sidelines, causing the market to thin out appreciably. Bid-offer spreads will widen, sometimes dramatically, and the number of resting orders behind the best market will decrease, making

Chapter 6 - Understanding Risk

it challenging to assess the depth and almost impossible to execute a large order without moving the market. Recall the bid-offer deck of a low-volume commodity from Chapter 5.

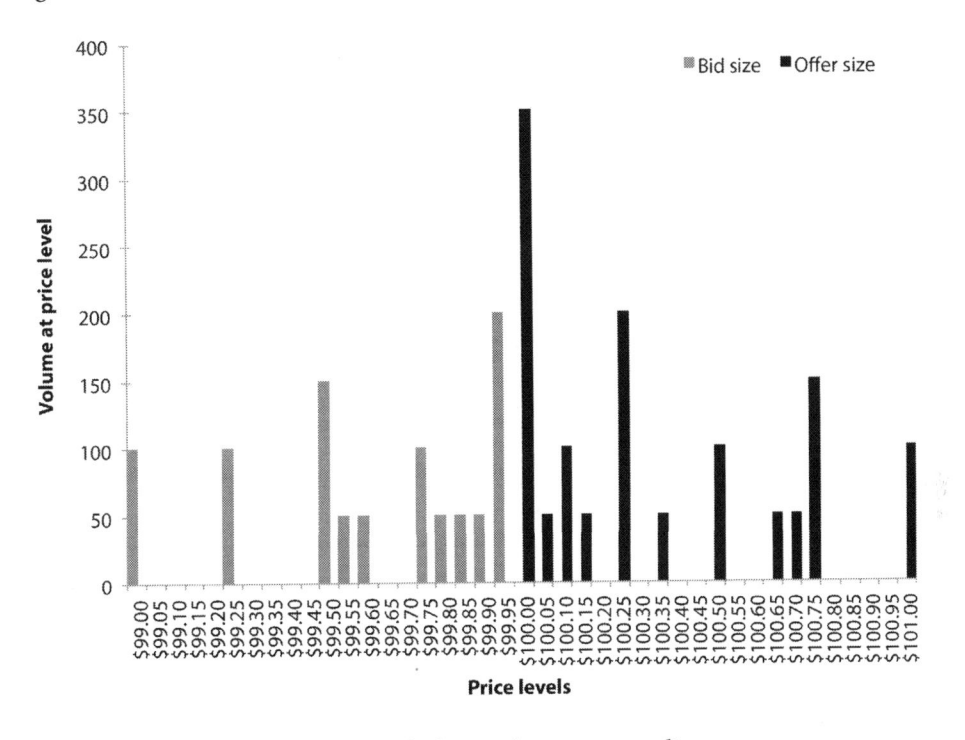

Figure 6.4 Bid-offer deck of a low-volume commodity.

Assuming a market in which this graph represented standard order sizes and dispersion, in a period of market stress or uncertainty the posted interest would likely deteriorate, yielding a stack that could look like the graph below.

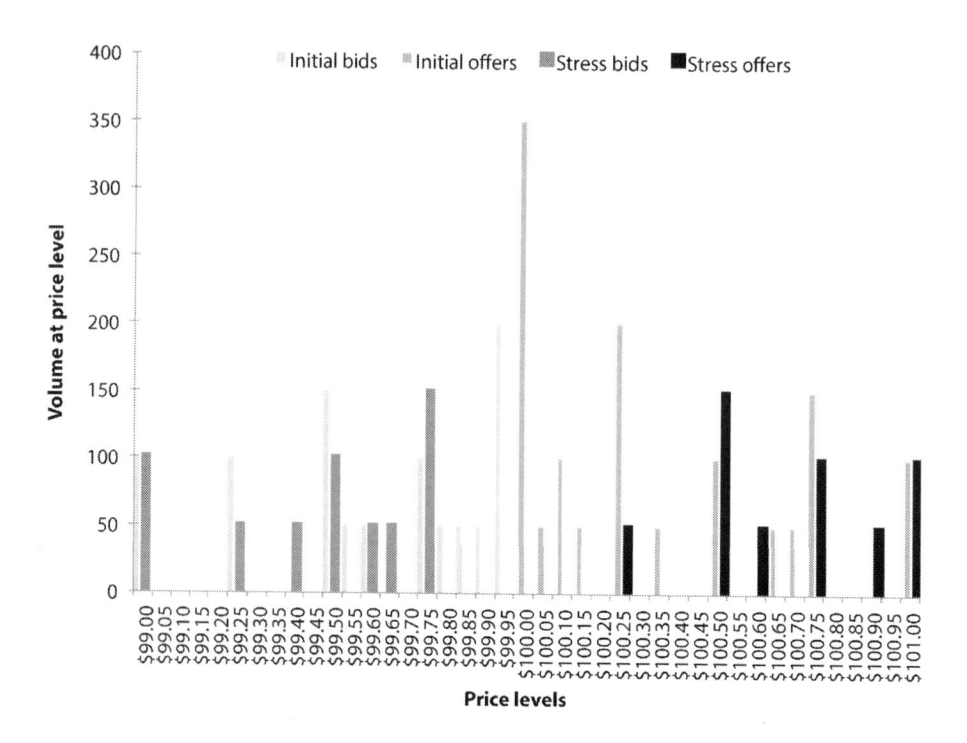

Figure 6.5 Deterioration of a low-volume bid-offer deck under stress or uncertainty.

The bid-offer spread has widened considerably, the volume available at the best market is lower, the increments between orders are larger and there are fewer orders and less total volume available. This type of symmetrical reduction in orders would be symptomatic of lack of interest, lack of participation, or a difficult-to-interpret change that resulted in general uncertainty. In most cases a disruptive event would have obviously bearish or bullish implications, which would unbalance the market and result in ample liquidity on one side and severely decreased participation on the other. An unexpected bullish surprise could lead to the following bid-offer deck.

Chapter 6 - Understanding Risk

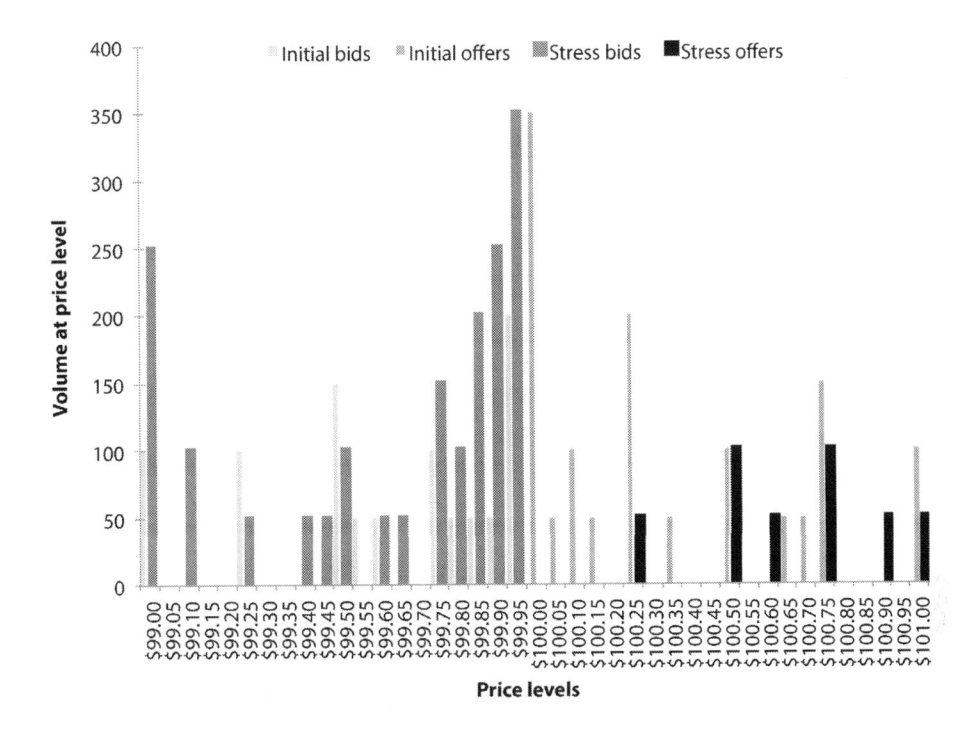

Figure 6.6 Shift in bid-offer deck in response to a bullish surprise.

The volume interest at the current price has sharply increased, the total bid interest has tripled, and the offer side of the market has all but disappeared.

Many firms, particularly those that do a significant volume of customer execution business, will maintain liquidity curves. A liquidity curve is a trader-provided estimate of the potential price impact of executing larger-sized transactions, typically visualized as a widening bid-offer spread for incremental units of volume.

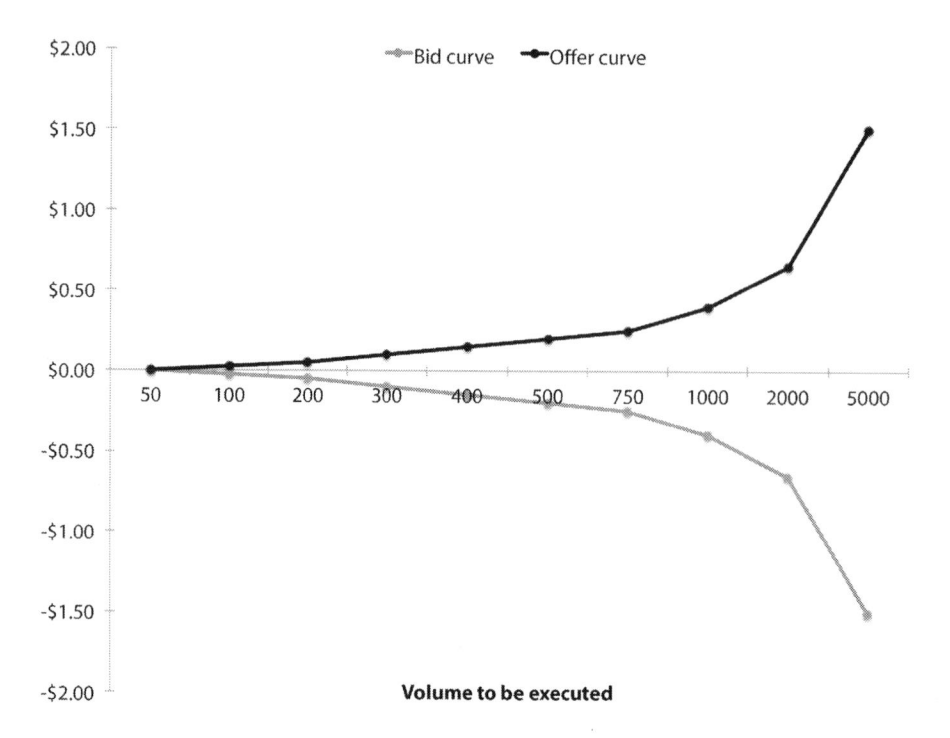

Figure 6.7 A liquidity curve estimating price impact per unit of volume executed.

Selling 50 to 100 lots should be possible at or near the posted market price, but a 750 lot order should be expected to move the market $0.25, and executing between 2,000 and 5,000 contracts could have up to a $1.50 impact on price. Liquidity curves are intended to measure impact of volume executed without allowing the market time to re-build depth. A patient trader with time to execute will frequently choose to break a transaction into smaller chunks sized to have a minimal impact when incrementally dribbled into the market. The skill lies in reading the market conditions and understanding which approach will yield a better average execution price.

A well-maintained set of liquidity curves is critical for originators and structuring analysts to correctly price the cost of executing hedges or laying off exposures for large proposed transactions. Senior executives and risk managers will also use liquidity curves to rank potential alternatives by executable volume at a price when contemplating risk-mitigation strategies.

A much more ominous aspect of liquidity risk, particularly in thin or volatile markets, is the real possibility that when a trader decides to execute a trade, there may not be anyone who cares to take the other side of the transaction. In theory, in a well-functioning market, there should always be someone willing to sell if there is a buyer present, the only question being at what price. In reality, during periods of extreme stress, there may not be any counterparties willing to transact, regardless of price. These liquidity gaps or holes (see Chapter 5 – Understanding Volatility) can be extremely destructive.

Product Risk
Product risk is a catch-all term, which can encompass default risk, prepayment risk, bankruptcy risk, and operational risk. It is the risk that a trader's inventory under future conditions changes materially without the trader's control, and usually not for the better. The quality and quantity of product risk depends on the market, the standard instruments, and to an extent on the choice of trade implementation.

While in some early-stage or physically driven markets it is impossible to completely avoid product risk, in most cases there are mitigation technologies available. These can range from paying slightly more to a more secure, creditworthy counterparty to execute a deal, using a financial clearinghouse to secure a trade, purchasing credit default swaps, or taking out an insurance contract to protect against the loss of critical production infrastructure. The incremental cost is proportional to the security desired, though in many cases the fees required for total risk mitigation can be prohibitive.

Volatility Risk
Volatility risk comes in several flavors. The market level of volatility will directly impact a position built out of options or option-like instruments. A net long option-based position should increase in value with higher volatility and decrease with lower volatility, all else being equal. A net short option position would lose value as volatility increased. Less obvious are the potential impacts on strategies where a certain range of market volatilities are expected, but do not materialize. This will be covered in greater depth in Chapter 10 – Option Trading Strategies.

Counterparty/Credit Risk
The early days of any new market can be pretty lawless and wild. Most if not all business will be executed as a bilateral contract directly with another company, exposing the trader's firm to its ability to honor commitments and pay debts (see Chapter 2 – Evolution of Markets). There is money to be made by the bold, and tremendous pressure to validate the firm's presence in the market by getting business done, regardless of conditions or counterparties. Taking no risk and making no money gets traders just as fired, in the long run, as getting stiffed by a counterparty that ultimately turns out to be a guy living in his parents' basement who tries to post a shoebox of comic books as variance margin. This combination of short-term desperation and lack of concern for long-term consequences engenders a certain level of transactional promiscuity, leading some firms to do business with anyone available. Eventually a firm will bite off more risk than it can chew and lose badly, defaulting on its obligations and forcing everyone else in the market to learn about credit and counterparty risk.

Counterparty risk assesses the likelihood that a particular firm will continue to be a going concern, active in the market and able to honor obligations and pay bills on time. The firm's credit manager will cross reference balance sheets with credit ratings and other publicly available information to determine the counterparty's cash position, estimated continued viability or ability to borrow as reflected by their credit rating relative to their obligations, and reasonable probability of default. Causes for concern include dwindling cash, a downgrade by one or more credit rating agencies, or a significant increase in the amount of money owed for new transactions. If the credit manager feels that there is a risk of nonperformance, she may recommend corrective action. The options available will be spelled out in the contracts governing the trading relationship between the firms, most commonly a master agreement, International Swaps Dealers Association (ISDA) contract, or other similarly thick, unreadable document. No two contracts are the same, but common solutions involve the impaired party agreeing to post additional collateral as surety, attempts to reduce the balance of money owed through offsetting transactions, cessation of trading until positions roll off the books, and cash prepayment for any new business.

Maintaining a web of individually negotiated master agreements, ISDAs, margining, and netting agreements will eventually become a drag on the system as a whole. Financial clearinghouses will emerge to stand between counterparties, guaranteeing all transactions from default and bringing efficiency and standardization to the marketplace.

Contract Risk – Grey Areas and Shenanigans
All traders operating in nonfinancial markets must be aware of any grey areas, loopholes, or wiggle room in their firm's contracts. In any market there are "generally accepted practices," and there can be latitude within those boundaries to do unpleasant things to the incautious, the unwary, and the imprecise. In a new market, it is tremendously advantageous to have traders, risk managers and support staff who have seen it all before, understand the pitfalls, and are prepared for all of the dirty tricks.

Clearing/Margin Risk – How It Impacts Traders
In the early going, access to credit will determine who can do business with whom and define the term and depth of the exposure each will be willing to entertain. This is particularly important for firms that do a significant volume of direct transactions and mid-marketing, structured, and origination deals. Below some threshold of financial well being, a firm will have difficulty executing new business. If there is any further deterioration, its counterparties may well start to unwind positions or seek mitigation through credit default swaps or other instruments. This is a less severe restriction now than in the past, as widespread adoption of cleared financial products can provide refuge for the chronically noncreditworthy. The consequences of a degraded credit rating would be felt in the surety provisions and amount of margin and/or collateral demanded by the clearing broker that warehouses the firm's trades. Credit has gone from being a binary access issue to an ongoing, fluctuating tax on execution.

Clearing brokers do not exist to allow traders to further their ambitions, they exist to hold positions and get paid a small stream of fees to compensate for the customer firm's default risk. If that default risk goes up, the fees charged will escalate proportionally, sometimes geometrically. Credit managers at clearing firms are not paid based on how much liquidity they provide, they are paid on how good they are at being stewards of their firm's capital. While a trading firm's struggles are the single most important thing to its employees, the clearing firm has several dozen (or hundred) others in its portfolio. From repeated practical experience, it will understand liquidity and solvency issues better than its clients, and will act dispassionately to protect its interests at the expense of any client, regardless of how "special" or "valued."

It is important for traders to understand both the initial collateral required to hold the transaction and the potential for that quantity to fluctuate after the position is on the books. There are two kinds of modifications to collateral required by clearing firms. Exchange-mandated adjustments are made to the standard rates required for each product that are a function of the volatility of the market. Company-specific adders/multipliers to that base level are applied to a particular firm based on its relative credit standing and net open position. If the amount of holding collateral expands significantly, a firm can be forced to liquidate positions at extremely inopportune moments. The clearing broker will favor speed and surety of execution over price, which makes sense, as it is spending someone else's money to get rid of a position it does not want to hold.

As the preponderance of business transacted in a market shifts from bilateral to cleared, the relationship between clearing broker and trading firm becomes ever more critical. The clearing broker becomes the lifeline between the trading company and the market. Many trading firms will maintain relationships with several, as a prudent diversification and to prevent any one firm from having undue influence over their business and knowledge of their positions.

The Trading Position Is Not the Credit Position
Just as firms will employ more than one clearing broker for diversification, many will do business through a variety of financial clearing mechanisms. It is possible to have direct exposure to a counterparty via negotiated transactions, to do financially settled direct swaps under a standardized ISDA, execute trades through a pit broker or on a screen that ultimately come to reside in a clearing broker's account, and execute OTC trades and then "block" the trades through to a clearing broker. At the end of the day, the credit and treasury function will have to come to grips with all of the various cash flow ramifications of each element of the firm's position. The firm can be completely flat on a delta and product basis but have material residual exposures due to the cash flow properties and relative surety of delivery of the various pieces of the puzzle.

Most firms indemnify traders from credit risk responsibility as long as they are transacting in an approved fashion with a vetted counterparty or using a clearing mechanism authorized by the firm. As a practical matter, it would be difficult if not impossible for an individual trader to understand how their actions aggregate with all of the other contemporaneous transactions to affect the firm's net credit position in real time.

Credit Efficient Trading
Most trading activity is financed with borrowed money. As capital constraints become tighter and collateral requirements more onerous, managing trading activity in a resource-efficient fashion becomes increasingly important. Extracting the maximum value per unit of credit and

collateral utilized is critical, both in terms of a trader's absolute and relative profitability. It does not pay to be a resource hog. Credit and collateral constrained markets tend to lead traders to more spread trading (when receiving favorable offsets), long option positions (minimal up-front payments), and a significant increase in intraday trading (limits are usually only enforced at the close of business). Directional trading, long-term buy and hold strategies and counterparty-direct origination, and structured transactions are very resource intensive and tend to fall quickly out of favor when the cost of financing and holding positions rises. This will be covered in greater depth in Chapter 12 – Evaluating Trades & Creating A Trading Plan.

Risk Management Challenges

Perfectly Inaccurate (Mark Risk and Mark-Induced Volatility)

One of the main problems facing an institutional risk manager at small and medium-sized firms is the strain the scope of the business puts on data collection, verification, and processing. Marking the book at the end of the day can be an extremely involved process, particularly in markets without a consistent, reliable stream of exchange closes, clearing/margining numbers and third-party, end-of-day prices. In markets with poor pricing visibility, the risk group is usually loathe to create its own curves and is unable, for control purposes, to rely on the in-house experts on the trading desk, due to the obvious conflict of interest. The unfortunate result is that frequently risk groups will only track pricing they are absolutely certain is correct, verifiable, and visible, which ends up being only a small subset of the total.

Trading management will never voluntarily self-restrict potentially profitable business because of the limitations of a risk or audit process.[32] Profitable trading ideas are frequently found where there is little price visibility. In early-stage markets the trading group will typically have a vastly wider purview and possess better market information than that available to the risk group. This will pose a variety of problems, as the traders will propose executing transactions in a new product and the risk group will immediately demand to know how it is defined, how it trades, how they should value it, how much liquidity is present to set position limits and how to build up a database of historical data to simulate V@R, etc. Most of this information will probably not be available, and definitely not in an audit-friendly form, so after some predictably tense meetings the Faustian bargain will be struck that New Product #1 (NP1) somewhat resembles Product #46 (P46), but is a little more valuable. How much more valuable? The trader thinks $2.00, or so. Risk will build a pricing reference into the deal capture system that marks NP1 = P46 + $2.00 and maintains this stable relationship until someone advises otherwise or the market at NP1 becomes mature enough to be observed as a stand-alone product. This is called marking to a pricing relationship or as a basis. Sometimes it may be logically correct to utilize a price relationship composed of a weighted formula of other

---

[32] Senior management frequently has to adjudicate between trading management who rightly want to book novel types of profitable business and risk management who rightly try to protect the firm. The revenue producer will tend to win about 95% of these arguments.

observable products, i.e., New Product #2 = 70% of the value of Product #46 and 30% of Product #48.

Market Participant Risk Perspectives

Though the basics of risk measurement and mitigation are common to all firms, each category of market participants has unique considerations that impact activities. Hedgers, merchants, financials, and speculators each have a distinct set of advantages that they can leverage and pitfalls that they must seek to avoid.

Hedger's Risks

Unlike other participants, hedgers have a core business that is not necessarily related to the market. A hedger's trades are risk-reduction actions, and cannot be allowed to add risk or the program will be discontinued. It is actually surprisingly easy for a hedger to add net risk to the firm if it is particularly unsophisticated and has exposures to volatile process inputs and output prices. Fixing the volume or price of either leg of what amounts to a spread or spread option position can have the effect of net decreasing optionality as it converts the proposition from a relative value play to an outright long or short position.

Hedgers also frequently operate at an informational disadvantage to the rest of the financial markets, and are prone to be surprised by large macro events, exogenous occurrences, and industry-wide shifts.

The Hedger's Dilemma – Cash Flow Timing

A much more potentially dangerous risk is the potential for mismatched timing of cash flows. Consider a corn farmer, who expects a great crop next year and likes the prices currently in the market. The farmer can sell a volume of corn equivalent to his expected production using financial futures, effectively locking in a margin against the anticipated harvest. If the market continues to go up, the farmer has a loss on the hedges, but the crop is theoretically increasing in value at an approximately equal rate. However, the farmer will be paid for his crop when it is grown, harvested, and delivered to market sometime next year. He will owe the clearing broker margin for the losses on the hedges at the close of business, today.

The farmer has a mismatch in the timing of payments, and if the market moves enough to generate near-term financial losses that he cannot cover, could ironically be bankrupted by prosperity. This is the classic hedgers dilemma. It is sometimes possible for a natural to avoid this trap by structuring a package of hedges with a bank or other financial intermediary that is willing to accept a lien on the underlying business or productive capacity in lieu of cash collateral. This service is typically only available to, and practical for, more sophisticated hedgers with a substantial physical asset base. Also, there is a fee.

Evolving Risk

Assume that a company has a set of risks A, B, and C at time T and that it is able to place a perfect hedge against each at a fair cost in a manner acceptable to its corporate governance, auditors, and accountants. Now, start the clock. Production schedules change, forecasts are revised, the macroeconomic climate shifts and the situation evolves in a complex and unpredictable fashion. As the underlying conditions evolve, risk A diminishes, B remains constant, and C definitely grows much larger. The unchanged hedge positions are out of balance with the exposures, and are no longer mitigating the underlying risk in a one-for-one fashion. The manager in charge has two options, either true up the position to current projections—which may be expensive, politically untenable, or just impossible—or live with the exposure imbalance.

Very few executives would identify this exact moment as the point that they launched an internal proprietary trading group. It happens every day, and to companies that would never be expected to be running material speculative financial exposures. More confounding for board members, regulators, and, ultimately, the shareholders and employees is that it is often impossible to distinguish between well-intentioned risk mitigation strategies that naturally drift and clearly out-of-bounds behavior designed to juice up profits (and bonus payouts) by building invisible casinos.

If the firm decides to proactively manage risks and seeks to reconfigure the hedge position, it faces a host of operational issues:

- The natural will have to incorporate forecast updates that impact the magnitude of the exposure to be hedged, and therefore the volume of hedges required.
- Assuming that the model is generating useful information, is it possible for the firm to make meaningful modifications to the hedge position given the available instruments and liquidity?
- Can the firm afford all of the explicit and implicit costs of making changes to the hedge positions, including brokerage, slippage, credit/collateral, etc.?

A Merchant's Risks
A cornerstone of the merchant business model is assuming long-term levered contractual obligations, and then seeking to enhance the exposure via aggressive optimization or extract fallow value not properly managed by original owner. There are a number of risks:

- The biggest risk lies in incorrectly assessing the quantity and characteristics of risk being sought or held.
- Asset-based deals are frequently highly complex and very committing.
- Misjudging the risks inherent in committing positions can be deadly, as the positions are large and difficult or impossible to exit.
- Merchants are also frequently thinly capitalization and assume a degree of implied leverage that frequently makes mistakes fatal.

A Bank's Risks
Banks are primarily customer-facing transactors that warehouse risk and earn a bid-offer spread as a fee for the service.

- A large warehouse of accumulated positions leads to high levels of complexity, difficult-to-model net exposures, and huge potential lead time to exit.
- As a net liquidity provider, a bank can find it difficult to access the liquidity it needs to enter/exit at will.
- Banks will develop critical exposures to a small handful of hedging instruments that they will use to balance the book against market movements.
- In the current environment there is large regulatory risk potential.

A Speculator's Risks

Speculators should have the most precise exposures, as taking risk is their primary business and they have no clients to service, legacy assets to optimize, or core business to protect. Speculators' risks typically concern access to markets and an ability to do business.

- Maintaining a capital base, as investors will tend to flee rapidly during periods of underperformance.
- Any breakdown in relationships with the exchanges, clearinghouses, banks, and counterparties that speculators rely on to implement their exposures, most commonly caused by poor performance, can prove devastating.
- Potential capital flight and continued market access makes liquidity risk the primary concern of any pure speculator.

Chapter Six Summary

Understanding how price data is translated into historical volatility and measurements of risk is critical for any trader. The risk management group will primarily concern itself with calculated metrics based on end-of-day price data, including the correlation matrix that will sit at the heart of the deal capture system, the value-at-risk that measures the probabilistic fluctuations and governs the size of the portfolio, and the daily P&L and applicable loss limits. The risk group will also be responsible for daily reporting to the trading group and senior management on the positions and profitability of the firm. The trading group will have different perspective on risk, focusing on the current volatility, the product risk inherent in the instruments of choice, contract and counterparty/credit risk, the available liquidity, and the potential for an unexpected disruptive black swan event.

Weighing and measuring the risks present in the market will play a large part in the trader's development of their view, explored in depth in Chapter 7.

Review Questions

1. Describe the importance of correlation in trading risk management.
2. What are the four limits that control a trader's activity?
3. What shortcomings of Value-at-Risk impact its utility as a risk management tool?
4. Describe three of the types of risk that traders are primarily concerned about.
5. What is a black swan? How should a trader incorporate black swan risk into their assessment of the market conditions?

Resources

- *Dynamic Hedging: Managing Vanilla and Exotic Options* by Nassim Nicholas Taleb
- *Value at Risk: The New Benchmark for Managing Financial Risk, 3rd Edition* by Philippe Jorion
- *Measuring Market Risk* by Kevin Dowd
- *When Genius Failed: The Rise and Fall of Long-Term Capital Management* by Roger Lowenstein
- *Rogue Trader* by Nick Leeson
- *The Vandal's Crown: How Rebel Currency Traders Overthrew The World's Central Banks* by Gregory J. Millman

Chapter 6 - Understanding Risk

Case Study: Product X Risks

As discussed in Chapter 2, Product X is in an early-to-middle developmental state, and has both a set of current risks occupying the attention of traders and a number of proto-risk factors that, while not currently present, will inevitably emerge as the market and its participants continue to evolve.

Product X Parametric V@R

Calculating the 1-Day 95% parametric V@R for a 1M ton FEB Product X position worth $105.29MM that has a 6.65% annual volatility is done by the following process:

$$\text{Daily volatility FEB ProdX} = 6.65\% / \sqrt{252} = 0.419\%$$

The standard deviation of the daily changes is the daily volatility multiplied by the notional value:

$$\$105.290M \times 0.419\% = \$441,289$$

Assuming a normal distribution, the trader can look up the value in a standard statistical table, in this case finding that:

$$N(-1.65) = 0.05$$

The N-value of 1.65 (in this example) is multiplied by the standard deviation:

$$1.65 \times \$440,903 = \$728,127$$

The 1-Day, 95% confidence interval V@R for 1M tons of FEB ProdX is $728,127.

The 99% confidence interval can be obtained by multiplying the standard deviation by the N value $N(-2.33)$, yielding $2.33 \times \$440,903 = \$1,028,204$ 1-Day V@R.

Product X Simulation V@R

Begin with the prior day closing price for the FEB contract ($105.29) and, using a spreadsheet or other looping randomized process, generate a sample of 200 day-over-day changes that form a price distribution. Simulated V@R based on a normal distribution would be problematic for most financial instruments, as it would tend to understate the tail risk present in the market. For a lower-liquidity, early-to-middle developmental stage market facing a potentially severe supply constraint, it could grievously understate the potential for high-sigma events. Allowing the simulation to incorporate the potential for larger, less expected moves in the FEB ProdX price yields the following distribution:

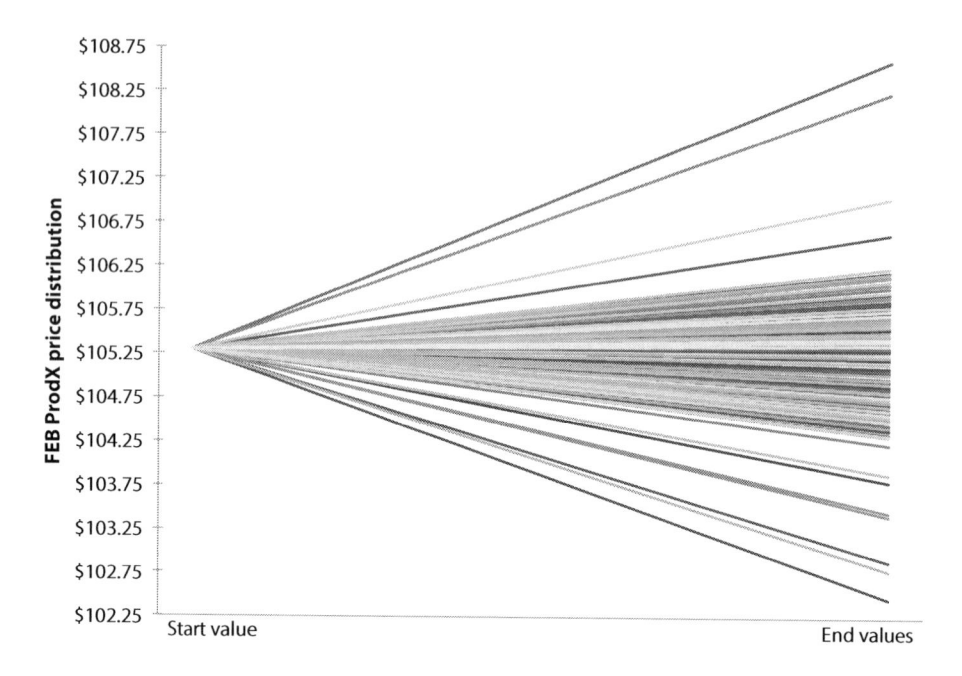

Figure 6.8 Monte Carlo simulation of FEB ProdX contract with potential for large price fluctuations.

With 200 data points, the 1-day 95% V@R would be represented by averaging the 10 lowest observations, with the 1-day 99% V@R defined by the two worst outcomes, as seen in the following table:

Data point	Observation	DOD change
188	$104.33	-$0.96
167	$104.33	-$0.96
117	$104.23	-$1.06
128	$103.89	-$1.40
46	$103.81	-$1.48
135	$103.45	-$1.84
101	$103.42	-$1.87
15	$102.89	-$2.40
165	$102.79	-$2.50
94	$102.46	-$2.83
Worst 10 average	$103.56	-$1.73
Worst 2 average	$102.63	-$2.66
1-day 95% V@R		$1,730,557
1-day 99% V@R		$2,663,632

Table 6.6 Simulated V@R for FEB ProdX contract.

Chapter 6 - Understanding Risk

The larger probability space yields simulated V@Rs for the FEB ProdX that are significantly larger than the parametric calculations.

Given the strong potential for the Product X market to increase in volatility, the historically-based parametric V@Rs are almost certainly understating the risk currently present in the market. The simulated V@R offers a more realistic perspective on the magnitude of potential price fluctuations, but is somewhat counterfeited by being determined by a set of random draws based on a user-defined probability distribution function. The parametric V@R is very precise about how risky the ProdX market probably isn't, and the simulation V@R yields some perspective on how risky things could be, if the market acts like the person running the simulation thinks it should. The trader should take both data points into consideration, but also be aware of the potential for larger price fluctuations brought on by unexpected events.

Black Swan Risk
Product X has existed as a traded financial commodity for a relatively short period of time, during a global recession and the subsequent recovery. The conservative economic backdrop and lack of speculative froth resulted in a period of depressed volatility for all markets, and against that placid backdrop Product X has never had the opportunity to go thermonuclear. It would be extremely foolish to think that this would not be possible in the future, and traders should be alert to the potential for conditions conducive to a volatility-led disaster.

The loss of the African production facility is not a black swan event. Mechanical failure, even extremely low-probability manifestations, should be always be factored into a physical market participant's decision calculus.

Market Risk
As the historical volatilities calculated in Chapter 5 will attest, the market risk in Product X has been relatively low. The recent outage-related tightening of the supply/demand balance combined with the potentially bullish/bearish return to service event path inflection point will almost certainly increase the going-forward volatility and the market risk for all participants.

Liquidity Risk
The liquidity risk present in the Product X market to date has been primarily a function of the wide bid-offer spreads and moderate transactional volumes present in the forward and futures markets. It is anticipated that, if the volatility increases on a going-forward basis, the prevailing normal level of liquidity will become interspersed with low-volume periods and the occasional panic or step-function move in prices on near-zero turnover.

Product Risk
The product risk in the Product X market is currently relatively low, with cleared futures products available in the United States and Europe to mitigate what little counterparty risk exists between large financial institutions, global natural resources conglomerates, and nation-state mining concerns. The entry into the market of less well-capitalized merchants and speculative entities and a probable near-term uptick in volatility will, all else being equal, increase the product risk.

Volatility Risk

The volatility of the Product X market is currently elevated relative to historical norms, but seems almost comically low when compared to the prevailing volatilities of almost any other established natural resource commodity. Numerous examples exist of sleepy commodity markets jolted out of their reverie by seismic volatility shocks (US power market prior to 1998, US coal market prior to 2001, etc.).

While it is possible that Product X returns to its sleepy, mid-recession fluctuation levels and the forward volatility declines back to the low, low single digits, both the normal evolution of markets and the omnipresence of black swan risk would seem to argue against that remote probability. Chapter 11 – Option Trading Strategies will examine how the price of derivative contracts to buy or sell Product X in the future reflects a market perception of the probability of increased volatility.

Counterparty/Credit Risk

The preponderance of transactions in the Product X market have historically been long-term, over-the-counter negotiated physical trades with direct counterparty exposure. Counterparty performance risk was poorly understood and the probability of default effectively priced at zero, which was not an entirely unreasonable assumption in an environment where all of the players in the space were nation states, global commodity players, and bulge bracket banks. The rapid growth of the financial market and an associated increase in volatility have brought in smaller, less permanent speculative entities with thinner capital reserves and no vested interest in the Product X market beyond its utility as a vehicle for profit generation. The development of standardized forward products and the margining requirements of ISDA-governed swaps introduced the concept of relative creditworthiness, with the advent of cleared financial futures contracts removing some barriers to participation and rigidly codifying the amount of capital necessary to hold a trading position.

Any material up-tick in volatility will lead to tightening of credit and clearing requirements, while at the same time the profit opportunities draw in small- to medium-sized speculative entities. This influx of thinly capitalized players with higher aggression levels and a need to transact to earn a rate of return will exacerbate price swings, leading to more volatility, which will tighten credit and margin requirements, which will put more stress on the counterparties with weaker balance sheets.

Contract Risk

The vast majority of historical Product X transactions were physical supply deals consummated via long-form, non-standardized contracts with direct counterparty performance risk and credit exposure. Performance risk is currently low to moderate (except for the defaulted African-based supply contract), but should be expected to increase materially with the influx of new market participants with a willingness to compromise on contractual performance standards to book business, and the anticipated uptick in volatility, which will increase the overall stress on the system.

Chapter 6 - Understanding Risk

Cleared financial products and futures contracts will provide a safe haven for firms willing and able to do business under the more stringent contractual and credit restrictions.

Clearing/Margin Risk

The gradual shift to ISDA swaps and, more recently, to futures is slowly acting to reduce the contract risk on the books, but has increased the reliance on the clearing broker(s) with no vested interest in the trader's firm.

Product X Risk Summary

As seen in Chapter 5, Product X has exhibited extremely low observed historical volatility during the study period. When translated into an estimated Value at Risk for the futures contracts, this yields a relatively low amount of risk for a nascent, mostly physical commodity. The lack of price volatility has also perpetuated an unusually low-stress environment for the participants to operate in. Given the anticipated event path for the Product X market, it seems extremely unlikely that this low-volatility, low-risk environment will continue into the future.

7

Developing a Cohesive Market View

Having a soundly constructed, well-reasoned view of the market is the primary job of any trader. Developing a view is not about waiting for a *Eureka!* moment, being knocked out by a falling apple, or receiving the gift of total consciousness. Crafting a perspective on the future of prices is a deliberate, methodical process of aggregation and interpretation. A view does not guarantee a position. If, after evaluating all available information there are no attractive opportunities, so be it. If the market is not conducive to activity, sometimes the only rational course of action is not to play.

Good scientists know that designing an experiment around a particular outcome will inevitably lead to data that reinforces the pre-experimental bias. For the same reason, a trader's view must be the end result of an analytical process, not the starting point. The process does not exist to validate a trader's preconceived notions. Poor experiment design usually leads to bad science and worthless results, predetermined conclusions lead to bad trading ideas and losing positions.

Developing a Market View

A market view is constructed by incrementally incorporating a trader's perspectives on:

1. Fundamental information and the current drivers impacting the market.
2. A technical analysis of price fluctuations.
3. The current volatility and anticipated risk environment.
4. An understanding of the current market conditions.
5. An assessment of the magnitude of the probable risks and the potential rewards.

Each step in the process serves to refine and sharpen the thesis. The fundamental information gives a sense of what the market may be worth in the future, or under different conditions. This fundamental value, when compared to the prevailing prices, provides perspective on potential market movements. Technical analysis uses graphical tools to examine market sentiment and assess the probability of a potential move, how far it may go, and under what conditions it may accelerate or decelerate. The prevailing volatility gives the trader perspective as to how swiftly the market could move, and how bumpy the road might be along the way. The market conditions color the trader's expectations as to the relative ease or difficulty of executing the strategy, holding the position and optimizing its performance. Comparing the probable risks relative to the possible rewards allows the trader to make a determination if the market justifies participation. In flowchart form:

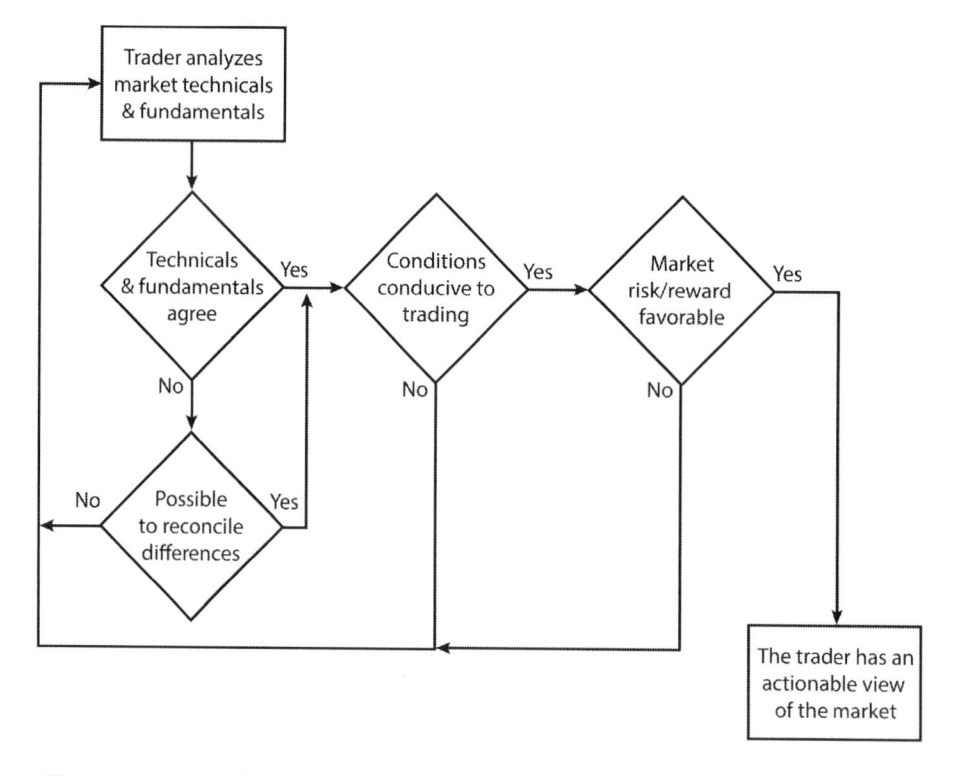

Figure 7.1   Flowchart of process of developing a view of the market.

Fundamental Information

The method for deriving information from fundamental data will depend on the trader's preference for a more or less structured decision-making process. Unstructured decision making is more common in markets that evolve rapidly or that have highly changeable influences. Structured decision making is more common in well-established markets where evolution and consensus have determined a set of variables that matter, each meticulously tracked and microscopically interpreted.

Chapter 7 - Developing a Cohesive Market View

Unstructured Information – Drivers and Forces
Old market or new, many influences or few, the fundamental drivers will rarely all point in the same direction at the same time. Of a hypothetical set of a dozen or so factors that could influence price at any given time, some may be bullish, a few will be bearish, and the rest neutral or inconclusive. Many traders deploy a sophisticated heuristic algorithm to assist with decision making under uncertainty called "making a list." The trader will free associate all of the drivers that appear to be impacting the market, from well-established data items to the news and events of the moment. He will go through item by item and categorize each as a bullish, neutral, or bearish influence on prices in isolation. This embarrassingly low-tech approach is extremely effective for two reasons. First, it forces the trader to consider all of the possible market drivers, not just the one or two that he has been obsessing about for the past few days. Considering each factor in isolation helps prevent any trader bias from bleeding from one driver to another. Examining the total sorted and categorized list forces the trader to weigh and measure the contributions of each factor relative to the others, and to the group as a whole. Does one bearish factor overcome two bullish items? Three?

The trader can sort the list of drivers in terms of traditional or ongoing importance, generally resulting in the balance sheet items or analog case variables at the top and the news of the day at the bottom. A trader concerned with shorter-term fluctuations might attempt to order the list based on his perception of the factors having the largest influence on market price right now, which may lead to a more random or counterintuitive ordering. A sorted list of market drivers can be a useful tool to examine change over time, as it forces the trader to contemplate and acknowledge the impacts of each incremental piece of information. Something happened: is the overall informational topology more bullish, increasingly bearish, or still inconclusive?

Structured Information – Measures and Models
Traders with a more systematic or rigidly defined decision-making methodology will typically have an established process for periodically refreshing their data and running it through a model, balance sheet, or other analytical tool.

Traders utilizing a balance sheet will be constantly updating estimates, continually logging observed data points, and continuously tweaking assumptions in an attempt to keep the predictive instrument finely tuned. With each evolution in the data, logic, or assumptions the trader will turn the crank on the machine and re-examine previous conclusions. Given the new data or fresh information, has the market become more or less oversupplied or undersupplied? Is it tighter or looser? Are the market drivers that have created this condition persistent, which would suggest the potential for an extended move, or will they manifest as a short-duration event with effects that will fade quickly?

Simple spreadsheet-based balance sheets easily answer the question whether the market will move but are generally silent on the magnitude of any potential move. Traders and analysts will create demand curves to intersect anticipated supply with projected demand to arrive at an estimate of the price that would clear the market under those conditions. More sophisticated analytical models will utilize an iterative process to evaluate the variable implications of user-defined binding assumptions or criteria.

Technical Analysis

Fundamental analysis gives the trader a perspective on what the market ought to be doing, given a set of observable or inferable data points and an approximation of value that may or may not bear any resemblance to current prices. With this information in hand, the trader will then create a rigorous, detailed, and entirely independent technical analysis of recent price action. While a detailed chart reading is interesting in its own right, the ultimate goal is to integrate the technical analysis with the fundamental thesis to provide context, timing, and measurement objectives.

To create a complete technical analysis the trader will deploy the analytical studies developed in Chapter 4.

Trend
A trader will first determine if the market is trending, how well defined the trend is, and under what time scale it is relevant. The trader will consider how the current price action fits within the macro-, intermediate-, and microstructure.

Support and Resistance
Are there areas of levels of obvious, well-defined support and/or resistance present on the chart that would either impede or assist future price movement? In a non-trending market, the proximity to support or resistance will inform the trader's selection of entry points and stop levels. The breach of a well-defined support or resistance level can serve as a trigger point for a breakout strategy designed to capitalize on an abrupt move away from a pattern or consolidation area.

Pattern
Are there well-defined patterns present in the chart that would impact an ongoing trend positively or negatively? Are any patterns statistically more symptomatic of continuation of the current move, consolidation at the current level, or a reversal of the trend in progress?

Studies
Do any of the standard studies add additional insight to the analysis? Do Bollinger Bands indicate the market is temporarily overbought or oversold? What do the moving averages say about the momentum? If the market is poised for a retracement, what Fibonacci levels are in play?

Measurements and Objectives
Do the trend, support and resistance levels, pattern analysis, and studies combine to imply a rational price objective that the market is capable of achieving?

Summary Technical View
What is the chart as a whole saying? Combine the trend, support and resistance, pattern, studies, and measurement and objectives perspectives into a cohesive analysis. It is no failure to conduct a detailed, thorough analysis and conclude that the current chart contains little usable technical information. The real failure lies in a trader seeing what he wants to see,

bending the rules or blurring his vision to attribute convenient significance to a chart that has none in order to facilitate a predetermined trade.

Comparing the Fundamental and Technical Perspectives

The first step in crafting a view of the market is comparing the independently derived fundamental and technical perspectives. The compatibility of the fundamental and technical perspectives provides the initial screen that separates productive and unproductive markets, as irreconcilable analytical differences cannot be overcome by any magic and are not worth the expenditure of time and effort.

Are the Fundamental Facts and Technical Analysis Aligned?

There are four potential scenarios when comparing the technical and fundamental information:

1. The fundamentals and technicals conflict.
2. One study has a strong perspective, and the other is inconclusive and provides no additional clarity.
3. One study has a strong perspective, and the other is neutral and implies no additional motivation.
4. The fundamentals and technicals are aligned.

The Fundamentals and Technicals Conflict

If the technical study is diametrically opposed to the fundamental analysis, the trader should do nothing until he understands the reason for the divergent interpretations of the market. There are many potential causes for conflicting fundamental and technical perspectives. Among the most common are:

1. The trader's internal fundamental information is leading or lagging the market.
2. There is a mismatch in the timescales of the technical and fundamental studies.
3. Non-fundamental price fluctuations.

If the trader is early with a fundamental insight, the firm's internal fundamental view may be ahead of the market and may not be reflected in the price action of the technical analysis. The trader will wonder why the price is not moving. If the trader is late with a fundamental insight, the internal fundamental view will lag the market and will not reflect a change that is propagating in the price action and visible on the technical analysis. The net result is that the technical chart will be moving in a static internal fundamental environment. The trader will wonder why the price is moving.

Leading the market may result in productive trading strategies, lagging the market never will.

It is also entirely possible that the trader may be completely unaware of a change in the fundamental thesis that is currently impacting the price (and therefore the technical pattern). Recall from Chapter 3 that it is impossible for any trader to form a complete fundamental picture of a market, there is simply too much information to absorb and process, and every participant acts on some subset of the total information space. This is particularly true of markets with a large number of information sources, as on any given day someone will be changing a forecast or issuing an update to an outlook, etc.[33] Inexplicable or unexpected price moves invariably send traders scrambling to their news screens, searching for some fresh piece of analysis or research that everyone else in the industry is currently acting on.

Traders should be wary of potential timing mismatch issues whenever the study periods of the fundamental and technical forecasts are materially different. Consider the following price chart of a fundamentally structurally bearish market:

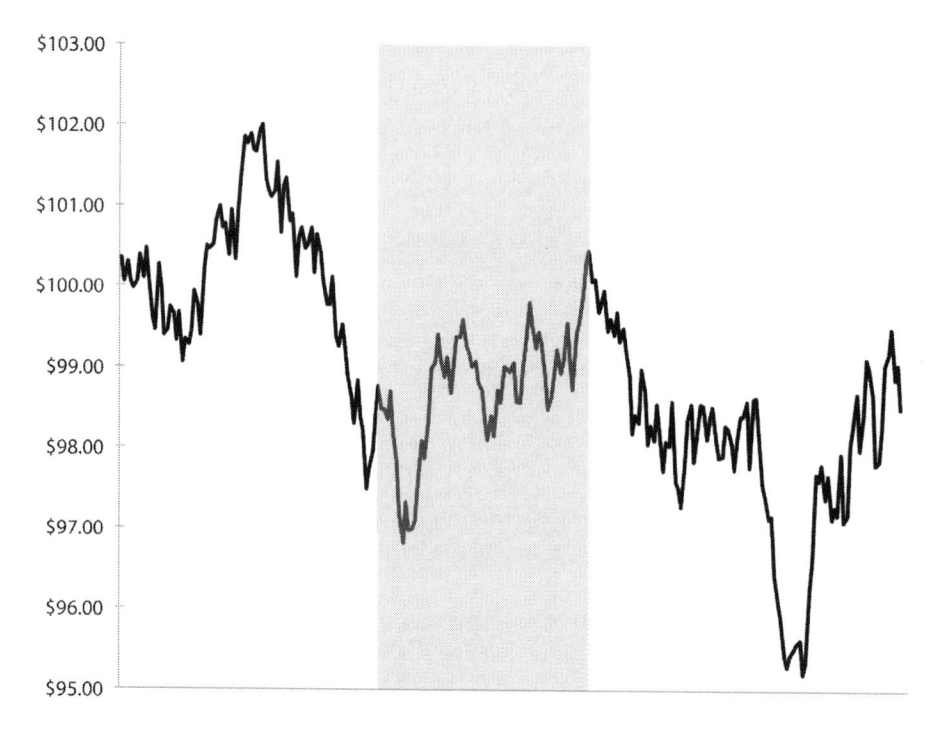

Figure 7.2   A mismatch of study timeframes can lead to conflicting fundamental and technical perspectives.

The long-term chart is also technically bearish, with a well-defined downtrend featuring sequentially lower highs and lower lows. A technician that had artificially confined his analysis to the highlighted period would quite rationally arrive at a bullish forecast, as the market makes a series higher highs and higher lows. A longer-term technical analysis would correctly

---

[33] This is one reason that many large, aggressive trading firms subscribe to all of the available research. Not because they value it for their decision-making process, but because other firms might deem it important, and they want to be aware of everything that anybody could possibly be factoring into their calculus.

Chapter 7 - Developing a Cohesive Market View

identify the shaded area as a bullish retracement or bear flag within a large, well-defined macro downtrend, which is entirely consistent with the fundamental information.

It is also common for longer-term fundamentals to be temporarily overcome by short-term drivers or one-off exogenous events. For example, large position accumulation or distribution in a thin market can create short, violent technical breaks in the chart of a product driven by clear, stable fundamentals.[34]

A contradictory fundamental and technical perspective does not rule out the possibility that there is a trade to be done, but may mean that there isn't a trade to be done immediately, under the current conditions. Patience is often a virtue, and good traders learn to distinguish temporary conflicts in otherwise productive scenarios that need time to evolve and clarify from obvious non-starter propositions.

One Study Is Neutral or Inconclusive
It is common for a trader to be faced with one piece of analysis that suggests a compelling opportunity only to have the corroborating study yield neutral or inconclusive results. Neutral and inconclusive are not interchangeable concepts, in this context. A neutral analysis implies that the trader understands the current disposition of the facts, but that his best assessment is that the market will not move or that the probabilities and potentialities are so symmetrical that there is no information to be gained about how it could possibly move and under what conditions. An inconclusive analysis results when the trader does not feel that he concretely understands what is motivating the market, or when the market appears[35] to be acting in a random, chaotic fashion.

In practice, it is very common for traders to need to reconcile a solid fundamental view with an inconclusive or neutral technical picture. The reverse, a solid technical picture with inscrutable fundamentals, is much more rare. There are several reasons for this. First, as seen in Chapter 4, most charts do not contain any actionable information for a large portion of their price history. It takes a lot of back and forth fluctuation to create a trend channel or a head and shoulders, and until a pattern is complete or a channel is defined it does not have predictive value. Fundamentals are much more conducive to partial or "working" interpretation, where the trader or analyst begins with rough assumptions and suboptimal data and iteratively refines the analysis as new or better information becomes available. Even a half-baked fundamental analysis is still a fundamental analysis, which will always trump a

---

[34] It is sometimes possible to estimate how much volume to expect to come to market based on the size of recent chart patterns and the accretion of open interest created during a consolidation pattern or area of congestion. For example, an unexpected rally in a fundamentally bearish market might do enough damage to a cluster of short positions that require coverage en masse, which accelerates the price spikes higher. A trader observing this from a distance may be able to ride out the panic by understanding that as soon as the stampede for the door stops, the market is still bearish. Knowing how many cattle are in the herd helps significantly, as it is one thing to dodge a few steers, quite another to stand in front of the running of the bulls.

[35] "Appears" is the key word. Just because the trader cannot determine the motivation or drivers of a market does not mean that they are not present and valid.

chart squiggle that is still trying to decide where it is going. This is doubly true when the analysis is generated by an internal resource, particularly one who carries a lot of weight with the firm. Woe to the trader who tries to refute the Head of Research's 438-slide presentation with a single sheet of printout and some hastily scribbled pencil lines.

The only time a trader would ever reasonably expect to be faced with a solid technical picture and an inconclusive fundamental case is if the research was done by a third-party analyst or is compiled from an amalgamation of multiple external sources. It is entirely possible for a trader to wade through a poorly written research report and finish with less understanding of the subject. Worse than that is trying to derive useful information from two contradictory vendor-provided forecasts with opaque, proprietary, analytical methodologies. These types of aggregation-under-uncertainty problems are very common to energy traders (multiple conflicting weather forecasts), equity traders (a plethora of quarterly earnings estimate forecasts), and agricultural traders (weather and crop report forecasts). It's enough to make anyone reach for a ruler and #2 pencil.

Partially offsetting perspectives can potentially yield a tradable thesis if one is extremely solid and the other ambiguous, or one implies a large move and the other offers only token resistance. Timing differences are again the most likely culprit, particularly if the firm has identified a fundamental thesis especially early or developed some unique informational insight ahead of the crowd.

A strong technical or fundamental signal combined with an inconclusive result from the opposite discipline should caution against an overly aggressive position relative to a trader's maximum capacity and normal risk tolerance.

The Fundamental and Technical Analysis Are Aligned
Having a robust, independently generated technical analysis that supports the fundamental view is the best possible starting point. A constructive technical analysis provides insight into the timing, measurement, and probability of anticipated future price fluctuations motivated by the evolution of the fundamental drivers. The question stops being "should the trader consider a position" and shifts to "what sort of a position should the trader consider?" With both primary informational vectors aligned, any trader worth her salt (or seat) should be planning to get involved.

The Degree of Support Informs Trade Sizing and Commitment Level
Depending on the alignment of the fundamental and technical perspectives, the trader will be faced with the following choices:

- Contradictory technical and fundamental analysis = **No exposure**
- Two neutral or inconclusive analyses = **No exposure**
- A bullish/bearish analysis + an inconclusive/neutral analysis = **Possible limited exposure, proceed with evaluation**
- Two aligned, well-developed analyses = **Moderate to Significant exposure**

Chapter 7 - Developing a Cohesive Market View

If the comparison of the basic directionality yields a workable thesis, the trader will seek to incorporate all additional relevant information from each discipline to gain perspective on the magnitude and timing of the anticipated market move. The trader will also take into consideration:

- Conviction – The confidence inspired by each of the analyses will contribute to the trader's relative weighting in the decision calculus.
- Measurability – How well defined are the price objectives and the respective technical and fundamental drivers that will interact to achieve them?
- Timing – Across what time horizon, and under what conditions, is the anticipated market move expected to occur?
- Triggers – Are there any imminent catalysts that are expected to start/stop a market move? Includes the fundamental event path and any technical breakout points. Are they well-specified in terms of chronology and market expectation?
- Targets – What are the reasonable objectives?

There is a tremendous difference in terms of predictive utility between:

- A market currently in a steep uptrend temporarily impeded by a large, well-defined continuation pattern that has just broken out to the upside, supported by bullish fundamentals and imminent forecast revisions that have a 90% chance of shifting the balance in an even more bullish direction.
- A market moving sloppily sideways that may be turning higher, but that has no trend, no discernable patterns, and no targets, and a fundamental picture that is constructive for price appreciation but lacks a specific motivating influence and has no impending news to alter perceptions.

One market has trend, drivers, triggers, a target and a near-term motivating factor that will alter the supply/demand balance and undoubtedly result in a price response. The other is the complete opposite, lacking direction and motivation and with nothing to generate interest and influence prices.

Volatility and the Risk Environment

The trader will take the fundamental information and technical analysis of the market and estimate the resources needed to maintain an exposure and the magnitude of potential P&L fluctuations. The analysis should take into consideration both standard risk metrics and experience-based, non-quantitative factors, particularly the trader's understanding of the potential ways the current market environment could evolve over time.

Measure Historical Market Volatility

The trader must calculate the historical volatility (or utilize the figures provided by the risk group) and have a sense of how the current observed levels compare to the recent past and longer-term norms. Is the market becoming more or less volatile? Does the trader expect the market to revert to more normal levels, continue as it is, or become even more violent? As seen in Chapter 3, the need to derive a market price via poor, observed data or a best-guess estimated midpoint can severely distort purely quantitative metrics, which will also be an issue when calculating the risk metrics that govern the trader's activities.

Characterize/Describe Risk Environment
If there is historical data, how are the returns distributed? Are they relatively normal, or intensely leptokurtic? How is volatility distributed: a relatively constant level of chop, or a low volatility environment with a few episodes of epic price spikes?

Market Conditions
The final step is to take the risk-derived perspective and apply an additional layer of real experience and observation-based assessment. This is an area where depth and breadth of market participation generally infer real, tangible advantages to the trader.[36] Traders without a deep reservoir of market- and product-specific experience will be forced to seek as many analogs as possible from the available historical record.

All markets have different characteristics:

- Current participants
- Transaction frequency and size
- Product standardization
- Bid-offer spreads
- Signal-to-noise ratio

None of these characteristics are constants. It is crucial to both understand the current market characteristics and have a sense of how they could potentially change, both through gradual evolution and exogenous shock. In particular, it is critical to understand that in times of stress, the number of participants and total volume of transactions will tend to decline, the bid-offer spreads and other transaction costs will tend to rise, the overall market volatility will rise and the "noise" around the central trend (if there is a central trend) will tend to increase.[37]

The trader must make a non-quantitative assessment of the current state of the market: how it is trading and what the price action looks like.

- Is it a good market, with ample volume, small tick-to-tick differentials, relatively continuous price action, and minimal overnight and intraday gaps?

---

[36] Experience that leads to open-minded decision making and inclusive probability spaces is generally a good thing, experience that leads to prematurely narrowed alternatives and biased decision making is most certainly a negative.
[37] In the case of a truly extreme market event, such as a natural disaster, geopolitical crisis, etc., trading may stop altogether. Unfortunately, just when a trader really needs to do something, it can suddenly be much more difficult to execute and cost significantly more.

Chapter 7 - Developing a Cohesive Market View

- Is it a challenging market, with less than optimal levels of liquidity, larger bid-offer spreads and price action that could be considered gappy, choppy, or otherwise discontinuous?
- Is it a dangerous market, with poor liquidity and price visibility, wide markets that imply huge entry and exit costs, and a level of noise the completely overwhelms any trend or direction impulse?

Risk-Reward Calculus

Risk-reward calculus impacts all aspects of the trader's decision making, with the evaluation and revaluation of the balance between peril and prosperity occurring at each successive step in the process. Risk-reward ratios are used to both craft the trader's view of the market and to evaluate potential implementation strategies. The importance cannot be overstated:

The ability to make a rigorous, intellectually honest assessment of the probable risks and the potential reward inherent in a proposition is the single most important determinant of long-term trading success.

Many traders have a tendency to select the best possible outcome while refusing to acknowledge the worst possible result, leading to distorted risk-reward ratios and poor trading decisions. Others see only risk, and this overly pessimistic outlook biases their assessments and makes it difficult to find positions they would feel comfortable holding. Traders must learn to see things as they are, not as they would have them be, or are afraid they could be.

There is a three-step process for refining the trader's assessment of the risk and reward:

1. Derive the risk-reward ratio of the market.
2. Add probability estimates for each outcome to yield the probability-adjusted market risk-reward ratio.
3. Examine the risk-reward ratio and probability-adjusted risk-reward ratio of each potential implementation strategy.

Deriving the Market Risk-Reward Ratio

The first step is to derive a basic risk-reward ratio for the market as a whole, giving the trader a sense of how far prices could potentially move in either direction from the current level. The trader will incorporate perspective derived from fundamental information, the technical analysis of price action, an assessment of the volatility and risk present in the market, and the current operating environment. The risks and rewards must be must be evaluated independently, with study time frames that are as similar as possible and relevant to the trader's intended holding period. The basic risk-reward calculus will yield the statement "the market could move X higher or Y lower from the current level."

As an example, consider a structurally bullish market that has spent the prior year constructing a large flat triangle, as seen on the following chart:

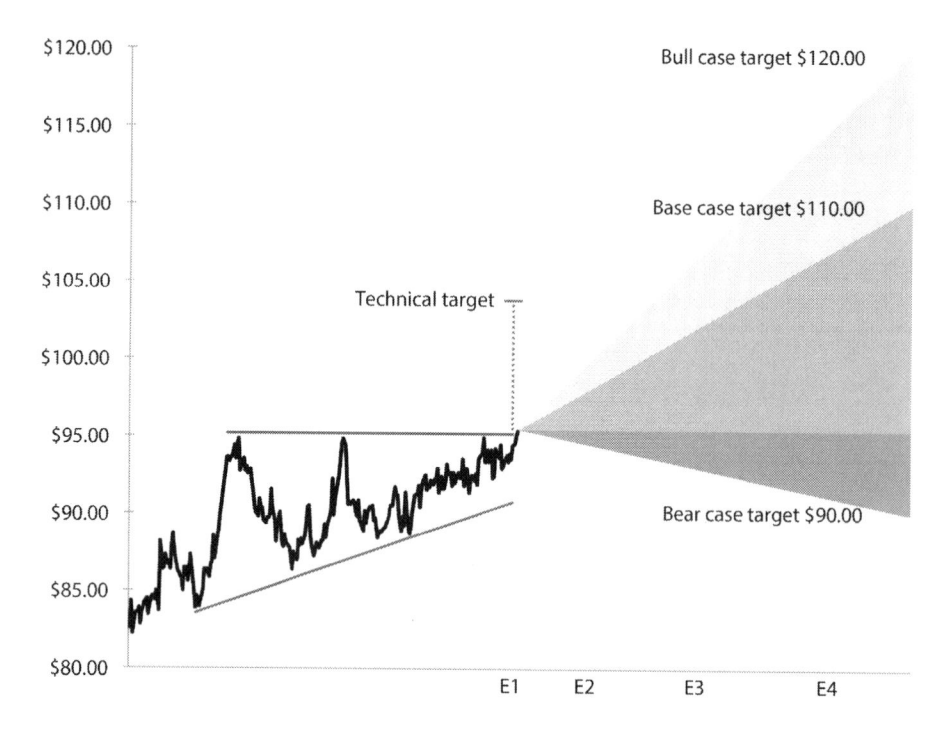

Figure 7.3 Deriving a market risk-reward ratio from fundamental case targets and technical analysis.

To derive the market risk-reward ratio, the trader will weigh the perspectives from the fundamental information, the technical analysis of price action, the assessment of the volatility and risk present in the market, and the current operating environment.

- The trader's fundamental analysis leads to three possible outcomes, a base case where year-end price rallies to $110.00, a bear case where it falls to $90.00, and a bull case where it explodes to $120.00.
- The well-defined flat triangle that comprises the majority of the prior year's price action features a clear upper resistance line at $95.00 which, having been breached, should trigger a rally with a price target equal to the height of the pattern, implying an $8.50 move higher to $103.50. If the breakout above $95.00 fails, it is likely that the market will re-establish within the triangle between the support and resistance lines, yielding a near- to medium-term floor of $91.00.
- The event path features four primary inflection points, the first of which (E1) has caused the market to breach the resistance level that forms the top of the triangle at $95.00. Event E2 is expected to reinforce the base and bull cases with a high level of confidence, with events E3 and E4 having equal probability of being bullish, neutral, or bearish.
- The market features a 20-day historical volatility that ranged between 8.9% and 24.8%, finishing the year at 15.6%. The day-to-day change is a reasonable +/- $0.69

Chapter 7 - Developing a Cohesive Market View

on average, but is prone to intermittently larger moves, with a peak observation of +$4.47.

A trader intending to take a long position with a medium-term, 3-4 month holding period to take advantage of the inflection point at E2 but avoid the uncertainty of E3 & E4 would arrive at the following market risk/reward:

- If the breakout fails, the bottom of the triangle should provide support at $91.00, with the longer-term bear case serving as an additional backstop at $90.00. If there were a more material difference between the short- and long-term risk levels, the trader should give extra weight to the near-term target to match the intended holding period. The only inflection path node during the trader's intended holding period (E2) is expected to be bullish, and should not factor into the risk evaluation.[38]
- To determine the potential reward the trader should only consider levels relevant to the holding period, ruling out the aggressive $120.00 year-end bullish target. The near-term technical target at $103.50 would provide a primary target, with the potential for the bullish development at (E2) to bring the base case target at $110 into play within the trader's anticipated holding period.

Using an intellectually pure short-term to short-term technical perspective, the market offers $8.50 of reward for $4.00 of risk, for a slightly better than 2:1 market risk-reward ratio. If the trader strongly believes the bullish inflection point at (E2) will accelerate the evolution toward the base case $110.00 target, he can make a case for using a $15.00 reward and arriving at a more compelling 3.75:1 market risk-reward ratio.

Deriving the Market Probability-Adjusted Risk-Reward Ratio
Incorporating the relative probabilities of positive and negative outcomes further refines the risk-reward ratio. The probability-adjusted risk-reward analysis yields the somewhat more actionable statement "the market has a 65% chance of moving X higher and a 35% chance of moving Y lower from the current level."

Consider an example where a trader is offered the opportunity to bet on heads on the flip of a coin:

1. Betting $1.00 to win $1.00 on the flip of a fair coin will, in the long run, earn zero dollars, as nothing is in the bettor's favor.
2. Betting $1.00 to win $1.00 on a coin that has odds of coming up heads of 60% and of tails 40% will profitable, as the odds are in the bettor's favor.
3. Betting $1.00 to win $2.00 on the flip of a fair coin will be profitable, as the payouts are in the bettor's favor.
4. Betting $1.00 to win $2.00 on a coin that has odds of coming up heads of 60% and of tails 40% will be very, very profitable, as everything is in the bettor's favor.

---

[38] A trader might choose to incorporate a small probability that E2 is not bullish and examine the potential impact on price.

The expected value (EV) is the amount a player should theoretically earn over an infinitely long series of iterations of a game. It is calculated by summing the value of each outcome multiplied by the probability of its occurrence. For the fair game (1) the expected value is zero, and there is no point in playing. The unfair coin with equal payouts (2) will pay the player $0.10 per game over time. The fair coin with unequal payouts (3) is worth $0.50 per game. The unfair coin with the unequal payouts (4) yields $0.80 per game.

A trader can accept symmetrical payouts with asymmetric probabilities or symmetrical probabilities with asymmetric payouts, but the very best trades have both favorable payouts relative to the risks and positively skewed probability of success.

A trader is seeking the game with the highest potential return per play, the trade with the greatest probability of being profitable *and* the largest potential profit. It doesn't matter if the basic risk-reward implies that the trader is risking $1.00 to earn $5.00 if the probability of winning is 1% and the chances of losing are 99%. The basic 5:1 risk-reward ratio is thoroughly counterfeited by the odds, yielding a horrible probability-adjusted risk-reward of 5:99 (0.01 × $5.00 reward to 0.99 × $1.00 risk). Well-defined, clear-cut examples like the coin flipping example are exceedingly rare, unfortunately. Most of the time traders will be evaluating opportunities with probabilities and potentialities that are much more difficult to ascertain.

Returning to the example of the bullish market breaking out of a triangle formation, we can see how the trader can derive the probability-adjusted risk-reward ratio:

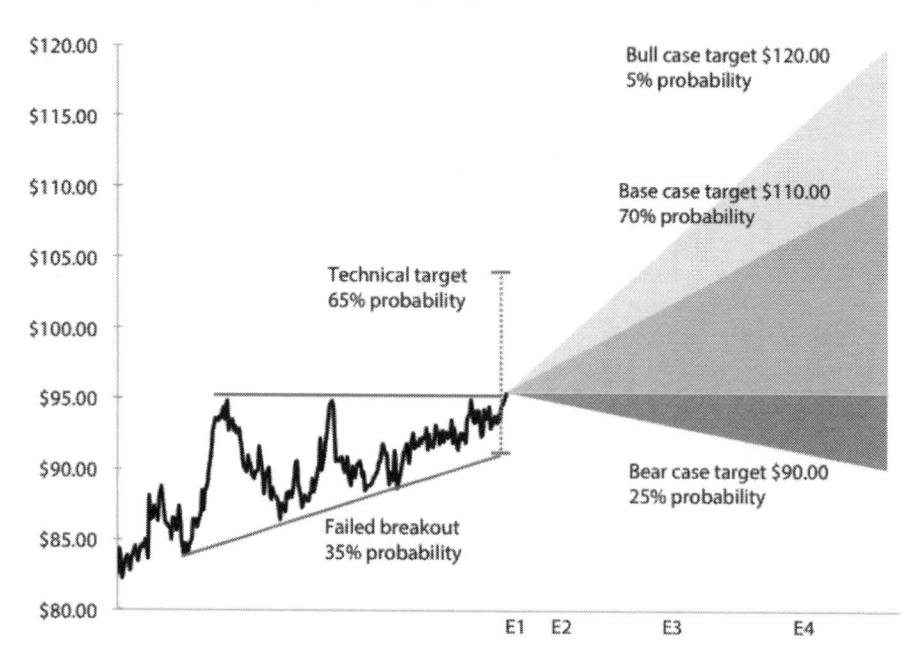

Figure 7.4 Deriving a probability-adjusted market risk-reward ratio from fundamental case targets and technical analysis.

- A properly defined base case should have the highest probability of evolving, and in this case the trader is confident enough in the underlying fundamentals to assign it a 70% chance of playing out in the market. The bear case receives a 25% probability, with the bull case given a remote 5% chance.
- A flat triangle will tend to break out in the direction of the prior trend, and though there are no exact percentages to apply, the trader feels comfortable assigning a 65% probability to a move higher and 35% to a failed breakout and return to the triangle pattern.

The trader's pure short-term to short-term technically derived market risk-reward ratio was a relatively uninspiring 2:1. When the probabilities of each outcome are taken into consideration, the 65% chance of earning $8.50 vs. the 35% possibility of losing $4.00 yields a much more favorable probability-adjusted risk-reward ratio of $5.53 to $1.40, or an approximately 4:1.

If the trader feels strongly enough about the bullish inflection point at (E2) using the $15.00 profit target from the accelerated realization of the base case, she will have to re-assign the probabilities of the positive and negative outcomes. If the trader elects to reduce the chance of the $4.00 loss to 30% and maintain the 70% probability of a $15.00 profit, she will arrive at $10.50 to $1.20, or and extremely attractive 8.75:1 risk-reward ratio.

Traders must be very careful to not overweight the positive probabilities and diminish the chances of a negative outcome when deriving the probability-adjusted risk-rewards of both the market and, later, the proposed implementation strategies.

As we will see in Chapters 8-12, the probability-weighted risk-reward ratio as a tool for position evaluation should incorporate a weighting for extremely unlikely events that may have outsized P&L impacts. A 1% chance of a $25.00 negative outcome doesn't seem terribly important, yet it will subtract $0.25 from the overall value of a trade. Evaluating extreme tail risk is an area where experience really does prove useful. The more a trader has seen in his career, the more he is able to incorporate into the calculus as unlikely, yet possible outcomes. The inherent, difficult-to-quantify tail risk in high-volatility products can be a significant percentage of the total risk in a transaction.

Deriving Strategy Risk-Reward & Probability-Adjusted Risk-Reward Ratios
Every potential means of implementing the trader's view will have unique risk and reward characteristics which will be estimated and used to derive strategy risk-reward and probability-adjusted strategy risk-reward ratios. The strategy risk-reward ratio is, by definition, a subset of the market risk-reward ratio, and is subject to the underlying market probability dynamics. The probability-adjusted strategy risk-reward ratio makes the highly specific statement that "given a market with 65% percent chance of going higher and 35% chance of going lower, the trade has a 65% chance of moving X higher and a 35% chance of moving Y lower from the current level."

The probability-adjusted strategy risk-reward ratios will be used to first exclude subpar trade ideas that do not meet a minimum trader-defined threshold, then as a tool to assist in the evaluation and selection of the optimal strategy to implement the trader's view. The strategy risk-reward and probability-adjusted risk-reward ratios will be explored in detail in Chapter 12 – Evaluating Trades & Creating A Trading Plan.

More Markets, More Problems
Traders with access to multiple uncorrelated markets will have to independently assess the risk and reward present in each, first deciding if participation is warranted and then evaluating a variety of implementation modalities to determine the most efficient means of expressing their view.

Is the Thesis Tradable?
There are 169 possible two-card starting hands in Texas Hold 'Em; the vast majority of them are not worth playing under any circumstances. Most professionals assert that, depending on the players and the texture of the game, only the top 10-15% of the hands dealt have any hope at a positive expectation when played to completion. Traders must also learn to filter. In the real world, when taking into consideration the explicit and implicit costs, most trades no longer meet a minimum threshold for potential profitability per unit risk.[39]

If the trader is able to generate an actionable view of the market, he will move on to examine potential implementation methodologies in four primary styles, directional, spread, option, and quantitative (Chapters 8-11). The best implementation strategy is the one that modifies the market probability-adjusted risk-reward ratio in the most favorable way to yield the best strategy probability-adjusted risk-reward ratio. Chapter 12 will evaluate the potential implementation options for efficiency of execution, probability of favorability of result, proximity to underlying motive stimulus, and refined risk-reward ratio. It will also generate a trading plan with primary, secondary, and tertiary implementation methodologies.

This Is My View. There Are Many Like It, But This One Is Mine
It is important to be mindful that the trader's view is entirely a product of his:

- Relative informational advantages and disadvantages.
- Acquisition, manipulation, and processing skills.
- Particular interpretation biases, strengths, and weaknesses.
- Access to incremental, going-forward information and the ability to feed it back into the decision loop.

As explored in Chapter 3, every individual in the market is working with a subset of the total available information. It is possible for different traders to begin with the same starting

---

[39] Some nascent markets do occasionally present seemingly infinite low-hanging fruit, but in any semi-developed market putting on anything like the majority of the potential trading ideas is a recipe for disaster.

Chapter 7 - Developing a Cohesive Market View

information and, through differences in technique and interpretation, arrive at very different views of the market. This disparity is exacerbated when, in most markets, traders and trading companies will start with widely different sets of information and possess varying degrees of observational and interpretational acumen. Every trader must understand that, of the factors that combine to create their view, they will have above-average skill with some, be even with the market in others, and lag behind with the rest. The trader must take into consideration, for each of the primary variables and key drivers that makes up his view:

- What he personally is good at or has a comparative advantage in?
- What he personally is bad at or has a comparative disadvantage in?
- What the firm is good at or has a comparative advantage in?
- What the firm is bad at or has a comparative disadvantage in?

The trader must make a clear and intellectually honest assessment of his skill and that of the analysts at their firm, relative to the market, or he deceives himself into a proposition where he is operating from a perceived advantage but an actual disadvantage. It is difficult, but possible, to beat the market with average information. To do so, the trader will have to compensate by leveraging other strengths to make up for the lack of an informational edge. His analysis will have to be better than the rest of the market's, his risk assessment superior, and his trade selection more creative. He will need superior position management skill and iron discipline.

It is probably impossible to be long-run profitable with consistently worse-than-market information. No amount of skill on the trader's part can be expected to overcome such a critical structural disadvantage.

Articulating the Trader's View

To remote observers a trader's market view is like an iceberg. The jagged part that does all the P&L damage is easy to see from a great distance, but the preponderance of the underlying rationale will remain hidden deep beneath the surface, impossible to gauge. A trader's view on the market, also like an iceberg, has a tendency to roll over and change direction with little to no warning.

An unarticulated view, regardless of how meticulously researched and reasoned, is invisible to management. Documenting a view and the underlying rationale pre-trade can be massively useful in the event that the position turns out poorly. For any unusually committing trade, either in terms of size, risk, or novelty, making management aware of the underlying reasons for the exposure in addition to the stop and profit targets should be considered mandatory.

For any position that requires management or senior management approval, the ability to clearly articulate the view will frequently be the primary reason that the authorization for the exposure is approved or denied. A trader that cannot clearly explain and justify why she wants to create a position will not be given the latitude to do so.

Implementing the Trader's View – Chapter 8-12 Preview
In Chapter 7 we have taken the trader's fundamental information, technical analysis, and assessments of the volatility, risk, and overall market conditions and distilled them down into a view on future prices. This view contains an assessment of the risk and reward inherent in the market at the current time, measuring the amount it could reasonably be expected to move in the trader's favor relative to the potential negative consequences.

There is a right tool for every job, and an optimal implementation methodology for every view. The next four chapters will investigate four common strategies used by traders to express their views on the market. Chapter 8 will cover directional trading, where the trader accumulates a position designed to profit from a move higher or lower in the market. Chapter 9 discusses spread trading, making a paired bet involving the purchase of one instrument and the sale of another, creating profit from the change in the price relationship between the two. Chapter 10 explores option trading, where traders employ instruments with non-linear performance characteristics that can be combined into complex structures that allow the trader to make very specific wagers on the future of prices. Chapter 11 provides an overview of quantitative trading, from simplistic implementations where machine tools are used to augment the user's decision-making process, to the extreme of granting faster-than-human artificial intelligences the discretion to develop and execute trades. Chapter 12 will focus on evaluating the trading strategies developed in Chapters 8 through 11 and identifying the best available alternative to implement the trader's view of the market.

Chapter Seven Summary
Deriving a view of the market by incorporating fundamental information, technical analysis, and the current volatility and market conditions is the primary function of any trader. The trader must have a sense of what he feels is going to happen. With a well-considered view of the market in hand, the trader will explore potential implementation strategies, starting with directional positions and progressing to the more nuanced spread-trading strategies, the non-linear characteristics of options, culminating in the complexity of machine-assisted quantitative strategies.

Review Questions

1. What is a view? Describe the steps involved in developing a cohesive view of the market.
2. How does the alignment between the fundamental and technical analysis relate to position sizing?
3. What is risk/reward calculus, and why is it important to a trader's success?
4. Name three impediments that could keep a trader's perspective on the market from being actionable.
5. How does the trader's and their firm's skill and breadth of knowledge relative to the market impact the quality of their view?

Chapter 7 - Developing a Cohesive Market View

Resources

- *Every Hand Revealed* by Gus Hansen
- *Market Wizards: Interviews with Top Traders* by Jack D. Schwager
- *The New Market Wizards: Conversations with America's Top Traders* by Jack Schwager
- *The Money Bazaar: Inside the Trillion-Dollar World of Currency Trading* by Andrew Krieger

Case Study: Developing a Cohesive View of the Product X Market

Product X Fundamental Analysis

Product X Drivers and Forces

Product X is a very economically sensitive commodity. It is used as an input to many GDP-sensitive industrial processes and in high-tech manufacturing that is inextricably linked to consumer demand. The supply of Product X is also subject to the fluctuations of the local and global economy, as the cost of labor, materials, leases or outright purchases of productive acreage, and the availability and cost of shipping all impact the volume brought to market and the price at which the tonnage is available.

The two primary historical drivers were the loss of African supply in June and the unexpected increase in demand from China beginning in August. Recall the prior year's balance sheet:

Prior year supply	Jan	Feb	Mar	Apr	May	Jun	Jul	Aug	Sep	Oct	Nov	Dec
United States	125	125	125	125	125	125	125	125	125	125	125	125
Russia	100	100	100	100	100	100	100	100	100	100	100	100
Mexico	40	40	40	40	40	40	40	40	40	40	40	40
India	45	45	45	45	45	45	45	45	45	45	45	45
South America	50	50	50	50	50	50	50	50	50	50	50	50
Africa	40	40	40	40	25	2	2	2	2	2	2	2
Canada	15	15	15	15	15	15	15	15	15	25	25	25
Australia	20	20	20	20	20	20	20	20	20	20	20	20
Total supply	435	435	435	435	420	397	397	397	397	407	407	407

Prior year demand	Jan	Feb	Mar	Apr	May	Jun	Jul	Aug	Sep	Oct	Nov	Dec
United States	175	175	175	175	175	175	175	175	175	175	175	175
Europe	135	135	135	135	135	135	135	135	135	135	135	135
China	65	65	65	65	65	70	70	80	80	90	90	90
Japan	15	15	15	15	15	15	15	15	15	15	15	15
Total demand	390	390	390	390	390	395	395	405	405	415	415	415
Net balance	45	45	45	45	30	2	2	(8)	(8)	(8)	(8)	(8)
Storage	1045	1090	1135	1180	1210	1212	1214	1206	1198	1190	1182	1174

Table 7.1   Product X prior-year balance sheet.

Consider a graph of the FEB ProdX prices overlaid with the two main historical market drivers:

Chapter 7 - Developing a Cohesive Market View

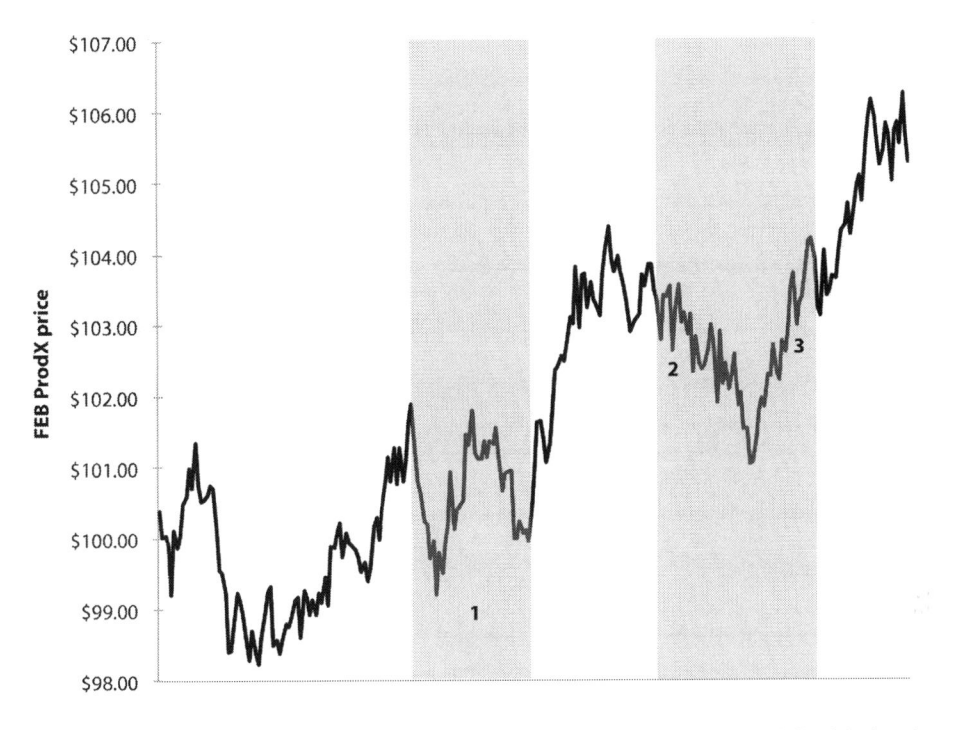

Figure 7.5 FEB ProdX chart with inflection points in the event path highlighted.

The operational problem at the central African processing facility began sometime mid-May, with output dropping severely and deliveries unfilled or rescheduled beginning in the second half of the month. By June, output had fallen to a baseline 2M tons per month and the return to service date for the facility had been pushed from "imminent" to "soon" to "sometime in the following year." It is unclear how rapidly the information was disseminated into the market and how it was initially interpreted, but sometime during the window between mid-May and the end of June (1), the global market became aware that the total output from Africa had precipitously dropped and would not be returning to service until the following year. The price response to the loss of 38M tons was immediate, with Product X breaking out of a consolidation pattern and trading up from just under $100.00 to $104.00 in slightly more than a month.

The second historical driver was the unexpected increase in demand from China. Though some additional consumption had been expected in the second half of the year, the jump from 70M to 80M tons in August (2), followed by an additional 10M ton increase in October (3) was enough to tip an already tight balance sheet into a slight deficit and begin drawing down storage to compensate. Additional Canadian supply was brought online in October to satisfy the incremental demand, but the increased tightness in the market was sufficient to push the price of Product X from the $102.00 range up to $106.00 in near-linear fashion.

The present day Product X market is tight, with demand outpacing supply by 8M/tons per month and growing uncertainty about the potential return-to-service date of the processing plant that controls African production and the magnitude of potential increases in Chinese demand. It is against that backdrop that traders and analysts must consider the future Product X market drivers.

Product X Measures and Models – The Balance Sheet
The Product X balance sheet starts the conversation. The trader's interrogation of the current facts and, most critically, the forward-looking assumptions underlying the balance leads to a perspective on the relative tightness or looseness of the market. When combined with a supply curve, it gives a sense of the potential future price of the market.

Consider a set of four simplified balance sheets showing the total supply, total demand, net balance and storage for the initial balance sheet and the bear, base, and bull case studies explored in Chapter 3:

Initial Balance
The initial balance contains the basic facts about the Product X market, without the benefit of any critical interrogation or analysis.

	Jan	Feb	Mar	Apr	May	Jun	Jul	Aug	Sep	Oct	Nov	Dec
Total supply	432	450	470	490	490	490	500	500	500	515	515	515
Total demand	450	460	460	470	470	480	510	510	510	545	545	545
Net balance	(18)	(10)	10	20	20	10	(10)	(10)	(10)	(30)	(30)	(30)
Storage	1156	1146	1156	1176	1196	1206	1196	1186	1176	1146	1116	1086

Current year - Initial balance

Table 7.2   Simplified initial balance sheet for Product X.

The initial balance depicts a market that starts with a short-term deficit that is remedied by a production response from both new supply and the return to service of a facility on outage. The market slowly builds storage through June, at which point demand from a resurgent economy is expected to outstrip supply and create a persistent shortage that will erode stocks of Product X and should lead to generally higher prices, all things being equal.

Base Case
The base case is intended to serve as the most probabilistically likely outcome resulting from an informed assessment of the starting conditions and likely on-the-run changes to the supply and demand.

The base case for Product X implies the following:

1. The global economy performs at target levels, leaving most estimates unchanged.

Chapter 7 - Developing a Cohesive Market View

2. China demand was somewhat overstated and is reduced to a maximum of 130M tons per month.
3. Production from Africa is partially restored to 20M tons per month by April.

	Current year - Base case											
	Jan	Feb	Mar	Apr	May	Jun	Jul	Aug	Sep	Oct	Nov	Dec
Total supply	432	440	445	470	470	470	480	480	480	495	495	495
Total demand	450	460	460	465	465	475	500	500	500	525	525	525
Net balance	(18)	(20)	(15)	5	5	(5)	(20)	(20)	(20)	(30)	(30)	(30)
Storage	1156	1136	1121	1126	1131	1126	1106	1086	1066	1036	1006	976

Table 7.3   Simplified base case balance sheet for Product X.

The base case depicts a market facing an initial supply constraint that is briefly alleviated by the partial return to service of African production, only to be reinforced and exacerbated by a combination of general economic growth and increasing (but still below-expectation) growth from China, the largest incremental consumer of Product X. By the end of the year, the Product X market is solidly in deficit and is drawing from storage at the rate of 30M/tons per month. The mechanism for rebalancing the market is price, and the Product X market will need to rally to incentivize incremental production, destroy any marginal price-sensitive demand, or (most likely) some combination of both.

Bear Case

The bear case reflects events that could be expected to increase supply or decrease demand, and is intended to put a relatively reasonable lower bound on expectations.

The bear case for Product X implies the following:

1. The global economy underperforms, which drops growth estimates for the U.S. to 185M tons per month and for Europe to 135M tons per month, and dramatically reduces growth targets for China to 100M tons per month.
2. Labor costs decrease and shipping is both cheaper and more plentiful, making the market as a whole more efficient globally and reducing the spread between markets.
3. African production returns to full output on schedule.
4. Higher-priced Canadian production is forced out of market, capping output at 35M tons per month.

	Current year - Bear case											
	Jan	Feb	Mar	Apr	May	Jun	Jul	Aug	Sep	Oct	Nov	Dec
Total supply	427	445	465	485	485	485	495	495	495	505	505	505
Total demand	435	435	435	435	435	435	435	435	435	435	435	435
Net balance	(8)	10	30	50	50	50	60	60	60	70	70	70
Storage	1166	1176	1206	1256	1306	1356	1416	1476	1536	1606	1676	1746

Table 7.4   Simplified bear case balance sheet for Product X.

The bear case begins with an initial negative net balance that is quickly remedied by the scheduled return to full output of African production. Later in the year the expected economic growth fails to materialize, leading to across-the-board declines in consumption and a net balance that balloons to +70M tons per month even after high-cost Canadian production is forced out of the market. The combination of both decreased demand and increased supply should lead to lower Product X prices.

Bull Case

The bull case reflects events that could be expected to decrease supply or increase demand, and is intended to put a relatively reasonable upper bound on expectations.

The bull case for Product X implies the following:

1. The global economy grows as expected during the period.
2. China achieves its aggressive growth and consumption target.
3. African production does not return to service during year.
4. Labor costs rise, and shipping becomes both more expensive and scarcer, widening market differentials.

	Jan	Feb	Mar	Apr	May	Jun	Jul	Aug	Sep	Oct	Nov	Dec
					Current year - Bull case							
Total supply	432	432	432	452	452	452	462	462	462	477	477	477
Total demand	450	460	460	470	470	480	510	510	510	545	545	545
Net balance	(18)	(28)	(28)	(18)	(18)	(28)	(48)	(48)	(48)	(68)	(68)	(68)
Storage	1156	1128	1100	1082	1064	1036	988	940	892	824	756	688

Table 7.5 Simplified bull case balance sheet for Product X.

The bull case depicts a market under stress. The year begins with a deficit condition that progressively worsens with each incremental event. Production does not return, economic conditions improve leading to more demand, and the largest swing consumer in the market meets an extremely aggressive growth target, necessitating significant incremental spot purchases. By the end of the year the market is facing a scary net 68M-ton monthly deficit and rapidly drawing down storage levels. As with the base case, the Product X market will need to rally to incentivize incremental production, destroy any marginal price-sensitive demand, or (most likely) some combination of both.

The bear and bull cases are not intended to represent barrier conditions. They are neither as bad or as good as it could theoretically get. Many analysts will also generate extreme bear and bull cases, where the underlying assumptions are pushed nearer to the limits of possibility in an attempt to capture more of the totality of the probabilistic outcomes. As explained in Chapter 6, while extreme cases are useful tools for understanding low-probability outcomes, they are not—nor will they ever be—black swan predictors.

A set of supply curves graphed on the same axis will give some sense of the impacts of the supply and demand shifts inherent in the three case studies, as well as the potential price consequences.

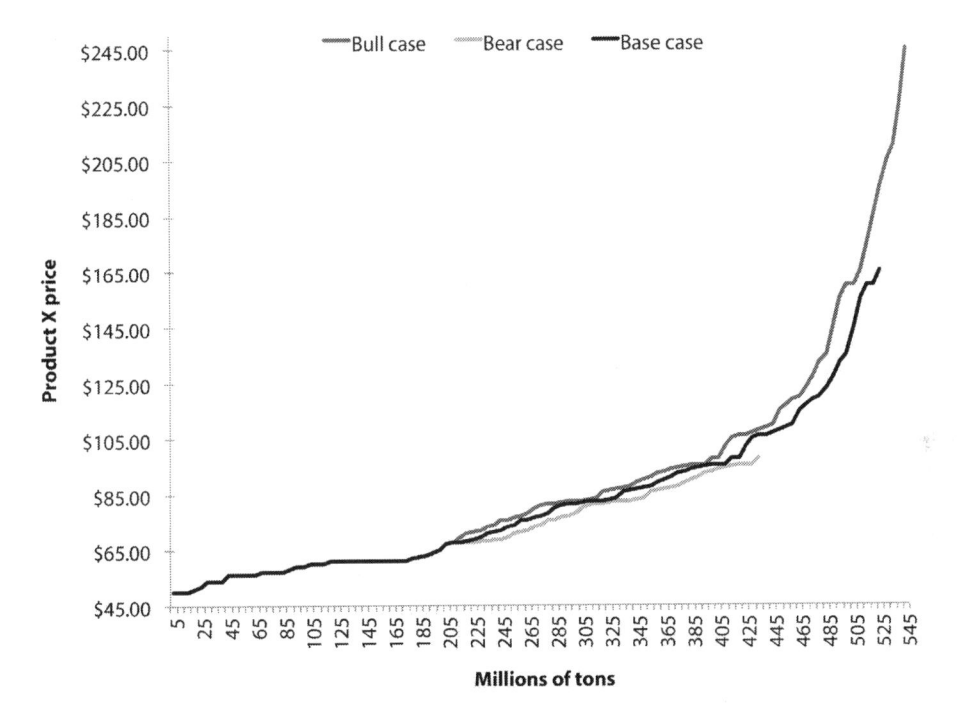

Figure 7.6   Year-end supply stacks for Product X base, bear, and bull cases.

A well-constructed set of fundamental cases should describe a wide range of price outcomes when contemplated across a medium- to long-term horizon. The fundamental analysis will function as the trader's strategic perspective, which will be refined with technical analysis to sharpen and tactically inform the decision-making process.

The Product X Event Path
The primary factors that will influence the price of Product X are:

January	Statistics on total demand. A reading below 450M tons/month would support the bear case, anything north of 450M tons/month leans toward either the base or bull cases.
February	Scheduled return to service of the African processing plant. Production unchanged at 2M tons/month supports the bull case, an increase to 10M tons/month would suggest the base case, and a ramp up to 20M tons/month or more argues strongly for the bear case.
March	Ramp up of African production. To validate the bull case, production remains unchanged at 2M tons/month. The base case calls for production to

	reach 15M tons/month, while validating the bear case would require a nearly full return to service of 40M tons/month.
April	Consumption from China expected to ramp up from a starting point of 95M in the bear case or 100M in the base and bull cases. An increase to 105M tons/month is in line with the base case, anything past 110M tons/month strongly argues for the bull case. Also, positive net balance argues for the bear case, where a negative net balance increases the probability of a bull case.
July	American and European demand is expected to increase during the summer, providing a second demand-based inflection point.

The first quarter of the year is dominated by supply considerations, with actual vs. projected demand taking center stage during the second quarter. By July or August it should be relatively clear from the evolution of the fundamental developments—and very likely the price action—which of the three initial cases is playing out in the market. The remainder of the year will be driven by successive refinements of that case, with each incremental data point examined and classified as helping or hurting.

Summary Fundamental Analysis of Product X

The base case is designed to reflect the analyst's and/or trader's best information, and the additive effect of the most likely outcomes for each branch in the event path. The trader defines her fundamental view by her level of confidence in the base case, and the degree to which she chooses to probabilistically incorporate or ignore the bull and bear cases. A trader can choose to utilize the base case in isolation, incorporate elements from the more extreme bull and bear cases, or adopt a more radical perspective and adopt the bull or bear cases as her fundamental perspective.

Product X Technical Analysis

Revisiting the technical analysis from Chapter 4, Product X has the following characteristics.

Trend

The Product X market is a reasonably well-defined uptrend marked by periods of consolidation, bounded by a wide trend channel. There is no clearly defined Elliott Wave count, but the Product X chart does exhibit structure characterized by a macro uptrend with intermediate retracements and constant micro-level fluctuations.

Chapter 7 - Developing a Cohesive Market View

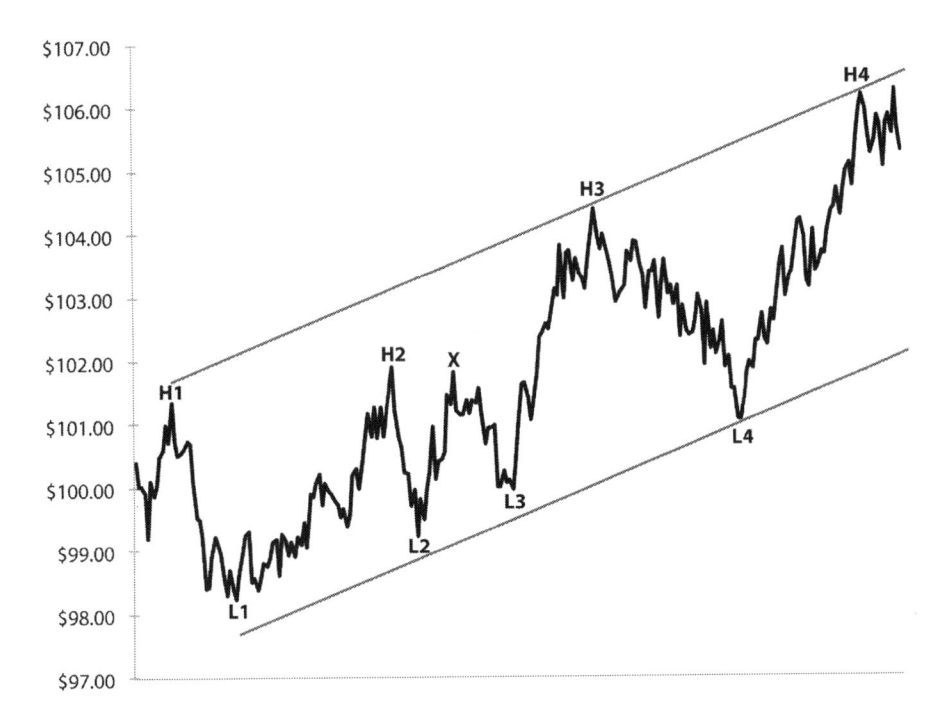

Figure 7.7   FEB ProdX chart making higher lows and higher highs defined by wide trend channel.

Support and Resistance

The impulse uptrend channel should provide the first support at or near the current price of $105.29 (S1). A close below the prior low of $105.03 would mark the end of the impulse wave and likely signal a more significant sell-off that would first find support at the prior peak at $104.39 (S2), then the bottom of the trend channel/triangle consolidation pattern around $102 (S3). A close below the prior low of $101.05 decisively ends the macro uptrend.

The only resistance level impeding the upward progress of Product X is the top of the macro uptrend channel, which would come into play somewhere between $106.00-$107.00, depending on the time taken to rally.

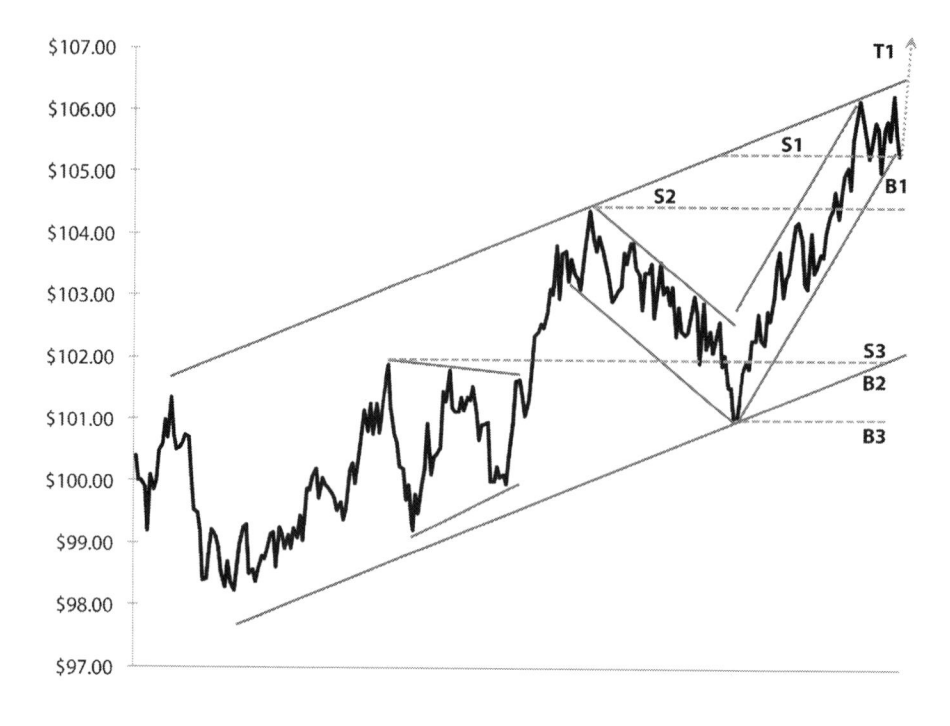

Figure 7.8 Combining the pattern and trend analysis of the FEB ProdX chart.

Pattern

Product X does not exhibit an overabundance of predictive patterns. Aside from the large, well-defined symmetrical triangle that served as a continuation pattern early in the price history, Product X has confined itself to tightly defined channels within the macro trend.

Chapter 7 - Developing a Cohesive Market View

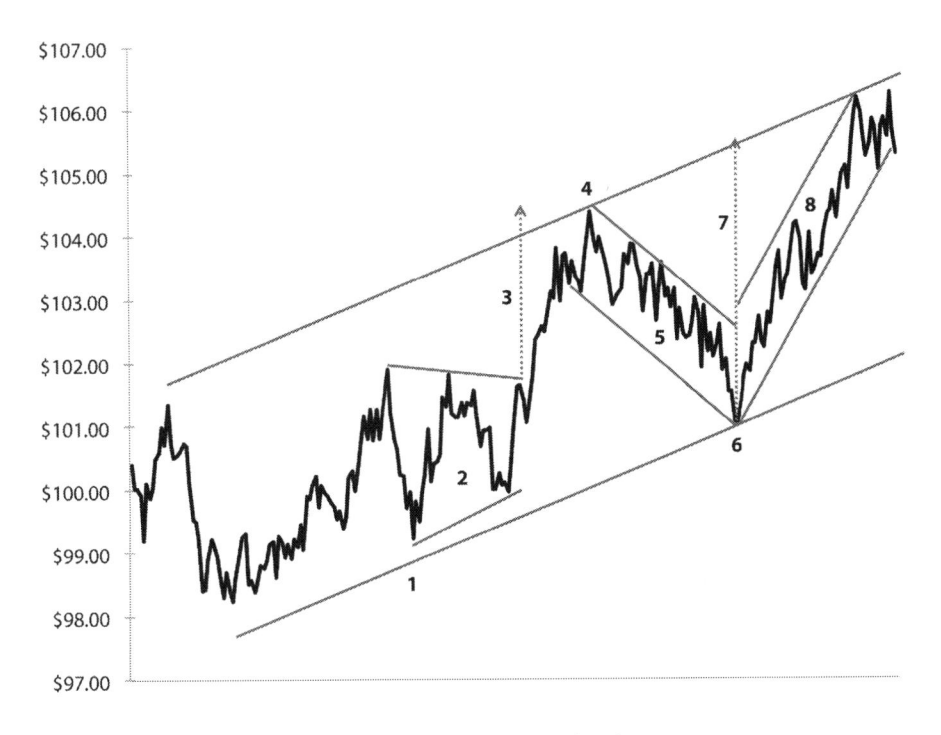

Figure 7.9 Pattern analysis of the FEB ProdX chart.

Studies
Product X is currently in a bullish state based on the moving averages, with a clearly defined cross of the 20-day above the 40-day that has maintained a constant gap width through the end of the chart. The Bollinger Band study shows Product X to be locally at or near "fair" value at the 20-day moving average. The Fibonacci analysis indicates that there is significant potential room for Product X to move lower, with the first stop on a study of the impulse wave being the 23.6% retracement and secondary support at the nearly overlapping 38.2% impulse and 23.6% macro levels.

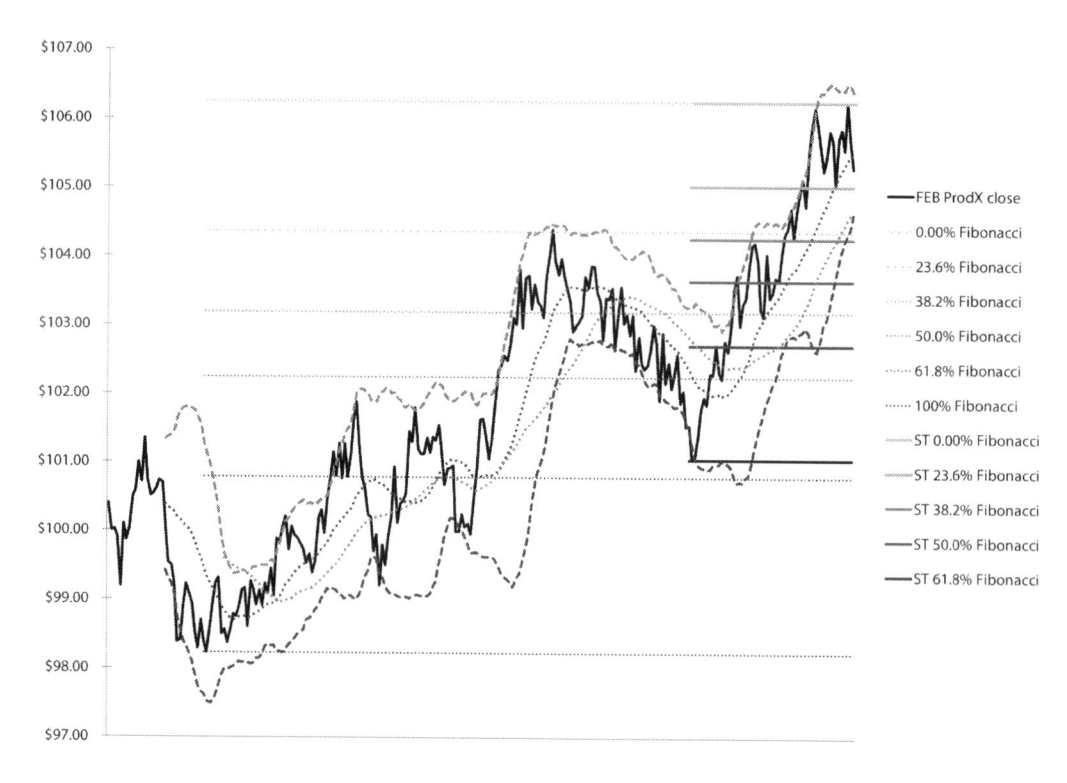

Figure 7.10 FEB ProdX chart with moving average, Bollinger Band, and short- and long-term Fibonacci retracement studies.

Measurement and Objectives
Product X is currently in a well-defined impulse wave that has recently made new highs, and then pulled back to the bottom of its narrow impulse trend channel. There are no obvious measurement objectives motivating the market higher, and the current position at the top of the macro trend channel leaves Product X vulnerable to a countertrend move.

Summary Technical Analysis of Product X
The Product X chart is in an interesting position: a bullish chart with no currently bullish motivation. Traders will frequently say that "a market needs motivation to rally, but can sink of its own weight." Given the position near the all-time high (for the study period), it is entirely reasonable to expect that Product X could experience a short, violent countertrend move. The degree to which this is a constructive, actionable piece of information depends on the trader's style and operational timeframe.

Anticipating a pullback in a well-defined bullish chart is not the same thing as being bearish. By attempting to trade the intermediate, downward-oriented countertrend in a bullish market the trader is intentionally taking the short end of the stick in every way possible. For a well-bounded uptrend the potential distance traversed to the downside will be less than the magnitude of a potential upward move. The countertrend requires everything to go right for the trader: the underlying macro impulse reaches some period of quiet or is temporarily overcome by one or more intermediate factors that combine to temporarily dominate the price action. The key word is "temporarily." By attempting to trade the countertrend the trader is looking for a particular response within a very well-defined window, a window that can, however, slam shut unexpectedly as the macro trend dramatically reasserts itself.

Disciplined traders with fast-twitch information acquisition, processing, and response times can attempt to trade the intermediate trend, but for most players it is more constructive to focus on extracting the maximum possible value from the macro trend. Countertrend movements to support offer the trader attractive opportunities to establish or add to a position. Logical points to establish a Product X position or add to an existing exposure would be:

- The bottom of the current impulse wave at $105.29 (point S1 in Figure 7.8).
- The first support level at the previous high at $104.39 (S2).
- The most solid of all is the bottom of the trend channel at $102 that coincides with the top of the large continuation pattern (S3).

Combining the Product X Fundamental and Technical Perspectives
The first step in combining the fundamental and technical studies for Product X is the initial test for directional compatibility.

Fundamentally, Product X will evolve through an event path during the year that will, depending on the impacts of each incremental market driver on the supply/demand balance, resolve itself in the direction of the base, bear, or bull case. The base case is, by definition, the most likely outcome. The base case for Product X depicts a market facing an initial supply constraint that is briefly alleviated by the partial return to service of African production, only to be reinforced and exacerbated by a combination of general economic growth and demand from China. By the end of the year, the Product X market is solidly in deficit and drawing from storage. The price will need to rally to incentivize incremental production and destroy marginal demand. The intersection of the Product X supply curve and the projected consumption level yields a $165.00 year-end price target.

Technically, Product X is in a relatively stable uptrend with well-defined upper and lower boundaries. While price does appear to be vulnerable to a pullback from the recent all-time highs, there are three prominent support levels that should check the decline at $105.29, $104.39, and $102.00. The only relevant resistance level that could impede upward price movement is the top of the macro uptrend channel. While certainly a valid indicator in isolation, with little price action above the current level the top of the trend channel is more of a psychological barrier and does not have the solidity of an overhead resistance or consolidation level created by a volume of pre-existing open interest. The short-term probabilities favor a pullback to support to points S1, S2, or S3 that will not impact the long-term macro uptrend. Barring a decisive break below the bottom of the trend channel, Product X should remain in an uptrend for the foreseeable future.

Both the fundamental and technical studies are long-term bullish on the price of Product X, with the only caution being that the short-term technical analysis indicates the potential for a non-destructive retracement to support. The Product X market clearly justifies participation, and the trader must consider what additional information can be extracted from the continued comparison of the technical and fundamental information.

Conviction
While the ultimate evolution of the event path is unknown at the start of the year, the price response to the events described in the base case should be extremely predictable.

Measurability
The fundamental base case provides a great deal of confidence about the long-term direction of the market, but little in the way of short-term guidance. The technical case is also long-term constructive, but appears vulnerable to a short-term retracement. This places the trader in the somewhat unusual position of having a high degree of confidence about where prices are ultimately likely to go with a somewhat murkier view in the short term. This is exactly the opposite of the normal state of affairs, but is consistent with a market where the trader's in-house fundamental perspective is leading the market.

Timing
The timing of accumulating a Product X position is slightly tricky. There is a desire to have an exposure for the initial, potentially bullish, data points on the event path, but a respect for the potential magnitude of the possible intermediate-trend pull back.

Triggers
The primary triggers will be the inflection points along the event path, first and foremost the anticipated return to service of the African production facility mid-February.

Targets
It is often constructive to compare the technical and fundamental objectives on an equivalent basis by plotting the price targets from the base, bear, and bull onto a price chart with the same scale as the recent history of Product X.

Chapter 7 - Developing a Cohesive Market View

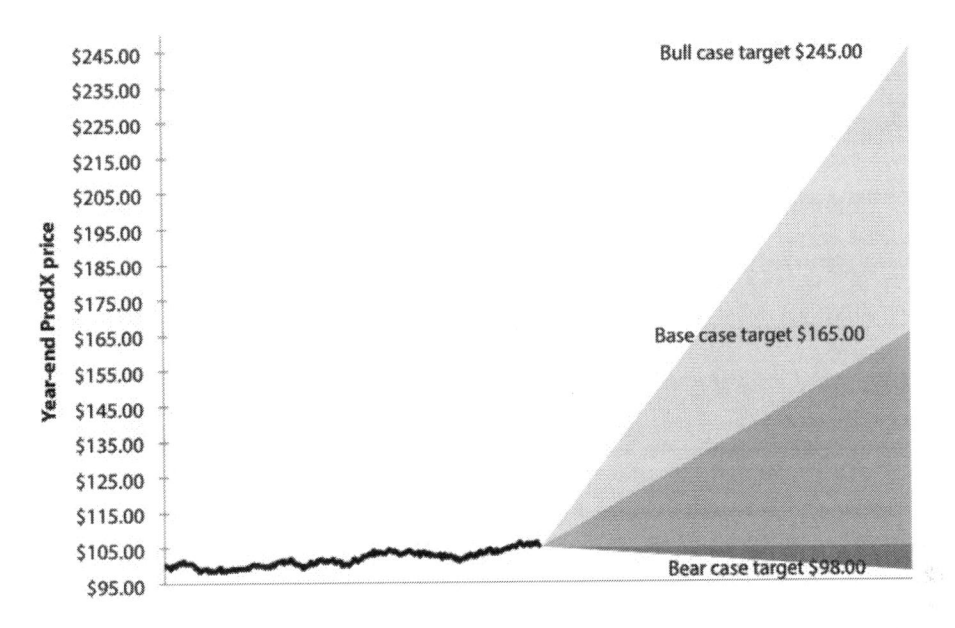

Figure 7.11   Comparing the Product X fundamental case study targets with the technical chart.

The magnitude of the moves implied by case-study price targets dwarf the price action to date and the technical considerations for Product X. While dramatic, this is not an unexpected state of affairs, given recent history and the evolutionary state of the market. Product X is currently emerging from a low-participation, low-demand, low-volatility recessionary environment and transitioning to an event-driven market with increased participation by aggressive speculative entities and a supply/demand balance that has tightened abruptly from a surplus to a net shortage that is forcing withdrawal from storage. It is reasonable to expect that the market will be increasingly volatile going forward.

The trader must remember that the case study price targets are based on end-of-year balance levels and anticipated supply/demand values. The $245.00 target in the bull case does not suggest that the market should immediately step-function to that level on January 1st. To reach that level the fundamentals will have to evolve significantly during the course of the year, as would also be necessary for the base or bear case to materialize. To have a sense of how each incremental data point will influence perception it is constructive to consider the timeline of anticipated events for the upcoming year. The event path for Product X contains impactful decision nodes beginning early and recurring on an almost monthly basis for the first half of the year.

Product X Volatility and Risk Environment

Characterize Product X Volatility
The volatility of Product X is impacted by the following factors:

1. The market is in an early-middle to middle development stage, where financially traded products bring transparency, price visibility, and begin to draw in aggressive players that net increase volatility.
2. Product X is emerging from a broad-based recessionary environment and exhibiting lower than normal volatility.
3. Recent fundamental events are net volatility increasing, and two of the three case studies should lead to both higher prices and higher volatilities going forward.

As discussed in Chapter 5, Product X exhibits elements of all of the volatility patterns. Most of the chart is eminently tradable, with consistently sized daily ranges and only moderate day-over-day gaps. Product X has some tendency toward gappy price action when traversing ground rapidly and seems to signal market turns or intramove consolidation areas with periods of choppy trading activity. Product X has also started to chop toward the end of the price chart, which based on its recent behavior could indicate either an imminent reversal or the consolidation of an in-progress move, both of which are consistent with a market at highs and at the top of a technical macro trend channel.

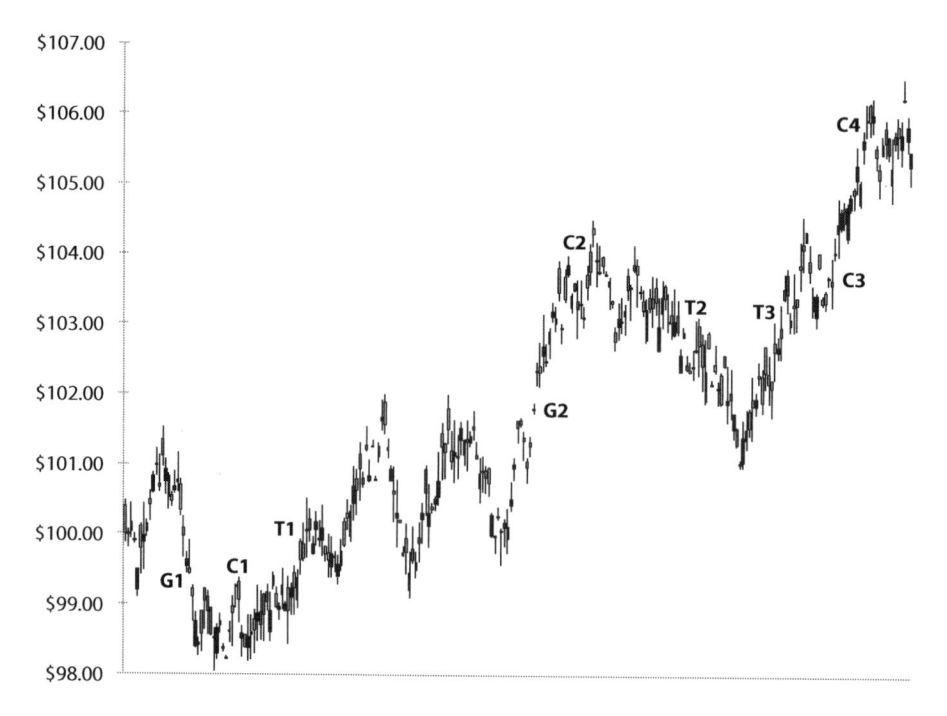

Figure 7.12   Volatility study of FEB ProdX candlestick chart with gaps, consolidation, and trends.

Chapter 7 - Developing a Cohesive Market View

With the exception of the sideways consolidation pattern, the majority of the Product X chart exhibits long, linear moves with day-to-day price fluctuations of similar size and overnight gaps that are not consequential relative to the overall distance traversed. Product X appears eminently macro-tradable, with only occasional instances where shorter-term strategies would encounter problematic chop or the potential for a gap move.

Measure Product X Volatility
Calculating the historical volatility of Product X by the straightforward process described in Chapter 5 yields the following chart.

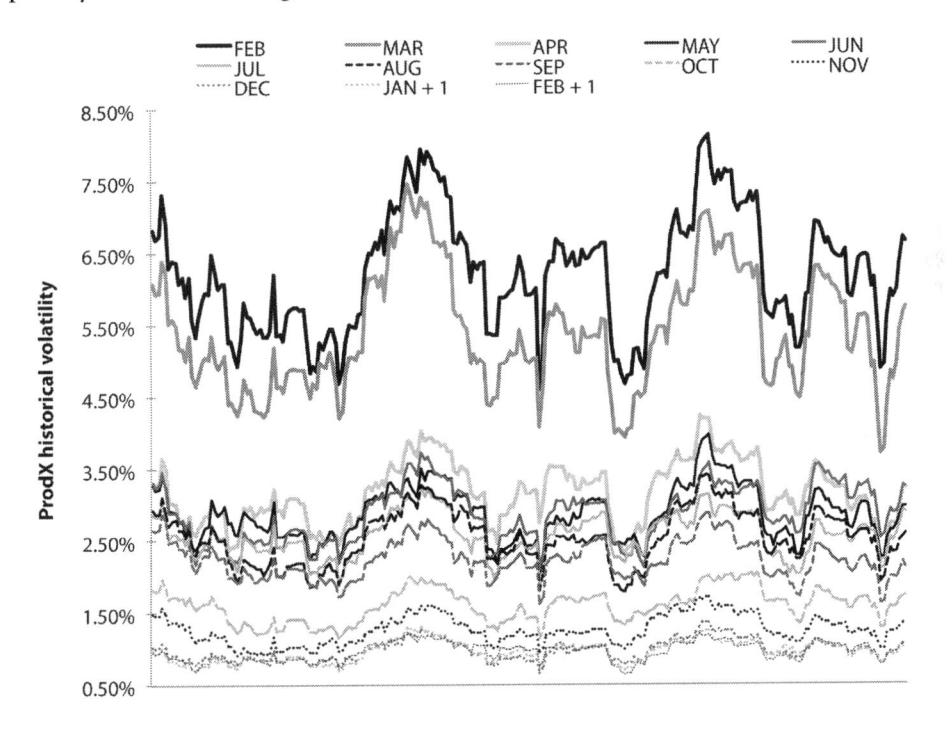

Figure 7.13   Historical volatility of all ProdX futures contracts.

Though low by comparison with other commodities (and financial products in general), the prompt month volatility for Product X is the highest of any contract month:

	Minimum	Maximum	Average	End of year
FEB	4.60%	8.14%	6.22%	6.65%
MAR	3.71%	7.48%	5.39%	5.74%
APR	2.19%	4.24%	3.16%	3.23%
MAY	2.05%	3.96%	2.86%	2.98%
JUN	2.10%	3.73%	2.87%	3.25%
JUL	1.86%	3.25%	2.56%	2.89%
AUG	1.79%	3.41%	2.54%	2.60%
SEP	1.62%	2.89%	2.23%	2.12%
OCT	1.14%	2.05%	1.60%	1.72%
NOV	0.92%	1.71%	1.26%	1.32%
DEC	0.65%	1.36%	0.97%	1.00%
JAN+1	0.70%	1.30%	0.96%	1.03%
FEB+1	0.63%	1.21%	0.96%	1.06%

Table 7.6 Max, min, average, and end-of-year historical volatility of ProdX futures contracts.

It is entirely reasonable for an oversupplied physical market to exhibit low observed volatility on both a relative and absolute level, particularly prior to the arrival of aggressive speculative entities. Though not yet filtered through to price, recent events in the Product X market clearly indicate the possibility (almost probability) for increased volatility going forward. The production disruption in Africa and unexpected Chinese demand have tightened the market into what will be, at the minimum, a short-term deficit. For long-lead, production-intensive physical commodity markets tightness usually sets the stage for bullish shocks, as demand is a relatively better-known constant and supply is the more unpredictable variable. Mines to not typically start up unexpectedly, for example, but do frequently close down due to an accident, strike, etc.

It is critical for traders to understand the volatility sensitivities of the market as a whole and the particular idiosyncrasies of the positions they are evaluating to implement the view of the market. This will be covered in much greater depth in Chapters 8-12.

The current volatility level and forward sensitivity of Product X is directionally aligned with two of the three possible cases.

Product X Risk Environment
Utilizing the parametric method from Chapter 6, the 95% confidence interval, the 1-Day V@R for a 1M-ton position of Product X was calculated to be $728,127. Extending the analysis for the other contract months yields the following V@R table.

Chapter 7 - Developing a Cohesive Market View

	Last price	Last volatility	95% V@R	99% V@R
FEB	$105.29	6.65%	$728,127	$1,028,204
MAR	$105.52	5.74%	$629,416	$888,812
APR	$104.95	3.23%	$352,727	$498,093
MAY	$104.82	2.98%	$324,578	$458,343
JUN	$104.43	3.25%	$352,646	$497,979
JUL	$103.96	2.89%	$312,356	$441,084
AUG	$103.76	2.60%	$280,509	$396,112
SEP	$103.48	2.12%	$228,498	$322,667
OCT	$103.28	1.72%	$184,850	$261,031
NOV	$103.02	1.32%	$141,870	$200,337
DEC	$102.77	1.00%	$107,259	$151,462
JAN+1	$103.25	1.03%	$110,219	$155,643
FEB+1	$103.08	1.06%	$113,178	$159,820

Table 7.7   Calculated V@R for ProdX futures contracts.

Note that the decreasing volatility from the APR contract onward has a material affect on the V@R necessary to hold a position. With only $113K of V@R required to own 1M tons of FEB+1, the trader could theoretically carry a position almost six and a half times notionally larger than he could with the prompt FEB contract, and expressing a view in MAY rather than FEB would allow over twice as large a position. It is highly likely that Product X volatility increases materially in the near term, the effects of which can be seen when the V@R for a FEB position is re-calculated at different levels:

FEB ProdX volatility	95% 1-Day V@R	99% 1-Day V@R
6.00%	$656,633	$927,245
7.00%	$766,071	$1,081,786
8.00%	$875,510	$1,236,327
9.00%	$984,949	$1,390,867
10.00%	$1,094,388	$1,545,408
12.50%	$1,367,985	$1,931,760
15.00%	$1,641,582	$2,318,112
20.00%	$2,188,776	$3,090,817
25.00%	$2,735,970	$3,863,521
30.00%	$3,283,164	$4,636,225
40.00%	$4,377,551	$6,181,633
50.00%	$5,471,939	$7,727,041

Table 7.8   FEB ProdX V@R calculated for a range of implied volatilities.

Product X Market Conditions
The market is in an early-middle to middle development stage, where newly-created financial products bring increased transparency, price visibility, and begin to draw in aggressive players that increase the initially extremely low volatility.

Product X Risks
The worst-case scenario for a long-biased view would involve a technical countertrend move that gathers strength, breaches the support at S1, S2, and (most critically) S3, and takes out the prior low at $101.50, which would signal the end of the macro uptrend. A technical breakdown is problematic in isolation, but in conjunction with a run of bearish data points early in the event path (strong return of African production, unexpected economic slowdown, etc.) would prove destructive to both the chart pattern and the base case as a viable model for the future of Product X fundamentals. A fundamental shift to the acceptance of the bear case would open the door to a possible move lower to the $98.00 target. The $98.00 fair value for the bear case does not imply that price cannot go below that level, as markets can become extremely over- and underpriced in the short term. Though impossible to predict or incorporate into the analysis, there is also some non-zero probability of a negative-outcome black swan event that could send prices far lower than any market participant would ever deem rational.

Product X Rewards
The best-case scenario for a long-biased view would involve a series of bullish fundamental data points (continuation of the African production outage, strong economic growth driving above-expectation demand from China, Europe, and the United States, etc.) The technical chart currently offers no particularly significant overhead resistance, so prices are free to appreciate as far as the fundamentals can take them.

To evaluate upside targets, the trader must consider both the base and bull cases. The base case has a year-end price target of $165.00, with the probable maximum upside being defined by the bull case's $245.00 valuation. As with the inherent risks, fair value does not imply that price cannot go above that level, as markets can become extremely over- and underpriced in the short term. There is also the potential for a black swan event that helps the trader's position, though this never seems to happen.

Product X Market Risk-Reward Ratio
Comparing the bear case's fair value vs. the base case's target yields a $7.29 decline and a $59.71 potential reward, for an approximately 8:1 market risk-reward ratio. Comparing the retracement to the trend channel vs. the base case's target yields $3.29 of risk and $59.71 of potential reward, for an approximately 18:1 ratio. This is a very favorable ratio, and is somewhat problematic due to the utilization of a short-term retracement level and a long-term fundamental target, creating an unequal comparison that looks good on paper, but is not reflective of real outcomes. The trader should likewise refrain from considering risk-reward ratios derived from the $59.71 potential reward from the base case and the lesser technical retracements to S1 and S2, which will generate metrics that are completely unrealistic.

Chapter 7 - Developing a Cohesive Market View

The 8:1 ratio around the current price defined by the bear case target of $98.00 and the base case fair value of $165.00 seems to offer the most reasonable representation of the market's potential over the coming year.

Product X Market Probability-Adjusted Risk-Reward Ratio

Although the base case is by far the most likely outcome, the trader must incorporate non-zero probabilities for other outcomes, both planned and unplanned. The practical problem lies in assigning the relative weights to each outcome. Trading is an inherently optimistic endeavor, and one of the many manifestations of this bias is the tendency to overweight possible but unlikely positive outcomes and minimize the chances of negative or exogenously bad scenarios.

Current FEB price	$105.29
Base case target	$165.00
Bear case target	$98.00
Bull case target	$245.00

In the near term, the primary inflection point on the Product X event path is the return to service of the African production facility. The owner-operator of the facility continues to stand by the initial Q1 return to service date, but in the absence of any additional or new information it would be optimistic to attempt to parse the probability of the facility coming back on-line as anything other than a 50/50 coin flip. A near-term 50% chance of a full return to service that tilts the market toward the Bear case and a 50% chance of a continued outage that brings the Base case target into play would lead to the following risk/reward assessment:

Reward	$59.71
Risk	$7.29
Market risk-reward ratio	8:1

Using a straight 50/50 probability split, the expected year-end value would be $131.50.

Product X Market View

The trader's fundamental information, technical analysis, and assessment of the current market conditions have led to the following conclusions:

1. Product X is cheap on an outright basis given the probable structural supply/demand balance that is expected to emerge toward the middle/end of the year in the base case, with a possibility that an inability to resume production from Africa in February could move the supply shortfall forward and create a violent price response.
2. Product X is very cheap on a volatility basis, with historical volatilities that can only reasonably be expected to move higher during the course of the year.
3. Traders should want to get positioned for the long term ASAP, with the only caution being a probable near-term retracement.
4. Evolutions to fundamental thesis to persist for the remainder of the year.

Given the favorable 8:1 risk-reward ratio present in the market with an unmodified 50/50 probability split, all of the components of the trader's view argue for aggressive positioning. The trader now needs to explore different strategic implementations of this view, which will be covered in subsequent chapters on Directional, Spread, Option and Quantitative trading.

Playing Devil's Advocate – Who Would Ever Sell Product X?
Given the seemingly obvious analysis that Product X is going higher and that the rewards seem to overwhelm the risks on both an absolute and probabilistic basis, it is worth examining the question: who would *ever* sell Product X?

1. A market participant with a radically different interpretation of the fundamentals, which would probably center around a strong belief that the African production facility will return to service and doubt about the continued increase in Chinese demand and future global economic growth.
2. Natural sellers hedging to hedge unsold future production at attractive levels or to gain cash flow and margin certainty to finance expansion.
3. Traders with in-the-money long positions exiting their exposures and booking profits.

While the second and third reasons make logical, intuitive sense, it can be harder for some traders to believe that a rational participant can arrive at a different interpretation of the same market. Recall that every market participant is operating with a unique subset of the total informational inputs, and that given a different set of starting assumptions it is absolutely possible to arrive at an alternate, opposing conclusion.

8

Directional Trading Strategies

According to football lore, in the 1970s a young National Football League coach named John Madden attended a seminar taught by living legend Vince Lombardi. The topic was The Power Sweep, an offensive formation perfected by Lombardi's team, the Green Bay Packers. Madden was the coach of the Los Angeles Raiders, a football prodigy known for emphasizing extreme attention to detail when preparing his team for a game. At Lombardi's seminar he was astounded to spend eight hours going over seemingly endless permutations of the same play, drilling deeper and deeper into the minutiae, examining pre-planned contingencies, shifts in responsibility and subtle variations designed to counter myriad defensive responses. Madden was staggered by the depth and complexity of what initially appeared to be, even to a highly educated observer, a relatively straightforward, bread-and-butter running play.

Directional trading also appears to be very simple. A directional trade is a position taken to capitalize on an anticipated price movement higher or lower. The up-or-down, buy-or-sell binary nature of directional trading lends itself regrettably well to uninformed comparisons to flipping a coin, or gambling at a roulette wheel. These are convenient, yet flawed metaphors. It is not the comparison to gambling that rankles, but the type. Directional trading is about proactively controlling risk, not passively accepting the consequences of fate or luck. Directional trading is most conceptually similar to no-limit poker, a game where players seek to draw their opponents into asymmetrical information confrontations where they alone understand the correct odds. To be consistently profitable requires a disciplined approach and a tremendous body of theory and technique.

Mastering the Minimum
In contemplating strategic alternatives to implement his view, a trader will, for the first time, begin to examine something other than historical data and future projections. The bridge

between the known facts of the past and the presumed trajectory of the future is a never-ending series of small events occurring in the present. All forms of trading are immersive, but directional trading demands the most intense focus on the current operational environment. The trader must observe and interpret the day-to-day, hour-to-hour, and minute-by-minute fluctuations of the market in response to each incremental piece of information that will, in aggregate, influence the perceptions of the participants and motivate them to action.

The relative simplicity of directional trading reduces the number of moving parts while dramatically increasing the relative importance of each remaining variable. By definition, every position is a trader-constructed subset of the total market risk-reward space. A directional position is unique in that it creates an unmitigated exposure to the totality of the market's price movement, unlike the inherent exposure limitations of an option or the self-hedging characteristics of a spread. Directional trading is about control and execution, and requires a degree of engagement and commitment not necessary with other, more limited forms of exposure.

Good directional traders are extremely skilled at the basic, unglamorous blocking and tackling that, while not flashy, is often the determining factor between winning and losing. For this reason, many of the basic topics covered in this chapter will be assumed as prerequisites for the sections on spreads, options, and quantitative trading that follow. The more complex strategies allow the trader to express subtler, more nuanced views of the market, but all either retain a directional component to their performance, or can also be used to express directional views.

Directional Trading Advantages

Directional trading strategies have a number of inherent advantages and disadvantages. The primary advantages are:

1. Precise, responsive exposures.
2. Available for use at any stage of market development
3. Ease of position accumulation, distribution, and risk modification.
4. No requirement that value be inherent in the transaction.
5. Conceptually straightforward.

Precise, Responsive Exposures
Directional positions have very straightforward performance characteristics. The notional volume of the trader's exposure will change in value linearly, tick-for-tick, with changes in its market price. A $0.10 increase per ton on the price of 1M tons of material will yield a $100,000 profit for a long position and a $100,000 loss for a short position.

Available for Use at Any Stage of Market Development
Directional trades can be implemented with most instruments, though traders will tend to gravitate to liquidity and linearity of response, when possible. The linear instruments like physical and financial forwards, futures, and swaps are typically the first to start trading,

allowing early-stage participants like naturals and merchants to mitigate risks until sophisticated players arrive and develop more complex, non-linear option products, etc.

For early-stage markets with predominantly bilateral physical trade, position size may be constrained by the actual production/consumption needs of the organic buyers and sellers. When a forward market develops, the number of "paper" or pseudo-financial transactions will typically increase to a multiple of production- and consumption-linked volumes. The advent of purely financial instruments and a robust clearing system that removes counterparty credit bottlenecks will lead to an explosion in trading volume (and shortly thereafter to the explosion of firms with poor risk-management cultures who are not ready for the transactional freedom).

Ease of Position Accumulation Distribution, and Risk Modification
The core forwards, futures, and swap products that form the foundation of the market will typically have the highest transaction volume, the greatest depth and liquidity, and the smallest bid-offer spreads. Paying away the bid-offer spread is a tax on the business, as is slippage risk associated with tick-to-tick differentials. This relatively low-friction transactional environment allows for rapid, frequent, efficient execution. A highly transactional environment with an ability to modify positions at will gives traders the confidence to accumulate significant positions and create exposure to material amounts of risk without undue fear of being trapped.

The trader must be mindful that intentionally straying from liquidity decreases some of the advantages of a directional strategy and increases the relative level of risk which, to make sense, must be accompanied by a material, anticipated, incremental benefit.

No Requirement That Value Be Inherent in the Proposition
A directional position does not have to be cheap or expensive on a relative basis to be a good trade. It is entirely possible for a trader to profit by purchasing something that is expensive, as long as she is able to sell once it has become even more expensive.

Conceptually Straightforward
A directional trade is a fairly straightforward concept, and as long as the trader's view is cogent and well constructed it should be relatively easy to explain both the position and its rationale. Management should be able to understand the trader's strategy and have a level of comfort with its implementation. The exposures are exact, the risk is linear and the metrics are simple to calculate given visible end-of-day marks and a reasonable amount of price history. Trades with more moving pieces and/or non-linear risk characteristics pose significantly greater challenges to obtaining management and risk group approval, as we will see in subsequent chapters.

Directional Trading Disadvantages

The inherent disadvantages of a directional strategy are, in many ways, the flip side of each of the advantages:

1. Full responsibility for risk mitigation lies with the trader.
2. The market will always be fairly priced, no inherent edge in the deal.
3. Prevailing volatility will impact or restrict usable strategies
4. Directional strategies are not V@R and collateral efficient
5. Directional trading is Neanderthal trading.

Full Responsibility for Risk Mitigation Lies with the Trader

A precise, responsive position is a great thing, until it starts to precisely, responsively lose money. The only thing protecting the trader from disaster if the market moves against him is his analysis of the situation, discipline, and execution skill. Traders that do not promptly and efficiently clean up their messes will not be traders for long.

It is worth noting that the generally accepted belief that other types of trading are somehow inherently "safer" is nonsense. Options and spreads typically exhibit less P&L volatility than a volumetrically equivalent directional position in the underlying, but in practice are typically accumulated in far greater size. The correct way to view any position is on a delta-adjusted or risk-weighted basis. A spread trade that is half as volatile as a directional position but ten times as big is still five times as dangerous. The implementation efficiency of different instruments will be covered in depth on a strategy-by-strategy basis in the relevant chapters and comparatively evaluated in Chapter 12 – Evaluating Trades and Creating a Trading Plan.

The Market Will Always Be Fairly Priced

In most markets, the basic forwards, futures, and swaps offer by far the most depth, liquidity, and price discovery. While these are positive attributes, the drawback is that there is almost no possibility that they will ever be materially mispriced. "Fair value" will be well established and widely known due to the number of participants, the volume of transactions, and the diverse interests brought to bear at all times. The price is the price, and directional trading strategies rely on correctly assessing what will impact and motivate that price in the future, as there will be no free lunch to be had in the present.

Prevailing Volatility Will Impact or Restrict Usable Strategies

What the market is doing is important, but how it is doing it also greatly impacts the trader's choice of strategy. The prevailing market conditions will, to a great extent, act to determine the types of trading strategies that can be productively employed at any particular point in time. Consider a graph of two price trajectories, one with high and one with low volatility, centered around the same sinusoidal trend:

Chapter 8 - Directional Trading Strategies

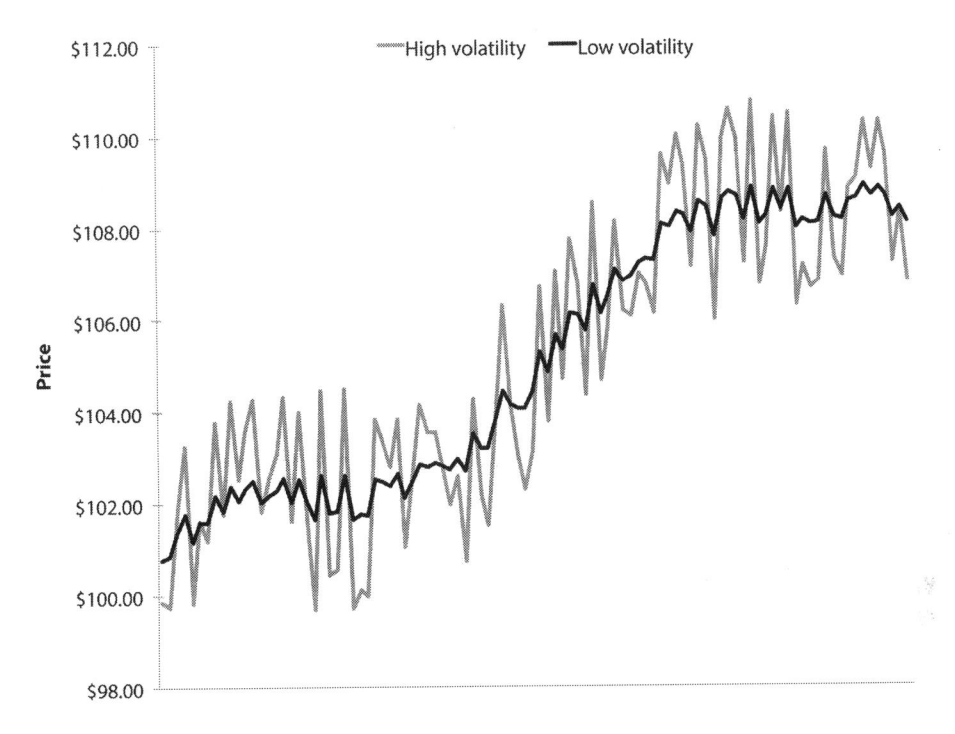

Figure 8.1 High and low volatility price paths around the same central trend.

In the low volatility case it is possible to establish a long position early and hold it with minimal suffering. The move from $101.00 to $108.00 is relatively linear, with no material pullbacks to cause doubt or inflict mark-to-market pain. When the market plateaus between $108.00-109.00 there is a prolonged period of time to evaluate the position and exit the exposure.

In the high volatility case the trader is faced with daily fluctuations ranging between $2.00-$4.00 that severely distort the appearance of the in-progress trend. With perfect execution, it is possible that a skilled trader who recognizes the choppy conditions and is proficient at operating in dangerous markets could buy at $100.00 and, after riding out a material amount of volatility, sell at $110.00. A less-skilled (or less lucky) trader could easily buy early in the trend at $104.00 and sell late in the move at $106.00, making a paltry $2.00 (or about half a typical day's trading range) for enduring a significant amount of suffering.

In a non-volatile market with tight bid-offer spreads there is often little difference between executing at the market bid or offer and exercising good tradecraft and negotiating a better price or providing liquidity by posting a two-way. The slight difference in price will not materially impact the profitability of the overall trade. In a volatile or panic-driven market the bid-offer spread can widen appreciably, forcing the trader to execute efficiently at both entry and exit or risk significantly eroding the potential inherent in the trade.

The prevailing volatility should be factored into the pre-trade risk-reward assessment, as seen in Chapter 7. The more volatile the market, the greater the skill necessary to execute and establish a position at levels that will allow it to be survivable. At extreme levels of volatility survivability becomes a key consideration, and the ratio between the amplitude of the daily and intraday fluctuations and the pain the trader can afford to endure before being stopped out of the position must be carefully considered. A market exhibiting daily swings that are wider than a trader's stop means that even with optimal execution there is a high probability that the trader could be forced out of her position within the next 24 hours. There is no magic formula to determine how much volatility is too much. Assessing the relative operability of the prevailing conditions comes down to the trader's skill, experience, and not infrequently, self-confidence.

Directional Strategies Are Not V@R and Collateral Efficient
While the trader should benefit from the lowest bid-offer transaction slippage and greatest liquidity with a directional trade, the post-trade maintenance costs are frequently more onerous than with self-hedging or loss-limited strategies. As with any trade, the firm will be required to post initial margin to a clearinghouse or counterparty. The funds necessary to finance the position will have a cost, usually charged back to the business unit and ultimately to the trader. A $100M notional position might require the firm to post $10M of initial margin, for which the trader will be charged. For a trader with an 8% internal cost of borrowing, financing the $10M necessary to hold the $100M notional position will cost approximately $800K per year, or around $3K per trading day.

Directional Trading Is Neanderthal Trading
In the early stages of most markets, the only exposures possible will be directional trades. Naturals will have to buy or sell, and traders will make money facilitating those transactions, providing liquidity, and warehousing risk to smooth out the interregnum when buyers and sellers are not concurrently present in the market. As time passes and the market evolves, non-linear instruments will develop and more complex strategies will become commonplace. With each incremental advance, the traders who have developed and mastered the new technology will look down on those that came before. This is logical, as novelty and technology are revered in trading circles, and differentiating oneself as a cutting-edge practitioner can do great things for a trader's career. Standing on the shoulders of giants requires using something (or someone) as a stepping-stone, and the simplistic, capital intensive, risky directional trading frequently provides a convenient foil.

Common Directional Trading Strategies
Directional trading strategies are commonly deployed in four basic market scenarios:

1. Breakout Strategies – A market that is in the process of making a move higher or lower from an equilibrium state or well-defined trading range. In an early stage, driven by fundamentals or a technical pattern.
2. Trend Strategies – Getting involved in a market move in progress. The skill lies in assessing how to ride the trend and when to close the position.

Chapter 8 - Directional Trading Strategies

3. Range-Trading Strategies – Making short-duration trades to take advantage of the oscillations of a market stuck between well-defined support and resistance.
4. Trend Reversals and Market Turns – Taking a contrarian view on a trend that has run its course and appears ready to retrace some or all of its prior progress.

Traders can deploy these basic strategies at every time scale, from the microsecond holding periods of a high-frequency trader to the multi-year positioning of long-term value investors. Regardless of how zoomed in or out on the fractal the trader is, what the market is currently doing will attract different types of players and be conducive to different kinds of strategies.

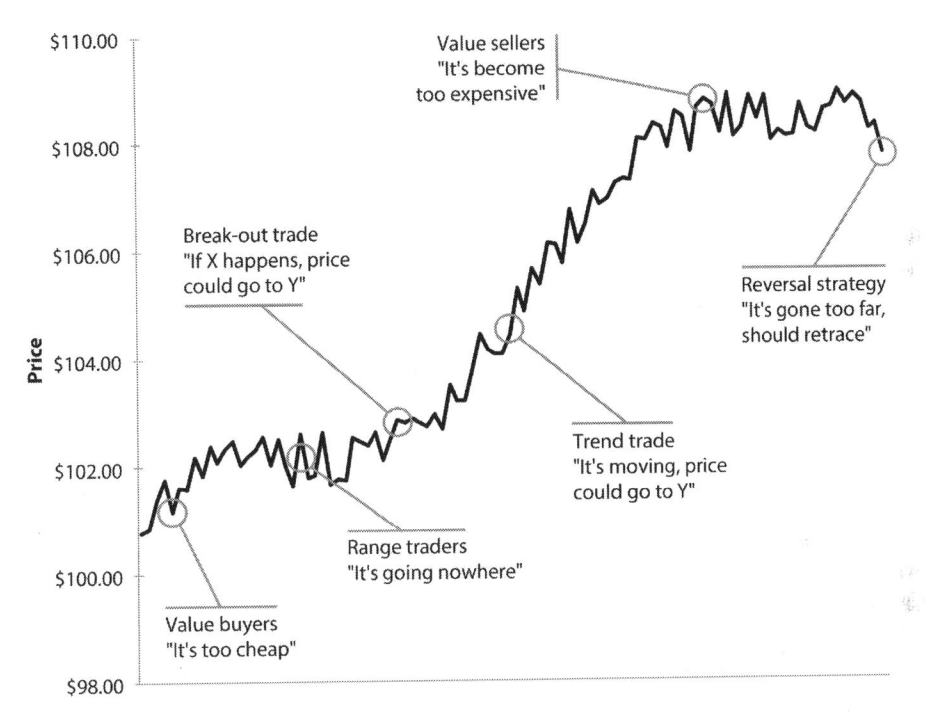

Figure 8.2 Strategies for different phases of a market move.

1. Breakout Strategies – A Market About to Go Somewhere

There are two types of breakout strategies:

1. Attempting to capitalize on the completion of a technical pattern with an easily observed breach/trigger criteria and a defined measurement objective.
2. Trades where the market is jolted out of a non-specific range by a seismic shift in a critical underlying fundamental variable. Trades with a potentially violent response to incremental information are sometimes called "explosion trades."

A technical breakout occurs when the market price completes a pattern or breaches a level deemed to be critical support or resistance. An obvious prerequisite is an interpretable pattern that has had time to develop a material amount of vested positional interest and clear breakout criteria, such as the violation of a trend line or taking out a prior high or low. If the trader's firm is leading on the fundamentals and has a strong view, it can be aggressive on the break. The clearer and more interpretable the pattern, the better sense of target levels and the transit time to target.

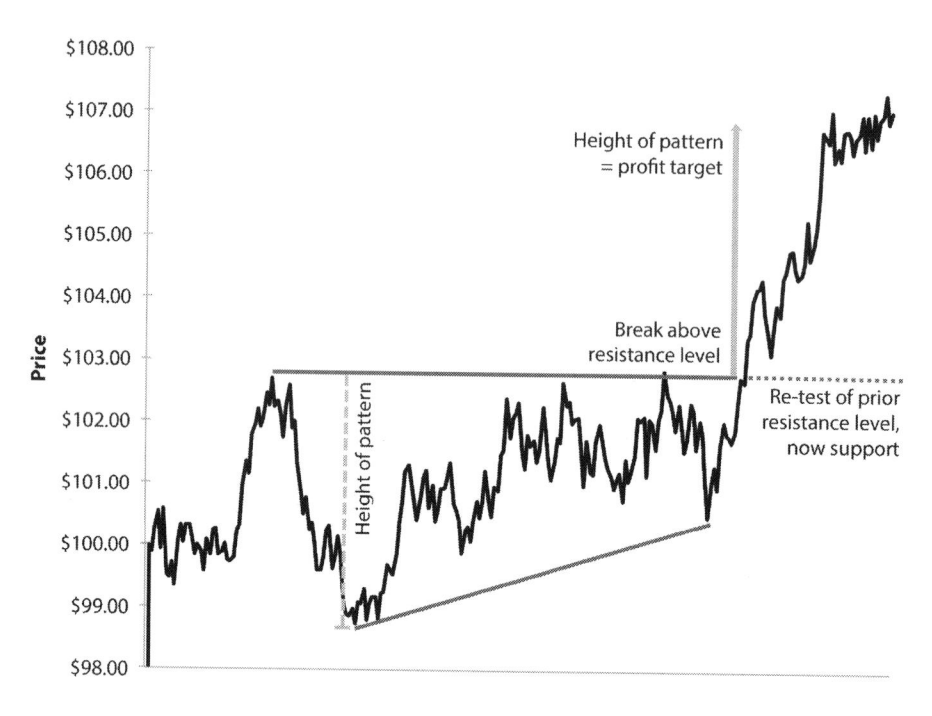

Figure 8.3 Technical break-out strategy.

The key to any breakout trade is the magnitude and duration of the market's initial motivating force, which must be sufficient to push prices out of and away from the recent trading range and incent a flurry of position covering. This surge of buying or selling will frequently be augmented by fresh money coming in off the sidelines to participate, creating increased localized competition for the available liquidity and exacerbating the severity of the price move. The trader should anticipate a possible retest of the former resistance level, which will function as a source of support going forward. The market must pass the retest test, or is not a breakout. A breach that does not gather a critical mass will fail, and the market will either seek a new equilibrium state around its current price or be beaten back into the pre-breakout range or pattern. These "false breakouts" are common, particularly with pattern-driven technical-only trades.

Technical breakouts from well-defined patterns frequently imply a short- to medium-term target level for the subsequent price action, which can be invaluable for assessing the risk-

Chapter 8 - Directional Trading Strategies

reward inherent in the trade and evaluating the trader's ability to participate. Using the same breakout of the top line of a flat wedge as an example:

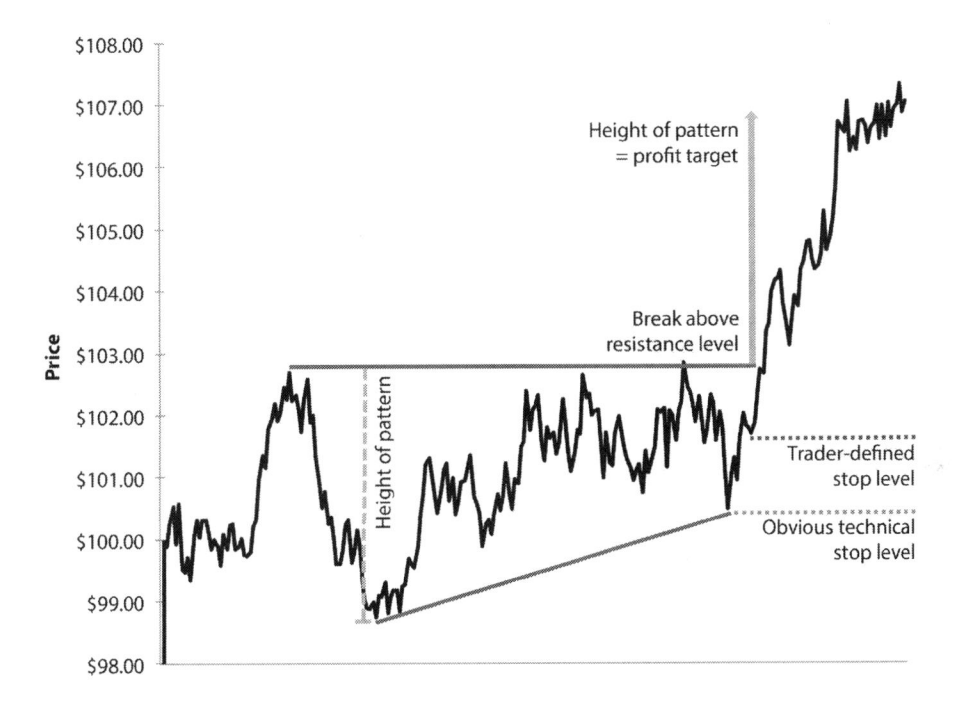

Figure 8.4   Setting stop-loss and profit target for technical break-out strategy.

The target implied for a flat wedge is equal to the height of the widest part of the pattern, in this case approximately $4.25, implying a move from the $103.00 breakout level to $107.25. With a probable maximum of $4.25 to play for, the trader must select a stop-loss level significantly smaller in order to justify the transaction.

The logical place to set a stop would be at either the prior low of the formation at $100.50 or the continuation of the support line that bounded the pattern, which would come into play somewhere around the $101.00 level (depending on how much time had elapsed). If the trader managed to buy exactly at the $103.00 breakout, with an expected $4.25 profit she cannot justify a stop level that would lead to a $2.00 or $2.50 loss and something like a 17:8 to 17:10 (or approximately 2:1) risk-reward ratio. The trader will have to define a stop that creates a favorable risk-reward, but that is also reasonable given the market conditions. Using a trader-defined $101.75 stop yields a $1.25 potential loss vs. a $4.25 potential profit, for a significantly more attractive 17:5 (or between 3:1 and 4:1) risk-reward ratio. The $1.25 stop is located at the approximate midpoint of the narrowing triangle, and is far enough below the former resistance level that any retracement back to the $101.75 level would be an unambiguous signal that the breakout had failed, invalidating the core thesis behind the trade.

It is critical that the trader also be either extremely decisive or extremely disciplined when establishing a directional position with a measurement-bounded upside and a self-defined downside. The 17:5 risk-reward ratio presupposes that the trader is able to get positioned at the $103.00 breakout level. Any additional slippage above that price will erode the headroom available under the profit target and increase the amount at risk relative to the stop-loss. Buying at the local post-break peak at $104.20 would shift the dynamic to a $2.45 loss vs. a $3.05 gain and an unattractive 6:5 risk-reward ratio. Technical traders must seek to identify potential breakout trades before they happen, then react instantly once the target level is breached. If the trader misses the original break, he must be disciplined and wait for a possible retracement to the former resistance level which may be tested as a support and offer a second opportunity to accumulate a position at constructive levels.

The principal difference between a fundamentally driven breakout and a non-patterned chart is that the market just moves, leaving behind a volume of open interest, one half delighted and the other half frantically attempting to cover their positions and, in doing so, creating the price response that is destroying them. Getting positioned before a fundamental breakout is only possible when the firm is clearly, unambiguously ahead of the market on a critical piece of analysis or information that, once revealed or realized, will lead to an abrupt revaluation (or step-function shift in price for an explosion trade).

A fundamental break out will not necessarily have an obvious pattern-derived technical price target, so the trader will have to utilize a fundamentally derived objective or rely on insight gleaned from monitoring the market momentum in an effort to suss out an exit point. Fundamental breakouts or explosion trades lack the visual cue of a support or resistance breach, but compensate the trader with more clarity as to the drivers underpinning the move, their relative severity, and the potential inferences going forward.

With both fundamental and technical breaks, the volume traded within a technical pattern or congestion range can offer some insight as to the magnitude of the post-break move. The larger the open interest created in a pattern or congestion area, the more incorrect trades need to be unwound. If there were 1,000 contracts traded in the ascending triangle pictured in Figure 8.4 and the immediate post-breakout volume was somewhere in the range of 200-300 contracts, it would be reasonable to infer that the market could continue to move higher, as there are a substantial amount of bad short positions that need to be closed. Conversely, if 950 lots changed hands just above the breakout level it could serve as an indicator that the short-covering appetite had largely been sated, and that a post-break move might not achieve its technical target.

2. Trend- and Momentum-Driven Strategies – A Market That Is Going Somewhere

Trading a market that is already in motion is a different proposition from anticipating and reacting to a breakout or explosion. A momentum-based directional strategy seeks to capitalize on a price movement in progress, riding it as far as possible and exiting when the trend has run its course. Ideally, the trader should understand the fundamental case for the movement and be using the technical indicators to gauge the probable magnitude. This type of mid- to late-move positioning has less risk of timing the move incorrectly (as it is already

Chapter 8 - Directional Trading Strategies

in progress), but a potentially decreased market risk-reward as some portion of the potential move has already occurred. The probability-adjusted risk-reward for the trade may have improved, however, as the probability gain applied to the trade may outweigh the market risk-reward giveaway. Successfully trading a trend is a matter of identifying it, entering the position as efficiently as possible, and defining the exit criteria.

Consider a chart of a robust, well-defined uptrend.

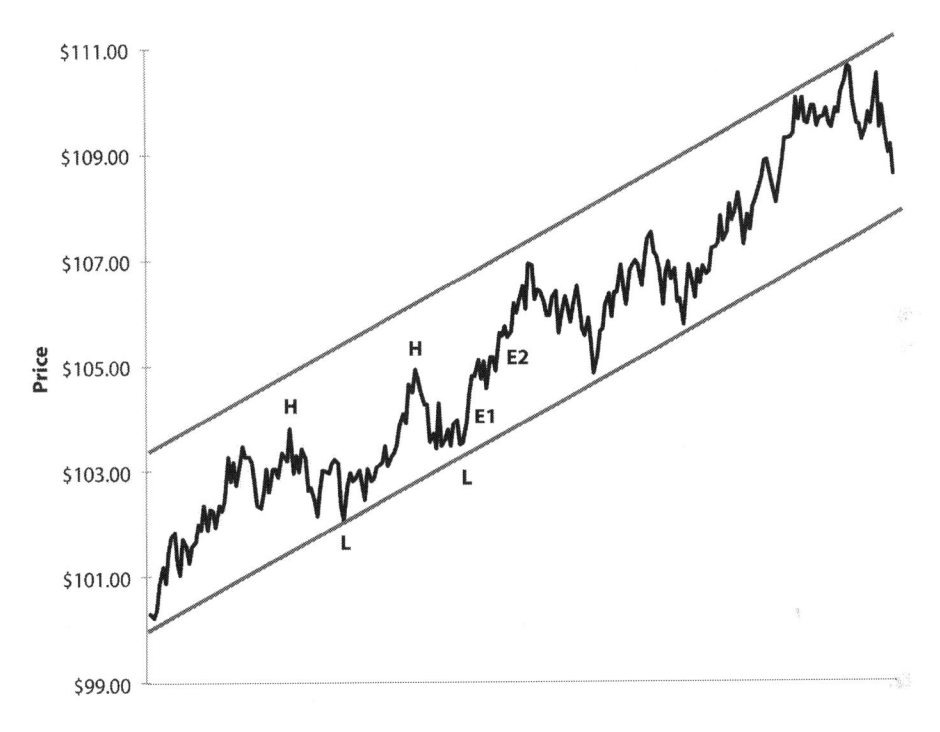

Figure 8.5 Trend strategy for a market in motion.

During the period of study the market makes a total move from a low of $100.00 to a peak just under $111.00. Though in retrospect the trend is well defined, stepping through the price action chronologically from left to right shows a market that made a initial push from $100.00 to a peak at $104.00, chopped lower to a bottom near $102.00, made a sharp rally to $105.00, then retraced and made a bottom around $103.50. Until the second bottom at $103.50 is defined at (E1), which occurs approximately 40% through the time series, the market had not fulfilled the basic definitional criteria of an uptrend by making higher highs and higher lows. That level is the first point that a trend-based technical trader could use to realistically, logically justify participation in the market. Many technical traders would wait until the previous high had been eclipsed (E2) as additional confirmation of the trend before entering a position.

Trading a trend also requires the patience to wait until a retracement has taken the price action to near the bottom or top of the trading range to allow the trader to extract the maximum possible risk-reward ratio relative to the obvious prior high/low stop and the trend channel itself. Buying the top of the trend channel in an uptrend will earn the trader a ticket to a probable retracement in the near future and maximizes the amount potentially lost if the market breaks a prior low and she is forced out of the position. The only exception to this rule would be if the trader feels that an imminent (most likely fundamental) event could steepen the trend channel or lead to a step-function move higher in the direction of their intended position.

Consider the differing consequences of entering a long position at the top and bottom of an uptrend channel.

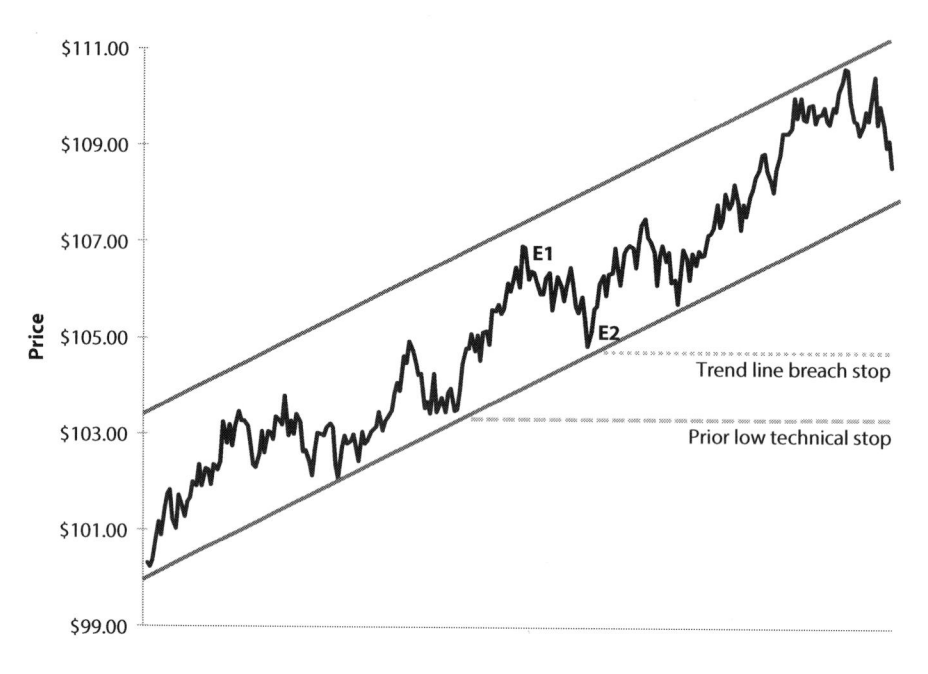

Figure 8.6   Setting stop-loss levels for trend strategy.

A trader taking a position at the local high point of the channel (E1) would have an entry point of $106.91, a trend break of $104.84 and a prior low stop of $103.43. A trader taking a position at the bottom of the trend channel (E2) the would have an entry point of $105.15, and the same trend-break level of $104.84 and prior low stop of $103.43.

Chapter 8 - Directional Trading Strategies

	Entry point	Trend break	Prior low stop	Entry-to-trend	Entry-to-stop
E1	$106.91	$104.84	$103.43	($2.07)	($3.48)
E2	$105.15	$104.84	$103.43	($0.31)	($1.72)

Table 8.1   Comparison of different trade entry points.

Using a $110 price target on the trade yields the following risk-to-reward ratios:

	Entry point	Prior low stop	Entry-to-stop	Entry-to-target	Risk-to-reward
E1	$106.91	$103.43	($3.48)	$3.09	0.9-to-1
E2	$105.15	$103.43	($1.72)	$4.85	2.8-to-1

Table 8.2   Risk-to-reward ratios for different trade entry points.

The near 1:1 risk-reward ratio created by buying at the top of the trend channel and using the definitive prior low trend-break as a stop is clearly a non-starter. A trader with poor intra-trend positioning will have to rely on a self-defined stop to improve the risk-to-reward ratio to an acceptable level, which may potentially force an exit from the position during a normal retracement or due to a problematic, but not necessarily fatal, trend break. While not incorrect in the strictest sense, it is clearly an example of making things more difficult than they need be, which in the long run usually leads to suboptimal performance.

The relative width of the channel that bounds the trend will greatly impact the trader's ability to optimize (or sub-optimize) entry and exit. Compare an uptrend with wide fluctuations with an extremely tight downtrend.

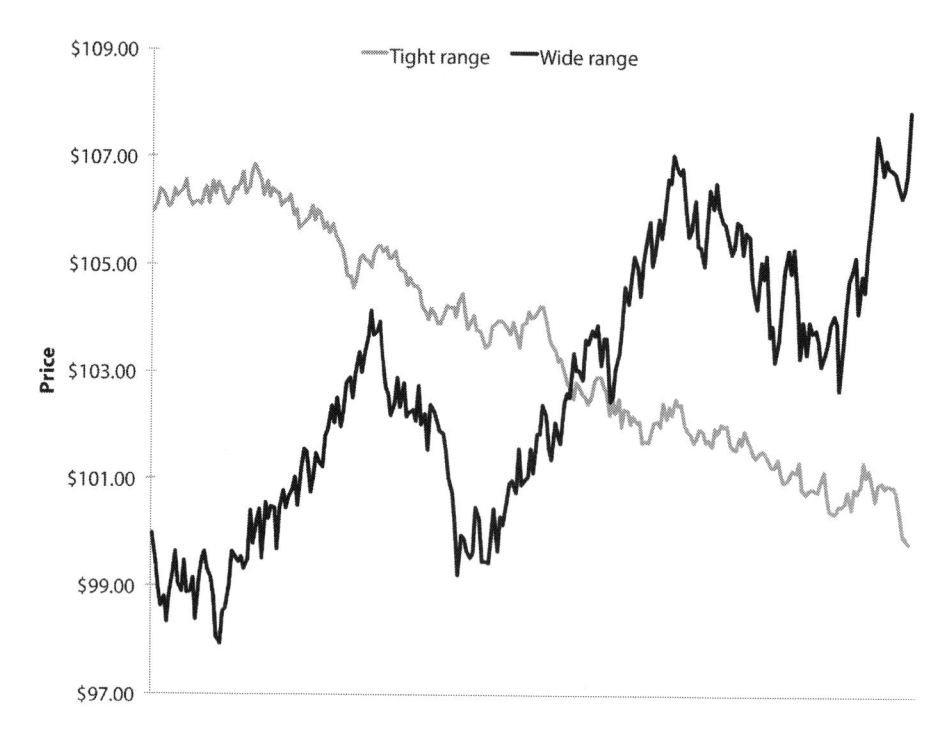

Figure 8.7 Trend channel width impacts the trade characteristics.

A trader attempting to participate in the tight downtrend would face relatively small consequences from suboptimal execution but would face an increased risk of being stopped out by a relatively small fluctuation in absolute dollar terms. Trading the wide uptrend would require good position entry and exit and an ability to tolerate significant P&L swings within the trend channel.

A trader deploying a momentum strategy is taking advantage of structural imbalance in the market that is manifesting as a protracted price response. The trader's goal is to ride the trend for as long as possible, and the focus must be on understanding when and under what conditions the motivating force may dissipate. The trader must also maintain good stop discipline around trend channel breaches and prior high/low violations that would signal that the trend is at an end.

3. Range-Trading Strategies – A Market Not Going Anywhere

If the trader has become convinced that the price is stuck between two levels she may attempt to trade the range, repeatedly buying and selling as the market goes back and forth between support and resistance. Though trading ranges are most often initially noticed on a chart, they are not purely technical phenomena, and the more fundamental information the trader can bring to bear, the easier it is to justify calling what can seem like an arbitrary turning point.

Chapter 8 - Directional Trading Strategies

As seen in Chapter 4, a trading range is a consolidation pattern where the market becomes trapped between two approximately equal, sustained buying and selling interests, as seen in the following chart.

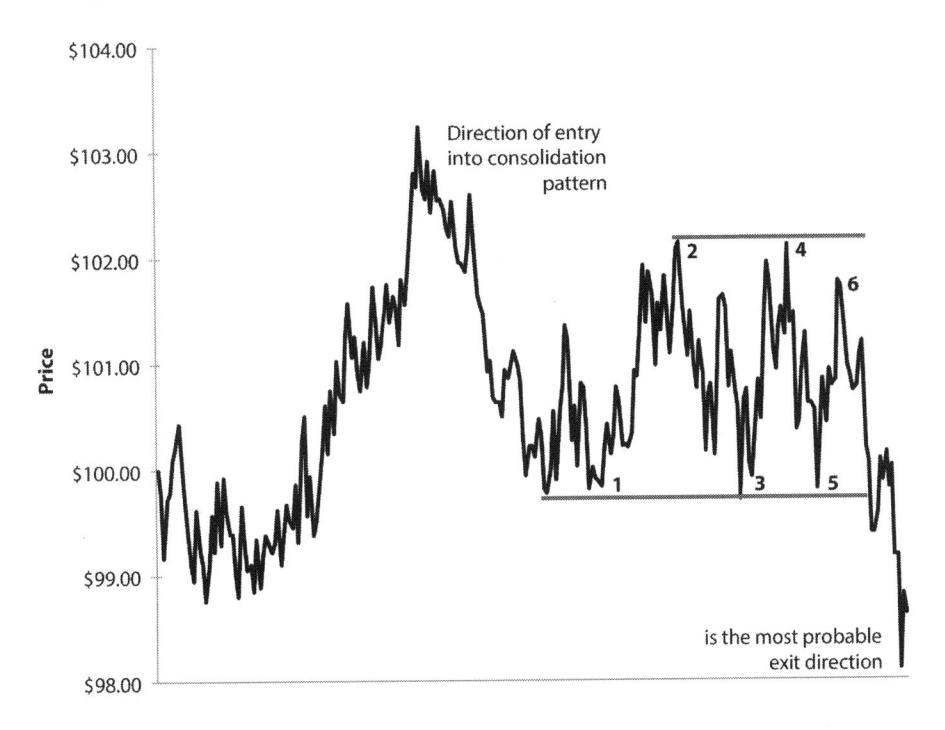

Figure 8.8 Range trading strategy in a consolidating market.

A trading range may have a well-defined uptrend or downtrend leading into the pattern. The trader must take the pre-range price action (if there is any of note) into consideration, as it will impact both the probable breakout direction and influence the speed of movement in the direction of the trend.

In this example the market approaches the $100.00 support level and $102.00 resistance level three times each, for a total of six movements. The trader must first wait for the range to define itself by making at least one bottom and top, more realistically two of each. It is possible to approach a range-bound market with varying degrees of aggression, which can manifest in a variety of trading plans.

The most conservative approach would involve starting from a flat position, waiting for the range to define itself with two tops and two bottoms, then selling after each turn off the top at $102.00 and buying back the short position as the price nears $100.00. The trader is positioned with the pre-range trend at all times, selling after the top of the range is re-defined then buying before the bottom is tested. This yields one to two tradable moves, #4 and #6.

If the trader was fortunate enough to maintain a core short position prior to the market becoming range-bound, he can add at the top of the range, then buy the incremental position back at the bottom of the range. This strategy is more vulnerable to a break higher (as there is a constant short exposure), but avoids lost opportunity costs from being flat in a break lower, as happens after the break and retest following #6. Having a core position with the trend can lead to greater participation, as the trader is more committedly bearish and will tend to add before the trend has completely defined itself, yielding two to three tradable moves (#4 and #6, and possibly #2) plus the profits from the core short position.

The trader can also attempt to catch both sides of the market's fluctuations by buying at the bottom of the range, selling out of that length and getting short at the top, and riding the short down to the bottom of the range before closing the short and re-instituting a long position at the bottom. This aggressive approach attempts to capture 100% of the price action. The biggest risk is the ever-present potential for the market to break higher or lower out of the range with the trader holding exactly the wrong position, long in a falling market or short in a rising market. This yields two to four tradable moves (#5 and #6 after the range is fully defined; #3 and #4 if the trader jumps the gun a little).

The riskiest strategy would involve starting from a flat position once the range is established and buying local lows, then closing the position at the top. The downside is that the trader is exposed to wrong-way risk relative the to pre-consolidation trend if the market breaks out to the downside. This yields one to two tradable moves (#5 and possibly #3 for an aggressive trader) and the strong possibility of not getting out of the #5 trade (as it did not make it all the way back up to the top of the channel and might not have reached a sale level) and riding the position downward into a loss.

The primary risk of a range-trading strategy is that the boundary conditions fail and the market gaps higher or lower, leaving the trader on the wrong side of a breakout trade. The trader must be aware of the technical levels and of what constitutes a range break, and be ready to be very decisive in mitigating the risk if caught out by an unexpected move.

Chapter 8 - Directional Trading Strategies

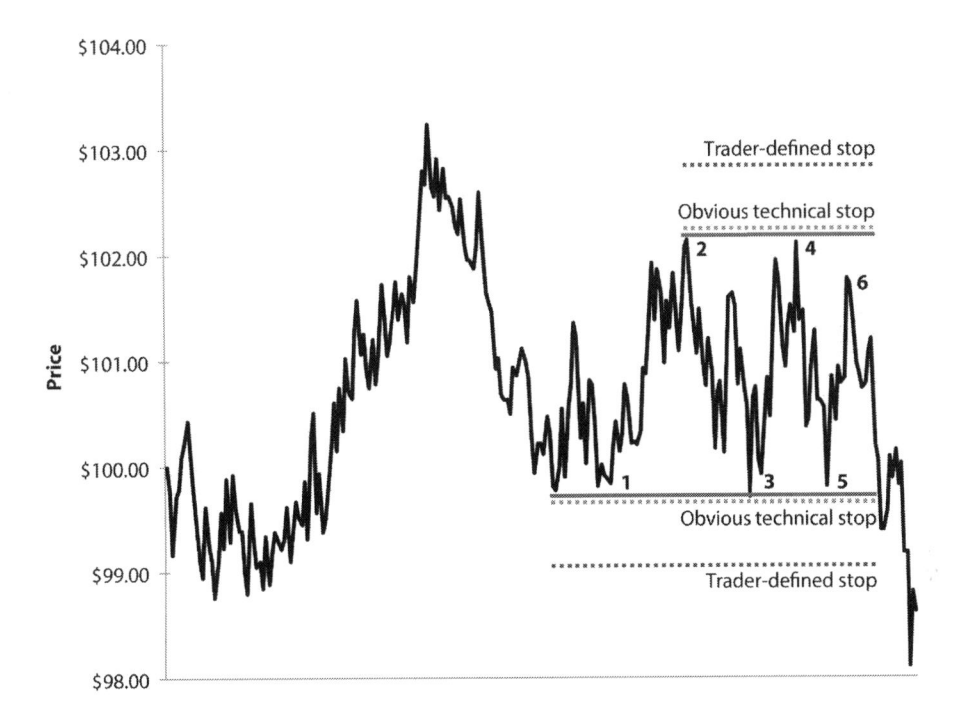

Figure 8.9   Setting stop-losses for range trading a consolidating market.

The trader-defined stop will need to be a small fraction of the trading range to create a productive risk-reward relationship and justify the exposure. Products with good liquidity, small bid/offer spreads and small tick-to-tick price differentials will permit the trader to employ a tighter stop, leading to a better risk-to-reward relationship and a more favorable trade.

Regardless of her chosen aggression level, the trader must establish or modify her position shortly before or immediately after the market encounters the support or resistance level and begins to retrace. Waiting until the chart has made a clear move significantly away from either boundary will increase the probability of a successful trade, but will significantly degrade the risk-reward characteristics when measured relative to the trader-defined stop and the price target formed by the opposite support or resistance level.

Unlike a trend or a breakout, with a range there is only so much money to be made. The wider the range, the more tradable it is. The bid-offer spread present in the market and the tick-to-tick differentials must also be a sufficiently small percentage of the expected range so as not to degrade the risk-reward calculus. When trading a well-defined range the trader has the opportunity to be a liquidity provider and earn the bid-offer spread by posting bids to buy at the bottom of the range and offers to sell at the top. This market making activity will both help facilitate execution and define the top or bottom of the range.

Trading a range is, in many ways, calling a series of small market turns that are created by boundary conditions, some of which are easily observed, like prior highs and lows, and others of which are more ephemeral, like the forward extrapolation of a trend line or support and resistance levels. Traders must learn to understand how the market acts when approaching, at, and beyond a boundary level. The difference between a breakout and the continuation of a trading range is how the market acted in that critical interstitial zone. Every trading range is a series of failed breakouts, and every breakout is a trading range or pattern ended by a compelling motive force. Traders must learn to sharpen their focus as the market approaches a critical trend line, support, or resistance level, taking in all of the available information to determine if the market is going to break out or retrace. To understand the difference, a trader must study how markets act at a turn.

4. Market Turns, Retracements, and Reversals

Understanding how a particular market changes direction is critical for every trading strategy. Turns, retracements, reversals,[40] and the creation of top and bottom patterns all involve a market changing direction, but differ in the magnitude of the potential movement and the implications for the chart as a whole:

1. A turn is the act of changing direction, and in so doing, making a local peak or valley on the chart.
2. A retracement within a trend is a move back to or toward an established support, resistance, Fibonacci level, or other technical feature of a chart.
3. A reversal breaks through an established support or resistance level or eclipses a prior high or low, with implications for the viability of the established trend.
4. A top or bottom is a definitive ending of a trend in motion, and has potential implications for the chart as a whole.

Markets can change directions for fundamental reasons, technical factors, or a combination of both.

Fundamental reasons for a change in the market direction:

- The market price has dropped below the incremental production cost for the product, reducing the supply offered to the market and potentially motivating a wave of financial short covering.
- The market has rallied to a level that brings on new supply, allowing hedgers to push volume into the market to lock in forward margins.
- A material change in the non-price factors that make up the supply/demand balance.

Technical factors for a change in the market direction:

---

[40] I am semantically differentiating a retracement from a reversal, but many traders use the terms interchangeably. I feel that there is enough nuance to warrant the additional clarity.

Chapter 8 - Directional Trading Strategies

- The market has approached a robust, well-defined trend line that has survived multiple prior tests.
- The market has reached an established support or resistance level, or re-approaches a penetrated support/resistance level that has switched significance and is now a resistance/support level.
- The market arrives at a congestion level of substantial prior trading activity, allowing previously incorrect traders to exit at near breakeven.
- The market is oversold or overbought relative to a Bollinger Band, Fibonacci level, moving average, or other technical study.

Consider the following graph, which shows the trending market previously seen in Figure 8.6 overlaid with a similarly scaled head-and-shoulders pattern that emerges out of a nearly identical trajectory. Based on the technical analysis techniques in Chapter 4, at what point was it possible to say that the market was possibly experiencing a turn, retracement, reversal, and, ultimately, had made a top?

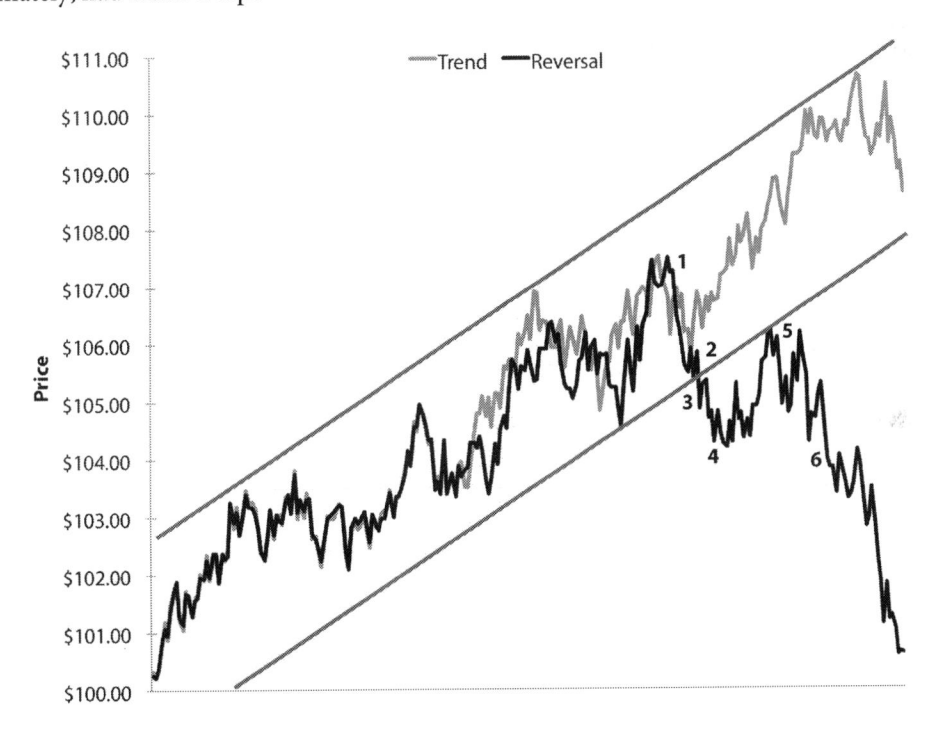

Figure 8.10   Identifying a trend break that evolves into a reversal.

Examining the price action, the market:

1. Makes a turn off the most recent local high.
2. Accelerates toward the bottom of the trend channel, indicating a probable retracement to support.

3. Breaks the bottom of the trend channel, indicating that the market may be in for a more serious reversal.
4. Takes out a prior low, and is now by definition no longer in a technical uptrend.
5. Rallies to test the bottom of the trend channel, which should be expected to function as resistance. Finds resistance and sells off, making a lower high.
6. Takes out the prior low at (4), and is now making lower highs and lower lows, which is the definition of a downtrend. Also, in doing so, forms a solid looking head and shoulders reversal pattern with a measurement objective of $100.50. The market has made a top.

As clearly illustrated by Figure 8.10, arbitrarily picking a point on a trend in motion and initiating a countertrend position is foolish. Waiting for a reversal signal/pattern will improve the trader's odds of success, which can be well worth the cost of giving away some portion of the potential move.

Market Turns
There are a number of technical indicators and non-technical signs that a trader can observe that indicate the potential for a market to turn back against its prior direction.

One-Day/One-Period Technical Signals of A Market Turn
Two extremely useful indicators of an imminent market turn are the hammer/hanging man candlestick pattern and the outside day up/outside day down. Both provide very strong, short-term reads into market sentiment.

The Hammer and The Hanging Man
The hammer is a unique one-period indicator that comes from a sub-discipline of technical analysis called candlestick charting. Candlestick charting focuses on recognizing small, highly specific combinations of up and down days in the price data in an attempt to divine the market sentiment and reaction to very recent history. There are a number of constructive reversal patterns; in my experience, the most pragmatically useful is the hammer, a one-day or one-period pattern created by a down-trending market that opens, immediately trades materially lower, then rallies to settle almost unchanged as a slight winner or loser on the day (winner or loser is irrelevant to the validity of the pattern).

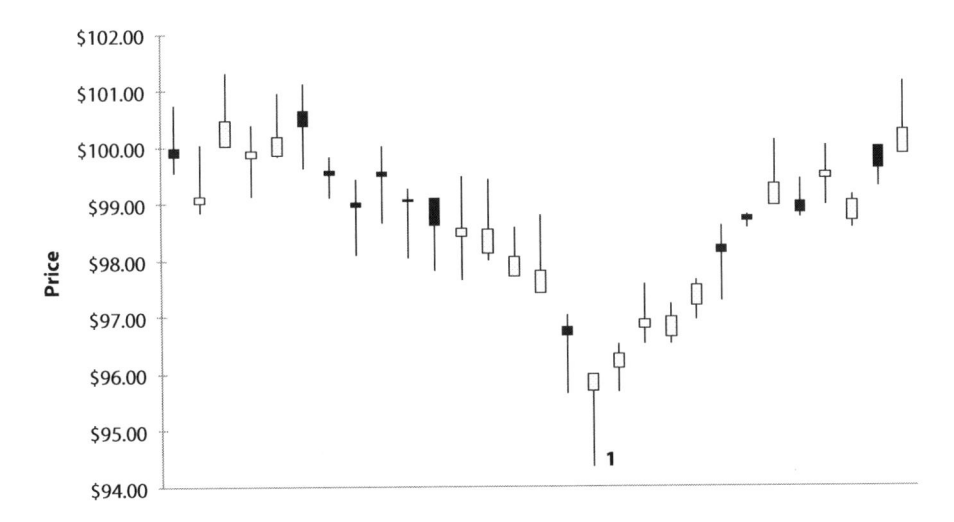

Figure 8.11 The hammer (1) one-period reversal indicator.

The result is an elongated intraday range bar with a compact open-close range at the top, which looks like the head of a hammer (1). The hammer forms in a market that has given up and sells off until it finds real, significant buying interest that triggers a powerful rally back to near breakeven. This is referred to as "hammering out a bottom." It does not matter if the market finishes net up or down, only that it has faced a significant sell-off and defeated it within the trading day.

The same one-period pattern can also signal a top after a multi-period rally, where the market opens a new high and traverses a wide intraday range, only to close slightly below its peak, disappointing long-side players. This topping indicator is referred to as a hanging man.

The Outside Day Up / Outside Day Down
Another powerful one-day reversal indicator is the outside day, which can manifest in either an upward or downward direction. An outside day down is created when the market opens higher than the previous day's range, then proceeds to sell off during the day to close below the prior day's range (1). The market's initial bullish impetus is beaten down throughout the day and ultimately reversed into a bearish close, and as such is a very powerful refutation of both the prior trading activity and the uptrend as a whole. An outside day up is the exact opposite, where a lower open is turned upward intraday to close bullishly higher (2).

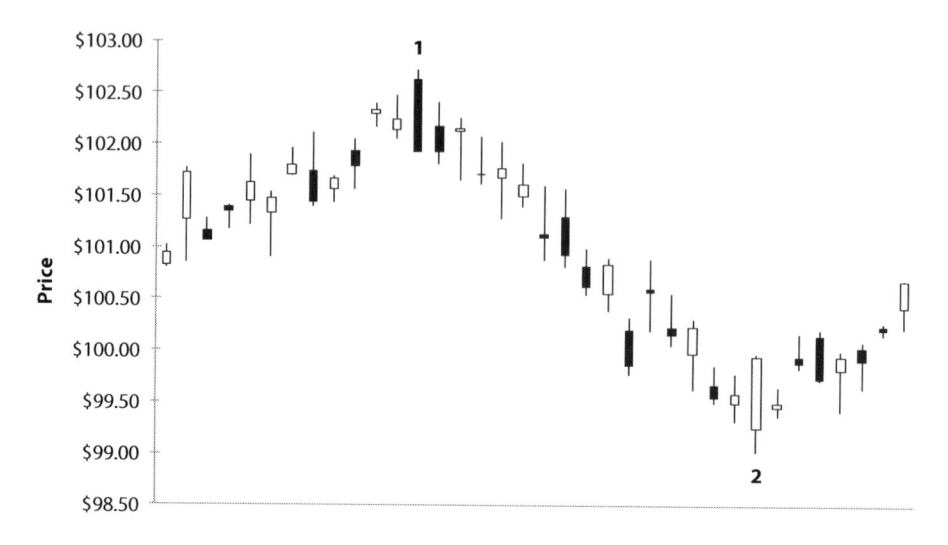

Figure 8.12 Outside day down (1) and outside day up (2) one-period reversal indicators.

An outside day is conceptually similar to the hammer, but differs by starting with a gap beyond the prior day's range that is reversed. An outside day is a symptom of a market move that is exuberant, but running out of steam and lacking real strength, which is revealed when a strong opposing force emerges and ultimately defeats and negates the momentum.

Non-Technical Signs That a Market Is Ready to Make a Turn
In the absence of a well-defined technical pattern, support or resistance, or other robust indicator, there are a number of signals that traders will look for to get a sense if a market is ready to make a turn:

1. Thinning volume and lack of participation.
2. Buyer/seller fatigue.
3. A shift in motivation between buyers and sellers, or more balance in interest.
4. Progress becomes harder to make after a period of easy transition.

1. Thinning Volume and Lack of Participation.
It is very common for volume to drop precipitously at market turns. This can be the result of a sharp, violent blow-off top or capitulation bottom, where losing traders exit their positions en masse, creating a spike in volume that clears out a significant percentage of the total open interest in the market. The next day (or days) the market is a ghost town with a price that has been pushed significantly higher or lower than normal, which often motivates fresh money to come in off the sidelines to bet on a reversion to the mean.

Chapter 8 - Directional Trading Strategies

2. Buyer or Seller Fatigue.

Buyer or seller fatigue is a result of one side of the market being unwilling or unable to chase the other higher or lower. Consider the following chart of a rally running out of steam over the course of an hour, with the bid-offer spread represented by gray squares (for market bids) and black squares (for market offers):

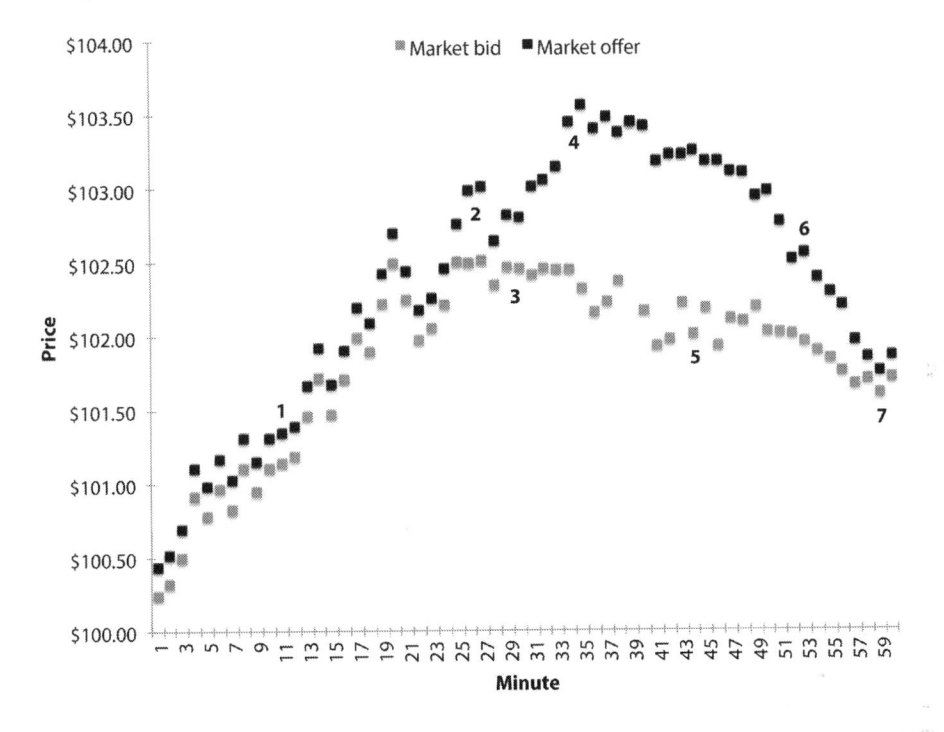

Figure 8.13 Post-rally buyer fatigue.

Stepping through the price action point by point:

1. The market is trading fairly normally, moving higher with reasonably tight bid-offer spreads and small minute-to-minute price differentials.
2. The sellers become aware that the market is in an uptrend and they have the psychological upper hand, which they attempt to use to extract extra value by backing up their offers to see if they will get lifted by an over-zealous buyer. This widens the bid-offer spread, making transactions more costly and difficult to achieve.
3. The buyers in the market refuse to pay more than $102.50.
4. The offers become greedy. The bid-offer spread widens precipitously, and the number of transactions decreases sharply as players without a vested interest refuse to jump across the spread.
5. The buyers in the market continue to be firm in their desire to not pay past $102.50. Some become disinterested, realizing that there are no willing sellers, and either remove their bids or back up, further widening the bid-offer spread.

6. The sellers realize that they have misinterpreted the level of motivation present in the population of buyers. As they do want to sell, they begin to drop their offers lower, which leads to sellers jumping in front of each other in line to get at the now demotivated buyers who see the offers dropping and sense that the tide may be turning back in their direction.
7. Motivated sellers finally drop their offers to a point where genuine buying interest returns. Transaction volumes increase once the bid-offer spread reaches reasonable levels.

These type of back-and-forth shifts in momentum happen continuously in every market, and reading and responding—or being smart or disciplined enough not to respond—to the current conditions is a large part of a directional trader's job.

3. A Shift in Motivation Between Buyers and Sellers

Shifts in momentum can be more subtly felt in the relative aggression levels of the buyers and sellers. Assuming a relatively constant, fair bid-offer spread is continuously present in the market (a marked contrast to the prior example), at any particular time are the buyers jumping across the spread to transact, or are the sellers willing to give up the margin to execute? This phenomenon has short-term self-reinforcing psychological characteristics. Most trading screens differentiate trades that are higher or lower than the prior print, and many will indicate if it was a bid that was hit or an offer that was lifted. Voice brokers will convey the same information in a much more dramatic fashion as they yell "Bid out! Gets hit! I still sell! Is anyone a buyer?" Players needing to buy or sell can easily be panicked into action.

This relative level of buyer or seller motivation is a tradable indicator. Consider the following chart that depicts transactions where the offer is lifted as black squares, transactions where the bid is hit as gray squares, and the running net balance between the two as a dashed line on the right axis:

Chapter 8 - Directional Trading Strategies

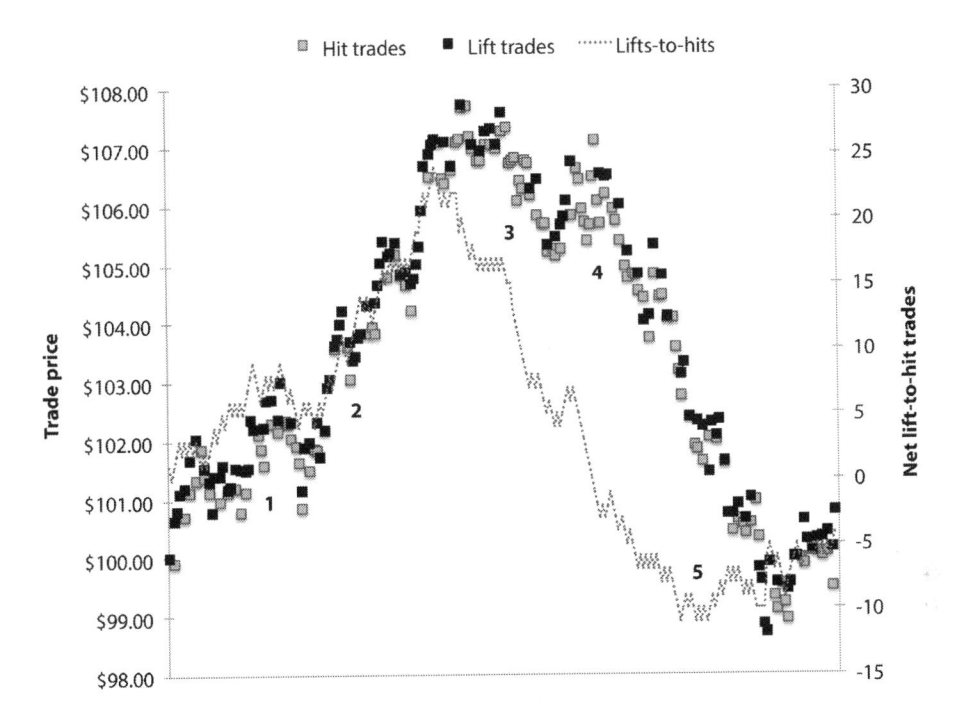

Figure 8.14 The relative balance between hit and lift transactions as a sentiment indicator.

The market begins in relative balance (1), but soon buying interest starts to overwhelm the selling interest as the move from $100.00 to $108.00 gains momentum (2). At the peak, the buying and selling interest become much more balanced, with an increase in bids hit after the market peak at (3). When the market breaks to $105.00 and fails to rally past $107.00 (4), the sellers return in force and overwhelm the buying interest, as can be seen by both the linear decline to $99.00 and the negative net balance in the number of buyers vs. sellers (5). After the market finds support at $99.00 and begins to chop back and forth, the buying and selling interest again becomes relatively balanced.

Traders rarely have the luxury of a chart showing recent net buying and selling interest in this fashion (it would not be possible in most markets), but they do develop a keen feel for the localized sentiment as an indicator of market momentum. Transitions from a world of aggressive buyers or sellers to a more balanced trading action can signal a period of consolidation or presage a market turn.

4. Progress Becomes Difficult. The opposite of buyer/seller fatigue occurs when an enthusiastic group of participants in a trending market run headlong into a lurking band of equally or more enthusiastic traders willing to get involved in the opposite direction. This is very common when the price hits a level at which hedgers become motivated, or a point on a price chart that represented a significant volume of prior trading activity that forms a support, resistance, or

congestion level. If a large natural had decided to be a seller of a significant volume of hedges at $107.00, the previous example might have looked more like this:

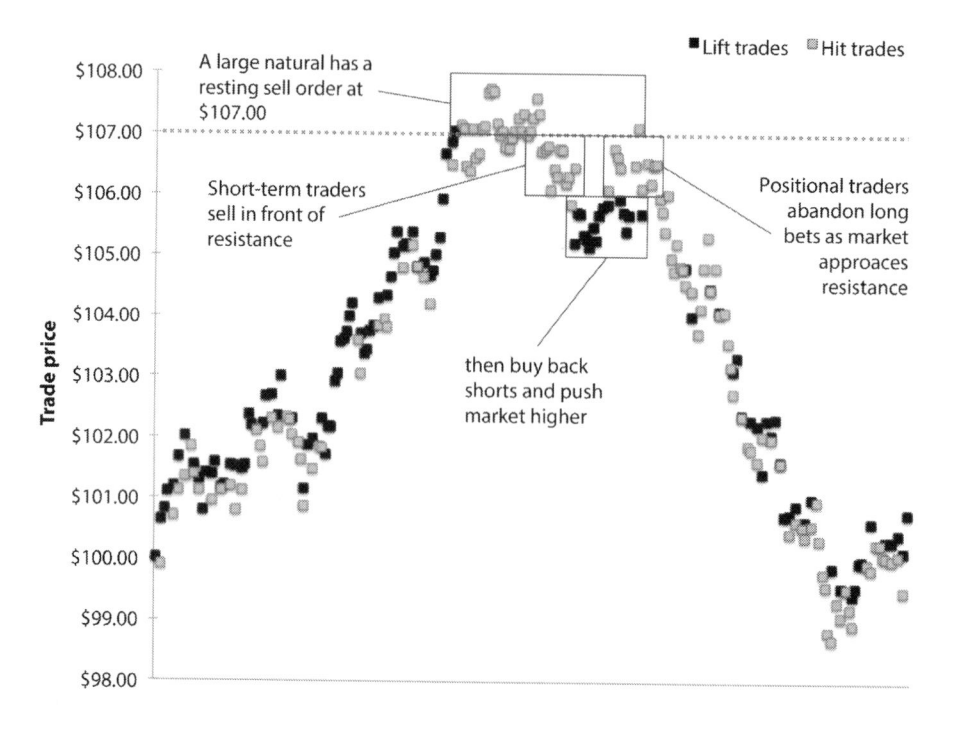

Figure 8.15 Concentrated selling interest as an impediment to an in-progress move.

The market has a relatively even distribution of buy and sell transactions during the rally from $100.02 to $106.88. Then, the market prints a trade at $107.05, triggering the natural's sell order. The next 39 consecutive trades are a flurry of bids getting hit until the price retreats back below the natural's $107.00 price target. There is a brief dip as short-term traders recognize the presence of a strong offer at $107.00 and jump in front of the natural's interest, selling in the mid-$106s and buying the positions back starting in the mid-$105s. The short-term buying interest moves the market back up into the mid-$106s, where positional traders who have been buying since $100.02 throw in the towel ahead of the probable resistance at $107.00 and start selling, turning the market decisively lower and starting an elongated move back to the initial levels.

Many of the turn indicators are intraday phenomena that can only be observed in real-time by a focused individual. This is one area where knowing the market conditions is critical, and simply checking in periodically to see what's going on simply will not do.

Market Retracements & Reversals

As discussed in Chapter 4 – Technical Analysis, a retracement is a non-destructive turn back against a defined trend, frequently as a result of price action that has gotten ahead of itself and become locally cheap or expensive. A retracement will traverse back to the nearest support line, trend channel, etc. and then either stop and consolidate or turn back toward the direction of the macro trend. A reversal is, effectively, a more destructive form of retracement where the price action violates a support, resistance, or trend line and/or takes out a prior high or low. Reversing a trend requires the cessation or exhaustion of the primary driver(s), or encountering a decisively stronger counter force at a particular price point. A significant reversal that gathers strength can ultimately evolve into a top or bottom, ending the trend completely and changing the conversation about the market entirely.

Market Tops & Bottoms
Market tops and bottoms can form in a variety of ways. They can emerge as slowly constructed consolidation patterns like rounding tops and bottoms, well-defined reversal patterns like a head and shoulders, and as low-volume, short-duration, v-bottom spikes caused by capitulation selling or blow-off tops due to panic buying. Each calls for a different approach:

1. Slowly emerging consolidation patterns offer an abundance of time for the trader to accumulate a position, but can prove unproductive if the market lacks an obvious, imminent trigger to jolt prices out of the pattern and motivate losing traders to exit positions.
2. Well-defined patterns like head and shoulders patterns have a high degree of tradability. As with any technical pattern, the trader must wait for it to fully form to have any predictive validity and then take into consideration the implied measurement objectives relative to any pre-existing support or resistance levels.
3. Sharp, spiky highs and lows caused by panic in the market can be extremely challenging to trade. The top or bottom can form very rapidly, and may traverse a wide range of prices on very low volume. Attempting to buy or sell a spike bottom or top requires an extremely high level of conviction and a willingness to stomach a potentially significant short-term swing if the trader is not somehow prescient enough to pick the exact high or low. Typically, the trader will have to decide on a level and hang out a bid or offer and hope that the market reaches his price.

A trader immersed in the ebb and flow of the market can much more easily contextualize the manner in which it changes direction, allowing her to distinguish between a meaningless series of turns caused by transitory imbalances in buying and selling pressure, a more meaningful retracement to support or resistance, or a reversal or top/bottom with potentially serious consequences for the chart as whole.

Constructing a Directional Trade
Directional trades are relatively straightforward to construct, once the trader has developed a view of the market. The value add, and what separates the good from the unemployed, are the nuances that add value, save money on execution, and protect against unnecessary losses.

Directional Trading Instruments

The advantage of being a Neanderthal is that any rock or stick can be used as a tool. Traders with a number of potential implementation instruments must evaluate which will yield the best response to the intended stimulus. Directional traders typically prefer instruments with linear risk characteristics and the maximum available liquidity. There is generally an evolution of the instruments used to express trades in the benchmark product that matches the evolution of the market as a whole, as seen in Chapter 2. Each has advantages and disadvantages.

Physical Products

Physical trades result in direct counterparty exposures that will necessitate pre-existing contract and credit relationships and can restrict the ability of the trader to efficiently enter and exit positions. This structural friction can make risk-reward assessment challenging and erode a significant portion of the value inherent in a transaction. In the early days of a market a physical position may be the only avenue for expressing a view, and traders may have to choose between a suboptimal position and none at all.

Forward Contracts

While still constrained by counterparty credit and contractual obligations, the open interest and transaction volume for paper products will typically be significantly larger than the physical market, leading to a greater ability to modify exposures.

Futures Contracts

Futures offer the trader standardized products with clearinghouse protection and a relatively high level of anonymity. The drawbacks include increased regulation, oversight, and potentially onerous or restrictive position limits for very large firms. Liquidity will tend to be concentrated in the front few months. Expiry conditions can increase the volatility of front month positions in the last days of a contract's life, as low liquidity and open interest combined with a need to execute to close positions exacerbates swings in price.

Swaps

Once evolved, the swap market should offer massive liquidity with no mandatory volumetric linkage to an underlying physical market. The biggest early-stage problem will be not having credit in place with sufficient counterparties to ensure access to the best bids and offers, which will ultimately be solved by a centralized clearing function.

Options

The loss-limiting characteristics of a long option position offer a huge advantage, which will be explored in greater depth in Chapter 10. Paying rent via the premium required to hold the position in a stagnant market is a drawback, as is the need to earn back the cost of the option(s) before starting to accumulate a profit, forcing the trader to not only be right about the direction, but also the timing and magnitude.

The type of strategy the trader is intending to pursue (breakout, trend, range, or reversal) and the scope (in time) and scale (in magnitude) of the anticipated market move will narrow the list of potentially usable instruments. The longer the time horizon and holding period and the greater the magnitude of the anticipated move, the wider the range of usable instruments. Short holding periods and/or small anticipated price moves mandate maximum liquidity and low transaction costs.

Determining the Risk and Reward Components of a Directional Trade
The trader's development of the market risk-to-reward ratio involved a detailed, unbiased evaluation of the potential rewards and the probable risks given the fundamental information, the technical analysis, and the current volatility and risk characteristics. The market risk-to-reward ratio defines a large probability space, within which the trader constructs trading strategies with unique risk-to-reward ratios that are subsets of the whole. The market risk-to-reward ratio describes what the market could do; the strategic risk-to-reward ratios define what the trader will allow the position to do.

The trader must take into consideration the inherent limitations of the market risk-to-reward ratio when defining the parameters of each potential strategic implementation:

- If the trader has a market-defined upside, he will have to self-define an appropriately proportional downside.
- If the trader has a market-defined downside, he will have to self-define an appropriately proportional upside.
- With no impediments in either direction and only a relative up/down probability to guide him, the trader will have to carve a risk-to-reward relationship out of thin air.

Market-defined upside and downside constraints will typically only be present in periods of unusually high/low prices, or in the presence of an unusually robust fundamental barrier to price evolution in a particular direction. The vast majority of the time, the trader will have to derive the strategy risk-to-reward relationship based on the market risk-to-reward ratio and their sense of the fundamental information and technical analysis of the recent price action. Deriving stops and profit targets and developing an implementation plan will be covered in Chapter 12 – Evaluating Trades & Developing a Trading Plan.

Directional Trading for Hedgers
The utility of directional trading strategies to a hedger will depend on the nature of the firm's primary risk(s), the liquidity present in the market(s) to modify exposures, the accounting flexibility available to the firm, and the commitment of the senior management.

The primary risk(s) to a hedger can be one-factor, two-factor, or multi-factor:

1. A plant with fixed inputs costs but a variable market price for finished output would have one risk factor—the price paid for finished goods.
2. A plant with variable input costs and fluctuating prices for finished output would have two-factor risk. Simultaneously mitigating both the inputs and outputs of the system requires some form of spread trading, which will be covered extensively in Chapter 9.

3. A plant with variable input costs and fluctuating prices paid for finished output that also experienced volatility on the costs of manufacturing would have multi-factor risk.

Depending on the relative volatilities and correlations of the input(s) and output(s), and the cost(s) of the process, a directional hedge can increase or decrease the initial level of risk. Determining the performance characteristics of an incremental position on the totality of the firm's portfolio can require quantitative tools and risk management processes that the natural may be unwilling or unable to contemplate. Putting on a risk-reducing hedge position can feel like directional trading to senior management, and will force the firm to deal with accounting, disclosure, reporting, and margin considerations that can bring a great deal of investor and regulatory scrutiny.

The liquidity available in the market can greatly impact the ability of a natural to mitigate exposures. For most players this is not a problem, but the largest companies or medium-sized firms operating in nascent or illiquid products often cannot simply rapidly accumulate or distribute a meaningful quantity of hedges without materially distorting prices.

Adventurous hedgers often utilize directional trading strategies to "enhance returns" or "optimize the portfolio" by intentionally over- or under-hedging their exposures in an attempt to catch intermediate or long-term trends in their input or output products. If the firm is lucky or skilled enough to catch a price move with an uncovered exposure they will re-set the hedge position and lock in profits by returning the system back to its initial state. This can be a profitable strategy in markets with defined trends or sizable and frequent enough fluctuations to justify the costs. Aggressive portfolio optimization can edge uncomfortably close to outright speculative activity for many managers, a line that is frequently visible only in retrospect.

Directional Trading for Financials
Directional trading at a financial can be done on a proactive proprietary or reactive customer-driven basis. Most large financial institutions will have a dedicated directional trader for each product that is required to make markets and quote prices for both internal and external clients. The directional trader's job is to bring order out of chaos, sourcing positions to balance the option desk's exposure and hedges for the origination desk's structured products, and aggregating the firm's deal flow to present one consistent transactional face to the market. This trader is usually said to be running the "flat price," "delta one," or financial book, and the poor unfortunate doing it usually looks like a battle scene extra from *All Quiet On the Western Front*, with less mud and more shell shock.

Proactively, a bank or insurance company may have a proprietary desk that leverages the existing analytical resources and the transactional knowledge gained from customer dealing to put on speculative directional positions in the market. Proprietary trading was once massively in fashion, but has fallen out of favor with new regulations designed to curtail speculative excess at financial institutions.

Chapter 8 - Directional Trading Strategies

Directional Trading for Merchants
Hedgers occupy a particular market niche, but generally lack financial sophistication. Financials are sophisticated generalists capable of operating in all markets to service the needs of their clients. Merchants are niche market experts with financial sophistication. Merchants typically make their most significant directional bets through their initial decisions around acquiring or divesting control of assets, then engage in hedging or enhancement and/or optimization trades during the lifetime of the transaction. Where hedgers might be disinclined to lock in a risk-enhancing leg of a spread-based physical position, merchants have no such qualms.

Directional Trading for Speculators
Directional trading is the most elemental means of taking risk, and is popular with every type of speculator, from individuals trading one-lots of agricultural futures to giant hedge funds riding multi-billion dollar exposures. Most speculative entities are extremely sensitive to their costs of funding, and may choose to use spread positions or long option strategies as leveraged, credit- and collateral-efficient exposures in lieu of the most standard forward, futures, or swaps.

Chapter Eight Summary

Directional trading is not about guessing which way the market is going and making a lucky buy or sell transaction. A directional position gives the trader direct, linear exposure to the totality of market fluctuations, and can be employed to catch a breakout from a well-defined pattern, range-trade a market that has become trapped between support and resistance, participate in a trend in motion, or seek to identify a market reversal and play the anticipated counter-move. Directional exposures demand the most from a trader, as without any inherent self-hedging or loss-limiting characteristics the full responsibility for mitigating risk lies with the trader.

Good directional traders are completely immersed in the market, as that level of focus is mandatory to sense a shift in momentum around a market turn, read the signs that differentiate a viable trend from an imminent reversal, and execute with maximum dispatch when a market breaks out higher or lower. These fundamental skills will be prerequisites for contemplating the more complex exposures that follow in Chapter 9 – Spread Trading Strategies.

Review Questions

1. Describe three advantages and disadvantages of directional trading.
2. How does the prevailing volatility impact directional trading strategies?
3. Why are directional strategies not limit-efficient?
4. Describe the four common directional trading strategies.
5. What are the four signs that a market is likely to turn?
6. What are the unique challenges to defining the risk and reward for a directional trade?

Resources

- *Reminiscences of a Stock Operator* by Edwin Lefèvre
- *Market Wizards: Interviews with Top Traders* by Jack D. Schwager
- *The New Market Wizards: Conversations with America's Top Traders* by Jack Schwager
- *Pit Bull: Lessons from Wall Street's Champion Day Trader* by Martin Schwartz

Case Study: Product X Directional Trading Strategies

Based on the trader's view on the evolution of the fundamental environment anticipated in the base case and the inflection points contained in the event path, the Product X market offers opportunities for two types of directional trades:

1. An explosion-type, non-technical break higher based on a fundamental triggering event early in the event path, most likely the African processing plant not returning to service in February.
2. Regardless of the return or failure to return of the processing plant, the market will face increasing demand from China, the US, and Europe in April and July, which should create a productive environment for a bullish trend-following trade.

Best Instrument to Express a Directional View

There are a variety of instruments that the trader could employ to express either strategy, ranging from a physical purchase executed directly with a producer to a financially settled option priced off the US futures contract. Each will have relative advantages and/or disadvantages:

- A physical position or OTC forward at either a producing or consuming market could be a productive means of expressing a long view, but entering and exiting the exposure would require a large amount of local market knowledge and pre-established contractual and trading relationships. A firm not currently active in the space would face severe challenges, which would be felt in extreme amounts of slippage and a lack of transactional liquidity.
- Using a long call option position as a leveraged forward with a downside limited to the initial premium expenditure would be an extremely attractive strategy, presuming that there is a counterparty willing to take the other side of the transaction. As we will see in Chapter 10, this is a common problem in the option market, particularly in early- to mid-market development stages.
- The US ProdX futures market offers the best liquidity available in the market, coupled with the security of centralized clearing and financial settlement. Though the domestic market may not prove to be as explosively price responsive as physical products delivered to short-market areas, the trader should still be able to meaningfully participate in all across-the-board price increases.

The US ProdX futures seem to offer the best combination of tradability and responsiveness.

Location of the Exposure Given the Available Futures Contract Months

There are currently 13 months of ProdX futures contracts available to implement the trader's view, starting with FEB of the current year and extending through the FEB+1 of the following year. Not all contract months are created equal, with differences in responsiveness and relative utilities that depend on the type of view to be implemented and the nature of the directional strategy. The trader must take into consideration the usability of each individual contract, as well as the recent performance characteristics.

First, the trader should consider the major inflection points on the event path to help determine where on the curve to locate exposure. To capture a price response for a particular event the trader will have to utilize the futures contract for settlement in the following month, as there is no financial means of trading intramonth delivery. The (non)return to service of the African production plant is anticipated to (not) occur in February, and would most directly impact the MAR contract. Any March post-start ramp-up of the African plant would affect the APR contract. The increase in Chinese demand is expected in April and would first influence the MAY contract. Incremental need from the US and Europe is expected to come on line in July and would manifest itself in the price of the AUG contract.

It is also possible to use contracts further out on the curve to express a view on earlier inflection points (using a JUN or OCT contract to play the February return of the African production facility, for example), but with theoretically decreasing levels of liquidity and response to the stimulus event.

Second, the trader must examine how the curve has moved in response to stimulus and use that information to inform the decision of where on the curve to place exposures. Consider the following chart of the Product X forward curves at the market low in February, at the end of the year:

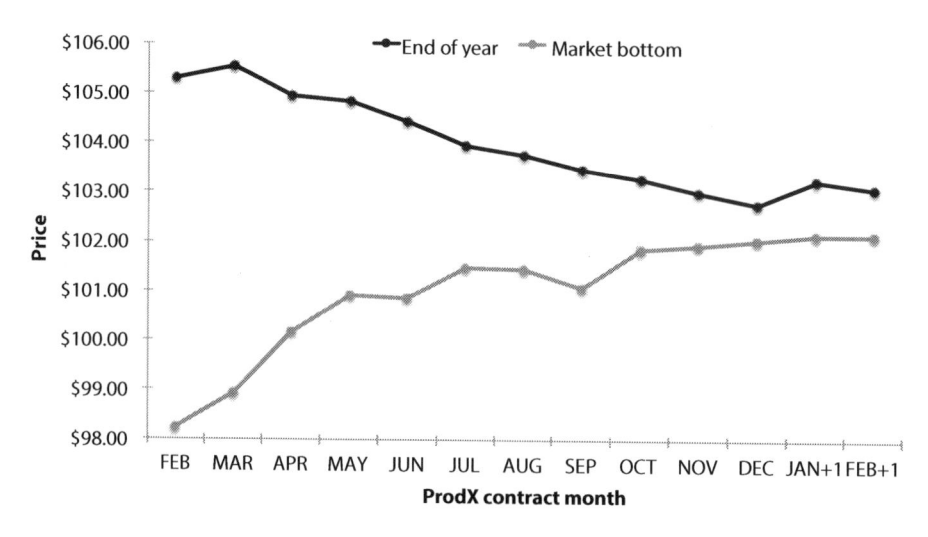

Figure 8.16 The ProdX futures forward curve at the market low and year-end.

Chapter 8 - Directional Trading Strategies

ProdX contract	Market bottom	End of year	Differential
FEB	$98.23	$105.29	$7.06
MAR	$98.94	$105.52	$6.59
APR	$100.16	$104.95	$4.79
MAY	$100.91	$104.82	$3.91
JUN	$100.87	$104.43	$3.56
JUL	$101.47	$103.96	$2.49
AUG	$101.44	$103.76	$2.32
SEP	$101.07	$103.48	$2.40
OCT	$101.87	$103.28	$1.41
NOV	$101.94	$103.02	$1.08
DEC	$102.03	$102.77	$0.74
JAN+1	$102.15	$103.25	$1.09
FEB+1	$102.16	$103.08	$0.92

Table 8.3 Comparing ProdX futures prices at market low and year-end.

The price response to the loss of the African production plant and the two unexpected increases in Chinese demand have been localized in the front of the curve, most dramatically in the first three months. In contrast, the relative lack of movement from the JUL contract onward could be an indication that market participants have interpreted the current tightness as short-term in nature, and are attempting to remedy the problem by bidding near-term prices high enough to flush out surplus material in the spot market. Looking at the year-end Product X supply stacks chart seen in Figure 3.11 it is clear that a $7.06 increase in price for the FEB contract (coupled with lesser responses in MAR and APR) will do little to incentivize producers. If the market needs to bring on incremental supply, and it certainly appears that it does, prices will have to rally across the curve to give producers an economic reason to ramp up and an ability to forward hedge, if they so choose.[41] It does not appear that the need for increased forward production has been priced into the market, either near term or in the forwards.

The relative lack of movement in the back of the curve is interesting with the October contract only moving $1.50 higher from the market low to the end-of-year peak and the further-out months barely averaging a $1.00 increase. This is worth considering for several reasons:

1. The back of the curve could offer better downside protection than the front. The front can drop $7.00, as it has proven, where the back of the curve has only ever been $1.00 lower than its current levels.

---

[41] One or two months of high prices will typically not be enough to incentivize a producer to bring on a new facility. To be profitable, the labor, materials, and other attendant start-up costs will need to be amortized over a longer period of time, and most producers think in terms of quarters and years, not months.

2. Back-of-the-curve prices should ultimately expire higher than the levels attainable by the front, as they will have more time to appreciate relative to the front and more ability to factor in what are expected to be bullish mid- to late-year developments.
3. Back-of-the-curve trades should benefit from lowest margin rates and lowest V@R, which could partially offset the extended holding period margin costs and the lack of liquidity.

By choosing a back-of-the-curve implementation, the trader would sacrifice liquidity and rapid price response for probable lower holding costs, greater upside potential and possibly a more limited downside. The front of the curve will be more trade-like, and the far forwards will be more investment-like, on a relative performance basis.

Taking Advantage of Directional Trading Flexibility: Position Timing

One main advantage of directional trading is an ability to control the timing of the exposure accumulation, distribution, and location on the curve to a much greater degree than possible with strategies like options or spreads that may require a great deal more patience in establishing a position and/or the assistance of market-making entities to enter and exit. The trader must take full advantage of this position timing flexibility to wring out every last bit of edge in the exposure.

The trader will want to be positioned prior to the major fundamental inflection points on the event path, the first being the February (non)return to service of the African processing plant. This gives the trader something like 20 business days to accumulate the desired exposure. Re-examining the FEB ProdX trend, targets, and support levels chart:

Figure 8.17 Pattern and trend analysis of the FEB ProdX chart.

Chapter 8 - Directional Trading Strategies

The Product X market is in a well-defined uptrend with a relatively high probability of a near-term pullback toward the bottom of the channel, which presents both a positioning challenge and an opportunity. A patient trader has up to 20 days to wait for a retracement to yield a better risk-reward entry point than currently available. The challenge arises from the fact that the trader does have a very strong fundamental view and desperately wants to be positioned.

- What the trader would ideally like to do is to buy the full size at S3 on Day 20 to get the best possible in-trend entry price and hold the position for the least amount of time to minimize the potential for exogenous events. The risk is that the price never gets to the S3 target level or that the triggering event (or some other circumstance) occurs earlier than anticipated, leaving the trader holding nothing as prices accelerate away.
- What the trader does not want to do is buy the full size at the current market price S1 on Day 1, potentially suffering the maximum P&L pain from a retracement and enduring the longest possible holding period exposed to event risk.
- What the trader really does not want is to not buy anything and watch prices rocket higher toward their fundamental target.

The question is not one of positioning, but of timing. The timing of accumulating and distributing positions will be discussed in much greater detail in Chapter 12 – Evaluating Trades and Creating A Trading Plan.

Trade Strategy #1: Short-Term Explosion Directional Trade
Long 1M notional tons, equivalent to 10,000 MAR ProdX futures to capture potentially extreme price response if/when African production plant does not return to service in February.

Position:	Long 1M notional tons, or 10,000 MAR ProdX futures.
Notional Dollars:	$105.52M
Initial Margin:	$10.55M
V@R:	$629k 1-Day V@R at 95%
	$888k 1-Day V@R at 99%

To determine the stop-losses and profit targets the trader must examine a chart of the MAR futures, which, while similar to the prompt FEB contract that has formed the basis of the analysis thus far, does have some differentiating nuances:

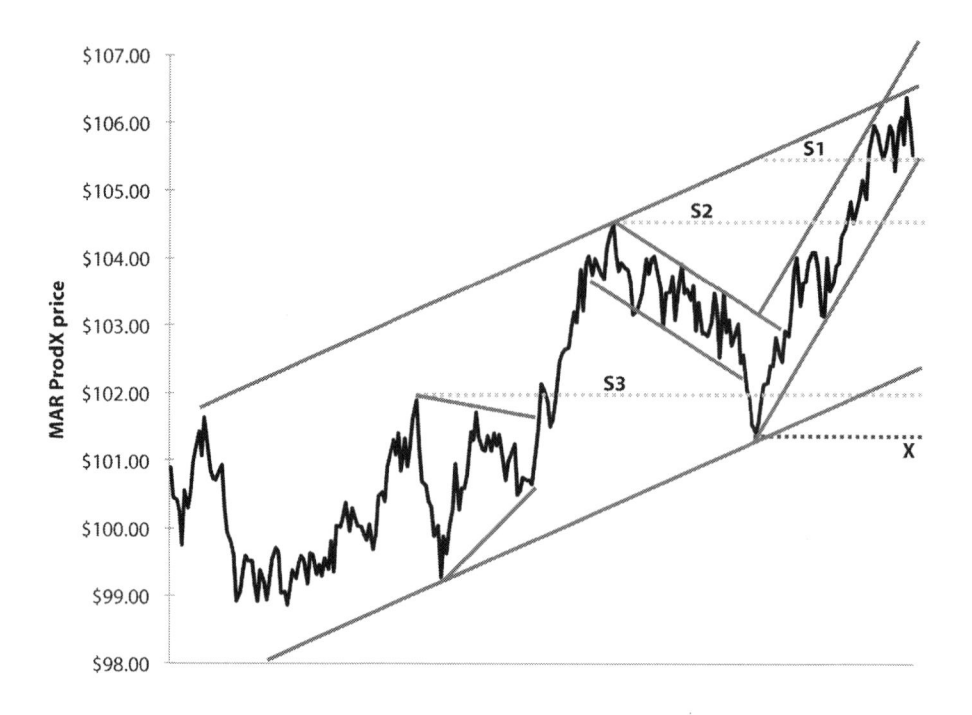

Figure 8.18 Pattern and trend analysis of the MAR ProdX chart.

The initial peak for the MAR contract is slightly higher than for the FEB, as is the subsequent trough, which in combination with the rest of the price action forms a slightly better-defined trend channel to the topside with slightly less clarity on the bottom. The trend channel as a whole is also moderately steeper, yielding a slight price differential between the bottom of the trend channel and the S3 support level defined by the top of the consolidation pattern. This increases the chances of a potentially short-term, non-fatal trend line break, which the trader will have to factor into the decision calculus.

As the trader is establishing what is intended to be a medium- to long-term position with a solid fundamental view bolstered by a constructive technical uptrend, the logical place to set the stop on the position is the level that decisively invalidates the trend, taking out the prior low at $101.43 (denoted by X). A trader would most likely pick a level somewhat lower than the prior low to ensure a true, material violation and round this level down to the nearest whole tick increment. For the MAR contract it would be reasonable to use $101.00 or $101.25, depending on how much latitude the trader cared to give the position. A trader using a $101.00 stop would be taking $4.52 of risk from current market levels.

The trader has no obvious technical price target to use as a benchmark, so all guidance will have to come from the fundamental analysis. The base case for the Product X market has an end-of-year fair value of $165.00, though it would be unrealistically optimistic to assume that that level is attainable in the near-term with just the stimulus provided by a non-return of the production facility. One certainty is that if the African facility does not return to service, Europe will be markedly shorter on an ongoing basis, which will immediately kick off a war with the United States for future supply out of South America, with the loser having to pay up to the low-to-mid $130s that will incentivize incremental Canadian production. It is more probable than not that the US will prevail due to its ongoing relationships with South American producers, but there is a strong possibility that US prices could approach the Canadian supply threshold and reach the $120.00-130.00 range as uncertainty disturbs the forward market. This level would serve as both a reasonable near-term price target for the base and bull cases and also a good level to take profits, as it is unlikely that the US prices above Canada in the short-to-medium term under any circumstances. Using $125.00 as a price target yields $19.48 of potential reward, and a favorable risk-reward ratio of slightly over 4.3-to-1:

Risk:	$4.52 or $4,520,000
Reward:	$19.48 or $19,480,000
Risk-Reward:	4.3-to-1

The trader will be operating with a defined time window between the mid-February return date of the African production facility and the expiry of the MAR contract at the end of the month. It is also possible to take a longer-term view of the evolution of the fundamental thesis with an exposure further out on the forward curve.

Trade Strategy #2: Long-Term, Fundamentally Driven Directional Uptrend
Long 1M notional tons, equivalent to 10,000 OCT ProdX futures, to capture long-term uptrend caused by the structural deficit in supply/demand balance.

Position:	Long 1M tons, or 10,000 OCT ProdX Futures contracts
Notional Dollars:	$103.28M
Initial Margin:	$10.33M
V@R:	$185k 1-Day V@R at 95%
	$261k 1-Day V@R at 99%

The OCT contract offers a reasonable balance between proximity to the motive stimulus (in this case, the cumulative effect of multiple stimuli between February and July described in the Product X event path) and being positioned far enough out on the curve to allow it time to work prior to the contract expiry. The OCT contract has also had a very muted response to stimulus thus far, settling at $1.41 off the contract lows and potentially offering the trader a "higher floor" and more downside protection. Consider the chart of the OCT ProdX futures contract:

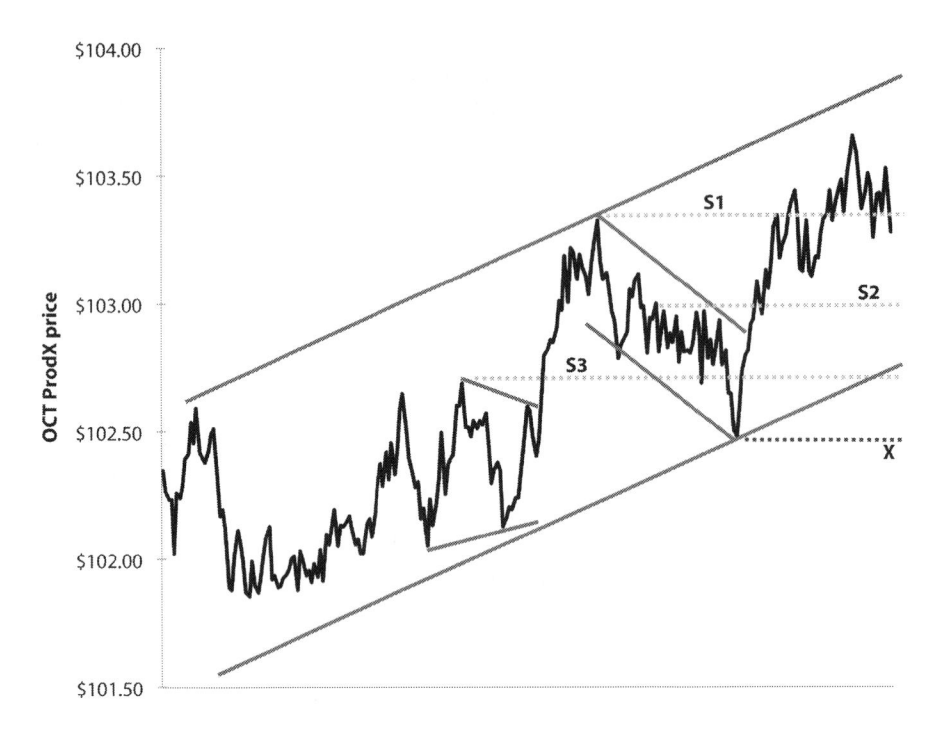

Figure 8.19 Pattern and trend analysis of the OCT ProdX chart.

There are several notable differences between the prompt FEB and second-month MAR contracts and the OCT ProdX futures. The general shape of the chart is similar, but the overall uptrend is flatter and the bottom support is less well defined. The initial consolidation triangle is present, but the bull flag countermove is less defined, with an area of significant congestion prior to testing the bottom of the trend channel. The final rally is stunted, falling well short of the top of the trend channel before making a choppy sideways consolidation with a most recent close below the S1 support level defined by the prior top. This type of lower-resolution, semi-degraded relationship to the front month chart is extremely common, particularly with products where most of the traded volume is concentrated in the first several contracts.

With the OCT position the trader is establishing what is intended to be a long-term position with a solid fundamental view bolstered by a constructive (if slightly less well-defined) technical uptrend. The logical place to set the stop on the position is again at the level that decisively invalidates the trend, taking out the prior low at $102.47 (denoted by X). A trader would most likely pick a level somewhat lower than the prior low to ensure a true, material violation and round this level down to the nearest whole tick increment. For the OCT contract it would be reasonable to use $102.25 or $102.00, depending on how much latitude the trader cared to give the position. A trader using a $102.00 stop on the position would be taking $1.28 of risk on the transaction.

As with the MAR futures position, the chart offers little in the way of technical targets to the upside to inform the trader's assessment of the potential rewards in the trade. The longer term fundamentals that are the primary drivers of an OCT ProdX position would argue for utilizing the $165.00 price target from the trader's base case, which would imply a $61.72 reward potential and an outrageous 48-to-1 risk-reward ratio. There is one major flaw in this representation of reality: the trader is using a short-to-medium-term technical target to derive the stop and a long-term fundamental thesis to support the potential profit target.

It is very possible that the trade does have $60.00+ of potential profit if held to maturity, but in committing to ride the position for the majority of the year it seems completely impractical to employ a stop that would be better suited for an exposure measured in days or weeks and that radically increases the probability that the trader will be forced out prior to expiry. The trader will have to decide whether to hold the position with a long-term, fundamentally based upside target of $60 that might require an arbitrarily derived, trader-defined $4.00-$6.00 worth of latitude to be held to maturity, or utilize shorter-term metrics with a technically derived $1.28 stop and a $4.00-$5.00 profit target based on the price response to the African production facility propagated across the curve. Ironically, both approaches yield trades that are definitely worth doing, but the lack of a clear definition of the risk and reward components is slightly troubling and will force the trader to be very clear about intentions and execution before committing to the position.

Short-Term Risk:	$1.28 or $1,280,000
Short-Term Reward:	$4.50 or $4,500,000
Short-Term Risk-Reward:	3.5-to-1
Long-Term Risk:	$5.00 or $5,000,000
Long-Term Reward:	$60.00 or $60,000,000
Long-Term Risk-Reward:	12-to-1

Challenges of Maintaining a Directional Position

Despite recent market fluctuations Product X volatility is still very low, so margin and utilized V@R should not be overly onerous constraints, but may prove to be a problem later as volatility increases and costs of holding position in terms of V@R, credit, and margin expand. As seen in Chapter 7, recalculating the V@R for the FEB ProdX contract with increasing volatilities yields:

FEB ProdX volatility	95% 1-Day V@R	99% 1-Day V@R
6.00%	$656,633	$927,245
7.00%	$766,071	$1,081,786
8.00%	$875,510	$1,236,327
9.00%	$984,949	$1,390,867
10.00%	$1,094,388	$1,545,408
12.50%	$1,367,985	$1,931,760
15.00%	$1,641,582	$2,318,112
20.00%	$2,188,776	$3,090,817
25.00%	$2,735,970	$3,863,521
30.00%	$3,283,164	$4,636,225
40.00%	$4,377,551	$6,181,633
50.00%	$5,471,939	$7,727,041

Table 8.4 FEB ProdX V@R calculated for a range of implied volatilities.

A FEB ProdX position that initially consumed $728k of 95% 1-day V@R at a 6.65% annual volatility would require $1.09M at 10% and $1.60M at 15%.

9

Spread Trading Strategies

Spread Trading Is a Correlation and Causation Game
A spread is a position created by the purchase of one instrument and the sale of another, yielding an exposure designed to profit from either the convergence or divergence of the initial price relationship. The degree of correlation and the stability of the relationship between the two products that comprise a spread structure will greatly influence the performance characteristics, as well as the impacts on the trader's limits and the cost of financing the position. Spreads can be constructed out of nearly identical or wildly dissimilar instruments, and allow the trader to express extremely nuanced views not possible with a pure directional trade.

Spread-Trading Terminology
Spread trades have a large number of unique pricing and quoting conventions that traders will need to be familiar with:

The spread between two products is expressed as the mathematical value of one subtracted from the other. The more expensive product is the premium, the cheaper is the discount. To avoid confusion when quoting markets, the established over-the-counter convention is to refer to the structure as the premium-to-discount spread, the premium/discount spread, or the premium-over-discount spread. Whatever the trader is doing to the premium product, they are doing to the spread. Buying the spread involves purchasing the premium product and selling the discount, and is a bet that the two component prices will widen. A trader selling the spread would sell the premium product and purchase the discount, believing that the differential will narrow.

For example, if apples cost $7.00 and oranges cost $3.00, a trader would say that the apple-over-orange spread was $4.00. A trader buying the apple-over-orange spread for $4.00 would profit if, in the future, apples became more expensive relative to oranges, regardless of the overall directionality of the apple or orange markets.

Each component position of a spread is called a leg. To put on or remove a spread trade one piece at a time is to "leg into it" or "leg out of it." A spread relationship that is derived from two individual product prices is quoted "on legs"; one that is expressed and traded as a pre-defined package is said to be "as a structure."

Occasionally, the prices in a spread will draw close to parity or invert. For market participants using the standard quoting methodology the price of apples dropping below that of oranges would result in the description of the spread changing from the apple-to-orange spread to the orange-to-apple (and back again, if need be). Electronic exchanges and the traders that depend on them are forced to initially define a spread as apple minus orange and keep it that way for consistency, regardless of price changes to either product. If the price of oranges spikes to $9.00 while the price of apples stays the same, it is simultaneously possible that over the counter brokers would say that the orange-over-apple spread is $2.00 (conventionally quoting the premium product first: $9.00 − $7.00 = $2.00), while on an exchange it would be shown that the apple-to-orange spread has inverted, and is now trading −$2.00 (using the established electronic convention $7.00 − $9.00 = −$2.00).

It can take some time to become comfortable thinking in spread market terms, particularly for traders that employ both voice brokers and exchange screens. It is always wise for a trader to verify what they are buying and selling before closing a transaction.

Advantages of Spread Trading

1. Spreads can be used to express a variety of market views.
2. The exposure can be, to some extent, self-hedging.
3. Spreads can be very credit and collateral efficient depending on margining method; very V@R and notional-limit efficient depending on calculation method and correlation.
4. Can offer very good risk-reward scenarios when betting on the disruption of a stable relationship or at/near barrier conditions. If motivational impulse fails to materialize (or disappoints), no big change and no big loss.
5. Spreads can work in both up or down markets.

Spreads Can Be Used to Express a Variety of Market Views
Spread trades can be used to express a wide variety of trading strategies, including:

- A sudden disruption in a traditional price relationship, or the reversion to normality of one that has become distorted.
- A gradual shift in value that plays out over a protracted period of time.

Chapter 9 - Spread Trading Strategies

- Differing levels of volatility that lead to unequal responses to a common stimulus.

Spread trades can be constructed out of:

- The same product, with each leg being a different future/forward contract.
- Two similar or closely related products, with some common fundamental drivers.
- Two different products governed by a statistical relationship.

The Exposure Can Be Self-Hedging

One major advantage of spread trades is the potentially self-hedging characteristics of being long one product and short another. Products that are highly correlated will yield a net spread exposure smaller than a volumetrically equivalent long or short position in either leg, which can be extremely useful in high-volatility markets that preclude directional trading.

Spreads Can Be Very Limit- and Resource-Efficient

To construct a spread position a trader will buy a volume of Instrument A, and sell a volume of Instrument B. The amount of cash, credit, or collateral paid out to maintain the long position in Instrument A will be offset, to some degree, by the amount of cash, credit, or collateral paid to the trading firm by the purchaser of Instrument B. The degree to which the payments net will depend on a variety of factors, among them:

- The similarity of the products. An A/B spread composed of contractually equivalent financially cleared futures will receive much more favorable treatment than a spread composed of a long physical A position with associated delivery and volume risk and a short position in B financial fixed-for-floating swaps.
- The degree of correlation between the products. The higher the correlation, the smaller the net exposure, limit burden, and margin requirement.
- The location of each leg of the position. A clearing broker holding both the long and short leg of the transaction will see the position as a spread, apply the correlation between the products, and margin accordingly. If the long position is held at one broker (or with one counterparty) and the short at another, each position will be margined as a stand-alone directional trade for a larger total capital outlay, forfeiting the efficiency inherent in the structure.

Spreads Can Offer Very Good Risk-Reward Mechanics

Some spread relationships will exhibit well-defined boundary conditions, particularly for products that are paired inputs and outputs of a production process or held together with a physical transportation mechanism. If the cost of shipping a product from B to A is $5, it will be difficult for the long-term spread between A and B to ever be materially less than that, barring a structural shift in the fundamentals of the market. It is common for spreads to erode to the fundamental minimums during low-volatility periods, only to gap wider once a fear or uncertainty premium returns to the market.

Spreads Can Work in Both Up or Down Markets

By betting on only the differential between two prices, the trader can be relatively agnostic as to how that change in valuation comes to pass, caring only that it evolves in a way that suits her position.

While it is possible for a spread to work (or not) in either an up- or down-trending market, many spread positions will have established, intuitively obvious performance characteristics. A spread that tends to work well in down markets is frequently referred to as a bear spread, while a strategy that generally profits during a rise in prices is called a bull spread.

Disadvantages of Spread Trading

1. With more moving parts, there are more opportunities for something to go wrong.
2. The trader may not get the desired price response, either due to an unexpected response to stimulus on one leg of the spread or an over/under correlation.
3. In extreme crisis, the correlation governing the spread can break down entirely.
4. Liquidity can be problematic, as a spread is only as transactable as its lower volume leg.

More Moving Parts Means More to Go Wrong

A spread involving a long and short position is a more complicated proposition than a simple directional position, with twice the opportunities for unproductive evolution to the fundamental or technical drivers, double the exposure to exogenous events, and an increased potential for a black swan event.

May Not Get Desired Price Response

A spread position will be intended to respond to one or more stimuli that will change the price relationship between the products. It is possible that the trader's anticipated market driver materializes as anticipated, but that it does not affect the spread as expected. A change in an environmental variable expected to impact one leg may instead influence the other, or perhaps both, reducing the efficiency of the position or destroying it altogether.

If one of the legs of a spread is free to fluctuate while the other becomes bound by a constraint, reaches a temporary or permanent barrier, or is otherwise prohibited from movement, the structure may start to perform more like a directional trade, albeit one with superior risk metrics and collateral usage.

In an Extreme Crisis, Correlations Can Completely Break Down

A spread trade will have a correlation between the two legs, which coupled with historical performance should provide some guidance to the trader as to the expected response to stimulus on a going-forward basis. Correlations and historical relationships are based on medium- and long-term averages, and in real time the two prices may not act in as rational or predictable a fashion as the trader would have anticipated.

A hard lesson learned in the 2008 financial crisis was that, in times of extreme crisis, the correlations and traditional relationships that govern the behavior of any spread can completely break down, leaving the trader with an unpredictable directional position or, in truly awful cases, an anti-correlated position where both legs hurt the trader at the same time.

Liquidity Can Be Problematic
The ability to modify a spread position will be limited by the volume transacted in the least liquid product. This can be particularly problematic for front-to-back spreads in markets that typically have structurally decreasing transacted volume for each month further out along the curve. Markets that trade infrequently or by appointment are particularly dangerous, as the trader can become caught in a position where one of the legs is effectively undefined and not transactable, creating massive mark-to-market challenges and taking what was a risk-reductive correlated trade and converting it into a much larger directionally sensitive exposure. This is a common trap, as traders often work into large spread positions a tiny piece at a time, but may want or need to exit the entire exposure rapidly, exposing them to the liquidity bottleneck that was always there, but that had not been a binding constraint.

Common Spread Trading Strategies

Spread trades are used to express views on the following market conditions:

1. Pre-shock explosion and post-shock mean-reversion, where prices gap apart and then snap back into alignment.
2. Drift trades, where one of the legs will under- or overperform over time.
3. Quantitative reversion, where prices that have diverged over time reassert a statistical relationship.

1. Pre-Shock Explosion and Post-Shock Mean-Reversion Trades
Traders can use a spread position to bet on the disruption of a stable relationship between two instruments caused by an exogenous event or abrupt fundamental shift in the market.

Accumulating a position prior to an explosion will typically involve a strong fundamental perspective on one or more specific drivers that will motivate an extreme price response. The explosion will typically be relatively short-duration, with the reversion occurring over a more protracted period. Explosions are difficult to forecast, and the magnitude of the price response can be difficult to gauge. The benefit of expressing an explosion trade with a spread (as opposed to the more intuitive directional position) is the ability to use the non-explosive leg of the trade to hedge as many risk factors as possible common to both products, leaving the volatility-responsive characteristic expressed in isolation. The trader can also bet on a common response with different magnitude price implications.

Consider the following chart of three similar path products with different volatilities:

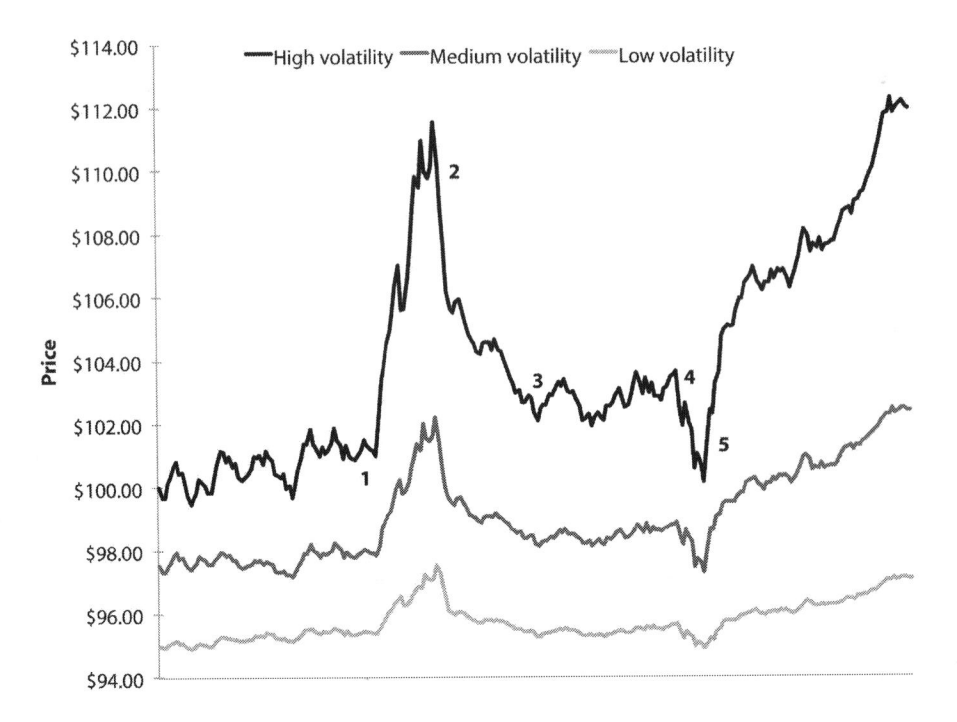

Figure 9.1 Explosion and reversion trades between high-, medium-, and low-volatility products.

The high-, medium-, and low-volatility products initially fluctuate in relatively close synchronization, moving sideways with relatively constant spreads between them. At (1) a market event occurs that dramatically impacts the price of the high-volatility product, with lesser effect on the medium-volatility and almost none for the low-volatility product. The spread between high and medium, which had been relatively stable between $2.25 and $3.50 blows out to $9.30 and the relatively less dynamic medium-to-low spread gaps out to $4.80.

Reversion trades are, in many ways, easier to frame intellectually, as something has already happened to change an established price relationship. The trader can analyze and make inferences as to the potential magnitude and durability of the motivational stimulus. One challenge with reversion trades lies in distinguishing between short-term exogenous events with little sticking power and true paradigm shifts with lasting if not permanent repercussions. If a motivational event is bad enough, even though it does not linger, it may have secondary or tertiary effects that do persist. It is also common for a motivational event to be partially permanent, where some of the effects quickly dissipate but the spread relationship establishes a new baseline at a different level. Once the initial motivation has dissipated (2), the high volatility product dramatically retraces and establishes a new set point at (3), compressing back to the original level (4) before encountering another explosive motivational event at (5).

Chapter 9 - Spread Trading Strategies

This example also serves to reinforce a point made in Chapter 8 about the fallacy of spread trading being inherently "safer" than directional trading. Graphing the absolute net change in value of the high-, medium-, and low-volatility products and the spreads between them from the initial starting point shows a surprising relationship:

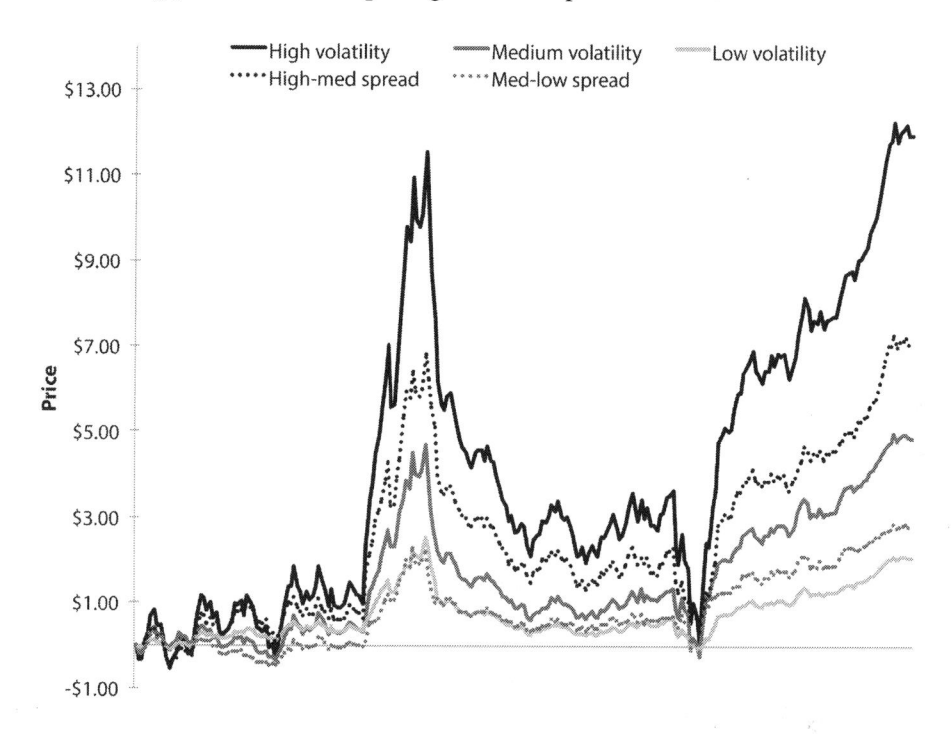

Figure 9.2   Comparing spread and directional volatility.

The high-medium and medium-low spreads are frequently more volatile in absolute terms than the lower volatility leg of the structure, and the high-medium spread is significantly more volatile than the medium product across its entire lifetime. Thus, given a large enough volatility differential between the two component products, the spread relationship can actually be more dangerous than the lower volatility product.

The opposite of an explosion trade is a compression trade, where the motivational force acts to dramatically narrow a previously stable spread relationship. The principles are generally the same, but compression trades have some unique characteristics:

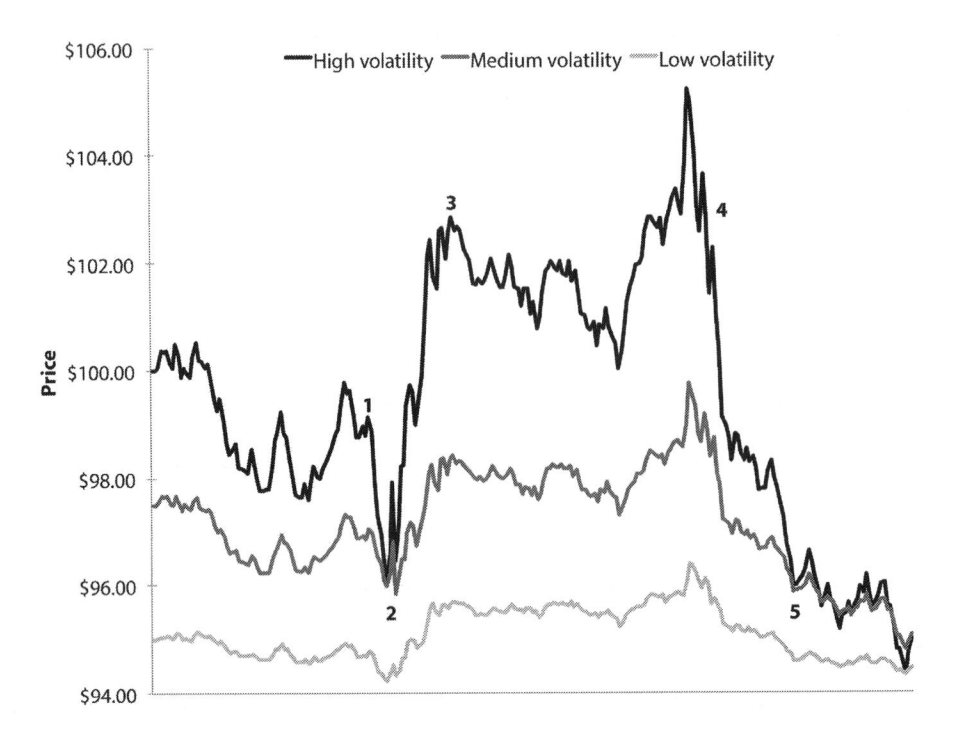

Figure 9.3 Compression trades between high-, medium-, and low-volatility products.

The price relationships initially fluctuate within reasonably well-defined relationships until a motivational stimulus occurs at (1) that principally impacts the high-volatility product, crushing the spread between it and the medium-volatility product down to near-zero at (2) while leaving the medium-low spread relatively undisturbed. The motivational force proves extremely transitory, and the high-medium spread explodes back outward to near $4.00 at (3). The high-medium spread maintains this higher orbit, fluctuating between $4.00-$5.00 for an extended period of time before encountering a second compressive force at (4). The second compressive force is both more powerful and wider reaching in its influence, as it both compresses the high-medium spread back down to zero and also drives the medium-low spread briefly below $0.50. The compressive effect between high and medium appears to have enduring properties, as the spread between them has remained near zero since (5), while the medium-low continued to contract until the end of the price series.

A spread relationship (particularly between similar physical products within the same market) can have delivery or transportation arbitrages that may bound the magnitude of potential price compression under normal, unconstrained conditions. This is common with products that have a point source of origin and are transported along a linear supply line to a succession of market areas. Financial spreads are typically much freer to fluctuate, particularly those constructed out of unrelated products.

2. Drift Strategies

The principal difference between a drift trade and an explosion/reversion trade is the elongated time scale during which the price action evolves. Explosion, by definition, implies rapidity and violence of movement. A drift trade is frequently the result of a more leisurely dissemination of information into the market and/or a gradual shift in consensus:

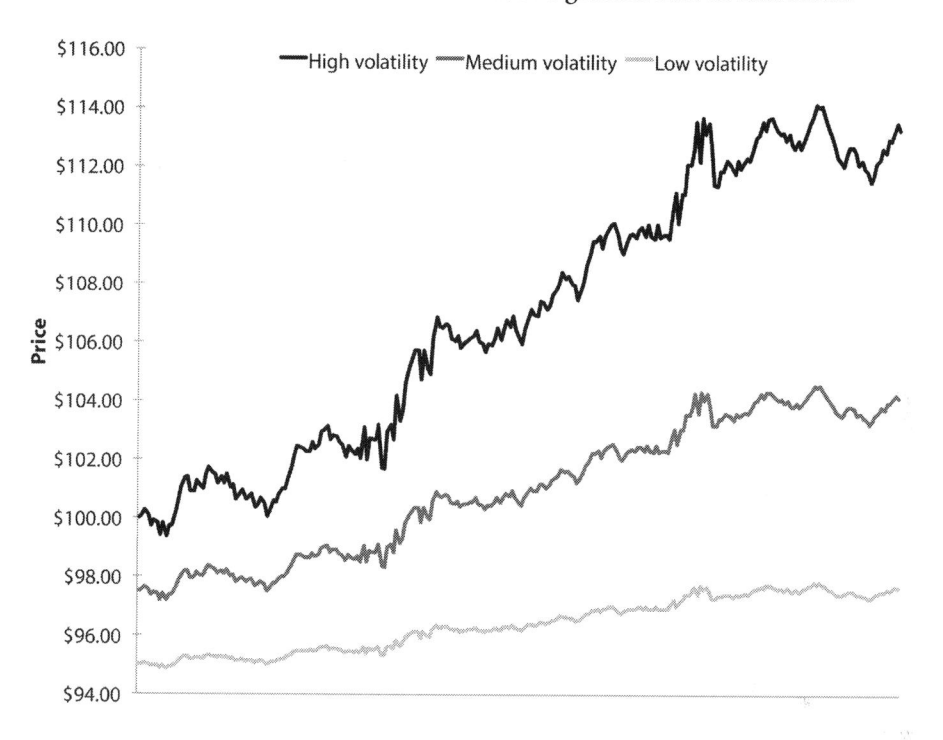

Figure 9.4 Widening drift trades between high-, medium-, and low-volatility products.

It is also possible to bet on a gradual erosion of price differentials:

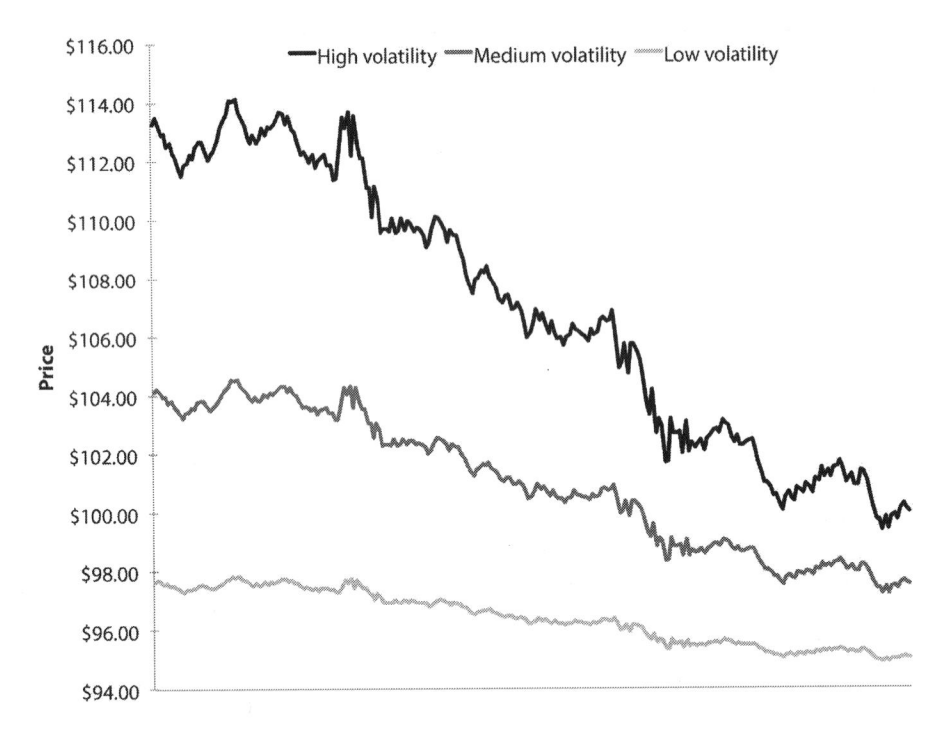

Figure 9.5 Narrowing drift trades between high-, medium-, and low-volatility products.

Drift trades tend to be more user-friendly than explosion trades, allowing more time to recognize the motivational impulse and initiate a position before the bulk of the potential move has occurred. A drift trade is somewhat intellectually analogous to a trend trade, where the value lies in establishing a position early and maintaining it as long as conditions are favorable, as opposed to the committing explosiveness of a breakout trade. In the prior explosion example it takes 22 days for the high-volatility product to move from the trough to the initial market peak $10.40 higher. In the drift trade it requires 216 days to span the $14.75 distance from bottom to top, providing much more opportunity to accumulate a position. Being a few days late to the explosion trade can result in a significant degradation in the risk/reward relationship given the poor entry level, but may not matter nearly as much to the drift trade.

The flip side of the more user-friendly decision-making environment is the necessity of maintaining an exposure for a prolonged period of time to achieve the target result. Staying in the trade to earn the maximum $14.75 means 216 days of financing costs that the trader must pay and 216 days of potential exogenous risks that the trader must worry about.

3. Trading Spreads Quantitatively

There two primary ways to trade spreads quantitatively:

- Model-based fair value trading, where the trader focuses on a small number of fundamentally understood spread pairs.
- Pure quantitative reversion on very large data sets.

The analysts at a trader's firm can construct a model to determine the fundamental "fair value" for a price relationship between two products, as well as a sense of the normal fluctuations around that level. If the market experiences a material divergence from fair value, the trader will buy the spread if it has become too cheap or sell it if has become too expensive, then wait for the market forces inherent in the fundamental view to prevail. This is, in many respects, a cousin of the standard mean-reversion trade. The principal difference is that the thesis is not built around a specific, observed motive impulse that is understood as a market driver. The trader does not really care why prices have deviated from normality, only that the traditional relationship reasserts itself with predictable price impacts. Making this type of trading decision requires a deeply ingrained confidence in the fundamental analytics. It also requires a really, really good model, which depending on the underlying market dynamics, can be extremely challenging to create and maintain.

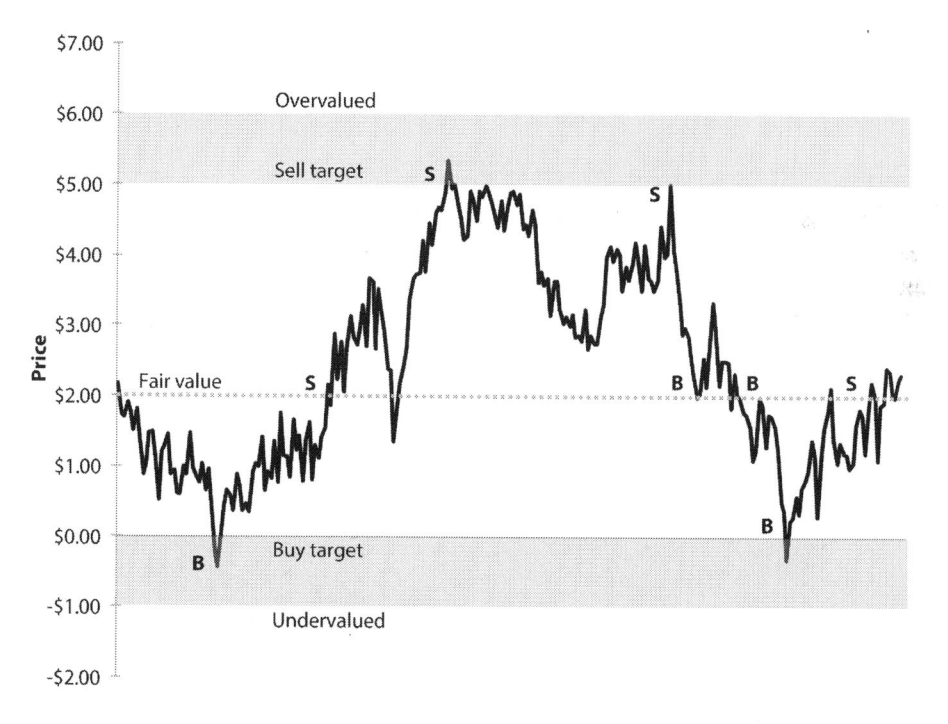

Figure 9.6   Using estimates of fair value to quantitatively trade a spread.

A second type of quantitative trading involves analysis of large data sets. Instead of deriving a fundamental fair value for a particular pair of prices, the trader's model will scan a universe of instruments and seek to identify combinations that have become statistically misaligned. This type of massively computational trading has only been possible with the development of cheap processing power and large volumes of reliable financial data.[42]

The underlying mechanics of this type of data-intensive spread trading will be discussed in greater detail in Chapter 11 – Quantitative Trading Strategies.

Spread-trading strategies require patience and good execution skills. Since spread trades are, in theory, less volatile propositions that transit less ground at a slower pace, giving away a few extra ticks to enter and exit the trade can be much more significant in percentage terms than would be the case with a directional trade. The trader may have to be a net liquidity provider, leaving bids and offers at productive levels to utilize the normal market micro-fluctuations, as opposed to hitting bids and lifting offers and paying away the spread.

Common Spread-Trade Structures

In constructing a spread position, a trader will typically be expressing a view on a particular driver (or set of drivers) that will manifest in one particular product or during one period of time, choosing instruments that are as similar as possible except for their exposure to, or ability to be influenced by, the driver(s). The desire for mostly offsetting characteristics (to create the self-hedging relationship) typically leads traders to express views via the spread between two products for the same time period, or two different time periods or physical locations for the same product.

- Spreads between two different time periods of the same product are called time spreads, calendar spreads, front-to-back spreads, and rolls.
- Spreads between similar products that are physically located in two different places are called basis spreads or transportation spreads.
- Spreads between different products are called cross-commodity or product spreads.

---

[42] Though difficult to pin down exactly, this convergence-arbitrage style (a taxonomic bastardization) likely reached a peak somewhere between the 1994 LTCM disaster and the 2007 financial crisis. During both events a large number of traditional correlation relationships between asset classes and instruments broke down dramatically as traders and investors dumped risk in a wholesale fashion and fled to safety. Though there will undoubtedly be profitable opportunities to deploy the strategy in the future, it remains to be seen if the strategy will ever regain its former popularity.

Chapter 9 - Spread Trading Strategies

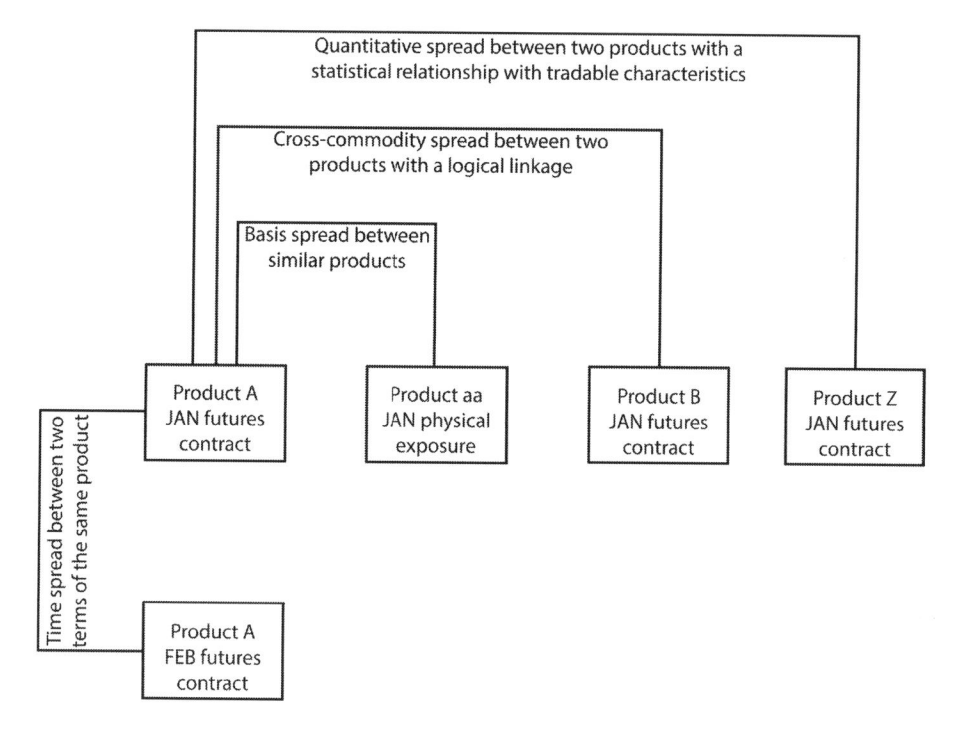

Figure 9.7 Comparing different spread-trade structures.

Time Spreads/ Calendar Spreads

Time spreads are positions that are constructed with a product that is deliverable in discrete time periods, and are commonly expressed using futures, swaps, options, and forwards. The trader will buy one maturity and sell another, creating a position that will benefit from the expansion or contraction of the initial price relationship. There are a few basic types of time spreads:

- Any spread where a month is traded against the next month is called a roll, from the practice of rolling the position forward as the prompt contract expires. The APR/MAY roll would involve transacting a volume of APR ProdX futures and taking an equal-sized opposing position in the MAY contract.
- The prompt/nearby spread is a roll between the front and second months, which is used to express a view on the short-term fundamentals that are affecting the expiring contract. A prompt/nearby spread in the ProdX futures would be the FEB/MAR spread.
- Front-to-back spreads are positions created between any two maturities on the curve. These types of trader-defined exposures are also called curve tilt trades, and can be used to express a wide variety of views on the market. Traders will also frequently utilize front-to-back time spreads as a more credit- and collateral-efficient means of expressing a directional view of the market. The leg of the trade positioned further out on the curve provides a measure of correlated hedge protection and, in so doing,

reduces the utilized V@R and can decrease the total amount of credit or collateral required by the clearinghouse or counterparty.[43]
- Calendar spreads involve creating a single or multi-month exposure in the same time period on a year-over-year basis, for example the FEB vs. FEB+1 spread. Multi-month calendar spreads are very common in physical markets, as traders combine contracts into quarterly, seasonal, and annual strips for easier execution.

Evolving Volatility in Time-Spread Positions

The degree to which the trader's preferred product has an established term structure of volatility or structurally increasing or decreasing volatility across the forward curve will need to be taken into consideration when deciding where to place the legs of a time spread. The relative volatility of the two legs of a spread can be a significant driver of the overall performance of the structure. A front-to-back spread position can also have evolving performance characteristics as each leg approaches or moves away from a localized high- or low-volatility pocket. Consider the performance characteristics of the A/B spread between a low-volatility product B and the premium product A that starts off with low volatility that gradually increases during the holding period:

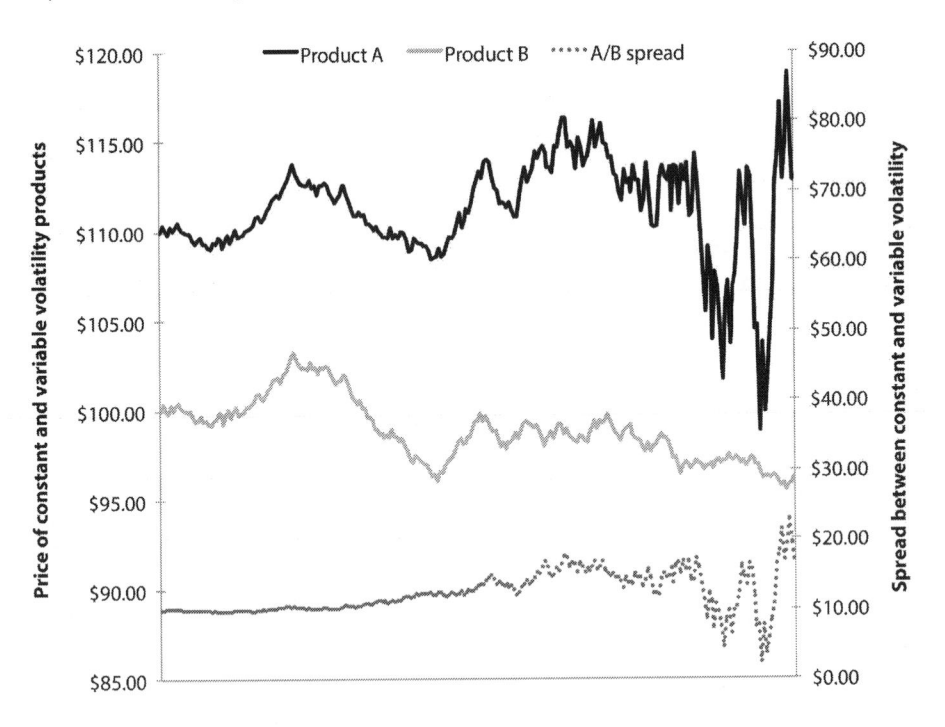

Figure 9.8   Evolving volatility in one leg of a spread position.

---

[43] The internally computed V@R should always decrease in the trader's favor, but the credit/collateral benefit will only be realized if both the long and the short position reside in the same clearing account or with the same counterparty, otherwise they would not acknowledge the offsetting position.

During the holding period the spread transitions from a highly correlated, low-risk position to a choppy, almost purely directional exposure as the increasing volatility of A overwhelms the contributions of the B hedge. Worse, what if the position in A was intended to be the hedge, and it has transitioned from being the risk-modifying enabler to the primary driver of the P&L of the position? That would almost certainly be a problem.

For spreads that have a defined motive leg that is expected to do the heavy P&L lifting and a correlated hedge position, the trader must carefully choose where to set each leg. The motive leg will generally be placed in close proximity to the anticipated stimulus event, either before, after, or in the pertinent delivery period. The location of the hedge leg is a trickier proposition, and will depend on the characteristics of the market and the view the trader is trying to implement. In most markets the near term, the delivery month, and the next one or two months have by far the highest informational density and the clearest picture of the fundamental landscape. Further out on the curve, the facts begin to diminish, replaced with projections and estimates. Further still, the estimates give way to "normals," an assumption that in the absence of any specific information the future will look approximately like the historical averages.

If the trader is betting on a different rate or magnitude of response to a common stimulus, she should set a motive leg as close as possible to the stimuli and choose a hedge leg slightly further away, but still within range of its effects. This would suggest intra-year positioning, playing the prompt month against the second or third, for example. If the trader is attempting to express a view on a stimulus causing a change from "normal" conditions, she will also want to position the motive leg close to the stimuli, but place the hedge leg far enough away that it should not be affected. Year-over-year spreads are particularly effective at expressing these types of market views.

Basis/Transportation Spreads

A basis or transportation spread is a play on the price differential between geographically separated products or markets. Basis relationships are defined by the real constraints of moving material from locations where it is produced to locations where it is consumed that evolve early in the development of a market. The physical delivery mechanism provides logical underpinnings to the relative value relationship and some semblance of structure to the potential price fluctuations in unconstrained, non-disrupted market conditions. Trading basis spreads involves understanding that transportation dynamic and the conditions under which it can become disrupted or congested, allowing prices to fluctuate independently or exhibit greater than normal volatility.

Cross-Commodity Spreads

Traders use cross-commodity spreads to express views on products that are substitutes, complements, or that have process-related linkages (the first may be a feedstock or material input into the production of the second). Cross-commodity spreads tend to have either a logical price linkage or a physical causality-derived relationship and tend to be traded by sector experts. Relationships can be factually based (it takes so much of X to make Y, therefore the prices should relate to each other) or historically derived (for the past decade the price of X has fluctuated within a 5% band around the price of Y). In the energy space, one of the most common cross-commodity spreads is the "crack spread," which relates the price of a barrel of oil to its component products. The most common structure for the trade is called a 3:2:1, where the trader spreads three crude oil contracts against two unleaded gasoline contracts and one heating oil contract, mimicking the inputs and outputs of an oil refinery.

Regardless of the structure of a spread, one of the legs will be more volatile than the other, and one of the legs will be more directionally sensitive. To not understand this relationship, and more importantly to be unaware that it will evolve through the intended holding period, is to ignore a significant portion of the total risk in the trade.

In any spread trade there are drivers that will be shared by both legs and one or more differentiating factor(s) that will act to alter the initial price relationship. The trader must understand which unique market drivers will be acting on each leg of the spread. The differences should be relatively straightforward for time spreads, given the common product, but can be significantly more subtle and complex for basis and cross-commodity positions that involve instruments with distinct (sometimes wildly different) performance characteristics.

Constructing a Spread Trade
Spread traders will tend to prefer instruments with linear risk characteristics, and will seek to employ the same physical forwards and financial futures and swaps as directional traders. Inherent non-linear risk characteristics can add additional complexity to a call or put spread trade, particularly when the strategy involves taking the structure to delivery or near-delivery, where a deeply out-of-the-money instrument can effectively cease to exist or a leg that is deeply in the money can perform like a piece of the underlying.

Ratio/Unbalanced Spreads
Spread trades can be constructed as balanced with volumetrically equal legs, or as intentionally unbalanced to protect against—or take advantage of—differing volatilities or rates of response to an anticipated market movement. Even within the same commodity equal notional values do not guarantee matched exposures, as one or the other of the legs will exhibit more sensitivity to fluctuations in the underlying market. The proper position sizing to achieve the trader's desired effect becomes more challenging when spreading different products against each other, particularly if there are wildly different volatility characteristics. Recent correlations will provide a starting point for relative initial position weightings, which may need to be adjusted to reflect actual performance characteristics during the lifetime of the trade.

Spreads can be constructed on a volume-weighted or risk-weighted basis. If X and Y have markedly different risk profiles, then an equal volume-weighted spread will perform like a smaller position in the riskier product and an extra directionality component will have been introduced. If that directional risk acts against the underlying motive force of the spread, it will underperform. If the risk is in the same direction, it will outperform. Risk weighting the legs can result in potentially significant differences in relative position sizes, but will ensure that the spread should be much more market neutral with respect to volatility or directionality.

Box Spreads

A box spread is a spread of spreads, a position defined by the price relationship between two different spreads. Box spreads have four legs in total, and are frequently used by traders to roll from one spread position into another, often in response to an approaching expiry of a near-term spread. This strategy tends to be more common in markets with a significant volume of spreads traded, or where the basic products are spreads, as is the case in the swaps market.

Spread Trading for Hedgers

It is often challenging for a hedger to execute desired volumes in his preferred product, forcing him to seek liquidity in correlated products and/or different time periods. A natural that has successfully executed a hedge package will now be in the business of managing a spread position between their organic exposure to Risk A and a hedge exposure to Product B, yielding a position in the A/B spread that will have positive or negative economic consequences. The natural can choose to maintain the position in the A/B spread indefinitely, add or remove incremental volumes of B as its A exposure changes, or slowly swap out of B and into A by executing offsetting transactions in the A/B spread as the market allows.

A hedger unable to access sufficient liquidity in the time period of its exposure can employ a method called a "stack and roll," where hedges are initially implemented in a liquid time period (typically the front of the curve), then rolled out to the desired risk-bearing period. The stack-and-roll method can cause problems for hedgers that must transact a massive amount of business relative to the normal traded volume in a narrow execution window, then seek to roll that large position rapidly into less liquid periods. In doing so, they can create huge temporary distortions in the normal pricing relationships and, ironically, create spread-trading opportunities for speculative mean-reversion traders.

The most infamous failure of a stack-and-roll hedging program occurred when the German commodity trading firm Metalgesellschaft attempted to mitigate the risks of long-dated petroleum product sales with a truly gigantic position in short-term crude oil contracts. The front contracts provided liquidity, but forced the firm to constantly roll the position forward on the curve, which they chose to do with what turned out to be very predictable regularity. As the market became aware of the firm's continued need to sell one month and buy the next, the relationship between the two would widen dramatically in anticipation, ultimately causing approximately $1.3B losses and nearly forcing Metalgesellschaft into bankruptcy. In the forensic examination that followed, academic luminaries debated the intellectual merits of the stack-and-roll hedge strategy, but there was little debate about it's practical value as implemented at Metalgesellschaft; it's hard to argue with a loss of $1,300,000,000.

The Metalgesellschaft incident permanently soured many industry participants on stacking and rolling as a valid risk management technique. Spread trades (and stepwise mitigation protocols, in general) can be optically challenging for senior management, forcing them to have a good story about why the firm produces A and could rationally be expected to sell A, but has instead sold B or C. Mistiming a transaction in the firm's core business area is professionally embarrassing, but having to explain hedging losses in what appears to be a completely unrelated position can be career ending.

The correlation between a firm's organic exposures and the risk mitigation instruments is critically important for naturals. Based on the prevailing generally accepted accounting principals (GAAP), there is a minimum correlation threshold required to designate a position as a hedge and employ hedge accounting. Hedge accounting has some extremely useful properties for the user, including the avoidance of daily mark-to-market accounting for the hedge position. Positions that do not qualify for hedge accounting are deemed to be not "hedge effective," and must be marked-to-market and the P&L disclosed in the firm's financial statements, which tends to lead to extremely pointed questions during the Q&A period in the quarterly corporate earnings calls with industry analysts.

Spread Trading for Financials
Financials trade spreads on both a proprietary and customer basis. Client-facing traders quote prices and execute trades based on the deal flow from their origination/sales group via direct customer contact. Depending on the transactional whims of their customer base, a bank trader may have the composition of the book change materially during the course of the day. The exposures that bank traders tend to accumulate will be in the less visible, less liquid products. The bank trader will frequently not be able to immediately source an equivalent product from the market, and will seek to put on a highly correlated, high-liquidity hedge to roughly neutralize the book and buy time to work out of the customer exposure.

Proprietary traders at a financial will use spread trades to more precisely target their desired exposures while simultaneously hedging out of undesirable product and market-specific risks.

Spread Trading for Merchants
Spread trading is an integral component of the core merchant strategy of controlling the value chain of a productive asset, particularly when the inputs and outputs are tradable products. Refineries with crude oil inputs and a basket of light products, power plants that burn natural gas to produce electricity, and processing plants that take raw ore and produce finished metal all allow a merchant to trade cross-commodity spreads to lock in profits or expose the asset to swings in the value relationship.

Merchants will trade locational or basis spreads to take advantage of the superior liquidity of benchmark instruments to set interim directional hedges, which they will roll into their preferred physical or low-liquidity products as market conditions allow.

Spread Trading for Speculators
Spread trading was the raison d'etre of the first hedge funds; firms that deployed a strategy called "equity pairs trading" and referred to their business as managing "hedged funds." "Equity pairs trading" involves buying one stock deemed undervalued and selling a closely related stock deemed overvalued by comparison. If, for example, Ford's valuation had become irrationally exuberant, it could be sold short against a long position in General Motors. Using

pairs that reside in the same industry or product category hedges out much of the directional market risk and a good portion of the risk that the particular sector will underperform.

Speculators continue to love spread trades for a variety of reasons. Small or resource-constrained players value the credit and collateral efficiency that allows them to participate in markets they would otherwise be unable to access. Traders interested in expressing a view on a reduced set of potential drivers like the self-hedging characteristics and the ability to chronologically bracket a particular stimulus or market-moving event. As we will see in Chapter 11, quantitative fund managers employ sophisticated models to study the fundamental relationship between small groups of like instruments and deploy statistical techniques on massive data sets to find mean-reversion spread trades.

Chapter Nine Summary

Spread strategies offer the trader the ability to create self-hedging, credit efficient positions that can be designed to knock out product, market, or seasonal risk. The downsides of spread trades are the increased potential complexity of response given two positional variables, potential liquidity issues on entry/exit if one of the legs of the spread trades significantly less than the other, and a reliance on the stability of the correlation between products to avoid wide swings in utilized risk limits. Spread trades can be used to bet on violent disruptions and/or dramatic resumptions of traditional price relationships, the gradual widening or narrowing of an instrument-to-instrument differential, or a quantitative overbought/oversold mean reversion. Spreads can be constructed out of any two instruments, but some of the more common thematic combinations are time spreads that span different terms of the same product, basis spreads that capture the value of transportation and local supply/demand forces, and cross-commodity spreads between products with a physical linkage to bind them or historical quantitative relationship.

Chapter 10 will ramp up the complexity even further and explore how to use options as an even more nuanced, sophisticated strategy for implementing the trader's view of the market.

Review Questions

1. Spreads are often referred to as "self-hedging". What does this mean, and under what circumstances might it not hold?
2. Explain the importance of correlation to spread trading strategies.
3. Name three types of spread structures and how they are commonly used.
4. How can the evolution of volatility impact the performance of a spread position?
5. Pick a commodity and generate three different spread trade ideas based on the forward curve and relationship to its market segment.

Resources

- *Charlie D. The Story of the Legendary Bond Trader* by William D. Falloon
- *Merchants of Grain: The Power and Profits of the Five Giant Companies at the Center of the World's Food Supply* by Dan Morgan
- *Metal Men: How Marc Rich Defrauded the Country, Evaded the Law, and Became the World's Most Sought-After Corporate Criminal* by A. Craig Copetas

Chapter 9 - Spread Trading Strategies

Case Study: Product X Spread Trading Strategies

Given the 13 contract months available in the six traded markets (ProdX and EurX futures and CanX, AusX, AfrX, and ChiX physical forwards) there are hundreds of potential spreads to contemplate. The trader must focus attention on the fundamental drivers of the event path and use the chronological and physical proximity to the motive forces as a filter to guide a search for value.

Types of Product X Spread Trades
There are two obvious types of spread trades that make sense given the current market dynamics and anticipated evolution toward the base fundamentals:

- Physical and financial basis spreads between countries that express views on the price impacts of the relative availability of supply, cost, and delivery reliability of the Product X.
- Financially settled time spreads in the US ProdX futures market designed to express relative valuation views within a single market area.

The trader has a fundamental view of the market that would favor a variety of drift trades with some potential for explosion in the most extreme circumstances.

The market for Product X is composed of financially traded products settling against the US and European benchmarks with physical basis markets located at producing and consuming countries. The first step in exploring basis-trading ideas for Product X is to examine how the relative levels of supply and demand are expected to change during the course of the year. The initial balance of trade for the base case looks like this:

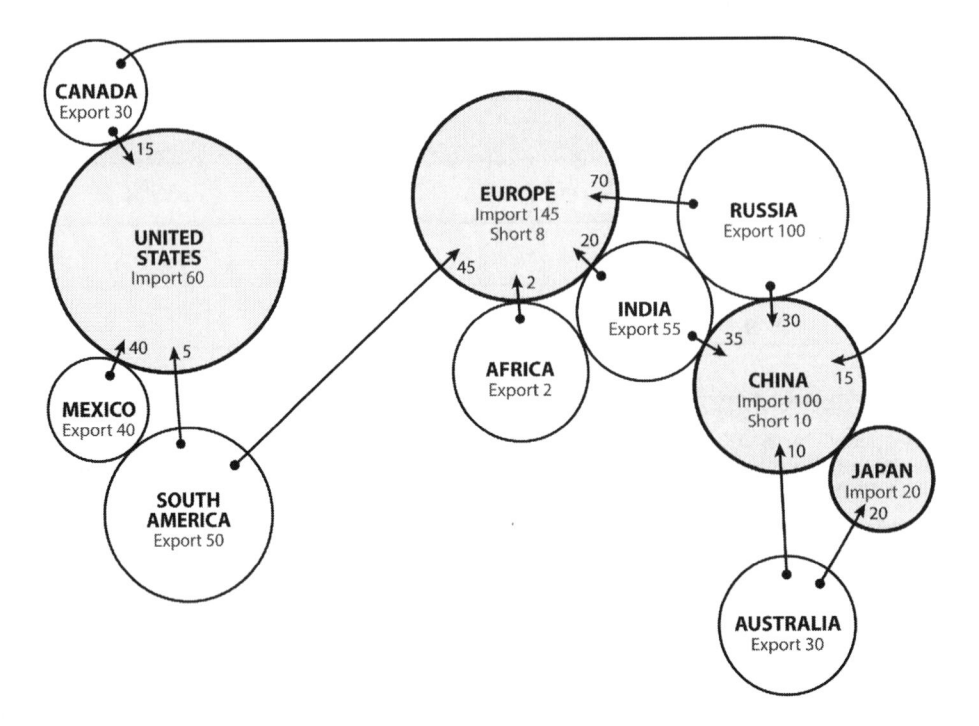

Figure 9.9 Product X base case initial balance of trade.

Which has led to the following price action in the local markets.

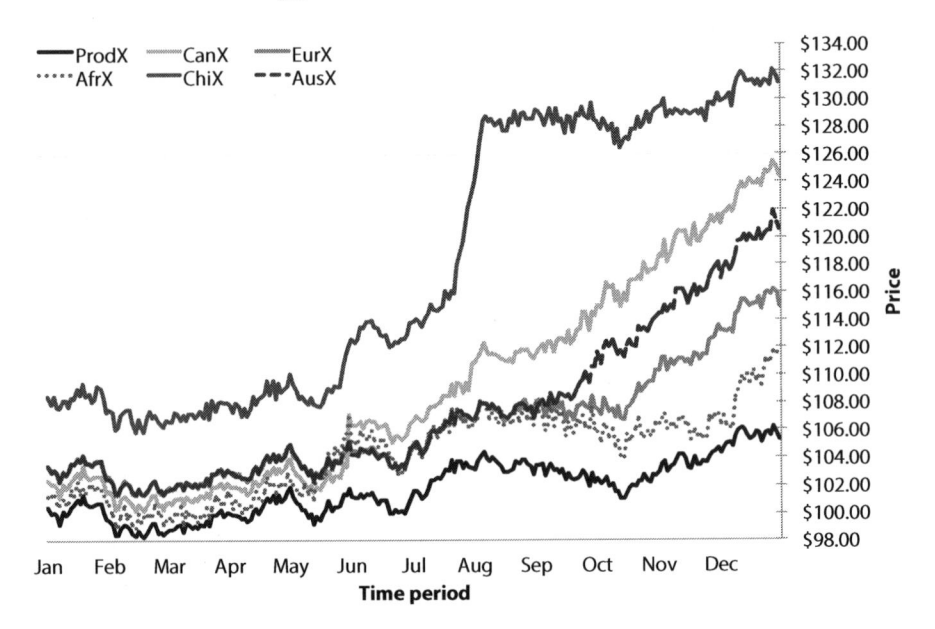

Figure 9.10 Global Product X FEB prices.

Chapter 9 - Spread Trading Strategies

With a projected 75M-ton increase in year-end demand in the base case offset by an estimated 63M tons of additional supply, the Product X market will almost certainly become tighter as the year goes on, forcing additional storage drawdowns, increased demand for high-cost marginal production, and a highly probable general increase in prices. Each of the four consuming nations (US, Europe, China, and Japan) will compete with the others for resources and bid up prices to incentivize incremental production.

- The United States will need to economically divert South American exports intended for Europe, or be forced to buy high-priced Canadian production to fill its incremental 20M-ton deficit.
- Europe desperately needs Africa to come back online or it will have to compete with US for South American and Canadian production to fill its additional 20M-ton shortfall.
- China (30M added demand) and Japan (net 5M shorter) will compete for the incremental 30M tons of Australian production, with the loser buying whatever Canadian production not scooped up by the United States and Europe.

Though it is impossible to know exactly how the market will attempt to balance, one scenario for the end of year incremental changes to the base case production and consumption volumes is shown in the following diagram.

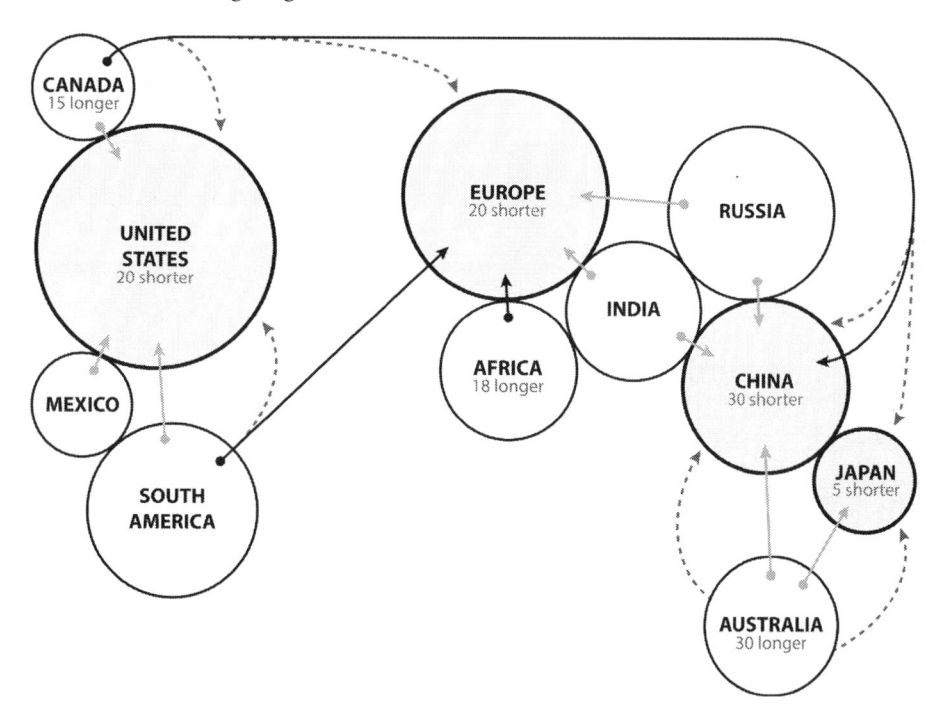

Figure 9.11   Product X base case potential year-end balance of trade.

The light gray arrows represent established producer/consumer relationships that are unlikely to change. The black arrows represent established producer/consumer relationships with a high probability of changing, with the dashed arrows indicating possible alternate destinations for production sourced from a particular country.

Physical and Financial Basis Spreads

Given the anticipated market dynamics there are four potentially interesting basis relationships:

1. The EurX/ProdX financial basis spread: a drift trade based on competition for South American and Canadian production in a short (possibly very short) market.
2. The AusX/AfrX physical basis spread: a drift trade based on the premium applied to surety of supply and the discount for non-performance.
3. The EurX/AfrX physical producer to consumer spread: an explosion trade based on the breakdown (and eventual resumption) of a traditional physical supply arrangement creating localized shortage.
4. The ChiX/AusX physical producer-to-consumer spread: an explosion trade based on a severe shortage that is seeking a price that will motivate additional supply to enter the market.

As visualized on a map:

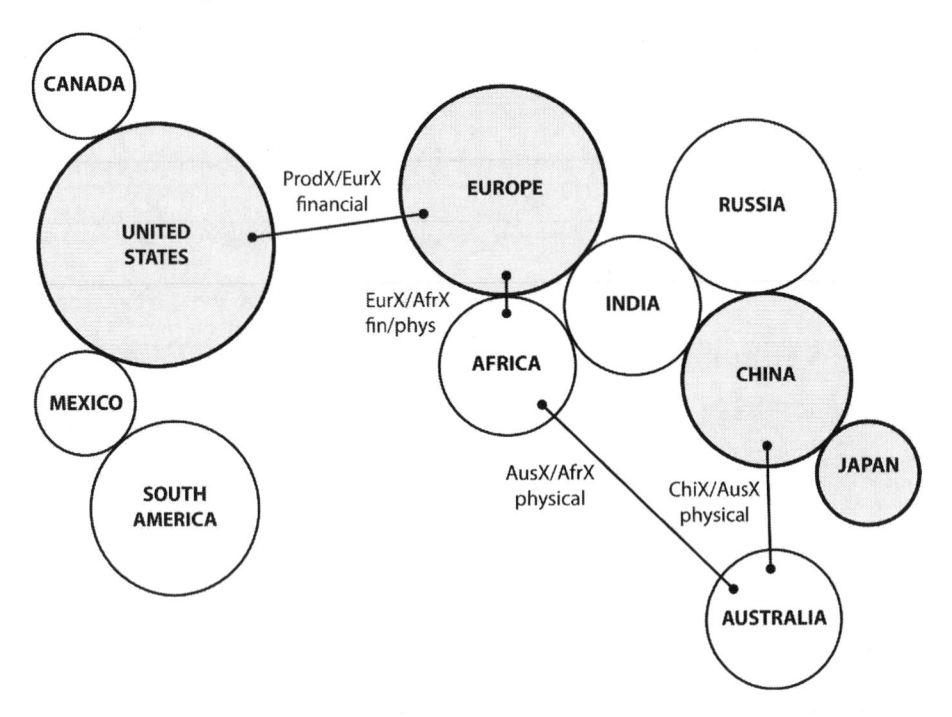

Figure 9.12 Product X spread-trade strategies.

Chapter 9 - Spread Trading Strategies

EurX/ProdX Financial Basis Spread: Differing Responses to Stimulus

The newly developed European EurX futures contract allows the trader to express a view on the locational basis differentials between Europe and the US with the benefits of visible pricing and standardized, cleared products. The EurX/ProdX spread is a classic example of a drift trade where a change in a fundamental variable is having a significantly larger impact on one of the two legs of a spread. The US was previously able to balance its market with local imports while the loss of African production tipped Europe into a persistent net deficit, pushing a spread that had been relatively stable at $3.00 out to $10.00 as seen in the following chart:

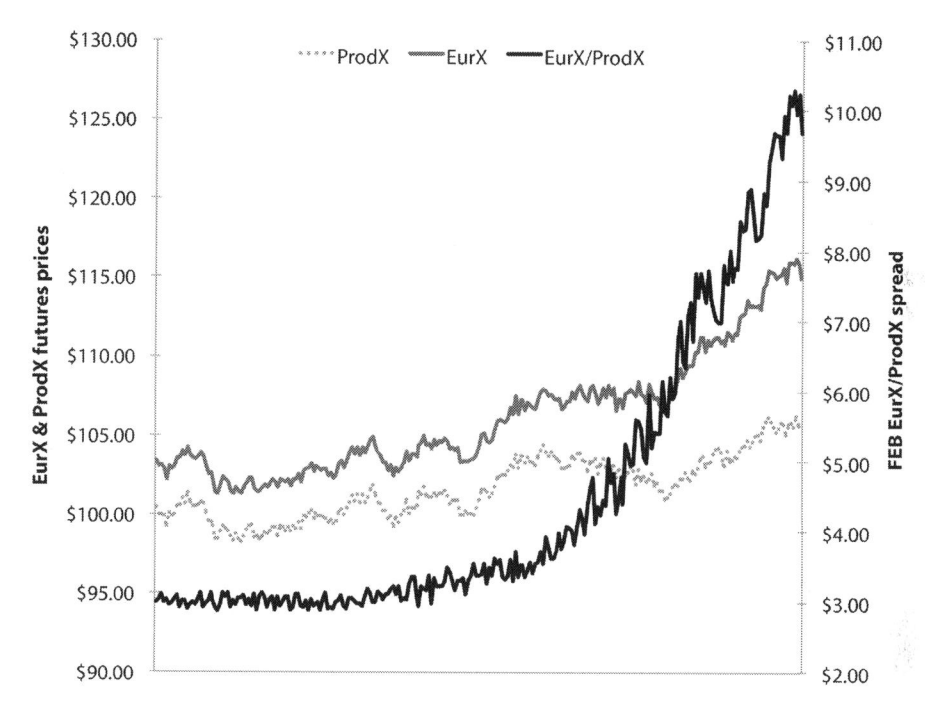

Figure 9.13 The FEB EurX/ProdX financial basis spread.

Buying the EurX/ProdX near the highs would be a bullish bet on both the overall direction of price and a play on the continued outage at the African facility and Europe's losing the battle with the US for future South American production, which could force EurX prices to the low-mid $130s to attract Canadian supply. A return to service in February and full output in March, or Europe decisively beating the US for South American production should collapse the spread back to near $3.00, making a sale of the EurX/ProdX a bearish bet on both price and supply. From the current $9.69 level the spread could possibly contract $6.50 to the $3.00 range or blow out over $20.00 to the low to mid-$30s, yielding a $20.00/$6.50 or approximately 3-to-1 risk-reward ratio.

The number of moving parts influencing the price relationship makes the EurX/ProdX a very complex exposure.

AusX/AfrX Physical Basis: A Reliability of Supply Spread

In times of volatility and crisis in a physical market surety of supply has tremendous value, and a proven ability or inability to deliver material will result in an immediate premium or discount applied to the price of future production. This can be seen in the Product X market by comparing the forward prices of African production given the processing plant disruption and the reliable Australian producers backstopped with additional surplus tonnage.

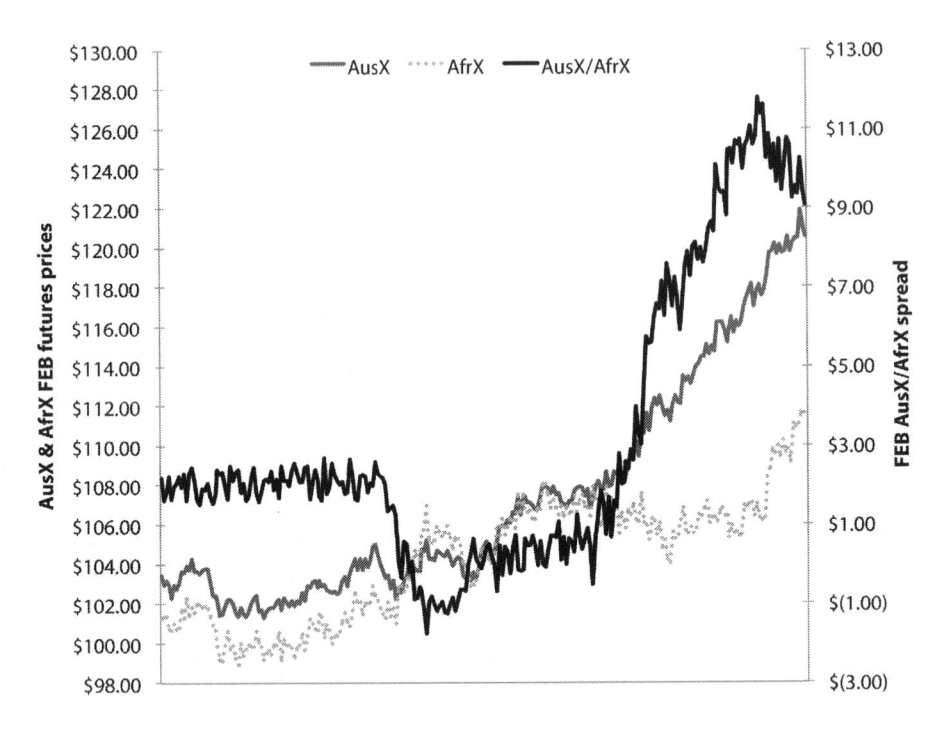

Figure 9.14 The FEB AusX/AfrX physical basis spread.

Balancing a physical market is, in some senses, a zero-sum game. A premium applied to one source will almost have to result in a discount being attached to another, though not necessarily of equal magnitude. When shippers delivering African-sourced material were unable to fulfill their obligations there was a brief spike in AfrX as short players scrambled to buy any spot tonnage available to meet their contracted volumes. This buying frenzy briefly lifted AfrX over AusX and inverted the spread before market participants lost faith in a resumption of service and the price of AfrX cratered to almost $12.00 below the much more reliable AusX market.

The return to service of African production in February should recompress the spread back toward the initial $2.50 level (for approximately $6.50 of risk), though it is probable that a residual performance discount will remain, yielding a more conservative $4.00-5.00 of downside risk. The failure to return to service should again widen the spread, but it is difficult to make a case that it should go much beyond the previously established peak, implying a maximum of $3.00 of reward and a sub-par 1-to-1.5 risk-reward ratio.

EurX/AfrX Physical Producer-to-Consumer Spread

The spread between the AfrX producing price and the EurX consuming price began the year as a straightforward transportation relationship where the price paid in Africa would fluctuate narrowly around the European price, less the cost of shipping. This changed dramatically when the central processing plant went offline, causing a sharp, short-lived spike in the price of AfrX supply as European consumers and merchants scrambled for any available spot tonnage to fill contractual shorts:

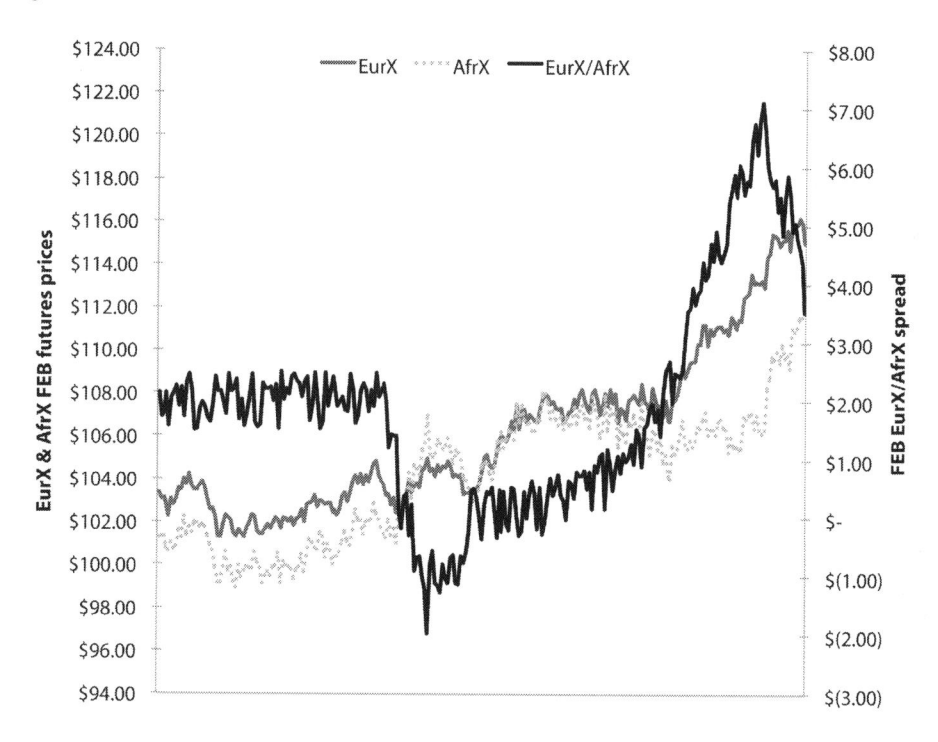

Figure 9.15 The FEB EurX/AfrX producer-to-consumer spread.

Once the immediate buying frenzy subsided and the market began to accept the fact that the processing plant was going to be offline for a significant period of time the implied price of the AfrX market began to sink relative to the EurX benchmark. This discounting of uncertain physical supply relative to a firm contractual obligation of a EurX contract peaked at $7.00 and has begun to contract as players position themselves prior to the anticipated return to service in February.[44] A restart of the facility should cause the spread to contract back toward

---

[44] This is an excellent example of why traders in different disciplines need to be aware of market events that superficially do not concern them. The recent narrowing of this spread would seem to be a clear signal that market participants anticipate the processing plant coming back on line in the

the initial $2.50 level (approximately $1.00 of risk), where failure to deliver would further erode confidence in the processing facility operator and likely push the physical uncertainty discount back to the prior $7.00 peak for a $3.50/$1.00 or 3.5-to-1 risk-reward ratio. There also exists the definite possibility that, if Europe is forced to price to the mid-$130s CanX market, the spread could explode higher, yielding extremely favorable risk-reward ratios of 15 or 20-to-1.

ChiX/AusX Physical Producer-to-Consumer Spread

The spread between physical producers in Australia and physical consumers in China was initially relatively stable around the $5.00 cost of shipping. China's unexpected uptick in demand in June widened the spread as suddenly short end users became aggressive buyers of material in the spot market to fill their obligations. The second demand increase in August blew the spread out to $21.50 as Chinese buyers effectively bid into thin air, having already absorbed all of the readily available tonnage.

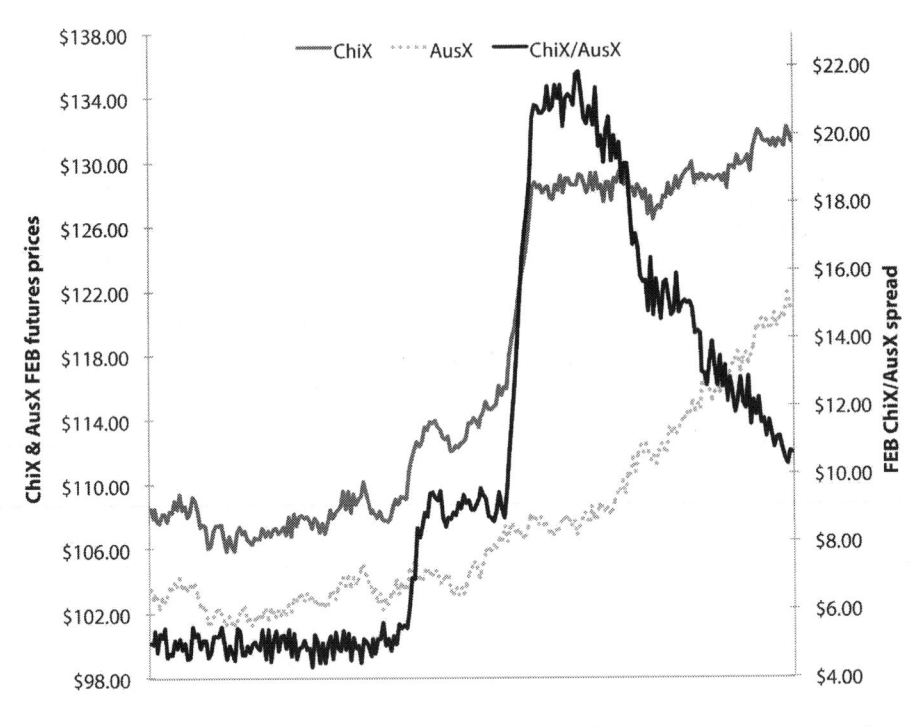

Figure 9.16   The FEB ChiX/AusX physical producer-to-consumer spread.

near future, with a small risk premium built in that has kept the spread at $3.82 and not its previous $2.00-2.50. This means that any failure to restart would, in fact, be a bullish development, as is theorized in the base and bull cases, as well as the thesis for long directional positions. A directional trader not bothering to look at the spread markets would be unaware of this important detail.

The contraction of the spread is a function of traders positioning themselves ahead of anticipated production increases that were, in large part, bankrolled by Australian producers selling into the forward market to lock in attractive levels and secure financing for upgrades to their production and export facilities. Australia is an extremely reliable shipper, and the spread probably contains almost zero discount for non-performance. If the Australian facilities come on line as anticipated, the spread should continue to narrow, potentially falling an additional $5.50 from the current $10.50 level to the initial $5.00 area. If Australia proves unable to meet its commitments and is forced to buy back the forward Chinese hedges in a market that Australia itself made shorter, the spread should blow out to well past the prior peak, yielding at least $10.50 of potential profit and an approximately 2-to-1 risk-reward ratio. It is possible to arrive at a more attractive 3-to-1 ratio by incorporating the reasonable assumption that persistent Chinese demand will keep the spread from ever reaching the prior lows, yielding only $3.00 of risk relative to the $10.50 potential reward.

The Need to Backstop Illiquid Physical Spreads With Transport
As the prior ChiX/AusX example illustrates, the ability to lean on physical delivery is critical when contemplating basis trades in new or highly physical markets. This is an area where first-mover merchants have traditionally earned a significant advantage, learning the physical market through trial by fire and emerging (those that emerge) with extremely valuable commercial information. For players without the ability to take possession of the physical material and move it via controlled or contracted shipping, a forward position is fraught with danger. Physical spread trading involves significant delivery risk, as the trader must be willing and able to execute the purchase-transport-deliver arbitrage as a last resort if they are unable to exit the position in the forward markets.

Imagine that a trader executed 5M tons of December sales to China and secured 5M tons of December production from Australia feeling that the spread would converge. The trader intends to take the position off prior to delivery and treat it is a pseudo-financial exposure. In this case the danger lies in being short a delivered physical commodity in a rising Chinese market, forcing the trader to source it at the point of delivery to meet the obligation or locate and transport tonnage to fill the contract. The problem is, this puts the trader in direct competition with the entity that is vacuuming up all of the excess volume, making sourcing at the local market all but impossible. But wait, it gets worse.

Shortly after the trader initiates his position, a Japanese consumer needing an incremental 5M tons of Product X for December delivery contracts for the last 5M tons of available shipping out of Australia, intending to wait for prices to decline to source the material from the Australian market. With no shipping available to move volume from Australia to China during the month of December, the trader is now stuck in a market that is net short of material—with an unfillable exposure that he cannot deliver against via a shipping arbitrage—and is long tonnage in a stranded market.

The trader is going to get destroyed.

The tonnage he is long in Australia will likely end up being sold to the Japanese end-user who can afford to wait until the very last minute for prices to drop, as it controls the only means of moving product. The trader will then have to attempt to either source material to fill the Chinese short, which should be all but impossible as he is bidding against a Chinese government who is also a motivated buyer and extremely price insensitive, or find a way to negotiate out of the contract at a substantial loss.

For traders without sufficient local expertise and/or intestinal fortitude for illiquid physical basis positions, it is also possible to express the trader's view with financial time spreads.

Financial Time/Front-to-Back Spreads in Product X
A financial time-spread position constructed with the US ProdX futures will have inherent advantages and disadvantages:

- Expressing the trade with a financially settled product removes all delivery risk, most performance risk, and, if cleared, counterparty and credit risk.
- While the US market is heavily influenced by global supply and demand fundamentals, there is no guarantee that ProdX futures prices will respond with the anticipated directionality and/or magnitude of price response to driver(s) potentially originating from conditions present in a local physical market.

Product X time spreads have been very sensitive to fundamental shifts in the global market:

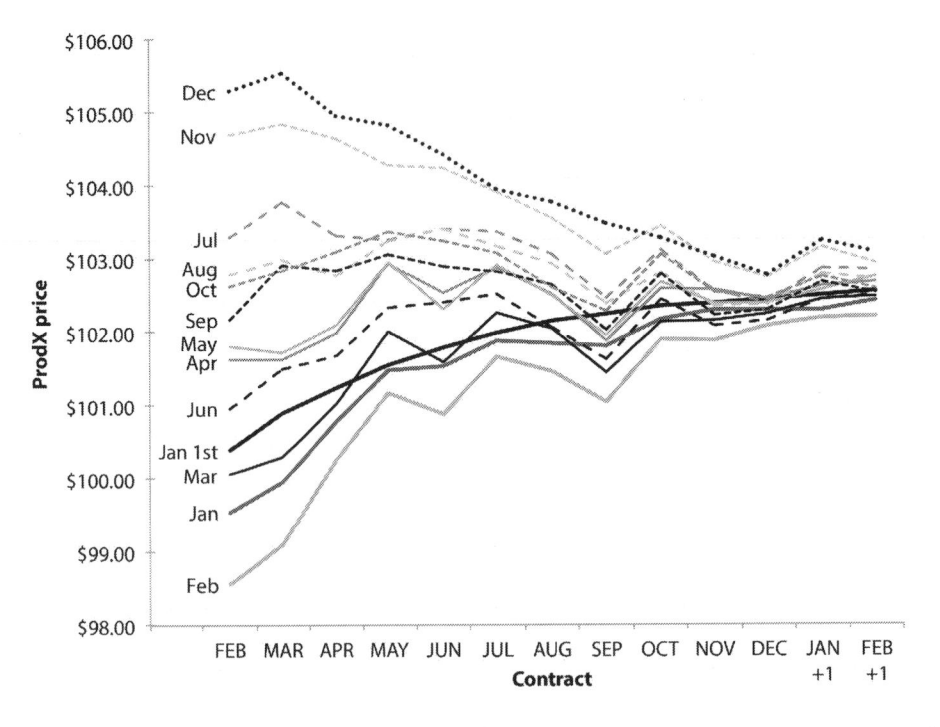

Figure 9.17   ProdX forward curve plots through time.

Chapter 9 - Spread Trading Strategies

The initial Jan 1st ProdX forward curve is in contango, which steepens dramatically toward the end of January and into February. March through October feature flatter curves that fluctuate between backwardation and contango, sometimes shifting abruptly from month to month, as seen between June and July. Ultimately, the ProdX curve develops a steep backwardation in November that persists until the final trading day of December. Examining the forward curve at the absolute market lows on Day 34 and contrasting it with the shape at the end of the year reveals three potentially interesting time spreads to express the trader's bullish view of the market.

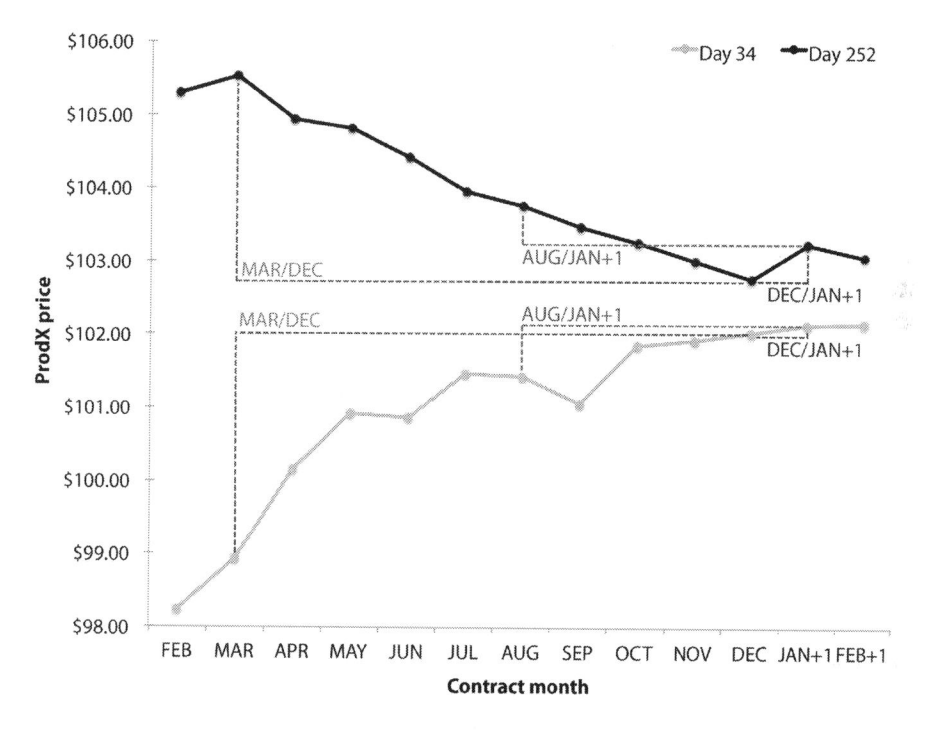

Figure 9.18   ProdX time-spread strategies.

Comparing the levels on Day 34 and Day 252:

Spread	Day 34	Day 252
MAR/DEC	($3.10)	$2.75
DEC/JAN+1	($0.12)	($0.48)
AUG/JAN+1	($0.71)	$0.52

Table 9.1   Comparison of ProdX time spread values.

The MAR/DEC Leveraged Outright Spread

The price response of the MAR/DEC spread is primarily driven by fluctuations of the MAR contract relative to the much more static DEC product. Following the year-long rally the MAR contract is the most expensive thing on the curve and will be the prompt contract at the time the African production facility does (or does not) return to service, exposing it to the highest potential volatility of response.

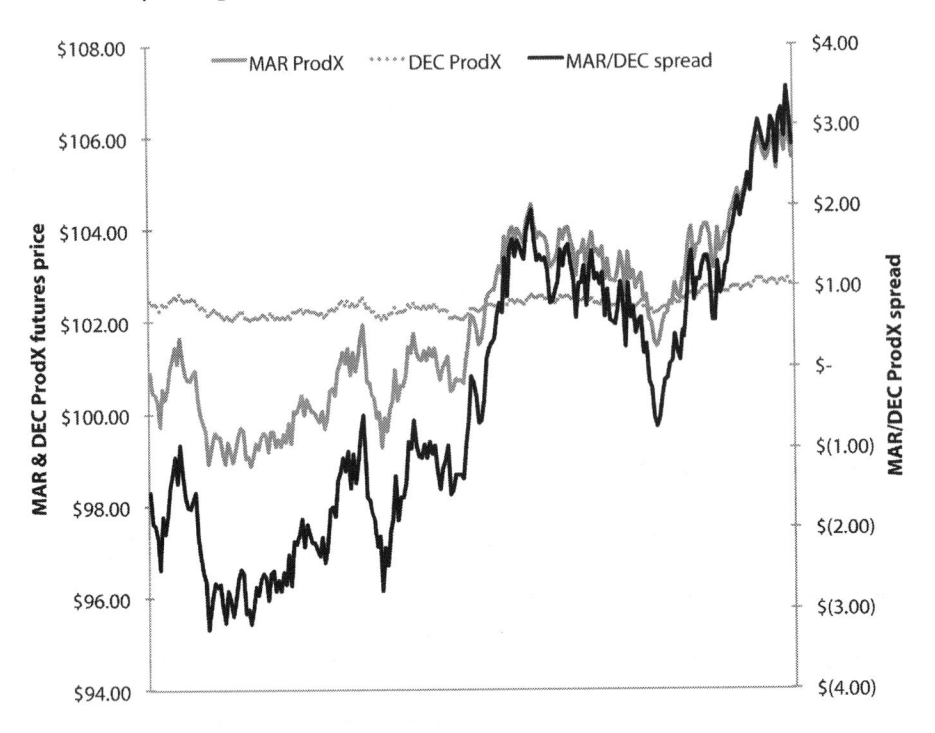

Figure 9.19   The MAR/DEC ProdX time spread as a leveraged outright trade.

The performance characteristics of the MAR/DEC spread offer the trader the opportunity to recast the short-term supply-shock explosion trade of Chapter 8 as a more tractable spread trade that has moved at approximately 80% of the velocity of the outright directional trade.

The DEC/JAN+1 Relative-Value Spread

The DEC/JAN+1 spread is a relative-value proposition, as there is no obvious reason why the DEC should trade at a material discount to the JAN+1. The DEC contract was a slight discount to the JAN+1 when the entire curve was in contango, but it is somewhat surprising that this relationship has not yet reversed itself given the shift to a largely backwardated curve.

Chapter 9 - Spread Trading Strategies

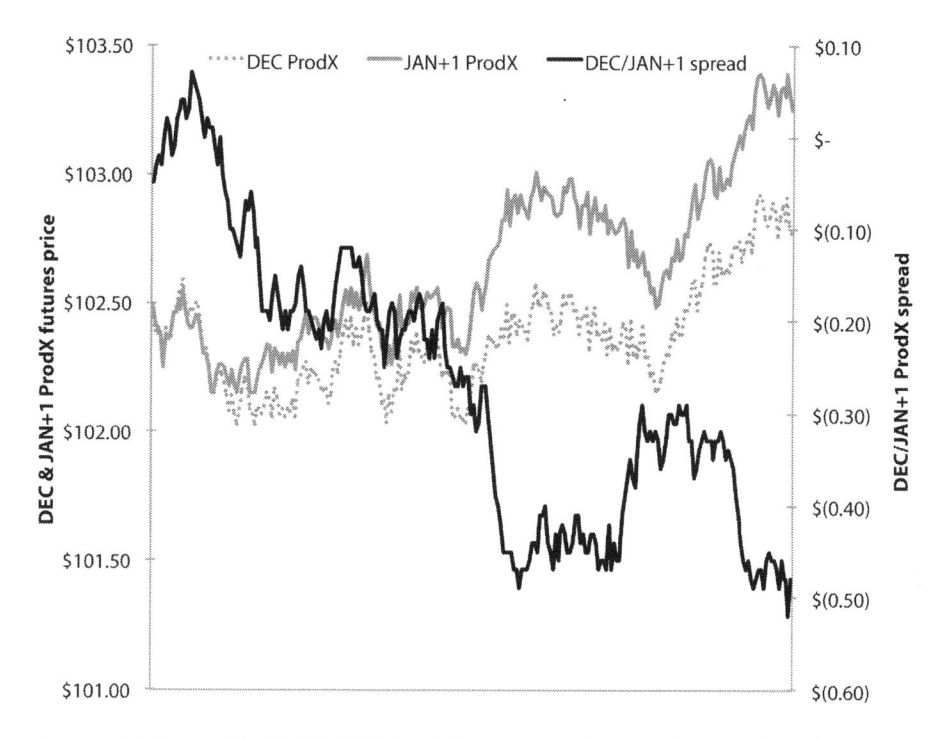

Figure 9.20 The DEC/JAN ProdX time spread as a relative-value play.

One possible explanation for the distortion between the DEC and JAN+1 contracts is a large number of market participants putting on positions in the MAR/DEC spread. Buying the MAR/DEC would involve selling the much less liquid DEC contract in the same volume as the highly liquid MAR, creating downward pressure that could be temporarily locally distorting the curve. This type of transitory positional consideration often provides an opportunity for spread trades as stable relationships are temporarily distorted.

The obvious question is what will be the catalyst for the spread relationship to change, and when and under what conditions the trader could expect this to happen. Without a trigger and a motive, it becomes more challenging to advocate for what appears to be a superficially interesting anomaly.

The AUG/JAN+1 Bull Spread
The trader can utilize the AUG/JAN+1 as a way to express a bullish view on the market by buying the AUG contract and selling the JAN+1, as seen in the following chart:

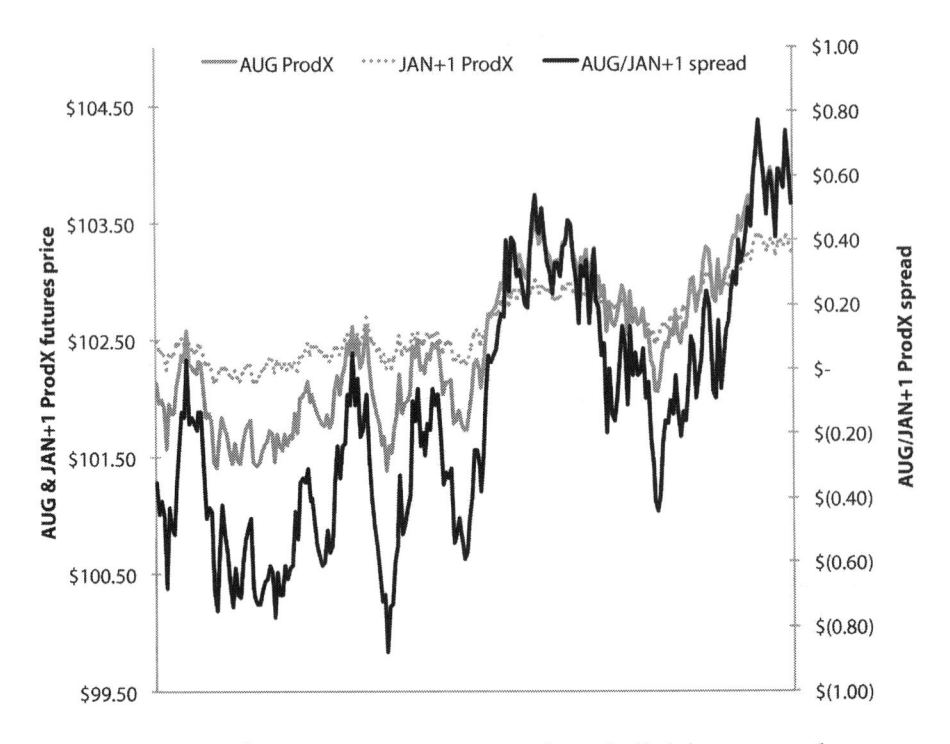

Figure 9.21 The AUG/JAN+1 time spread as a bullish long-term play.

The AUG/JAN+1 is participating the rally led by the FEB contract, but has only moved from a low of ($0.71) to a recent high of $0.77 and finishes the year at $0.52, a total move of $1.23 relative to the $7.00 move for the FEB contract. It is difficult to imagine that, barring a complete change in fundamentals toward the bear case, the spread ever reverts with the AUG trading below the JAN+1, implying a maximum of $0.50 to perhaps $0.75 of downside risk in the transaction. The profit potential is more challenging to assess, but considering that the previously examined MAR/DEC is currently trading $2.75 it is entirely possible that the AUG/JAN+1 trades out to that level, if not higher. This would imply a risk-reward ratio of $2.25 to $0.75 or 3:1.

The principal advantage of expressing a bullish view with a more long-dated front leg of the spread is that it allows significantly more time for the trade to be productively influenced by developments in the anticipated event path.

Of the seven basis and time spread trades considered, the three best options to implement the trader's view are the EurX/ProdX financial basis spread, the EurX/AfrX producer-to-consumer spread, and the AUG/JAN+1 bull time spread.

Trade Strategy #3 – EurX/ProdX MAR Financial Basis Spread
Long 1M notional tons of the MAR EurX/ProdX financial basis spread to express the view that the European market will outpace the US higher in an across the board price increase.

Chapter 9 - Spread Trading Strategies

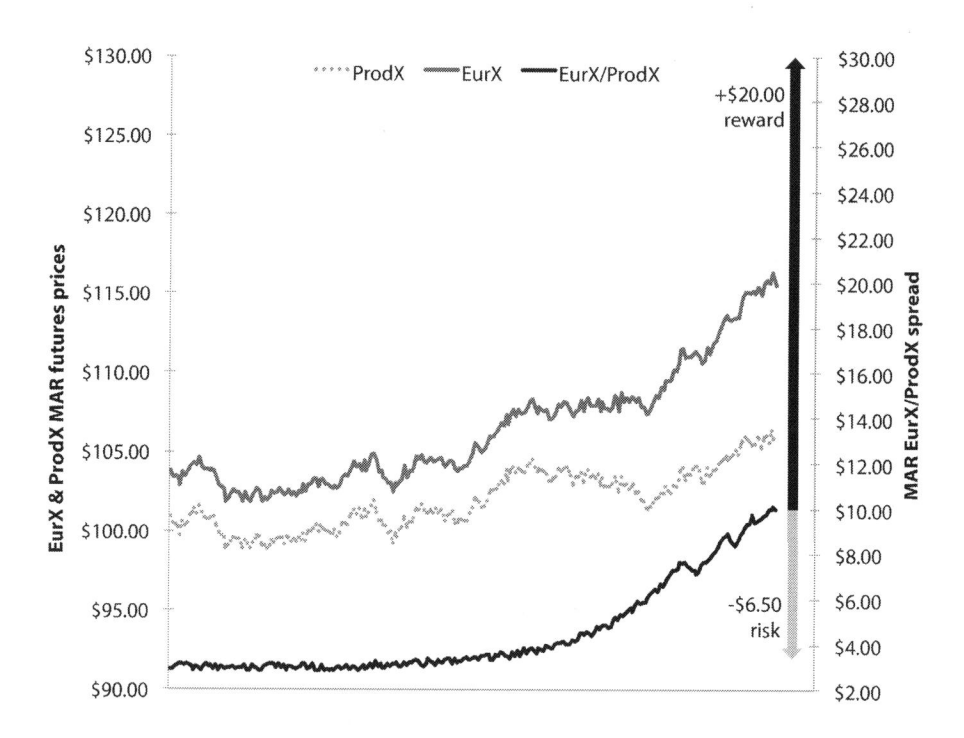

Figure 9.22   Evaluating the risk/reward of the EurX/ProdX strategy.

Position:	Long 1M notional tons MAR EurX futures at $115.53
	Short 1M notional tons MAR ProdX futures at $105.52
	Establishing a MAR EurX over ProdX spread position at $10.01
Notional Dollars:	Variable
Initial Margin:	Variable
V@R:	$456K 1-Day V@R at 95%
	$649K 1-Day V@R at 99%
Risk:	$6.50 or $6,500,000
Reward:	$20.00 or $20,000,000

The attractiveness of the EurX/ProdX spread is predicated on the assumption that the United States will win the battle for South American shipments and that Europe will have to price to a level that incentivizes incremental Canadian production, dramatically widening the spread. The trade has both positive and negative characteristics. The fact that both EurX and ProdX are financial futures contracts increases the available liquidity, lowers transaction costs and slippage, and reduces the cost of funding the position. The principal downside of the EurX/ProdX spread is the complexity of the response to the anticipated shortage due to the difficulty of handicapping the battle for South American production. The notional dollars and initial margin required to hold the exposure will be a function of the ultimate location of the component exposures, with a smaller net position and lower margin if the positions net with the same counterparty or clearing broker, and a more onerous limit burden if they reside with different firms.

Trade Strategy #4 – EurX/AfrX MAR Physical Producer to Consumer Spread
Long 1M notional tons of the MAR EurX futures vs. a short position of 1M notional tons of MAR AfrX physical volume as a play on the non-return to service of the African processing facility.

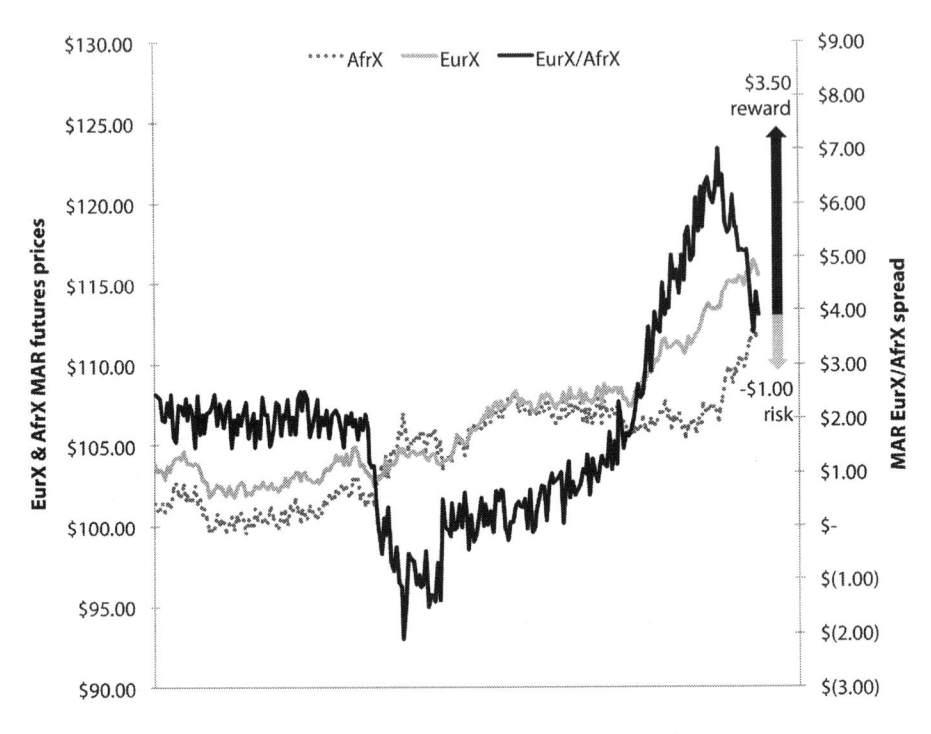

Figure 9.23 Evaluating the risk/reward of the EurX/AfrX strategy.

Position:	Long 1M notional tons MAR EurX futures at $115.53
	Short 1M notional tons MAR AfrX physical volume at $111.63
	Establishing a MAR EurX over AfrX spread position at $3.90
Notional Dollars:	Variable
Initial Margin:	Variable
V@R:	$828K 1-Day V@R at 95%
	$1.176M 1-Day V@R at 99%
Risk:	$1.00 or $1,000,000
Reward:	$3.50 or $3,500,000

The EurX/AfrX spread has a relatively low post-shutdown correlation of 0.718, which leads to a large V@R impact. The correlation for this spread has been as low as 0.099 and as high as 0.888, which would imply 95% 1-Day V@R figures of $1.237M and $603K respectively. Recall

Chapter 9 - Spread Trading Strategies   331

that as seen in Trade Strategy #1 a pure directional position in the financial MAR ProdX futures had a 95% 1-Day V@R of $629K, so the EurX/AfrX spread is actually more dangerous, which makes intuitive sense as both products are more volatile and the relationship between them is highly unstable. As with the EurX/ProdX spread, the notional dollars and initial margin required to hold the exposure will be a function of the ultimate location of the component exposures.

Trade Strategy #5 – The AUG/JAN+1 Bull Spread
Long 1M of the AUG/JAN+1 ProdX futures as a relatively loss-limited directional exposure with significant time to work prior to the expiry of the AUG contract.

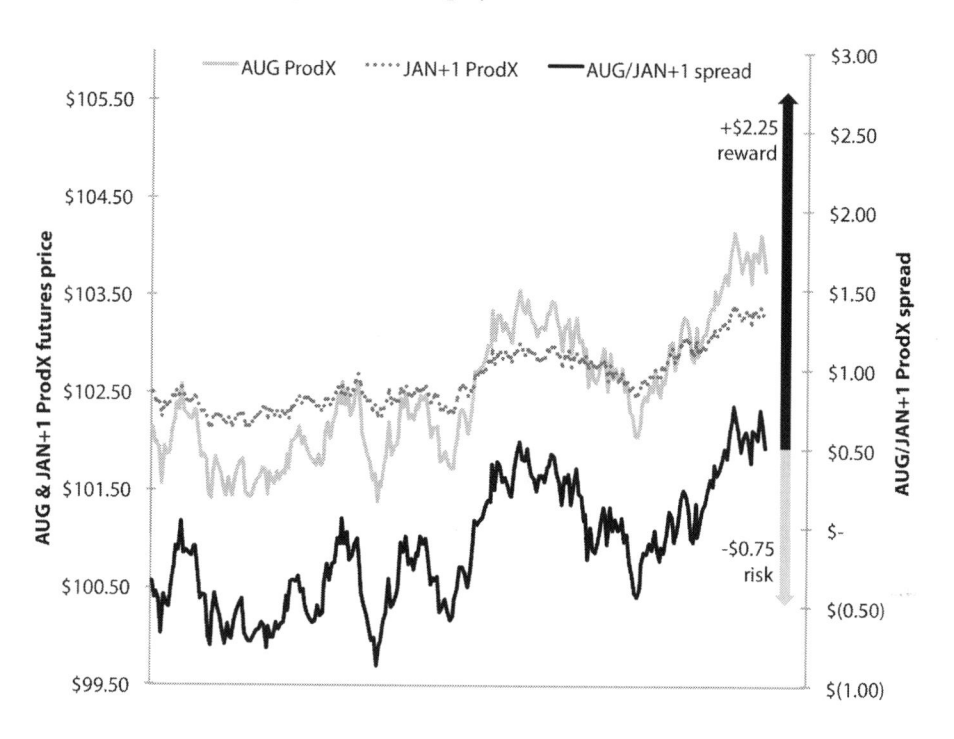

Figure 9.24   Evaluating the risk/reward of the AUG/JAN+1 ProdX strategy.

Position:	Long 1M notional tons AUG ProdX futures at $103.76
	Short 1M notional tons JAN+1 ProdX futures at $103.25
	Establishing a ProdX AUG over JAN+1 spread position at $0.51
Notional Dollars:	Variable
Initial Margin:	Variable
V@R:	$181K 1-Day V@R at 95%
	$257K 1-Day V@R at 99%
Risk:	$0.75 or $750,000
Reward:	$2.25 or $2,250,000

The AUG/JAN+1 offers the trader a way to play an increase in the overall level of Product X prices with what appears to be a very limited downside. The AUG/JAN+1 is also extremely limit friendly under the current market conditions, though it would be rational to expect that the low $175k 95% V@R number would increase both as a function of the anticipated general increase in volatility affecting both contracts and the pickup of the AUG relative to the JAN+1 as it moves closer to being the prompt month. The low V@R and small expected-price response would also make this exposure attractive for traders at risk-averse firms or those desiring a less aggressive position. As seen with the other spread positions, the notional dollars and initial margin required to hold the exposure will be a function of the ultimate location of the component exposures.

10

Option Trading Strategies

The invention of modern derivative securities is frequently compared to the discovery of fire, albeit with more pedestrian, less Promethean origins. Derivatives are a class of incredibly useful financial instruments that, when conscientiously employed by a knowledgeable practitioner, allow nearly infinite risk customization. When utilized in a haphazard, reckless, or negligent manner, the end result is often conflagration and disaster. The term "derivative" arises from the fact that the securities derive their value from another product, index, or observable data point. Every derivative will have a defined contractual linkage between the instrument and its pricing referent, which is called the underlying security. As the underlying fluctuates in response to market conditions, its price mathematically impacts the derivative security, changing its value.

Though there are many kinds of derivatives, traders typically divide them into two groups, vanilla and complex. The principal vanilla products are swaps[45] and options, and they are the common building blocks of all complex structures. Much like the basic square and rectangular Lego bricks, they can be stuck together in any number and combination to create sturdy structures or fanciful creations that appear solid but explode dramatically when impacted by unforeseen events (or dropped on the floor).

Options
As seen in Chapter 2, options are contracts that grant the purchaser the right but not the obligation to buy or sell a particular product for a predetermined price at or before a specified

---

[45] Previously covered in Chapter 2.

point in time. The option seller has an obligation to accept or deliver the product at the agreed-to price and time. To compensate the seller, the buyer pays an up-front fee called a premium. As the price of the underlying moves, the price of the option will change by a relative but not necessarily equal amount, the rate of which fluctuates due to a variety of variables. This variable rate of response is called non-linear risk, and adds significant complexity to the valuation of options. The same property, when understood and productively applied, exponentially increases their utility as financial engineering products.

Basic Building Blocks – Calls and Puts

As explored in Chapter 2, the basic building blocks of all option strategies are two instruments: calls and puts.

- A call grants the owner the right, but not the obligation, to buy a specified product at a predetermined time and price.
- A put grants the owner the right, but not the obligation, to sell a specified product at a predetermined time and price.

The owner of an option has the choice to exercise or allow the contract to expire worthless. The seller has an obligation to perform, regardless of market conditions. This asymmetry of commitment is one of the key characteristics of the option market.

- The maximum amount that the buyer of an option has at risk is the total dollar amount paid for the contract, called the premium. The amount that the buyer can gain is theoretically uncapped. The owner of the put or call is said to be long the option.
- The maximum amount that a seller of an option can make is the dollar amount of the premium received for the contract. The amount the seller can lose is theoretically uncapped. The seller of the put or call is said to be short the option.

Both calls and puts share a common terminology:

- The expiry date and expiration time on that day define the deadline when the trader must elect to take action or forfeit the right.
- Some types of options require that the trader exercise the option by informing the counterparty of the intent to buy the product (for a call) or sell the product (for a put). Others are financially settled against a predetermined index or posted price, triggering an exchange of payment, if applicable.
- European options are exercisable only on the expiry date at any time prior to the expiration time. American options are exercisable at any point prior to the expiration time on the expiry date.
- The strike price (or simply, strike) of an option is the predetermined level at which the owner buys (for a call) or sells (for a put).
- The premium is the price the trader must pay as an upfront fee to the counterparty for purchasing the option.

Chapter 10 – Option Trading Strategies

- The notional volume is the amount of the product the buyer of the option has the right to transact with the seller.

All of the above will be listed in a detailed document that describes the option product called the contract specification.

Advantages of Option Strategies

1. Long option positions have a fixed, known downside equal to the premium paid for the position.
2. It is possible to combine puts and calls at different strike prices into structures and complex portfolios designed to express very sophisticated market views.
3. Option positions have non-linear characteristics that let the trader express views not possible with purely directional instruments.

Known Downside of Long Option Positions

A trader entering into a long option position enjoys a rare risk-taking luxury, knowing from the start exactly, mathematically, how bad things can get. The total amount of premium paid for the contract is the maximum amount the buyer can lose, which will only occur if the option is not exercised or is allowed to expire worthless. The beyond-expectation losses that are an ever-present fear for directional and spread traders should never trouble an option trader deploying a leveraged directional strategy.

Ability to Combine Into Structures

A trader with an exposure to a linear risk really has only three choices: add to it, subtract from it, or keep it the same. The position is easily volumetrically modified at the current price point, but its basic characteristics will remain constant. In a reasonably developed option market there will be puts and calls present at multiple strike levels above and below the current price that can be combined into structures that allow for both volumetric risk modification and control of the rate of change of risk accumulation/reduction. This will be explored in greater depth in the section on Simple Combinations and Common Structures.

Non-Linear Risk

Option positions have inherent non-linear risk properties, and the value of an option can—and will—be affected by much more than just the up or down fluctuations of the market. Options are inherently complex instruments, and the forward price of a pre-expiry call or put will be influenced by the prevailing interest rates, the volatility present in the market, and the time remaining until expiry, among other things. More non-linear attributes reveal themselves when options are combined into simple structures and complex portfolios. It is critical for any option trader to understand the non-linear risk characteristics of potential option strategies across the full range of potential outcomes. This will be covered in detail later in the chapter.

Disadvantages of Option Strategies

1. Poor liquidity: the option market for most products will generally be smaller than that of the underlying product, which can make accumulating and distributing positions challenging, and may imply high bid-offer transaction costs.
2. Options may be generally too cheap or too expensive to be useful: it is possible for market conditions to make options across the board "cheap" or "expensive," which can make render some strategies unproductive.
3. The trader must pay to play, with a premium payment required to establish a long position.
4. Increased complexity in value determination: multiple factors influence price, and a productive thesis can be defeated by an unexpected change in any variable.
5. Option markets take time to develop, and may not be present in the early development stages.

Poor Liquidity

The option market is, in most cases, a secondary market that sits atop the trading that occurs in the underlying security. The total traded volume of options will generally be significantly smaller and will be divided across the range of put and call strikes, each accounting for a fraction of the whole. Traders needing to accumulate sizable exposures may need to work into them over time or risk distorting the market in the short term.

Many options are sold by market makers, who must sell above fair value to earn a margin for taking the risk of providing liquidity. They immediately hedge their exposure and have little or no intention of ever buying anything back unless it is at a discount to fair value. As a result, the bid-offer spreads present in the option market will typically be wider than in the corresponding underlying market, implying higher costs to enter or exit a position. Additionally, option strikes fall into and out of favor as the underlying fluctuates in price. A $100.00 call that may have been near par and widely traded may now be so hopelessly out of the money with the underlying at $42.00 that it is rarely, if ever, quoted. A trader wanting to exit a position in the now-dormant $100.00 strike would likely end up groveling to the friendly neighborhood market maker, which would probably not be a pleasant experience.

Options May Be Generally Too Cheap or Too Expensive to Be Useful

All things being equal, in periods of increasing market volatility options will become more valuable. Volatility is factored into price both explicitly and implicitly. Wider than normal swings in the price of the underlying increase the probability that an out-of-the-money option may become an in-the-money option at some point during its lifetime, which increases its value. Perversely, just as traders most want to buy options, they become more expensive. In extremely volatile conditions the price of an option can become very high relative to the potential market fluctuations, making them poor risk-reward trades from the buy side (but potentially good sales). Conversely, in periods of extreme quiet when the market becomes trapped in a narrow range, option prices will rapidly decrease as traders assume that there is little probability of them ever coming into the money, making them an interesting buy (but probably a terrible sale).

Chapter 10 – Option Trading Strategies

The Trader Must Pay to Play
Directional and spread trades are generally executable with little to no cost of entry other than the implied tax of crossing the bid-offer spread. The purchaser of an option must pay the seller the up-front premium to assume the risk in the transaction. The premium represents the total amount at risk to the owner of an option, but also the amount the market must move in the trader's favor for the transaction to break even if held to expiration.

Increased Complexity in Value Determination
Determining the value of a position in the underlying security is a straightforward exercise, whether it is a stock, bond, or commodity. Options present a more complex valuation proposition, particularly if the bid-offer spread is wide (or non-existent). Traders will use a variety of pricing and valuation models in an attempt to determine the fair value of an option from the other variables present in the market.

Options Markets Take Time to Develop
Options are not necessarily always available during the initial growth of a market, and will typically only become common instruments when sophisticated players arrive on the scene.

Common Option Strategies

Options can be utilized in very simple, straightforward strategies, combined into structures, and aggregated into complex non-linear portfolios with whatever properties the creator desires and can afford to pay for. Broadly speaking, there are four main varieties of option strategies:

1. Single-option strategies are designed to profit if the market moves in a particular direction within a specified time period. A call or put can be held to the expiration date and used to express a view on the market's ultimate evolution during that time horizon. An option position can also be treated like a leveraged forward contract and closed out prior to expiry, allowing the trader to take advantage of the known downside and the non-linear nature of the risk to profit from an anticipated market movement.
2. Structures are created from a combination of different options that are designed to profit from a specific set of market circumstances, either in terms of market timing, direction, or both.
3. Volatility-based strategies use options to express a view on the relative level of future market fluctuations.
4. In managing a portfolio of options, success is predicated on understanding the nuances of the market, an ability and willingness to warehouse risk, and access to customer flow and significant liquidity. A portfolio is generally most profitable for market-making entities, as they have a significant structural advantage. Complex, non-linear portfolios require sophisticated model support.

1. Single-Option Strategies and Payout Diagrams at Expiry

The first step toward understanding options is to examine how they perform at the end of their lives. A payout diagram is a chart of the value of an option at expiration graphed across a range of possible underlying prices, considering the total premium paid out or received. For example, consider the following chart of a $90.00 call option that was purchased for $4.00.

Figure 10.1 Payout at expiration of a long $90.00 strike call with a $4.00 premium.

At any price below $90.00, the option has no value, leaving the buyer out of pocket the $4.00 initial investment. At prices above $90.00, the option begins to accrue value in a linear fashion, increasing dollar for dollar with the change in price of the underlying. Between $90.00 and $94.00 the net payout is still negative, but the profits from being slightly in the money are starting to offset the cost of the option. Above $94.00 the option has completely paid off the premium cost and now participates dollar-for-dollar in the price increase of the underlying, with a theoretically infinite upside.

The payout diagram is inverted for the seller of the same option.

Chapter 10 – Option Trading Strategies

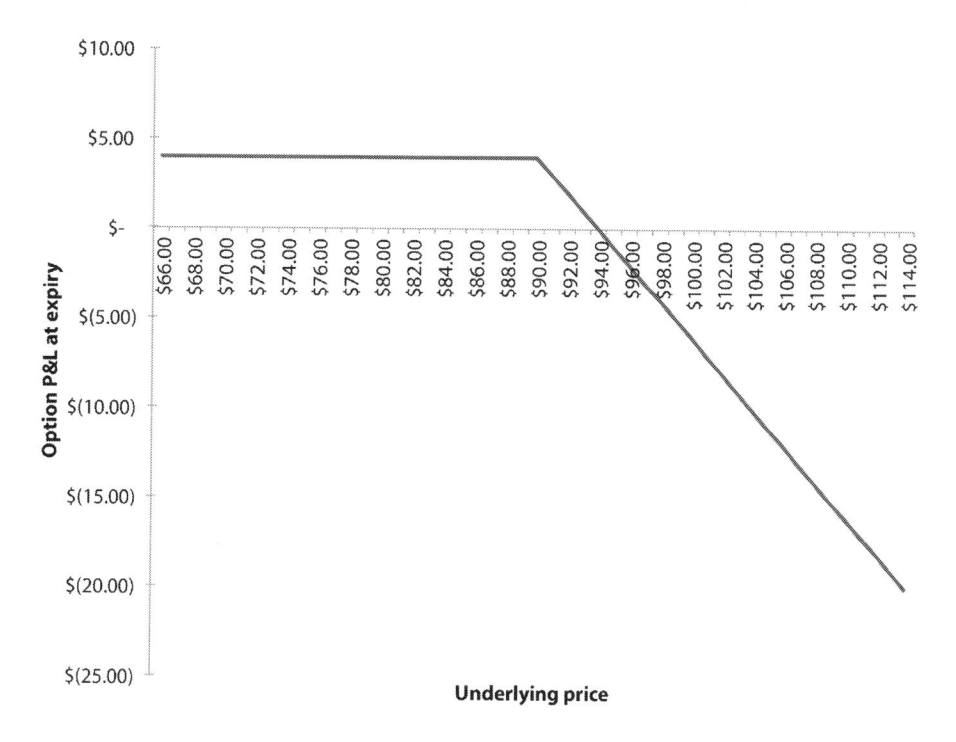

Figure 10.2 Payout at expiration of a short $90.00 strike call with a $4.00 premium.

The maximum profit for the seller of a $90.00 strike call option exactly matches the $4.00 maximum loss for the buyer and occurs at prices below $90. Between $90 and $94 the seller is still profitable, but margins erode as the option moves into the money. Above $94 the seller is losing money, and that loss will increase linearly as the price rises. Where the buyer of an option has a known downside and an uncapped upside, the seller has a known upside fixed at the inception of the trade with a theoretically infinite exposure to potential losses.

If the trader had wished to bet that prices would decline and purchased a $90.00 put for $4.00, the payout function would look like this.

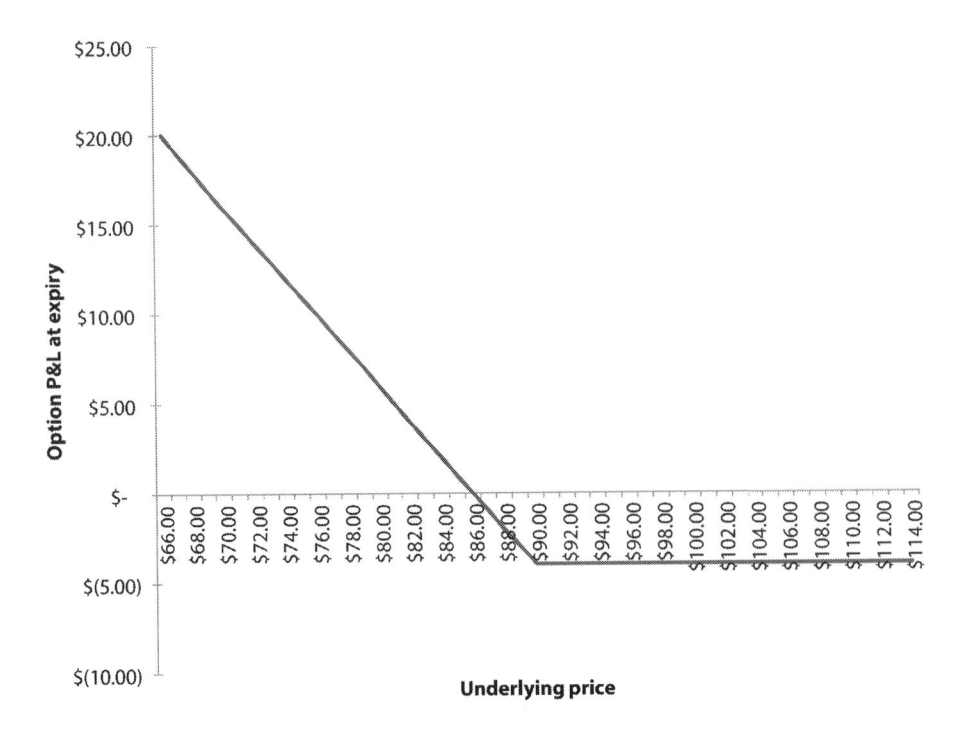

Figure 10.3 Payout at expiration of a long $90.00 strike put with a $4.00 premium.

Above $90.00, the put is worthless, and the trader has lost the $4.00 premium payment. Between $90.00 and $86.00, the option begins to increase in value to offset the cost, but the net payout is still negative. Below $86.00 the value of the option has completely offset the cost of the premium and now participates linearly in the decrease in price of the underlying. Unlike a call, a put option usually does have a maximum possible value, the difference between the strike price and zero.[46] This structural difference in maximum potential payout is one of the reasons that calls will tend to have a slightly higher value than similar strike-price puts in most markets at most times.

So Many Options to Choose From
The number of options quoted in a market can vary widely, from price-by-appointment illiquidity to developed, sophisticated, exchanged-based menus of strike prices and maturity terms. For those that need still more variety, the over-the-counter market contains market makers willing to price non-standard strike levels, odd-lot volumes, and elongated tenors, for a fee.

---

[46] There are rare exceptions with products that can encounter storage or delivery constraints so severe that the owner may have to pay a counterparty to take the product off their hands, implying a negative selling price. In general, it is safe to assume the lower boundary is zero.

Chapter 10 – Option Trading Strategies

A call option with a strike price well above the underlying's current price (or a put well below) is said to be out of the money. Options struck at or near the current price are at the money or par. A call option with a strike well below the current market price (or a put well above) is in the money. Out of the money, at the money, and in the money are clearly subjective measures and vary from market to market; they are generally used as casual shorthand by traders to refer to a range of strike prices.

Options as Levered Forwards

In markets that offer good depth, liquidity, and small bid-offer spreads it is possible to utilize long options positions to replicate the equivalent exposures in the underlying product. This is a very attractive strategy, when feasible. The trader's maximum loss is fixed at the premium expended and is known at the trade's inception, yielding perfect clarity on the downside of the transaction, a great advantage when assessing the risk-to-reward ratio. Removing the potential for disaster can be very liberating to a trader's psyche, leading to better on-the-run trading decisions. The known downside can give the trader additional patience to let the trade work and allow greater latitude for a position to fluctuate.

The principal challenge when using options as leveraged outrights is the need to call not only the direction of the market move, but also the magnitude and the timing, which adds several degrees of difficulty. The profit will have to overcome the premium paid out to assume the position, which will necessitate a larger market move. Risking $1.00 to make $3.00 on a forward position that can be exited at a $1.00 profit can still be considered a productive trade. An option with the same strike price that cost $1.00 would have just broken barely even with the same move in the underlying if taken to expiry. If exited prior to expiry, it is highly probable that after paying away the bid-offer spread on the option the trader would have lost money on the transaction.

Using an option as a levered, known-downside forward position is only possible for long option positions where the trader is purchasing the call or put and controls the exercise/no exercise decision. Selling a put or call does not yield the opposite exposure, as the potential profit is capped at the premium harvested and the potential losses are, in theory, unlimited.

The usefulness of options as levered forwards is also contingent on the general level of option prices being productively low, within the context of the market move the trader hopes to capture.

Put/Call Parity and Using Underlying to Convert Option Positions

A trader holding a call or put can use a volume of the underlying to change the payout of the combined position. As discussed in Chapter 8, a directional position in the underlying has linear performance characteristics. A trader owning par puts who has changed her view and now believes that the market is going higher could purchase a notionally equivalent volume of the underlying product. The combined long put, long underlying position will perform like a call with a similar strike price, as seen in the following payout diagram of a $90.00 put that cost $4.00 combined with a long position in the underlying security trading $90.00:

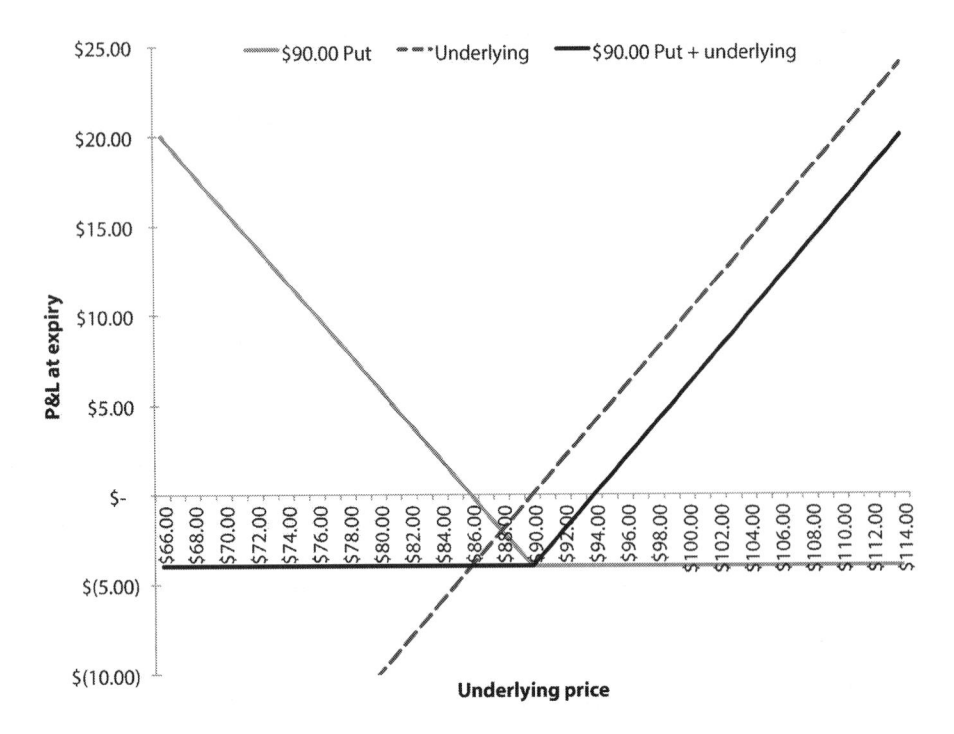

Figure 10.4 The combined payout of a $90.00 put plus a long position in the underlying at $90.00 is equivalent to the long $90.00 call payout seen in Figure 10.1.

Modifying the payout of an option with a volume of underlying is called a conversion, and is the simplest example of an option structure. The most common combinations are:

- long call + short underlying = long put
- long put + long underlying = long call
- short call + long underlying = short put
- short put + short underlying = short call

The combined exposure created by converting an option is called a synthetic put or call. The ability to use the underlying to convert calls into puts and vice versa creates a price relationship between the values of par options known as put/call parity.

Consider an example where the underlying market is trading at $90.00, the $90.00 strike call is trading for $6.00 and the $90.00 strike put is trading for $3.00. It would be possible to synthetically replicate the $90.00 call option by buying the $90.00 put for $3.00 and buying the underlying. The owner of the $3.00 put + underlying synthetic call could, if they choose, sell

Chapter 10 – Option Trading Strategies

the $6.00 call option and lock in a virtually riskless $3.00 profit.[47] The more efficient the market, the faster the conversion arbitrage will erode any price differential. Put/call parity equates the prices of par options and underlying in an arbitrage-free environment.[48]

Put/call parity is often mathematically expressed:

$$P(t) + S(t) = C(t) + B(t)*X$$

Which states that at time t, a portfolio of a put with a strike price of X plus a share of stock trading at X must be equal in value to a call with a strike price of X plus X dollars of a zero coupon risk-free bond that matures at expiry. Any material difference between the put + stock and call + risk-free bond portfolios would create an arbitrage opportunity.

2. Common Option Structures

One of the main advantages of options as trading instruments is the ability to select performance characteristics by choosing a strike price, premium, and exposure direction that best suits the trader's needs from the menu of calls and puts available in the market. It is possible to assemble a position out of options with different strike prices and directionalities that has a customized payout structure designed to profit from a particular expected market movement. The most common structures are called straddles, strangles, collars, vertical spreads, ratio spreads, and iron butterflies. Each has distinctly different properties and uses.

Straddles

A straddle is constructed out of a call and a put with the same strike price. Straddles can be purchased to bet on an abrupt price movement away from the common strike level or an increase in the general level of volatility. If sold, they are a gamble on a lack of volatility leading to an expiry at or near the strike. The price of the structure is the sum of the premiums paid if long, or the total received if short. The total cost of the options relative to the anticipated movement in the underlying frames the risk to reward proposition inherent in the trade.

Below is a payout diagram for a long $50.00 straddle composed of a $3.00 call option and a $3.00 put option.

---

[47] Almost riskless, because the trader could have execution risk around the exercise, depending on the type of option traded.
[48] Put/call parity is technically only formulaically valid for European options, but the concept generally applies to all options.

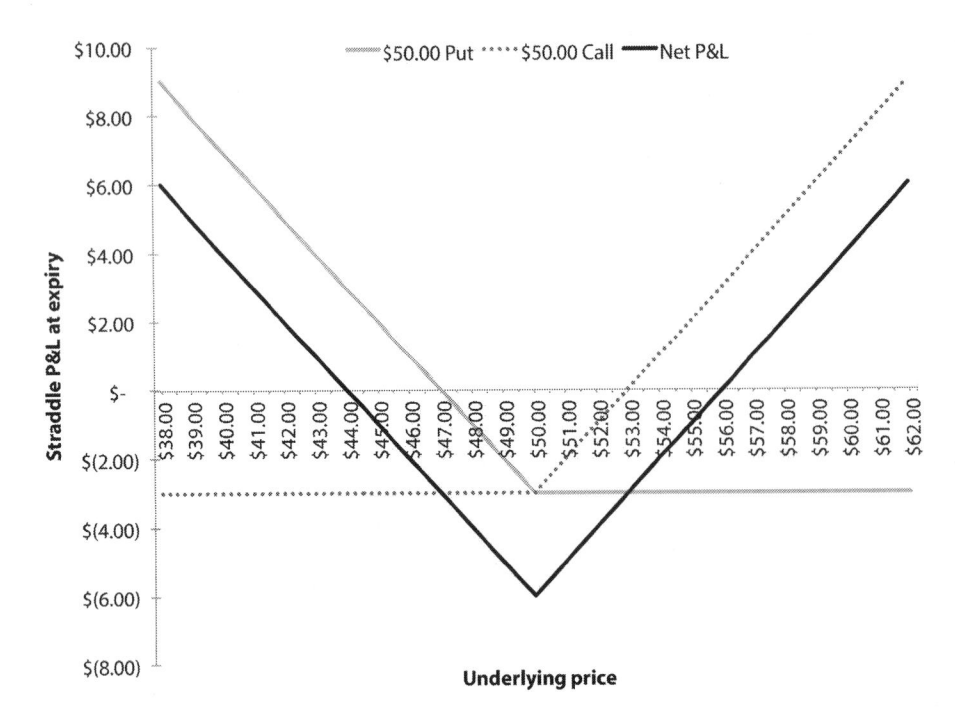

Figure 10.5 Payout at expiration of a long $50.00 straddle with $6.00 total premium cost.

The combined P&L at expiry is the simple sum of the individual component option payouts. Since a long straddle is a bet that prices will move away from a predefined level, it should come as no surprise that the maximum $6.00 loss ($3.00 for the call, $3.00 for the put) occurs at $50.00, where both options are effectively worthless. As the position moves in either direction away from $50.00, one of the options will remain worthless, but the other will start to contribute value to the structure. The breakeven level for a straddle is equal to the sum of the premiums above or below the strike price, in this case $44.00 to the downside or $56.00 to the upside. Below $44.00 or above $56.00 the straddle will pay the owner in a linear fashion dollar-for-dollar with the move in the underlying. A straddle is unprofitable for a range of 2x the total premium paid around the strike price, which necessitates a fairly significant price move away from that level to justify the cost and imply a workable risk-to-reward ratio if taken to delivery.

A short straddle with the same components would have the following expiry graph:

Chapter 10 – Option Trading Strategies

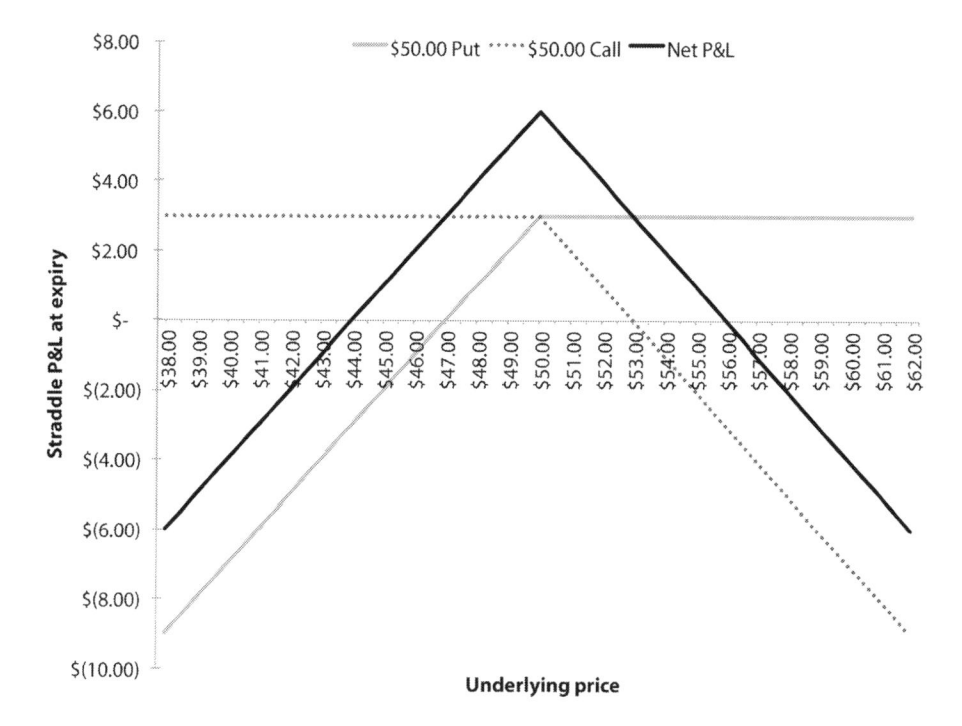

Figure 10.6 Payout at expiration of a short $50.00 straddle with $6.00 total premium cost.

Selling a straddle is a bet that prices will not move away from the strike price, in this case $50.00. The structure is profitable across a distance of 2x the total premium received, losing dollar-for-dollar if the price drops below $44 or rises above $56.

Converting Near-Par Calls and Puts Into Straddles

As seen in the previous section on conversions, it is possible to reverse the directionality of a near-par option position by adding an equivalently sized long or short position in the underlying. It is also possible to modify a par option position into a synthetic straddle by converting half of the notional volume and leaving the rest to function as originally intended. Assuming a 100-lot option position, the most common combinations would be:

- 100 lots long call + 50 lots short underlying = 50 lots long straddle
- 100 lots long put + 50 lots long underlying = 50 lots long straddle

Straddle Prices as Volatility Measurements

Straddles are typically priced and traded with near par strike prices. Since the trader profits if the market moves in either direction, the value inherent in the proposition is a bet on the probability of a large move occurring within a pre-defined timeframe, and is therefore a statement about the anticipated level of volatility in the market. The current price of a par straddle for a particular maturity will be used as the benchmark volatility for the period.

Getting a straddle run from a broker across a product term is a common way to see where the relative volatilities are being priced in the market and make period-to-period and day-over-day comparisons.

Call and Put Skew

In the previous straddle examples I have arbitrarily assigned the same price to both component options. In reality, one of the legs would generally command a premium over the other. The imbalance in price between calls and puts of the same strike price is referred to as the skew. Most markets will have a slight structural skew toward calls, as their theoretically unlimited upside would always warrant a higher valuation. The day-to-day change in the relative skew is watched as an overall market sentiment indicator, with a shift in value toward the call or put side potentially signaling an imminent move in the underlying. Client-facing traders at banks and merchants will also closely monitor shifts in customer requests for quotes on bullish or bearish strategies as a window into market sentiment.

Strangles

A strangle is a structure that is conceptually similar to a straddle, but with a gap between the strikes of the call and put options that leads to a flattened payout distribution between the two prices. The component options are further away from par (and therefore cheaper), which lowers the total cost of entering the position.

Consider a strangle composed of a $45.00 strike put and a $55.00 strike call, both of which cost $1.50.

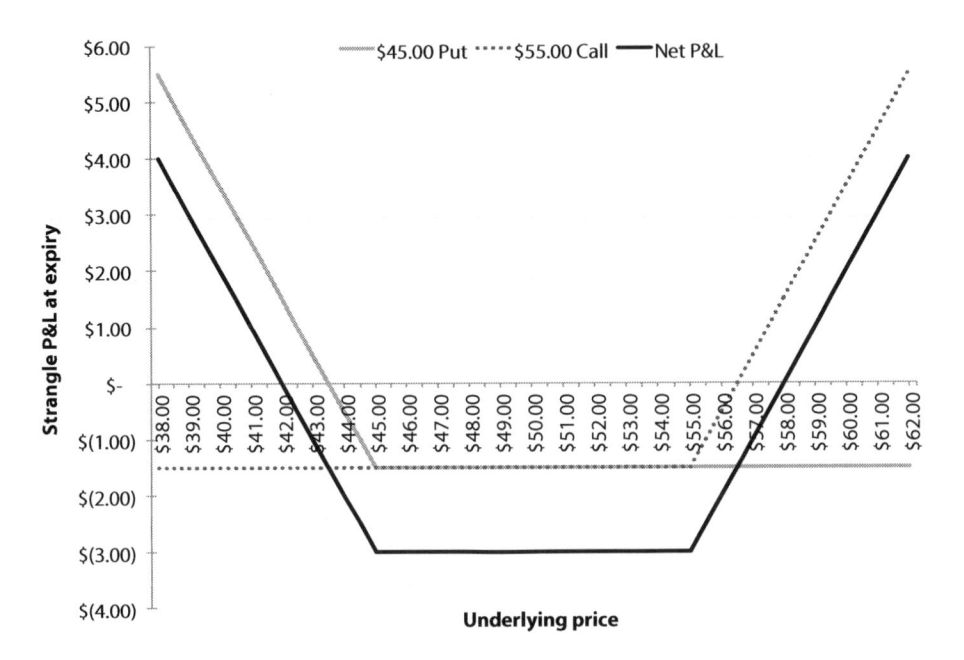

Figure 10.7   Payout at expiration of a long $45.00/$55.00 strangle with $3.00 total premium cost.

The maximum possible loss is again equal to the sum of the option premiums. In a straddle it is only present at the coincident strikes of the options, but in a strangle it spans the entire distance between $45.00 and $55.00. If the price of the underlying drops below $45.00 or rises above $55.00 at expiry, one option will remain worthless and the other will start contributing value in a linear fashion. A strangle is therefore unprofitable for a range equal to (call premium + put premium + (strike 1 − strike 2)) around the midpoint of the structure. Strangles are used to bet on large moves or to reduce the cost of entering the position.

Collars

A collar is created by selling a slightly out-of-the-money call and buying a slightly out-of-the-money put. The proceeds from selling one option partially finance the purchase of the other. Collars are a structure useful for entities that have a natural long position that they are seeking to hedge in a cost-effective fashion. A power generator who is long energy, for example, might want to buy puts to protect the value of its output and is willing to finance that protection by selling the right to have it profitably called away if prices rise.

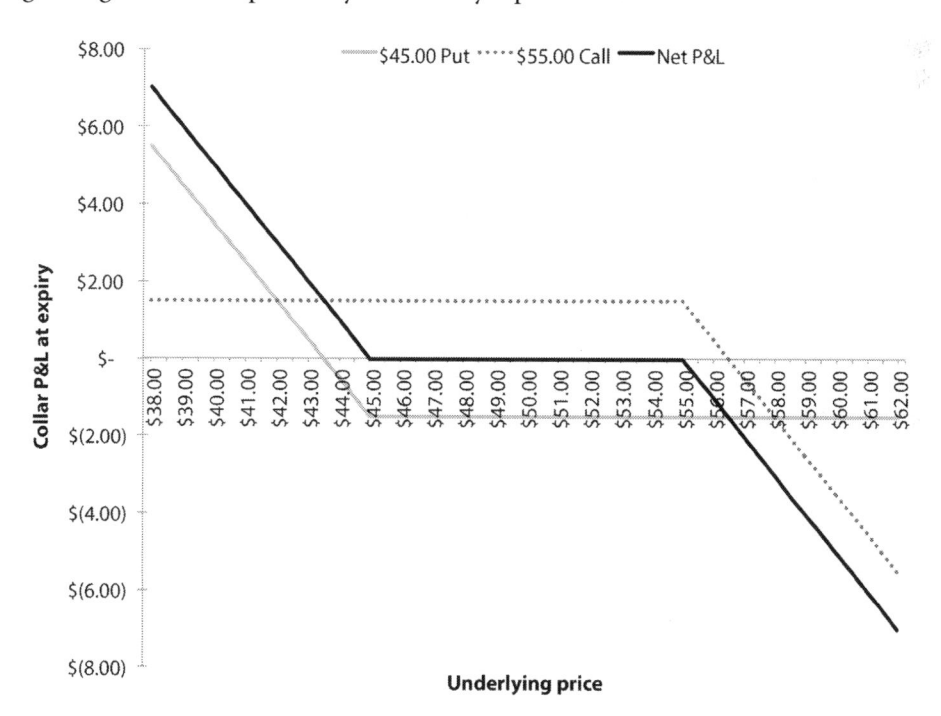

Figure 10.8 Payout at expiration of a long $45.00/$55.00 collar with zero net premium cost.

Combining the $45.00 put/$55.00 call collar with an equivalent notional volume long position leads to a payout diagram at expiry that looks like:

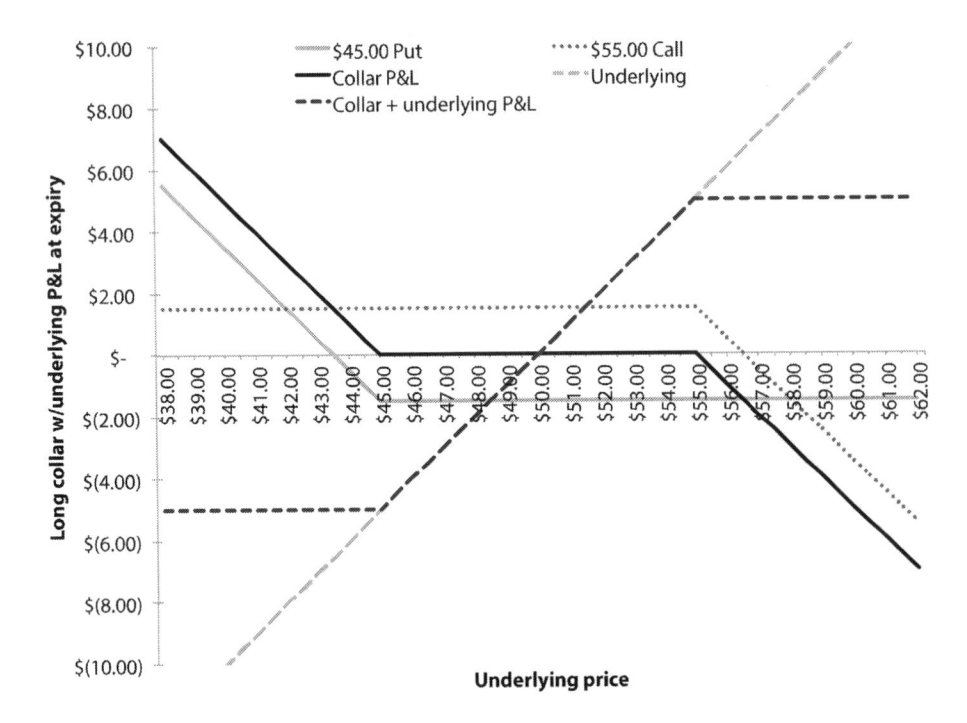

Figure 10.9 Payout at expiration of a long $45.00/$55.00 collar with zero net premium cost combined with a position in the underlying.

The payout of the collar combined with the natural long position in the underlying creates a P&L floor below the put strike price, which is paid for by the loss of the upside above the call strike.

Collars are extremely popular among naturals, as they can be made costless by adjusting the strike prices to achieve a net zero cash outlay for the purchaser. Collar purchasers must beware the component pricing, however, as traders love to sell collars to unsophisticated clients, who eat up the zero cost of implementation and ignore the edge for the seller created by over-valuing or under-valuing one of the options. Financial players looking to call a turn in the market also use collars as a way to be long volatility with directionality.

The payout diagram for a seller of a collar:

Chapter 10 – Option Trading Strategies

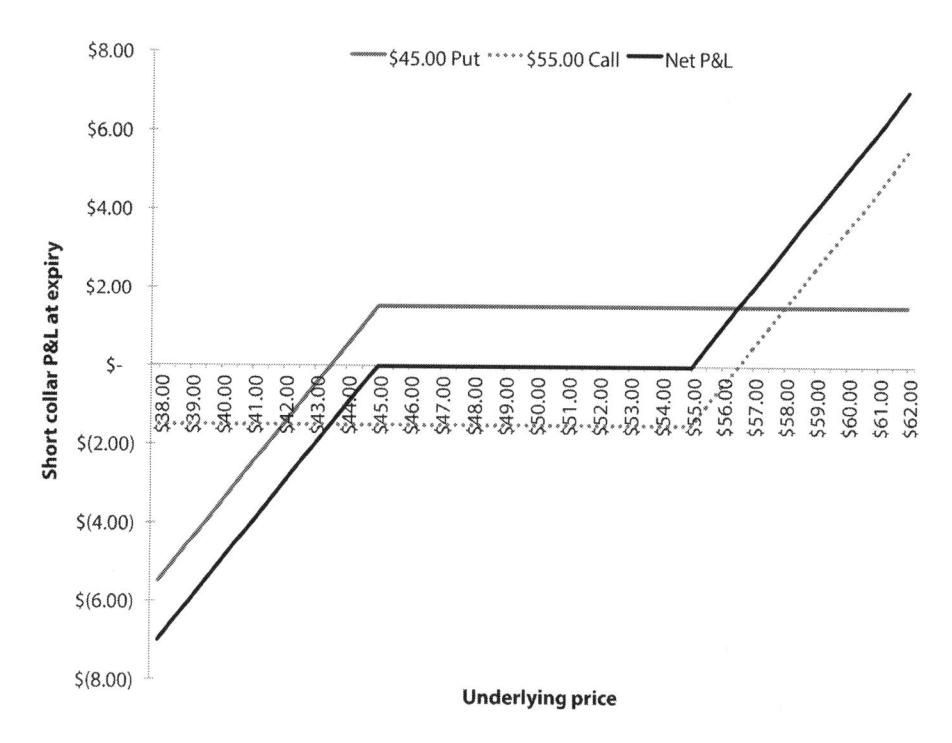

Figure 10.10 Payout at expiration of a short $45.00/$55.00 collar with zero net premium cost.

Vertical Spreads

A vertical spread is a combination of two calls or puts with the same expiration date but different strike prices. They are designed to capture a directional market move with reduced costs of implementation relative to an outright call or put purchase. A bullish vertical spread involves purchasing a call with a near-the-money strike price and selling a further out-of-the-money call. The premium collected from the sale of the higher strike option partially finances the purchase cost of the more expensive near-the-money option. A bearish vertical spread involves buying a near-the-money put and selling an out-of-the-money put against it. Vertical spreads are also frequently referred to as call spreads or put spreads.

A $55.00/$65.00 bullish vertical spread, involving the purchase of a $55.00 call for $3.00 and the sale of a $65.00 call for $1.50, would have the following payout at expiry:

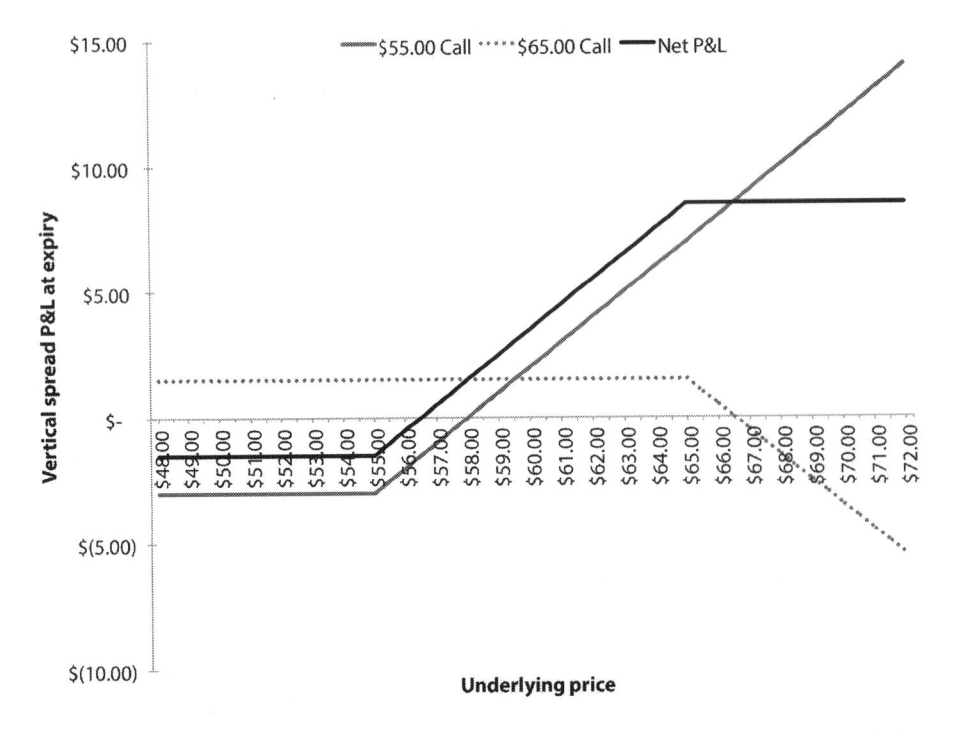

Figure 10.11 Payout at expiration of a long $55.00/$65.00 call spread with $1.50 net premium cost.

The structure loses the total net premium at prices below the lower strike, and then starts to accrue value linearly between the lower and upper strikes. The maximum value occurs at or above the higher strike, beyond which the now in-the-money short call option prevents any additional appreciation in value. The total potential profit is equal to the distance between the strike prices, less the total net cost of putting on the structure. This very visible relationship between the maximum loss of the premium paid and the potential profit presents an unusually clear risk-reward assessment opportunity for the trader.

Ratio Spreads

A ratio spread is conceptually similar to a vertical spread, with the added complexity that the volumes of options at each of the strike prices are different and can vary according to the whims of the trader. A typical ratio-spread call construction would involve selling two or three out-of-the-money calls for each near-the-money call purchased, making the structure cheaper, but ultimately much riskier.

The payout diagram for a ratio call spread involving the purchase of one $55.00 call for $3.00 and selling three $65.00 calls for $1.50 each looks like this:

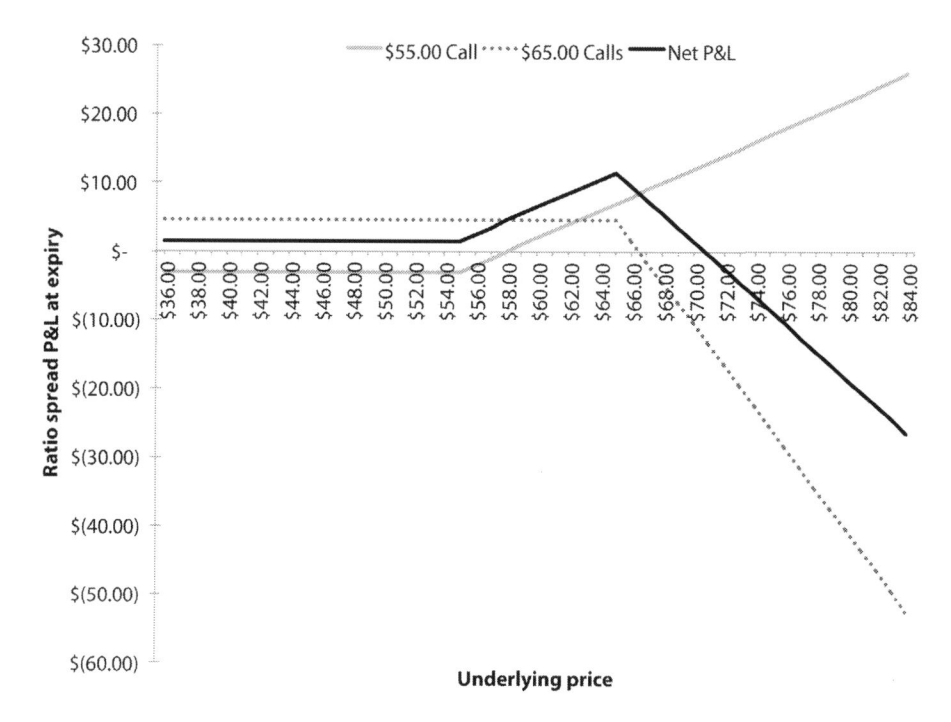

Figure 10.12 Payout at expiration of a long 1x3 $55.00/$65.00 call spread with $1.50 net premium inflow.

The first critical difference is that this particular structure results in a net premium inflow, in that the trader is paying $3.00 for the $55.00 call but taking in a total of $4.50 from the sale of the three $65.00 calls. The structure is therefore profitable at the net premium level until the lower option strike, at which point the $55.00 call starts contributing value up to the point of maximum profitability at the $65.00 strike price. Above $65.00 the three short calls come into the money and start subtracting value at a rate of $3.00 per $1.00 movement in the underlying. This asymmetry of profitability around an inflection point is a very significant risk and one of the key attributes of ratio spreads. The ability to reduce or eliminate the cost of funding is a powerful tool, but traders must always remember that there is no such thing as a free lunch.

Iron Butterflies

An iron butterfly involves four component options, two calls and two puts spread across three strike prices. A short iron butterfly position consists of a long out-of-the-money put, short at-the-money put, short at-the-money call, and long out-of-the-money call. A short iron butterfly can be conceptually decomposed into a put and a call vertical spread at the same strike price, or as a short straddle surrounded by a long strangle. The par call and put are frequently referred to as the body of the structure, and the out of the money call and put are the wings. The payoff diagram for the structure composed of a $45.00 put that cost $1.25, a $50.00 put that cost $2.50, a $50.00 call that cost $2.50, and a $55.00 call that cost $1.25 would be:

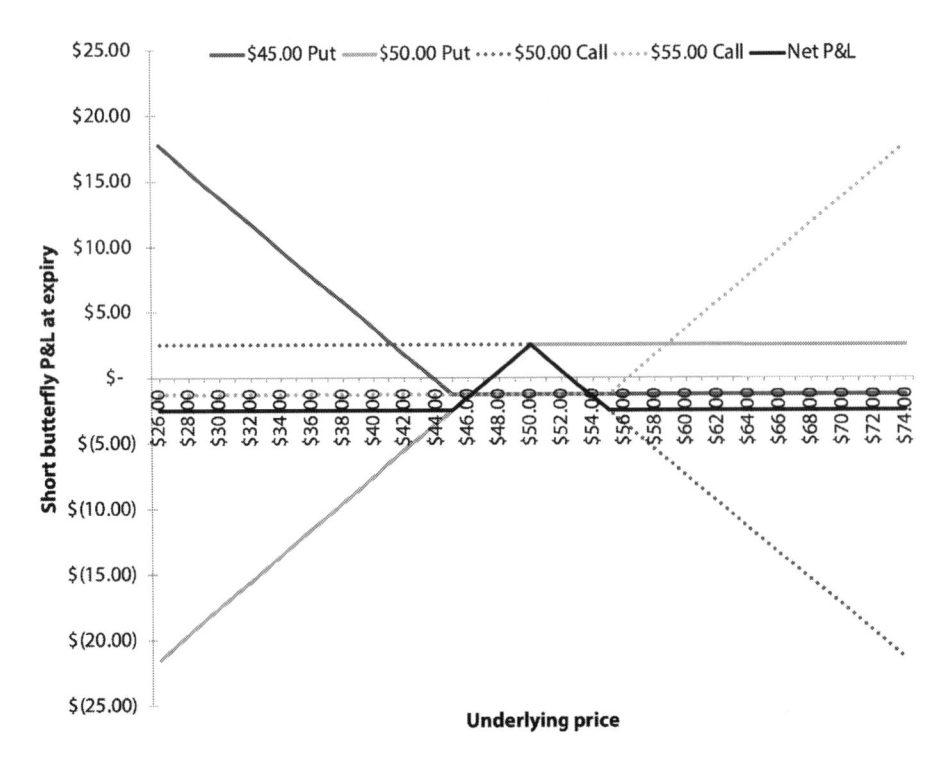

Figure 10.13 Payout diagram at expiration of a short $45.00/$50.00/$55.00 iron butterfly with a net $2.50 credit.

Like a short straddle, a short iron butterfly is a bet on prices expiring close to par, but with markedly different performance characteristics. The premium inflow from the sale of the par call and put finances the cost of the wings, reducing the maximum loss to $2.50 in this case, but capping the potential profit at $2.50.

The payoff diagram for a long $45.00/$50.00/$55.00 iron butterfly with the same underlying cost structure designed to profit from a move away from par would be:

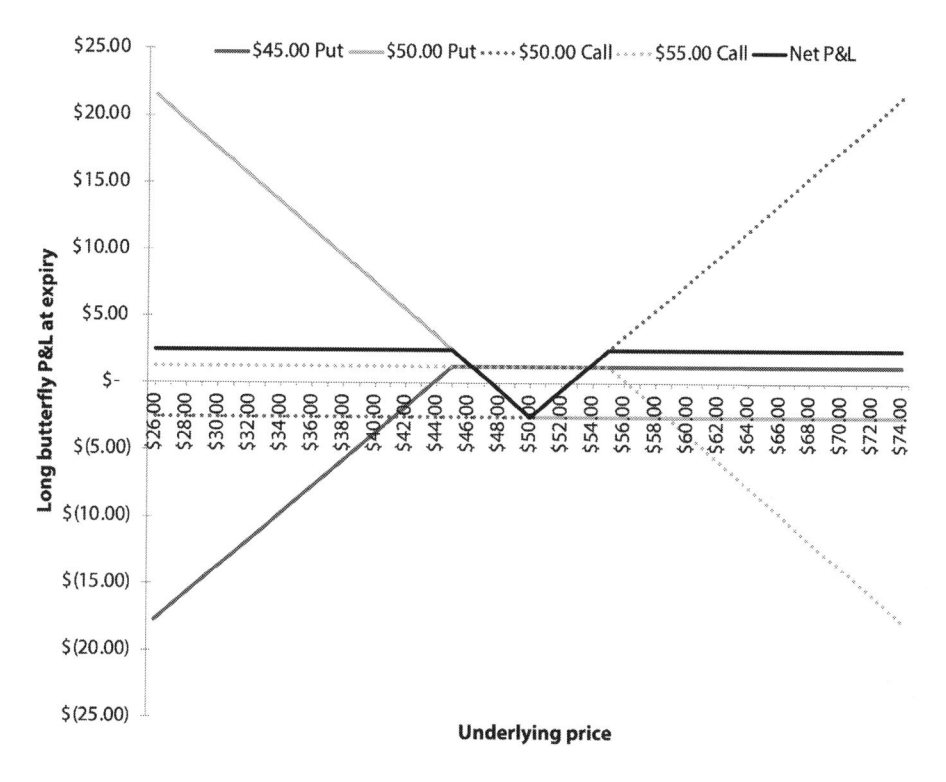

Figure 10.14 Payout diagram at expiration of a long $45.00/$50.00/$55.00 iron butterfly with a net $2.50 cost.

Quotation and Execution of Structures

Popular option structures are frequently quoted and traded as packages for convenience and ease of execution. There are occasionally benefits to legging into a structure one option at a time, which is generally done to avoid showing the trader's strategy to the market, or to avoid drawing attention to a particularly under/overvalued combination. It is sometimes possible in very inefficient markets to leg into a structure at a different cost than the quoted price of the package, providing a cheaper means of entry or, in extreme cases, arbitrage profits.

The utility of the standard option structures depends heavily on the interrelationship of the available strike prices and premiums of each of the individual components. There is a proportionality that must be maintained to be a good risk-reward trade, both in isolation and when combined with the anticipated market movement. If the prices of the wings of an iron butterfly are very low relative to the cost of the body, then the money taken in by selling them will be poor compensation for the loss of upside, making the structure a poor purchase. Option traders quickly develop a keen sense of relative value, and if an option or structure is significantly mispriced, will quickly step in to buy or sell until equilibrium is restored.

As with individual options, structures can be entered into with the goal of taking the position to expiration and delivery or financial settlement, or of trading out of it beforehand. The added complexity of a structure can create additional liquidity problems for traders intending to deal out of the exposure, particularly if the market has traded to a level where some (but not all) of the component options are either deep in or out of the money, which can lead to a lack of transactional interest and worsen bid-offer spreads and executable volumes.

Modeling Non-Linear Option Risks

From the time of the Greeks until the dawn of disco, a basic structural knowledge of the market and an understanding of potential payoffs at expiry would have encompassed the sum total of the practical knowledge on option trading. In 1973, everything changed. Fischer Black and Myron Scholes published "The Pricing of Options and Corporate Liabilities" in *The Journal of Political Economy*. In that groundbreaking work Black and Scholes derived a model for pricing options using simple, market-observable values, giving practitioners an ability to calculate a theoretical "fair value" for any option. The paper represented a seismic shift in the conceptual understanding of risk and, in conjunction with follow-up work by Robert Merton, won for its authors the 1997 Nobel Prize in Economic Sciences.[49]

In tandem with theoretical developments of the day, the rise of (relatively) cheap, (relatively) easy to use desktop computers revolutionized the industry by putting the analytical horsepower necessary to run the Black-Scholes model and all its descendants in the grubby, ape-like paws of the average trader. Wall Street banks immediately started an all-out nerd arms race, which peaked in the mid-1990s as the Masters of the Universe frantically bid for the very same chess team captains and math club members they'd spent the majority of their formative years locking in lockers and picking last for dodge ball.[50] Every firm believed it needed a trading floor full of astrophysics PhDs to out-calculate the applied math weasels from across the street. Having a lowly mechanical engineer pricing your deals was like bringing a knife to a gunfight, and firms stopped bragging about their private jets and started bragging about the number of petaflops their newest supercomputer could handle. Eventually, nuclear finance (aided and abetted by some good old-fashioned poor decisions) fulfilled its taxonomic destiny and nearly destroyed the global banking system a couple of times, most notably in 1994, the early 2000s, and the Mother-of-All Crashes in 2007-9.

Option model sophistication has evolved as a function of time, computing capability, and the ever-more-complicated valuation challenges. Though the state of the art varies widely from industry to industry and the level of sophistication is different from firm to firm, things tend to start off simple and get complicated very quickly. At the low end of the spectrum or in the early days of a market, dealers will rely on street smarts, a pencil, and a legal pad. At the upper

---

[49] Unfortunately, Fischer Black passed away in 1995, prior to the Nobel award.
[50] The advent and aggressive expansion of quantitative trading methodologies based on machine learning, data science, and alternative data has made the hiring frenzy for elite intellectual talent in the 1990s seem tepid by comparison. Some top-tier finance firms currently have open postings for hundreds of coders and quants, and in the process have bid up the price of talent to where the heads of data science teams are commanding larger guarantees than mid-career traders. Anybody know where I can get a Kali Linux hoodie and a Fields Medal?

end of the range are the super quants that surgically dissect exotic derivatives at banks and hedge funds, deploying strategies that are only possible to implement using options and that seek to exploit (rather than avoid) the complex, non-linear nature of the inherent risks. While it is possible to trade options as end-state investments or leveraged forwards without taking into consideration the underlying mathematics, deploying more sophisticated strategies requires an understanding of how options are valued and how that value changes with the fluctuations of the market. For this, it is necessary to understand the basics of option pricing models.

Option and Derivative Pricing Models
Options and other derivative securities can have complex, formula-derived relationships to their underlying products, in some cases making it impossible to make more than a semi-educated guess at their value without employing some form of mathematical model. Moreover, not all derivative pricing models are the same, due to their basic underlying assumptions, the parameters considered, the method used to arrive at a valuation, and the robustness and sophistication of the algorithm employed. A product designed and priced by the structuring group with Model X may, when evaluated by the trading desk with Model Y seem to be a big winner, but when marked by risk with Model Z appear to be a huge loser. Models are, by definition, simplified versions of reality. The simplifying assumptions influence the performance characteristics of the model and its outputs.

Broadly speaking, option models break down into familial classes:

1. Closed-form solutions, like the venerable Black-Scholes model and its progeny.
2. Tree-based structures that begin at a starting point in time and evaluate branching paths forward into the future, then sum the results to create a present value.
3. Simulation-based methods that generate large numbers of randomized future price paths, and then either sum the results or create sub-valuations based on price trajectory characteristics. These so-called Monte Carlo methods are very popular with path-dependent securities like mortgage derivatives.

A significant amount of research and development has gone into building successive iterations of the Better Mousetrap Model. Each approaches the valuation problem from a different angle, but all come equipped with unique assumptions and flaws of their own. Unless they are modeling a product for which an alternate methodology offers clear, demonstrably superior performance, most traders will run their pricing tools off a robust, fast Black-Scholes engine and do whatever fudging is necessary to yield market-actionable pricing.

Everyone's First Option Pricing Model – Black-Scholes
The Black-Scholes model has remained the benchmark for option risk valuation and assessment since its creation. The basic Black-Scholes model has been iteratively improved several times, with the most commonly used variants being the Black-Scholes-Merton and the Black-76 models. I will use the Black-Scholes model to represent both the original and, unless explicitly stated otherwise, all subsequent refinements and variants. For most traders, Black-

Scholes will be a black box that will exist as an Excel add-in, stand-alone spreadsheet, or feature of their risk system.[51] As an end user, it is critical to understand the data inputs to the model, the idiosyncrasies inherent in its approach, and the impacts on the pricing and metrics it produces.

Inputs to the Black-Scholes Model
One of the main reasons for the rapid acceptance and near-universal adoption of the Black-Scholes model is its extreme ease of use. The primary inputs to the model are:

1. The derivative instrument, put or call.
2. The price of the underlying security.
3. The strike price of the option.
4. The time remaining until the date of expiry.
5. The risk-free interest rate.
6. The prevailing market volatility of the underlying instrument.

All of the inputs to the Black-Scholes model are readily observed facts, with the exception of the prevailing volatility of the underlying instrument. What should the trader use for this value?

What Volatility Should the Trader Use?
As seen in Chapter 6, risk managers principally rely on historical volatility calculated from a series of end-of-day closes to generate their backward-looking metrics. Plugging this value into a model would tell the trader what the option was worth, or could be worth if the same conditions were expected to persist. Historical volatility is typically only used for products that have not yet developed a robust, visible forward-option market, and any trader forced to use it as an input must be cognizant that any change from the established levels of underlying price fluctuation could have serious valuation implications.

In developed option markets that feature robust, visible pricing it is possible to use the posted bids and offers for a particular product to calculate the implied volatility. The implied volatility of an option is the value that, if plugged into the Black-Scholes (or other) model, would solve for the current market price. The actual calculation methodology lies outside the scope of this text, involving a recursive process (commonly a Newton-Raphson search or similar method) that iterates to converge to a solution. Though not a technically accurate description, it feels like running the model in reverse[52]: instead of using volatility as an input to derive price, price is an input to derive volatility. Option traders will spend a great deal of effort monitoring the market, noting the implied volatility levels derived from the executed trades and posted bids

---

[51] The actual derivation of the Black-Scholes model lies outside the scope of this text. Those interested should locate a copy of "The Pricing of Options and Corporate Liabilities." by Fischer Black and Myron Scholes, from *The Journal of Political Economy*, May 1973, Volume 81, Issue 3. Published by the University of Chicago Press.
[52] It is not possible to run a closed-form model in reverse, hence the fancy Newton-Raphson search and the previously mentioned math that 99% of all traders could care less about.

Chapter 10 – Option Trading Strategies

and offers, and archiving the information for future reference. Good option traders develop a keen sense of how the different volatilities of the products they follow relate to each other, and are able to infer that if the volatility for one has increased by X, and another by Y, that the third should probably be about Z. The "implied vol" is something that a serious option trader should just know.

For most traders, this data will be entered into a pre-fabricated spreadsheet or pricing engine, which will look something like this:

Generic option calculator	
Option type	c
Current underlying price	$90.00
Strike price	$100.00
Today	1/1/17
Expiry date	1/31/17
Time-to-expiry (days)	30
Interest rate	3%
Implied volatility	50%
Option price	$1.82

Figure 10.15 A spreadsheet interface to the Black-Scholes model. **Note:** All model-based option analytics in *Trader Construction Kit* were created with the software tools (VBA code and Excel spreadsheets) accompanying Espen Gaarder Haug's *The Complete Guide to Option Pricing Formulas – Second Edition*, (New York: McGraw-Hill, 2007).

The trader's model will take as inputs whether they are pricing a call or a put, the current market price, the strike price of the option, the time remaining until maturity, the risk-free interest rate, and the pertinent prevailing implied volatility and derive a price for the option. It is very likely that the price may not match up exactly with what the trader is seeing in the market. Some of the reasons for a potential discrepancy are functions of the limitations of the pricing model.

Limitations of the Black-Scholes Model
Black-Scholes is far from perfect. As with any model, the ultimate utility is contingent on the degree to which the problem under consideration readily translates into an idealized theoretical paradigm. The more closely a model resembles reality, the more likely the trader will get usable results. Black and Scholes identified seven core assumptions about the market that were necessary to allow their model to properly function:

a) The short-term interest rate is known and constant through time.
b) The stock price follows a random walk in continuous time with a variance rate proportional to the square of the stock price. Thus the distribution of possible

stock prices at the end of any finite interval is log-normal. The variance rate of the return on the stock is constant.
c) The stock pays no dividends or other distributions.
d) The option is "European," that is, can only be exercised at maturity.
e) There are no transaction costs in buying or selling the stock or the option.
f) It is possible to borrow any fraction of the price of a security to buy it or to hold it, at the short-term interest rate.
g) There are no penalties to short selling. A seller who does not own a security will simply accept the price of the security from a buyer, and will agree to settle with the buyer on some future date by paying him an amount equal to the price of the security on that date. 53

The bulk of the practitioner criticism directed at the model stems from the assumption of a statistically normal distribution.[54] As discussed in Chapter 6 – Understanding Risk, most securities markets have "fat-tailed" or leptokurtic probability distributions, with a smaller than normal number of observations near the mean and a larger than expected amount clustered at statistically improbable levels. This skewed distribution generally leads to a systematic underpricing of the potential for extreme events, and therefore of risk in general.

Given this major structural flaw, why has the Black-Scholes model even survived, let alone thrived?

1. It was first.
2. It is fast.
3. It is relatively stable.
4. It is computationally manageable on both the input and processing side.
5. It fails in predictable, easy-to-understand ways based on the initial assumptions.

The Greek Risks

In addition to solving for a theoretical price, most modern derivative models also generate risk metrics that describe different non-linear performance characteristics of the option. There are four primary risks, each named after a Greek letter: delta, gamma, vega, and theta. We will examine each risk in turn, using a common example of a $100.00 strike price call option with 30 days until expiry and an implied volatility of 50%.

Delta

---

[53] Fischer Black and Myron Scholes, "The Pricing of Options and Corporate Liabilities," *The Journal of Political Economy*, May 1973, Volume 81, Issue 3, p 640. Published by the University of Chicago Press. Excerpt reprinted by permission.
[54] The requirement of frictionless, zero-cost trading is usually given a pass as an unrealistic yet necessary contrivance. The ability to easily add and subtract options and hedges from the portfolio without eating up all of the potential margin in fees and transaction costs varies from market to market.

Chapter 10 – Option Trading Strategies

The delta of an option measures the relative percentage amount that the value of the option should be expected to move for a $1.00 move in the price of the underlying. It is often constructive to think of the delta as the speed or velocity of a call or put, as it defines how fast the option is moving (change in the price of the option) relative to the surrounding market (the change in the price of the underlying). Delta values range from almost zero (0%) for options that are far out of the money to near 1 (100%) for an option that is so deep in the money that it has effectively become a piece of underlying.[55] The delta for an at-the-money option will typically be around 0.5 (50%). The delta of an option is a reasonable proxy for the probability that it will ultimately expire in the money.[56] Delta values are positive for long option positions, negative for short option positions, and can be summed across an option portfolio to generate the net delta of the entire position.

Consider the following graph of the deltas of a range call options with different strike prices:

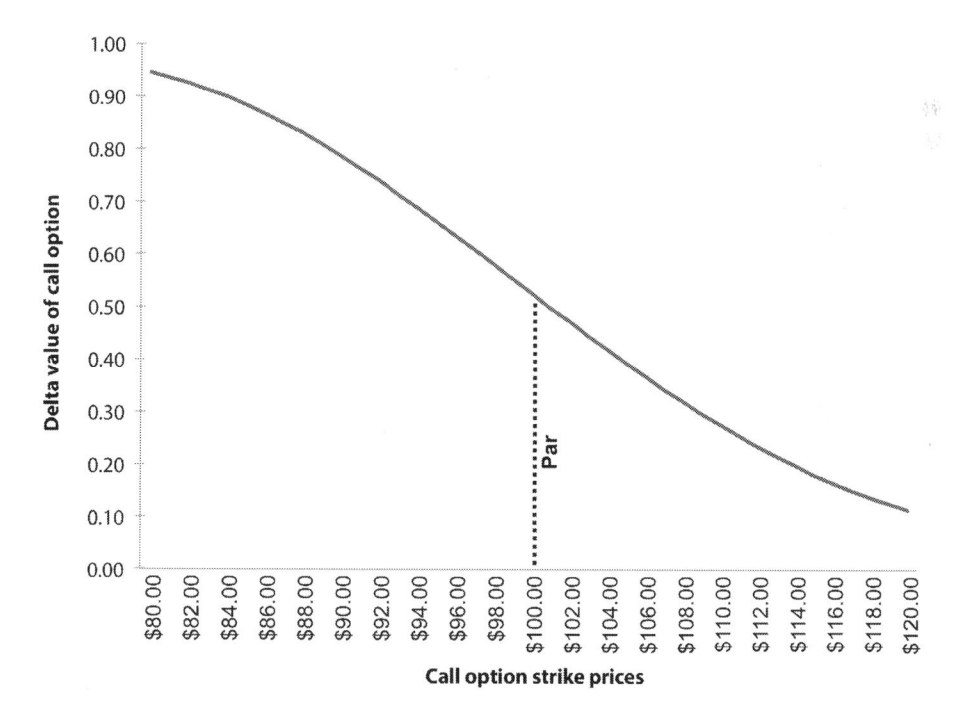

Figure 10.16   Delta values of a range of long call option strikes with a $100.00 underlying price.

---

[55] Option deltas are frequently referred to as round numbers, not percentages or decimals. Thus, a par option would be called a "fifty delta option" not 0.50 or 50%.
[56] It is common to hear jargon-obsessed traders referring to any probability as a delta, frequently dropping the decimal or percent convention, as in "I'm 90 delta you miss this putt." This makes them look like a jerk 100% of the time, or a 100 delta jackass, bro.

All else being equal, if the price of the underlying increased from $100.00 to $101.00, the price of a deep in-the-money $80.00 call should increase by approximately $0.95, a near-par $100.00 call by $0.53, and an out-of-the-money $120.00 call by around $0.11.

As a model-derived risk measurement, the delta of an option will change as the inputs fluctuate in value. Delta values are also not constant through time, and will evolve in different ways as a function of the strike price relative to the market as the option nears expiry. Consider the following graph of a par $100.00 strike call option with 30 days to expiry and 50% implied volatility.

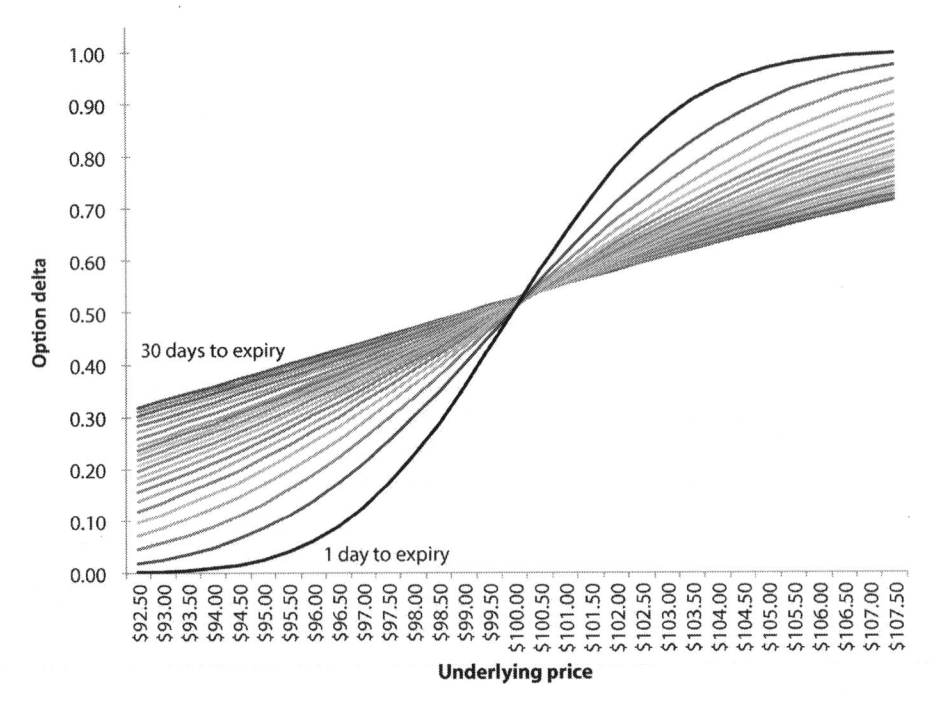

Figure 10.17   Evolution of delta for a long $100.00 strike call option with 30 days to expiry.

The delta is initially relatively linear with respect to change in the underlying at the time the trade is initiated, but steepens appreciably around the strike price and gains significant curvature away from it as the time to expiry decreases. The delta of an option can speed up or slow down as a function of time, strike price, and other variables. The rate of change of the delta is itself a Greek risk, called gamma.

Gamma
The gamma of an option is the rate of change of the option's delta per unit of movement higher or lower in the underlying. If delta is the velocity of an option, gamma is the acceleration, increasing or decreasing the rate of change of the option price per unit of change in the price

of the underlying. Option gammas are much smaller than deltas; this makes sense as they are rates of change, and are positive for long option positions and negative for short exposures. The gamma for the $100.00 strike call option with 30 days to expiry at 50% implied volatility looks like:

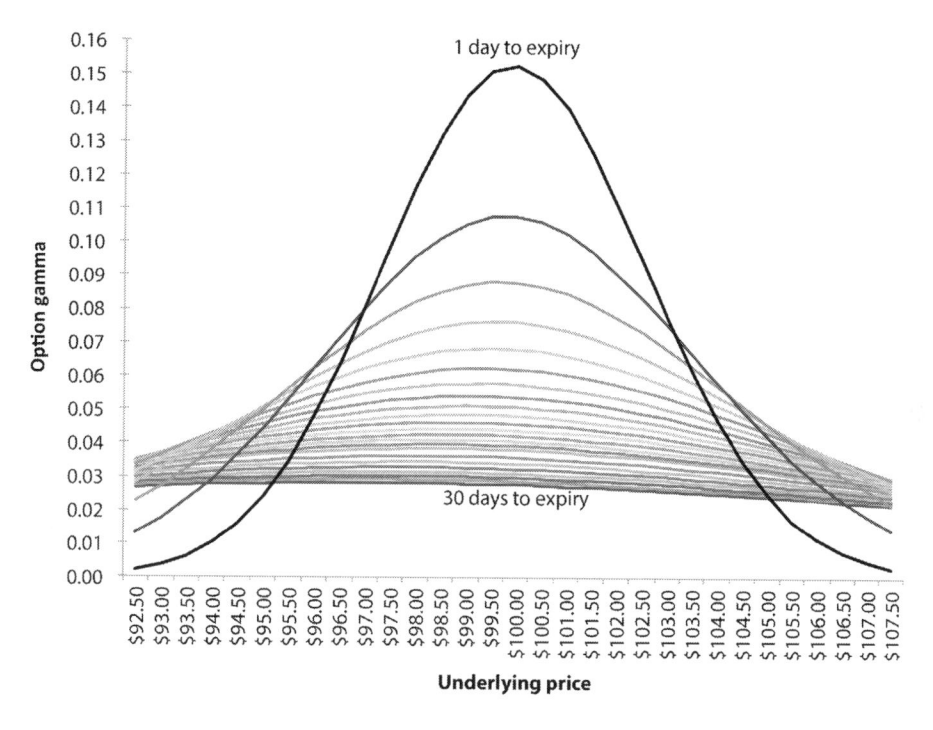

Figure 10.18   Evolution of gamma for a long $100.00 strike call option with 30 days to expiry.

The gamma for the option is initially relatively small in percentage terms and does not vary significantly, which is why the initial delta graph from Figure 10.8 is almost (but not quite) a straight line. As the option moves closer to expiry, the gamma starts to both increase and develop more curvature around the near-par strikes, implying that the option will start to gain and lose value more rapidly around the inflection point where it will or will not ultimately be worth something. With one day left until expiry the gamma curve has become extremely steep around par, with any move toward or away from the strike price having large impacts on the delta of the option. The impact of the large near-expiry gamma can be seen in the delta graph, which is very steep around par as expiry approaches.

Traders (and their management) have a relatively easy time understanding delta and its effects on an option or portfolio of options, as it allows them to pretend that the book is a smaller amount of underlying and make reasonably accurate back-of-the-envelope risk calculations based on that assumption. Gamma is somehow intrinsically scary, as it disrupts that convenient approximation in unpredictable ways. Being long gamma, which in practice means long options, is fine, as it means that the trader's exposure is getting larger by accumulating increasingly larger deltas as the trade moves into the money, which is generally a positive state of affairs. Short gamma positions that result from selling options are dangerous for exactly the same reason, that is, the obligation grows larger as it moves against the trader. Misunderstanding or mismanaging this property of short option positions has ended many careers, and large short gamma positions are the root cause of many stories of financial disaster.

Vega
The vega of an option is the sensitivity to changes in the volatility of the market and represents the change in value per unit of increase or decrease in the forward implied volatility of the underlying. A long option position is a bet that the underlying price will breach the strike price prior to the expiration of the contract. The more volatile the underlying market, the greater the likelihood that the option will move into the money at some point during its lifetime. A decreasing level of volatility implies that prices are more likely to remain static, rendering all bets on price movements less valuable. Vega is positive for long option positions and negative for short exposures. The vega for a $100.00 strike call option with 30 days to expiry and a 50% implied volatility can be seen in the following graph.

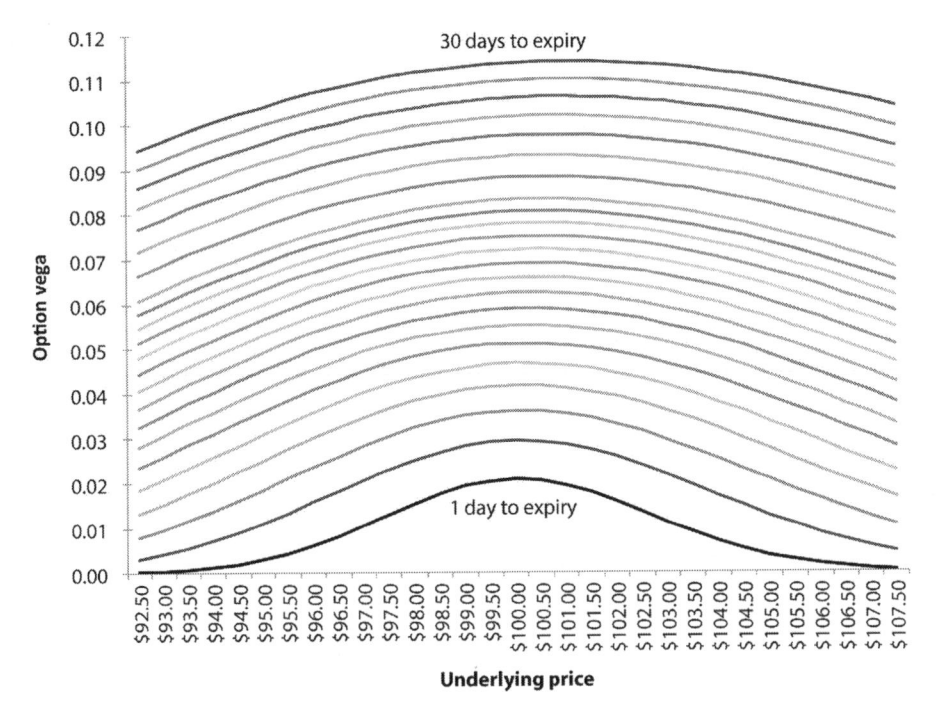

Figure 10.19 Evolution of vega for a long $100.00 strike call option with 30 days to expiry.

Chapter 10 – Option Trading Strategies   363

Changes in the volatility of the underlying security have more meaning for options with longer relative time remaining until expiry, as each additional day represents another opportunity for the trade to potentially cross the strike price and accrue economic value. With 30 days until expiry the vega of the call option is relatively flat around par with slightly steeper curvature for lower out-of-the-money strikes. With 15 days until expiry the responsiveness per unit of volatility has decreased, with the curvature for out-of-the-money strikes increasing slightly. With only one day until expiry the overall sensitivity to volatility has declined precipitously, with the only material changes occurring right around the strike price of the option.

While not as intrinsically horrifying to management as a short gamma position, being outright short vega is also fairly uncomfortable, as it leaves the trader and the option portfolio vulnerable to the entire universe of unexpected, exogenous events that will inevitably increase volatility in the market and damage the position.

Theta

By purchasing an option the trader is making a bet that the market is going to move during a particular, pre-defined period of time prior to expiry. Theta is the amount by which the value of an option erodes per unit of time passage, and is negative for long option positions and positive for short exposures. Theta is also frequently referred to as "decay" or "bleed." The theta for a $100.00 strike call option with 30 days to expiry and a 50% implied volatility looks like:

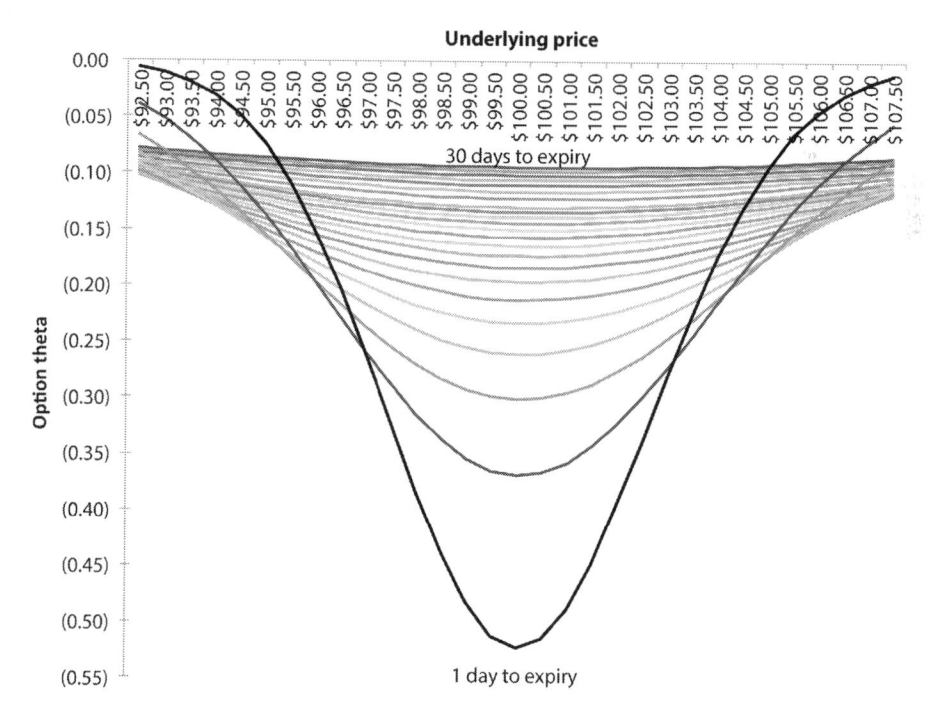

Figure 10.20   Evolution of theta for a long $100.00 strike call option with 30 days to expiry.

The longer the period of time before the option expires, the greater the chance that the market is able to pass through the strike price and accrue value. With 30 days left, the call option will only lose a small amount of value per day, and the decrease is relatively constant across the range of underlying prices. The level of value erosion does not materially change with 15 days left until expiry. With one day left until expiration the curve has steepened significantly around the par strikes, implying that the value of the remaining optionality will be decreasing rapidly as the call option evolves to an expiry end-state of being in or out of the money.

Practically speaking, the rapid erosion of value toward the end of an option's lifespan is something that traders employing long options as leveraged directional plays must understand and take into consideration when planning the holding periods of their positions. This is seen in the following chart of an in-the-money, at-the-money, and out-of-the-money option approaching expiration.

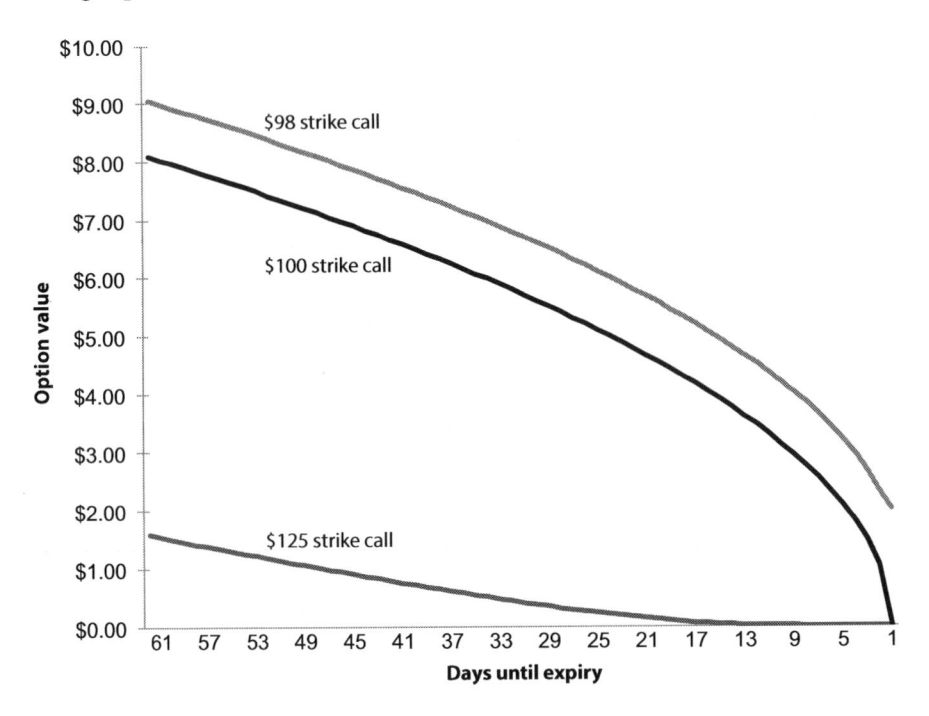

Figure 10.21 Erosion of long $98.00 strike, $100.00 strike and $125.00 strike call values.

The $125.00 call did not start with much value in a $100.00 market, so its erosion is relatively gradual and by midway through the time period it has effectively become worthless. The $100.00 call has some potential to finish in the money, and its value erodes in a fairly linear fashion with relatively constant theta until just before expiry, at which point its value falls off a cliff. The $98 strike call option is in the money for its entire life, which leads to a similar erosion trajectory of the value of its additional upside potential before diving toward the $2.00 intrinsic value at expiration. A trader deploying a long leveraged outright strategy by buying

Chapter 10 – Option Trading Strategies

calls would probably prefer to exit the position before the theta bleed starts to significantly erode the value, and will need to know when this model-derived inflection point is approaching.

Localized Greeks
The standard graphs of Greek risks experience rapid topographical evolution at certain key stress points, most commonly around par and near expiry. Though many practitioners may never experience those conditions, all traders in the option markets need to understand the influences of the Greek risks on their position (however minimal at the time). Most measurements of Greek risks are best used like a flashlight, to illuminate a trader's current surroundings and to allow them to see the path immediately ahead.

A trader running a more complex book of options with an assortment of strikes spread across a multi-period forward curve will need to be much more aware of both the initial and near-terminal Greek properties, as they will be experiencing them in some combination or on a continuous basis.

The Rest of the Fraternity – The Lesser Greeks
Delta, gamma, vega, and theta are the primary risks that traders and risk managers monitor and manage. There are secondary Greek measures and a plethora of hybrid, esoterically specialized metrics that sophisticated option traders will calculate and ponder. Exotic derivative traders must, out of necessity, monitor and respond to risks that dealers in less-developed markets will not even be remotely aware of. Having said that, I have never heard of an option-related debacle that started "He didn't hedge (insert obscure proto risk metric here) and before you know it, Capitol City was burning." Most disasters are a result of bungling one (or more) of the big four Greek risks, and traders and risk managers should make sure they have delta, gamma, vega, and theta well under control before worrying about secondary and tertiary risks.

2 + 2 = 5
Greek risks are weighed and measured as individual component risks but act in concert on an option (or portfolio of options) simultaneously, often with confounding offsetting influences. Countless traders (and managers) have been vexed by a complicated options position that they thought should have been profitable on a given day, only to prove a loser because of a changing perception of forward volatility combined with an abrupt shift in the underlying and the normal passage of time. Good option traders become adept at estimating the P&L implications of the various interacting forces and reporting material day-over-day changes to management to avoid blindsiding them with an unexpected mark-to-market report.

Volatility and Option Prices
The discussion thus far has focused on what options are worth, either as a known quantity at the end of their life or as a mathematical model-derived value mid-way through their term. There can be (and frequently is) a significant difference between what an option ought to be worth and its actual price in the market. There are two principal reasons for the gap: market-making margins and differing views on volatility.

Traders generate option prices, and traders typically like to make money. Market makers tend to offer above fair value and bid below fair value in an attempt to earn a spread by buying and selling and be paid for providing liquidity and warehousing risk. As long as the demands are not egregious, this is a normal, completely reasonable cost of doing business.

Differing perceptions of volatility is a much more subtle variable, and one that is more common in developing markets or markets with massively illiquid products. It is normal for traders to have an excellent understanding of the implied volatilities and prices for a wide variety of call and put strikes in the nearby months, with moderate visibility in the popular strikes for several calendar years forward. The problem arises if a trader is asked to make a market on, for example, a five-year strip of options starting five years forward for a customer, or as part of a structured transaction. Total clarity in Year 1 and decent indicative straddle markets by month for Years 2 and 3 do not necessarily tell the trader much about volatility or price in Years 6, 7, 8, 9, and 10. A natural requesting quotes from three different firms may—and probably will—get radically different pricing back due to the variance in the educated volatility guesses of the market-making traders.

Using Implied Volatility as a Pricing Tool
In mature markets where the majority of the variables that determine an option's price are readily observed, brokers and traders will switch to an informal shorthand and quote options in terms of the implied volatility. This saves the effort of re-calculating and re-quoting the value of the option with every fluctuation in the price of the underlying. The convention also allows the broker and trader to converse about general option prices as opposed to re-quoting each term and each price every time the trader wants to refresh pricing or the market moves.

Traders will usually build a spreadsheet or use a pre-packaged application that tracks several core products and uses that observed data to create and populate indicative prices for a range of other strikes and maturities. It is then incumbent on the trader to tend his garden, weeding out old prices and obsolete assumptions, lest an old relationship lead to a new mispricing.

A typical pricing spreadsheet for a trader keeping an eye on the MAR ProdX options might look like:

Chapter 10 – Option Trading Strategies

MAR ProdX calls								
Strike	Vol	Implied price	Live bid	Live offer	Delta	Gamma	Vega	Theta
$110.00	7.40%	$0.13	$0.15	$1.00	0.09	0.05	0.07	(0.00)
$109.00	7.20%	$0.21			0.14	0.07	0.09	(0.01)
$108.00	7.00%	$0.36	$0.25		0.21	0.10	0.12	(0.01)
$107.00	6.80%	$0.58			0.31	0.12	0.15	(0.01)
$106.00	6.60%	$0.91	$0.50		0.44	0.14	0.17	(0.01)
$105.00	6.50%	$1.39	$1.25	$2.00	0.58	0.14	0.17	(0.01)
$104.00	6.60%	$2.03			0.71	0.12	0.15	(0.01)
$103.00	6.75%	$2.81			0.81	0.09	0.11	(0.01)
$102.00	6.90%	$3.66			0.88	0.06	0.08	(0.00)
$101.00	7.05%	$4.58			0.93	0.04	0.05	(0.00)
$100.00	7.20%	$5.53			0.96	0.02	0.03	(0.00)

MAR ProdX puts								
Strike	Vol	Implied price	Live bid	Live offer	Delta	Gamma	Vega	Theta
$110.00	7.20%	$4.56			(0.91)	0.05	0.06	(0.00)
$109.00	7.05%	$3.65			(0.86)	0.07	0.09	(0.00)
$108.00	6.90%	$2.80			(0.79)	0.10	0.12	(0.01)
$107.00	6.75%	$2.04			(0.68)	0.12	0.15	(0.01)
$106.00	6.60%	$1.38			(0.56)	0.14	0.17	(0.01)
$105.00	6.50%	$0.87	$0.75	$1.65	(0.42)	0.14	0.17	(0.01)
$104.00	6.60%	$0.52			(0.29)	0.12	0.15	(0.01)
$103.00	6.80%	$0.30			(0.19)	0.09	0.12	(0.01)
$102.00	7.00%	$0.17			(0.11)	0.06	0.08	(0.00)
$101.00	7.20%	$0.09			(0.07)	0.04	0.05	(0.00)
$100.00	7.40%	$0.05	$0.10	$0.75	(0.04)	0.02	0.03	(0.00)

Figure 10.22   Sample option-tracking spreadsheet.

In both the put and call screen the trader is tracking a range of strike prices around par, each with a straddle-derived estimated implied volatility used to derive a Black-Scholes valuation of the price of the option. The screen also includes a data entry section where the trader can make note of live bids and offers and compare them to the volatility-derived prices. It is interesting to note that the volatility of in and out of the money strikes is different from the par options, a phenomenon called the volatility smile.

The Volatility Smile

The volatility level implied by the par straddles is only relevant for close-to-the-money options. The volatility smile is a curvature away from the benchmark near-par levels typically exhibited by deeply in or out of the money options. Most instruments will exhibit increasing implied volatility for both higher and lower strike prices. As options get further out of the money, the model-implied value decreases, often to near-zero levels. Traders generally frown on selling something for nothing, and will increase the cost above the model-derived level to a price deemed worthy of transacting. Out-of-the-money strikes can have a markedly higher implied volatility than in the money, yielding a skewed smile. Some products will have an almost one-sided curvature is called a smirk. The degree of curvature varies by market and product and the shape of the smile can be different for different maturities, particularly for products that have a pronounced term structure of volatility.

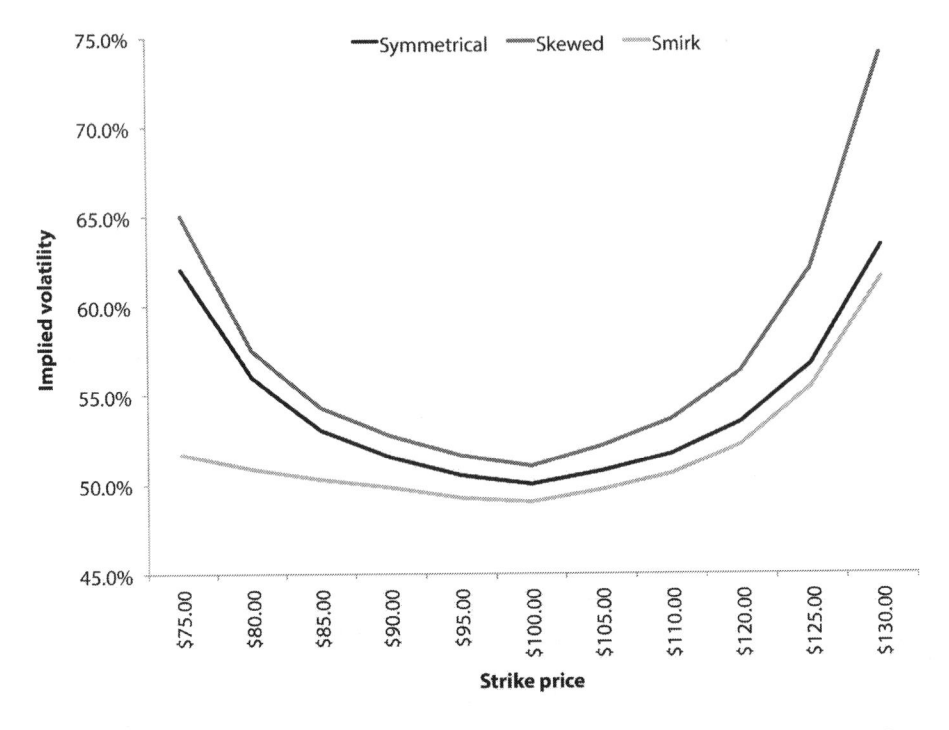

Figure 10.23   Curvature of a symmetrical implied volatility smile, a skewed smile, and a smirk.

In an illiquid market the smile can become extremely exaggerated, and the lack of transaction volume at some strikes can severely distort the shape and cause large day-to-day changes in estimated volatility levels. Traders contemplating positions in illiquid, out-of-the-money strikes must prepare themselves (and their management) for potentially larger than normal P&L fluctuations.

A Room Full of Models: Sounds Like Fun, But Not Always a Good Thing
Black-Scholes is by far the most common, but by no means the only, option-pricing model in use at trading firms. While a trader may come to trust the ease of use and robust nature of a standard Black-76 spreadsheet, an analytics or structuring group may need to deploy or, in extreme cases, develop internally, more complex models that mimic the real characteristics of the instruments they are attempting to value. The risk group will default to the engine built into the deal entry system, with any additional pre- or post-processing done with audited, approved industry-standard models. While there are valid reasons for each group to use a particular model for a specific purpose, in practice it creates the possibility for a firm to arrive at multiple, possibly wildly divergent, valuations for the same instrument.

Chapter 10 – Option Trading Strategies

The most common areas of model conflict are:
- Trading vs. risk on mark-to-market of a position.
- Origination/structuring vs. trading and/or risk on the value of a deal.
- Risk/credit vs. a counterparty or clearinghouse on margin calculations.

Most trading vs. risk conflicts center on the end-of-day volatility marks, with a disconnect between the trader's live quoted prices relative to risk's audited close numbers. A secondary area of conflict will arise if a trader's position is composed of unusual products or contains a structured transaction(s) with significant embedded optionality, which may not value properly with risk's approved toolkit of models.

A similar problem will occur when the origination and structuring group value a deal with its own model, then attempts to get trading to buy into the valuation. This becomes particularly contentious if the firm employs transfer pricing between origination and trading when the deal is booked, where a price must be agreed on to transfer the risk from one group to the other. Origination will want to value the deal as richly as possible to get the most credit for producing value, and trading will want to buy it as cheaply as possible to build a cushion for the risk of managing the position. This dynamic can become very contentious when each has their own valuation tool, creating an irreconcilable difference between two parties with extremely vested interests.

Risk and credit can disagree with the valuation of positions when reconciling margin payments with a clearinghouse or directly with a counterparty. Disagreements with the clearinghouse are usually short lived, as it is "their way or the highway" with respect to model valuations. Counterparty discrepancies can be very challenging to reconcile, as the marks, volatilities, and model of record can all be different.

The Difference Between Price and Value
It may seem like a semantic splitting of hairs, but there is a difference between price and value. The price is what a trader must pay to buy or is paid for selling an option, and is a pure manifestation of the prevailing market conditions. Value is what the trader feels the option is ultimately worth. If they were the same, there would be no reason for transacting, outside of position maintenance considerations. The further apart price and value are, the more compelling the transaction becomes. The price belongs to the market, while the valuation is proprietary and will vary significantly from trader to trader and firm to firm. Most valuation differences stem from differing perceptions of forward implied volatility and its probable manifestation as price distributions.

Intrinsic and Extrinsic Value
Options have two types of value, intrinsic and extrinsic. An option's intrinsic value is defined as the economic difference between the strike and current market price, and represents the amount that could be earned by exercising the option and exiting the resulting exposure. A $100.00 strike call in a market currently trading $105.00 would have $5.00 of intrinsic value. A $110.00 strike call would have no intrinsic value, but a $110.00 strike put would have $5.00. Only in-the-money options have intrinsic value. Par and out-of-the-money options typically

have most of their price determined by model-derived and trader-imputed extrinsic value based on the potential for the option to ultimately finish in the money. Extrinsic value depends on the remaining time to expiration, the volatility of the market, and a host of other factors. Consider a $100.00 strike call with 30 days to expiry. In a market with a 50% implied forward volatility that is currently trading at $105.00, the call will be valued at $8.67 by the standard Black-Scholes model. Of that value, $5.00 is intrinsic and $3.67 extrinsic. By varying the implied forward volatility and the number of days to expiry and re-running the model, we can see the effects on both the price of the option and in extrinsic value component.

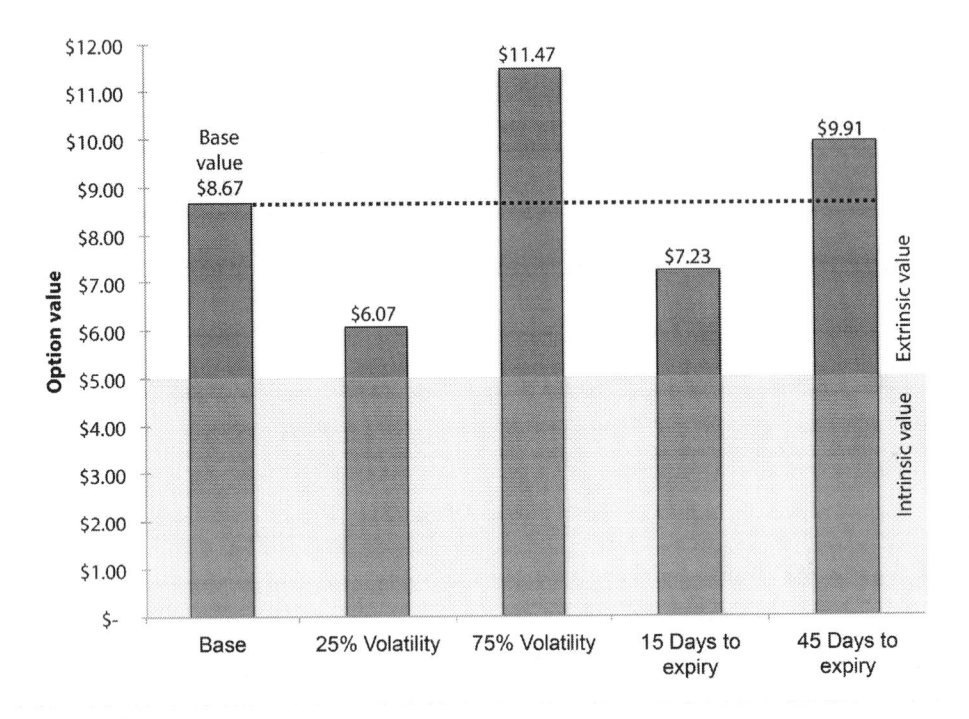

Figure 10.24 Comparing the intrinsic and extrinsic value of a $100.00 long call as a function of volatility and time to expiry.

Compare this to a $110.00 strike call option in the same $105.00 market:

Chapter 10 – Option Trading Strategies

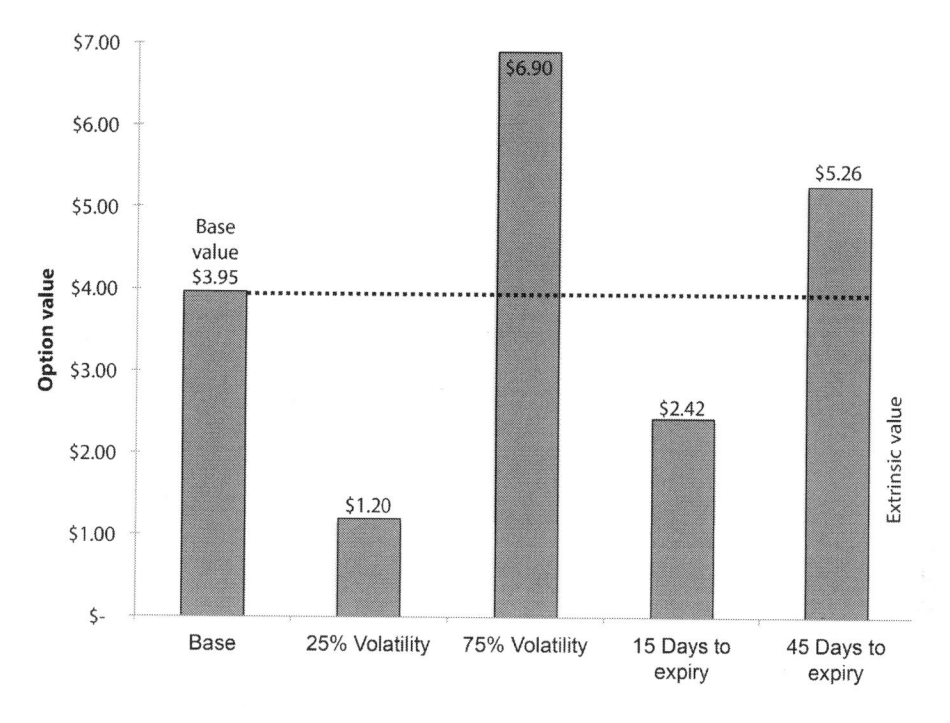

Figure 10.25 Comparing extrinsic values of a $110.00 long call as a function of volatility and time to expiry.

The $110.00 strike call is out of the money and has no intrinsic value, so the changes in the extrinsic value caused by the volatility and time to maturity lead to much larger percentage changes in the price of the option.

3. Volatility Strategies

As seen earlier, option prices are both explicitly (via pricing models) and implicitly (through heuristic trader pricing) impacted by changes in the current and implied level of market volatility. Option traders have the ability to use this property to speculate on the future trajectory of the implied volatility of the market, which is not possible with any other instrument. While any long option position should theoretically benefit from an uptick in implied volatility, in practice options are complex enough instruments that it is possible that the net gain due to vega could be subsumed by a directional delta exposure. For this reason, traders typically remove the directionality of the trade by buying and selling par or near-par straddles and strangles where the combination put and call roughly self-hedge the delta exposure, leaving the vega exposure the trader desires and theta bleed that she will have to live with.

4. Managing Option Portfolios

Many types of traders will use options as the best tool out of a range of alternatives to facilitate a particular strategy. For pure option traders, the instruments are the strategy, and they must to learn to understand the behavioral characteristics of gobs of the things glued together into a portfolio. This type of book running is mostly seen at banks and specialized dealers, and requires a steady volume of customer deal flow willing to give up edge and a pool of counterparties to provide liquidity. A market-making option trader wants to buy cheap, sell expensive, and repeat as many times as possible. That trader will warehouse product while attempting to maintain delta, gamma, and vega neutrality and some sort of constructive, minimally drifting position. A book that veers away from this ideally neutral strategy and intentionally builds risk positions is trying to call some aspect of the market.

Most traders, whether they admit it or not, lack the scale and experience to profit from running an option book. Their book will be too small to properly manage the Greek risks or they will have insufficient access to deal flow to harvest value.

For those who dare, the good news is that component Greek risks are additive and a snapshot of the position can be taken and the exposures easily analyzed. The bad news is that the sub-risks are interrelated in extremely counterintuitive, non-linear fashions that change as a function of price and time. When dealing with different maturities, different strike prices, and different volumes of buy and sell transactions within each strike things can get far more complex than any trader can easily keep track of. Option traders are extremely reliant on technological infrastructure to do their jobs, and face significant challenges managing the portfolio, generating actionable trading information, and marking the positions to market.

At a minimum an option trader will need a robust risk system capable of booking the myriad transactions she will undertake and digesting an ocean of non-standard end-of-day marks, the majority of which will be difficult to observe and process. From there, the risk system will have to internalize the data set and generate position-solid, reliable metrics, including net deltas, gamma, vega, and theta.

Measuring Exposures & Managing the Portfolio
The first potentially tricky part is that the risk system may utilize an internal option-pricing engine that does not function well with the products in question. As an example, Black-Scholes tends to break down with products that feature very high, implied volatilities and a distribution with significant tail risk, as is the case with the energy commodities. This market-to-model gap is particularly common with new products and new markets, as the necessary tweaks to the standard pricing formulas are works in progress or completely non-existent. In many cases the risk group will have to fudge things to get results that are close to expectations, telling the trader and management that they will have to live with the discrepancy until the position is closed out. This will make management extremely uncomfortable.

The trader will often export the portfolio positions into a gigantic spreadsheet and run it through either a proprietary third-party model or some homebrew of his own devising. This invariably gets ugly very quickly, as there will now exist two sets of positions, two sets of Greeks, and two sets of daily P&Ls, one of which is by definition official, and the other which the front office believes to be the truth. If the risk group is required to source its data and marks from particular audit-approved resources and forced to exclude better market-observed information that might not be as "robust," there can be valuation disagreements between well-intentioned parties that are flatly unresolvable. The Solomonic compromise for short- and medium-term holding periods is for the trader to live with the ugly marks and let the ultimate P&L come out in the wash when the position is closed.

Marking to Market – Model vs. Risk vs. Reality
Most option models (the Black-Scholes in particular) presume continuous time and frictionless hedging capabilities. Lack of continuous time is felt in overnight and intraday market gaps, which causes a step function in the inputs to and outputs from the valuation model without allowing an opportunity to make changes to the portfolio. The bid-offer spread the trader must pay to modify the position is an additional tax. Depending on the model-to-reality gap, the practical modifications to the ideal strategy can be significant. Most traders will, out of necessity, allow Greek exposures to accumulate to some minimum threshold level before taking any action, living with the P&L fluctuations and risk implications in the interim in exchange for reduced execution risk, slippage, and transaction costs. The standard transaction size and bid-offer spread present in the market will impact the trader's ability to effectively hedge, as there will be some minimum ratio of the size of the option portfolio and resultant incremental Greek risk changes to the standardized trading block and transaction costs present in the market.

Managing the other Greek risks involves trading additional options, frequently at a variety of strike prices and maturities. In an environment with a severe smile, an unwillingness to quote price further out the curve, or liquidity-induced wide bid-offer spreads for out-of-the-money options, the ability to manage gamma, vega, and theta may be severely impaired. The option book must also be significantly larger than the size of the incremental hedging instruments or the tail will effectively be wagging the dog. It is easier to manage a very large book of options in a highly traded market with small contract size than to attempt to do so in a thinly traded product with large standard transaction sizes.

Managing Greek Risks – An Extremely Simple, Semi-Practical Example
A newly minted equity option trader at a bank gets a client call asking for a price on par call options expiring at the end of the month on a stock currently trading around $100.00. The trader consults the pricing model and determines that, given the prevailing implied 25% forward volatility and with 21 business days until expiry, the option is worth around $2.40. The trader offers the customer $100.00 strike call options on 10,000 shares for an up-front premium of $4.00. The customer agrees, and they book the transaction.

The trader is now short call options on 10,000 notional shares with a theoretical $1.60 profit relative to the model-derived fair value. The goal is to capture as much of that margin as possible, given the market conditions. There are a number of potential ways he can choose to manage the position.

The trader can elect to retain all of the option risk, hoping that the market will expire below the $100.00 strike price, rendering the calls worthless and allowing the trader to pocket the entire $4.00 premium for a $40,000 total profit. The downside is that the trader is completely unhedged. If the market rallies above $104.00 he will start losing money in a linear fashion with the losses theoretically uncapped and limited only by the whims of the market.

The trader can choose to mitigate the directional risk of the position by buying an amount of the underlying sufficient to neutralize the initial risk exposure, then adding or subtracting volume as necessary to compensate for the day-to-day fluctuations, a strategy called delta hedging. For this to be productive, the trader must have access to a deep, liquid hedging instrument with minimal transaction costs. The size of the option position relative to the smallest common denominator in the underlying market impacts the ability to productively delta hedge, and the trader must book enough business to have hedge volumes be market-standard size, lest the additional tax for odd-lot execution and additional reduction in liquidity prove disruptive.

Assume that the trader holds the short option position for the 21 days until expiry with the following underlying price trajectory, implied option value, and associated Greek risks:

Chapter 10 – Option Trading Strategies

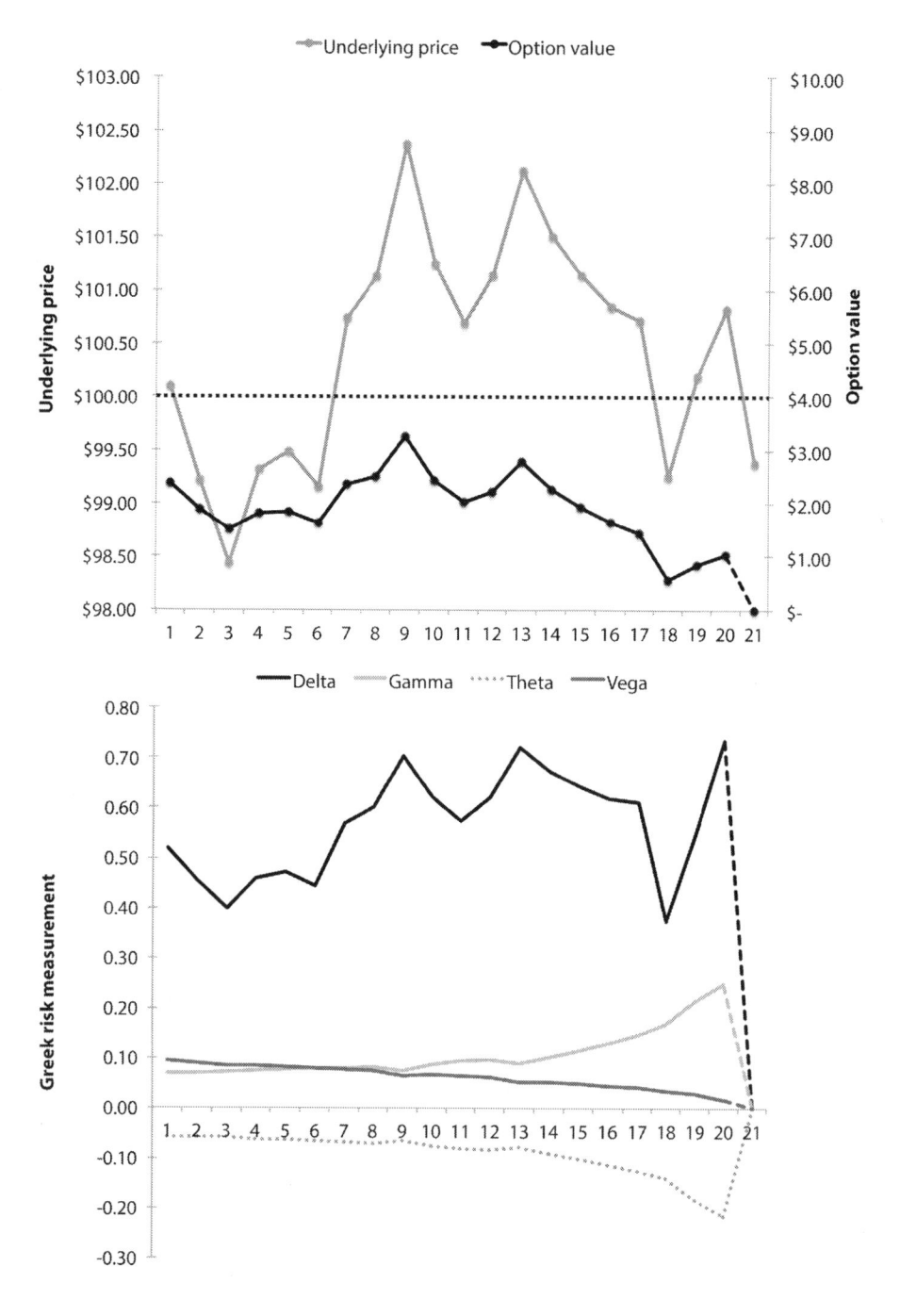

Figure 10.26 The evolution of the option value and delta, gamma, vega and theta Greek risks of a long $100.00 strike call option with 25% implied volatility and 21 days to expiry.

At the end of each day, the trader will rerun the option-pricing model with the current market price, which will yield a new set of Greek risk metrics. Pay particular attention to the change in delta relative to the fluctuation in the underlying price.

	Underlying	Option value	Delta	Gamma	Vega	Theta
Day 1	$100.11	$2.38	0.5177	0.0679	0.0932	-0.0580
Day 2	$99.21	$1.89	0.4550	0.0699	0.0896	-0.0587
Day 3	$98.43	$1.50	0.3979	0.0705	0.0842	-0.0583
Day 4	$99.32	$1.82	0.4594	0.0739	0.0849	-0.0622
Day 5	$99.49	$1.83	0.4707	0.0763	0.0827	-0.0644
Day 6	$99.16	$1.62	0.4432	0.0785	0.0793	-0.0659
Day 7	$100.74	$2.35	0.5684	0.0795	0.0774	-0.0689
Day 8	$101.13	$2.51	0.6024	0.0807	0.0735	-0.0704
Day 9	$102.36	$3.25	0.7039	0.0743	0.0640	-0.0663
Day 10	$101.25	$2.43	0.6202	0.0865	0.0668	-0.0756
Day 11	$100.69	$2.02	0.5739	0.0940	0.0653	-0.0813
Day 12	$101.14	$2.21	0.6208	0.0957	0.0603	-0.0836
Day 13	$102.12	$2.78	0.7201	0.0889	0.0508	-0.0790
Day 14	$101.51	$2.27	0.6728	0.1026	0.0507	-0.0902
Day 15	$101.13	$1.93	0.6430	0.1150	0.0483	-0.1004
Day 16	$100.85	$1.64	0.6186	0.1291	0.0450	-0.1122
Day 17	$100.71	$1.44	0.6117	0.1453	0.0404	-0.1260
Day 18	$99.25	$0.57	0.3736	0.1683	0.0341	-0.1419
Day 19	$100.20	$0.84	0.5460	0.2137	0.0294	-0.1836
Day 20	$100.82	$1.03	0.7347	0.2484	0.0173	-0.2160
Day 21	$99.38	$0.00	0.0000	0.0000	0.0000	0.0000

Table 10.1 Option value and delta, gamma, vega and theta Greek risks of a long $100.00 strike call option with 25% implied volatility and 21 days to expiry.

When the trader books the position on Day 1, the risk system will show a net exposure of −5,177 shares, the 0.5177 model-derived delta multiplied by the short 10,000 share notional volume. The trader will mitigate this risk by buying 5,100 shares at the close of the market, leaving a relatively minor 77-share net short exposure overnight.[57]

On Day 2, the market for the underlying stock drops by $0.90 to $99.21. This decreases the model-derived value of the short options to $1.89, increasing the mark-to-market profit for the trader. The lower underlying price impacts the calculated Greek risks, most critically the delta, which drops to 0.4550. This change leaves the trader with a delta equivalent −4,550-share short option position against which there is a 5,100-share long hedge position, effectively making the position net long 550 shares of stock. The trader will have to sell 500 shares of

---

[57] The trader could also have chosen to buy 5,200 shares and be net 23 long overnight if bullish, or have paid an odd-lot premium to transact exactly 5,177 to be as flat as possible. Traders will usually embed their overall view into even these types of micro-decisions.

Chapter 10 – Option Trading Strategies

stock at the close of the market to get back to a relatively neutral 50 share, long position overnight. This process will repeat itself daily, with the trader monitoring the market, recalculating the exposure, and rebalancing the position to hedge out the majority of the directional risk. Extended across the 21-day holding period the process would look like:

	Underlying	Option value	Option delta	Delta volume	DOD delta chg	Dvol - HP	Daily hedge	Net pos	Hedge pos
Day 1	$100.11	$2.38	0.5177	(5177)			5100	(77)	5100
Day 2	$99.21	$1.89	0.4550	(4550)	627	550	(500)	50	4600
Day 3	$98.43	$1.50	0.3979	(3979)	572	621	(600)	21	4000
Day 4	$99.32	$1.82	0.4594	(4594)	(615)	(594)	500	(94)	4500
Day 5	$99.49	$1.83	0.4707	(4707)	(113)	(207)	200	(7)	4700
Day 6	$99.16	$1.62	0.4432	(4432)	275	268	(200)	68	4500
Day 7	$100.74	$2.35	0.5684	(5684)	(1252)	(1184)	1100	(84)	5600
Day 8	$101.13	$2.51	0.6024	(6024)	(341)	(424)	400	(24)	6000
Day 9	$102.36	$3.25	0.7039	(7039)	(1014)	(1039)	1000	(39)	7000
Day 10	$101.25	$2.43	0.6202	(6202)	837	798	(700)	98	6300
Day 11	$100.69	$2.02	0.5739	(5739)	462	561	(500)	61	5800
Day 12	$101.14	$2.21	0.6208	(6208)	(469)	(408)	400	(8)	6200
Day 13	$102.12	$2.78	0.7201	(7201)	(993)	(1001)	1000	(1)	7200
Day 14	$101.51	$2.27	0.6728	(6728)	473	472	(400)	72	6800
Day 15	$101.13	$1.93	0.6430	(6430)	298	370	(300)	70	6500
Day 16	$100.85	$1.64	0.6186	(6186)	245	314	(300)	14	6200
Day 17	$100.71	$1.44	0.6117	(6117)	69	83	0	83	6200
Day 18	$99.25	$0.57	0.3736	(3736)	2381	2464	(2400)	64	3800
Day 19	$100.20	$0.84	0.5460	(5460)	(1724)	(1660)	1600	(60)	5400
Day 20	$100.82	$1.03	0.7347	(7347)	(1887)	(1947)	1900	(47)	7300
Day 21	$99.38	$0.00	0.0000	0	7347	7300	(7300)	0	0

Table 10.2 Hedging the changing delta exposure with underlying for a long $100.00 strike call option with 25% implied volatility and 21 days to expiry.

Examining the hedge trades and total position in isolation yields the following chart:

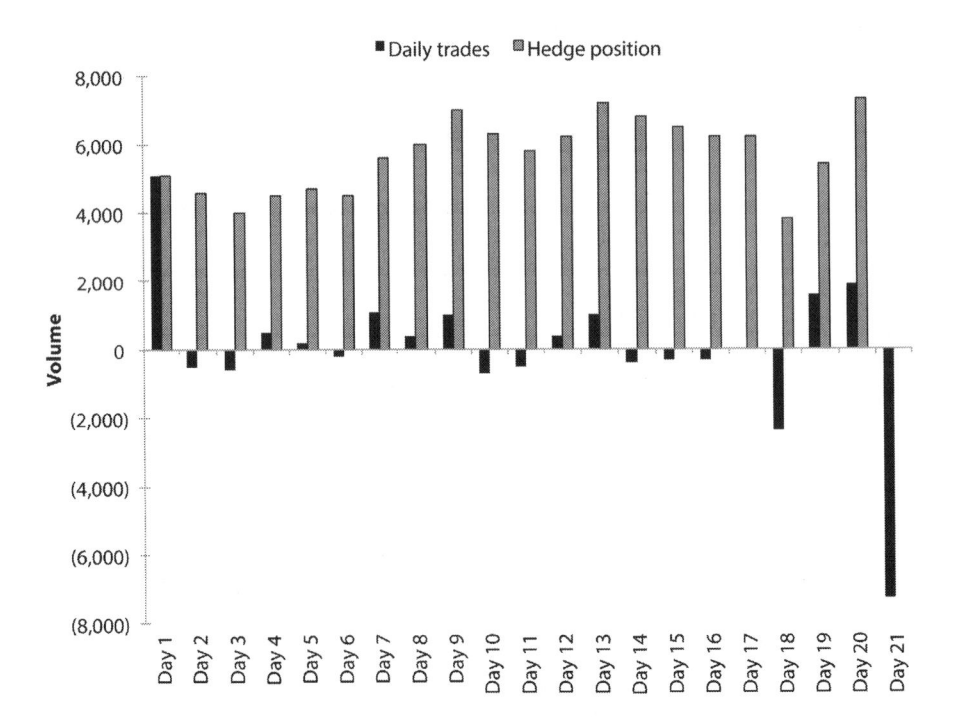

Figure 10.27 Daily trades in underlying necessary to hedge delta exposure of long $100.00 call option.

The largest hedge transactions occur on the first and last days, when the option is booked and creates the exposure to be mitigated, and when the position expires and the trader must remove the hedges that would now act like an outright long position. The three days prior to expiry also involve relatively large hedge trades of −2,400, 1,600, and 1,900 shares. This is partially due to the fact that the option is near the money and crosses and re-crosses the $100.00 strike price barrier, but also due to the fact that the gamma has been increasing as the option nears maturity, from just under 0.07 at inception to 0.168 on Day 18, 0.213 on Day 19, and peaking at 0.248 on Day 20. Recall that gamma is the rate of change of delta as a function of the movement of the underlying. Since the trader is short the option, he is short gamma, which means that not only will the option position be generally more responsive to market fluctuations, it is particularly sensitive to upward movements. As the market rallies the trader will get shorter, faster. The end-of-day price on Day 17 is $100.71 compared with $100.82 on Day 20 (a net $0.11 change), but on the Day 18 drop, the trader was forced to shed 2,400 shares, only to have to buy back a total of 3,500 across the next two days as the market re-rallied.

All of this position management comes with a cost. Even in the simplest possible theoretical case, transacting at the market close in round-lot sizes with a zero bid-offer spread, the trader will be buying in up markets and selling in down markets, leading to small losses throughout the hedging process. Of the 5,100 shares initially purchased at $100.11 on Day 1, the trader will have to sell 500 at $99.21 on Day 2 to re-balance the delta position, leading to a realized

$450.00 loss. The trader will sell an additional 600 shares on Day 3 at $98.43, only to buy 500 back again on Day 4 for $99.32. This daily "sell low, buy high" value destruction is part and parcel of any hedging process and erodes the initial booked margin of the trader's option sale to the client. Remember, hedging increases surety, and eliminating risk always has a cost.

Managing the delta risk of an option position is fairly standard practice. Depending on his relative level of sophistication and tolerance for risk, the trader can also choose to attempt to mitigate additional Greek risks that influence the price of the option. By being short call options to the customer, the trader is short gamma, short vega, and long theta, which give the position the following characteristics:

- The short gamma position creates a potentially dangerous exposure where the delta position increases in size as it moves against the trader, effectively making the short larger as it gets worse.
- By being short vega the trader is exposed to increases in the volatility of the stock.
- In this example, the trader is long theta, meaning that the bleed of the option value as a function of time is working in his favor, so he would be unlikely to want to mitigate that risk.

Adding and subtracting underlying shares will only impact the delta exposure of the portfolio. Modifying the gamma, vega, and theta risks of the position involves trading a variety of other options, creating a portfolio of instruments each designed to fine tune one or more of the Greek exposures. The challenge for the trader is that a call or put that may help flatten the gamma may exacerbate the imbalance in the vega, and when compensating for the imbalance in the vega, upsets the delta or the theta, etc. Attempting to neutralize the Greek risks involves substantially increasing the number of transactions per time period, as the trader will have to potentially buy and sell several different options and a volume of underlying, only to repeat the process whenever the market moves beyond a threshold that forces a recalculation of the exposures. Most option traders will reach a point where, to keep from having to transact at a nearly infinite rate, they develop a sense of how their book will generally respond to anticipated price moves and learn to live with being slightly out of balance on some of their Greeks.

The Challenges of Managing a Greek Book and the Profitable Customer Myth
Delta hedging a portfolio of options is a strategy designed to preserve a theoretical margin built into the portfolio of options. If the trader has not been buying cheaply and selling dearly, there will be no margin built into the portfolio, and therefore nothing to preserve. Paying customer rates ensures that every product will be sold below and bought above fair value. The bid-offer spread paid for frequent balancing trades in the underlying and options will erode any margins, if there were any to begin with. Running a long-run profitable Greek book demands that the trader continually find and harvest "value," options that are either under- or overpriced by an appreciable margin relative to their theoretical value. To do this, the book runner will have to seek out and trade with less sophisticated players who unwittingly surrender value or counterparties (frequently hedgers) willing to give up edge for execution. This is why Greek books are more properly the domain of the sell-side or trading shops that have the wherewithal to be market-making entities. For a bank or a large, sophisticated

merchant or hedge fund, selling options to customers and managing the resultant Greek book can be a profitable business. The firm should be getting paid to put on the option position and have real, tangible margin to protect and enhance. This is particularly true with complex, structured transactions or options embedded in a deal.

It is all but impossible to make money as a bottom-of-the-food-chain option trader by managing pure Greek risks. I believe that most successful customer-side option books are perpetually net delta long or short and profiting from directional trading (with the options as, effectively, a very complicated excuse or facilitation utensil) or engaging in massive intraday spec trading around the core position. Another mistake is assuming that it is possible to pay customer rates, but make up for it by exploiting the inherent trade-around value in a portfolio of options that drift in and out of the money. It is possible, but in that case what the firm is really profiting from (or not profiting from, as the case may be) is the trader's ability to call short-term directional fluctuations in the market. While an option position may be providing a backstop to that trading activity (for which the trader has paid a fee), it is really only justification for maintaining a near-par straddle position, not a large Greek book.

Establishing a Greek book is an extremely committing decision. It takes a long time to build up and an even longer time to wind down, if the firm decides to exit the business. There is a point, some number of options, where it makes sense to treat them as a book and manage the Greek risks. Once an option book reaches a certain size and crosses that ambiguous threshold it takes on a life of its own and requires constant tending, lest it run rampant or die off from neglect. Traders also need to prune back their books from time to time to keep them healthy, as growing like a weed invariably leads to a giant, tangled mess.

Option Trading Instruments
There are three principal categories of options that are traded: physical options, options on forward contracts, and financial options.

Physical Options
Physical options are most commonly traded in the early days of a market, and are frequently embedded within the contractual language of the structured deals and asset-based transactions that merchants so desperately crave. The option will rarely be clearly, explicitly defined, and will instead often be expressed as a flexibility of supply, demand, or an acceptable level of variation in one or more parameters of the deal. Frequently what the contract language does not say creates substantial interpretive wiggle room that allows canny traders to manufacture optionality where none was intended to exist. Not all optionality has value, but some most certainly does.

Physical options are infrastructure intensive. Even the simplest, most clearly defined physical options can require person-to-person notification of exercise and extensive logistical and operational support to coordinate scheduling and production or receipt of the contracted notional volume.

Chapter 10 – Option Trading Strategies

Options on Forward Contracts
Options on forward contracts tend to be relatively more contractually specific, as both the option itself and the resulting security must be defined. There is still flexibility, particularly for OTC transactions executed directly between two counterparties, but any non-standard conditions or specifications will need to be agreed to, defined, and documented.

Financial Options
Financial options are a huge class of instruments, encompassing the following sub-categories of instruments:

- Options that settle financially against a predetermined price, index, or data point, where the counterparties exchange payments relative to the differential between the strike price and the settlement value.
- Options that are exercisable into a futures contract.
- Options that are exercisable into a financial swap contract, also commonly called options on swaps or, for super derivatives nerds, swaptions.

Financial options can be standardized, exchange-traded cleared products, or customized, negotiated instruments executed between two counterparties. While non-standard structures can be extremely challenging to price and trade, standardized options on futures and swaps are extremely common and utilized by every type of market participant.

A Little Exercise Is Good for You, Too Much Will Kill You
Depending on the relative evolutionary state, sophistication, and structure of a market, the majority of the options traded may be either physical or financial products. Financial options can automatically settle against a pre-defined index, be triggered by a contractual provision, or be exercised through a counterparty or clearinghouse notification. A physical option will typically require verified notification of exercise to an authorized representative of the option seller at or before a predetermined time and date. This can create significant operational risk for both the buyer and seller of the option, as traders scramble to execute while simultaneously responding to incoming option notifications from other counterparties. Most markets mature to the point that the operational bottleneck of managing physical options will begin to strangle the business. When faced with the reality of making and/or accepting dozens of phone calls over the space of a few minutes, most market participants begin to see the need for a financially auto-exercised contract that settles relative to a robust pre-defined index.

Successfully exercising an option can also bring its own perils. In most cases, a firm will have to pay for or post margin on the newly created underlying position. This is not something that is typically given much consideration when buying cheap out-of-the-money calls or puts, as the premium expended is small and the initial collateral needs are typically relatively inconsequential. If the option moves into the money and a trader exercises into a larger dollar-value notional exposure, the firm may have to post significant amounts of incremental margin to hold the position. Converting the position from a risk-limited option to a directional position in the underlying also exposes the trader to a material increase in risk. The newly created position in the underlying will need to be dealt with efficiently, particularly if the trader intends to immediately exit and book her profits, as liquidity frequently decreases sharply around option expiry. The difficulty of locking in gains and the additional costs of collateral frequently motivate traders to trade out of profitable option positions near expiry, theoretically realizing most of the gains they could achieve through exercising. In practice, the discount for exiting a position may be material, as option market makers extract value from counterparties that want to flatten out exposures at the eleventh hour.

It's NOT Cool to Be Fashionably Late to the Option Party

The business plan for most nascent options desks will invariably be something along the lines of: "The firm will leverage its core competency in trading by expanding into a new, exciting market where undoubtedly all sorts of customer-types are waiting around to surrender cash in the form of wide bid-offer spreads, cheap volatility, and exotic, high-value structures." The problem is, just because the trader's firm has discovered this brand-new market does not mean that everyone else just showed up at the party. In an established market a new entrant may be operating at a significant information and experiential disadvantage, with no institutional knowledge base or built-up comfort level with the product and its unique risk requirements. Remember, if you can't spot the sucker in the option market, you are the sucker in the option market.

Options in New Markets

There can be epic opportunities in the early days of any new product as a mass of uninformed participants simultaneously attempt to learn the market starting from an informational tabula rasa. Options in new products can be significantly mispriced relative to the prevailing (or potential future) conditions, as the natural players are often unfamiliar with the nuances and underlying mathematics of option pricing, the term structure and distributions of volatility, and the lack of an appreciation for how dramatically a market can shift character, rendering previously useless instruments extremely valuable to the holder. Traders with prior experience from other developed markets will enjoy a significant early advantage, particularly merchants, whose core business is leveraging previously acquired knowledge in early-stage markets. The entrance of new money and aggressive speculative entities tends to increase volatility, all things being equal, which means that optionality is often systematically underpriced at the advent of a new market. Whether or not a firm is able to capitalize, given the transactional comfort levels of newfound counterparties and their appetite for doing business that they may not fully understand, is open to debate.

Options in new markets are frequently embedded in structured transactions or packaged in what appear to be standard products. Correctly pricing optionality involves first recognizing that the transaction contains non-linear risk, and then analyzing and pricing it. Options embedded in structured transactions or customer deals will be covered in greater depth in Chapter 15 – Pricing and Hedging Structured Transactions.

Options for Hedgers

The natural inclination is to assume that hedgers would be net buyers of options, as the ability to mitigate risk with a controlled exposure should be extremely attractive to generally risk-averse entities—and it is, in theory. In practice, hedger-sized volumes of options are frequently impossible to accumulate in all but the most liquid products. In the more volatile and/or less visible markets, the premium charged for the protection may be so onerous, particularly in size, that the hedger may be unable to justify the expense. Option strategies that are designed to be exited prior to expiry can also be optically problematic, as this can look too much like speculation. For these reasons, naturals tend to prefer structures like collars that suit their organic long position and that can be made costless by adjusting the relative strike price of the component options.

It is possible for naturals with one-factor risks to be sellers of options. The key for a natural that intends to be a seller of optionality is to enter into transactions that result in a beneficial outcome if the options end up in the money. This is intellectually similar to a covered call strategy, a common technique in the equity markets where call options are sold against a long equity position. The short calls are struck at a level where the trader would be happy to sell the stock and take profits. A hedger with locked-in costs but an exposure to its finished product (making it net long) might sell options against future production at price levels above the current market. If the market rallies through the strike price the options would be exercised and the hedger would sell at a favorable level. If the market decreases, the premium taken in would help to cushion the blow. A covered call strategy would not be as productive for naturals with both variable input and output prices, as selling options against non-locked in costs could result in capping the upside of the finished goods price while allowing margins to be squeezed by increases in un-hedged input costs.

Options for Financials
Banks are typically in the business of selling options to customers and managing a sizable Greek book to warehouse the risk. They have all of the possible advantages: state of the art analytics and infrastructure, pricing resources, an origination group to aid in accumulating/distributing positions, a store of institutional knowledge on similar deal pricing and experience decomposing of structured transactions, a willingness to execute customer business and a transactional mindset, top-notch trading talent, and a profound ability to warehouse large volumes of risk at low costs of funding.

The problems at financials are often the result of taking a well-running, moderately profitable option market-making business and attempting to juice up the returns to hit an expanded target by attempting to call the market and intentionally amassing a large delta, gamma, or vega exposure.

Options for Merchants
Merchants are frequently able to be buyers of cheap optionality early in the development of a market, usually through contractual control of productive assets and highly structured transactions. A merchant's core business of owning leveraged control of physical assets will generally result in long physical option and long volatility positions. Merchants covet "trade-around value," the ability to use an option-like position as a backstop for buy and sell transactions designed to capture small fluctuations in the market. Merchants also profit from longer-term evolutionary increases in market volatility that add to the value of their leveraged long option positions. The principal downside of first-mover physical options positions and

asset-related transactions is significantly increased optimization challenges and performance risks not present with financially settled transactions.

Options for Speculators
Speculators will deploy the full range of option strategies, tending to adopt a sophisticated customer role and expecting to be serviced by the large market-making financial players. Speculators tend to prefer to be long options as a rule, as they value the long gamma and long vega exposures. Hedge fund traders will generally only want exposures to financially settled products for safety and liquidity purposes. Institutional fund managers like to purchase options as relatively cheap insurance against declines in the value of the less-liquid portions of their portfolios in times of increased market uncertainty.

Chapter Ten Summary

Option strategies represent one of the most nuanced methods for a trader to express a view of the market, offering an unparalleled ability to manage and modify risk for traders willing to learn the complexities of the products and structures. The trader must first understand the basic properties of calls and puts, which create the option but not the obligation to buy or sell a specified volume of a product at a pre-determined price and time. Puts and calls can be combined together into structures designed to profit at expiry from general directional movements higher or lower or precise shifts in value of the underlying toward or away from specific price ranges.

Option prices are impacted by shifts in the underlying, the time remaining until expiry, the volatility of the market, and a host of other variables, forcing the trader to use a pricing model to value the on-the-run exposure. The Black-Scholes model and its variants are the most common valuation tools. Most option models generate risk metrics, the most common of which are the delta sensitivity of the option price to moves in the underlying, the gamma rate of change of the delta per unit of movement in the underlying, the vega sensitivity of the option to volatility, and the theta erosion of value as the option moves toward expiration. Option traders will monitor these Greek risks and, if managing a large portfolio of calls and puts, may seek to hedge them by adding/subtracting exposures to the underlying product or additional options.

Option traders rely on pricing models to allow them to value the instruments they buy and sell. Option models are one type of quantitative trading tool, but by no means the most sophisticated employed by traders. Quantitative strategies will be discussed in detail in Chapter 11.

Review Questions

1. Draw a payout diagram for the following structure: short $95 put, long $100 put, short $105 call, long $100 call. What is this called, and what exposure does it create?
2. What are the four primary Greek risk factors of an option position, and what does each represent?

Chapter 10 – Option Trading Strategies

3. How are delta and gamma related?
4. What is the primary challenge that customers as a class will have in extracting profits from a portfolio of options?
5. Pick an equity or commodity and examine the curvature of the smile by looking up or deriving the implied volatility of near-par and deeply in and out of the money strikes.

Resources

- *Options, Futures, and Other Derivatives* by John C. Hull
- *Option Volatility & Pricing: Advanced Strategies and Techniques* by Sheldon Natenberg
- *Dynamic Hedging: Managing Vanilla and Exotic Options* by Nassim Nicholas Taleb
- *The Complete Guide to Option Pricing Formulas* by Espen Gaarder Haug
- *Options Markets* by John C. Cox and Mark Rubinstein

Case Study: Product X Option Trading Strategies

The Product X market exhibits many characteristics of a new or recently developed option market, including a lack of traded volume, poor price transparency, and volatility that is low relative to recent historical norms and on an absolute basis. All of the fundamental scenarios for Product X involve end states that would imply substantially higher volatility, which would suggest that almost any long-option, long-volatility position would potentially be interesting and that that any short-volatility strategy would be extremely dangerous.

Given the trader's long directionality bias and long volatility-biased view and the developmental state of the ProdX market, the most logical option strategies would be:

- Long calls as leveraged outright long positions to implement the trader's bullish view of the market with a known, limited downside.
- Long straddles that will profit from a general increase in the prevailing volatility.

To evaluate the potential trading strategies the trader will first have to use the historical and prevailing market volatility to estimate the market prices of the component options, then see what is actually available in the market to construct the trades.

Forward Option Markets and Volatility

Over the prior year the ProdX futures market had exhibited an historical volatility that ranged between 7-12% for the front contracts and decreased month by month further out on the curve, as seen in the following end-of-year chart calculated via the method described in Chapter 5 – Understanding Volatility:

Contract	Historical vol
FEB	6.65%
MAR	5.74%
APR	3.23%
MAY	2.98%
JUN	3.25%
JUL	2.89%
AUG	2.60%
SEP	2.12%
OCT	1.72%
NOV	1.32%
DEC	1.00%
JAN+1	1.03%
FEB+1	1.06%

Table 10.3 Historical volatilities of Product X contracts.

From this historical starting point, the trader will have to either observe or estimate the current market-implied volatilities. Observation is clearly preferred whenever possible, but verified trade prices can be hard to come by in a developing market like Product X's. In the absence of market data the trader will have to make educated estimates and adjust based on any observable data points. It would be logical to assume that the current implied volatilities for Product X will be higher than the historical values, the question being how much higher. By calling around to several OTC ProdX brokers, the trader is able to discover that the par straddles for FEB were last seen trading at an 8% volatility "a few days ago," MAR was "somewhere between 6-7%" and that April was "a little below that."[58] Based on this enlightening exchange, the trader decides to use 6.50% for MAR, puts APR down as 5.00%, and re-scales the rest of the months higher, resulting in the following estimate of the implied volatilities:

Contract	Historical vol	Implied vol
FEB	6.65%	8.00%
MAR	5.74%	6.50%
APR	3.23%	5.00%
MAY	2.98%	4.00%
JUN	3.25%	3.50%
JUL	2.89%	3.00%
AUG	2.60%	2.75%
SEP	2.12%	2.50%
OCT	1.72%	2.25%
NOV	1.32%	2.00%
DEC	1.00%	1.75%
JAN+1	1.03%	1.50%
FEB+1	1.06%	1.50%

Table 10.4   Deriving implied volatilities for Product X contracts based on isolated market observations and historical volatilities.

The historical and implied volatilities apply to at-the-money puts and calls. To value options and multi-option structures with strike prices above and below the current market, the par implied volatilities will need to be contoured into a volatility surface, a series of month-specific smiles plotted together to allow the trader to visualize the changes in implied volatility as a function of strike price and expiry date. Gathering information about the curvature of the volatility surface necessitates another round of calls to the trader's option brokers, yielding a few data points scattered across the front of the curve, from which they are able to rough out a grid of implied volatilities:

---

[58] This is actually a very common conversation between a trader and OTC broker, particularly in an undeveloped or illiquid market. Sometimes the best you get is a stale quote, some sort of a range, or a referential estimate.

	Par - $5	Par - $4	Par - $3	Par - $2	Par - $1	Par	Par + $1	Par + $2	Par + $3	Par + $4	Par + $5
FEB	11.81%	10.27%	9.25%	8.57%	8.16%	**8.00%**	8.24%	8.73%	9.61%	10.86%	12.81%
MAR	9.78%	8.51%	7.66%	7.10%	6.70%	**6.50%**	6.76%	7.23%	7.96%	8.99%	10.61%
APR	7.81%	6.73%	6.01%	5.51%	5.20%	**5.00%**	5.25%	5.67%	6.29%	7.17%	8.54%
MAY	6.24%	5.38%	4.81%	4.41%	4.16%	**4.00%**	4.20%	4.54%	5.03%	5.74%	6.83%
JUN	5.46%	4.71%	4.21%	3.86%	3.64%	**3.50%**	3.68%	3.97%	4.41%	5.02%	5.98%
JUL	4.68%	4.04%	3.60%	3.31%	3.12%	**3.00%**	3.15%	3.40%	3.78%	4.30%	5.12%
AUG	4.37%	3.73%	3.30%	3.03%	2.86%	**2.75%**	2.89%	3.12%	3.49%	4.02%	4.82%
SEP	4.05%	3.46%	3.06%	2.78%	2.60%	**2.50%**	2.63%	2.86%	3.20%	3.69%	4.42%
OCT	3.71%	3.14%	2.78%	2.53%	2.36%	**2.25%**	2.39%	2.60%	2.91%	3.35%	4.02%
NOV	3.42%	2.87%	2.52%	2.27%	2.10%	**2.00%**	2.12%	2.33%	2.64%	3.06%	3.70%
DEC	3.01%	2.51%	2.20%	1.98%	1.84%	**1.75%**	1.86%	2.04%	2.31%	2.67%	3.24%
JAN+1	2.79%	2.23%	1.94%	1.73%	1.59%	**1.50%**	1.61%	1.78%	2.03%	2.38%	2.97%
FEB+1	2.98%	2.29%	1.98%	1.75%	1.61%	**1.50%**	1.62%	1.81%	2.09%	2.46%	3.32%

Table 10.5 ProdX implied volatility grid by contract and strike price.

Seen in graphical form:

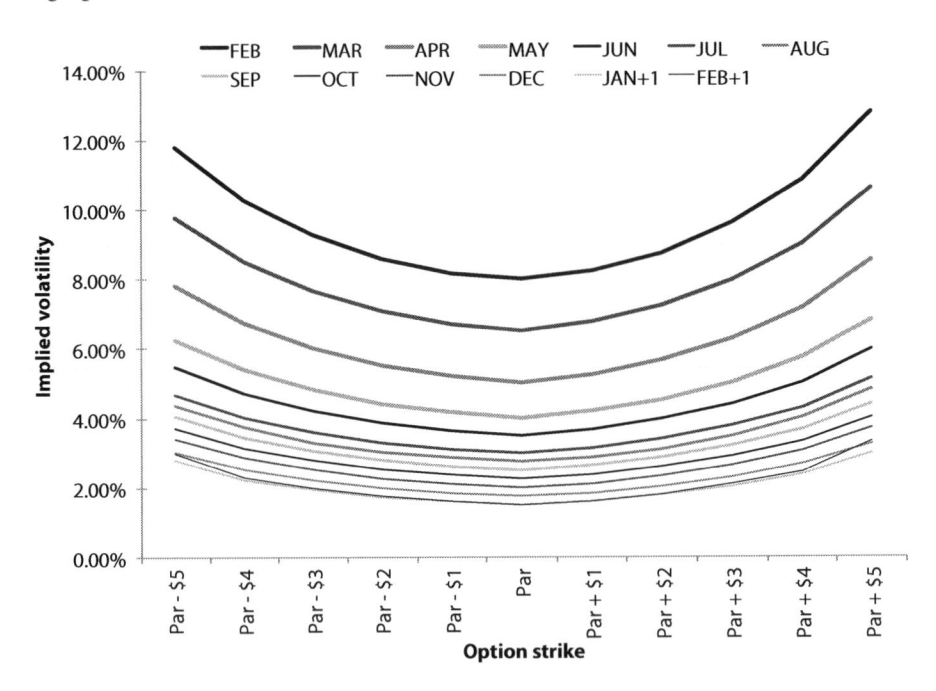

Figure 10.28 Product X volatility smiles by contract.

This would solve (via the Black-Scholes model) for the following grid of estimated option prices for Product X:

Chapter 10 – Option Trading Strategies

			Put strike prices				Straddle		Call strike prices				
	$100.00	$101.00	$102.00	$103.00	$104.00	$105.00	$105.00	$105.00	$106.00	$107.00	$108.00	$109.00	$110.00
FEB	$0.10	$0.11	$0.16	$0.26	$0.47	$0.83	$1.94	$1.12	$0.69	$0.42	$0.29	$0.23	$0.23
	$100.00	$101.00	$102.00	$103.00	$104.00	$105.00	$105.00	$105.00	$106.00	$107.00	$108.00	$109.00	$110.00
MAR	$0.17	$0.18	$0.23	$0.34	$0.53	$0.87	$2.25	$1.39	$0.94	$0.65	$0.48	$0.41	$0.42
	$100.00	$101.00	$102.00	$103.00	$104.00	$105.00	$105.00	$105.00	$106.00	$107.00	$108.00	$109.00	$110.00
APR	$0.21	$0.22	$0.28	$0.42	$0.67	$1.06	$2.07	$1.01	$0.65	$0.44	$0.33	$0.28	$0.31
	$100.00	$101.00	$102.00	$103.00	$104.00	$105.00	$105.00	$105.00	$106.00	$107.00	$108.00	$109.00	$110.00
MAY	$0.16	$0.18	$0.24	$0.38	$0.63	$1.04	$1.91	$0.87	$0.53	$0.34	$0.24	$0.20	$0.22
	$100.00	$101.00	$102.00	$103.00	$104.00	$105.00	$105.00	$105.00	$106.00	$107.00	$108.00	$109.00	$110.00
JUN	$0.19	$0.21	$0.29	$0.46	$0.77	$1.24	$1.91	$0.67	$0.39	$0.24	$0.17	$0.15	$0.17
	$99.00	$100.00	$101.00	$102.00	$103.00	$104.00	$104.00	$104.00	$105.00	$106.00	$107.00	$108.00	$109.00
JUL	$0.10	$0.11	$0.16	$0.28	$0.50	$0.88	$1.73	$0.84	$0.49	$0.29	$0.20	$0.16	$0.17
	$99.00	$100.00	$101.00	$102.00	$103.00	$104.00	$104.00	$104.00	$105.00	$106.00	$107.00	$108.00	$109.00
AUG	$0.12	$0.13	$0.18	$0.31	$0.56	$0.97	$1.71	$0.74	$0.42	$0.25	$0.17	$0.14	$0.16
	$98.50	$99.50	$100.50	$101.50	$102.50	$103.50	$103.50	$103.50	$104.50	$105.50	$106.50	$107.50	$108.50
SEP	$0.10	$0.11	$0.15	$0.25	$0.46	$0.83	$1.64	$0.81	$0.46	$0.27	$0.18	$0.15	$0.16
	$98.00	$99.00	$100.00	$101.00	$102.00	$103.00	$103.00	$103.00	$104.00	$105.00	$106.00	$107.00	$108.00
OCT	$0.07	$0.07	$0.10	$0.17	$0.34	$0.65	$1.57	$0.92	$0.53	$0.31	$0.20	$0.16	$0.17
	$98.00	$99.00	$100.00	$101.00	$102.00	$103.00	$103.00	$103.00	$104.00	$105.00	$106.00	$107.00	$108.00
NOV	$0.07	$0.07	$0.10	$0.19	$0.37	$0.72	$1.45	$0.73	$0.39	$0.22	$0.14	$0.11	$0.13
	$98.00	$99.00	$100.00	$101.00	$102.00	$103.00	$103.00	$103.00	$104.00	$105.00	$106.00	$107.00	$108.00
DEC	$0.06	$0.06	$0.09	$0.18	$0.38	$0.78	$1.34	$0.56	$0.27	$0.13	$0.08	$0.06	$0.07
	$98.50	$99.50	$100.50	$101.50	$102.50	$103.50	$103.50	$103.50	$104.50	$105.50	$106.50	$107.50	$108.50
JAN+1	$0.05	$0.04	$0.07	$0.15	$0.33	$0.72	$1.20	$0.48	$0.21	$0.10	$0.06	$0.04	$0.06
	$98.00	$99.00	$100.00	$101.00	$102.00	$103.00	$103.00	$103.00	$104.00	$105.00	$106.00	$107.00	$108.00
FEB+1	$0.06	$0.04	$0.06	$0.12	$0.26	$0.58	$1.23	$0.65	$0.32	$0.16	$0.10	$0.08	$0.14

Table 10.6 Product X volatilities translated into option prices by contract and strike.

At first glance, options on ProdX futures look cheap—very cheap—in dollar terms. The question is, do these apparently inexpensive instruments translate into a superior means of expressing the trader's view?

Long MAR Call Options as Leveraged Outrights

The most straightforward means of employing an option to express the trader's view of the Product X market is as a leveraged outright to simulate the performance characteristics of a directional trade. Buying a par option on the MAR contract will allow the trader to participate in any rally caused by the African processing facility's failure to return and subsequent bidding war for supply between the US and Europe with the additional advantage of a known, fixed downside. Consider the following chart of a $105.00 strike call option with a premium of $1.39.

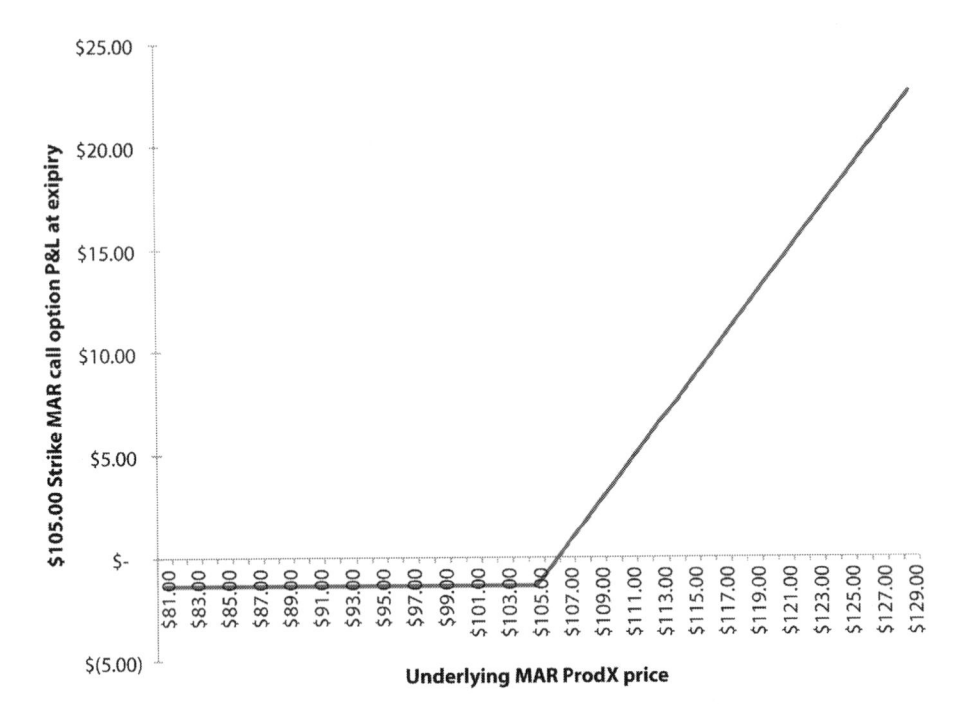

Figure 10.29 Long MAR Product X $105.00 strike call option payout diagram at expiry.

With a maximum downside capped at $1.39 and an upside that could easily exceed $20.00+ if the US is forced to price at a level that incentivizes Canadian supply, the MAR $105.00 calls seem to offer the trader a gaudy 10:1 to 15:1 risk-reward ratio.

The principal challenge with implementing the strategy with MAR options is extracting value within the anticipated operational environment. The success or failure of the return to service of the African production facility will impact the market in mid-February, leaving only two weeks, at most, for the price to respond and the trader to extract whatever value possible before the option expires at the start of the delivery month. This short holding period also greatly increases the probability that the trader will be unable to exit the position and will need to exercise the option, taking delivery of the ProdX futures and selling them to lock in the differential between $105.00 and the prevailing market price. This will significantly increase the potential slippage and risk inherent in the transaction, as well as force the trader to post additional margin for the futures. Some of this risk could be avoided by utilizing APR (or further out on the curve) call options with a longer time to expiry, though with reduced liquidity and a slightly dampened price response.

Trade Strategy #6 – Long MAR Call Options as Leveraged Outrights
Long 2M notional tons of $105.00 strike MAR ProdX call options as a loss-limited directional position with some additional benefit if the general level of volatility increases.

Position:	Long 2M notional tons $105.00 strike MAR call options at a price of $1.39 or better.
Notional Dollars:	$2,780,000 total notional exposure.
Initial Margin:	$2,780,000 initial margin for option contracts.
V@R:	$2.78M 1-Day V@R at 95%
	$2.78M 1-Day V@R at 99%
Risk:	$1.39 for a total loss of $2,780,000.
Reward:	$18.61 for a total profit of $37,220,000
Risk-Reward Ratio:	13-to-1

The MAR $105.00 call options will have 42 business days until expiry, which in combination with the current $105.52 market price and 6.50% implied volatility will yield the following initial Greek measurements:

Delta:	0.575
Gamma:	0.139
Vega:	0.167
Theta:	−0.009

The 0.575 delta means that the 2M notional-ton position will act like a 1.15M net long position for small price changes from the current level. The gamma number of 0.139 implies that the rate of change of the call option value will decrease or increase sharply for moves lower or higher in the underlying MAR ProdX contract.

The $2.78M V@R at both a 95% and 99% level may seem egregiously high, but is the result of a principled risk management approach where, in the absence of verifiable options markets and observable implied volatilities, the safest, most conservative approach is to assume that the entire value of the long option position is at risk.

The change in value between the January to February, first half of February, and second half during which the anticipated return to service will occur is shown as:

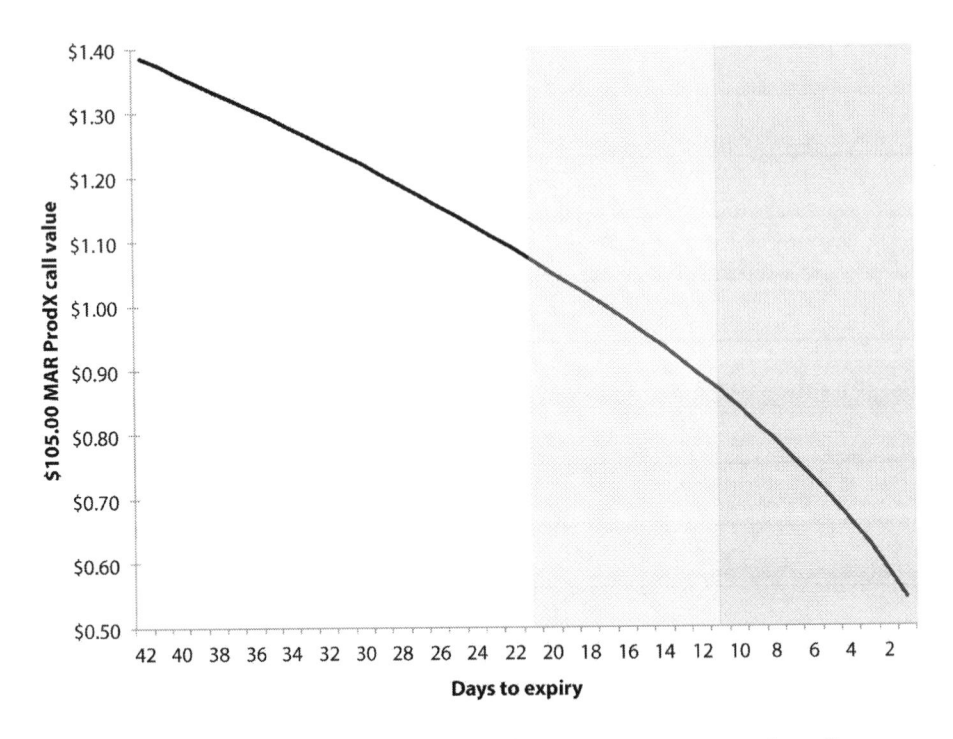

Figure 10.30 Erosion of value of long $105.00 strike MAR ProdX call option.

The value of the option initially decays slowly for the first half of its existence, then accelerates before dramatically increasing in the final 11 days until expiration, as seen in the following table:

Days to expiry	$105.00 Call value	Change in value
42	$1.384	
21	$1.072	-$0.313
11	$0.866	-$0.205
1	$0.544	-$0.322

Table 10.7 Change in value of long $105.00 MAR call as a function of time.

A trader intending to hold a long option position as a leveraged directional must be aware of how much the theta will cost per each additional day of the intended holding period, a value that varies across the time remaining until expiry.

Long OCT Straddles as a Volatility/Directional Position
Regardless of the outcome of the February re-start of the processing facility, the trader has a view that the Product X market will continue to tighten as the year goes on, leading to a structurally short supply/demand balance that results in a tradable uptrend. While the economics of a long call position are very favorable (as seen with the MAR long call strategy),

Chapter 10 – Option Trading Strategies

it is possible to express a view on both the relative level of volatility and the direction of the market by buying par straddles toward the back of the curve. The trader could choose to locate exposure in either the SEP or OCT contract to take advantage of the totality of the potential bullish information in the Product X event path. The advantage of the OCT contract is that it would expire at the end of September, giving the trader an additional month to participate in any rally and putting less execution pressure on the exit of the position.

The par OCT $103.00 straddle has the following payoff diagram at expiry:

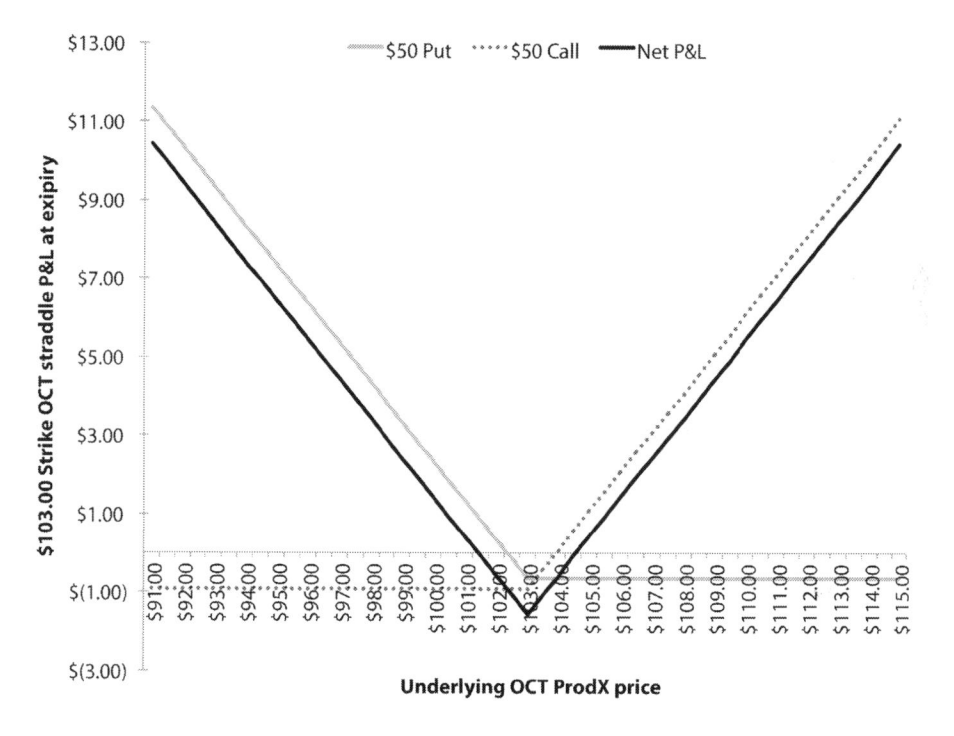

Figure 10.31 Long OCT Product X $103.00 strike straddle payoff diagram at expiry.

The trader will have to pay $0.92 for the call and $0.65 for the put, for a total price of $1.57 for the structure. The trade is profitable for prices below $101.43 and above $104.57, losing money at all points in between, with a maximum loss equal to the cost of the straddle.

The majority of the other trading strategies described thus far require a specific triggering event, set of circumstances, or evolution from the current status quo. If the anticipated factor(s) do not line up, the trade will not work. The advantage of a long volatility strategy is that it does not matter what happens, only that something sufficiently impactful occurs prior to the expiration of the options. The long $103.00 OCT straddle has a number of ways that it can win:

- If prices rally, as the trader's deeply convicted view would suggest, the straddle will be profitable above $104.57.
- If the trader is wrong and the bear case develops, the straddle will be profitable if prices fall below $101.43.
- If the general level of volatility increases, the straddle will become more valuable due to the increased probability of an in the money expiry, which can be seen in the following chart.

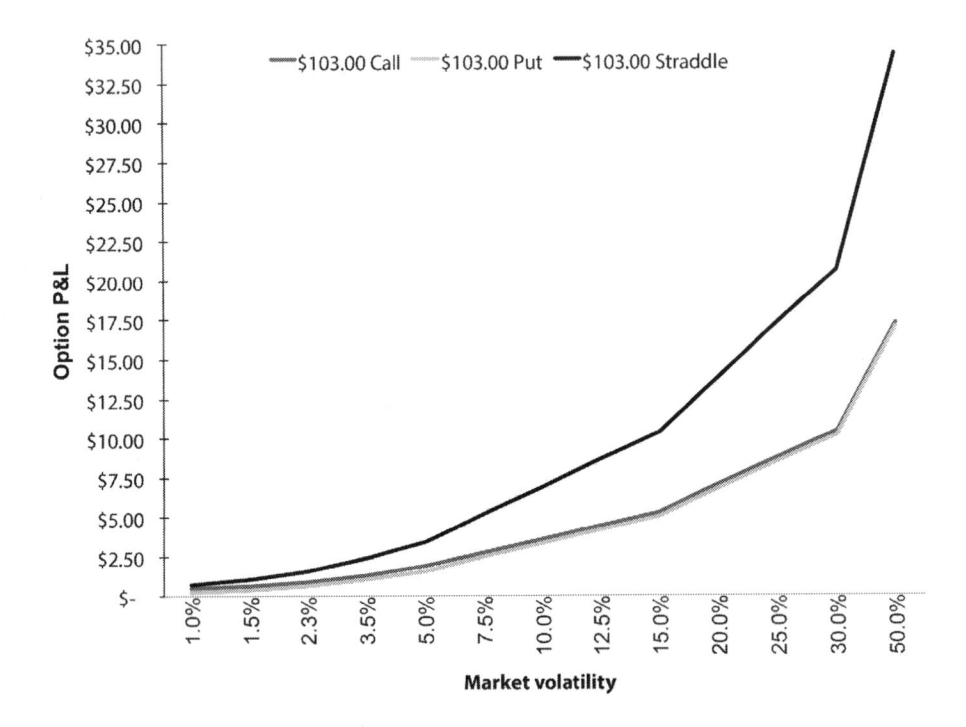

Figure 10.32 P&L evolution of long $103.00 OCT ProdX straddle for changes in implied volatility.

The trader will make money if she is right, if she is really, really wrong, and if volatility increases, which is can be a byproduct of prices rallying or selling off, but also a product of increased chop around a particular level. The only way the straddle does not work is if the market remains in exactly the same place and fluctuates less going forward; that seems incredibly unlikely, given everything that is expected to happen in the Product X market during the year.

The total amount the trader has at risk in the transaction is the $1.57 total premium paid for the structure. The profit potential from an upside price move is similar to that of a pure long call position, with $20.00+ available if the market prices to Canadian production. The downside profit potential is more challenging to assess, as the contract has never traded materially below the current levels. Additionally, the trader can also profit if the generalized level of volatility increases enough during the event path to offset the erosion of time decay. Trades with multiple ways to win are rare and wonderful things, and traders must factor this into the decision calculus, either as an increased probability of success when calculating the probability-adjusted risk-reward ratio or via some other non-quantitative method. This will be covered in greater depth in Chapter 12 – Evaluating Trades & Creating A Trading Plan.

Trade Strategy #7 – Long OCT Straddles as a Volatility/Directional Position
Long 2M notional tons of $103.00 strike OCT calls and puts as a play on an increase in the general level of volatility and the price of the ProdX futures moving away from that level in either direction prior to expiry.

Position:	Long 2M notional tons $103 strike OCT call options at a price of $0.92 or better.
	Long 2M notional tons $103 strike OCT put options at a price of $0.65 or better.
Notional Dollars:	$3,142,407 total notional exposure.
Initial Margin:	$3,142,407 initial margin for option contracts.
V@R:	$3.142M 1-Day V@R at 95%
	$3.142M 1-Day V@R at 99%

The OCT straddle will have 189 business days until expiry, which in combination with the current $103.28 market price and 2.25% implied volatility, will yield the following initial Greek measurements:

	OCT $103.00 call	OCT $103.00 put	OCT $103.00 straddle
Delta	0.5427	(0.4277)	0.1150
Gamma	0.1903	0.1903	0.3805
Vega	0.3425	0.3425	0.6849
Theta	(0.0013)	(0.0013)	(0.0026)

Table 10.8   Greek risks of a long $103.00 OCT ProdX straddle.

The delta values of the option partially offset, leaving the trader with small, residual, net long position sensitivity. The same-sign gamma numbers are locally equivalent, which means that the trader will rapidly get longer in a rally and shorter in a sell-off. The positive vegas for both options indicates that any increase or decrease in the implied OCT volatility will have a significant impact on the value of the straddle.

Deriving the risk leg of the OCT straddle is a straightforward exercise, as the maximum the trader can lose is equal to the $1.57 premium paid to the counterparty (or counterparties) for the call and the put. As with the OCT ProdX futures directional position contemplated in Chapter 8, it is challenging to derive a profit target for the OCT straddles. As the position will have a longer time to benefit from the entire Product X event path, it seems reasonable to allow for the possibility that sometime during the period under consideration the OCT contract could have to price to the mid $130.00s (if not higher) to incentivize Canadian production, given the base case fundamentals. Using a $130.00 target minus the $103.00 strike price and $1.57 premium cost, the straddle would have a maximum upside of $25.43.

Risk: $1.57 for a total loss of $3,142,407.
Reward: $25.43 for a total gain of $50,860,000.
Risk-Reward: 16-to-1

As with the MAR call options, the trader would have the entire $3.142M premium expenditure count against their utilized V@R at both a 95% and 99% level. In the absence of verifiable options markets and observable implied volatilities, the safest, most conservative approach is to assume that the entire value of the long option position is at risk.

The trader can synthetically replicate the MAR calls and the OCT straddle by buying puts (which should be easier to secure in a market that everyone is sure is going up), then buying the underlying to convert the volume (or half of the volume for the straddle) into synthetic calls as described earlier. This is not as metric efficient, but has a similar payout profile and superior ease of position accumulation, although it does present trickier exit dynamics.

Clearly, expressing the trader's view via either a long call option or long par straddle or both would be an extremely attractive strategy. The challenge will be finding someone willing to sell options to the trader, given the evolutionary state and current conditions of the Product X market.

When the trader pings a number of large financials that act as market makers, either directly or via a broker, he should not be surprised to get back quotes with the bid price relatively close to the current market-implied volatility but with an offer significantly higher. This can be due to an inherent desire on the part of market makers to purchase volatility, a desire to not sell volatility, or, more likely, both. Option market makers at large financial institutions tend to be extremely sophisticated operators, and will be well aware of the low absolute level of volatility present in the Product X market and the relative risk-reward ratio. If the trader cannot buy volatility or long option positions from sophisticated financial players, there may be other ways to arrive at the same or similar position.

A trader with good industry relationships or a strong origination group may be able to source options from a natural. The trader will face two challenges, finding naturals willing and able to deal, and those with exposures that they are willing to modify in the short to medium-term. Naturals frequently hedge their exposures well ahead of time, rendering them disinclined to make any substantial positional changes close to delivery. If the trader were looking for options on the next calendar year (or further out), a natural would express considerably more interest in pricing the product.

For a natural, executing an option trade is often a novel, interesting exercise (pun intended), which can require a great deal of back and forth discussion. Even if the trader is fortunate enough to locate a willing counterparty and successfully negotiate a transaction, there can be significant performance and credit risk inherent in buying options from a producer. There can also be significant performance risk in buying financial options from thinly capitalized players, as they may not fully anticipate the magnitude of their liability and incur losses too large for them to bear, leading to default, bankruptcy, or both.

The most likely scenario is that the trader will have to severely overpay on a volatility (and therefore price) basis to secure a long option position, but given the magnitude of the move expected, this is more of an inconvenience than a deal-breaking problem. The trader will have to endure significant mark-to-market pain in the short-to-medium term, as the model built into the risk system will very probably use a lower vol or a mid-market from a wide bid-offer spread that will be below the offer side the trader had to transact against.

Traders are able to take advantage of the flexibility inherent in a high-liquidity directional position to modify the exposure at the time and price of their choosing with the maximum efficiency. The option market can, particularly in low-liquidity, early-stage markets, be the exact opposite, requiring the trader to execute when he can, sometimes to the extent of being somewhat price insensitive. The trader may need to buy Product X options whenever they are for sale and from whoever is willing to sell them, then neutralize the net delta position with a volume of underlying and wait. When the trader likes the market, he can then remove hedges (directionally) or keep as-is and get paid on probable volatility increase.

11

Quantitative Trading Strategies

Quantitative trading strategies use one or more computer-based tools to extend and/or enhance the capabilities of the human operator, either via the capacity to do work or in terms of raw processing speed. In some cases the human operator is replaced altogether by a decision engine and an execution interface linked to one or more exchanges. There are obvious advantages and disadvantages to a machine-based trading strategy:

The Advantages of Model-Based Trading

1. There can be a huge first-mover advantage.
2. Model discipline can compensate for human flaws.
3. Productive strategies are scalable to other products and markets.

Huge First-Mover Advantage

The principal advantage of machine-enhanced or model-based trading systems is that there are real, tangible benefits to being either first or fastest. Deploying a cutting-edge analytical tool can materially improve the decision accuracy or efficiency of a human operator's trading strategies. Even the large potential gains to the productivity of a trader are childish when compared to the crushing advantage a faster execution platform or algorithm will have over older, slower competition. While a human trader can easily gain a non-trivial edge over peers, a state-of-the-art arbitrage robot hooked up to the most direct means of market access should, in theory, displace slower agents to the back of the transactional queue 100% of the time.

Model or Robot Discipline Can Compensate for Human Flaws
Human beings are deeply flawed decision makers, as generations of evil cybernetic movie villains and countless robotic sidekicks never tire of pointing out. Organic traders often lack discipline, can be indecisive in moments of crisis, and take forever to analyze and respond to information. A self-aware trader who has identified a persistent flaw in his technique may be able to compensate with a model-based solution. In some cases, it is actually possible to turn a weakness into a strength with a well-designed and creatively implemented tool. One of my many deficiencies early in my career was an inability to follow multiple markets; I just couldn't keep all the numbers straight in my head. To compensate, I built a spreadsheet that allowed me to track the best bid and offer for the common products in my market, with built-in macros to archive and time-stamp trades. I quickly accumulated a sizable amount of historical data, which at that point in the market's evolution was a rare and valuable resource. My spreadsheet—and the work ethic necessary to maintain it—turned a data deficit into a decisive informational advantage.

Expandable
There are a finite number of markets a human operator can watch, and a limit to how much time they can sit in the seat and continue to productively function. Machines don't get tired, and a quantitative strategy can be deployed 24/7/365 in as many markets as the firm can afford servers, routers, and bandwidth.

The Disadvantages of Model-Based Trading
There are a number of disadvantages to model-based trading strategies:

1. Machine strategies are very infrastructure intensive.
2. Measuring risk and reward for high-speed strategies is challenging, if not impossible.
3. Very data-intensive, and data-sensitive.
4. Back testing can lead to developing the perfect strategy for yesterday's market.
5. It is an arms race.
6. Bad or improperly checked code can result in non-economic or nonsensical trades executed at a high rate of speed.

Infrastructure Intensive
More than any other style of trading, machine-based quantitative strategies require a structured approach and a market that will remain functionally the same over time. Some strategies are deployable in early and early-medium market environments, but most highly automated systems will require late-stage market infrastructure, including electronic exchanges with machine-capable interfaces, massive amounts of automated or automatable data delivery and cheap computational resources. There is also an implied requirement that the market conditions that lead to the theoretically profitable trading conditions be somewhat persistent in nature. It is certainly possible to deploy a massively computational model-based solution on a single, one-off problem if the potential reward is deemed worth the expenditure of effort, but developing a trading engine pre-supposes some minimum level of ongoing transactions to justify the effort.

Chapter 11 – Quantitative Trading Strategies

Measuring Risk and Reward for High-Speed Strategies
As seen in Chapter 6, industry-standard risk metrics are calculated using day-to-day price changes. Rarely, if ever, is any effort made to capture and quantify inside the day price fluctuations, let alone risk events that happen almost too quickly to be observed and responded to. Ultimately, a whole new set of tools will have to evolve to measure the intraday, intrasecond, market microecology.

The trader faces similar issues from a more commercial perspective. How does a human operator assess the risk and reward inherent in a transaction when he can observe neither?

Data Disasters
Data quality issues can be particularly problematic for unsupervised algorithmic systems. A human operator, upon seeing a price stream reading $19.90 $19.90 $19.90 $1990 $19.90 would immediately assume that another human being had botched the input process and disregard the anomalous $1990 price. An algorithm might be triggered into taking action. Any algorithm making decisions based on the midpoint of a bid-offer pair is similarly vulnerable to data fragility issues, as poor or non-existent market data could be misinterpreted as a meaningful event and trigger a response.

It's Difficult to Drive Using the Rear-View Mirror
One of the biggest dangers from machine systems that attempt to derive actionable patterns from historical data is a tendency to over-fit or over-learn from the past. This is a common problem for both rules-based systems programmed by a human operator and neural networks that "learn" from pre-selected data sets. A human operator will tend to err in building in preconceptions about how to best operate in the future market environment, which may not apply going forward. A machine learning system is capable of determining the exact optimal strategy for the past, but will be unable to cope with a future that unfolds in random and unexpected ways.

Over-fitting to historical data is particularly problematic in markets prone to shocks, upheavals, etc. This is true of all heuristic-based trading methodologies.

It's an Arms Race
Human and model-based trading share three principal constraints: speed and ability of acquiring information, speed and ability of processing information into actionable strategies, and speed and ability of executing on actionable strategies. Algorithmic traders, who exist in a much less chronologically forgiving environment, are much more cognizant of, and dedicated to, wringing out every possible inefficiency. Algorithmic traders tend to fix their processing problems with money, upgrading hardware and software the second it becomes obsolete, and aggressively recruiting star programmers and electrical engineers in an effort to stay on the bleeding edge of the state of the art. Think a laptop and free coffee-shop Wi-Fi can compete with that?

Bad Code Can Result in Non-Economic or Nonsensical Trades
Quantitative systems are only as smart as the people that design them and, more importantly, the people that test them for obvious and potentially devastating flaws. A decision engine will not stop to question if a particular action makes sense unless it has been programmed with some sort of a fail-safe. The problem is, it is almost (if not actually) impossible to envision all of the possible market calamity scenarios and program responses to them. For example, an entirely rational circuit breaker, designed to protect against bad data by preventing an algorithm from trading if the price moves beyond a pre-specified amount from the prior point, could fail in a panic, when prices actually move faster than the calibrated level, and shut down the algorithm. Even more subtly, if the circuit breaker is expressed as a constant number and not a percentage, an increase in the general level of prices over time or a rise in volatility could cause the tick-to-tick trade differential to be larger than the hard coded number, locking the algorithm out of normal market conditions.

The challenges of designing and maintaining a state of the art automated execution platform were graphically illustrated on August 1st 2012, when market-making firm Knight Capital inadvertently reactivated a piece of dormant code while installing an upgrade, causing their order routing system to spew out millions of alternating orders to buy at the offer and sell at the bid on 148 different NYSE stocks. Giving away the bid-offer spread is bad business, particularly thousands of times a second. It took 30 minutes for Knight to get their rogue system under control, during which time it managed to lose over $400M, imperiling the firm and leaving the rest of the Street scratching their heads as to where the fail-safes, automatic cut-outs, or control processes were.

Quantitative Strategies

A quantitative trading strategy is a slightly different concept than a directional, spread, or option strategy. For other types of trading, the strategy is a method of operating designed to profit from a particular set of market conditions. A quantitative strategy is a method of operating in a particular set of market conditions using a specifically designed tool. The quantitative tool makes the market operable and allows the trader to express a view of the market. There are five principal categories of quantitative strategies:

1. Operator Assistants: Simple tools that broaden the purview or solve computationally challenging problems for a human user, who then acts on the resultant information.
2. Deep Thinkers: More complex tools that go beyond superficially examining large data sets or computational problems and seek to solve for some underlying valuation proposition.
3. Executors: Tools used to operate in the market with superhuman vigilance, speed, or complexity to achieve the best price possible.
4. Arbitrageurs: Autonomous agents that operate simultaneously in multiple markets looking for and transacting on profitable price discrepancies, enforcing the law of one price.

5. Algorithmic Trading Systems: Sophisticated machine agents that leverage ultra low-latency responses to information or deploy complex analytical processes to autonomously execute trading strategies.

Assistants, deep thinkers, and executors are means of compensating for or overcoming the limitations of the operator. All allow the trader to be more human than human, both in terms of capacity to do work and capacity to do harm. Autonomous arbitrageurs and algorithmic systems replace the human operator, allowing for total operational customization and infinitely disciplined execution of the pre-determined strategy. Good when it results in buckets full of money, not so good when it unexpectedly becomes self-aware and starts stealing launch codes instead of trading soybean futures.

1. Basic Operator Assistants – Extending the Trader's Reach
Operator-assisting tools directly address the trader's limitations, and can be as simple as a data-logging spreadsheet used to track markets or as complex as a sophisticated suite of option pricing models. There are two types of reach extenders, those that improve the trader's breadth of information and those that help increase the depth of the trader's information. Operator-assisting tools have no particular need to be fast, efficient, or even particularly good, as long as the net contribution to the trader's insights and actions results in increased productivity and profitability.

In an early-stage market there will be no established, widely distributed a la carte menu of analyst reports and vendor services to serve as the basis for decision making. Information will be found in niche industry publications, company reports, and obscure regulatory filings, and the very best traders and analysts will seek out and assimilate as much as they can. Analysts will utilize a variety of retrieval and aggregation tools (web scrapers, news readers, etc.) to pull together disparate sources of data to yield a set of internal summary reports or a single cohesive, interactive dashboard or tool.

As a market matures the challenges will shift from basic data collection and analysis to processing and value-added interpretation. Once standardized, readily available, third-party data sets exist, traders and analysts will compete to extract the most usable information from the basic figures. Basic data-retrieval tools using structured query language facilitate the preparation of historical cases based on specific prior criteria (for example, retrieve all instances where the high temperature was between 90 and 95 between 3PM and 6PM during July for the years 2002-2005) for comparison against the current environment. Data visualization tools are currently a very hot topic as quants explore their artistic sides and discover non-traditional ways of deriving information from graphical representations of complex data sets.

Operator-assisting tools are frequently constructed on-desk by a trader or analyst, which allows for a great deal of specialization, rapid prototyping, and constant evolution to meet the requirements of the moment. My initial data-entry spreadsheet has, at various times, also calculated spreads, tracked positions, and generated real-time option pricing indications. Since I was intimately familiar with its construction, modifying it to handle my immediate needs was a relatively straightforward process. An ability to develop on the desk without relying on the comparatively less motivated IT department is a huge advantage for any trader or analyst.

Poorly designed, badly tested operator-assisting tools can be counterproductive at best and devastating at worst. This problem is particularly common at large financial institutions that maintain extremely complex systems that can, over time, develop significant legacy code issues. A core engine that was initially intended to do A, B, and C may in the future be re-purposed for use on D, E, and F without consideration (or comprehension) that the core logic does not work for those products and/or circumstances.

2. Deep Thinkers – Data Mining and Pattern Recognition
Analysts and traders use machine tools to manipulate very large data sets and deploy complex analytical techniques.

In developed markets with a large number of tradable instruments it is common to see traders rendering gigantic amounts of price data into the historical statistical tendencies of each instrument, as well as the relationships between pairs and groups of instruments. This type of statistical, correlation-based analysis leads to a large number of potential trade strategies, among them:

- Instruments that have become cheap or expensive relative to their historical range will be bought or sold under the presumption of a reversion to the mean.
- If a pair of instruments have experienced a temporary shock to what was once a previously stable price relationship they will be spread against each other under the presumption of a reversion to the mean.
- If an instrument has become cheap or expensive relative to a peer cohort, the trader will construct a spread between a volume of the variant product and a basket of the other securities, assuming that the traditional price relationship will re-assert itself.

The downside of simple computer-driven reversion strategies is that there may be an extremely valid reason for a divergence from a traditional price relationship, which may persist (making the trade unproductive) or become more exacerbated (making it a loser).

Models: Make or Buy?
Traders attempting to understand the interaction of a large number of interrelated dynamic variables may need to utilize a highly complex, purpose-built model. The firm will face the choice between building their own in-house tool, commissioning a bespoke solution from a vendor, or purchasing an off-the-shelf package and modifying it as needed. There are plusses and minuses with either approach.

In-house development of a model or decision-support tool allows for total control of the product, but exacts a heavy cost in terms of front-office bandwidth that might be more constructively deployed on revenue-producing activities. The development effort will be constrained by the skill sets and proficiencies of the firm's development team, as well as their skill in articulating the problem to be solved and sophistication in designing and implementing a software solution.

Purchasing an off-the-shelf solution will provide the firm with a readily available, robust tool, the utility of which will largely be determined by the degree to which it is a workable solution for the particular problem(s) faced by the firm. The trader will have to determine if there is utility in a 70%, 80%, or 90% effective solution available now relative to the development time necessary to achieve 95% or 100% of their needs.

If the trader finds off-the-shelf solutions lacking, but does not have the capacity for internal development, she will have to contract a custom-built solution. This tends to get expensive and inevitably takes longer than anticipated, and as with internal development, the ultimate success of the project is highly contingent on the trader or analyst's ability to define what she wants out of the delivered product.

Neural Nets and Machine Learning
A neural network is a program that is "trained" on a set of data, which involves feeding it a curated library of precursor historical information that leads to a price response and allowing the model to make complex, sometimes counterintuitive, causal relationships between the historical facts and the market response. The principal challenges lie in properly training the model. Giving the neural network too much information to consider is often just as bad as giving it too little, and it is very easy for the human operator to sub-optimize the cognitive development of the program by building a bias into its informational inputs. There is also an ever-present worry that the causal linkages the neural network intuits are ultimately proven to be an example of correlation without causation.

Neural networks were extremely fashionable in the 1990s into the 2000s, but have fallen somewhat out of favor. As with all machine intelligence systems, they are massively vulnerable to exogenous shocks and paradigm shifts.

3. Executors
Executors are tools that are used to compensate for the transactional deficiencies of the human operator. The execution tools available are largely dependent on the market and its relative developmental state. The most common are:

- Simple order executors.
- Conditional and combination order executors, either linked to spreadsheets or a decision engine. Usually single platform driven.
- Multi-market/semi-autonomous engines that specialize in order routing to minimize slippage.

The Rise of the Computer
The first and most common computer assist a trader will utilize will be the order handling functions resident in the online exchange(s), which can range from extremely basic to complex

and feature-laden, depending on the sophistication and evolutionary state of the market. A trader wanting to purchase 500 FEB ProdX futures at $105.25 would open the preferred exchange screen and enter an order:

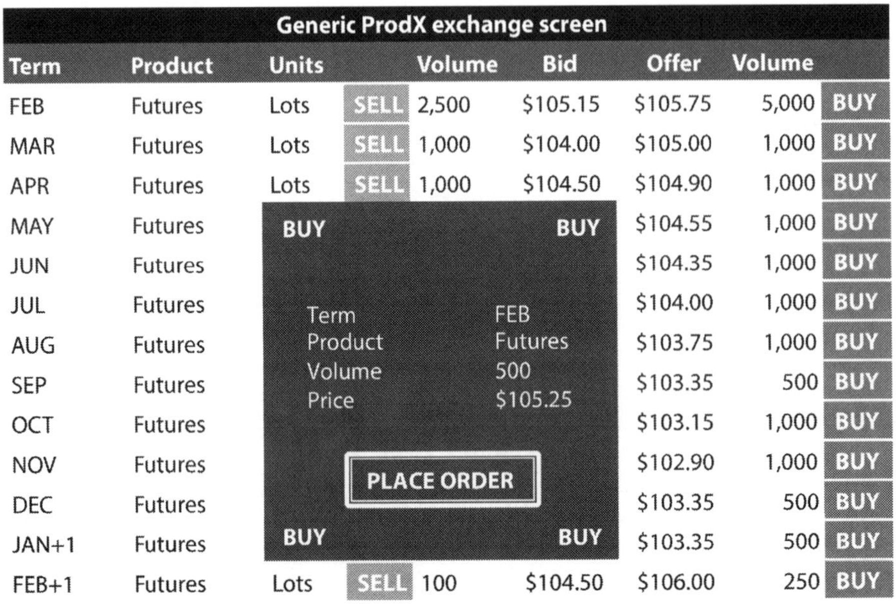

Generic ProdX exchange screen							
Term	Product	Units	Volume	Bid	Offer	Volume	
FEB	Futures	Lots	SELL 2,500	$105.15	$105.75	5,000	BUY
MAR	Futures	Lots	SELL 1,000	$104.00	$105.00	1,000	BUY
APR	Futures	Lots	SELL 1,000	$104.50	$104.90	1,000	BUY
MAY	Futures				$104.55	1,000	BUY
JUN	Futures				$104.35	1,000	BUY
JUL	Futures		Term	FEB	$104.00	1,000	BUY
AUG	Futures		Product	Futures	$103.75	1,000	BUY
SEP	Futures		Volume	500	$103.35	500	BUY
			Price	$105.25			
OCT	Futures				$103.15	1,000	BUY
NOV	Futures		PLACE ORDER		$102.90	1,000	BUY
DEC	Futures				$103.35	500	BUY
JAN+1	Futures				$103.35	500	BUY
FEB+1	Futures	Lots	SELL 100	$104.50	$106.00	250	BUY

Figure 11.1 Generic exchange screen, with posted bids, offers, and volumes.
Note: All graphical representations of trading screens, exchange platforms, order processing systems, and other trading infrastructure are the generic fictional creations of the author. Any similarity to real-world screens, exchanges, tools, or products is purely coincidental.

As the previous market for FEB ProdX is $105.15 bid, offered at $105.75, the trader's new order would not immediately result in a transaction. The $105.25 bid would replace the 2,500 lots at $105.15 as the best price in the market and remain there until it trades, another participant posts a better bid that supplants it, or the trader loses interest and cancels the order.

The advantage of a simple execution system is that, once given an objective, it will not swerve from its assigned task. This is a tremendous boon for traders trying to watch a large number of markets and products at the same time. It would be virtually impossible, for example, for any sort of a large-scale equity trader (watching from a few dozen to a few hundred stocks) to function without a trading system loaded with executable orders. Computer orders can also be used to compensate for any discipline problems a trader may have. Closing out positions when they reach profit targets or stop levels is one of the hardest things to do consistently. If this is a persistent problem, let the computer take care of it. The trader can decide on exit points at the inception of the trade, enter them into the system, and then sit back and see what happens without the mental stress of having to sweat out the decision.

Chapter 11 – Quantitative Trading Strategies

The principal danger of using an electronic platform is self-inflicted damage. The trading system does not know what the trader was trying to do, it only knows what the trader told it to do. The most common errors result from inattention due to screen fatigue or fat-fingering data entry. Sitting, staring, and squeezing a stress ball to death are surprisingly mentally tiring. It is extremely common for traders to go screen blind, enter some kind of transactional fugue state, and click on the wrong product, hit "Buy" instead of "Sell," or not pay attention to the indicated volume and execute ten times the size intended. Fat-fingering a trade occurs when the trader accidentally enters a wrong product code, price, or volume, leading to a trade that is larger or smaller than intended, done at the wrong price, or in a completely different product. Both types of errors can have extremely serious consequences. While most trading systems have some sort of procedure for voiding or breaking clearly erroneous trades, in practice most transactions done on an electronic system are binding.

Many modern trading platforms will have conditional/combination functionality resident in the software. In this case, the trader is entering an order to sell 1,000 FEB ProdX futures at $106.00 if the market transacts at that level.

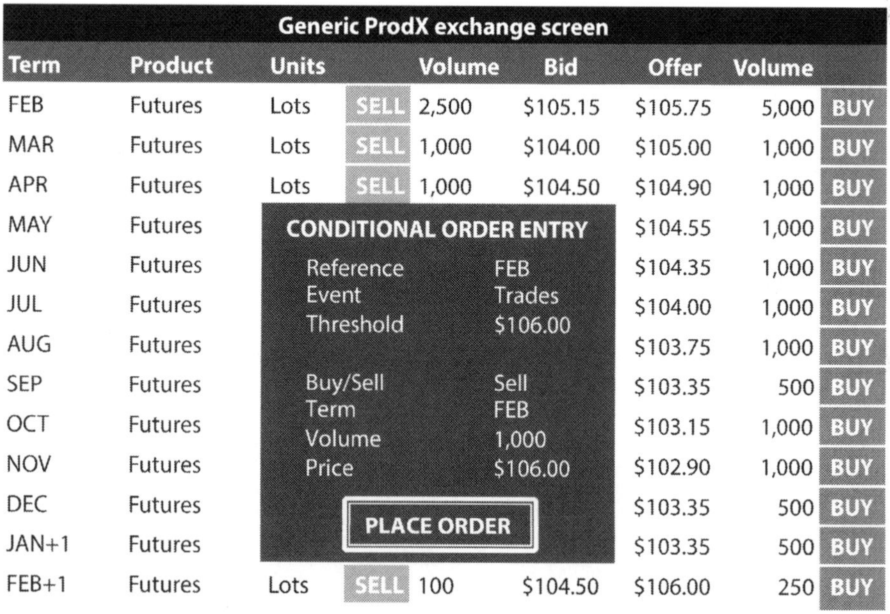

Generic ProdX exchange screen							
Term	Product	Units	Volume	Bid	Offer	Volume	
FEB	Futures	Lots	SELL 2,500	$105.15	$105.75	5,000	BUY
MAR	Futures	Lots	SELL 1,000	$104.00	$105.00	1,000	BUY
APR	Futures	Lots	SELL 1,000	$104.50	$104.90	1,000	BUY
MAY	Futures				$104.55	1,000	BUY
JUN	Futures				$104.35	1,000	BUY
JUL	Futures				$104.00	1,000	BUY
AUG	Futures				$103.75	1,000	BUY
SEP	Futures				$103.35	500	BUY
OCT	Futures				$103.15	1,000	BUY
NOV	Futures				$102.90	1,000	BUY
DEC	Futures				$103.35	500	BUY
JAN+1	Futures				$103.35	500	BUY
FEB+1	Futures	Lots	SELL 100	$104.50	$106.00	250	BUY

CONDITIONAL ORDER ENTRY
Reference: FEB
Event: Trades
Threshold: $106.00
Buy/Sell: Sell
Term: FEB
Volume: 1,000
Price: $106.00
PLACE ORDER

Figure 11.2 Conditional order entry on exchange screen.

Most executors operate on some variation or combination of core "if," "or," and "and" statements, taking action if the criteria are met and remaining inert otherwise. Some of the more common triggering criteria are:

- Execute ABC units of X at price Y if the price of X trades at or above Y
- Execute ABC Units of X at price Y if the price of A trades at or above B

- Execute up to ABC Units of X at price Y, showing only a portion of the volume to the market. If shown volume is executed, create another order until total volume ABC executed.
- Monitor the relationship of X and Y, either the difference or the ratio, and execute an order to trade X and Y if the relationship meets or exceeds Z (requires the ability to execute as a spread or place conditional orders).
- Multi-leg trades: the executor monitors a combination of markets, remaining inert until a set of AND-based criteria is met.

Many execution platforms are able to interface with a spreadsheet or external pricing engine to accept and execute computer-generated buy and sell orders. At this point, the level of complexity is only limited by a trader's ability to write creative code and chain together logic operations, the computer's ability to crunch numbers, and the amount of order flow the trading system will accept.

One of the challenges unique to large-scale institutional traders is how to accumulate or distribute volume while minimizing slippage and other execution costs. Every trader wants to be efficient, but asset managers, hedgers, large banks, and hedge funds frequently have exposures or build positions that could be market moving if handled badly. In a centralized market the principal issue is calibrating the executed volume per unit of time to avoid oversaturating the available buying or selling interest and pushing the price. A decentralized market structure increases the degree of difficulty, as the trader will have to locate the best price from an array of alternatives, calibrate execution intensity to the particular market conditions, and constantly scan for better prices or superior liquidity elsewhere and stand ready to instantly shift focus to any superior market conditions. Consider a trading firm attempting to monitor six different markets:

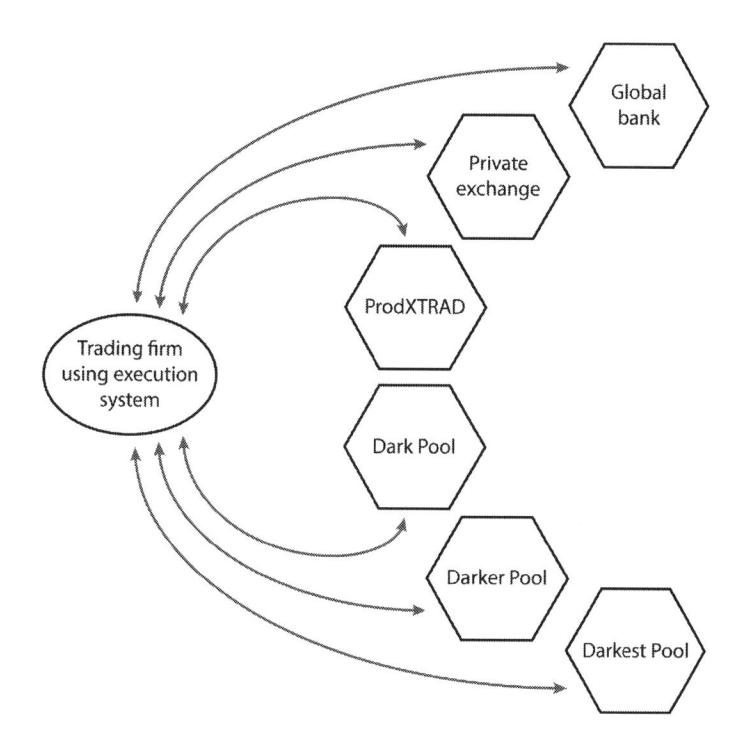

Figure 11.3 Execution system connected to multiple exchanges in a decentralized market.

In slowly moving markets it may be possible for a human trader to monitor multiple platforms (which is why every trader has so many screens). Faster, more dynamic markets with significant machine penetration will require the trader to deploy a software agent to monitor activity across multiple platforms and optimize execution. The multi-platform order-processing system will have an interface that looks something like:

Fictional multi-exchange execution system				
Active orders				
Product	Volume	Bid	Offer	Volume
FEB Product X Fut			$105.75	35,000
FEB Product X Fut			$106.00	50,000

Detail order view				
Product	Volume	Bid	Offer	Volume
FEB Product X Fut			$105.75	35,000
Order increment				2,500
Monitored exchanges				ALL
Executing exchanges				ALL
Resting orders				<ON>
Resting order routing				ProdXTRAD
				Dark Pool
Order re-routing to best bid/offer				<ON>

Live exchange monitor – FEB ProdX futures				
	Volume	Bid	Offer	Volume
ProdXTRAD	2,500	$105.15	**$105.75**	**2,500**
Dark Pool	2,500	$105.25	**$105.75**	**2,500**
Global bank	1,000	$105.00	$105.85	1,000
Private exchange	500	$104.00	$106.50	500
Darker Pool	5,000	$105.10	$106.00	1,000
Darkest Pool	10,000	$104.50	$106.25	5,000

Figure 11.4 Fictional multi-exchange execution system.

The Active Orders window displays the products the trader is attempting to buy or sell. The trader is currently attempting to sell a total of 85,000 contracts of FEB Product X, with one order of 35,000 lots offered at $105.75 and an additional 50,000 at $106.00.

The second Detail Order View window shows the execution details of an order highlighted in the Active Orders window, in this case the initial 35,000 sale at $105.75. The Order Increment determines the size that the execution system will send as a bid or offer to an exchange. By only displaying a portion of their total interest the trader can conceal the full extent of his intentions. If the initial 2,500-ton block trades, the execution system will check the volume of the remaining order and, if there is size left to go, post another offer. The executor is monitoring all of the available exchanges for changes in the bid-offer spreads and will attempt to execute at any exchange where the posted bid reaches the program's selling target. The system is capable of acting as a liquidity provider by posting bids and offers for the market to see and respond to, or staying invisible and only reacting when the market price reaches the predetermined level. The execution system is currently showing orders and providing liquidity

Chapter 11 – Quantitative Trading Strategies

at ProdXTRAD and Dark Pool and monitoring Global Bank, Private Exchange, Darker Pool, and Darkest Pool for bids that reach the $105.75 trigger threshold. The system is set to automatically re-route orders, so if an aggressive buyer suddenly appeared at Global Bank or Darkest Pool the system will pull unexecuted volume from ProdXTRAD and Dark Pool and attempt to sell it wherever the buying interest is strongest.

Even this relatively simple executor will be engaged in a constant process of monitoring each individual exchange and retrieving price data, processing it with the decision engine, then transmitting orders for any necessary action back to the relevant exchange for execution.

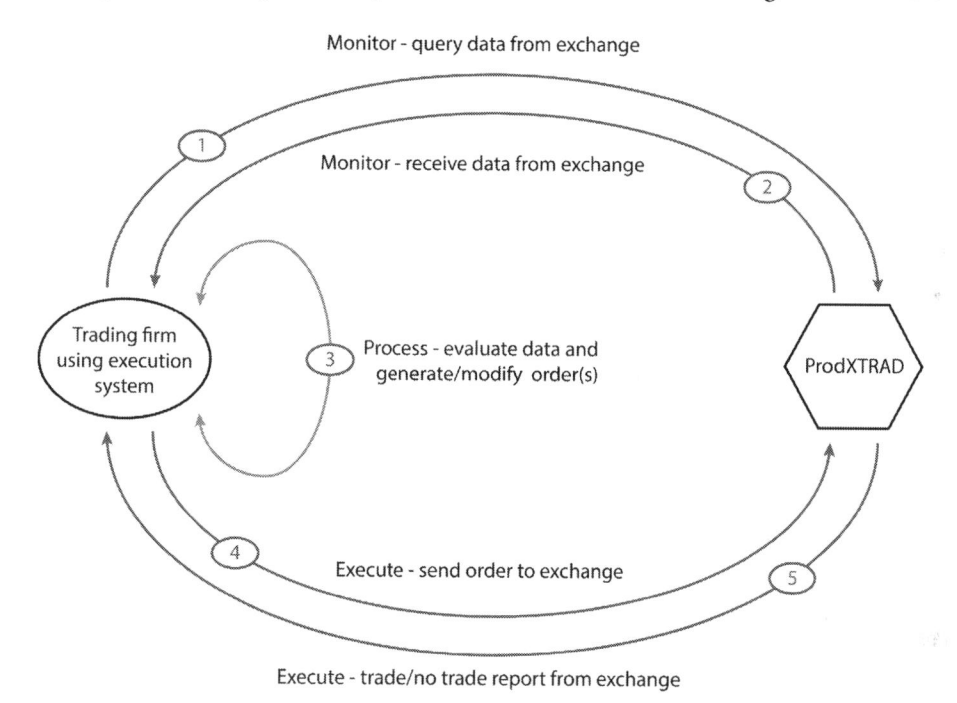

Figure 11.5 The monitor-process-execute loop for an execution platform.

Depending on the number of exchanges and the complexity of the trader's desired execution strategy, the monitor-process-execute procedure can become extremely complicated. Each sub-step will take time, and each additional microsecond spent processing or waiting for a return on a data query increases the probability of sub-optimal execution. Adding to the complexity of the problem, the signal transmission time (and therefore the total speed of the monitor-process-execute loop) will vary as a function of connection speed and the physical distance between the location of the trader's firm and the exchange servers. The differences can be extremely non-trivial, particularly when dealing with exchanges that are physically spread across a large geographic area.

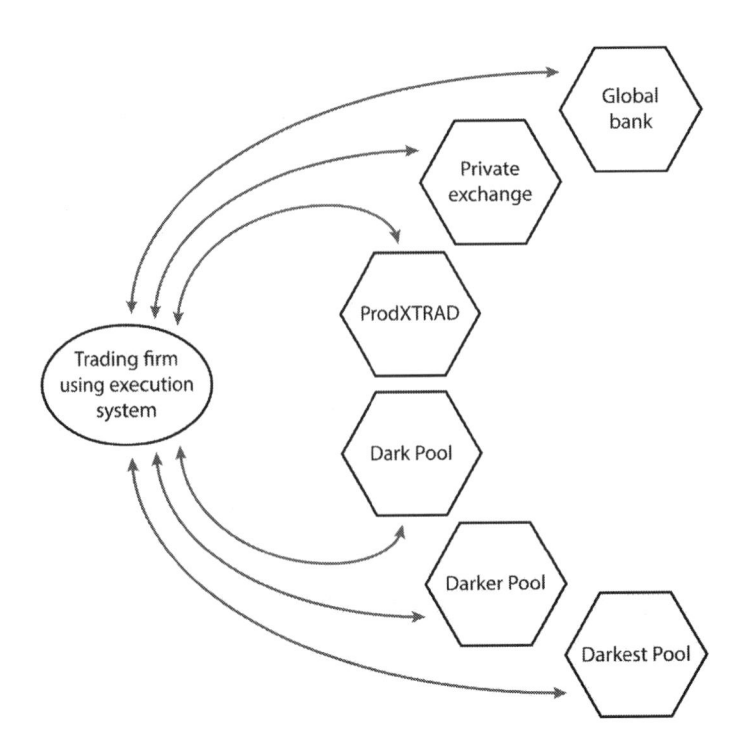

Figure 11.6 Execution system connected to multiple exchanges with signal latency visualized as vector length.

The introduction of multiple exchanges adds complexity to the process loop. Depending on the trader's preferences and the dictates of the firm, there may be a fairly elaborate set of constraints to navigate, including (but not limited to) differing brokerage rates at different exchanges, different margin rates at different exchanges, maximum credit exposures to various exchanges, a preference for offsetting transactions at a particular exchange, minimum contractual volume requirements per period, etc. Executing at the best available price will (should) always trump other considerations, but in the case of multiple equivalent bids or offers the decision engine may have to work through a lengthy process and weigh a variety of factors before choosing order routing.

Execution systems can either be bought off the shelf or custom-coded. Buying a standardized package should offer tremendous advantages over a human operator and have significant reliability and support advantages, but it will, by definition, only be as fast and reliable as any other trader using the same package. Custom building a system will offer traders (and their firm) an opportunity to create or destroy a lot of value. Cutting edge is neither cheap nor easy, but can be well worth the effort. A sub-optimal implementation is a great way to waste a lot of development time and money, and then add in additional losses on an ongoing basis by getting chumped by every trader with a superior pre-packaged solution.

Execution systems are extremely vulnerable to data glitches that lead to transactions, particularly if linking to a multiplicity of markets. A bad print in the price in the heating oil pit can cause the trader's robot to think the crack spread is misaligned and take action. As discussed previously, by far the biggest non-catastrophic risk to an execution system is other, faster machine agents.

For 99% of all traders, the sum total of their first-person, hands-on experience with computer trading will be via operator-assisting tools, deep-thinking models, and possibly an execution system. Going forward, almost every trader operating in a market that features electronic trading infrastructure will have to understand and deal with the practical implications of arbitrage agents that constantly transact to enforce the law of one price and ultra low-latency algorithmic trading systems that lurk in the shadows, waiting to pounce on any exploitable opportunity. Traders can choose their own level of involvement with their machine tools, but they cannot choose their level of involvement with other traders' machine tools.

4. Arbitrageurs

Economists refer to the law of one price, which states that the same asset should trade at the same price in all markets simultaneously. The presence of arbitrage opportunities indicates an informational or operational inefficiency within a market or between multiple markets for the same product. Arbitrageurs are the primary enforcers of this "law," eliminating persistent discrepancies by buying cheap and selling expensive and, by doing so, pushing prices back into alignment.

This phenomenon was common to the Chicago and New York commodity markets, where in the large pits traders would, out of necessity, focus on the activity immediately around them, allowing a product to trade at multiple simultaneous prices at different physical locations within the swarm due to poor information dissemination. Traders situated between pockets of price divergence would step in and buy from one group and sell to the other until a common price prevailed. The original low-latency co-located arbitrage bots were 45-year-old men with high school diplomas, quick reflexes, and good sight lines to both sides of the trading pit. The primary difference lies in the fact that the arbitrages in a large pit or a simple market were perceptible and actionable by humans.

There have historically been five main categories of arbitrage opportunities:

- Counterparty Arbitrage. Most common in early-stage, dealer-to-dealer markets with no centralized information or transaction exchange, where the scrappiest trader who collects the most bids and offers directly from counterparties can sometimes find a buyer at $35.00 and a seller at $34.00 who were too lazy to pick up the phone and call each other.
- OTC-to-Exchange Arbitrage. A typically short-lived opportunity that will exist when some, but not all, market participants have access to the electronic exchange, allowing prices among the uninformed to diverge from the central trading location.
- Intermarket Arbitrage. The classic case, where two fungible instruments trading in different physical locations become temporarily mispriced. This is less of an

informational gap and more of a latency and execution issue, as traders in either market will certainly be aware of the price differential but may not be able to act quickly enough to close it while dealing with localized market conditions.
- Composition/Decomposition Arbitrage. For complex products that are composed of tradable sub-instruments it is sometimes possible to buy the component pieces cheaper than the market price of the structure (or to sell them more dearly). The number of moving parts makes this type of arbitrage particularly challenging. It is most commonly seen in the option and bond markets, and tends to involve some execution/slippage risk (and is therefore not a pure riskless arbitrage).
- Interexchange Arbitrage. The widespread utilization of single-exchange trading platforms and explosive growth in the number of invitation-only pools and matching systems allows localized buying and selling to push prices out of alignment, creating opportunities for machine-based arbitrage.

Only two types of arbitrage are, realistically, machine actionable: the limited opportunities available in the niche specialization of composition/decomposition trading and the booming growth market in electronic interexchange arbitrage.

Over the last decade the number of tradable locations for financial products has exploded, with the advent of electronic exchanges of every size and shape, private subscriber matching services, and invitation-only "dark pools," closed marketplaces with no transaction information transmitted out to the general market.[59] If each were allowed to trade in a vacuum, the bid-offer spreads for any particular stock, bond, currency or commodity would inevitably drift rapidly out of alignment as each exchange sought an equilibrium price based on localized buying and selling activity.

The argument for constant machine arbitrage is a simple matter of math. Assuming a universe of 36 possible trading venues, there would be 36 x 35 = 1260 possible exchange-to-exchange arbitrage pairs for a single security. No human could even begin to recognize, process, and act on even a small fraction of that information in real time. Without some form of autonomous arbitrage agent resident in the market, prices would immediately begin to drift apart. The current financial markets, which are massively more complicated, cannot function without the presence of large numbers of efficient, arbitrage-based, algorithmic trading robots.

---

[59] As in Las Vegas, what happens in the dark pool stays in the dark pool. The opposite of a dark pool is a "lit market."

Chapter 11 – Quantitative Trading Strategies

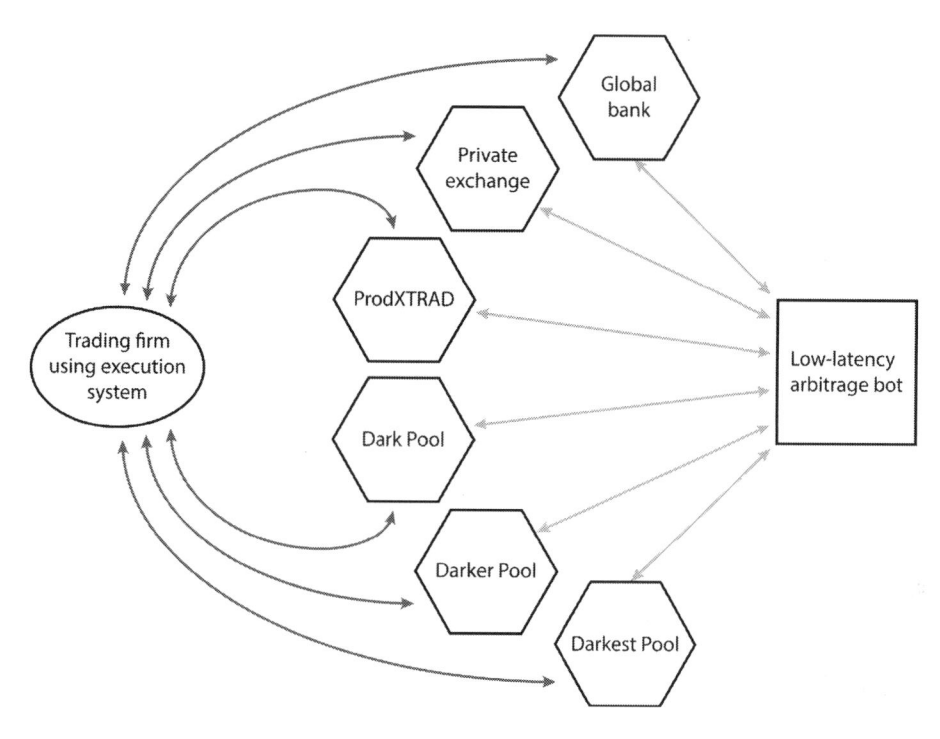

Figure 11.7   A trading firm and arbitrage bot connected to the same exchanges, signal latency visualized as vector length.

Figure 11.7 depicts a two-agent market space, with a trading firm utilizing an automated trading system connecting to the same six electronic exchanges as a dedicated arbitrage bot. While the trading firm's execution platform patiently waits for prices to reach a threshold level that triggers a trade signal, the arbitrage bot constantly scans and compares prices of every security at each exchange, pouncing if the bid in one location is ever above the offer in another. The arbitrage bot is able to do this because it is a highly specialized, highly efficient tool with faster processing times, simpler decision metrics, and shorter connection paths to the exchange, making it capable of recognizing, responding to, and executing before the trader's system notices the opportunity.

Arbitrage is a theoretically risk-free business, and as such tends to produce commensurately small returns when practiced at human-scale timeframes. At cutting-edge computer speed, however, it is a completely different value proposition. A human trader who can successfully execute one arbitrage per hour that makes $100 will make $800 per day, $4,000 per week, and around $200K per year, which would almost certainly not pay for their seat on the desk or exchange. A computer agent might be able to make $100 per minute ($12M per year) or $100 per second ($720M per year).

5. Algorithmic Predators

The seeds of what would ultimately evolve into low-latency algorithmic trading have been present for decades in arguably the lowest tech market, the trading pits of New York and Chicago. In the futures pits, the first high frequency traders used to make their money by seeing customer deal flow cascading into the market from the brokers on the top step and getting ahead of the resultant buying/selling pressure for a few ticks, then quickly exiting. This same behavior resurfaced in the late 1990s as NASDAQ's Small Order Execution System allowed traders to stare unblinking at their screens sixteen hours a day, grinding their teeth and waiting for significant imbalances in the posted buying and selling volumes in a particular stock at a particular decimalized price point. The SOES Bandits, as these people were called, would then hit the small bid or lift the small offer and hope for the momentum of the unfilled larger order to move the market fractionally in their direction. The SOES Bandit would then close the position and pocket a small profit, then get back to staring at the screen and grinding his teeth.

Eventually, enterprising traders figured out that C++ code was cheaper than Adderall and dental work and replaced the frazzled human traders with algorithms that could do the same thing at picosecond speeds across all markets simultaneously, leading to the rise of algorithmic trading.

Autonomous algorithmic trading agents are the current bleeding edge of financial technology[60], lurking in the market waiting for the conditions their creator has anticipated, then executing their pre-programmed strategy. Such "predatory algorithms" kill in a variety of ways, either by pure speed, superior exploitation of the mechanics of modern trading infrastructure, or pattern recognition and game theory.

A predatory algorithm has to be the fastest or the smartest, for the same reason that any other hunter must be quicker, stronger, or smarter than its prey. Execution systems exist to facilitate position accumulation and distribution more efficiently than a human operator, which is a low hurdle. The need to buy or sell in size can imbalance the local market, creating profitable price discrepancies for the arbitrage bots that clean up the mess, rebalance the system, and enforce the law of one price. The machine ecosystem exists because of the needs of executors and is maintained by the custodial actions of arbitrage bots. Predators are not guaranteed a place, and have no necessary market niche to fill. A predatory algorithm must displace some other less-efficient market participant, either out-speeding an arb bot or defeating the logic of an executor.

---

[60] The sheer volume of money, time and quality of intellectual capital being deployed in machine learning, artificial intelligence, and alternative data analytics has (as of this writing) completely eclipsed the cutting-edge primacy of high-frequency trading, which has seen its profitability (and therefore level of interest) decline from an estimated peak of $7B/yr of profits across the industry just over $1B in 2017.

Chapter 11 – Quantitative Trading Strategies

The most obvious difference between a predatory algorithm and a more pedestrian arbitrage bot or execution system is speed differential in the components of the monitor-process-execute loop, represented as the vector length in the following graph:

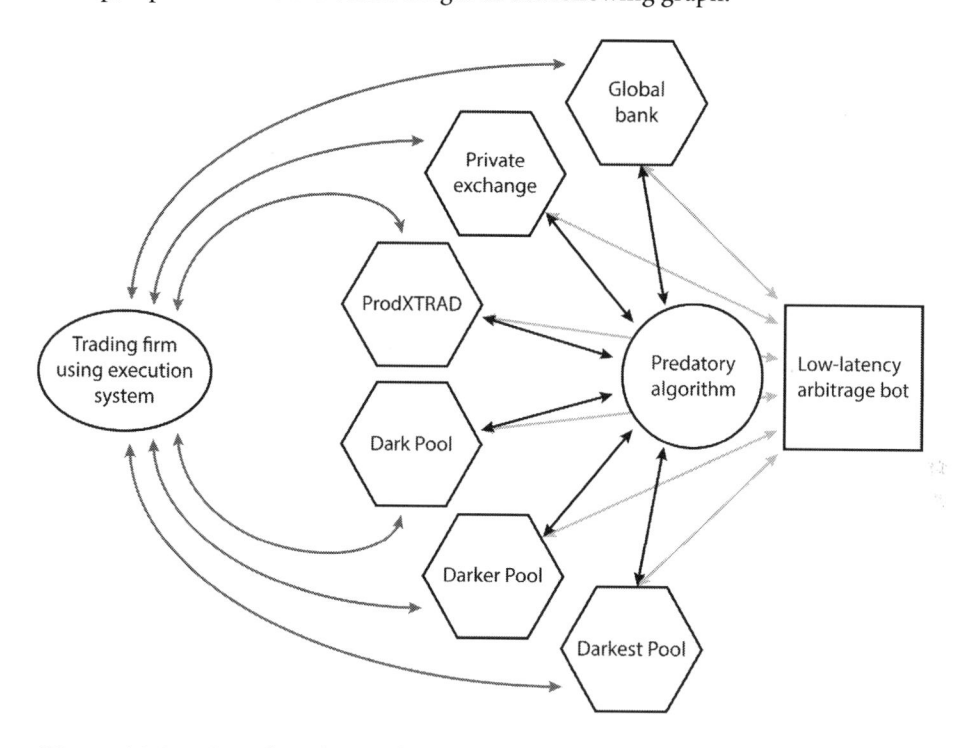

Figure 11.8 A trading firm, arbitrage bot, and predatory algorithm connected to the same exchanges; signal latency represented by vector length.

One of the most common ways that predatory algorithms defeat execution systems is by leveraging their speed advantage to exploit a latency differential in the order routing and processing functionality. Consider a scenario where a trading firm attempts to simultaneously execute on four resting $100.00 bids at different exchanges.

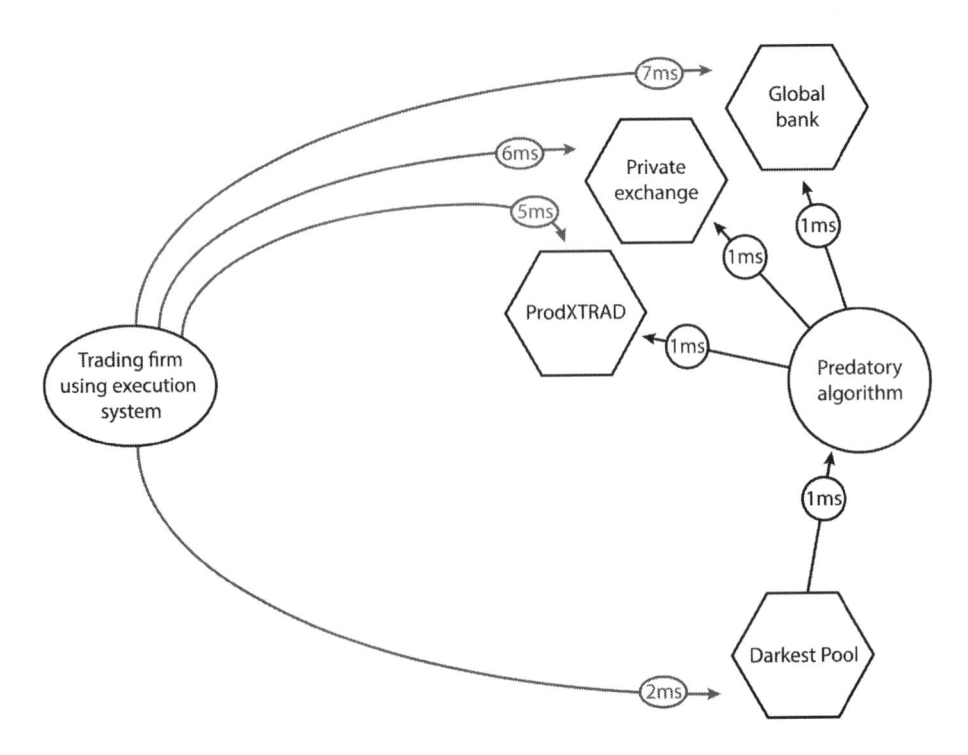

Figure 11.9 Signal latency as a determinant of execution success.

Trading Firm (TF) sends four orders to sell $100.00 to Global Bank, Private Exchange, ProdXTRAD, and Darkest Pool. Stepping through the activity millisecond by millisecond:

1ms TF sell orders en route to exchanges.
2ms TF sell order arrives at Darkest Pool and is executed at $100.00.
3ms Predatory Algorithm sees executed $100.00 trade at Darkest Pool and sends sell orders at the same level to all other exchanges.
4ms Predatory Algorithm Sell orders arrive at ProdXTRAD, Private Exchange and Global Bank and are executed at $100.00. Trader at TF gets trade report from Darkest Pool.
5ms TF sell order arrives at ProdXTRAD but $100.00 bid is no longer there. No trade.
6ms TF sell order arrives at Private Exchange but $100.00 bid is no longer there. No trade.
7ms TF sell order arrives at Global Bank but $100.00 bid is no longer there. No trade.
10ms Trader at TF gets first no trade report.
12ms Trader at TF gets second no trade report.
14ms Trader at TF gets third no trade report (screams profanity).

Once the dust settles, the predatory algorithm would hold a 3-unit short position at $100.00 and the trading firm would be 3 units longer than it intended to be (and extremely frustrated, as it was only filled on 25% of its intended transaction). Low latency traders typically transact for small incremental gains as often as they can, attempting to hold a position for absolutely as little time as possible to reduce the possibility of exogenous shock or change in the

Chapter 11 – Quantitative Trading Strategies

underlying variables. The predatory algorithm needs to quickly monetize its 3-unit short position. To do that, it can utilize a mix of game theory and an understanding of the design of execution systems.

Execution systems can send a wide variety of orders to the exchange,[61] the most common of which are some variation of limit orders or market orders. There are pros and cons to each order type. A limit order is safer, but might not result in a trade and will waste communication cycles as the engine fumbles around trying to locate a bid to hit. A market order will result in a trade, but with an uncertain price. The execution system's designers may attempt to compensate for its slower latency by utilizing market orders. The algorithm might, after it had hit the $100.00 bids at ProdXTRAD, Private Exchange, and Global Bank leave behind slightly lower bids at $99.90 in the same places, just in case some or all of the slower orders cascading into the exchange were market sell transactions. Any market sell order would execute against the predatory algorithm's $99.90 bid, booking a $0.10 profit per unit in a few thousandths of a second.

Earning $0.10 on 300 shares of a stock in 7ms is only $30, but there are 1,000ms in a second, 60,000 in a minute, and 3,600,000 in an hour. Is making $15,428,571 or so per hour interesting?

It is worth exploring why the predatory algorithm has 1ms latency to and from each exchange while the trading firm has a range of slower speeds that start at 2ms and range out to 7ms. The answer is complex, and speaks to the core of the predator vs. prey conflict.

The trading firm maintains a set of servers that communicate with each exchange through the pre-existing telecommunications infrastructure. It is fairly safe to assume that the trading firm's criteria for locating their physical infrastructure had more to do with human-centric concerns like the lease rate on their office space and the proximity to parking and public transit than machine-centric concerns like minimizing the fiber optic path length and the number of switches necessary to connect the server to the exchange.

Algorithm designers put significantly more effort into developing and leveraging an understanding of the physical operational characteristics of the order transmission and execution systems of the exchanges where they do business. Algorithmic trading firms reverse-engineered the telecommunications grid to ensure that they placed their physical infrastructure in places with the shortest, simplest (and therefore fastest) path to the exchanges they were trading. Optimizing the available infrastructure was a significant advantage at first, but soon every low-latency wannabe was poring over routing maps and ordering custom-shortened cables for their co-located servers. That is when the truly big-money players raised

---

[61] Modern, high-frequency-trading-friendly exchanges can accept a thoroughly insane number of customized orders. The reason for the incredible diversity is speed. The more functionality codified and resident in the exchange, the less that needs to be handled with a time wasting back-and-forth between the execution engine and the exchange.

the stakes of the game by constructing their own state-of-the-art, no-expense-spared communications networks to link their servers and the exchanges.

Nobody Does Anything New
Many of the things that high-frequency and algorithmic traders are pilloried for are, or have been in the past, common behavior. There have always been latency differentials between traders, and rewards have always accrued to those who understood the plumbing and wiring of the financial system better than the rest.

There is a big difference between faster, smarter players doing things that slower, more established entities do not like (but probably once did to people that were slower than them) and intentionally disrupting the market. At the time of this writing, there are a number of algorithmic trading strategies that are unambiguously interpreted by regulators as efforts to manipulate the orderly operation of the market. The most common are spoofing, layering, and quote stuffing.

Spoofing is a trading strategy that seeks to utilize an extreme speed advantage to present market participants with bids and offers for just long enough to observe and respond to, but not long enough to consummate a transaction. Each participant in the market will have an individual monitor-process-execute loop, some of which will be faster or slower than others. A spoofing algorithm will place and remove orders that will be visible and, in theory, able to be transacted. Slower algorithms and execution systems will observe the spoofer's orders and may take action in response, either by attempting to transact at their price or modifying their own orders to respond to the change in market condition. While each slow agent is occupied with processing the implications of the spoofed price and generating and transmitting an execution order, the fast algorithm issues a cancellation of the spoofed price, removing it from the market before any of the orders it elicited have arrived back at the exchange for processing and execution. The algorithm will monitor the responses to its spoofed price and seek to exploit the slower order traffic, which can be done in a number of ways, as seen in the following example:

Chapter 11 – Quantitative Trading Strategies

Price	1ms Offer volume	2ms Offer volume	3ms Offer volume	4ms Offer volume	5ms Offer volume	6ms Offer volume	7ms Offer volume	8ms Offer volume
$100.25	50	50	50	50	50	50	50	50
$100.20	30	30	30	30	30	30	30	30
$100.15	15	15	15	15	15	15	15	15
$100.10	25	25	25	25	25	25	25	25
$100.05	75	75	75	75	75	75	75	75
$100.00			50	offer out	50	50	50 trades	
$99.95		50	50	50 trades		50	bid out	
$99.90	5	5	5	5	5	5	5	5
$99.85	25	25	25	25	25	25	25	25
$99.80	75	75	75	75	75	75	75	75
$99.75	35	35	35	35	35	35	35	35
	Bid volume	Bid volume	Bid volume	Bid volume	Bid volume	Bid volume	Bid volume	Bid volume

Figure 11.10 Spoofing algorithm.

Stepping through the events millisecond by millisecond:

1ms   The market is visible on the screen at $99.90 bid for 5 lots, with 75 offered at $100.05.

2ms   The spoofing algorithm posts a $99.95 bid for 50 lots, becoming the best buyer in the market.

3ms   The spoofing algorithm posts an offer for 50 lots at $100.00 and immediately issues an order cancellation. Some algorithmic agents see the market tighten to a one-tick, $0.05 width and send sell orders to hit the bid, others send buy orders in an attempt to lift the offer.

4ms   The spoofing algorithm is hit on its $99.95 bid for 50 lots. The buy orders from the other market participants find that the spoofer's offer has been cancelled and receive no-trade notifications.

5ms   The spoofing algorithm posts an offer for 50 lots at $100.00.

6ms   The spoofing algorithm posts a $99.95 bid for 50 lots and immediately issues an order cancellation. Some algorithmic agents see the market tighten to a one-tick, $0.05 width and send sell orders to hit the bid; others send buy orders in an attempt to lift the offer.

7ms   The spoofing algorithm is lifted on 50 lots at $100.00. The sell orders from the other market participants find that the spoofer's bid has been cancelled and receive no-trade notifications.

When all is said and done, the spoofing algorithm has earned a nearly riskless $0.05 on 50 lots, a process that it is likely to repeat as long as there are other easily duped algorithms to play with.

There is obviously no issue with being faster than other participants, and nothing per se problematic about placing and removing orders before they can be transacted. The regulatory infraction is in the intent to manipulate using speed to avoid economic peril.

Layering is another method of manipulating the appearance of the market without the intent of transacting, this time using volume as the primary means of deception. Both human traders and machine execution systems frequently take into consideration the depth of the market around the best, posted bid-offer. A market with 50 lots on the bid and 5,000 on the offer will look bearish. A trader thinking of selling may be more inclined to take action and hit that available bid while it is still there, before someone else jumps ahead. This is particularly true in markets where there is a large gap between the best bid or offer and the next best one behind. Traders are well within their rights to post a bid for 50 and an offer for 5,000, as long as they intend to stand on both prices. A fast algorithm may not be so inclined, and can post a huge offer for just long enough for it to be noticed and reacted to with a wave of sell orders, then pull it long before any of them (or an actual order to buy) hit the exchange. The algorithm can post a small bid and scare the market into hitting it with a massive sell order, then get out of the position at a profit by posting a small offer against a gigantic bid. This process will be repeated over and over again, until the regulators come knocking at the door.

The strategy is called layering because some algorithms will chose to simultaneously post multiple large bids or offers to make it look like there a several large entities interested in selling or buying at the same time.

Price	1ms Offer volume	2ms Offer volume	3ms Offer volume	4ms Offer volume	5ms Offer volume	6ms Offer volume	7ms Offer volume	8ms Offer volume
$100.25	50	50	50	50	50	50	50	50
$100.20	30	30	30	30	30	30	30	30
$100.15	15	15	15	15	15	15	15	15
$100.10	25	25	25	25	25	25	25	25
$100.05	75	75	75	75	75	75	75	75
$100.00			5000	offer out	50	50	50 trades	
$99.95		50	50	50 trades		5000	bid out	
$99.90	5	5	5	5	5	5	5	5
$99.85	25	25	25	25	25	25	25	25
$99.80	75	75	75	75	75	75	75	75
$99.75	35	35	35	35	35	35	35	35
	Bid volume	Bid volume	Bid volume	Bid volume	Bid volume	Bid volume	Bid volume	Bid volume

Figure 11.11   Layering algorithm.

Stepping through the events millisecond by millisecond:

1ms   The market is visible on the screen at $99.90 bid for 5 lots, with 75 offered at $100.05.

2ms   The layering algorithm posts a $99.95 bid for 50 lots, becoming the best buyer in the market.

3ms   The layering algorithm posts an offer for 5,000 lots at $100.00 and immediately issues an order cancellation. Some algorithmic agents see the market tighten to a one-tick, $0.05 width and send sell orders to hit the bid; others send buy orders in an attempt to lift the offer.

4ms   The layering algorithm is hit on its $99.95 bid for 50 lots. The buy orders from the other market participants find that the layering algorithm's offer has been cancelled and receive no-trade notifications.

5ms   The layering algorithm posts an offer for 50 lots at $100.00.

6ms   The layering algorithm posts a $99.95 bid for 5,000 lots and immediately issues an order cancellation. Some algorithmic agents see the market tighten to a one-tick, $0.05 width and send sell orders to hit the bid, others send buy orders in an attempt to lift the offer.

7ms   The layering algorithm is lifted on 50 lots at $100.00. The sell orders from the other market participants find that the layering algorithm's bid has been cancelled and receive no-trade notifications.

As before, the layering algorithm has earned a nearly riskless $0.05 on 50 lots, a process that will be repeated as long as there are easily duped algorithms to play with.

A layering algorithm can post as much size as necessary to motivate market players, as it has no intention of ever transacting on the large, scare-inducing bid or offer. As before, neither speed nor the desire to place unbalanced orders is necessarily problematic in isolation, but the intent to use both to manipulate the market is clearly inappropriate.

A certain amount of temporal inefficiency is present in the interexchange market at all times, which creates small price discrepancies that are continually cleaned up by arbitrage bots. Quote stuffing is the practice of creating and exploiting artificial arbitrage opportunities by bombarding an exchange with so much message traffic that it cannot process incoming bids and offers in a timely fashion, creating a lag in the posting and removing of orders that leads to exploitable price differentials. The approach is similar to a denial of service (DoS) attack used by malicious hackers to disrupt Internet traffic. While it may be theoretically possible to justify posting and removing orders at an extremely rapid pace and having radically unbalanced bid-offer sizes, there no plausible defense for intentionally lagging an exchange server and just happening to be there to profit from all of the pricing inefficiencies.

Understanding Implications of Machine Trading in The Market

Even if a trader is perfectly happy with his legal pad and slide ruler, it is still important to be aware of the ramifications of the proliferation of programmable tools and autonomous agents in the market.

For semi-autonomous execution systems, arbitrage bots, and predatory algorithms, the trader must bear in mind:

1. Diffuse market structure (particularly in equities) is forcing end users and their transactional intermediaries to develop machine-based execution methodologies to efficiently move volumes of positions.
2. Diffuse market structure is principally held together by a sub-lattice of myriad arbitrage bots that enforce the law of one price and distribute liquidity throughout the system.
3. The lack of any designated market-making activity in the system means that all of the liquidity is provided on a voluntary basis by buy/sell side execution interest and an enormous volume of infinitesimally small, short-duration arbitrage trades.
4. In any localized market disruption, the voluntary liquidity providers will either dramatically worsen their bids and offers or remove them from the market altogether, leading to hyper-fast liquidity vacuums.
5. The interconnectedness of the system and the presence of logic-based (but not common sense imbued) robotic agents allows for a Herstatt-like cascading of "panic" from point to point in the topography.

The probability of severe dislocation is exacerbated by the possibility of self-reinforcing feedback loops to be created and play themselves out in incomprehensibly small timeframes.

How to Tell if Robots Are in the Market:

- Obviously linked prices, where A and B are moving in tandem.
- Flickering bids and offers as the price changes hundreds of times per second.
- Inexplicably fast price movements and liquidity-gap induced volatility.
- Prices appearing and instantly trading, or prices not even seen to appear on the screen before printing to the executed trades ticker. Even a dangerously over-caffeinated trader will take a second or two to respond to a price, make a decision, and manually execute. Anything faster than that and there are robots afoot.

Can Human Traders Compete with Computer-Based Strategies?
Market participants have adopted a range of responses to the evolution and expansion of algorithmic trading. Some have fallen back on the tried and true methods of whining that it is not fair (because markets have always been fair, apparently) to lobbying for regulatory change to outlaw HFT, curtail speed and market access, limit the volume of quotation/transaction, or a combination of all of the above. Others have chosen to take matters into their own hands and develop order execution systems designed to efficiently execute in the current machine-heavy environment.

It is possible to negate some of the tactical and speed advantages of an algorithm by reverse-engineering the strategy used in a standard latency arbitrage and developing execution techniques to compensate for the lag built into slower, less sophisticated execution systems. In the prior example, the predatory algorithm was able to sense and respond to a potential

Chapter 11 – Quantitative Trading Strategies

wave of selling based on the execution of the first of four orders sent from a trading firm that had a pronounced difference in routing times. If the trading firm studies its own routing system and learns the transmission time to exchange along each path, it can intentionally delay orders on faster systems by amounts sufficient to ensure that the package arrives at all of the relevant exchanges at the same time. This results in the predatory algorithm receiving information about all of the trades at the same time, generating no actionable information.

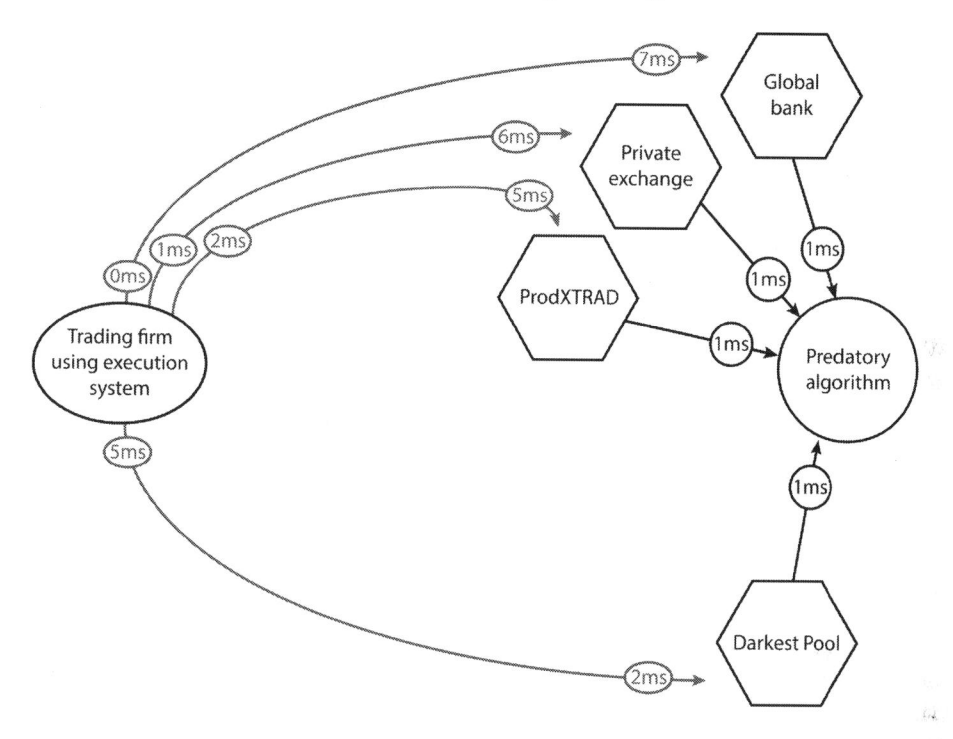

Figure 11.12 Defeating predatory algorithm with lagged order dispersal.

While not all firms have the financial or technological resources to develop proprietary counter-algorithmic systems, human traders can always choose to develop strategies that play to their individual human strengths and away from the strong points of computational agents. A human trader can creatively outthink and out-interpret an algorithm, reverse-engineer and seek to confound the underlying logic, and exploit repetitive patterns in its market activity. If human traders can't win the algorithm's game, then they should seek another game to play.

Generally speaking, computationally intensive solutions are brought to be bear on slow markets and transactional systems are designed to operate in fast markets.

- Analytical quantitative tools are deployable on any instrument, regardless of the evolutionary state of the market, as a human operator will bear the responsibility for digesting the information and facilitating any necessary transactions.

- Machine execution systems can only be deployed for products that have sufficient infrastructure to allow for automated order processing and execution, which will tend to be the more developed markets.

A trader uses an operator-assisting tool to interact with, or inform interactions with, the market. With more complex, machine-driven strategies, traders will be defining how they want the machine to operate, then allowing it to run within those pre-established parameters. One material difference lies in the ability to scale a robust machine-driven quantitative strategy. A successful strategy can (theoretically) operate on and be ported into as many markets as the firm has bandwidth to handle and capital to support, something not possible with a human trader.

Operator-assisting quantitative tools are frequently brought to bear on other, non-quantitative trading strategies. Directional traders will use complex fundamental models to determine "fair value" prices for securities and seek to position themselves ahead of a short- or long-term market revaluation. Spread traders will statistically analyze giant universes of data looking for pricing discrepancies and placing trades to capture anticipated mean-reversions. Option traders develop incredibly complex models to value increasingly esoteric instruments, and then attempt to buy them cheaply and sell them dearly.

It is far more likely that most traders will utilize one or more quantitative tools than develop an autonomous machine agent in their spare time.

Quant Strategies for Hedgers
The quantitative tools created and deployed by hedgers will primarily be reach-extending tools, with a bias toward proven, off-the-shelf solutions for enhanced analytics, data visualization, and efficiency that allow the firm to do more with less and increase management's ability to understand the risks inherent in the business.

As arguably the least sophisticated players in the market with the smallest amount of dedicated front-office infrastructure, it is unlikely that a natural would embrace the cost of building out customized execution tools, again preferring to go with pre-existing, industry-standard solutions.

Quant Strategies for Financials
Banks and large insurance companies develop and deploy huge amounts of sophisticated proprietary technology, but face significant legacy and obsolescence issues that are frequently compared to the challenge of repairing an airplane mid-flight. Nobody wants to shut down a profitable money-making machine, even for the short time necessary to upgrade, for fear that, when switched back on, it won't work as well.

Financials will utilize the entire spectrum of quantitative tools across their various businesses: decision support tools, enhanced analytics and data mining, execution systems, and in some cases algorithmic trading tools. Some large banks have developed and operate proprietary dark pools that function as invitation-only matching systems for favored clients. Given the complexity of their various businesses and the need to accumulate, distribute, and leverage massive quantities of information across the firm, it would be impossible for any large financial player to exist without significant quantitative infrastructure.[62]

Quant Strategies for Merchants
The merchant's business model is more early stage and deal-centric, and its usage of quantitative tools will typically be limited to enhanced analytics to leverage its extensive knowledge base and reach extenders to increase execution efficiency. The principal merchant machine advantage lies in its ability to translate stable, productive sub-state-of-the-art strategies from developed products into new and early-stage markets, where yesterday's proven technology becomes game-changing magic from the future.

Quant Strategies for Hedge Funds
Hedge funds deploy the full spectrum of quantitative trading strategies, from the simplest reach-extending models in early-stage markets to bleeding-edge algorithmic technology in highly liquid developed products. Hedge funds have numerous advantages in developing trading technology, foremost among them the will to ruthlessly innovate and an unparalleled ability to throw money at development issues, hiring whoever it takes and paying whatever it costs to win.

Chapter Eleven Summary
Quantitative tools allow the trader to increase his capability to observe the market, process data into information, and operate a more efficient analytical, decision-making, and/or execution process. Deploying innovative trading technology can confer huge first-mover advantages, compensate for the flaws inherent in a human trader's discipline, and be scaled into multiple products and markets. Developing quantitative tools is not without challenges, among them the infrastructure demands of development and ongoing operation, the potential for implementation defects that can lead to flawed analysis or trading losses, and the arms-race nature of innovation. Computational aids range from operator-assisting tools that allow the human operator to access and process information more efficiently, to complex models that operate on large data sets, to execution tools that facilitate transaction. Most traders will never develop arbitrage robots or code algorithmic trading systems, but will very likely come into contact and transact with such agents created by other entities, so it behooves them to understand the basics of their operation.

After developing directional, spread, option, and quantitative implementations of their view of the market, the trader will now evaluate the candidate strategies, which will be covered in depth in Chapter 12.

---

[62] As previously mentioned, the bank model is rapidly shifting away from human flow traders and market makers toward platform-based algorithmic execution systems. While there is still room for human intermediation in "high-touch" and non-standard products, the current business model is to replace a floor full of expensive traders with a room full of expensive servers on a floor full of expensive quantitative strategists and programmers.

Review Questions

1. What are the primary advantages and disadvantages of machine-based trading strategies?
2. What should a trading manager be concerned with when evaluating a decision to build a cutting-edge model or buy an industry-standard product off the shelf.
3. What are the primary advantages and disadvantages of an automated execution platform?
4. Why is the presence of arbitrage agents critical to the function of a modern financial market?
5. Is it possible for a human trader to compete successfully in the same market as algorithmic agents and machine execution systems? Why or why not, and how?

Resources

- *Advances in Financial Machine Learning* by Marcos López de Prado
- *Flash Boys: A Wall Street Revolt* by Michael Lewis
- *The Man Who Solved the Market* by Gregory Zuckerman
- *A Quantitative Primer on Investments with R* by Dale W.R. Rosenthal

Chapter 11 – Quantitative Trading Strategies

Case Study: Product X Quantitative Trading Strategies

The current evolutionary state of the Product X market will greatly determine the relative utility of the five principal categories of quantitative strategies.

Operator Assisting and Augmenting
In an early-medium development stage market there should be a huge edge available to traders who build or acquire state-of-the-art (such as it is) aggregation and analytical tools. There should be very little tech in place across the market as a whole, so any incremental development can yield a huge advantage. A trade capture and aggregation system that scrapes broker and counterparty messages for live quotes and electronic exchanges for executed trades will allow the trader to have as close to complete coverage of the totality of price information as possible.[63] The ability to store and search for esoteric or seldom-seen products and maturities is a great tool, particularly in an illiquid market pricing information on some exotic products or atypical terms that may be rarely observable.

Deep Thinkers
Product X is an early-stage market that is still primarily driven by the needs of physical producers and consumers. The one thing that unites both is the need to ship product, which is something traders can use to build a model that can help them achieve a significant informational advantage. As explored previously in Chapter 9 – Spread Trading, one of the keys to the future of regional price spreads is determining which country has failed to source cheap incremental supply (or wrest it away from another consumer) and is forced to bid the market up to incentivize incremental Canadian production. For the winner, that will mean a change in shipping from one producing nation to its ports, while the loser will be booking freight from Canada to its terminals. Merchants understand this dynamic intimately, as it is one of their key business activities, but with the development of GPS-tracked shipping and services that post route and location information for trains and vessels, it is increasingly possible for all types of industry participants to build a transportation-based model to interface with their supply/demand balance sheet to gain additional perspective on the drivers impacting the market.

Trade Strategy #8 – Real-Time Shipping Tracking Tool
Develop a tool (or adapt an existing package) to enhance the fundamental analytics around shipping Product X from producers to consumers to improve understanding of changes in traditional producer-consumer relationships and assess the impacts of incremental supply.

Resources:	1 Programmer	
	1 Fundamental Analyst	
	Live GPS tracking data	
Development:	3-6 Months	
Projected Costs:	Programmer	$37.5-75K
	Analyst	$25-50K

---

[63] At the time of this writing, these types of products are commercially available in many markets.

Data	$35K
Total	$97.5-$160K

Strategies Impacted: Physical/financial basis spreads
Directional positions
Option strategies

Executors
It is very likely that traders will employ the conditional order-handling tools built into the electronic exchange(s) they use to access the Product X market. For anything beyond simple execution triggers the trader may need to investigate a third-party platform that interfaces with the exchange and allows greater order generation flexibility and the added functionality of being able to link market activity to different price and event triggers. For firms with truly extreme execution needs, either in terms of speed or complexity, it may be necessary to custom build a system. The cost in terms of dollars and time spent in development will likely prove too onerous for most, who will stick to off-the-shelf or exchange-provided solutions.

Arbitrageurs
There are several electronic exchanges that transact physical and financial Product X forwards, swaps and futures, so it should be possible to create a rudimentary arbitrage agent. The main problem, coding and testing aside, is that it would probably sit idle 99.9% of the time waiting for an inefficiency to be created by the ebb and flow of market activity. It should be minimally profitable, but it would be highly unlikely that the arbitrage bot would ever be able to make enough money per year to justify the costs of operating it, monitoring it, and (most important to management) worrying about its potential to freak out and start destroying value before someone can find the off switch.

Algorithmic Trading Systems
Low-latency algorithms have less practical application in the Product X market than arbitrage bots. There simply isn't enough deal flow to interpret, or bid-and-offer stack depth to profitably read and respond to at this stage of the market. It would certainly be possible to create a predatory algorithm that would sense mismatched buying and selling interest and attempt to transact based on this information, but most algorithmic systems are based on the principle of being the fastest to react in a group of responsive entities. Observing that there are two bids and one offer, then lifting the offer is useless if the two bids remain stationary and do not improve, leaving the algorithm with a long position can only result in the loss implied by the bid-offer spread.

It would also be possible for the trader to create a rules-based trading system that utilizes fundamental and/or technical inputs to derive trading inputs. This "slow" algorithmic system would be a better match for the current market conditions (low turnover, minimal electronic infrastructure, and good discipline characteristics).

Chapter 11 – Quantitative Trading Strategies

Trade Strategy #9 – Rules-Based Automated Trading System
Use an off-the-shelf analytics platform and pre-existing market data feeds to create a rules-based system that leverages the basic fundamental analysis to determine conditions of structural surplus or shortfall, then deploys a trend following technical methodology to find entry and exit points for directional and leveraged, directional option positions.

Resources:	1 Analyst	
Development:	1-2 Months	
Projected Costs:	Analyst	$8.5-17K
	Analytics Platform	$25K
	Total	$33.5-42K
Strategies Impacted:	Directional positions	
	Option strategies	

There are two principal challenges inherent in contemplating the development any of the models or trading systems described:

1. The time required to conceptualize, design, construct, test, and implement as a production-ready tool used in live markets. Barring the discovery of an off-the-shelf solution that miraculously meets traders' needs and interfaces with all of their systems (analytics, exchange(s), etc.), the trader will almost certainly miss the February return to service inflection point on the event path.
2. Unlike the directional, spread, and option trading strategies, the quantitative strategies for Product X do not yield immediately actionable positions for evaluation. The trader must instead evaluate the potential for a tool, once developed and implemented, to produce information that will result in productive trade ideas. This compound utility probability problem of weighing the development costs against the potential future incremental contribution to the P&L is one of the principal barriers to the development of quantitative tools, and will prove challenging to evaluate relative to the other options available. This will be dealt with in greater depth in Chapter 12 – Evaluating Trades & Creating a Trading Plan.

12

Evaluating Trades & Creating a Trading Plan

Archimedean Trade Selection
Visualize the market risk-reward as a partially filled bucket, where some portion of the total volume is risk (water) and some is reward (air). Now imagine each possible strategic implementation of the trader's view as an opaque balloon, varying in size relative to the total amount of exposure inherent in the trade. Each strategic balloon will be filled with some volume of risk (water) and some quantity of reward (air). If the trader were to place the balloons into the bucket, each would sink to the degree to which they were filled with water. The heavier, mostly-water balloons would sink low in the bucket and the mostly-air balloons would sit with most of their volume above the surface. The relative proportion of risk and reward inherent in each transaction would be easily observed and the best strategy would, literally, float to the top.

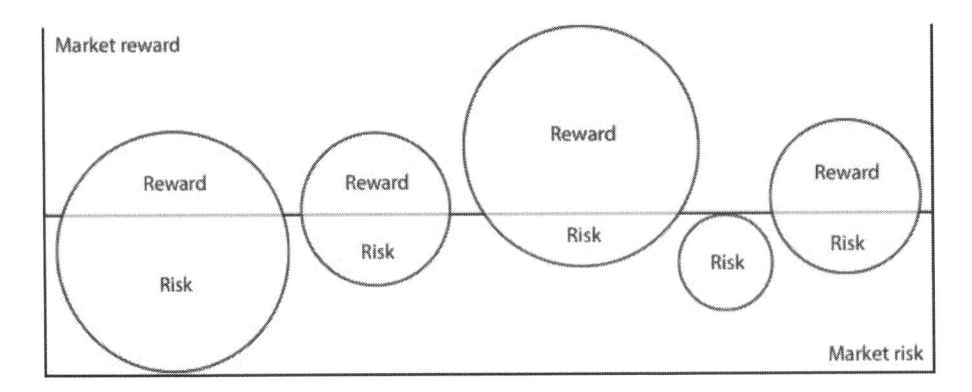

Figure 12.1 Archimedean trade selection.

Unfortunately, assessing the relative merits of an array of strategic alternatives is not nearly as scientifically straightforward.

The evaluation process begins with the trader's view of the market and a set of potential implementation strategies. From there, the trader must determine:

1. What can be done, given available resources
2. What could be done, given the current P&L relative to goals
3. What should be done, by evaluating strategies
4. What will be done, by selecting the best implementation
5. How it will be done, by developing a trading plan.

The first step is for the trader to make an assessment of her capacity to put on new positions.[64] This initial practical consideration is necessary, as the headroom under the trader's risk limits and current P&L can greatly influence the relative attractiveness of the various methods of expressing the view. Strategies that do not fit the trader's current risk appetite should be discarded immediately. Strategies that cannot be sized to fit within the trader's current available limits will require management approval. Limit expansion will generally require a recent positive P&L to justify the increased risk exposure and management buy-in to the specific strategy to be deployed.

1. What Can Be Done, Given Available Resources
The first set of constraints on any hypothetical position are the trader's initial allocated limits, the operational parameters that define maximum allowable exposures. As previously covered in Chapter 6 – Understanding Risk, the primary metrics that quantify a trader's exposure are the notional volume, stop-loss, V@R, and credit/collateral limits. The trader must be

---

[64] It is arguable that the trader should determine the headroom for new positions earlier in the process, before considering possible trade strategies. I feel that doing so artificially constrains the trader's thought process, which could lead her to overlook a high-value strategy that could potentially be accommodated with a temporary exemption or a permanent limit expansion.

cognizant of both the current utilization of individual limits and the available capacity to do business under firm-wide limits, particularly when multiple traders have the capability to accumulate risk in the same books, products, maturities, and/or strategies.

Consider a firm that employs four traders, each of whom could, at his sole discretion, accumulate a 250-lot position in a particular product. The firm itself, not wishing to be too exposed to any one instrument, has set a 400-lot limit on the total net position in the product. Trader 1 feels that the market is bullish and buys 144 lots, followed closely by Trader 2 who purchases 121 lots, and Trader 3 who accumulates 81, making the firm as a whole long 356 lots.

Trader 4, after engaging in somewhat more lengthy analytical process, also decides to be a buyer of the market and plans to purchase 150 lots, which is well below both his personal limit and the firm's established maximum exposure cap. When he queries the risk system to check the current position and verify his ability to execute the trade, he is dismayed to find that there is only a paltry 44 lots of space available until the firm hits its position limit.

Depending on the headroom available under the firm's limits a trader may or may not be able to utilize some portion (or any, in extreme cases) of her allocated resources, or may find that her ability to implement one type of strategy is severely reduced where another may not be impacted. The inability to use allocated limits due to blockage by other traders or overly restrictive firm-wide limits is one of the primary reasons traders are forced into utilizing secondary and tertiary implementation strategies. If all of the good stuff is taken, the trader may be faced with a decision to use what's available or stay on the sidelines.

Any to-be-executed position will consume some portion of the trader's limits. Directional trades have straightforward notional impacts and easily calculated V@Rs. The limit burden of spread and option positions can be significantly less intuitive and will require applying correlations and running a dedicated model, either using the trading system to generate a "what if" scenario based on a non-commercial sample trade or having the risk group calculate an intraday estimate of the probable limit impacts as of close of business.[65]

The prevailing market conditions will impact which limit is more likely to be the binding constraint on the trader's activities:

---

[65] Most risk- and deal-capture systems have the capability to process "test" or "proposed" deals, non-economic transactions that allow the trader and risk group to study the potential exposures and find problems before a live trade is executed. Unless the risk group and traders are very detail oriented about this process, the simulated exposures may not be reflective of the official risk reports that will run overnight. In any case where a trader intends to get close to her limits, it is always advisable to create and retain email correspondence with the risk group to show that the trader understood the issues, attempted to utilize the resources available, and acted with appropriate supervision. It may not stop the trader from violating a limit, but it may keep her out of trouble for it.

- In a relatively low-volatility time period the notional volume limit will usually be the primary constraint.
- High-volatility periods and products with more risk per unit of volume will push against the V@R limit and/or the amount of credit or collateral required to hold the position first.

The trader's current inventory will also impact his ability to take on additional positions, particularly if the extant trades are consuming a significant amount of any one metric. Traders considering adding additional exposures to an established book must be aware that an incremental position may not be problematic in isolation, but could prove to be a catalyst for a limit violation when folded into the existing portfolio. If this is even a remote possibility, the trader should have the risk group run a simulation of the current book plus the proposed addition prior to execution.

2. What Could Be Done, Given the Current P&L and Available Stop-Loss

Money management is a critical, yet ironically underappreciated, aspect of being a professional trader. The quantity of money between a trader and his annual stop-loss is his most valuable resource, and to a great extent determines both the quantity and quality of trades he can execute.

It is frequently said that a trader shouldn't trade her P&L, meaning that the evaluation of a particular new opportunity should not be influenced by the trader's recent profitability or lack thereof. The intellectually correct decision should be the same in all cases, whether up or down money, riding a huge winning streak or mired in endless losses. I completely agree with this, in theory. In practice, the actual state of the trader's P&L has too many implications to exclude it from the decision-making process.

The trader will be allocated a certain amount of money that he is allowed to lose during the course of the year, called the annual stop-loss. Some trading firms will also impose a shorter-duration stop-loss, usually monthly. The annual stop-loss exists to protect the firm from the trader; the monthly stop-loss exists to protect the trader from himself.

A trader who is currently winning will have the opportunity to increase the size of his business, sometimes dramatically. This is logical, both in terms of building on past successes and because the trader is probably seeing the market drivers clearly and has a better-than-average perspective on future price movements. As seen in the example below, the trader who has generated a significant YTD P&L can use the totality of his allocated limits without fear of a negative result damaging his year.

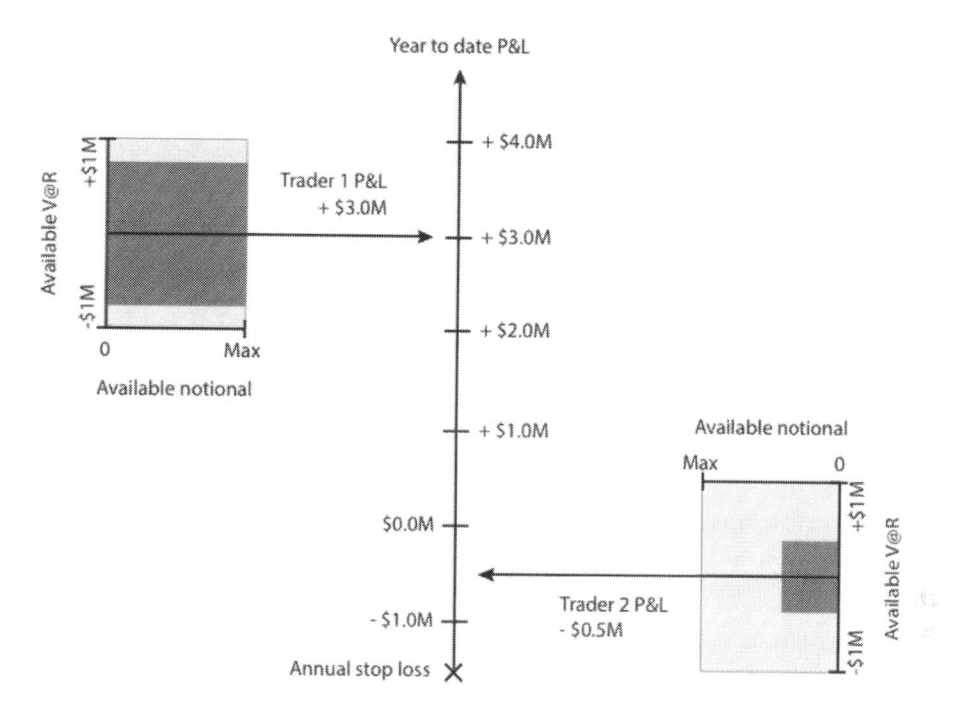

Chapter 12 - Evaluating Trades & Creating a Trading Plan

Figure 12.2 Trader's current P&L determines usability of allocated trading limits.

The other trader's poor YTD performance has left her down money and much closer to her annual stop-loss. Taking on a full position could, if it turned out negatively, potentially stop her out for the year. She will, out of practical necessity, have to limit her position sizes and V@R utilization until she can build up a larger P&L, which is, ironically, significantly harder to do with less ability to do business.

A trader who is losing may find himself being slowly strangled by a reduced capacity to put on risk that prevents him from ever earning back what he has lost, either due to short-term stop-loss headroom erosion or a proactive decision by management to restrict the trader's activity. If the market is too volatile, the trader may not have deep enough pockets to survive the swings to get back to profitability. When nearing a monthly or annual stop-loss limit, traders must preserve their remaining ability to do business, tightening their individual position stops and implementing stricter trade selection criteria to ensure that their strategies have superior risk/reward characteristics.

Stylistic Considerations That Impact How Much Risk to Deploy on a Thesis

Most traders heuristically evolve their trade-sizing criteria as a function of their personal style and risk tolerance, the relative abundance or scarcity of interesting trade ideas, and the characteristics of the market they inhabit.

Some traders with well-defined, systematized approaches prefer to allocate small amounts of capital to individual positions, never letting any one trade account for more than X% of the notional book or Y% of the total risk. Others will take a more ad-hoc approach, allowing the relative attractiveness of the proposition to determine their level of investment.

The expectation of the number of potential trades per unit of time in the market also plays a part in determining position size. An equity trader with thousands of individual securities, ample volatility, and deep liquidity is free to add and subtract exposures at will, concentrating her risk into as few or as many positions as she likes. A trader with a narrow mandate and a small set of usable instruments will be forced to express all views with the tools at his disposal, however restrictive they may be. When all you have is a hammer, everything looks like a nail.

This extreme specialization is more common among "professional" traders assigned a particular product set to ensure firm-wide diversification and coverage of an entire market, and are expected to be both subject matter experts on their area of operations and P&L generators. A trader stuck in a market with poor liquidity, minimal volatility, and a handful of products to choose from may have to concentrate risk into the few large ideas per year that (hopefully) present themselves.

The greater the certainty about a trader's ability to efficiently enter, exit, and modify a position, the more of the allocated monthly or annual stop the trader can feel comfortable putting in play. This factor, called the controllability of the position, is covered in greater depth in the next section.

Don't Forget About the Goal: What the Trader Is Trying to Achieve
Limits govern activity, but goals—and ultimately the compensation for achieving them – drive behavior.

The size of a trader's ultimate goal will impact initial choices on levels of risk needed to achieve it, and inform strategic trading decisions. If the trader needs to make a pile of money to justify his seat he will have to be aggressively risk seeking. If the trader has already booked an excellent year and is in cruise control until bonus time, she may elect to only entertain extremely conservative exposures with superior risk-reward characteristics. When combined with liquidity considerations, the trader's risk seeking/aversion behavior will steer the implementation in one direction or the other.

3. What Should Be Done – Evaluating Alternative Strategies
Selecting the optimal means of implementing the trader's view can be far from straightforward, and can vary significantly from market to market. If there are no simple, direct instruments available, or the ability to utilize them has been internally consumed, the trader will have to seek out causally connected or highly correlated products in an attempt to capture some portion of the potential market move. The key to utilizing secondary or tertiary instruments lies in the trader's ability to weigh the benefits of improved visibility, liquidity, and execution against the risks of correlation breakdown or other unpredictable fundamental influences that can degrade or complicate the performance characteristics of the strategy.

Chapter 12 - Evaluating Trades & Creating a Trading Plan

The trader must evaluate each potential implementation strategy with respect to five subjective performance characteristics:

1. Proximity – the number of links in the causal chain between motive and the instrument chosen to implement the view.
2. Complexity – the number of potential influences to the price.
3. Responsiveness – the degree to which the anticipated stimulus will impact the position.
4. Liquidity – the relative ease and cost of entry and exit.
5. Controllability – the relative ease of managing the risk inherent in the position.

Proximity

The proximity of an implementation strategy is a qualitative measure of the closeness to the primary driver(s) of the trader's thesis. Closeness can be a literal measure of distance in the case of trading strategies with a physical or geographic component, or an assessment of how many dominoes are lined up from the motivation to the reaction the trader is anticipating. In a case of transitive causality, each link in the chain can potentially have an unpredictable response to the upstream influences that can propagate down the line. The more links in the causal chain, the greater chance of an unpredictable or under- or overstated response.

Complexity

A strategy can have a single primary influence or be impacted by changes in a number of factors. The trader must be aware of not only how many drivers exist beyond the primary one he is seeking to exploit, but also the relative strength of the influence on the price of the instrument chosen to express the view. Complexity can also be structural, as is the case with options and derivative securities that have multiple mathematical price inputs and risk sensitivities (delta, gamma, vega, theta, etc.)

Responsiveness

From her ongoing observation of market conditions, a trader will develop a set of expectations that an anticipated stimulus X should produce a result Y of a particular magnitude. The responsiveness of a position is the degree to which the result is proportional to stimulus, which may be greater or less than the trader's expectation. If she were to throw a large rock into a lake, she would expect to see a big splash. Throwing a large rock into a lake only to watch it disappear without a ripple would be less responsive than anticipated; seeing the lake explode and the surrounding trees catch on fire would be a somewhat excessively responsive result.

Some of the potential implementations of the trader's view will be more or less responsive to the primary driver of his thesis. This can be a result of the complexity of the position (having many potentially offsetting influences that interact unpredictably) or a consequence of its construction or inherent properties (spreads that exhibit a muted response due to the hedge leg of the transaction, options that move only as fast as their current delta and the underlying will allow, etc.). The responsiveness of a position can also be greatly affected by the current market dynamics. A long position will respond differently to an incremental piece of information that acts as a catalyst to break the market out of a trading range (very responsive), adds fuel midway through an in-progress trend (responsive), or arrives as the rally has run its course and is encountering resistance (minimally responsive).

Liquidity
In this context, liquidity is a catchall criterion that includes transaction costs to be paid on the entry and exit of the position, the relative volume traded, and the frequency of transaction, as well as the depth present in the market and the ongoing interest of the entities present in the marketplace.

Controllability
The controllability of a position describes the degree to which a trader is able to proactively manage the risk inherent in the transaction. Controllability encompasses liquidity and a high degree of continuous, gap-free trading, but is also a statement about the anticipated conditions the trade and the trader are expected to endure over the planned holding period. A small foreign exchange position that can be traded out of 24 hours a day, seven days a week offers the trader near infinite opportunity to make proactive risk management decisions in ways that event-driven positions or trades with significant intraday or overnight or weekend gap risk do not. A bond trade initiated in the minutes before an interest rate announcement by the Federal Reserve will offer scant opportunity for the trader to manage risk, as the first indication of winning or losing will be an instant step-function move in price after the announcement.

Ideally, the trader would prefer an implementation that is proximal to the main driver of his view, has no complications that could interfere with the extremely responsive nature of the trade, and has excellent liquidity and controllability to facilitate position and risk management. This is rarely, if ever, possible. In reality, the trader will be forced to weigh the various characteristics of the attributes of each implementation strategy. Different traders will give primacy to different attributes depending on their strengths, weaknesses, and personal trading style.

Traders with discretionary authority and the latitude to transact in multiple markets must evaluate directional, spread, option, and quantitative implementations of their views in each, radically increasing the complexity of the decision calculus. When evaluating the optimal instrument to implement a trader's view of the market it is critical to remember that the trader is also trying to execute within a specified timeframe in order to be positioned for an anticipated holding period. The question is not really "what is the best possible implementation strategy?" but rather "what is the best possible implementation strategy that is actually implementable?"

Factoring In Real Costs
The trader must also take into consideration the costs of executing and maintaining the position. Some will be fixed, known fees and others will depend on the market conditions and the time horizon over which the trader intends to hold the position. The principal costs are the bid-offer spread, slippage, brokerage and exchange fees, and the holding cost of credit or collateral.

The bid-offer spread acts as a transaction tax; the amount paid is a function of the market conditions and the trader's skill. In general, traders assume that under normal conditions they will have to pay one full bid-offer spread, half when entering the position and half on exit. It may be possible to pay less in a negotiation-friendly market, or if a sudden uptick in interest acts to temporarily narrow the spread. In contrast, market-making traders attempt to earn the bid-offer spread by posting numbers that they hope other market participants will hit or lift, allowing them to get paid for putting on positions.

Slippage is the amount of value wasted between the time a trader starts executing and the time he amasses or distributes the desired exposure. A certain amount of slippage is unavoidable, unless the trader somehow manages to do 100% of the volume transacted in the market during the execution window and gets it all done at the same price. Slippage is almost impossible to quantify in advance, but the more deeply immersed in the market the trader is, the better he is able to gauge the potential impacts of transactional activity.

Most trades will involve paying a fee to the trading platform or brokerage for arranging the transaction. The trader may have to pay exchange fees for processing the transaction and clearing fees for routing it to the clearing broker. In most evolved markets the brokerage, exchange, and clearing fees will be a non-trivial but not onerous cost to the trader.

Credit and/or collateral costs can vary significantly from strategy to strategy, and have a large impact on the relative attractiveness of an array of alternatives. Unlike transaction-based fees that are paid once, the cost of financing the trader's position across the anticipated holding period will depend on a host of factors, including the volatility of the product (which will impact the base-level margin requirements set by the exchange), the firm's credit rating (which will impact the extra or the multiplier the clearing broker applies to the basic exchange margin requirements), the directionality of the exposure relative to positions already held by the clearing broker, etc.

Consider a trade with a potential $3.00 of upside and $1.00 of downside and a two-month intended holding period. A 3:1 risk-reward ratio would generally be a proposition that any trader would immediately seek to execute. When evaluating the relative attractiveness of the exposure the trader must also take into consideration the $0.25 bid/offer spread that she will have to pay away to a market-maker, a $0.01 brokerage charge and $0.01 clearing fee on both the buy and sell transactions, and $0.13 per month of financing costs to maintain the position. The $0.55 (= $0.25 + ($0.02 × 2) + ($0.13 × 2)) total that the trader must pay away in fees and costs adds to the cost of a loser and subtracts from the profits of a winner. In reality, the trader is risking $1.55 ($1.00 projected loss + $0.55 costs) to make $2.45 ($3.00 possible gain - $0.55 costs) for a risk-reward ratio of 2.45-to-1.55, which most traders would typically not entertain.

Traders have a tendency to underestimate the fees and costs inherent in their transactions for a variety of reasons. Some, like the bid-offer spread and the slippage, are difficult to fully assess without actually attempting to execute the transaction. Others, like the financing cost of holding the position, frequently end up being larger than expected as the trader clings to an exposure that with the hope that it will pay off someday.

4. What Will Be Done – Using Probability-Adjusted Strategy Risk-Reward Ratio

In Chapter 7 the trader derived a probability-adjusted risk-reward ratio for the market as part of the process of developing a view on the future of prices. The market risk-reward defines a probability space, with each individual strategic risk-reward ratio occupying a subset of that space. The best trade is the one that gives the trader the largest potential amount of market reward and the least exposure to market risk with the best odds of success. The proximity, complexity, responsiveness, liquidity, and controllability properties of each potential implementation must be incorporated into the assessment of the probability-adjusted risk-reward ratio for each strategy.

For each potential implementation strategy the trader will begin with the probability-adjusted risk-reward ratio, then:

1. Add in the real-world costs relevant to their anticipated holding period.
2. Assess the proximity, complexity, response, liquidity, and controllability of the strategy and, if necessary, adjust the risk-reward ratio.
3. Rank each strategy by the modified risk-reward ratios. If there are any candidate strategies that are close, use the subjective performance characteristics as a determinant. In markets that are intrinsically less liquid or more challenging to operate in, give more weight to the subjective performance characteristics.

The inclusion of the subjective performance characteristics may seem to transform what is meant to be an intellectually rigorous process into a non-quantitative interpretive exercise. In reality, the basic unmodified risk-reward calculus will almost always clearly delineate the superior strategy. If the trader is faced with several alternatives with nearly equivalent risk-reward ratios, the non-quantitative factors like proximity, complexity, response, liquidity, and controllability can serve to differentiate the optimal strategy from the others.

Having determined the strategy she wants to deploy to implement her view of the market, the next step is to decide how much of an exposure to accumulate, given available limits, and develop a trading plan.

Determining Potential Trade Size

The capability to deploy usable trading limits will provide an initial exposure cap to bound the trader's deliberations. Determining where to be on the range from zero to maximum exposure is largely a function of the probability-adjusted risk-reward ratio relative to the controllability of the risk inherent in the proposition, the presence or absence of alternative strategies, and the trader's goal for the year.

- The better the probability-adjusted risk-reward ratio, the more the trader should feel comfortable putting at risk.
- The more controllable the exposure, the more the trader should feel comfortable committing to the strategy. A lack of controllability would strongly argue for a smaller risk allocation.

Any potential exposure must be evaluated relative to any alternative strategies available to the trader. In a late-stage, highly liquid, extremely developed financial market there may be boundless opportunities to do 2:1 trades with 3:1 risk-reward positions frequently available, all with good controllability and well-defined risk-reward parameters. In that environment, the trader should feel very comfortable passing on 2:1 and 2.5:1 trades and waiting for the next 3:1 or better opportunity. In a less liquid early-stage market, the trader may have significantly fewer opportunities that may offer a combination of better risk-reward but lower controllability. In those circumstances, the trader would have to be (or become) comfortable taking more risk on fewer strategies per year.

The trader's goal for the year also factors heavily into the decision calculus. Traders expected to make a significant P&L contribution will either have to take a lot of small risks continuously or accumulate a smaller number of significantly larger, riskier positions.

Size of the Exposure vs. Size of the Market
Traders with sizable exposures to accumulate or distribute must often take into consideration the liquidity available in a particular strategic implementation. For traders in deep, liquid markets where desired size is an infinitesimal percentage of the daily turnover, this is not a consideration. Traders operating in an illiquid market or attempting to implement a high-volume strategy may not be able to execute the desired size in a timely fashion or without undesired market-moving consequences. To avoid counterproductive slippage the trader may need to entertain second and third options, living with basis and/or correlation risk in exchange for amassing a larger, if somewhat less optimal, position.

Special Situations
Occasionally a trader will develop a rock-solid view of the market then, when evaluating implementation alternatives, discover an opportunity that is egregiously, improbably, almost impossibly good. These types of lay-up trades are extremely few and far between. They can be a function of an absurdly skewed probability distribution, a near-zero loss possibility balanced against huge potential gains, a persistent structural imbalance, an early-stage market where value has not yet been recognized, or some combination of all four. If the trader is fortunate enough to discover the market equivalent of a winning lottery ticket, the thought process should shift away from a question of percentage utilization of individual limits to a group-wide discussion of how much of the firm-wide limits need to be allocated to the trade. Strategies outside the normal limits are typically dealt with via special board and/or risk management committee authorization and the creation of a special-purpose book or trading account to hold the transaction and facilitate monitoring and reporting to the sure-to-be-engaged senior managers.

Large, committing positions lead to a concentration of risk that leverages the success or failure of the group to one position and one view of the market. It also very probably bets the career of the trader that proposed it on the eventual outcome, which can be somewhat problematic when the extra cooks that have been invited to the kitchen (other traders, management) start to weigh in on how to optimize the exposure.

Once the trader has determined the preferred exposure size, they must plan how to accumulate the position.

5. How It Will Be Done: Generating a Trading Plan
A trading plan defines the conditions under which the trader intends to accumulate an exposure, the operational parameters that will govern the execution process, and the stop-loss and profit targets. The specificity and formality will vary, but almost all successful traders form some sort of a trading plan prior to taking action, whether they choose to articulate it or not.

The key phrase is "prior to taking action." The development of the trading plan is the last time the trader can be truly unbiased in his assessment of a potential position. Once the deal is booked, the trader is committed emotionally, intellectually, and financially to its success and will be unable to view it in a detached, clinical, unbiased state. A well-constructed trading plan will help the trader organize his thoughts and bolster his discipline. Plan the trade; trade the plan.

A thorough trading plan includes:

1. A summary of the view, the primary drivers, and the expected market response.
2. The proposed position, including risk metrics (notional, V@R, credit/collateral required to hold, etc.)
3. Execution strategy including entry point, stop-loss, and profit target.
4. Plan for hedging any unwanted risks, if necessary.
5. Any other exit or position modification conditions.

The metrics necessary to hold the position would be calculated either on the desk (and therefore be estimates) or developed in conjunction with the risk group (and be semi-official). The remaining steps for the trader to define are the execution strategy, the stop-loss and profit targets, and any additional exit or modification criteria.

Determining an Entry Point
The trader's entry strategy will be dictated by the prevailing market conditions and the urgency inherent in her view. The trader must ask herself, given what she knows about the current state of the market, if there is time to use her execution skills to get a better price or if the trade needs to be positioned now, before it runs away from her.

For markets with an imminent anticipated move or shallower trends, there may be time to attempt negotiated mid-point pricing and/or opportunities to use the micro or intermediate trend to facilitate superior execution. Being patient enough to wait for a retracement and/or skilled enough to work the market for a better fill can improve the risk-to-reward ratio and increase trade survivability dramatically. For trades with a lot of inherent risk, or a very thin potential reward, it may be necessary to achieve a better-than-current market entry point just to make the trade worthwhile. This type of enhanced execution ability is typically only possible for traders that are immersed in the market and follow the price on a tick-by-tick basis. The principal risk of trying to play things too cute is not getting positioned and missing the move, and the trader must always take into consideration the value of an extra tick relative to the much larger move she is trying to capture.

Sometimes the trader will determine that she must be positioned immediately, with maximum efficiency at the best price possible at the moment. This is common in a sharply trending market, where there is no ability for the trader to negotiate a mid-point price, and any delay represents lost opportunity cost and a worsening of the risk-reward relationship. Maximum execution aggression is also optimal when there is only a small amount of a product to be had (relative to the needs of the market participants), and the first mover has the best chance of securing the needed volume before the market goes away.

The trader can also employ an event-based entry trigger that is based on an evolution of the fundamental or technical thesis. If A, B, or C happens, the trader puts on the position. The trader's definition of the trigger criteria should result in a better risk-reward scenario, imbue the trade with a higher degree of confidence of success, or both. As is the case when attempting to enhance execution by negotiating or waiting for a retracement, the principal danger is missing the trade. This is particularly true for highly observable trigger points with obvious, dramatic price implications.

A trader intending to wait or work the market for better pricing should make sure that the current technical environment is conducive to the plan of action. A retracement to better levels to buy or sell is unlikely if the market is sitting on rock-solid support or resistance, and the market is unlikely to hang around if it has just broken a material trend line or completed a large, well constructed pattern.

Determining an Exit Point – Stop-Losses and Profit Targets

Once the trader has determined the entry point and execution plan for the trade, he must determine the exit criteria, which means defining a stop-loss and a profit target. In some cases the contemplated strategy will have structural properties that make deriving the stop or target straightforward, as would be the case with a long vertical call spread where the maximum risk is the net premium paid and the maximum profit is the distance between the option strikes. If the strategy under consideration contains functionally unbounded risk, the trader must begin by deriving a profit target from his view of the market, then manufacturing a reasonable stop-loss relative to the potential profitability of the trade.[66]

---

[66] It is reasonable for a trader to have a principled view of the market that leads him to believe that there is X profit to be had, then derive a stop-loss set at some fraction of X. I do not think that the converse, deriving a profit target from a stop, is valid. A trader cannot say with any reasonable logic that, if his maximum risk is Y then somehow he should be able to make a multiple of Y through unspecified means. There is a large difference between saying:
- Based on the trader's view, the market could move X dollars higher, and he is willing to hold the position until it is 1/3 X against him to allow the trade latitude to work.
- Based on the trader's view, he cannot lose more than Y dollars, and he is willing to lose Y dollars in the hopes that he will somehow make several times Y.

Deriving stop-loss and profit targets is another area where the characteristics of the strategy will influence the decision process. The controllability, in particular, is important to factor into the calculus.

Deriving a Profit Target Level

A profit target should be something that is achievable, given the trader's view, and should represent the level where she would be satisfied removing the exposure and booking her P&L. The trader can arrive at a profit target via a fundamentally derived objective or a measured technical move from a pattern with good forecasting ability. Ideally, a trader will use inputs from both disciplines, letting the fundamentals describe the totality of what the market is capable of and letting the technicals speak to what is possible given the current sentiment and areas of vested interest manifest in the chart patterns (if any). Consider the following chart:

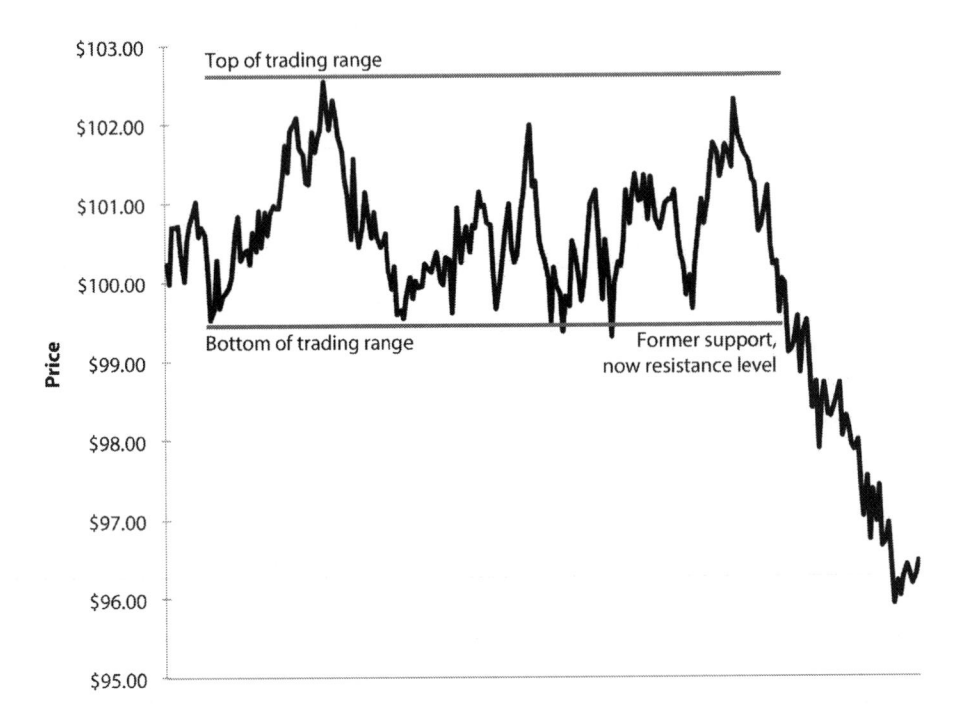

Figure 12.3 Using technical information to derive a profit target for a long position.

The chart depicts a market that has been stuck in a relatively well-defined trading range between $99.50 and $102.50 for the majority of the time horizon, recently breaking lower in a measured move to just below $96.00 before rebounding slightly. A trader contemplating a long position at $96.50 feeling that the market is grievously oversold must take the prior price action into consideration when setting a profit target.

- Anything above $103.00 is delusional in the absence of compelling fundamental information (which may exist), as the market has not traded above that range in its

recent history and attempts at that level have been extremely short lived, as seen in the three sharp peaks and immediate sell-offs.
- Something in the range of $99.50 to $102.50 is intellectually defensible, as the market has spent the majority of its time in that range. There is just one problem.
- The bottom of the trading range at $99.50 has been approached seven times prior to the breach that ultimately led to the sell-off to the $96.00 level. That is a lot of combat around that level, and a lot of vested interest created. A robust support level that is breached tends to act as stout resistance if/when the market retraces to that level, as there will be a lot of traders with bad positions looking to get out around breakeven. Setting a profit target at $99.50 makes good sense, as that is as high as the market should reasonably be expected to go, unless the fundamentals are truly compelling. There is just one more problem.
- Every trader with a chart and a pair of eyes can see the resistance level lurking at $99.50, which means that anyone contemplating selling will look to offer slightly below that level, perhaps the $99.40s or $99.30s, to ensure that they get filled, with the $99.50 resistance above acting as protection for players initiating fresh short positions.

Based on the technical analysis alone, the trader's profit target should be circa $99.25 unless the fundamental component of his view is strong enough to blow up the chart, which again, could very well be the case.

In this example, the technical analysis acted as a boundary on the trader's ambition. In reality, the technical perspective can act to modify the fundamental price target inherent in the trader's view in either direction, suggesting a reduced goal or opening up the possibility of a much more significant price move caused by a trend in motion or an explosive response to the violation of a prior high/low or support/resistance level.

Deriving a Stop-Loss Level
The starting point for the stop-loss calculation is the recently established profit target, as the stop must be a fraction of that figure; ideally, a small fraction. The trader should utilize the fundamental information and technical analysis to derive the best place to put (and best places not to put) the stop-loss levels. The trader will want to set a stop at a level where it is reasonable to expect sufficient liquidity to exit the position with minimal slippage costs. Of particular interest are trend lines and support/resistance levels where the market may pause temporarily or reverse, offering the trader a window of time and liquidity to operate. Congestion patterns can also offer pockets of transactional interest as traders with previously established positions seize the opportunity to unwind them at breakeven.

If the trader disregards the obvious technical danger signs and sets the stop at an obvious support or resistance break point or above/below a new all-time high or low, it would be prudent to assume a degraded liquidity environment and a larger than normal amount of slippage during execution. For example, consider a trader pondering a long position in the following market:

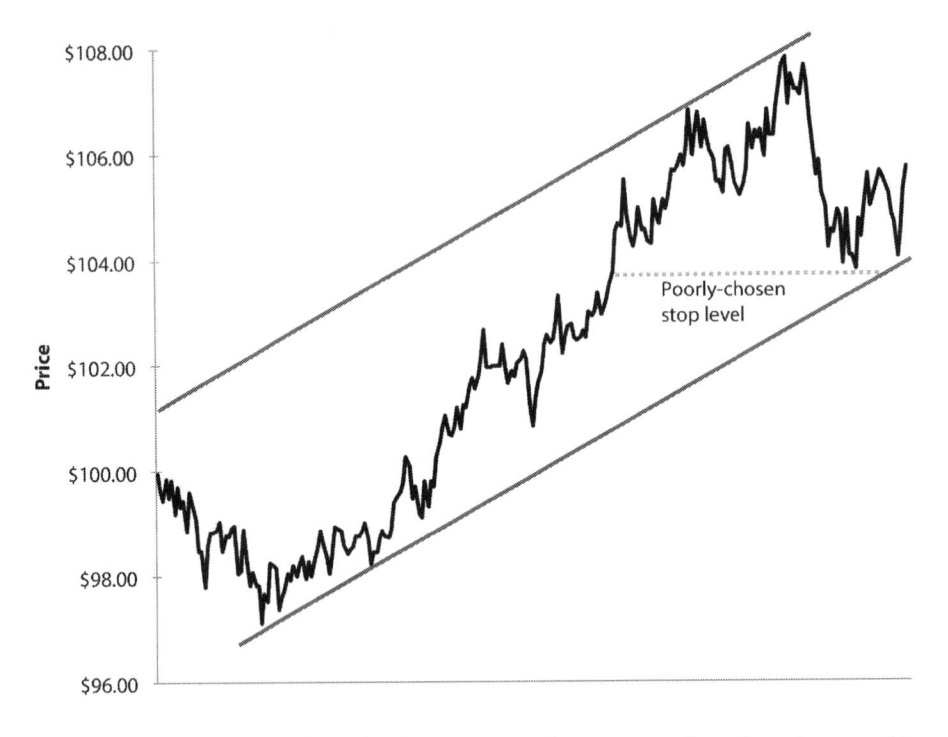

Figure 12.4 Using technical information to derive a stop-loss for a long position.

By attempting to buy at $105.75 near the bottom of a poorly organized trend channel the trader feels that he will have the opportunity to ride the trend up to the $108.00-$110.00 upper boundary, earning $4.25 with a $2.00 stop-loss set just below the prior low at $103.75. The just-better-than 2:1 risk-reward ratio isn't great, but the real problem lies in the trader's choice of stop.

- By trading down to $103.75 the market will have taken out the bottom of the trend line and the prior low, which is decisively bearish. This is a logical, obvious place to set a stop. This is, paradoxically, bad.
- Conclusively ending the uptrend with a support and prior-low violation will turn every long technical trader into a seller. This is very bad.
- All of this probable selling interest will have nothing of substance to slow it down or check its progress, as there are no prior congestion levels, support areas, or patterns to arrest the decline. There really isn't a level prices can't fall to. This is the worst.

Attempting to use a $103.75 stop will result in a risk-reward ratio that is actually, in practical application, possibly 1:1 at best. The trader may have to set an artificially tight stop (perhaps at the $104.75 to $105.00 trend break level) to justify the position, which ironically would substantially improve the risk-reward ratio of the strategy.

Some traders will tend to err on the conservative side with stop levels, artificially throttling down the amount of risk to be assumed. Other traders will allow a position more latitude to fluctuate, setting the stop wider in an attempt to hold the position.

- A tight stop will restrict the position to a smaller loss, which will improve the risk-reward ratio of the trade, but also increase the probability that the trader is stopped out of the position by market chop.
- A wide stop will lead to a greater degree of P&L volatility, allow for greater loss potential and result in a worse risk-reward ratio for the trade, but will reduce the probability that the trader is stopped out of the position.

Tight stops are more common in developed, liquid markets. In low-volume, early-stage markets, a trader may have to allow a position more latitude, as it will be harder (or impossible) to exit the core exposure. Tight or loose, any realistic stop is better than no stop at all.

There are three common types of stop-losses:

1. The hard stop.
2. The trailing stop.
3. The event stop.

The Hard Stop
The most common type of stop-loss is the hard stop (frequently just called a stop), a predetermined exit if the price of a security reaches a threshold level. There are two kinds of stops, one that is triggered if the market trades at a level, and a stop if the market trades through or breaches the level. Every position should, at a minimum, have a hard stop.

The hard stop is a solid basic position management tool, but one that lacks flexibility. If employed in isolation on a productive position, the trader will progressively risk more and more as the trade moves into the money and toward the price target for less potential reward. If the underlying motivating factors of the trade change, a hard stop will offer no protection until prices travel back to its level. To provide additional protection traders will often use stops designed to respond to and evolve with post-trade market fluctuations and incorporate changes to the trader's view.

The Trailing Stop
A creative way to manage risk is to deploy a "trailing" or "rolling" stop to protect profits. If the trader was willing to initially risk a maximum of $2.00 on a trade, using a trailing stop he would continuously reset the stop level $2.00 below current market as the position moved in his favor. If the trader entered the position at $100.00, he would initially plan to remove the exposure if prices traded below $98.00. If the market trades up to $101.00, the stop would reset to $99.00 and continue to track higher as the price moved in the trader's favor. If the market went to $103.00 the stop would move to $101.00, if the rally continued to $105.00 the trader would exit the position if the market retraced to $103.00, etc. A trailing stop acts to protect the trader's profits, preventing him from rationalizing giving away mark-to-market gains. Traders

with discipline problems around booking profits or a tendency to allow trades too much latitude to perform should consider employing a rolling stop to protect their positions from that flaw in their decision-making process.

The trader must take into consideration the magnitude of the normal market fluctuations relative to the size of the move she is trying to capture when setting a trailing stop. If the trader is trying to make $25.00 in a market that fluctuates $2.00-3.00 per day, a $0.50 trailing stop will likely result in an almost immediate exit from the position and a missed opportunity.

The Event Stop
If there is a material negative change in the primary driver(s) of the trader's view in general and the position in particular, the trader must strongly consider exiting the exposure immediately, even if it continues to perform well in the market. This is an extremely challenging, extremely disciplined move, and one that can be extremely painful in the short term if the trader exits and the position continues to improve. If the trader has good clarity that the primary driver of the market is no longer motivating the price action there are a number of possible reasons for its continuing improvement:

1. Another driver has emerged, taken over the motivational workload, and is currently pushing the price. If the trader can somehow identify and understand this new (or newly important) driver, he might be able to make a case for maintaining an exposure, but how much trust should the trader place in a variable he didn't see, doesn't understand, and/or chose not to factor into the initial decision calculus?
2. The market is being motivated by purely technical considerations, which can certainly drive price for a period of time in a fundamental vacuum. This should be fairly obvious to the trader, as any pattern- or trend-based movement should be readily apparent from the chart.
3. The market has reached a point where the price action has triggered a rolling stop out of participants who are being forced out of positions, which moves the price, which stops out more traders, which moves the price, etc.

Unless the driver that has been subtracted from the trader's view has been replaced with something that the trader understands equally well or better that will unambiguously strengthen the position, the prudent move is to immediately eliminate the exposure.

Properly employed stop-losses allow the trader to ration available resources and preserve risk capital for future trade strategies. Keeping losses limited allows the trader to remain an active participant in the market and reduces the size of the hole that they will ultimately have to dig themselves out of.

Pre-Planned Defensive Hedging As An Alternative To Maintain Exposures
For traders that specialize in illiquid markets and accumulate a book of exotic non-standard structured products it may be more constructive to attempt to neutralize the position rather than haphazardly chucking it overboard in times of crisis. This is particularly common for large, deal-based transactions where there would be no ready market for the totality of the

Chapter 12 - Evaluating Trades & Creating a Trading Plan

trader's exposure. It is more or less impossible to stop out of a refinery lease or a controlling interest in a power plant. This type of "un-exitable" position and messy defensive hedging is most common among merchants (for whom it is a core business) and banks that are paid to warehouse risk (no matter how grotesque).

A defensive hedge will not lead to a zero-risk position, only an approximately offsetting exposure designed to neutralize the current directionality of the market. The trader will block in a volume of the most liquid, highly correlated instrument available to temporarily stabilize the book, resulting in a misshapen Frankenposition that must be cleaned up as quickly as possible before it gets loose and terrorizes the village.

Execution Strategy

The trader has defined an entry point, a stop-loss level, and a profit target, which combine to define the risk-reward ratio of the implementation strategy. The trader's ability to execute at (or better than) her entry level is critical, as every tick given up in accumulating the exposure adds to the probable risk and subtracts from the potential reward. If the trader severely botches the execution or mistimes the entry she may end up with a position that is no longer worth having. To define the execution strategy, the trader must decide on:

- Price target – The price target is the level that the trader is hoping to achieve, which may in fact be lower/higher than the current market price.
- Execution window – The time period during which the trader will accumulate/distribute the exposure. The time period will be defined by the market conditions (a placid market granting more time, a volatile one allowing less), the size of the exposure (larger positions take more time), and any other considerations that need to be taken into account (must finish before the weekend, the release of a data item, the lunch-time lull, etc.) The execution window exists to allow the trader to achieve the price target, giving space to use the intraday fluctuations and time to work the market to get the best possible fill.
- Contingency plan – If the trader is unable to locate willing counterparties for the desired instrument at the preferred price within the execution window, he may have to consider utilizing a correlated instrument as a sub-optimal but still potentially constructive alternative.

For many large market participants, the ability to accumulate or distribute a position within a desired time window is simply not possible without unacceptable market-moving consequences. This problem is most common for naturals attempting to set large hedge positions in a specific instrument and banks seeking to backfill a significant customer transaction or unload a large amount of warehoused risk. If there is a stable correlation between the preferred mitigation instrument and a more liquid benchmark product, the trader can seek to offload the risk into the higher liquidity market, then seek to roll the position into the instrument of choice as quickly as is practical. The key to this strategy is the stability of the correlation during the strategic time horizon. The correlation risk must be lower than the feared directional and liquidity risk the trader is seeking to avoid. This will almost always be the case, making this a very common strategy.

Extreme illiquidity can necessitate a multi-stage rolling process. This approach is frequently necessary in the niche power markets, where a trader may need to set the position in the highly liquid natural gas market, roll it into benchmark power, then finally spread it into the desired end-state product. Managing liquidity will be discussed in Chapter 13 – Trading Mechanics, and multi-stage hedge implementation will be covered in greater depth in Chapter 15- Pricing & Hedging Structured Transactions.

Hedging Unwanted Risks
If the trader is only able to implement a view with a second or third choice (or otherwise sub-optimal) instrument, or is attempting to employ a strategy that has a multiplicity of potential drivers, it is sometimes advantageous (if possible) to hedge away some of the unwanted risks inherent in the transaction. For example, a trader is considering a long spread between two power products that should fundamentally expand, but that is directionally sensitive to gas. The trader could calculate the change in the historical value of the position per move up and down in the natural gas market and sell a volume of natural gas futures intended to neutralize that component of the exposure. The P&L from the short natural gas futures would compensate the trader for any damage a sell-off would cause to his spread position, and likewise subtract from the profits if the market rallies.

It is important to understand that hedging has not removed any risk, just transformed the initial risks inherent in the transaction into a different, hopefully more productive form. Hedges also have costs, both implicit and explicit. There will be additional brokerage fees, costs for paying across the bid-offer spread, and possible margin or collateral implications if the hedge position is not determined to be risk reductive. The hidden cost will be the degree to which the hedge erodes the profitable side of the transaction relative to the protection it offers from negative outcomes.

Traders will generally seek to hedge risks that are clearly defined with readily quantifiable, stable price relationships with the desired exposure, allowing the trader to set a position size that will offer relatively predictable performance results. No trader would seriously consider adding an incremental position that increases risk or decreases certainty due to the unpredictability of the hedge instrument.

Other Exit or Modification Criteria
It is impossible to predict beforehand every potential scenario that could transpire or influence that could impact the proposed trade. Most trading plans will include a catch-all condition to the effect that, if market conditions change or unforeseen events transpire the trader will at a minimum re-evaluate the exposure and, in all likelihood, reduce or remove the position.

Chapter Twelve Summary
To evaluate the candidate strategies the trader will first determine the portion of allocated limits available for use, requesting additional authorization if necessary to entertain a particularly compelling exposure. The trader's year-to-date P&L will factor into the position-sizing calculus, with recent profitability affording more latitude to contemplate larger

exposures and a string of losses forcing a more conservative risk allocation. With an understanding of his positional capability, the trader will begin to evaluate candidate directional, spread, option, and quantitative strategies. The trader will consider the proximity to the primary driver(s) of the thesis, the complexity of the strategy's influences, the price responsiveness to changes in the fundamentals, the available liquidity, and the controllability or exposure. The trader will also take the real-world costs of accumulating and distributing the exposure into consideration when evaluating the probability-adjusted risk-reward ratios of each potential strategy. The trader will rank the strategies and develop a detailed trading plan that includes his view, choice of exposure(s), execution plan, stop-loss, and profit target.

From here, the trader will explore how to execute their trading plan in Chapter 13.

Review Questions

1. Describe the primary elements of a trading plan.
2. How do a trader's resources and current P&L impact their trading plan?
3. What are the five characteristics of an exposure that the trader must take into consideration when evaluating candidate trades?
4. What costs must the trader factor into their evaluation of trading strategies? Why is this critical?
5. What are the three types of stop losses a trader can employ, and how do they function?

Resources

- *Every Hand Revealed* by Gus Hansen
- *Market Wizards: Interviews with Top Traders* by Jack D. Schwager
- *The New Market Wizards: Conversations with America's Top Traders* by Jack Schwager
- *The Money Bazaar: Inside the Trillion-Dollar World of Currency Trading* by Andrew Krieger
- *Reminiscences of a Stock Operator* by Edwin Lefèvre

Case Study: Evaluating Product X Trades & Creating a Trading Plan

There are nine candidate trades that have been identified as being productive methods of implementing the trader's view of the Product X market. Each strategy will have different advantages and disadvantages:

	Strategy	Risk/Reward	95% 1d V@R	Advantages	Disadvantages
#1	MAR ProdX futures	4.3-to-1	$629k	Ease of implementation. Direct, linear price response.	Direct exposure to adverse price movements.
#2	OCT ProdX futures	3.5-to-1	$185k	Linear price response. Excellent price appreciation potential.	Direct exposure to adverse price movements.
#3	MAR EurX/ProdX fin spread	3-to-1	$456k	Easiest basis trade to implement. Best liquidity & controllability.	Many potential drivers, unpredictable price response.
#4	MAR EurX/AfrX fin/phys spread	3.5-to-1	$828k	Favorable Risk/Reward ratio, possibly very favorable.	Severe liquidity challenges around physical AfrX leg.
#5	AUG/JAN+1 bull time spread	3-to-1	$181k	Non-voaltile with a relatively well-defined loss scenario.	Far-forward contracts may mute price action, impede execution.
#6	MAR call option	13-to-1	$2.78M	Extremely favorable Risk/Reward ratio. Risk-limited.	Liquidity & lack of counterparties make positioning difficult.
#7	OCT straddle	16-to-1	$3.142M	Extemely favorable Risk/Reward ratio, multiple ways to profit.	Extreme illiquidity makes positioning all but impossible.
#8	Shipping tracking tool	Undefined	N/A	Applications to diverse trading stratgies & time periods	Not ready to be deployed, no guarantee of productivity.
#9	Rule-based automated system	Undefined	N/A	Applications to diverse trading strategies & time periods.	Not ready to be deployed, no guarantee of productivity.

Table 12.1   Characteristics of nine candidate Product X strategies.

Each potential trade strategy has a different operational time horizon that will allow it to be affected by different portions of the event path.

Chapter 12 - Evaluating Trades & Creating a Trading Plan

Strategy
#1 Long MAR ProdX futures
#2 Long OCT ProdX futures
#3 MAR EurX/ProdX fin basis
#4 MAR EurX/AfrX phys basis
#5 AUG/JAN+1 time spread
#6 Long MAR call option
#7 Long OCT straddle
#8 Shipping tracking tool
#9 Automated trading system

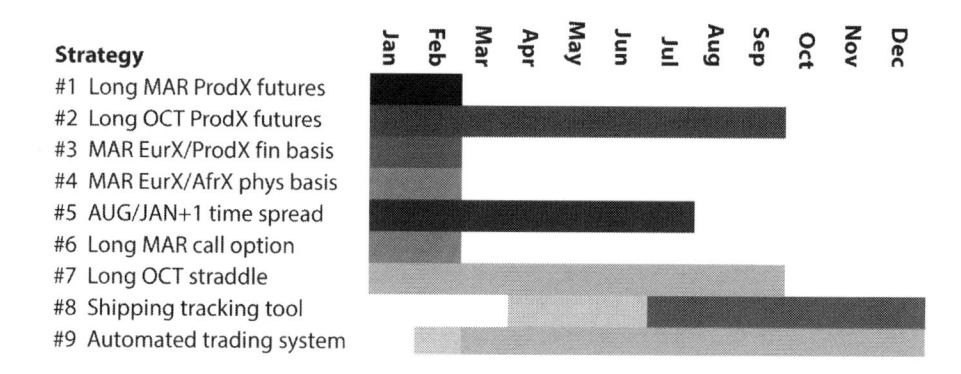

Figure 12.5 Operational time horizons of Product X candidate strategies.

Nine trades is a bit much for a deep evaluation, so in order to focus the analysis the trader should eliminate the least productive strategies and those with problematic properties to concentrate on the best starting sample. In doing so, the trader may discard perfectly good strategies that might be extremely productive in other markets at other times, but are not a good match for the current circumstances and prevailing conditions. Based on the initial set of candidate strategies, the trader's view and the current state of the Product X market, it makes sense to discard:

Strategy #8 – Real-Time Shipping Tracking Tool
Strategy #9 – Rules-Based Automated Trading System

The model-based trading tools are conceptually very interesting, but both will require time and resources that most traders would be unwilling or unable to commit to at the beginning of a new year.

Strategy #3 – EurX/ProdX Financial Basis Spread

The EurX/ProdX financial basis spread has a lot of inherent advantages, including cleared futures products with good liquidity and a respectable 3-to-1 risk-reward ratio. The problem arises from the uncertainty about the anticipated battle between Europe and the US to avoid having to rely on Canadian production. It is possible that the trader could call the market correctly (African processing plant does not return, battle commences, prices go up in general) but still lose money if Europe emerges victorious in the battle for cheap supply, forcing the US to pay up and causing the spread to contract. The risk-reward inherent in the trade, while reasonable in isolation, does not justify the complexity of the exposure unless the trader's firm as a specialist has insight into the dynamics of South American production and shipping.

Strategy #5 – AUG/JAN+1 Time Spread

Strategy #5 also features cleared financial products and a decent 3-to-1 risk-reward ratio, as well as a fairly well-defined, maximum-loss scenario. The principal problem with the AUG/JAN+1 spread is the lack of a specific driver to motivate a change in the price relationship in the near term. The position may well work in the future, but may act like dead money until successive contract expirations moves the AUG closer to the front of the curve and it begins to participate in the (hopefully) increased volatility.

Strategy #2 – Long OCT ProdX Futures

Perhaps a slightly surprising choice given the robust risk-reward ratio that lies somewhere between 3.5 and 12-to-1. For the first two months of the year Strategy #1 contains all of the same drivers and is a cleaner implementation. If the question was which trade would perform better from now until the end of the year, it is probable that Strategy #2 would be in and #1 would be out, but that is not the question. It is what is the best trade to hold now.

This leaves the trader with the four strongest ideas: long MAR ProdX futures, long MAR EurX/AfrX financial/physical basis spread, long MAR ProdX call options, and long OCT ProdX straddles.

Ranked in terms of risk-reward ratio:

Risk-reward	Strategy
16-to-1	Long OCT ProdX straddle
13-to-1	Long MAR ProdX call option
4.3-to-1	Long MAR ProdX futures
3.5-to-1	EurX/AfrX financial/physical basis spread

Compared visually in terms of millions dollars of risk and reward inherent in the proposed notional volumes for each trade:

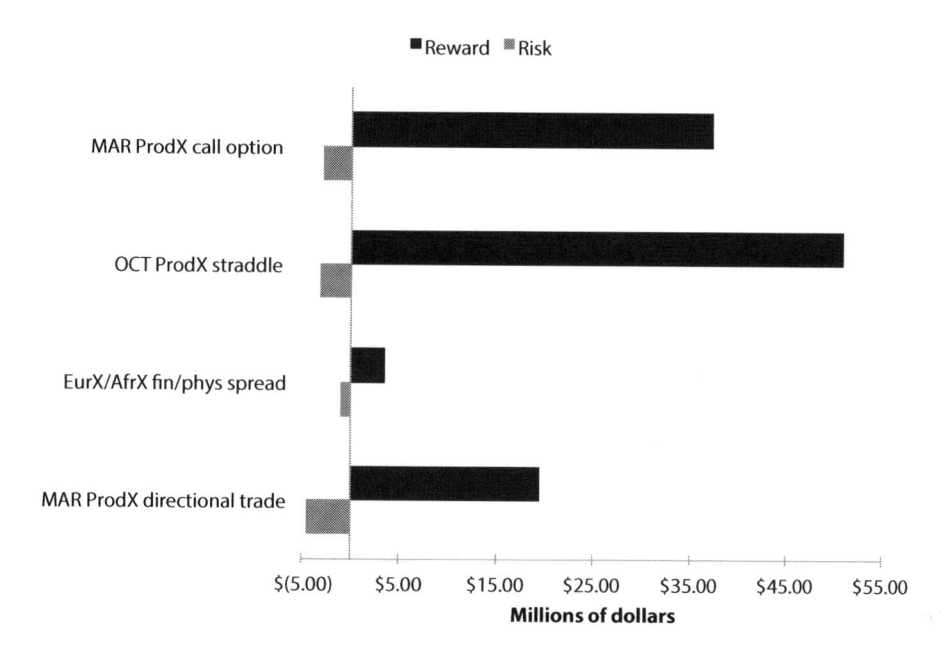

Chapter 12 - Evaluating Trades & Creating a Trading Plan

Figure 12.6 Risk/reward in dollar terms for the four best Product X trading strategies.

The trader must evaluate each remaining Product X implementation strategy with respect to the five subjective performance characteristics:

1. **Proximity** – the number of links in the causal chain between motive and the instrument chosen to implement the view.
2. **Complexity** – the number of potential influences to the price.
3. **Responsiveness** – degree to which the anticipated stimulus will impact the position.
4. **Liquidity** – relative ease and cost of entry and exit.
5. **Controllability** – relative ease of managing the risk inherent in the position.

Proximity (high to low)	Complexity (least to most)	Response (best to worst)	Liquidity (best to worst)	Controllability (best to worst)
EurX/AfrX spread	MAR ProdX directional	EurX/AfrX spread	MAR ProdX directional	MAR ProdX directional
MAR ProdX directional	MAR ProdX call	MAR ProdX directional	MAR ProdX call	MAR ProdX call
MAR ProdX call	OCT ProdX straddle	MAR ProdX call	OCT ProdX straddle	OCT ProdX straddle
OCT ProdX straddle	EurX/AfrX spread	OCT ProdX straddle	EurX/AfrX spread	EurX/AfrX spread

Table 12.2 Characteristics of Product X trade strategies.

Strategy #4 – EurX/AfrX Financial/Physical Producer to Consumer Spread

Proximity	Best of all strategies. Closest proximity to the initial inflection point on the event path.
Complexity	Worst of all strategies. Complexity arising from the uncertainty inherent in the US vs. Europe battle for South American production, with the loser getting to pay $130+ to incentivize Canadian producers.
Responsiveness	Best of all strategies. Should be very responsive.
Liquidity	Worst of all strategies. Very low, due to need to transact a physical AfrX sale directly with a counterparty.
Controllability	Worst of all strategies. Very low, due to the illiquidity of the AfrX sale and the complexity of the response to stimulus.

The EurX/AfrX has quite a dispersion of characteristics, rating either the absolute best or worst in every category. The spread should be extremely responsive and has excellent proximity to the initial inflection point on the event path, but lowest ratings in terms of liquidity and controllability (mostly due to the physical nature of the AfrX leg of the spread) are extremely problematic. The factor that makes this trade a candidate for implementation is the very possible near-term pricing of European futures to Canadian supply, which would blow the risk-reward ratio out from a very respectable 3.5-to-1 to a mega 15-to-1 or higher.

It is interesting to note, and somewhat problematic, that the EurX/AfrX spread consumes $828K of 95% 1-day V@R, making it by far the riskiest position of the available strategies (excluding the artificially conservative option V@Rs). This also brings into question the notion that the trader can hold the potential losses to the $1M defined in the risk-reward ratio, particularly given the low controllability.

The majority of the problems with the EurX/AfrX position are due to the physical AfrX leg of the trade. In the event of the return-to-service problems that are the primary value driver of the position the trader might not be able to deliver against her short AfrX if she cannot source supply. As a physical transaction the AfrX leg will involve direct counterparty exposure with (potentially) non-standardized, negotiated contract terms. This could be either a help or a hindrance. If the trader is able to contractually protect against being short and unable to cover—via a force majeure or facility-contingent clause or pre-negotiated, non-destructive penalty for non-delivery—the EurX/AfrX may be a very attractive transaction. The mandatory level of local market knowledge and comfort with non-standard transactions suggest that this would be an interesting trade for an aggressive merchant, but that might prove too challenging for other market participants.

Strategy #1 – Long MAR ProdX Futures as a Short-Term Explosion Directional Trade

Proximity	The MAR ProdX is one step removed from the primary driver affecting the EurX market.
Complexity	Best of all strategies. The structural complexity is as low as it gets.

Chapter 12 - Evaluating Trades & Creating a Trading Plan

Responsiveness	The responsiveness should be good, with some potential for a slightly muted response to the return to service of the African plant.
Liquidity	Best of all strategies. A ProdX futures exposure near the front of the curve will have the most liquidity available in the market.
Controllability	Best of all strategies. Maximum liquidity in the most commonly traded product will equate to excellent controllability, which will be needed given the trader-enforced nature of the stop and profit target.

The directional MAR ProdX futures position grades out very well, ranking either first or second with respect to every performance characteristic. The V@R requirement to hold the position is somewhat high at $629K, and the potential stop-loss of $4.52M is the largest of the trades under consideration, both of which are in line with the generally limit-intensive and risk-centric nature of directional positions.

One huge advantage of the MAR ProdX futures is the massive liquidity available, which will allow the trader maximum flexibility to optimize the timing of the accumulation and distribution of the exposure, as well as charging the minimum penalties for bid/offer spread and slippage. The MAR futures offer the trader maximum controllability, which will increase her confidence in assuming a large exposure and her ability to manage the position to conform to the 4.3-to-1 risk/reward ratio.

Strategy #6 – Long MAR ProdX Call Option as Leveraged Outright

Proximity	One step removed from the primary driver, with the added distance of a derivative contract with non-linear properties.
Complexity	Some complexity due to the structural performance characteristics of an option.
Responsiveness	Slightly muted responsiveness that should approximate the current delta of the call option.
Liquidity	Liquidity will be extremely poor, rivaling that of the EurX/AfrX trade.
Controllability	The controllability will be helped by the fixed and known amount of risk equal to the premium expended, but limited in every other way by transactional challenges.

Strategy #6 is effectively a much more efficient implementation of Strategy #1, with similar potential upside but radically reduced risk due to the fixed premium paid to the option seller. The downside is that it is, in effect, a committing strategy, as the lack of liquidity and the bid-offer spread demanded would likely be punitive in the extreme if the trader decided to exit. The $2.78M V@R consumed by the position is problematic, but as it is the result of a principled stance by the risk group and, by definition, encompasses 100% of the total potential risk inherent in the transaction, it will likely be heavily discounted by the trader.

The trader may have to rely on put/call parity with the near-par underlying and work into the desired exposure by finding counterparties willing to sell put options, which the trader will then convert into calls by purchasing a volume of the underlying. This will not read as cleanly from a limit perspective, but the trader will have the exposure he is seeking.

Strategy #7 – Long OCT ProdX Straddle as a Volatility/Directional Position

Proximity	Worst of all strategies. Position is in a market one step removed from initial primary driver, located toward the back of the curve, and expressed via a derivative contract with non-linear properties.
Complexity	Some complexity due to the structural performance characteristics of an option.
Responsiveness	Worst of all strategies. Proximity issues combined with the net delta of the position.
Liquidity	Liquidity will be extremely poor, rivaling that of the EurX/AfrX trade.
Controllability	The controllability will be helped by the fixed and known amount of risk equal to the premium expended, but limited in every other way by transactional challenges.

The OCT ProdX straddle has a superior risk-reward ratio to the MAR directional call option and a radically better probability-adjusted risk-reward ratio, as the trade wins if the market goes up, if it goes down, or if it gets more volatile. The only material performance issue is that an OCT position is not a play on the front of the curve, like the other three trades, but should compensate for exposure to the remainder of the event path. The OCT straddles do consume an extremely large $3.142M of 1-day V@R, but as with the MAR call options, the trader will definitely consider the exposure to be far less risky than its metrics suggest.

The principal challenge with the OCT straddle will be getting positioned, as this will be the trade that counterparties, particularly sophisticated market makers, will least want to sell. As with the call options, the answer may be to utilize put/call parity and the current proximity of the underlying to purchase a volume of put options (counterparties afraid to sell calls because they think the market is going up can sometimes be persuaded to look at selling puts) and then convert them into straddles by buying half of the notional volume of the underlying at near par. This implementation will not be as credit and collateral efficient, but the exposure will be approximately equivalent.

Clearly, the option trades are the superior implementation strategies of both the short- and long-term aspects of the trader's view, with the directional position a strong second place by virtue of the controllability of the risk inherent in the exposure.

The trader is faced with an extremely frustrating situation, desperately wanting to be long option-based structures that, in all probability, will be fantastically difficult to acquire. In the short term, he is left with the unpleasant choice of paying an extremely above-market rate or waiting in the hope that a seller emerges before the anticipated market move materializes. The logical course of action is for the trader to accumulate a position in the best available instrument, MAR ProdX futures, and then roll as much of the exposure into the preferred option strategies as counterparty interest and market conditions permit.

Chapter 12 - Evaluating Trades & Creating a Trading Plan

Product X Trading Plan

Summary of the View:
The trader's view of the market is that the return to service of a major African production facility will be only partially successful at best which, combined with a structurally tightening market as the year progresses, will lead to a shortage-led increase in Product X prices to levels necessary to incentivize incremental production, estimated to be between $130.00-135.00/ton in the near term.

Proposed Position(s) Listed in Order of Preference:

1. Long 2M notional tons $103.00 strike OCT ProdX straddles at $1.57.
2. Long 2M notional tons $105.00 strike MAR ProdX calls at $1.39.
3. Long 1M notional tons MAR ProdX futures at $105.52.

Execution Strategy:

- Accumulate a 1M notional ton position in the MAR ProdX futures at or below $105.29.
- Maintain a resting bid for both the MAR ProdX $105.00 calls and the OCT $103.00 straddles. If the trader finds a willing seller, execute as much volume as possible up to the 2M notional exposure target for the option position, then take off a proportional amount of the MAR ProdX futures. The trader will be able to bid the $105.00 MAR calls with a $105.00 cross in the underlying futures, giving the seller of the option a packaged delta hedge, which should be attractive and may help facilitate execution.

Profit Target:
$125.00 for the MAR ProdX contract. Exit all option-related exposures if this threshold is reached.

Stop-Loss:
$101.00 for the MAR ProdX contract. Exit all option-related exposures if this threshold is reached.

Risk/Reward:
4.3-to-1

Hedging Unnecessary Risks:
None Required.

Exit or Position Modification Conditions:
If African production facility verifiably returns to service and exceeds 20M tons output, exit any MAR ProdX length. If there is good liquidity, seek to exit any long MAR ProdX call positions. If there is no option liquidity, seek to sell a delta-equivalent amount of MAR ProdX to neutralize the position. Maintain any Oct ProdX straddles and re-evaluate, since the bearish

put portion of the position should be contributing value, as will the probable net increase in volatility.

13

Trading Mechanics

Good Mechanics
The ability to efficiently operate in the market is a skill, one that will take time to develop and effort to maintain. The benefits of efficient execution are lower costs of entry and exit in docile markets and an enhanced ability to accumulate and distribute volume in volatile markets. Transactional technique is particularly valuable in the early- to middle-stage markets when lower volume, wider bid-offer spreads, and higher volatility act as an ineptitude tax on the lackadaisical and less proficient.

The trader will start with the position rationale, stop-loss, and profit target developed in the trading plan, then take into consideration:

1. The current market conditions, and how they impact the plan.
2. An understanding of the available liquidity and depth.
3. Intraday events (if any) that need to be factored into the plan.
4. The available execution options, including direct counterparty contact, OTC brokers, and electronic screens and the types of orders available, given how they define the execution process.

Implementing the trading plan to accumulate or distribute a position is the first time that the trader will interact with the market, and in doing so expose himself to both economic and regulatory peril. Efficient execution is a matter of deploying crisp, expedient transactional technique while operating within the rules, regulations, and laws that govern the market and all activities within it. Industry participants must be cognizant of the current state of play and understand what is, and significantly more important, is not considered an allowable action by all of the various regulatory bodies that oversee the trader's market. The trader's best resource, short of keeping current on tens of thousands of pages of ever-changing rules and regulations, is to work as closely as possible with the compliance group at the firm. Interacting with the compliance group will be covered in depth in Chapter 16 – Navigating the Corporate Culture.

1. Current Market Conditions
First, the trader must find the market by locating the best available price and the greatest amount of transactional interest. Depending on the evolutionary state of the market, this may involve multiple rounds of direct phone calls to counterparties to piece together a sense of the available interest one price at a time, obtaining a quote from a dedicated market maker, or looking at the best posted bid and offer on an electronic exchange screen. For thriving markets with multiple execution platforms and an active OTC broker market, the location of the best bid and offer can jump rapidly from place to place as traders shift their prices to seek out willing counterparties or endeavor to disguise their transactional intent.

Once the trader has located the best market for her product of interest, she needs to watch how it is trading. There are pronounced differences between negotiation-friendly markets that encourage a back-and-forth dialogue to determine price and hit-or-lift or runaway markets, where any interaction other than a consummated trade will likely lead to an instant (usually adverse) adjustment in price.

Negotiation-friendly markets are common when players have a vested interest in collaboratively transacting, which is most often the case in medium-liquidity markets with a small number of participants. If two players understand that they need each other to transact it is much more likely that they will take a negotiation-based approach. Prices will start with wide bid-offer indications that gradually narrow with successive rounds of compromise on the part of both parties. Skilled traders develop an understanding of how far to push, but also how much to concede to get the business done. Being "a dick for a tick" profits a trader little if, instead of paying up to close the deal, he exposes his position to significantly larger intraday or overnight risks. Negotiation-friendly markets typically occur in sideways or slightly up- or down-trending markets where participants feel comfortable taking positions without undue fear of looming exogenous risk.

Willingness to negotiate is often directly related to the number of competing bids and offers, price level, and the inclination to respond to shifts in the market dynamic. One bidder facing five offers will not be motivated to improve the price, and may even back away if approached aggressively en masse. Conversely, each of the five offers staring at the single bid will feel pressure to improve their price and recast the market dynamic as a one-bid, one-offer negotiation on more equal terms.

A hit-or-lift market is the opposite of a negotiation-friendly space, where traders post numbers and expect others to deal on them without countering. This strategy is common with mature, highly liquid screen-based markets with little or no broker intermediation, or among traders who have hard threshold levels above or below which they cannot (or will not) transact. Hit-

or-lift conditions can be a perpetual state, a temporary degradation in liquidity from a more collaborative market, or a response to panic in the market.

When a market has embarked on a clearly defined linear trend, trying to get the winning side to negotiate is usually a fruitless endeavor. If the market has been up for six days, no seller is cutting a potential buyer a break, and a trader will either have to pay the asking price or hope that conditions change. In a steep trend in a fast moving market, merely attempting to counter an offer with a better bid can reek of enough desperation to cause the seller to pull back to a higher price or motivate another more desperate buyer to lunge in front and pay up.

In a runaway or panic-driven market liquidity typically evaporates completely as casual players looking to make small money from intraday trading cease activity, leaving only the traders with vested interests and significant winning or losing positions. The losers in a runaway market are often being hurt quite badly, and may be seeking to get out at any price. In disastrous cases, a trader in dire straits who has violated an internal loss-limit threshold may be temporarily relieved of duties. In that case, the responsibility for closing the problematic position is given to another trader or assigned to the risk management group.

A substitute trader unfamiliar with the nuances of a particular market will frequently make a mess unwinding a bad position, as he will be motivated to fix the problem as quickly as possible and not be personally concerned about the financial implications, which are presumably on the original trader's tab. Unless the risk manager assigned to close the position has prior trading experience and a familiarity with the market, it is highly likely that the attempt to close the position will be an unmitigated disaster. A risk manager is simultaneously personally unconcerned about the financial impacts and intensely aware of the need to reduce risk at any price. In a market with any sort of interpersonal dealing culture, the brokers and traders will be very aware of not only what firm has been buying and selling, but which individuals at the firm have been most active. If the trader who has just exploded is, "in a meeting," "off the desk", or mysteriously unreachable, and some new guy from the risk department who can barely work the telephone starts asking everyone in the market for prices, that is like waving the largest possible red cape in front of a very angry bull.

Even in anonymous electronic markets there is information to be gleaned from the transactions themselves. Traders learn to look at the size and frequency of the printed deals and how the bids and offers respond to them as a clue to the overall market disposition. If the best bid in the market gets hit and everything behind it disappears or backs up, that is a sign of weakness. If the best bid in the market gets hit and it immediately comes back re-bid for the same size, only to be joined by two other players for equal or greater volume, that is a sign of strength. Large bids or offers that disappear out of the market when partially filled could indicate an uncommitted or indecisive trader. Large orders that sit there nonplussed as they are slowly whittled away by smaller transactions are often hedgers with significant volume to transact and a patient approach to the market. The nuances vary from market to market, but there is always a pattern.

2. Understanding the Available Liquidity and Depth

The normal daily transactional volume in most markets is not a continuous, evenly distributed flow that starts at the open and continues undiminished and uninterrupted until the close of business. Every market will have its own intraday transactional rhythm. In the most general terms, markets often open with a burst of activity as traders respond to overnight events. Volume decreases in the late morning, undergoes a period of quiet during the traditional lunch hour, followed by a swell of interest in the afternoon into the close of the day, which can either go out with a bang or a whimper. At a more granular level, within each ebb and flow of interest there will be minutes and seconds of complete quiet and furious activity.

The trader must have a timeframe for expected execution, based on the size of the exposure to accumulate or distribute, the current market conditions, and the amount of slippage she is willing to live with to fill the order. The trader will need to know how to work with the available intraday liquidity to maximize execution efficiency.

Liquidity Does Not Equal Depth

Traders and risk managers frequently use "liquidity" and "depth" as near synonyms referring to the capacity of the market to absorb transactions. They are similar, but not equivalent concepts. Liquidity is a measure of the total volume and frequency of transactions, and is a function of bid-offer spread and decision latency. The growth of high-frequency trading has produced a dramatic uptick in the number and speed of transactions, but has not produced a concomitant increase in the amount of positions that trading firms are willing to hold at a particular point in time.

Depth is an attempt to quantify how much of a particular product the market can absorb in a relatively short period of time without significantly altering the prevailing price. Depth is a measure of how much of a position the aggregate market participants are willing to hold (or how much they are willing to modify their positions) at a particular time, and is a function of capital base, risk tolerance, and transactional interest. A trader intending to break a large transaction into many small pieces that will be executed over a span of time is more concerned with liquidity, a trader needing to move size in a short period of time will worry that there is enough depth to accommodate the transaction without moving the market.

It is important to distinguish the character of the volume transacting in the market. Who is out there doing business? What percent are day traders who churn like crazy but carry minimal positions, providing liquidity but no real depth? What percent are hedgers, who set a position and intend to keep it forever? How many positional traders are there who have significant interest that they will accumulate, hold, and eventually distribute?

Adding Liquidity or Taking Liquidity

The rise of high-frequency trading has also called attention to the distinction between trading activities that add liquidity or take liquidity. Liquidity is added when traders place real, usable bids and/or offers in the market for other participants to see, interact with, and ultimately transact. Taking liquidity is transacting on a posted bid or offer without placing any resting orders in the market. A liquidity adder provides numbers and the liquidity taker executes on them. What should be immediately apparent is that any viable market desperately needs liquidity adders. This market function can take many forms, from an unstructured group of participants with a vested, proprietary interest in a product to a structured specialist system where firms have exchange-granted monopolies in a product in exchange for an obligation to make a price at all times.

The balance between net liquidity adders and takers and their relative activity levels at any point in time will, to a great degree, define the market conditions.

It is also critical to understand under what conditions, and with what observable signs (if any), market making entities that are traditionally liquidity adders shift roles and become liquidity takers, as would be the case if a large, highly transactional player decided to materially alter their position. In a space dominated by few large liquidity providers the loss of one will be felt and the conversion, temporary or permanent, to a liquidity taker will have dramatic consequences for other market participants, particularly small- and medium-size players. A big firm seeking to rapidly close out a significant position may need to account for a significant percentage of the total volume traded in the market. The entirety of the OTC broker market will be drawn to the outsized commissions to be earned facilitating the big-hitter's transactions, which generally results in reduced service for the rest of the market. This will seem unfair to the degree that a particular trader is going in the same direction as the large player. A trader trying to buy at the same time as a gigantic, aggressive bidder may be unable to find an offer that hasn't already been lifted away by the monster hovering up all of the volume. A seller, in contrast, would have access to all of the liquidity he could ever want.

How Deep Is It?
Assessing the amount that a trader can reasonably expect to buy or sell without moving the market can be challenging, particularly if contemplating a larger-than-normal position or one that would necessitate an aggressive execution plan. Many exchange-traded products will have volume statistics compiled on an intraday basis that can be viewed as a study on a standard price chart. The challenge then becomes assessing how much of the posted intraday or daily volume the trader can expect to represent without being a distorting influence on price. OTC traders will have a more difficult challenge, and will need to observe the trades printed to the market by their brokers and attempt to form a picture of the actual transaction volume, size, and frequency. This is yet another area where constant immersion in the market pays huge dividends, as a trader who has watched the market print all day, every day will have a much better feel for the volume traded in both normal and abnormal conditions.

Industrial-Size Execution Challenges
For most small and medium-sized traders that operate in developed financial markets the difference between excellent and terrible execution is a primarily a question of being disciplined, having a plan, understanding the market conditions, and intraday trade timing. Large institutional traders must also gauge the capacity of the market to absorb their intended transaction volume without materially distorting prices. Efficiently accumulating and distributing mega size is a very real challenge, which has become increasingly difficult with

the regulatory and technological evolution of the markets in the last decade. Large traders face two primary challenges:

1. The need to manage the available depth and liquidity in the current HFT/small-order environment.
2. The need to conceal positions from aggressive firms that would seek to front-run (which acts like a small incremental tax) or push the market against them (a far more dangerous situation).

One characteristic of a modern diffuse, yet massively faster trading environment populated by myriad machine agents is transaction sizes have gotten smaller as they have grown in number and frequency. The need to financially clear transactions and the migration of liquidity to electronic exchanges has forced large players to funnel their business through platforms with smaller standard-sized transactions. A million-share transaction that formerly would have been negotiated privately between two counterparties might now have to be executed 1,000 shares at a time over a thousand individual trades. A million-share deal is an event that is over before other traders hear of it. A stream of a thousand transactions is a process that will be observed by and responded to by other market participants.

This highly visible stream of price and volume information generated by the stepwise execution of a large transaction is dangerous for large traders for two reasons. First, algorithmic processes will attempt to jump in front of the firm's order flow, costing the trader a small amount of slippage per transaction that can quickly add up to a significant dollar amount over time. Much more troubling, particularly for traders that run very large books or deal in markets with extremely illiquid products, is the potential for other aggressive players in the market to deduce the trader's intent and current inventory and use that information to push the trader out of the position at a significant loss.

Almost Too Easy
Early in my career it was possible to trade electricity futures contracts by calling down to the floor of the NYMEX and talking to a broker standing on the top step of the boiling cauldron of insanity that was an open-outcry pit. One day I wanted to buy some June PJM West Hub contracts and, still fascinated by the novelty of trading against people with names like Streets and Iron Mike, called my broker to see how the market was looking. He informed me that it was something like $46.00 bid, probably offered at $46.50, but that nothing was going on. It was quiet. I told him that I would be a $46.25 bid for a standard-sized 20-contract order and waited excitedly on the phone as he yelled my price into the void. $46.25 bid for 20 June! The void yelled back instantly, as seemingly every trader in the pit screamed SOOOOOOLD! at the top of their lungs. My exact words back were, "So, ummm, they hit me pretty fast, there, didn't they?" as the trader sitting next to me on the desk had a good chuckle at my obvious predicament. Who was I going to sell to if the entire market had just tried to sell to me?

The relative ease or difficulty of accumulating a position can be a valuable clue to the overall market sentiment. If there are more motivated buyers than sellers at a particular point in time it will logically be difficult for an incremental trader to purchase anything. Difficulty

Chapter 13 - Trading Mechanics

accumulating a position perversely makes it more likely that the position will be a winner, and ease of entry can mean that the trader is swimming against the current of market sentiment and will end up with all he wants of something that he will, very shortly, not want at all.

Reading and responding to this type of market condition is a common trading strategy deployed by ultra short-term day traders and some species of algorithmic agents that study the posted volume on the bid and offer and attempt to predict the next market microfluctuation caused by an imbalance of buyers and sellers. For positional, longer-term traders it can also be a valuable input, particularly if the conditions persist.

Good execution is a matter of recognizing and correctly responding to the market conditions of the moment, taking advantage when they are favorable and utilizing any available latitude to try to avoid an unproductive environment. An experienced trader will try to:

- Take advantage of any available latitude (time to execute, product choice, etc.)
- Take advantage of liquidity & depth provided by large orders.
- Have a sense of how executing a large order affects the market. Know when to stop executing to avoid moving price and worsening fill levels.

A trader will develop a sense for the normal volume present in the market, which will be periodically interrupted by temporary droughts and pockets of intense transactional interest. The market's transactional tempo will determine how much volume the trader can push into or pull out of the market in a given minute, hour, or day. If the trader decides to push through the available liquidity and bid or offer into air, the price will respond.

Recall the market turn example from Chapter 8, where the sellers in the market held back in the hopes that the buyers would pay up, only to be thwarted by stubborn bidders unwilling to pay more than $102.50.

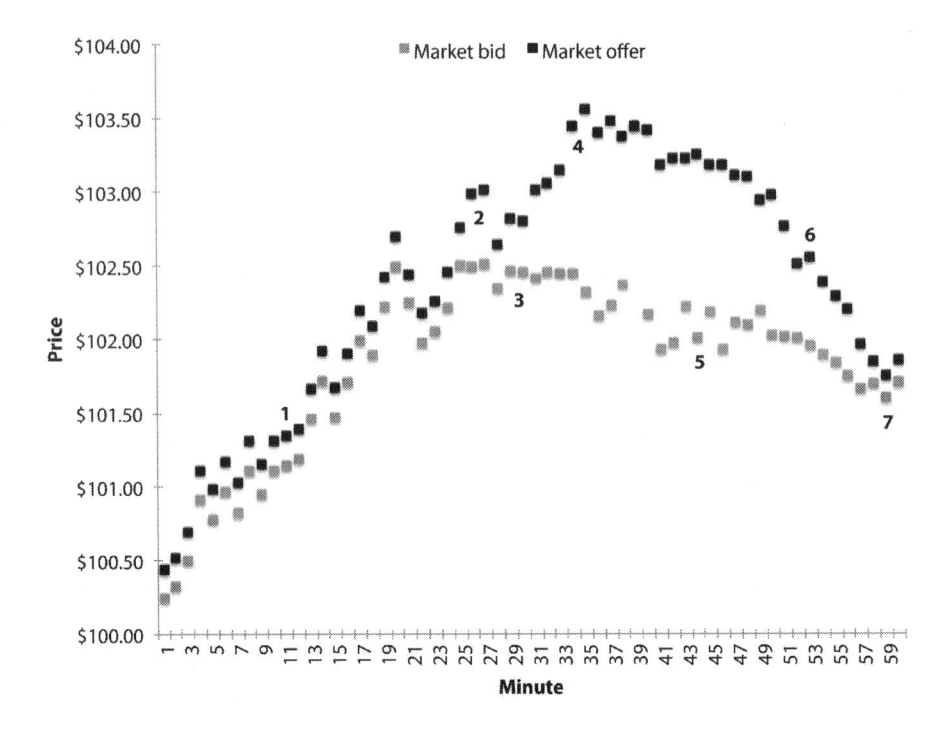

Figure 13.1 Post-rally buyer fatigue.

This type of ebb and flow of buyer and seller motivation and transactional density is extremely critical for traders, particularly when attempting to execute significant volume orders. It would clearly be easy to be a seller at (1) and a buyer at (7), but between (3) and (6) it would prove challenging for either to get anything done.

Just as there are unproductive times to trade, there are also isolated islands of extreme liquidity built into the intraday volume, as was seen in the market reversal example from Chapter 8:

Chapter 13 - Trading Mechanics

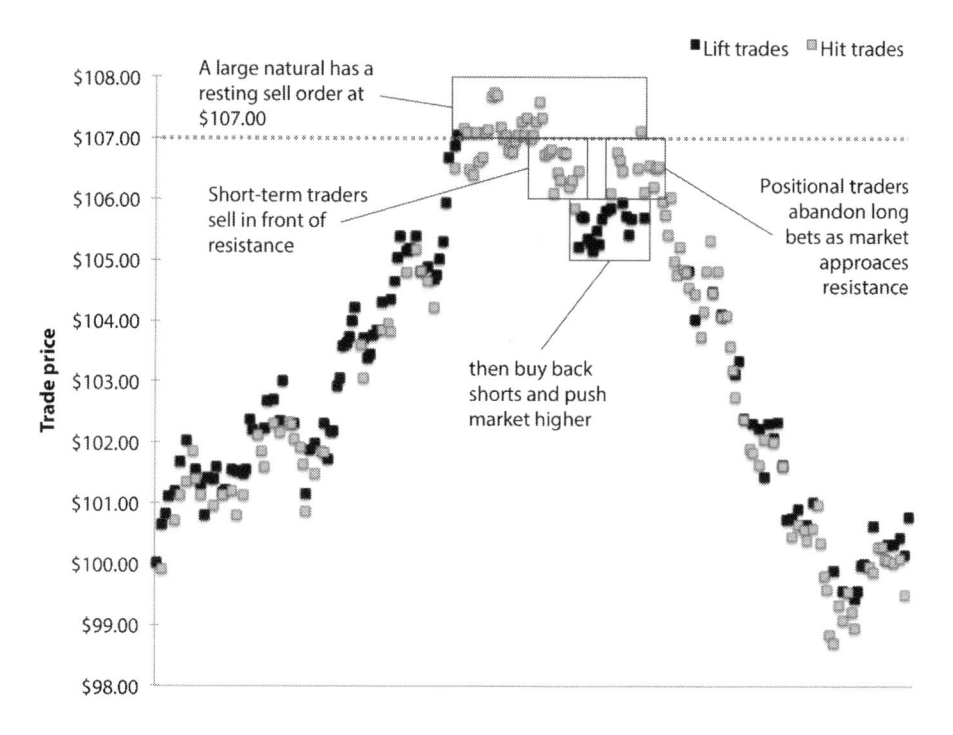

Figure 13.2 Concentrated selling interest as an impediment to an in-progress move.

A trader that needed to be a buyer in size would be challenged by the linear, low-volume rally from $100.02 up to $106.88. Being a resting bid for size would be unproductive, and being an aggressive buyer would only chase the market higher and accelerate the in-progress trend. This all changes when prices hit $107.00 and the natural initiates a hedging program and becomes an aggressive seller. This sudden entry of a motivated seller in size is exactly what the buyer has been waiting for, and he should take full advantage of the available liquidity at the price.

Two of the most valuable things a trader can have on her side are time and the patience to utilize that time. The latitude to wait out short-term market illiquidity, wide bid-offer spreads, and general market malaise is extremely valuable, and the trader should be prepared to utilize the entire duration of their execution window, if need be.

3. Intraday Events That Need to Be Factored Into the Plan

It is critical to understand the typical distribution of liquidity present in the market, but also be cognizant of any intraday consideration that could cause traders to want or need to execute at a different time of the day or prevent them from transacting entirely. Examples would include:

- Early market closures or late market opens.

- Release of scheduled economic statistics or other industry/product relevant data items.
- Results from an auction of supply or demand or the awarding of a particularly prominent piece of business to one or more counterparties.
- Time periods before an elongated break from trading, such as Friday before a weekend, Thursday/Friday before a long weekend, midweek holidays, and any holiday or event that creates a multi-day period of market closure.

In many cases announcements will cause a temporary decrease in liquidity, followed by a possible reactionary flurry immediately afterward as traders act on the fresh information. Pre-weekend, pre-holiday trade tends to thin out the afternoon of the day prior. In unusual cases where the holiday falls one day away from the weekend, as is the case with Thanksgiving in the United States, traders may be faced with a Wednesday close, no trading on Thursday, a partial unofficial holiday on Friday and then the normal Saturday and Sunday weekend. In cases like this the volume of short-term trading tends to dry up on Tuesday, making the Wednesday a low-volume day that will be absolute torture for any trader needing to modify a medium- to large-size position. Having to enter or exit a large volume position in a low-liquidity period is a recipe for extreme slippage, and the lack of cover provided by absence of incremental intraday buyers and sellers will make it significantly easier for other firms to figure out the trader's position and exploit their need to execute.

4. Available Execution Options
Depending on the desired exposure, the instruments necessary to achieve it, the current state of the market, and the active participants, there are a number of ways that a trader can seek to execute a transaction:

1. Negotiate directly with a counterparty.
2. Work with a broker to execute the trade.
3. Utilize a trading screen or exchange-provided platform.
4. Employ an automated execution system.

Each approach has advantages and disadvantages.

Dealing Directly With a Counterparty
Early-stage markets feature primarily physical business executed directly with a counterparty. Even in developed financial markets it can still be beneficial to negotiate directly, particularly for non-standard transactions. Characteristics of direct transactions:

- Direct counterparty contact means no anonymity.
- The trader must give up a lot of information about his interest (including product, price, volume, term, and direction) with no guarantee of a deal.
- The trader must be careful of the firm-to-firm relationship, particularly when contacting a critical counterparty. A trader never wants to anger a major trading partner.

- Direct transactions are transactionally inefficient, as the trader may have to contact a large number of firms to find a willing counterparty.

Working With a Broker
Brokers constantly survey the traders they cover, searching for interested buyers and sellers and aggregating bids and offers into the best available market to communicate back to their clients. Brokers also provide a buffer between traders, taking much of the sting out of rough negotiation and conducting rudimentary pre-trade credit and contract screening to vet counterparties. Characteristics of broker-intermediated transactions are:

- Relatively conflict-free negotiation.
- Broker-assisted, pre-trade credit and contract screening.
- A reasonable assumption of anonymity when not dealing with cleared products; significant anonymity in a post-clearing market.

Using an Electronic Exchange Screen
Once a market gains a certain level of participation and sophistication the business will inevitably migrate to electronic trading platforms that offer seamless credit/contract screening and total pre-trade anonymity. With less ancillary information circulating through the transactional space, the trader must learn to read the rhythm and pattern of transactions as they are printed to the market. Characteristics of electronic exchange transactions are:

- Stable, robust anonymous trading.
- Credit and contract validation built into the system, as are any clearing mechanisms present in the market.

Deploying an Automated Execution System
As seen in Chapter 11, markets that have developed electronic exchange platforms with the capability to interface with external spreadsheets or decision engines allow the trader to develop automated agents that will post bids and offers and execute based on conditional logic that can be as simple or complex as its creator desires. Automated systems offer a number of advantages:

- Faster than human reaction times.
- Infinitely vigilant and disciplined execution.
- Rational, to the extent that the underlying decision logic is sound.

Regardless of the trader's preferred execution modality, the trader (or intermediary) will interact with other participants via the types of orders they place in the market.

5. Types of Orders
Traders use a variety of orders to communicate both the price and the conditions of transaction to other participants in the market. Each market has its own nuances and terminology, but the basic concepts are the same.

Market Order

A market order is an instruction, usually to a broker or other intermediary, to buy or sell a defined volume of a product at the best available price. Even in the most efficient market there will be a lag between the pre-trade indication of the bid-offer spread and the available depth, and the actual price and volume when the trader's order reaches the market. A trader wanting to sell 1,000 lots in a market that was initially bid at $100.00 might find that they have sold their volume at $99.97, which may be either a single transaction or a weighted average of a number of small deals. For this reason, market orders are most commonly utilized in highly liquid markets with a large number of players and a very granular dispersion of price points, where within the execution time horizon price may deviate from the initial quotation, but is unlikely to vary significantly. Material variations are possible, as the 2010 Flash Crash in equities so dramatically illustrated. This outcome uncertainty is the primary reason why, typically, only small and/or unsophisticated players use market orders.

Limit Order

A limit order is a more precise instruction where the trader defines the transaction's specific price and indicated volume. Continuing the prior example, a trader using a limit order would want to sell 1,000 lots at $100.00. If the price was not available in the market at the time, the trader would have to decide if he wanted to cancel it, or allow it to remain in effect in the hopes that a willing counterparty would emerge. Limit orders result in greater price surety, but also an increased probability of an unfilled or partially filled order if the specified price is not currently available in the market and in the trader's desired volume. It is common for traders using limit orders to allow them to rest in the market for a period of time, adding liquidity and increasing the chances that the market will reach the specified price.

Contingent Orders

There are a wide variety of orders that indicate a trader's willingness to buy or sell a particular volume based on a relationship to a price, another order, or a desired execution timeframe.

- One-look or fill-or-kill orders require instant execution or the order is withdrawn from the market.
- Good-'till-cancelled orders remain in effect until the trader explicitly cancels them by declaring that they are "out" or "off of the price."
- A time-limited order, where the trader agrees to be a bid or offer for a specific period of time.
- One-cancels-other instructions indicate prices for two (or more) separate instruments where a transaction in one instantly voids the resting order for the other(s). OCO orders are used when the trader has several acceptable trade alternatives, but only wishes to execute on one of them.
- All-or-nothing orders indicate that the trader is willing to transact for a particular volume that is typically a multiple (sometimes a significant one) or the standard market size, but no lesser sub-divisible amount. All-or-nothing orders are most commonly seen when a trader or broker is trying to piece together a non-standard package and requires a specific volume to complete the structure and facilitate the trade.

Linked Orders

Many electronic exchanges give the trader the ability to link one order to another price posted on the system, creating a formulaic relationship that automatically updates the linked price based on changes to the referent. This functionality has many uses, including creating a stable spread relationship where the live order tracks the referent through intraday fluctuations, having an order that is a multiple of the referent, or changing the order price at an accelerated or decelerated rate. The complexity available to the trader is contingent on the flexibility built into the exchange platform, though many systems do allow the trader to port data back and forth from a spreadsheet or decision engine, allowing almost infinite customization.

Machine-Friendly Complex Orders

The growth of sophisticated execution platforms and the rise of high-frequency trading have led to a dramatic explosion in the number of types of executable orders. Recall the generalized monitor-process-execute loop of an automated trading system from Chapter 11. One potential way of cutting cycles out of the process, particularly in volatile markets, is utilizing orders that contain more complex instructions. Instead of sending a market or limit order, waiting for a report on its success or failure, computing a response, and transmitting an update, the trading system is able to say to the exchange, effectively, "do A, and if A is not possible, do B, C, etc." This theoretically creates a great deal of flexibility and efficiency, which are net positives. The problem with complex orders is that they are complex, and that complexity of interaction with other orders will manifest itself in a timeframe that is not human-observable, except forensically long after the algorithm has executed, or not executed, the transactions. A trader choosing from a vast menu of potential execution instructions must be sure that the order they are choosing to employ does exactly what he intends, no more and no less, else there is potential for it to generate unexpected results when interacting with other complex orders.

Partial Fills and Odd Lots

Every market has a standard transaction size. In financial markets this will typically be a round number of tradable units or notional volume, like 100 shares of stock, 10,000 barrels of oil, or 1 million dollars of USD/EUR. Physical markets tend to utilize more irregular sizes drawn from the needs and constraints of the underlying businesses.

An odd-lot transaction is any order that does not conform to the market's standard size convention. In a market designed to efficiently process 100 share blocks or $1M notional currency trades, trying to find a buyer or seller for 63 GE or $137,924 of the USD/EUR can be challenging. Odd lots will frequently gum up the market as brokers struggle to find a trader willing to accommodate the unusual size and take on the future challenge of disposing of the weirdly shaped position. Odd-lot players are often charged an execution premium to compensate the counterparty for assuming the non-standard size, which can vary from a token amount to a meaningful discount/premium.

If the trader is attempting to buy or sell more than one common unit in a particular order, it is possible that he may get a partial fill, where some but not all of the trade is done with the counterparty, leaving the remainder unexecuted. A trader bidding for 500 shares of stock may get 300 if partially filled in standard size 100 share increments or 256 if particularly unlucky with an odd-lot fill. Partial fills are a pain, particularly odd-lot partials, as the trader is now left with a problematically sized position that will probably cost extra to clean up at some point in the future.

Making Things Complicated – Multi-Product Execution
Things can be somewhat more complicated if the trader is attempting to accumulate or distribute an exposure that requires multiple transactions to create a spread or an option structure like a straddle or iron butterfly.

If the trader's desired structure is quoted as a package with all of the component pieces pre-assembled and priced as a complete unit, so much the better. A single package price can be explicitly quoted by the counterparty or assembled behind the scenes by an OTC broker or exchange matching system. A structure quoted as an explicit package by a single counterparty will generally be much more stable and easy to transact. An iron butterfly or box spread cobbled together by a broker may only have all of the component options line up intermittently during the day, and any change to one of the legs mid-negotiation will change the price of the package and potentially cause the structure to fall apart entirely.

Often, a trader will attempt to achieve a better price by piecing together a structure from individual products obtained from counterparties who may not be aware of the overall value relationship. This is often done when the trader feels that she has identified a material mispricing and is loathe to educate the market by completely defining it. This type of opportunity frequently occurs when a counterparty misprices a spread leg or option strike so egregiously that it makes it possible to assemble other positions around the mispriced product and create a structure with favorable risk-reward characteristics. This component mispricing can be born out of ignorance or a desire to execute significant volume without regard to small inefficiencies created for others to exploit. A hedger seeking to execute a huge volume of options at a particular strike and price would probably be completely unconcerned that, in doing so, it had created a small profit opportunity relative to theoretical value for traders looking a vertical spreads, straddles, and iron butterflies.

The inherent danger of self-assembling structures is the possibility that the trader gets some but not all of the products he needs, leaving a misshapen position with potentially dangerous performance characteristics. Legging into a spread or structure is also a fantastic way to waste a huge amount of time chasing a tiny performance improvement, which can easily be lost in slippage trying to execute two or four trades in a moving market instead of one clean transaction.

Common Execution Mistakes
There are a number of ways that a trader may self-sabotage execution:

1. Not having a clear idea of what he is trying to accomplish.
2. Incorrectly identifying the current market conditions and/or selecting an inefficient execution strategy.

Chapter 13 - Trading Mechanics

3. Lack of urgency when conditions are favorable.
4. Indecision in a fast-moving market.
5. Panicking, and either freezing or thrashing around in the market.
6. Accidentally transacting at an unintended price or incorrect volume by fat-fingering, mis-clicking, or out-trading.
7. Being a passive participant in the market.

Not Having a Clear Idea of What He Is Trying to Accomplish
The trader must know the volume he intends to transact and the price that would trigger execution, both of which should have been predetermined in the trading plan. Attempting to sell 1,000 lots at the trader's $100.00 price target if the market prints at that level is vastly different from wanting to "sell a little, if prices get a bit higher."

Incorrectly Identifying the Current Market Conditions
Traders who are not active, regular participants in the market are at increased risk of misreading the subtle cues that indicate participant interest, or lack thereof. How is the market trading? Is the intraday trend, if one exists, constructive for the trader's position and execution plan? How much volume is going through at each price point, how wide are the bid/offer spreads, and how large are the trade-to-trade gaps? If the market is granular enough to observe individual transactions, are bids getting hit or offers getting lifted? How is the market re-framing after each transaction?

If the trader needs to be a buyer and the last 47 trades in the OTC market have been a seller hitting the bid and aggressively trying to get them to double the ticket, there is no need to wade in and start lifting offers like a madman. It would be more productive to sit on the bid and wait for the selling interest to work down to their level.

Conversely, if the trader needs to be a buyer and the last 47 trades in the OTC market have been offers getting lifted and the buyer aggressively asking to double the ticket, sitting on the bid will be unproductive. The trader will have to compete for offers with the aggressive buying interest, or wait on the sidelines until the sentiment changes and motivated sellers emerge.

There is no substitute for market feel, and no shortcut to acquiring it, so in its absence a trader should not attempt to outsmart herself. She should find the best price and the best liquidity and execute as efficiently as possible. Traders that are immersed in the market and in tune with its rhythm will be better able to recognize favorable conditions, allowing them to utilize more of the intraday ebb and flow to wait for better prices and identify pockets of liquidity.

Lack of Urgency When Conditions Are Favorable
Squandering favorable market conditions is the most perplexing, frustrating execution error. Assuming that the trader has a defined plan and is engaged and paying attention to the market, there is no excuse for failing to hit a bid or lift an offer at the desired price and volume. Most commonly, the trader is either assuming that the market will hang around at his preferred level until he deigns to transact, or he is hoping that the price will continue to improve. More

often than not, the market will move away from the trader's target level or another, more aggressive participant will deal on the price.

Indecision in an Unfavorable, Fast-Moving Market
Trying to efficiently execute a runaway market is one of the most frustrating things imaginable, particularly if the trader isn't 100% clear on the objective. In any proper market explosion or meltdown there will be an inflection point where the price action goes from bad but still orderly to a disorderly melee, with any offer getting lifted or any bid getting hit, regardless of quality. A trader attempting to accumulate a position has the ability to sit on her hands and wait out the madness. A trader trapped in a bad position has no such option, and will have to shift from an idealized "buy/sell at X" to "buy/sell anything better than Y," and if the market blows past Y, start considering Z, ZZ and ZZZ.

Panicking
No trader is immune to panic, and sooner or later a combination of a bad position in bad market conditions will test the discipline of even the strongest, most iron-willed risk-taker. Most commonly a trader will either freeze up and become a passive participant in his own demise, or fall prey to the fight-or-flight instinct and hack and slash his way out of the position, irrespective of the P&L damage.

Fat-Fingering, Mis-clicking, and Out-Trading
Things can get hectic on a trading desk, particularly when the market is moving rapidly and/or the trader has an unusually high level of stress. When a fast market meets a distracted trader, the result is often a fat-finger, mis-click, or an out-trade:

- Incorrectly entering a component of a trade when posting an order to an exchange is called fat-fingering, and commonly manifests itself in a misplaced decimal (buy 1,000 shares at $5,900), a trailing zero added or subtracted (buy 100 or 10,000 shares at $59.00), or the transposition of two numbers (buy 1,000 shares at $95.00).
- A mis-click occurs when a trader scrolling around on an exchange screen for some unknown reason randomly presses a mouse button and executes an unintended trade. Bonus points are awarded for mis-click trades caused by spilling a drink on the keyboard or having the mouse hit by a thrown object. A different, less clumsy variety of mis-click occurs in a fast-moving market, where it is possible for the best bid or offer to disappear in the time it takes a trader to physically depress the mouse button. Unless the trader is quick enough to notice that something is different and stop, she will transact on whatever price and volume is next in the stack, no matter how large or small, cheap or expensive.
- An out trade is the verbal over-the-counter equivalent of a mis-click, and occurs when the broker and trader have not communicated properly about the product and/or price under negotiation. There are endless varieties of the out-trade, but the most common are price discrepancies, trading the wrong instrument or maturity, or both parties thinking they are the buyer or seller in the transaction.

Fat-fingers, mis-clicks, and out-trades are purely mechanical errors that can and should be preventable, if the trader has time to verify that what he is actually doing is what he thought he was doing.

Being a Passive Participant in the Market
If there is no bid-offer spread at all, the trader will have to decide if it is worth the risk to act as a market maker to add liquidity and provide some structure to the market. The trader who makes the market should get the first look at any countering bids and offers from interested participants, drawing transactional volume toward the market maker's prices.

The easiest path to good execution is having a sense of the plan of action and implementing it as efficiently as possible at the first opportunity.

Good Trading Mechanics Are Universal
The desire for crisp, efficient execution of a trade should not vary if the trader is employed at a hedger, financial, merchant, or speculator. The transactional protocols and accepted norms will vary from market to market and instrument to instrument, and can depend greatly on the evolutionary stage of the industry. While the basics are constant, there are differences in the execution challenges and methodologies employed at various industry participants.

Execution by Participant Type

Execution at a Hedger
Execution at a hedger is often an involved, collaborative process. Multiple layers of management will want sign off and veto power. There can also be significant internal constraints on the type and size of business possible. Unless the firm's business and organic exposures are large enough to justify a dedicated team of professionals who monitor the market on an ongoing basis, placing and removing hedges will be someone's part-time job, most commonly located in the Chief Financial Officer's group. Part-time trading is not trading. Not being an active market participant means that information about the prevailing conditions will not reach the decision makers. The person(s) involved in the hedging decision process may not have direct market access, which means that all trades need to be done via an intermediary, often a bank or other financial. A lack of activity will further retard the ability of the decision maker to assess the current state of the market. A natural will frequently have little to no analytical support, and many hedgers are spoon-fed the entirety of their information from customer-facing intermediaries. This is a sure prescription for sub-optimal performance.

A hedger may make the rational choice to be an inefficient executor under certain circumstances. Banks will demand a fee for execution (sometimes a hefty one), but it may be one worth paying, particularly if the bank is able to facilitate the business on credit- or collateral-efficient terms. Replacing margin with a lien on assets can allow cash-strapped firms to mitigate risk with little cash out the door, which can be very attractive to the CFO, particularly given the margin requirements of a hedger-sized package of positions that will have to be obtained from a business not traditionally accustomed to posting large amounts of margin.

Recall the hedger's dilemma: If the market rallies its business is good, but it ends up being bankrupted by the short-term cash needs of supporting its unprofitable hedge position. Most CFOs would gladly pay a premium over fair value to avoid this potential trap.

Taking a more aggressive, proactive approach and establishing a transactional market-facing group comes with significant costs, both in real terms and in the potential for the reputational risk of being seen as a "trader" in the market. Naturals traditionally have great difficulty attracting real trading talent, as they lack the ability to compensate producers at anything resembling market rates. Setting up a group cannot (or certainly should not) be done on a lowest-cost basis. Hiring second- or third-tier traders may save a little money in the short term but ultimately cost the firm much, much more, as its bench-warming talent is obliterated by someone else's varsity team.

Execution at a Financial
Bank traders generally have state-of-the-industry execution and position-management skills. Facilitating a near-constant stream of customer orders, aggregating the exposures, and crafting the resultant position into a profitable book requires quick, sharp, disciplined traders. The constant market interaction will give the trader an excellent sense of the available liquidity and the positioning of a wide cross-section of industry participants, which will be assimilated into his view of the market. One of the biggest challenges for liquidity-providing, market-making traders is finding willing counterparties when they want to (or need to) materially modify their positions.

Execution at a Merchant
Merchant traders tend to be experts in their specific niche market, and will possess an unparalleled ability to get business done within that space. Where a bank trader will tend to have arms-length relationships with a wide variety of market participants, merchants will generally be in very close contact with a small number of counterparties with a vested interest in the same physical products. Merchant traders walk a fine line between trying to extract maximum value from the market while not damaging what need to be long-term relationships with their critical counterparties.

Where a bank trader will have their meticulously calibrated book unbalanced at the whims of their clients and salesmen, a merchant is much more liable to be made unexpectedly short or long by a logistical event or sudden change in an operational characteristic of a controlled asset or structured transaction.

Execution at a Speculator
Most speculators are customers, albeit highly sophisticated customers with, in some cases, state-of-the-art execution skills. Speculators generally do not aspire to be supportive participants in the market, caring only about their own ability to transact efficiently when they choose, with the expectation that some other market participant(s) will provide liquidity and

make prices. For some extremely specialized high-frequency trading/algorithmic firms the bulk of their profits are derived from market making and liquidity providing activities.

Chapter Thirteen Summary

Poor execution mechanics act like an invisible tax on the trader's P&L, quietly eroding it a tick at a time via sloppy buying and selling or gouging chunks of it away through indecision at a critical moment of market panic. Efficient execution starts with a solid trading plan that spells out the conditions and trigger points for position modification. From there, the trader must take into consideration the current market conditions and any intraday events that could impact the available depth and liquidity. Depending on the evolutionary state of the market, the trader may have to weigh the relative benefits of direct counterparty negotiation, employing an OTC broker, or utilizing an electronic exchange or automated order routing system. The trader will precisely communicate his price, volume, and transactional interest to the counterparty or intermediary via the choice of order, which will spell out the exact conditions under which he will deal.

Review Questions

1. What are the advantages and disadvantages of employing a rolling stop loss?
2. What should the trader take into consideration when seeking to implement their trading plan?
3. What is the difference between liquidity and depth, and why should an institutional trader be concerned with the distinction?
4. What are the primary challenges facing an institutional trader attempting to execute a large order?
5. Why is being immersed in the market critical for the trader to efficiently execute?

Resources

- *Charlie D. The Story of the Legendary Bond Trader* by William D. Falloon

Case Study: Product X Trading Mechanics

The trader plans to employ stepwise execution, purchasing a 1M long position in the MAR ProdX futures as an interim substitute for a long exposure in MAR $105 calls and/or OCT $103 straddles, whichever she is able to opportunistically accumulate. Any purchased options will allow the trader to sell back a proportional amount of the MAR futures to maintain an approximately equivalent exposure throughout the holding period.

The MAR ProdX futures should be relatively straightforward to accumulate through some combination of screen-based exchange bids combined with orders places at a few large OTC brokerages. The challenge for the trader will be sourcing the options.

At the current developmental stage of the Product X market, options are less of a liquid instrument and more of a priced-by-request product. The trader will have to directly contact the banks active in the space, as well as any sophisticated merchants and naturals, to gauge their relative level of interest. Since the trader has a price in mind at which he would like to transact, it would probably be most efficient to leave resting bids for a portion of the desired volume with any reasonably serious counterparty, hoping for a slight pull-back in the market that might motivate them to become a seller of calls or straddles. Failing that, the trader might be able to synthetically replicate either the call or straddle position by finding a bullish counterparty unwilling to sell calls or straddles who would be willing to sell puts. MAR puts could be booked against the trader's pre-existing length to create calls, but purchasing OCT puts would require establishing a long position in OCT futures. This could be cleverly done by trading the MAR/OCT spread to simultaneously deplete some of the long MAR placeholder position and establish the OCT position the trader needs to synthetically create the straddles.

14

Managing Positions & Portfolios

At big-money poker tournaments it is common to see a player make a critical decision for all of his remaining chips then disengage from the game and wander away from the table, commiserating with friends as his fate is dealt out card by card. Some traders put on positions and then assume that their work is done, becoming passive participants and waiting to see how everything turns out. This is foolish. Trading is not a coin flip, a spin of the wheel, or a roll of the dice where a gambler makes a committing decision and finds out in an instant if he is a winner or a loser. Most trades take time to go from A to B, and in that interval when anything is possible the trader must manage the position.

Managing a position involves monitoring its performance in the market relative to expectations and evaluating its continued productive utility in light of a constant influx of new information. It is a continuous loop, in which the trader acquires information, re-evaluates his thesis, and modifies the position if necessary. To manage the position, the trader must stay plugged in to the market. One of the side effects of this ongoing immersion is stress.

Managing the Effects of Stress
There is a tremendous difference between the theoretical challenge of developing a view pre-trade and the visceral response to the fluctuations of a live position. Pre-trade views can be developed at leisure, debated at length, and contemplated in an antiseptic intellectual vacuum. Once the thesis goes from ethereal abstraction to contractual reality, even the most Vulcan-like traders become intimately invested in the moment-by-moment fluctuations.

Most traders experience a stress-related degradation in analytical and decision-making capabilities ranging from slight impairments of judgment to a complete inability to process incremental information. It is important for every trader to know where he lies on this spectrum and how heightened stress situations erode his cognitive abilities.

Poker players refer to themselves as being good before-the-flop or after-the-flop players, seeking to steer the bulk of the decision making toward the area where they have an advantage and away from where they have a disadvantage. Traders prone to mid-trade self-sabotage must learn the patterns of their own frailty and maneuver their decision making away from those areas. One common solution is to do as much what-if analysis as possible when constructing the trading plan to increase the number of scenarios with a ready, pre-planned response and decrease the potential for explosively bad improvisational sub-optimization.

Regardless of their fragility, all traders must be able to monitor their positions and execute their trading plans at the predetermined stop-loss and profit-target levels. Traders that are able to coherently, productively process new information must continually interrogate their view and stand ready to modify the exposure, if needed, to reflect the improvement or degradation of the initial thesis.

The trader can choose to modify the position based on an evolution in the fundamental drivers or technical factors that underlie the view, a change in the market conditions that impacts the attractiveness of the trade, or any other development that leads to a material shift in the risk-reward relationship.

Depending on style, mandate, and resources, a trader may hold:

1. A single position.
2. A thematically cohesive portfolio of positions designed to profit from a single market view.
3. A thematically diverse portfolio of positions, where each position expresses a particular view. A portfolio can be diversified across markets, or operate in the same market but embody trades that are designed to profit at different times or different conditions.

We begin with the simplest challenge, managing a single position, and then incorporate the incremental complexity of managing a portfolio.

Managing a Single Position
With a single position, there should be nothing to distract the trader's focus from processing all of the pertinent environmental variables that impact its risk-reward relationship.

Evolution of the Fundamental & Technical Thesis
The evolution of the fundamental and technical picture, both in terms of its pace relative to expectations and the impact of the new information need to be carefully monitored. For each incremental piece of information, or in each discrete period of time the trader must ask:

1. What has changed, is changing, or may change in the future?

2. Are the net changes helping or hurting the view in aggregate?
3. What is the impact on viability of the specific position? Positive, neutral, negative?
4. Has there been an appropriate price response?

The fundamental picture can shift during the holding period as incremental information alters the trader's perception of the magnitude of the potential losses, probable gains, or both. Any material change in the fundamentals should force a reconsideration of the risk-reward ratio and a re-evaluation of any impacted positions.

The technical picture can also evolve during the holding period. It is uncommon (though not impossible) for the technical picture to swing from fully supportive to fully contradictory (and vice versa), but it is very common for a supportive or contradictory technical environment to shift to neutral, or an inconclusive picture to clarify into a constructive or destructive pattern.

Evolution of the Risk Environment
The risk environment can evolve in a number of ways that positively or negatively impact the trader's ability to hold the position.

- Changes in volatility that create P&L swings beyond what the trader can endure, or that the risk group and/or management will allow.
- Changes in market volatility that impact the V@R consumed by the position, potentially causing problems relative to the trader's allocated limits.
- Changes in correlation that create sizing problems relative to the trader's allocated limits or performance problems for trades held in inventory.
- Changes in volatility, correlation, or both that impact the amount of credit/collateral necessary to hold the position.

Traders entering into near limit-max exposures must be particularly cognizant of the potential for negative evolution in the risk environment.

Evolution of the Risk-Reward Calculus
As with market characteristics, risk-reward ratios change as a trade evolves. What the ratio was when the trade was put on may bear no resemblance to what it is in the current moment. The risk/reward ratio can be impacted by positive or negative changes to the fundamental facts, the technical analysis, or shifts in the probabilities of favorable/unfavorable outcomes.

The risk-reward can also shift with the movement of price over time. Consider a position entered into at $100.00 with an initial $5.00 of downside and $35.00 of upside for a very favorable 7:1 risk-reward ratio. The market moves in the trader's favor and earns $10.00 from the entry point. The trader is now risking $15.00 ($5.00 initial possible loss + $10.00 unbooked profits) to hopefully make another $25.00, if everything goes as planned. The downside is that the risk-reward ratio has eroded significantly, from 7:1 to 5:3. As a position nears the profit target, the ratio can become skewed toward risking (much) more than could possibly be incrementally gained. In this case, when the price reaches $130.00 the trader is risking a total of $35.00 ($5.00 initial possible loss + $30.00 unbooked profits) for only an additional $5.00

gain, for a thoroughly terrible 1:7 risk-reward ratio. Paradoxically, great trades with favorable risk-reward characteristics that perform perfectly will have, at the end of their life, evolved into bad trades that should be taken off immediately.[67]

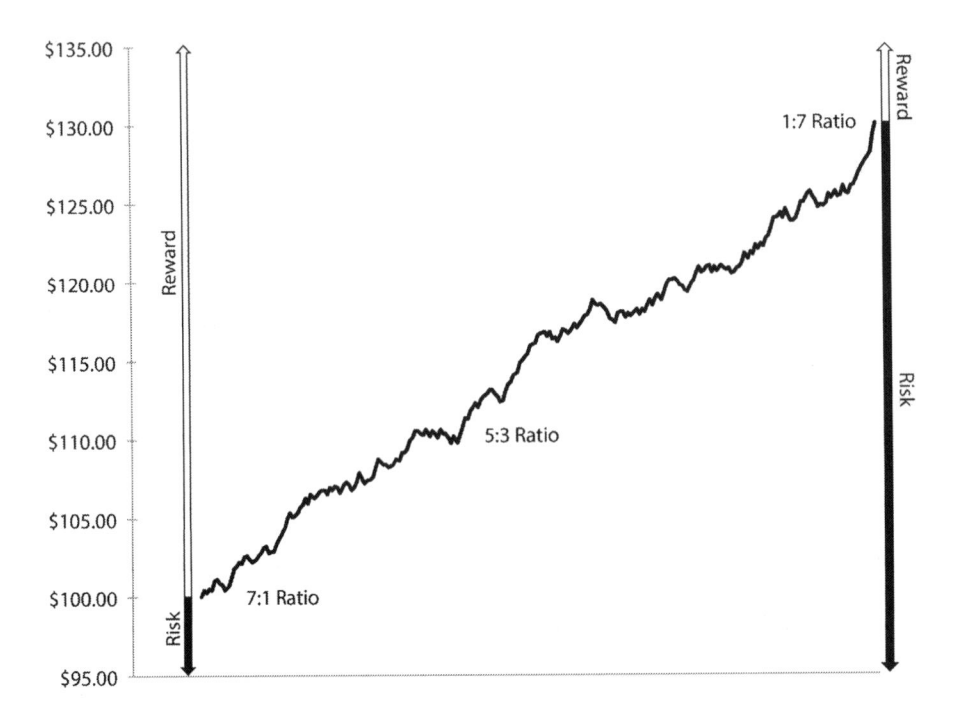

Figure 14.1 The risk-reward ratio of a trade will evolve during the holding period.

Taking Action – Modifying the Position Size

Depending on the evolution of the fundamental variables, the technical indicators, the risk environment, and the risk-reward ratio, the trader may be motivated to modify the size of the position. Most typically, traders will choose to increase the size of the position if the conditions are improving, decrease it if they are deteriorating, and trade around a core position if they feel they have a particularly good read on both the short-term and long-term price drivers.

1. Increasing Position Size

There are three principal reasons why a trader would add to an exposure:

1. The fundamental facts, technical indicators, or both have evolved from initial pre-trade dispositions to materially improve the risk-reward ratio.
2. The trader is continuing to build the position, per the original trading plan.
3. The trader is trading around a core position, and the market is locally cheap.

---

[67] The trader can (and should) use a rolling stop-loss to control degradation of the risk-reward ratio and protect profits.

If the probability-adjusted strategy risk-reward ratio has materially improved and the trader has the limits available to accommodate incremental volume, she may be able to justify accumulating a larger exposure. This calculus is easier if the market price is relatively unchanged or slightly in the trader's favor, as the incremental volume would not seriously alter the weighted average cost of the position. This is generally only possible if the firm is leading the rest of the participants in accumulating and processing information. If the price has responded, then the trader will have to assess if the probability-adjusted risk-reward of the incremental position meets the minimum hurdle rate for participation in a vacuum.

Traders will frequently plan to add incremental tranches of their total desired exposure across a defined time horizon as part of a predetermined execution strategy. This stepwise execution is called scaling into/out of a position or buying/selling on a scale. Using a scale allows the trader to chronologically diversify, and should yield an approximation of the weighted average price for the execution period.[68] It can also be done as a risk-management exercise if the trader is concerned about having the full exposure on the books in the event of a potential near-term adverse price fluctuation prior to the anticipated fundamental or technical trigger.

If managing a large position or faced with unfavorable market conditions the trader may not have the luxury of picking a price and a time and accumulating or distributing their desired volume. The trader may have to camp out on the bid or offer for multiple days, accepting whatever fluctuations occur in the interim in an effort to be part of any consummated transactions. Even in liquid markets, the trader may choose to average in over a period of time to reduce the possibility of misjudging the depth and unintentionally distorting the price.

Traders also incrementally add and subtract from a core position if they feel that the market has become temporarily mispriced. This is called trading around a position, and will be covered later in the chapter.

Traders frequently say, "never add to a losing position." While there can be valid reasons to add to a position that may currently be negative (as seen above), it is never permissible to add additional volume purely in an attempt to "double down," making the position twice (or more) as large so that it only has to regain half of the negative price move to return to profitability.

2. Reducing Position Size and Closing Positions

There are five possible reasons why a trader might reduce the size of a position or eliminate it entirely:

1. It has hit profit-target or stop-loss level.
2. The fundamental or technical drivers have been exhausted, or eroded severely.
3. To avoid event risk.
4. The position is not responding as expected to market stimuli.
5. The trader is trading around a core position, and the market is locally expensive.

---

[68] This type of scale-in/scale-out position accumulation/distribution is very popular with hedgers, for whom a result approximating the average price over a period of time is frequently good enough.

If the trade reaches a profit-target or stop-loss level (either predetermined in the trading plan or subsequently revised due to incremental information), traders will immediately remove the position with the maximum possible efficiency given the prevailing market conditions.

If the fundamental case erodes, or if the technical study is invalidated by post-trade price fluctuations, the trader needs to examine the justification for maintaining the position, even if the P&L is not yet problematic. No justification for a position should result in an expedient exit of the exposure. It is all too easy to delude oneself into deciding that, since nothing terribly wrong is happening to the position, it is reasonable to maintain it in the hope that something productive might occur. The key word is "hope," which should not be part of the trader's lexicon. Positions are proactive expressions of the trader's view. "No view" means "no position," period.

It can also be prudent to temporarily take off exposure, even in a favorable fundamental and technical environment, to avoid event risk around an economic announcement or gap risk over a night or weekend. This has less to do with the quality of the trade and more to do with prudent risk management.

If the position is not acting as the trader expected given the prevailing market conditions, she may elect to remove some or all of the exposure. This will be covered in greater depth later in the chapter.

Trading around a trend involves maintaining a core exposure in the direction of a trend, opportunistically adding incremental volume on countertrend retracements that is later closed out once the trend has re-established itself and the macro impulse wave has reached resistance. Trading around a trend will be explored in a separate section later in the chapter.

Managing Stop-Losses and Profit Targets With Gap Risk
In an infinitely liquid, continuous market, monitoring a stop-loss on a position would be a straightforward exercise. In practice, traders must deal with a variety of discontinuity-producing events, ranging from news items, economic data, and industry statistics, as well as overnight and holiday/weekend cessations of trading. The trader must develop a feel for the "normal" overnight and intraday gap risk as a percentage of total daily volatility.

Some portion of the total volatility will be "tradable" and some will be "untradeable." The less of the volatility that is tradable, and the more that occurs overnight or in short-duration step-function moves intraday, the greater the danger will be for a trader holding a position when her ability to proactively manage risk is degraded. Compare three different distributions of volatility, one where the bulk of the price fluctuations occur during the day session, one where the majority of the price move for the period happens overnight, before the trader is in the office, and one where a mid-day surge accounts for most of the day's trading range:

Chapter 14 - Managing Positions & Portfolios

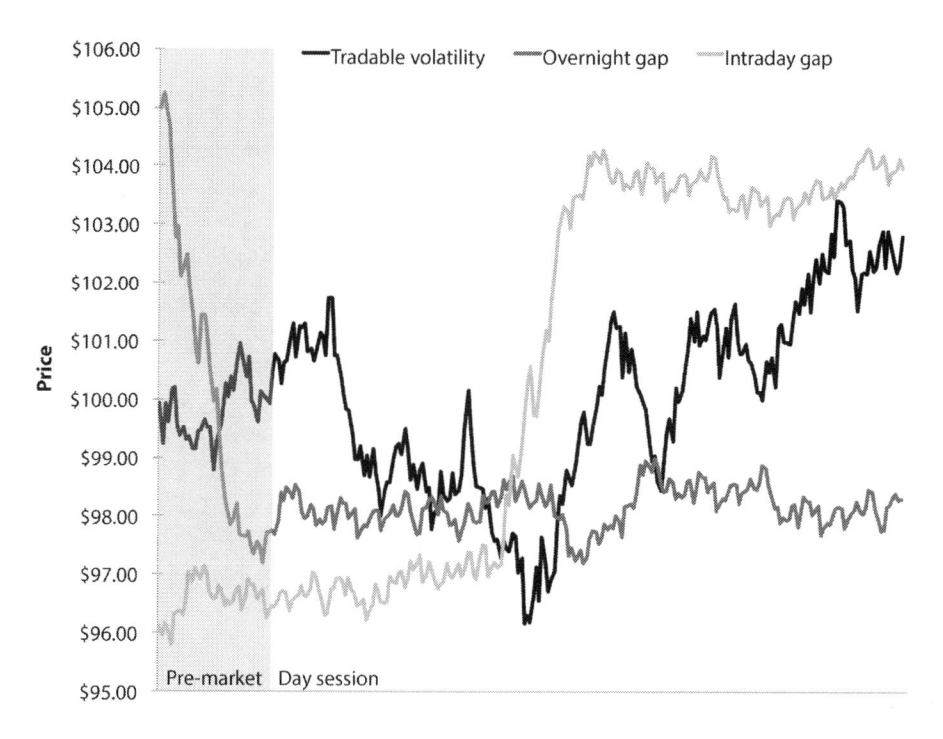

Figure 14.2 Volatility can be concentrated in the pre-market, during a brief window intraday, or be relatively constant throughout.

Markets with a tendency to express the majority of their fluctuations outside of normal trading hours or in one epic mid-day surge are extremely challenging. A trader holding a long position during the overnight gap lower would have no opportunity to mitigate risk until after the entirety of the sell-off had occurred. A trader short during the intraday rally could theoretically manage the position, though only if prescient enough to recognize the market conditions and aggressively execute in the narrow window available.

Managing gap risk can be extremely challenging, particularly if the trader is holding a position that is near, but not through, a stop level. The trader should:

1. Assess the gap potential present in the market.
2. Compare the gap potential to the remaining headroom under the stop-loss limit, particularly if there is any probability of a very large move.
3. Acknowledge that the gap and its potential effects on the market mean that the trader cannot control the risk in the trade, given the market conditions. Controllability has decreased significantly.
4. Give serious consideration to reducing the trade size, to allow the remaining position more room to breathe, in dollar P&L terms.

Managing stop-losses is particularly tricky overnight or over a weekend, where the trader must allow for the possibility that the market may open at a completely different level than the prior day's closing price. Consider a trader managing three positions on a Friday afternoon, each with a hard $110.00 stop-loss. The first trade trades above $110.00 shortly before the close, and on breaching that threshold the trader immediately closes out the position (X). In the dying minutes of the day the trader faces an interesting decision with respect to the two remaining trades, the first currently at $108.72 and the second printing $102.25. The trader estimates that there is an approximately equal chance that either trade opens up $4.00 higher or $4.00 lower on Monday morning. When graphed relative to the closing prices, the trader faces the following potential outcomes:

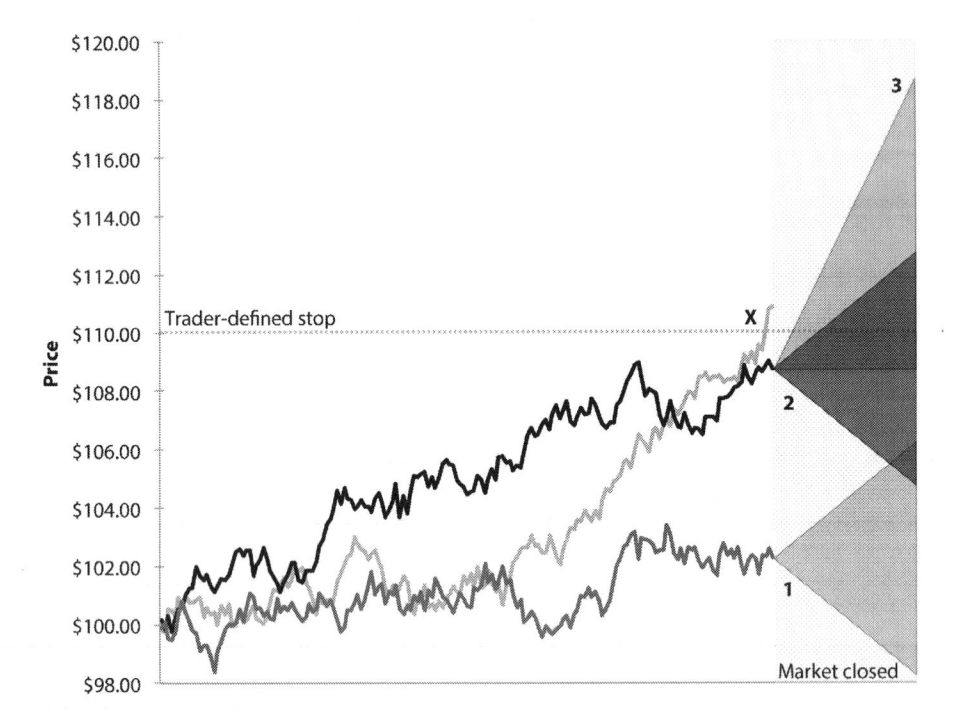

Figure 14.3 Managing a stop-loss with overnight gap risk.

The range of possible outcomes for the $102.25 trade (1) does not endanger the $110.00 stop-loss on the position. The $108.75 trade (2) is much more problematic, and is in legitimate jeopardy of opening well through the trader's stop first thing Monday morning, which forces some interesting calculus before the weekend. The math becomes even more interesting if the trader feels that there are asymmetrical probabilities of an up or down weekend gap. If the trader determines that he can lose $10.00 but possibly only make $4.00 (3), then he may be forced to close out a position that has not yet violated his predetermined stop-loss level purely because of the probability that it might, coupled with the lack of controllability brought on by the potential gap risk.

Unexpected, intraday event-driven gaps must be dealt with on a best-efforts basis, with the trader reading and responding to the situation as it unfolds and doing his best to limit the damage.

Incorporating Volatility/Market Conditions Into Stop-Loss and Profit-Target Levels
The trader must consider short- and medium-term volatility, available liquidity, and the prevailing market conditions when setting stop-loss levels. There is no point in setting a $0.05 stop on a position if the market trades in $0.10 increments. There is no point in setting a one-tick stop, as the first negative print will force the trader out of the exposure. Recall the example of evolving market volatility from Chapter 5.

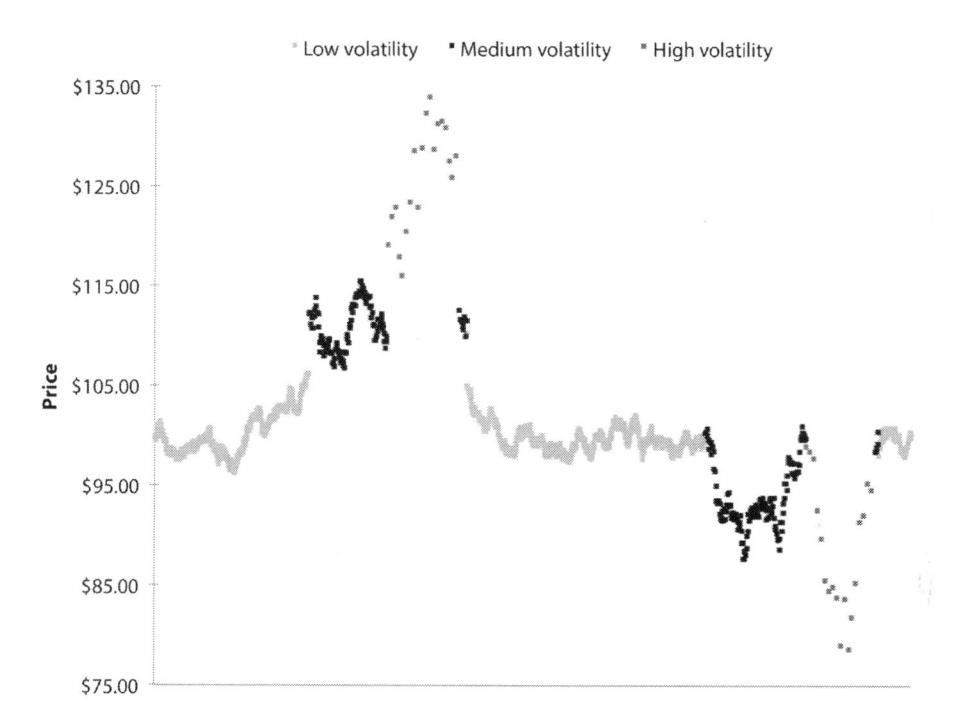

Figure 14.4 A market transitioning back and forth between low-volatility/high-liquidity and high-volatility/low-liquidity states.

The notion of a stop-loss calibrated in $0.10 or $0.25 tick increments may well make sense when the market is in a low volatility phase, but would clearly be unrealistic with medium volatility and completely absurd during periods of high volatility.

3. Trading Around a Trend
Trading around a trend is an extremely productive strategy that involves holding a core position aligned with the direction of the macro trend, then opportunistically adding incremental volume following intermediate retracements that is exited when the macro trend has re-asserted itself and is approaching resistance. Trading around a trend requires a well-

formed technical channel and a productive, but not excessive, level of intermediate and micro-level fluctuation. Too much chop, and a trader could potentially be scared out of an incremental position that would otherwise be profitable. Consider the chart of a well-defined trend:

Figure 14.5 Trading around a trend.

A trader with a fundamentally bullish view of the market and core long position would observe a trend in motion in a well-defined channel, the width of which is defined by the alternating higher lows at (L1) and (L2) and higher highs at (H1) and (H2). When the market retraces to support, the trader would purchase an incremental volume (B1), which he would hold with a tight stop, re-selling once the market reached the top of the trend channel at (S1). This process would be repeated at (B2) and (S2), and continue for as long as the trend remained viable. When market reaches the profit target or the trend ultimately ends, the trader would exit both the core position and any incremental trades held at the time.

Trading around a trend has several advantages:

1. The trader maintains a core positioned with the trend, and is incrementally adding in the direction of the trend and decreasing the position size prior to potential countertrend moves.
2. The trader buys "cheap" and sells "expensive" within the context of the trend.
3. There is a good balance between aggression and risk-reward.

The principal risk of trading around a trend is that, if the trend abruptly fails immediately after an incremental addition, the trader will be taking losses on a larger-than-core position.

The relationship between the size of the core position and the magnitude of the incremental trades is also important. If the core position is not materially larger than the incremental buys and sells, the trader will effectively be attempting to derive the majority of the P&L by trading the swings in the market and not the more predictable central trend.

It is also common for a trader wanting a larger core exposure to use retracements to add permanent volume to the position, with the hope of carrying the additional weight for the full duration.

Response to Stimulus

The trader will need to monitor and evaluate the degree to which the position responds to the underlying fundamental and technical motivators. It is possible that the trade will outperform the trader's expectation, perform as expected, underperform, or have a problematic negative outcome or puzzling non-response.

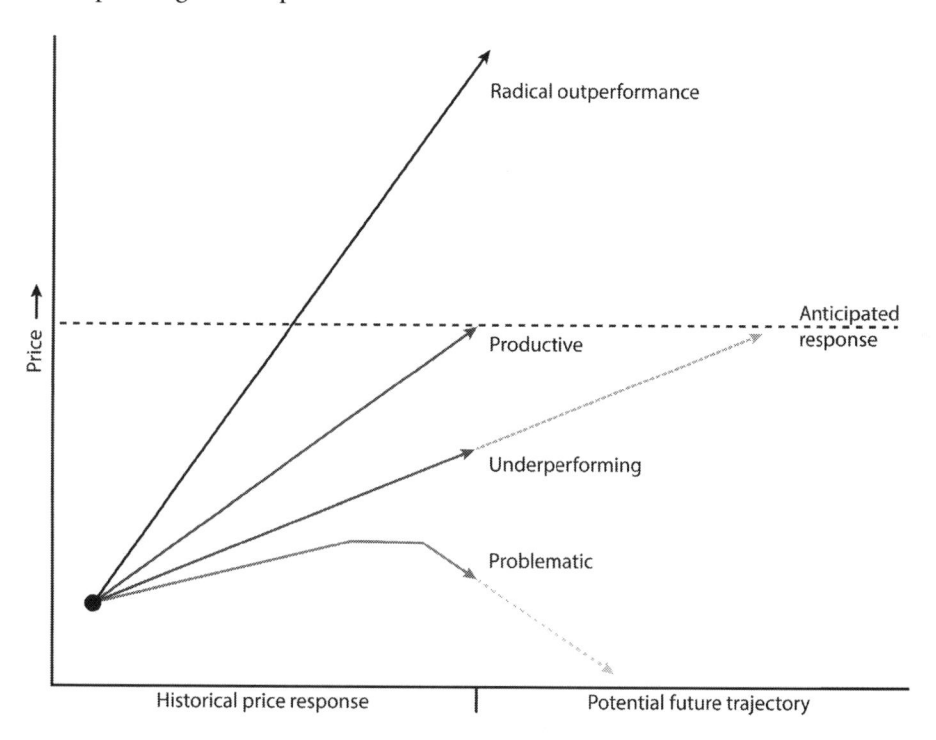

Figure 14.6   Potential performance trajectories of trade performance.

It's Working Too Well – Radical Outperformance
If the trader is in the enviable position of holding a position that has radically exceeded the profit target in a step-function move or at an highly accelerated pace, the only real question is whether to immediately exit the position and book the profit, or take the time to determine if something has fundamentally or technically changed such that the market is now capable of moving further beyond the goal. The danger in taking time for analysis is that the market may just as quickly reverse direction, potentially costing the trader some or all of the recently acquired profits. If the trader does decide to maintain an exposure, it would be prudent to consider lightening up by closing a portion of the position, adding a protective option position, and/or setting a tight rolling stop to prevent giving away windfall profits.

It's Working Like It Should – Productive Response
If the trader's position has reached the profit target set in the trading plan due to the anticipated evolution of the fundamental or technical landscape, then he should exit the exposure in as efficient a manner as possible, book the P&L, and start looking for the next idea.

It's Not Working Like It Should – Underperforming
If the fundamental and technical landscape has developed as the trader anticipated and the market's reaction was positive but decidedly uninspiring, the trader will face a challenging decision. It is possible that the market has yet to fully assimilate the new information and that additional gains may be forthcoming, but it is also possible that the incremental drivers were not nearly as impactful as the trader was anticipating. Unless the trader can make a compelling case that the new information is not priced into the market, it may be more productive to take the (small amount of) money and run while there are still profits to be had.[69] If not, the trader risks being forced to make a decision on a breakeven or negative transaction, which is an altogether worse state of affairs.

It's Slightly Negative or Not Really Doing Anything – Problematic
Positions that underperform or hover around breakeven through a productive fundamental or technical development are a warning sign for experienced traders. If the market can barely rally in the face of bullish information, the most logical explanation is that the overall sentiment is significantly bearish. This is problematic for a trader with the underperforming position, because if the market barely budges higher with bullish development, how far is it going to fall if something materially bearish occurs?

Slightly positive and break-even trades are psychologically easier to give up on, as the trader can exit with only the opportunity cost of utilized limits. Slightly negative positions are the bane of every trader's existence. It is all too easy to hang on to a small loser in the hopes that some unspecified, to-be-determined event will push prices back in the trader's favor, allowing

---

[69] One of the most frustrating aspects of evaluating on-the-run trading strategies is assessing the propagation of motive impulse across the market, and how capriciously the balance can shift from grudging refusal to respond to an exaggerated price movement long after most traders have grown tired of waiting.

an escape at breakeven. This is a trap. If a trader is unwilling to take a small loss on a position, the reward is usually a large loss realized at a later date.

Maintaining an unproductive position can be hazardous and expensive. The longer the trader sits on the position, waiting for something beneficial to happen, the greater the chance of an exogenous event impacting the market. Even if the market remains docile, there are nontrivial credit and collateral costs associated with holding a position. Paying rent on an unproductive exposure while waiting for a black swan to make things bad enough to exit is foolish.

Don't Let a Trade Turn Into an Investment
A well-structured trade should have an expected time horizon during which (or by which) some triggering event or paradigm shift should alter the value proposition and impact the market price of the position. If that does not occur, as with an underperforming trade, there is a temptation to keep the trade, to wait just a little bit longer to give it time to work. There can be reasons to extend the time horizon of a trade, particularly if the trigger is a defined event that has been delayed or rescheduled. If the anticipated trigger event has disappeared into the ether or come and gone without yielding the desired result, and the trader must admit that the exposure lacks a primary motivator, jettison the position, and move on to the next idea.

Managing Another Trader's Position
Traders are frequently responsible for managing positions that they do not own, either on behalf of the firm, or to assist other traders. If a trader is forced to be away from the desk or out of contact with the market, it is good risk management to ask a colleague or manager to watch the positions and either notify the trader of any material fluctuations or execute on his behalf. Senior traders and desk heads frequently put on positions and permanently delegate the maintenance to more junior traders. A trader with a particular expertise may be handed the firm's entire book of business in a product and be expected to aggregate the longs and shorts and execute on the residual position. A trader tasked with managing a colleague's position should:

- Make sure that the owner is aware that the trader's style and market view may not align completely with hers, and that she is comfortable delegating under those conditions.
- Remove all ambiguity from the process. Know exactly what the owner of the position wants done with it, what thresholds or limit levels will motivate execution, and under what conditions she expects reporting. Does she want the trader to close the position if the market trades at $45.00, or trades through $45.00? Do not agree to sell "some" if prices "go down" or if the economic statistic "isn't good." Without a specific action plan and defined trigger points, the trader is setting himself up to be someone else's excuse if things go poorly.
- Document everything in a permanently recorded medium, preferably via email. This should include the original execution plan, any mid-course status updates, and a final summary including fill prices, volumes, and market conditions.

This undoubtedly seems like overkill at best and paranoia at worst. The fact is, trading is a stressful, competitive business where, under enough performance pressure, otherwise honest, forthright people will exploit whatever opportunities available to blame others for their mistakes.

Managing Shared Positions
Optimizing the trading plan and execution strategy for an exposure that has multiple owners can be extremely challenging. It is critical to predetermine the entry criteria, the underlying thesis, and the exit strategy, and get documented buy-in from all participants. There should be a documented statement of ownership and control of the risk that spells out the percentage of the risk allocated to each trader before the position is accumulated. A single trader should be nominated to monitor and execute on the strategy, acting in accordance with the agreed-to plan and providing reporting to the other interested parties.

The degree of coordination required is proportional to the ease of execution and the divisible nature of desired exposure. Two people deciding to each buy 100 shares of an extremely liquid equity can easily go their own way if the partnership proves unwieldy. A consortium of eight firms with different resources and agendas that form a temporary alliance to buy a stake in the unproven mineral reserves of a developing nation face a significantly more committing proposition. In general, good, shared positions involve similarly aligned traders sharing a clearly defined strategy or a single dominant market expert and what amounts to a group of passive investors.

Any shared exposure where the interests, market views, or pain thresholds of the participants are not aligned is a recipe for disaster. Having one or more members of the group prepared to risk significantly more or who can afford to lose significantly less than the others can alter the group dynamic, potentially allowing the outlier(s) to exert undue influence on the plan of action. The lack of a clearly defined plan and predetermined execution delegation can also prove deadly, as achieving consensus in the midst of a crisis will be all but impossible.

Managing Herd Mentality
At firms that grant significant latitude to traders, individuals with similar market perspectives and informational resources frequently arrive at a kind of positional groupthink. The trade of the moment seizes the collective imagination and quickly becomes the position to have in the book. This presents a number of problems for the traders, the risk management group, and the management of the firm. As seen in Chapter 6, trading shops allocate V@R across portfolios and books with the assumption that the limits will be deployed into non-correlated positions, such that the total firm-wide risk exposure will be less than the sum of the individual portfolio V@Rs. Under normal circumstances the positional diversification and associated non-correlation will be sufficient to keep the firm-wide metrics within allowable boundaries. If, however, all of the fish start swimming in the same direction and every sub-portfolio is a mirror image of the others then the firm can easily breach its V@R limit with all of the individual traders below their allocated limits. The risk group needs to be cognizant of the positions accumulated above and beyond the basics necessary for reporting, and must notify

senior management whenever the risk on the book starts to become concentrated around a particular theme.

Herd positions are challenging for senior management, particularly in cases where the manager does not typically exercise a great deal of influence over the day-to-day risk-taking activities or does not feel it appropriate to intervene in individual trader decisions. It may be necessary to mediate between traders and institute an ad-hoc temporary cap on the maximum allowable exposure in a particular product to prevent a firm-wide V@R breach.

Herd positions are very challenging for the trader who functions as the firm's constant presence in the market that has so recently become fashionable. Trading with the herd can be a frustrating exercise, as uncoordinated traders ignore each other's interest in the market, execute at silly levels, and generally muddy the waters for the product specialist. Even a firm composed entirely of small traders can look very big to the outside market, in aggregate, when they are all trying to buy or sell at the same time. If something spooks the internal herd it can stampede, leading to a large amount of completely self-inflicted damage as traders unwilling to coordinate and aggregate their positions front-run each other to the door.

Expressing a contrarian point of view and betting against a herd can be challenging. Herds do not like to hear dissenting opinions, and herd members typically feel very confident in their view of the market as long as others share it.

A Time To Trade
One of the most unexpected day-to-day issues a trader can face is having the time to watch the market, plan strategies, and execute trades. Traders go to, or are involved in, a surprisingly large number of meetings. They will gather to discuss strategy, have brainstorming sessions with their immediate desk mates, attend briefings on fundamental market conditions, have regular updates with the risk group, give periodic updates to senior management, and have infinite one-off discussions about in-progress or proposed deal structuring and pricing. While technology has made it much easier to stay informed via laptop, tablet, or smartphone, there is still no substitute for being immersed in the market. Texting a broker under the table while suffering through a 264-slide deck is not the same thing.

The number of meetings is somewhat proportional to the type of firm and the responsibilities of the trader. Naturals will have more strategy sessions, management updates, and review meetings. Financials will have more briefings and a tremendous amount of deal-related mini-meetings to discuss strategy and pricing. Merchants will have a lot of fundamental review meetings. Traders at speculative firms should have the least number of demands on their time, as their primary focus is on the creation of value to the exclusion of all else.

Ideally, the firm will understand that the need to transact trumps all other considerations, and a trader can find ways to manage the competing demands on his time.

Managing the Trader's Emotions While Holding a Position

As discussed in the chapter introduction, a trader must learn to manage the emotional aspects of the stress of riding a position and minimize the effects on the decision making process. Bad trades hurt, and losing money sucks, there is no use pretending otherwise. When things get bad and the trader's fight-or-flight instincts kick in there can be a very powerful, visceral desire to flee, get out, and run away. The easiest path to not hurting any more is closing the trade, and many good positions are prematurely thrown under the bus by weak traders looking to do something, anything to make the pain stop. The challenge lies in constructing a cognitive framework or developing a tolerance to suffering such that the fear and greed are compartmentalized and dealt with separately from the fundamental information, technical analysis, and risk-reward characteristics of the market and the position.

In any given year a trader's P&L will largely be shaped by a small number of key positions. Mismanaging a large position is usually extremely damaging to the trader's year, and could potentially be career ending, if sufficiently ugly. The trader will need to, over time, understand her reactions to favorable and unfavorable circumstances and how this change from the baseline thought process affects her decisions around live, impactful positions.

Dealing With Large Losing Positions

Sooner or later, even a highly disciplined trader with a fundamentally sound, well-constructed position will experience a large enough exogenous market shock to step-function prices through their stop-loss levels. Large losses can also occur as a result of a discipline breakdown, where a small- to medium-sized losing trade is neglected or mismanaged until it becomes a legitimate problem. Regardless of whether the damage is self-inflicted or the result of a low-probability event, the trader needs to deal with the problem as efficiently as possible and prepare for the inevitable consequences.

If there is time, the trader needs to immediately notify management and the risk group as to the position, the estimated P&L impact, and the mitigation plan. This demonstrates that the trader is aware, engaged, and to the extent possible, managing the position. Managers hate losses, but they will never forgive being blindsided by a trader. Just as a trader has to deal with the immediate market consequences, the manager has to deal with the subsequent organizational consequences, which may involve shifting exposures or requesting additional resources if the trader's loss is impactful to the firm as a whole.

With the immediate reporting taken care of, the trader needs to fix the problem. There is no point in hashing through the logic, re-examining the underlying rationale, or engaging in any other time-wasting activity. The exposure that is currently destroying the P&L is no longer a decision item; it is a problem that needs to be solved as quickly and efficiently as possible. In the aftermath of an unusual market event there is only a certain amount of liquidity to be had, typically significantly less than normal. The trader needs to capitalize on whatever narrow execution window exists to take off or neutralize the position before the market becomes untradeable.

Once the exposure has been mitigated, the trader needs to start working on organizational and career damage control. There will be questions from management about the decision-making process, the size and composition of the exposure, and the overall handling of the risk. The trader should pre-empt these as much as possible by giving the rationale, the market events that unfolded to impact the trade, the P&L estimate, and the lessons learned going forward. By providing this information before it is asked for, the trader appears engaged and in control of the situation. This is critical, because senior management will certainly be reevaluating the trader's future risk-taking activities in terms of both size and scope, and possibly his future on the desk. They may stop by to have a chat to see how the trader is doing. They do not care how the trader is doing, they are checking to see if the trader is broken, defective, or is worn out and needs to be replaced. It is permissible to be unhappy, it is never permissible to be out of control, throwing a tantrum, or acting like a child. Management will want to see that the trader has accepted responsibility, understands what happened and why the trade was not successful, and has a plan for incorporating this information into going-forward analysis and future risk taking.

Once the dust has cleared, some traders immediately want to jump into the market and try to earn it all back as quickly as possible. This is a temptation that most traders should probably resist, as their decision-making process is likely highly compromised and their market view cannot be robust. There will also be a temporarily skewed personal risk-reward relationship, where making back some small quantity of money is marginally useful, but losing incremental dollars while under heightened management scrutiny will look very, very bad.

A trader's first post-disaster trade should be a model of risk-reward assessment, clear analysis, and flawless communication about the rationale, goals, and execution strategy. It should be appropriately sized for the trader's new economic reality and standing relative to allocated limits and goals. This can be frustrating, particularly if the trader had been running well and accustomed to larger bets with the house's money. Starting from zero, which is in many ways what every trader is doing post-disaster, is all about rebuilding credibility and confidence along with P&L. Large losses are part of the game, and on a long enough timeframe they will eventually happen to everyone. Having a career as a professional trader is highly dependent on developing good crisis management skills to ensure that the first bad position isn't the last.

Dealing With Large Winning Positions
Many traders sub-optimize the performance of their best positions by relaxing, losing focus, and counting their chickens before they hatch. If I had a nickel for every trader who prematurely joked about the Ferrari he was going to buy with his gigantic bonus, I'd have a Ferrari. Mismanaging a large winning position will be devastating to a trader's psyche, credibility, and standing within the firm, and will likely severely damage his performance for the year and ruin his bonus. A trader must understand that a large winning position is just as serious a matter as a career-threatening loser, and that whatever resources the trader can bring to bear, now is the time to put forth maximum effort.

Large winning positions are usually the result of prescient market calls and crisp execution, often followed by significant mid-course volume additions as the trader's thesis improved. As the trade got better, the position got bigger. If the trader is running a considerably larger position than at initiation (potentially several times over if they have been adding aggressively), it will not take much of a retracement to severely erode or completely wipe out the mark-to-market profits and start creating losses at a rapid rate. As discussed in Chapter 12, the trader should have one or more stops as a part of the trading plan, ideally both a trailing stop to protect the unbooked profits and an event stop to cover changes in the fundamental thesis.

As seen in Chapter 13 – Trading Mechanics, the degree to which the trader is going to have to finesse the execution is proportional to the trader's exposure size relative to the normal market volume. If operating in a deep and liquid market where his volume will only represent a modest amount of the daily turnover, the trader is free to attempt a very precise exit at a specific price point or chosen time. In an illiquid market, or for very large positions, the trader may have to take maximum advantage of pockets of intraday volume to get as much as possible done when conditions are favorable, even if it is not at the absolute best price of the day. At some point during the position's volumetric evolution the trader should have developed a defensive hedging strategy as part of an amended trading plan to protect the P&L in the event of unfavorable market conditions.

Managers tend to get involved with positions that they have a real or imagined vested interest in, and their input can be an unwanted distraction for the trader. This is particularly true for trades that required an expansion of limits and/or management trust and buy-in beyond the trader's normal ability to do business. Managers also tend to unfairly retro-trade large positions, viewing the high water mark of the P&L in hindsight as the logical exit point, with any subsequent giveback seen as trader underperformance. The trader will also have to deal with a lot of input from the other members of the desk, who will have all sorts of allegedly constructive ideas about what the trader should do, when, and how.[70]

So far we have discussed managing a single, concentrated exposure. The remainder of this section will consider the unique demands of managing a group of positions.

Managing a Thematically Cohesive Portfolio

A thematically cohesive portfolio is a trader-constructed group of positions accumulated to express a particular view of the market. The individual trades can be slight variations on the same theme (long highly correlated directional positions, long front-to-back spreads with a strong directional component, and long call options all in the same product) or a basket of varied exposures designed to function in different ways but in aggregate produce a desired response. To the extent that every position in the book is leveraged to a core thesis, the performance of the book will largely be determined by the validity of that insight.

A trader managing a cohesive portfolio will need to be constantly evaluating both the evolution of the central thesis and the response relative to expectation of each of the positions.

---

[70] Strangely enough, nobody rushes over to associate themselves with the terrible trades.

The trader will generally seek to rebalance the initial exposure weightings over time, pruning out underperforming strategies and maintaining or adding to the most productive positions.

Managing a Thematically Diverse Portfolio

Managing a diversified portfolio of positions is a completely different exercise from constructing a book around one specific view of the market. Each position will be expected to stand on its own merits, and will have its own rationale, stop, target, etc. Diverse portfolios are generally only seen at speculative entities like hedge funds, money managers, and the proprietary desks of large financial institutions.

There is a significant difference between holding an assortment of carefully considered positions and trying to create a basket of intentionally uncorrelated exposures. An extreme example is a market-neutral portfolio, a strategy common in the fixed income markets, where the trader attempts to hedge out all of the directional risk via a calibrated set of long and short exposures leaving only the relative yield advantage of the securities. A trader constructing an uncorrelated portfolio cannot count on any central driver and must either rely on each trade proving out on its own merits or have an advantage in accumulating positions at favorable prices to create realizable value.

Correlation Is Causation

Regardless of thematic considerations, managing a portfolio of positions with a correlation component (so, pretty much every portfolio) demands constant vigilance. If the historical relationships begin to come unglued the trader can find himself quickly blowing through position limits and forced to close out of exposures. This is particularly dangerous for highly correlation-dependent portfolios that feature significant volumes of spread positions designed to exploit relatively fine differentials between instruments. The small performance delta is compensated for by supersizing the position, and if the correlation goes from 98% to 95%, what was a reasonably sized net delta position can explode, both in terms of utilized risk limits and observed P&L fluctuations.

With a thematically cohesive portfolio the risk is that the correlation degrades: that the basket of trades that are designed to work together (or in direct opposition, in the case of hedges) stop pulling in the same direction and start wandering around randomly.

A thematically diverse portfolio is the complete opposite, where the trader has presumably assembled a basket of positions that are designed to operate independently, the worst thing that can happen would be if they all did start acting in concert, which would likely immediately explode every risk limit governing the portfolio and, shortly thereafter, the P&L.[71]

Managing a Position at a Natural

Managing a position at a natural has a few interesting wrinkles not present anywhere else in the industry, one of which is, ironically, figuring out what position the trader is trying to

---

[71] This is more or less what actually happened in 2007-2009 to, well, everyone.

manage. A natural will have an organic risk that the trader will attempt to partially or totally mitigate with some volume of hedges. The hedges are correlated risk-reducing exposures, but will feel like a position in their own right. Management will worry about the financial performance of the hedges, badger the trader about the hedges, and generally forget that if the hedges are looking good the exposure that is an organic part of the firm's business is looking bad. Unless the firm is taking an extremely aggressive approach to placing, modifying, and lifting hedges as a value-creation exercise, most naturals would be better served letting their hedges be hedges.

Even for naturals who remember which is the hedge and which is the exposure, every position modification decision will involve significant amounts of management input, red tape, and hoops to jump through prior to taking action.

Managing a Position at a Financial
Banks are in the business of earning a margin on a stream of customer deal flow and optimizing the net position, which requires a decisive trader with elite execution skills. Due to the need to warehouse risk, banks and other financials will accumulate by far the largest, most complicated exposures that will need to be proactively managed.

Managing a Position at a Merchant
A merchant will tend to have a core position built on control of an asset or long-term transaction, around which the trader is expected to create value-capturing and opportunistic revenue-enhancing transactions. Unlike a bank trader who is expected to respond to the transactional caprices of clients, a merchant trader will tend to have exposures that persist, allowing a much better feel for the performance characteristics of the position and its nuances over time. A merchant trader will tend to be making small incremental tuning adjustments to a very large position, as opposed to partially or completely mitigating transactions on a case-by-case basis. A merchant trader will need to have elite physical execution skills to operate in early-stage physical markets where the consequences of sub-optimization can be extreme.

Managing a Position at a Speculator
Position management at a speculative entity will be a matter of dividing time between shared positions, firm-wide obligations, and the trader's individual book of business. A speculator should be operating with the fewest possible organizational constraints, but may face significant transactional challenges if lacking capital, access to credit, or counterparty diversity.

Chapter Fourteen Summary
The key to efficiently managing a position lies in understanding that everything changes. The trader will shift from clinically impartial observer to emotionally committed participant. The fundamental drivers and technical patterns will immediately begin to evolve, altering the initial risk/reward relationship and potentially triggering a modification to the trader's exposure(s). Managing a position is frequently more about managing oneself than the mechanics of monitoring a stop-loss, evaluating intraday gap risk, etc. Efficient position

management is an exercise in intellectual honesty, and the trader must see things as they are, not as the trader would have them be. If the trader is unable to process incremental information or unwilling to accept its implications for her exposures, there is little hope that she will be able to extract the maximum value.

Review Questions

1. Explain the effects of stress on the position management process, and what can be done to understand & mitigate its effects.
2. How does gap risk impact the trader's management of stops and profit targets?
3. What is trading around a trend, and why is it a constructive strategy?
4. What should the trader do when faced with a large losing position?
5. Describe how the evolution of the fundamental & technical thesis, risk environment, and risk/reward ratio impact a trader's decision to maintain an exposure.

Resources

- *Charlie D. The Story of the Legendary Bond Trader* by William D. Falloon
- *Reminiscences of a Stock Operator* by Edwin Lefèvre

Case Study: Managing Product X Positions & Portfolios

The Product X case study has been built around the assumption that the trader would develop a view of the market, then evaluate an array of alternatives before selecting the optimal implementation strategy. In reality, for most traders the end-state would not be a single perfect position. Real-world liquidity, sizing, and timing issues frequently force traders to assemble a basket of similar, individually sub-optimal positions designed to replicate a larger, more efficient exposure that is currently impossible to accumulate.

If, as is entirely likely, a trader cannot accumulate her desired exposure in long-dated par straddles and near-term call options in the ProdX market, then she may choose to construct a risk-equivalent thematically cohesive portfolio from the available alternatives. The trader would begin by accumulating volumes of the positions she can execute (directionally long MAR and/or OCT ProdX futures, long the AUG/JAN+1 time spread, long either the EurX/AfrX or EurX/ProdX basis spreads, etc.), then roll out of those positions and into the preferred option strategies as efficiently as the market allows.

15

Pricing & Hedging Structured Transactions

Structured Transactions
Structured transactions can be found at both ends of the sophistication spectrum: seemingly simple products that contain difficult-to-disentangle organic risks, or obviously complex synthetic structures. Organic structured transactions frequently originate from naturals, who bring the risks that they would like to shed to banks and other financial intermediaries for pricing, hedging, or outright sale. At first glance the exposures can appear simple, but may contain complex risks arising from the physical attributes of the customer's core business that could require a lengthy process of decomposition and pricing. Often there is no established methodology to value particularly esoteric products, with no historical data and no point of reference to use as a baseline. Naturals will also sell or lease the rights to entire facilities to merchants, particularly in early-stage markets, as they are the premiere optimizers of physical systems and have a real appetite for the exposures.

At the opposite end of the spectrum are structures born in a lab at a financial institution and intended for sale to customers as "risk management products." The rise of exotic derivative markets in the 1990s exponentially increased the level of complexity of the products on offer by ushering in the practice of creating and pricing highly customized solutions—often for problems end-users did not necessarily know they had. There is a price for everything, and in that intellectually adventurous and unfettered atmosphere risks were cut apart and sewn together in expensive and avant-garde combinations. The lack of standardization precluded evolved, well-vetted modeling, as practitioners could not justify the time to develop rigorous valuation methodologies for a product that may only ever trade once, if at all. The challenge for the prospective customer/victim of some of these esoteric products was the same one faced by the protagonist in every sci-fi movie who stumbles across the piece of bizarre alien technology: Who made it? What does it do? How does it work? What happens if I push the shiny, shiny red button?

A trader evaluating a structured transaction must attempt to re-model, reverse-engineer, or deconstruct and price the product based on the provided description or term sheet and his knowledge of the market space. The challenge is that the constructor almost invariably has superior information, greater familiarity with similar structures and their value, and better analytical resources. One unique aspect of structured transactions is that neither the buyer nor the seller generally has any interest in transacting near fair value, as each will want to build in a margin to protect from the risks he knows he cannot model and hedge. If the deal is worth X, the seller will only transact for X+ and buyer must buy for X- to allow room for sub-optimization, particularly for physical deals. Structured deals get done because the two counterparties have different information, different analytical and pricing capabilities, different forward projections, and different perceptions of value, all of which lead to different prices.

To handle all of this fancy deal flow a new species of hybrid employees called structurers evolved at both buying and selling institutions. A structurer has some of the commercial knowledge of the originators and traders combined with the analytical acumen of the quant and risk groups. The structuring group is tasked with examining complex deals, decomposing them into their component risks, routing each piece to a quant for valuation or a trader for pricing, then re-assembling the entire monster for presentation to the client or evaluation by management. In flowchart form the process looks like this:

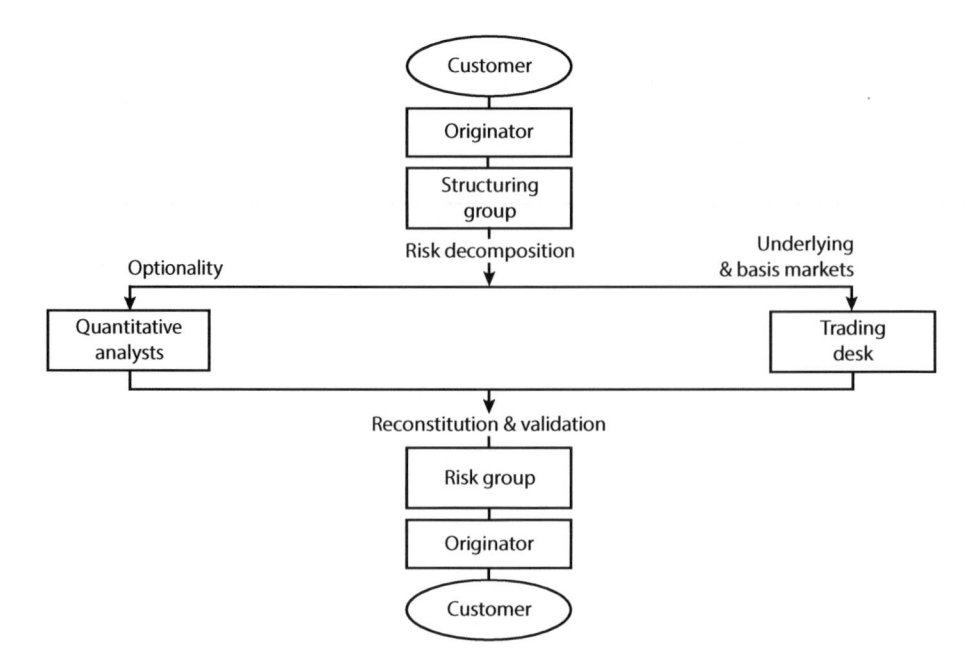

Figure 15.1 Flowchart of the origination and structuring process.

The process frequently starts with a conversation between a customer (generally a natural) and the originator that covers it for a bank or financial institution. Most complex, highly structured deals begin with a customer inquiry, either in the form of a Request for Quotation (RFQ) or Request for Proposal (RFP).

An RFQ is a straightforward request for a market in a particular product broadcast to a range of counterparties, either a select pre-screened group or the market as a whole via an electronic platform. A natural might issue an RFQ for a volume of flat price directional hedges to a small group of banks, for example. An RFQ would typically bypass the structuring desk and go directly to the trading desk for pricing and execution. An RFQ request is also a green light for a good originator to attempt to up-sell the client on a more sophisticated risk mitigation strategy.

An RFP is a request for pricing of a more complex transaction, often one that is structured around the operational properties and constraints of an actual physical asset or production facility that cannot be cleanly hedged with standard, readily available products. For example, a hedger might issue an RFP to buy a structure that would let it lock in a portion of the current margins around a metals processing facility while allowing it to participate in a percentage of the upside price appreciation of the end-use product.

Modeling a Deal
The originator will take his notes or the customer's RFP to the structuring desk to get a sense of the complexity of the valuation challenge, generally involving the trader with the most relevant experience. Evaluating proposals for structured transactions is a little like appraising the first cards dealt during a hand of poker. Most should be discarded immediately. Some are workable, and will usually be passed around for comment and possibly some light analysis to determine if there is anything worth doing. A rare few are clearly, unambiguously valuable and merit immediate attention and the expenditure of resources to evaluate and price.

If the proposal is interesting enough to price, the structuring group will begin to break it down into its component risks. For proposals similar to previously executed transactions, this can be a well-established exercise with the only minor wrinkles caused by the specific requirements of the customer. For truly novel pieces of business the structuring group will have to convene a small working group of analysts, a trader or two, and representatives from risk management in an attempt to intellectually crowd-source a solution to the problem. Typically the division of labor breaks down as:

- The structuring group will quarterback, making sure that it has the necessary information from each specialty and handling the more commercial modeling for the deal, including a framework for valuation that will source inputs from trading and quantitative analytics.
- The trader will source all market price, depth, and liquidity information, including live forward price quotes for futures, options, and spreads.
- The quant or analytics group will start to model the non-standard risks, which can require extensive simulation or the development of a valuation framework.

- The risk management group will ideally be present from the start to give the deal team insight into how the trade will be modeled in the deal capture system and the valuation challenges inherent in its mark to market. Very complex transactions that involve novel products and price locations may require the risk group to design new templates within the system to accurately model the nuances of the transaction.
- The credit and collateral group will have to compute the estimated funding requirements for booking the transaction and the associated hedges. The deal team will have to take this cost into consideration when pricing the transaction.
- Management will be brought in on any large, novel, or P&L impacting transactions, as they will ultimately have to approve the deal and its pricing before it is shipped to the client, and may have to proactively obtain approvals from senior management for any unusual risks or novel products/instruments inherent in the transaction.

The Trader's Contribution – Pricing, Depth, and Availability of Products

Once the deal is broken down into component pieces, they will be shipped across to the trading group for pricing, either directly out of the market or via analogs to similar products. Frequently, traders will be expected to make markets in uncommon products or particularly illiquid securities. The implicit and sometimes explicit assumption is that the traders should be willing to take the exposure onto their books at the price they are quoting.

The trader will also be expected to advise the structuring group on the depth of the market to calibrate the assumptions of how much slippage and execution risk to build into the pricing. This is relevant on both an initial hedge basis (what will it cost to place a volume of hedges on Day 1) and as an ongoing optimization exercise (what will it cost going forward doing optimization-related transactions).

The trader will also comment on the reasonableness of the transaction assumptions built into the valuation and the associated hedge plan. It may be possible, given normal levels of liquidity, to expect to execute a large volume of option hedges at the benchmark product in the market. The quant group may utilize that benchmark option price to derive the price of a similar option in the market most applicable to hedging the transaction. It is the trader's job to inform the quant and structuring group that, while its valuation makes intuitive sense, it does not guarantee that there will be counterparties willing to transact in the local market for any size, let alone the volume needed at the price imputed by its calculations.

Traders with an affinity for structured customer business become expert at understanding value differentials between standard benchmark products and illiquid, non-standard instruments, and develop a level of comfort compensating for uncertainly with price adjustments. The trader will start with what she knows and can observe, the product closest in performance to the puzzle piece she is trying to replicate, and then incrementally add or subtract value based on the characteristics of the product she is trying to simulate. When in doubt, the trader will err on the side of caution, as building in too much margin and missing the deal is preferable to building in too little and booking a loser.

Chapter 15 - Pricing & Hedging Structured Transactions

Embedded Options

The trading group and the structuring group will both evaluate the transaction to ensure that all of the embedded optionality is discovered and accounted for. There are several varieties of embedded optionality.

There is straightforward economic optionality, where if a price or volume reaches an established threshold the holder of the option can exercise and modify the conditions of the deal as specified in the contract. This acts like a vanilla put or call submerged in the contractual language of the deal.

For example: A coal producer agrees to sell a power generator 1 million tons of coal at the prevailing price of $100 per ton, with contract language that increases the total size delivered to 2 million tons if the price drops to $95 prior to the start of delivery. It is relatively easy to see that this transaction is actually a 1M-ton sale with an associated 1M-ton $95 strike put option sold back to the coal producer by the power generator. The put is fairly straightforward to price, the only question being whether the power generator correctly valued the option and seeks an equivalent discount to the cost of entering into the contract.

Non-economic options can be highly difficult to recognize and all but impossible to model, particularly those having to do with operational and reliability characteristics of a physical asset. A need to bring a production facility down for maintenance will certainly impact a deal predicated on its ability to generate output, but at the same time may not be driven by or correlated with any particular economic signal.[72] A driveshaft or furnace does not consider the marginal cost of the output of the facility before snapping or tripping offline.

Once the deal team has identified all of the optionality present in the deal, there is the minor problem of figuring out how to model and price it. Recall the exploration of the standard Black-Scholes model in Chapter 10 and its many inherent structural limitations. While it is possible to bend the rules slightly and achieve reasonable results for plain vanilla calls and puts, most of the non-standard characteristics of a complex physical option would invalidate the underlying economic underpinnings of the model.

As a result, risk managers and high-level quants will assemble a collection of specialized options models to choose the most applicable tool to price the risk inherent in the transaction.[73] "Most applicable" is the key term, as some of the types of organic optionality commonly found in structured transactions cannot neatly be modeled by anything, forcing the firm to go with the closest thing in the arsenal and attempt to understand and live with the discrepancies, or to home brew a solution. Neither is optimal, and traders and managers will often have to spend significant time laying siege to Castle Math deep in the non-Euclidian

---

[72] Some maintenance decisions in certain industries are definitely driven by economics, which can make the calculus even more challenging.

[73] There are a lot of different option models. Once the trader moves past the well-understood general solutions like Black-Scholes, binomial models, or Monte Carlo simulations things tend to get very product and circumstance specific.

forests of Quantsylvania in an attempt to decide whether they would prefer to go with something they know is slightly wrong (but hopefully only slightly) or something that could be completely right or completely wrong.

Recall the discussion of multiple internal valuation methodologies from Chapter 10; it is possible for different groups to value an option with different models and arrive at a completely different answer. This is extremely common with structured deals, and is another reason to have good coordination between structuring, the quantitative analysts, and risk from the beginning. The people doing the commercial valuation must know how the deal will be booked and how the risk group will generate valuation and issue P&L reports on the exposure. The risk group is beholden to approved modeling methodologies and the trading system of record (and whatever engine it uses), in contrast to the more intellectually unfettered commercial groups. Traders may feel that an option is too cheap based on gut instinct, and quant/structuring may agree based on a cutting-edge model or something of its own creation, but if risk is only approved to use Black-Scholes or a binomial tree, neither of which is designed for the product in question, there will be severe internal valuation problems.

Deal Mispricing Errors
Complex structured deals are difficult to creatively envision, challenging to construct and price, and incredibly difficult to evaluate and trade. While there are myriad opportunities for errors, mistakes, and misinterpretations that can materially affect the price of the deal, there are several common types of problems:

1. Being unable to correctly price the transaction.
2. Failing to understand fundamental nuance(s).
3. Getting too greedy on pricing.
4. Missing something.

1. Being Unable to Correctly Price the Transaction
Specialist knowledge of esoteric risks inherent in a structured transaction gives an expert practitioner an enormous advantage over a less-sophisticated participant. The informational advantage becomes nearly infinite when one counterparty designed the instrument in question, or built and operates the asset offered for sale. It is entirely possible for the customer to know significantly more about a market space in general and a specific transaction in particular than the banker or merchant on the other end of the telephone.

2. Failure to Understand Fundamental Nuance(s)
For physical deals with large amounts of embedded optionality and non-standard performance and delivery characteristics, knowing the minutiae of the marketplace becomes critical. While an initial rough-cut valuation can make any number of simplifying assumptions, at some point prior to the final pricing the specific parameters need to be quantified and taken into consideration. A small mispricing on one variable may not be material, but being systematically off on several can be devastating. Much more damaging are situations where a firm inadvertently promises something it is not capable of delivering, or

agrees to accept delivery only to find that it is not logistically or contractually able. Buying back out of an impossible transaction can be extremely punitive.

3. Getting Too Greedy on Pricing
There is some real artifice involved in pricing some of the esoteric sub-risks in a structured transaction, because if the firm tries to go completely rich across the board, it will end up with a bombproof structure that it can't possibly lose on, and be laughed out of the client's office. A radical mispricing can also occur as a result of a poorly coordinated process at a firm with P&L silos for both the trading and origination desks, where each party independently builds in a margin for its own book, the combination of which makes the product non-competitive relative to the customer's alternatives.

Conversely, if the firm gets too aggressive it is likely to book insufficient margin to pay for all of the very real risks assumed in the transaction. A bank, merchant, or other financial intermediary should get paid something for assuming risks the client wants to off-load. Warehousing risk and providing liquidity are valuable services. Firms that do a lot of structured business and profit by it tend to have a very good handle on certain aspects of the risk equation (or a natural ability to mitigate them) and can build in some needed margin on the parts they do not understand or cannot easily hedge.

4. Missing Something
This is the one that keeps traders, originators, structurers, quants, and managers – especially managers – up late at night: the potential to have overlooked some critical detail in the valuation or the mechanics of the underlying transaction that could have massive price or operational (which ultimately lead to price) implications.

Booking the Deal
While the decomposition and component pricing of structure was a collaborative effort between structuring, trading, and the quant and risk groups, the construction of the transaction model in the deal capture system is entirely up to the risk group. No commercial function will have input, and whatever limitations exist in terms of system sophistication, applicable models, or data quality will be impossible to avoid or overrule. The representation of the structure in the deal capture system is critical, as it will generate the informational outputs that the risk group will use to monitor and report on the transaction. This is one of the primary reasons to invite risk to the party in the first place, as the commercial group must have a sense of how the risk model of the structure is going to perform relative to the commercial reality of the transaction.

If the deal is sufficiently novel or dauntingly complex it may require an extremely creative implementation in the trade capture system. If the firm is using an industry-standard, off-the-shelf risk management system, chances are that it has already had development work done to accommodate the same or similar product, making the challenge adaptation of an existing template instead of wholesale creation.[74]

Managing the Deal
When the deal is done and the risk group has booked the transaction, the position will be formally handed off to the trading desk for hedging and value extraction.

Hedging Methodology
To hedge the transaction the trader will work through the risk list, first layering in directional exposures to achieve a basic neutralization of the exposure, then circling back to eliminate secondary and tertiary risk elements as quickly and efficiently as market conditions allow. Unless the transaction was very straightforward or the firm was able to close the deal with a large amount of baked-in value, the trader will very likely not be able to afford to hedge out all of the component risks without paying away most or all of the margin. Once the trader has stabilized the position to the best of her ability, she will turn to the more challenging issue of how to extract the remaining value in the transaction.

Post-Hedging Value Extraction
Once the transaction has been hedged into whatever configuration the firm is comfortable with, the trader will then have to extract the remaining value, which can occur in a number of ways:

1. Work out of the exposure with maximum efficiency as market conditions allow, shedding hedges as needed along the way.
2. Manage the exposure as part of a portfolio designed to reflect the trader's view of the market.
3. Extraction of operational value for physically based deals. Can also be outsourced to a specialist firm for entities without physical expertise.

In each case the firm will be trying to wring the maximum value out of the transaction, the difference being the method used to do so.

Working out of the Exposure
Some firms prefer to maintain a relatively clean book, rolling positions and hedges through as quickly and efficiently as possible, seeking the surety of locking in smaller margins rather than holding an exposure and betting on it achieving its full valuation potential.

---

[74] Most software firms that build, maintain, and charge exorbitant amounts for risk management systems are generally fairly good about making sure that novel system modifications designed in response to one client's needs ultimately filter out to the general user base. Some do not, however, forcing the client to hire an even more expensive deal implementation SWAT team (at rates that would make a Ferrari mechanic blush) to get the transaction modeled and booked.

Chapter 15 - Pricing & Hedging Structured Transactions

Managing the Position as Part of a Portfolio
If the trader's firm does a significant volume of customer business, the incremental transaction and its hedges will likely be aggregated with the other positions when booked into the risk system. The trader can then focus on understanding the performance characteristics of the now re-made portfolio, seeking to modify it to align with their overarching view of the market. Firms with a propensity to retain and manage positions tend to grow very large, complicated exposures that require a great deal of finagling to remain profitable. In this case the profitability of a specific transaction becomes something of a moot point, with the overall P&L of the book over time being the primary consideration.

Extracting Operational Value
Firms skilled in physical transactions may elect to hold the hedged exposure to delivery, trusting in their superior operational acumen to wring the last bits of value out of the position. Large, skilled operational groups are a luxury not available to all firms, and many smaller or purely financial players will subcontract this service from a niche industry participant.

As a practical example, consider a deal that was extremely common in the energy space in the late 1990s, a natural issuing an RFP to sell contractual control of one of its generating plants for a multi-year forward term.

Example – Complex Physical Energy Deal

Request For Proposal (RFP)
A Power Company (PowerCo) requests proposals for the physical tolling of one of its three 500MW gas-fired generating units. "Tolling" a plant is the process of delivering fuel to the facility and taking the electricity generated for sale into the market. Tolling deals were extremely popular in the early-to-middle development stages of the US electricity markets. The details of the proposed transaction are:

Unit:	PowerCo Unit Number 1
Capacity:	500MW peak output
Gas-to-Power Ratio:	Deliver 7 units of natural gas to receive 1 unit of power.
Type of Service:	Unit-contingent physical power
Electrical Receipt Point:	Station grid interconnection point.
Gas Delivery Point:	Facility interconnection off GasCo lateral pipeline.
Term of Deal:	3 Years

PowerCo will evaluate tendered offers with the goal of entering into contractual negotiations with the winning party no later than the month prior to commencement.

The Seller's Perspective – Why PowerCo Would Execute This Transaction
From PowerCo's perspective, this is a very straightforward transaction. It owns a power plant that it would like to opportunistically remove from its portfolio for a period of three years. It

would like to know what the market is willing to pay for the right to operate the facility, earn whatever profits there are to be earned, and hand back the keys at the end of the third year. There are a number of potential reasons why PowerCo would consider the transaction:

- It is highly probable that PowerCo has a figure in mind that it believes it can extract from the asset based on its analysis of the market and understanding of its operational characteristics, beyond which it would be quite happy to lock in a riskless result.
- PowerCo could also be looking to sell because it fears that the spread between power and natural gas will contract, reducing profit margins.
- The owner may feel that the market will experience reduced volatility, which will decrease the value of the long spread option that underlies the value of the plant.
- PowerCo may need to secure financing, and locking in a portion of its cash flows will make the company as a whole more stable, lowering the cost of funding.

In many cases, the owner does not really intend to enter into a transaction. RFPs are often circulated to help the owner establish the current value of a particular asset, sometimes to validate internal valuations or to aid in obtaining financing for the project in specific or the entity as a whole.

The Buyer's Perspective – Evaluating the PowerCo RFP

The first question for any trader contemplating an RFP is what does the customer know that the buyer does not? Why is the owner and most knowledgeable entity about the facility trying to off-load it for the next three years? A good originator will know the customer, understand its core business and motivations, and be able to provide some context for the RFP for the members of the trading desk.

Once the buyer has determined that the proposed transaction is worth evaluating, it must break it down into its component risks. Tolling transactions have a lot of optionality inherent in their structure. In the simplest sense, a power plant is a spread option on the cost of fuel inputs that the trader must purchase and deliver relative to the price of the power output that it will receive and sell. The strike price of the option is the ratio at which it converts fuel into power. In the case of the PowerCo transaction, the facility will burn 7 units of gas to generate 1 unit of power. That 7:1 ratio means that delivering $3.00 gas would produce $21.00 power, $4.00 gas would equal $28.00 power, and so on. The actual PowerCo power plant will have a host of other operational costs to consider, but the purchaser of the RFP is not being exposed to them in this contractual agreement, which is good from both a deal-modeling and risk-management perspective. There are plenty of other risks to quantify and manage.

Valuation Challenges

The primary valuation challenge lies in correctly valuing the spread option between the natural gas inputs and the power outputs. To do that, the trader will need to use a spread or cross-commodity model, which will use as its main inputs:

- The forward price of the fuel that the counterparty must supply to the plant.
- The forward price of the power that the counterparty will receive from the facility and sell into the market.

Chapter 15 - Pricing & Hedging Structured Transactions

- The volatility of each product.
- The correlation between the two products.
- The cost of carry of each product.
- The prevailing interest rate.

The primary value drivers are the forward prices, the forward volatilities, and the correlation between products, with the cost of carry and the prevailing interest rate having a lesser effect on the ultimate price of the option.

The PowerCo plant is geographically situated between local markets for natural gas and power and remote financial hubs that offer access to liquidity and pricing visibility, yielding six possible price points for the trader to use to evaluate the transaction:

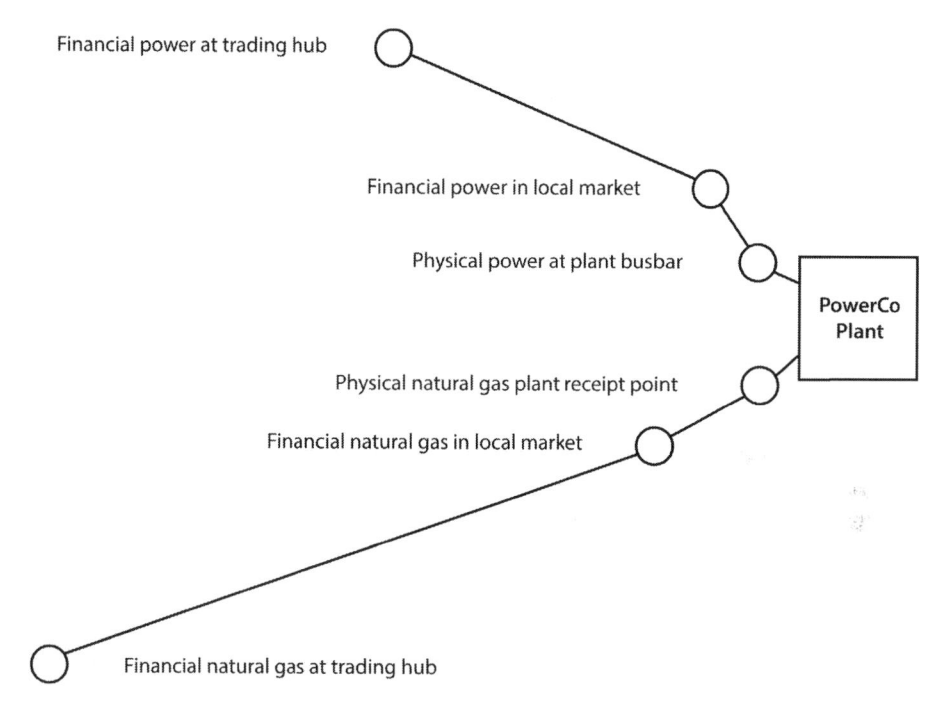

Figure 15.2 The six price points available to price and hedge the PowerCo deal.

The trader will have to decide what power and gas products to use to model the deal, which would normally be done in one of three ways:

1. Financial gas at the hub vs. financial power at the hub.
2. Financial gas in the local market vs. financial power in the local market.
3. Local-market physical gas vs. local-market physical power.

Financial Gas at Hub vs. Financial Power at Hub

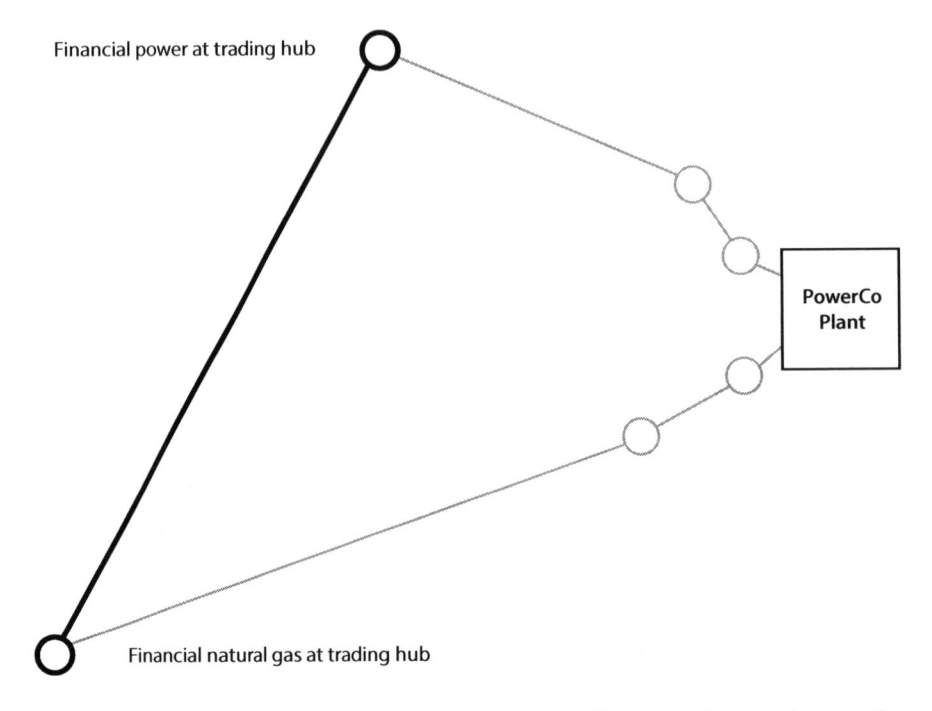

Figure 15.3 Pricing the PowerCo deal as a spread between financial gas and power.

Using these price points would allow for the best estimation of the underlying price of each leg, the historical volatilities, and the correlation between them. The trader will also be able to observe the implied volatilities of any traded options, which can be plugged directly into the valuation model.

The financial hub markets will have the highest liquidity and the lowest bid/offer spreads present in the market, allowing the trader to be extremely accurate about pricing of the transaction. Comparing the benchmark hub natural gas forwards against the observed power prices yields the following valuation:

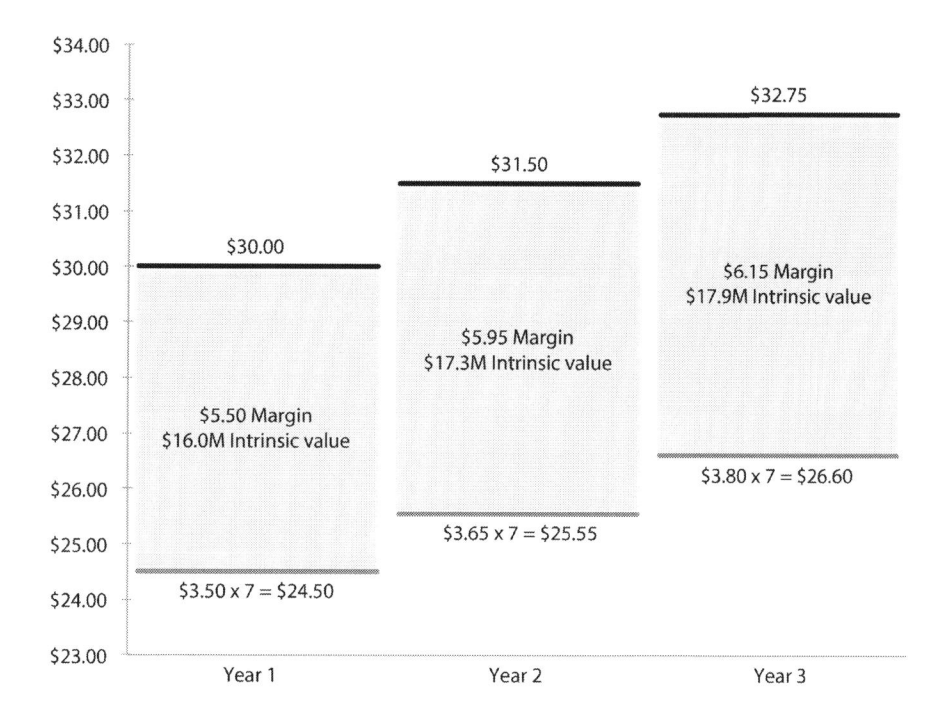

Chapter 15 - Pricing & Hedging Structured Transactions

Figure 15.4 Calculating the intrinsic margin of the PowerCo deal based on point estimates of financial gas and power prices.

The spread between the scaled fuel inputs and the power outputs creates a significant positive margin in each year of the deal, and a simplistic calculation of the intrinsic value of the transaction shows that there is at least $51M of value to be captured without taking into consideration any extrinsic option value. To obtain the full value of the transaction, the trader must take the forward prices, the observed implied volatilities for each product, and the correlation between the two and plug them into a spread option model:

	Year 1	Year 2	Year 3	Total
Power price	$30.00	$31.50	$32.75	
Implied natural gas price	$24.50	$25.55	$26.60	
Power volatility	60%	55%	49%	
Natural gas volatility	51%	47%	44%	
NG/Power correlation	0.85	0.85	0.85	
Option value	$6.84	$8.19	$8.89	
Total premium	$19,972,800	$23,914,800	$25,958,800	$69,846,400
Intrinsic value of spread	$16,060,000	$17,374,000	$17,958,000	$51,392,000

Table 15.1 Valuing the spread option between financial gas and power.

The option model values the spread option at $19.9M in Year 1, $23.9M in Year 2 and $25.96M in Year 3, for a total of $69.85M.

The primary challenge is that the result does not realistically depict the economic conditions that the plant, and therefore the tolling deal, is exposed to. Using the hub prices allows the trader to be extremely precise about an extremely imprecise model of the deal economics.

Financial Gas in Local Market vs. Financial Power in Local Market

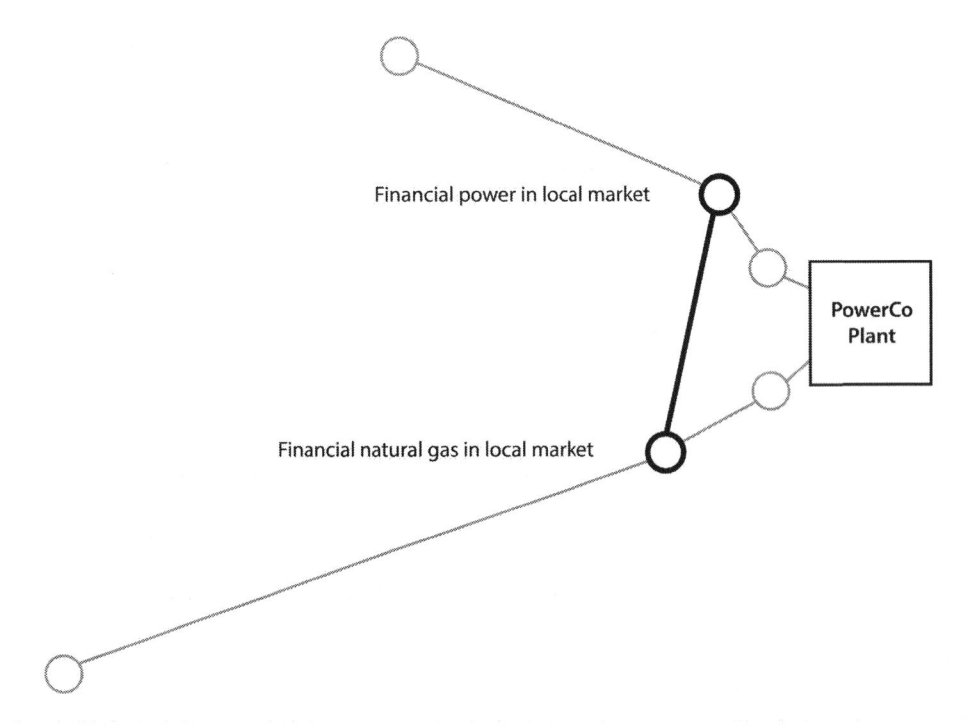

Figure 15.5   Pricing the PowerCo deal as a spread between local market financial gas and power.

The local financial markets are more operationally similar to the plant's gas pickup and power drop-off points, and have a limited amount of forward price visibility to allow for estimation of the volatilities and correlations.

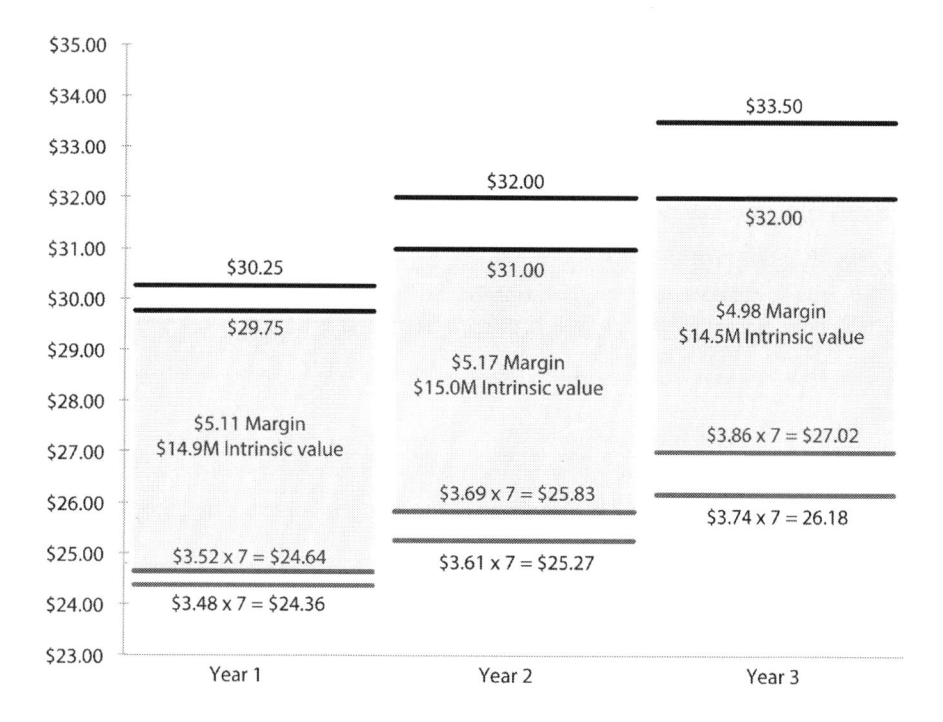

Chapter 15 - Pricing & Hedging Structured Transactions

Figure 15.6 Calculating the intrinsic margin of the PowerCo deal based on the market bid/offer spreads for financial gas and power.

The primary difference between the benchmark prices at the hub markets and the local financial markets is the greater deal of uncertainty about the prevailing forward prices. Instead of a known value, the trader will have a range bounded by either the observable data points of a market-maker's indicative spread or the trader's own sense of fair value relative to the hub market. At the local market surrounding the PowerCo plant the forward natural gas has bid/offer spreads starting at $0.04 that widen out to $0.12 for the third year, with estimated power price ranges of $0.50 for Year 1, $1.00 for Year 2, and $1.50 for Year 3. Taking a conservative valuation using the cheapest power prices against the most expensive gas prices yields the following intrinsic spreads and option valuations:

	Year 1	Year 2	Year 3	Total
Power price	$29.75	$31.00	$32.00	
Implied natural gas price	$24.64	$25.83	$27.02	
Power volatility	60%	55%	49%	
Natural gas volatility	51%	47%	44%	
NG/Power correlation	0.85	0.85	0.85	
Option value	$6.55	$7.64	$8.09	
Total premium	$19,126,000	$22,308,800	$23,622,800	$65,057,600
Intrinsic value of spread	$14,921,200	$15,096,400	$14,541,600	$44,559,200

Table 15.2 Valuing the spread option between local market financial gas and power using the gas offer and power bid, resulting in the lowest valuation.

Using the highest fuel price and lowest power price minimizes the value of the plant. To estimate the maximum reasonable valuation the trader can price the spread option with the cheapest natural gas and the most expensive power, yielding a significantly higher deal valuation:

	Year 1	Year 2	Year 3	Total
Power price	$30.25	$32.00	$33.50	
Implied natural gas price	$24.36	$25.27	$26.18	
Power volatility	60%	55%	49%	
Natural gas volatility	51%	47%	44%	
NG/Power correlation	0.85	0.85	0.85	
Option value	$7.14	$8.75	$9.72	
Total premium	$20,848,800	$25,550,000	$28,382,400	$74,781,200
Intrinsic value of spread	$17,198,800	$19,651,600	$21,374,400	$58,224,800

Table 15.3 Valuing the spread option between local market financial gas and power using the gas bid and power offer, resulting in the highest valuation.

The uncertainty around the forward prices of gas and power at the local market combine to create a potential valuation range of $65.05M to $74.78M for the PowerCo deal.

In both the best- and worst-case scenarios at the local market the volatilities and correlations have been kept constant and at the same levels as the financial trading hub. Ultimately, the trader will have to make inferences as to the implied volatilities and the correlation, scaling the observations from the hub markets up or down as needed, which will have additional valuation impacts.

Chapter 15 - Pricing & Hedging Structured Transactions

Physical Natural Gas at Plant vs. Physical Power at Plant

Physical power at plant busbar

PowerCo Plant

Physical natural gas plant receipt point

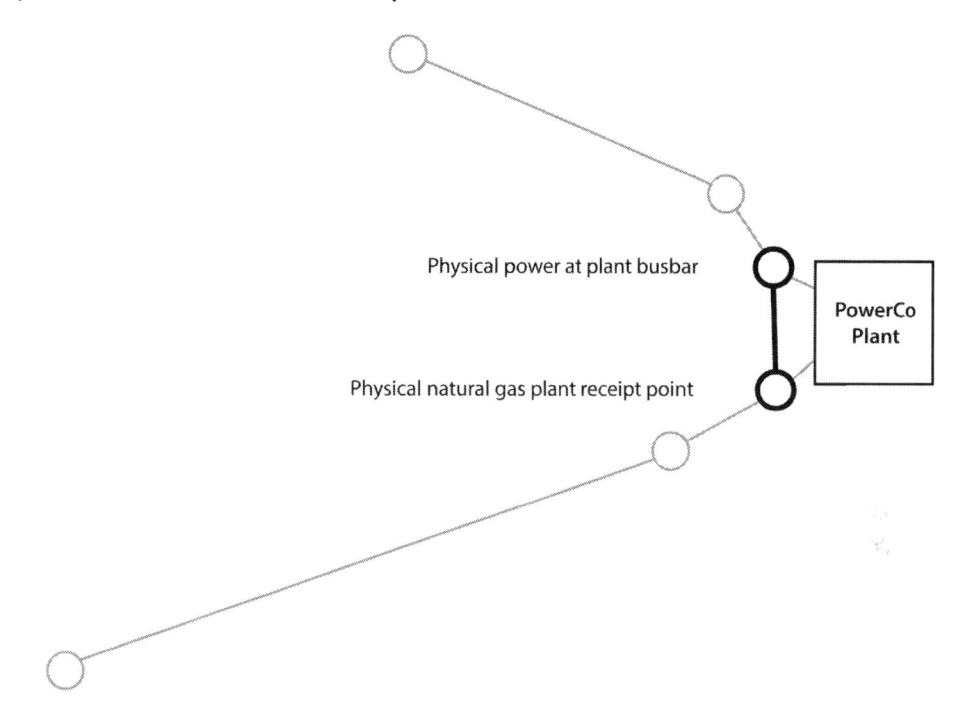

Figure 15.7   Pricing the PowerCo deal as a spread between physical gas & power.

This is the truest representation of the economic reality of the tolling deal, but will prove incredibly hard to value, as the forward underlying prices will be based on extremely wide two-way quotations, making the marks sub-optimal and the resultant volatilities and correlations suspect.

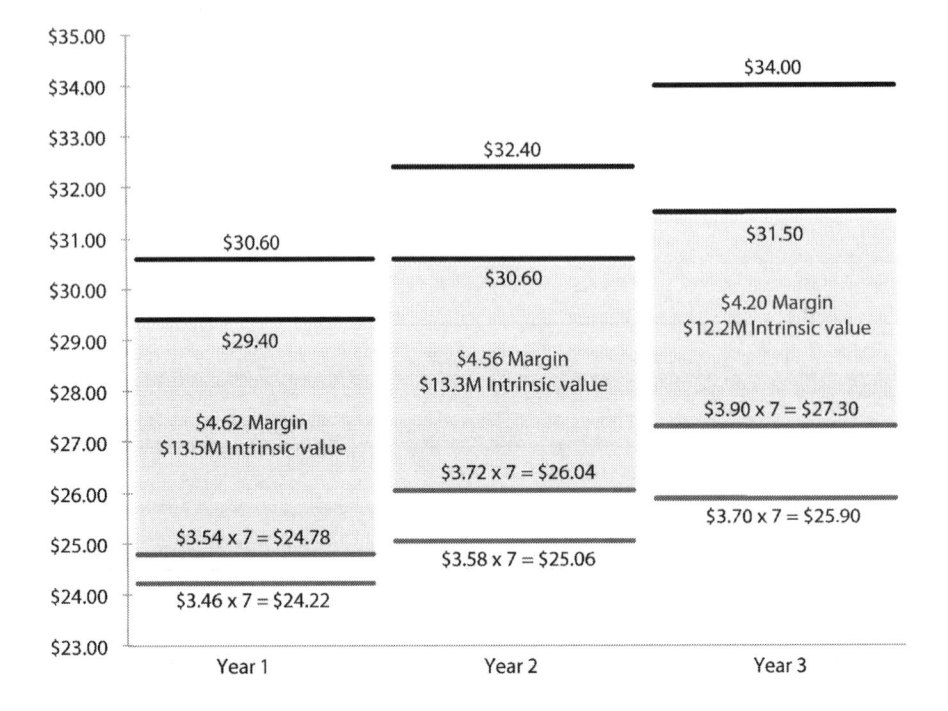

Figure 15.8 Calculating the intrinsic margin of the PowerCo deal based on the market bid/offer spreads for physical gas and power.

	Year 1	Year 2	Year 3	Total
Power price	$29.40	$30.60	$31.50	
Implied natural gas price	$24.78	$26.04	$27.30	
Power volatility	60%	55%	49%	
Natural gas volatility	51%	47%	44%	
NG/Power correlation	0.85	0.85	0.85	
Option value	$6.19	$7.22	$7.58	
Total premium	$18,074,800	$21,082,400	$22,133,600	$61,290,800
Intrinsic value of spread	$13,490,400	$13,315,200	$12,264,000	$39,069,600

Table 15.4 Valuing the spread option between physical gas and power using the gas offer and power bid, resulting in the lowest valuation.

Chapter 15 - Pricing & Hedging Structured Transactions

	Year 1	Year 2	Year 3	Total
Power price	$30.60	$32.40	$34.00	
Implied natural gas price	$24.22	$25.06	$25.90	
Power volatility	60%	55%	49%	
Natural gas volatility	51%	47%	44%	
NG/Power correlation	0.85	0.85	0.85	
Option value	$7.52	$9.20	$10.29	
Total premium	$21,958,400	$26,864,000	$30,046,800	$78,869,200
Intrinsic value of spread	$18,629,600	$21,432,800	$23,652,000	$63,714,400

Table 15.5 Valuing the spread option between physical gas and power using the gas bid and power offer, resulting in the highest valuation.

As was the case with the local market pricing, uncertainty around the forward prices of gas and power at the plant combine to create an even wider potential valuation range of $61.29M to $78.86M for the PowerCo deal.

The trader will again have to infer the implied volatility, this time from the prior estimate from the basis market.

Regardless of the modeling convention the trader choses to adopt, to arrive at the forward prices for gas and power, forward implied volatilities for gas and power, and the correlation between gas and power to plug into the pricing model, the trader will have to make a number of modifications to the initial observations and inferences:

- The physical natural gas that the plant consumes is subject to delivery constraint, and the trader may need to consider buying "firm" service to ensure supply during periods of stress, which will be more expensive.
- The power generated by the facility is unit contingent, meaning that if the plant is not able to operate, there will be no power for the trader to sell into the market and no financial recourse. Unit-contingent power is less valuable than firm power or power with financial liquidated damages, so the trader will need to discount the price of their forward power before plugging it into the model.
- The trader will be observing market-implied volatilities based on forward power contracts, most likely calendar strips, which give the trader the right to buy and sell the entire year as a package on one expiration date. The actual power plant operates on a daily basis, effectively acting like a strip of 365 individual options, giving the trader far more opportunities to capture market events and, consequently, commanding a significantly higher implied volatility. The trader will have to take observations at the hub or imputations of the basis or local market implied volatility and re-scale them higher to account for the extra value.

The extra cost of gas and the decreased value of the power output will narrow the spread between inputs and outputs and reduce the modeled value of the plant. Using a daily implied volatility instead of a one-time volatility for a calendar strip will increase the modeled value of the plant.

The trader's unique valuation assumptions will have a meaningful impact on the ultimate price of the spread option, and therefore the value of the PowerCo RFP.

The buyer's preference for modeling the deal will be influenced by its capabilities and plan for extracting value from the plant. The trader and originator must always be mindful of ways to extract additional value in the forward markets prior to the delivery or during the operational period. If the transaction in question is a purely financial construct, there may be limited opportunities to creatively optimize, or they may take entirely different forms than would be expected with a purely physical asset. It is simpler to transact financially and easier to settle financially, but this simplicity comes at the cost of a reduced potential for creativity.

The seller will almost certainly be valuing the plant at its full physical capability, as it has full operational control, but may not be correctly incorporating forward volatilities into the analysis.

Identifying the Risks Inherent in the Transaction
In any complex transaction the first goal is to understand and correctly value the inherent risks in the transaction.

1. Reliability Risk – The trader will own the rights to a physical, unit-contingent plant, against which they will place a package of financial hedges. If the plant is not able to run, the firm will be long financial gas hedges and short financial power hedges, but unable to convert physical gas to physical power to offset them and earn a margin.
2. Basis Risk – Depending on how the firm decides to hedge the transaction, there could be several possible permutations of forward basis risk between traded gas hedges and the plant, as well as forward basis risk between traded power hedges and the plant.
3. Cash-flow Risk – The trader will owe variance margin on the hedge positions at the close of business each day, but will not pay for the gas and be paid for the power generated until after the fact, possibly several months later, depending on the settlement and billing process. This discrepancy between payments, called the Hedger's Dilemma and initially discussed in Chapter 6, could potentially be disastrous in periods of high prices and volatility.

Sometimes, after carefully considering and pricing all of the inherent risks, a potential buyer simply can't afford do the deal. Much more commonly, the firm can't be competitive on price due to an inability to mitigate some physical constraint, an internal accounting issue (mark-to-market accounting instead of hedge accounting, for example), or an inability to compete on cost of capital, particularly if the treasury department of the firm charges the business unit a high internal interest rate.

Chapter 15 - Pricing & Hedging Structured Transactions

Risk Mitigation Plan

A firm that intends to physically optimize the PowerCo plant may be unable to find ready buyers of forward-delivered, unit-contingent power and sellers of delivered physical natural gas on the day it closes the transaction and assumes responsibility for the risk. The firm may choose to place a volume of hedges at the most liquid points, then roll the exposures closer to the desired delivered products as market conditions allow, as seen in the following diagram:

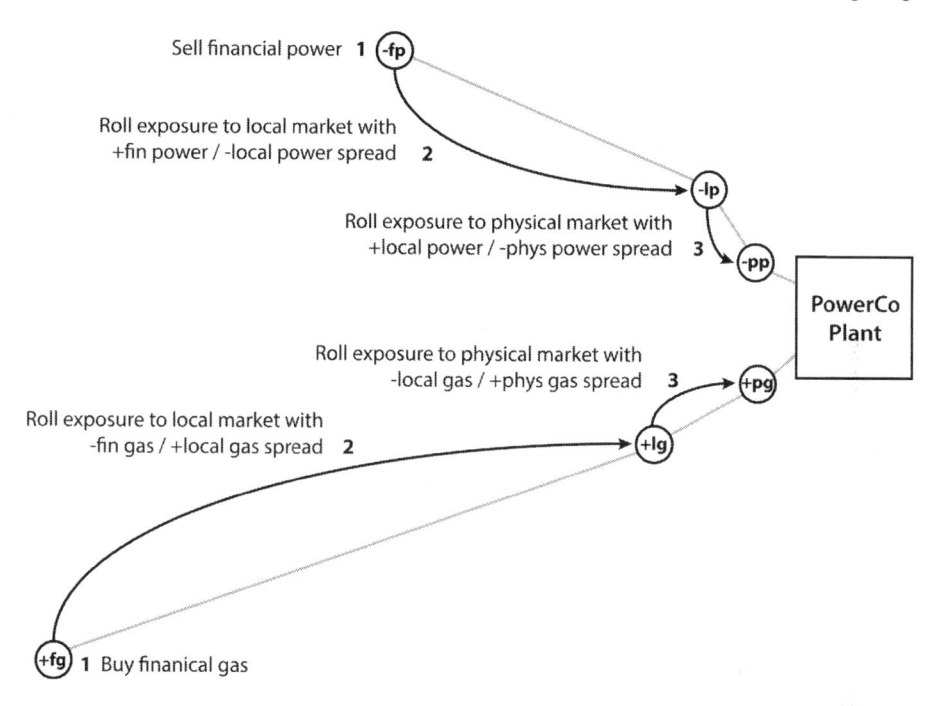

Figure 15.9   Rolling financial hedges at the trading hubs into physical hedges at the PowerCo plant.

The firm would start by (1) purchasing financial gas and selling financial power at a 7:1 ratio for a three-year forward term, possibly executing the transaction as a spread trade. The firm would then opportunistically buy the fin power/local power spread and sell the fin gas/local gas spread (2). Once the hedge position had been reconfigured into a short local power/long local gas spread, the trader would again seek to roll the exposure, buying local power/physical power spreads and selling local gas/physical gas spreads as market conditions allowed (3). The end result is a package of hedges that closely match the plant exposures.

Extracting Value from the PowerCo Transaction

The PowerCo transaction has a non-trivial amount of extrinsic value due to the optionality inherent in the transaction, measured at $18.45M in the hub market analysis, between $16.56-$20.49M in the local market, and $15.15-$22.22M at the plant delivery points. This value would be forgone if the trader were to lock in a hedge position around the plant and ride it until settlement. Unless the trader is able to buy below intrinsic value, which is highly unlikely, he will have to find a way to extract value from the optionality inherent in the position to earn a profit on investment. The means of value extraction will vary with the type of industry participant.

The PowerCo Deal for a Natural
Acquiring or divesting contractual control of a generating station is a bread-and-butter transaction for a natural, and might be something it might be negotiating from either the buy or sell side with various counterparties on an almost ongoing basis. The PowerCo RFP is being offered to the market by a natural, and may be of interest to other generation owners in the space, depending on the size and composition of their asset portfolios.

A natural's understanding of the mechanics of the optionality inherent in the transaction will probably be less sophisticated than that of a financial, merchant, or speculator, but its knowledge of the physical market and the plant's operational characteristics would be far more advanced. Accordingly, it would be much more likely to incorrectly price the transaction, but have a definite edge in extracting value from the operation of the asset.

A natural's value-extraction and optimization plan would almost certainly be built around physical operation of the plant, either as a stand-alone asset or folded into a portfolio of other generating stations. It would most likely hedge with a package of hub futures obtained from a bank or other financial player and live with the basis risk to the plant until delivery, when it would remove the hedges in the cash market and open up the plant into a long spread option in an attempt to capture the maximum potential volatility. This strategy amounts to a bet that cash volatility will be higher than the forward implied volatility of the spread option of the plant, after accounting for basis risk and hedging costs.

The PowerCo Deal for a Financial
A bank or financial player would see a continuous stream of deals like the PowerCo RFP from generation-owning clients in the energy space.

A bank might manage the financial risks, sub-contract the operation to a third-party for a fee and hope that it prices in enough to cover the physical risks. Bigger firms that are committed to the space may have built out a physical presence, with an operations and scheduling desk to support complex transactions. Doing so would be expensive, but would provide a significant advantage in executing on more complex transactions and providing experience-based pricing information.

A financial would be more inclined to employ its superior execution skills to roll the position from the hub market into the local market to mitigate the forward basis risk.

The PowerCo Deal for a Merchant
Merchants would be interested in the PowerCo deal for several reasons. It gives them productive control of a physical asset, which they can use to play the natural gas, power, and spread markets. A merchant can also fold the deal into its existing portfolio, which could

Chapter 15 - Pricing & Hedging Structured Transactions

include gas off take/production deals, or transactions that may involve an electricity short like a metals processing plant or other industrial concern.

A merchant would have a variety of ways to extract value from the PowerCo RFP, depending on its aggression level and current portfolio, and would place value on flexibility and the ability to re-configure the exposure to match its view of the market.

A merchant with a portfolio of other assets would be able to co-optimize the plant. Delivering gas to the facility and taking the power output are risks that a bank or hedge fund would need to quantify and manage. For a merchant that controls a natural gas storage facility and operates a scrap metal facility with an electric arc furnace, those risks become opportunities to extract value across the entire value chain:

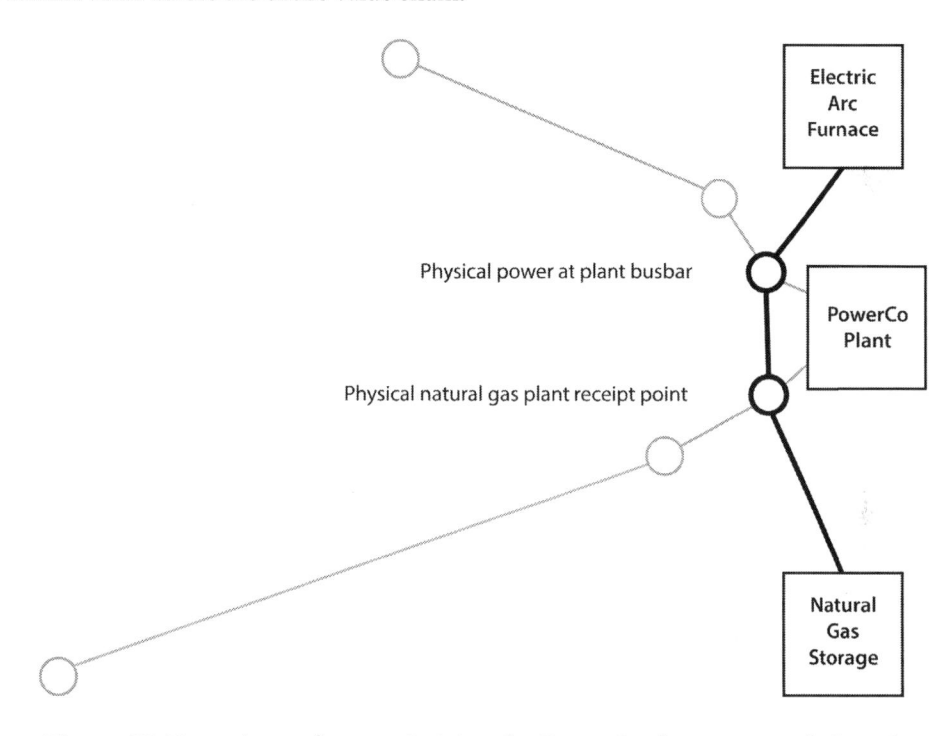

Figure 15.10 A merchant optimizing the PowerCo plant as part of a broader asset portfolio.

The PowerCo Deal for a Speculator

A purely speculative entity like a hedge fund would generally have little to no interest in assuming a large, illiquid exposure with a variety of difficult to price risk elements. These types of deals are very attractive to private equity firms that seek to buy them when asset prices and volatilities are depressed, contract out for easily-unwound financial hedges from a bank and operational services from an industry participant (with short-notice termination contracts), then ride the package like a position that they intend to re-sell once it has increased in value.

To this end, preferred deals have a far-forward start and/or a longer term to allow more time for value appreciation.

The primary value driver for a private equity firm is not a mis-pricing relative to the current market conditions, but a strategic view that volatility, the spread between inputs and outputs, or asset prices in general will trend in its direction.

Chapter Fifteen Summary

All traders should understand the basic mechanics of pricing and hedging structured transactions because, as the PowerCo PFP example illustrates, a single transaction can impact, or be impacted by, the entire continuum of risk:

- Another natural may bid for the transaction as a way to diversify its asset portfolio. If it does not get the deal, it may end up providing operational services to the entity that does.
- One or more banks will bid for the transaction. The winner would very likely sub-contract out the operational risk to a merchant or natural active in the space while looking to lay off forward power and natural gas hedges to speculative clients or other naturals with offsetting needs.
- A merchant will bid for the transaction and try to source a hedge package from a bank to allow it to take the deal to delivery, where it can leverage its skills in the physical market. If a bank or speculator wins the deal, it may contract out its services for a fee.
- A speculator will bid for the transaction and source hedges from a bank and operational support from a merchant. If the speculator does not get the deal, it will likely end up consuming pieces of another entity's hedge package as speculative positions.

As complicated as this example seems, it is still a simplification of the actual challenges inherent in pricing a relatively vanilla structured transaction. To manage the complexity, a trader will have to rely on the structuring group to model the exposure and disaggregate the risk into components that can be priced. As part of the process, the trader will develop a hedge plan to reconfigure the risk and a value-extraction plan for either monetizing the value inherent in the position or warehousing the exposure until it can resell it at a profit.

Review Questions

1. Describe the steps in the origination process. What is the trader's role?
2. What are an PFQ and an RFP, and what is the difference between them? How are they handled differently?
3. How does the location of the risk within the firm impact the types of deals that are closed and the relative level of risk taken?
4. Describe the primary inherent conflicts between origination and trading and origination and risk when pricing and hedging structured transactions.

5. Describe the relative advantages of banks and merchants when attempting to price and hedge structured transactions.

Resources

- *Fiasco: The Inside Story of a Wall Street Trader* by Frank Partnoy
- *The Vandal's Crown: How Rebel Currency Traders Overthrew The World's Central Banks* by Gregory J. Millman
- *Metal Men: How Marc Rich Defrauded the Country, Evaded the Law, and Became the World's Most Sought-After Corporate Criminal* by A. Craig Copetas
- *The Smartest Guys In The Room: The Amazing Rise and Scandalous Fall of Enron* by Bethany McLean and Peter Elkind

16

Navigating the Corporate Culture

Trading Desk Organizational Chart in Relation to the Firm as a Whole
The organizational chart of most trading groups is a fairly standard, pyramid-shaped hierarchy.

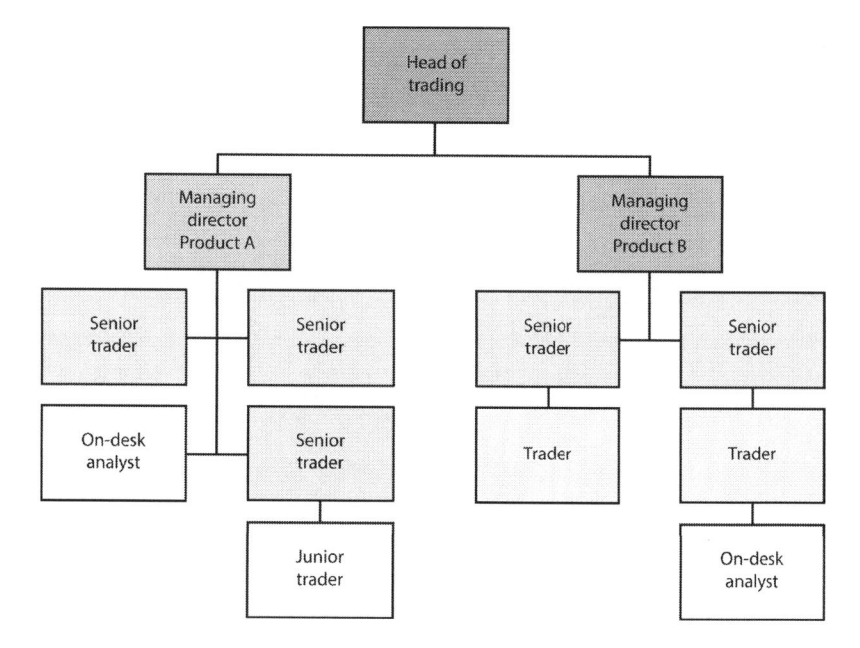

Figure 16.1 Organizational structure of a typical trading desk.

That sits within the larger group, as seen in the generic bank organization structure from Chapter 2:

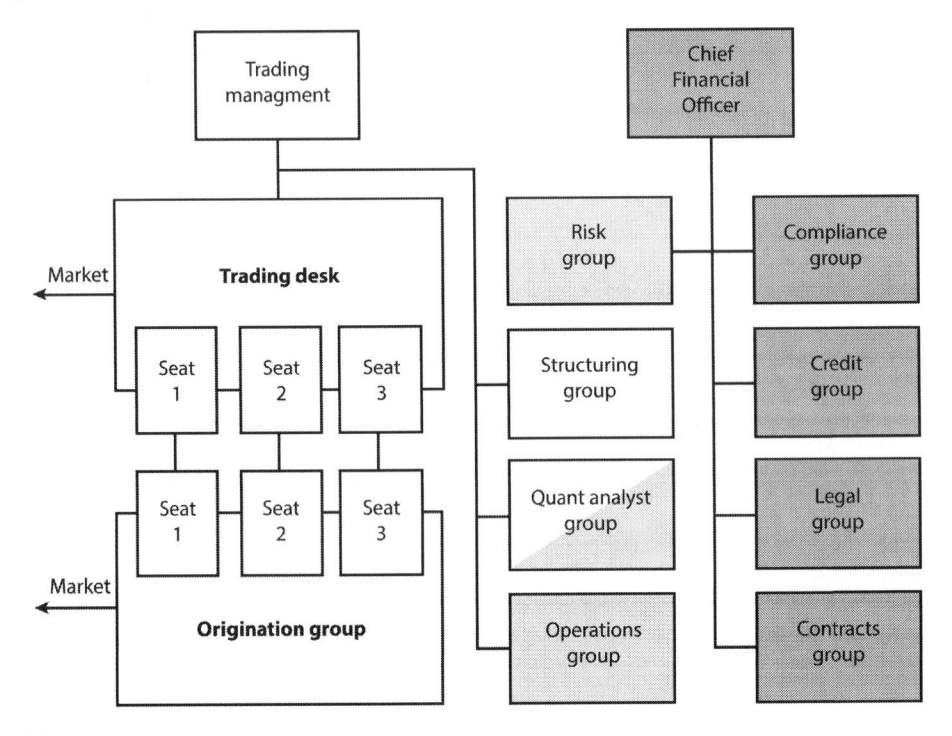

Figure 16.2 Generic trading-group organizational structure at a bank or merchant.

Getting a Trading Job

For those not currently in the industry it is important to internalize the cold, hard truth that absolutely no one gets hired into a firm as a trader without prior market and product-specific experience. Most aspiring traders are brought into a firm in a support function, which are commonly grouped into front office, middle office, and back office roles.

The front office is the commercial function of the firm, and will encompass the entire trading and origination desks and personnel that work closely with it, including dedicated on-desk analysts, members of the structuring group, and senior fundamental and quantitative analysts. Front-office jobs often function as unofficial training rotations, ongoing interview opportunities for bright employees who have done their time elsewhere in the firm to demonstrate that they should get a shot at advancement. The closer a support function works to the trading desk and the more day-to-day interaction with the shot callers, the better.

The middle office is engaged in the primary business of the firm, but may not have much direct contact with the trading desk and its management. Middle office functions include the risk group (though it is technically outside of the trading reporting chain), the portion of the analytics groups that does not report directly to trading, and the operations group that handles the scheduling and delivery of physical transactions. It is more difficult to get onto the desk from the middle office, as it requires jumping over all of the front office people in line.

The back office handles purely administrative functions, and is composed of the credit group, the legal group, the contract administrators, and the compliance group. There is no obvious development path that leads from the back office to the trading desk, and it is best avoided unless there are no other options available.

Pick Me! Pick Me!
There is one huge misconception that prevents people from being hired onto a trading desk from some other area of the company: aspirants believe that some innate quality of theirs will shine through as they toil away on the cover sheets for their TPS reports, that senior management will somehow identify it through unspecified means and, in a stirring act of trust and belief, whisk the employee off into a fairytale world of four-screen desks, turret phones, and lavish compensation. It does not work like that. Anyone seeking to escape support-staff hell will have to do the following:

1. Make the management of the trading desk aware that he really wants to be a trader and would strongly consider anything up to and including murder as a means of career advancement.[75]
2. Make sure he understands the requirements of the position he is seeking, and show that he is attempting to evolve in that direction, to the maximum extent possible. This is the crux of the matter. Nobody cares how good of a confirmations analyst or accounts payable coordinator the anonymous drone from down the hall is; it has no bearing on their capability to fill a trading seat.
3. Be engaged in the firm's business, show interest, initiative, and make the most of any opportunity. It is difficult for a person in a support function to be current on the market, but he can at least know which markets the firm participates in, etc.

A trader's first job in the industry will be based on the current needs of the firm or desk, as he will not yet have developed any unique skills that that would make him valuable as an individual. The needs of the firm will depend on the current evolutionary state of the market.

The Evolutionary State of the Market and Job Prospects
As seen in Chapter 2, markets have a life cycle and an evolutionary process. The types of jobs available will depend on the business the firm is currently engaged in and, crucially, the business it is engaged in building.

Early-stage markets are heavily deal-focused, as aggressive merchants carve out a niche doing structured transactions with naturals and attempt to protect themselves by laying off exposure to a few courageous and prescient financials and the occasional speculator with a taste for

---

[75] I would hope that I would not need to clarify this for anyone, but this is a joke. Do not murder anyone. This is not *American Psycho*.

outré products. This is, by and large, no place for beginners, and there will be very few junior trader jobs and even fewer support positions available.

Early-to-medium-stage markets will start to trade on a regular basis, and the space will start to attract a full complement of merchants, banks, and speculators to join the now transactional naturals. The market will still be defining itself, and there will be opportunities for junior people to wedge their way into the industry, mostly by being extremely proactive and able to carry more than one responsibility. Most of the future leaders of the industry will cut their teeth during this period.

Medium-stage markets are extremely transactional and are solidly in growth mode. The participants will have developed an understanding of the market and their position within it, and will be seeking to aggressively expand into whatever end state their singular manifest destiny would imply. Growth and aggressive expansion plans mean across the board hiring, and this is the absolute best time for a non-industry person to snag an analyst, structuring, operations, risk, or (for the very lucky few) junior trading position.

Medium-to-late-stage markets are all about production. The firms in the market have defined the structure of their trading groups and will seek to fill positions and make incremental additions on an as-needed basis only. There will be an established knowledge base and an idealized template for each piece of the puzzle on the trading floor, and trainees will be required to spend time in apprenticeship support functions to merit a look at a junior trading seat. It is still possible to earn a seat, but it will require specialist knowledge and an ability to add value almost instantly.

Late-stage markets are attempting to hold onto their former glory as the number of opportunities decreases, profitability declines, and firms start leaving the industry for greener pastures (pun intended). Industry headcount will shrink, and hiring will stop except for critical backfills. It is perversely possible to make rapid progress within a firm at this point, as traders flee for better opportunities and senior managers slash expensive experienced headcount and advance (but not necessarily promote) junior personnel instead. At every level, aspirants will compete with legions of displaced employees from other firms, many willing to take a step backward in career for a steady paycheck. Late-stage markets are no fun.

Add Value to Add Headcount
At every evolutionary stage of the market, the key to getting a shot at a junior trader position is the ability to add value to the desk, the traders and senior traders, and the head of trading who runs the group. Value is first added by helping a senior trader be more productive, then once the junior trader is established, building out a revenue- and profit-producing business of her own. Initial duties will include aggregating, analyzing, and reporting market information and managing small positions delegated to the junior trader for efficient execution. These are tests of the junior trader's ability to immerse herself in a market and operate within it, and should be viewed as an extended competency examination. Once the junior trader has proven that she has basic competency it is time for her to start working herself up the growth curve.

Chapter 16 - Navigating the Corporate Culture

The Lifecycle of a Trader

Traders evolve and mature over time, just like the markets they inhabit. There are a number of evolutionary states that traders will pass through as they transition from fresh-faced trainee to grizzled veteran.

Phase 1 – Ignorance Is Bliss

0-3 Months. Trainees know nothing. The fact that they know nothing is not a problem, per se, but the continual demonstration of this fact to their superiors is generally cause for some amusement and, if repeated often enough, scorn. At this stage a wise trainee will keep her mouth shut and her ears open. The entire goal of the first months on the desk is to figure out how things function. What does the firm do? What does the trading group do within the firm? How do the individual traders and their support staff accomplish this? How are decisions made? What resources are utilized create strategy, to implement it, and to do risk and management reporting?

Phase 2 – Boundless Enthusiasm

3-12 Months. Having learned how things work at the firm, the trainee must learn how to process the flow of information and begin to think about how it can be used to make decisions and create actionable strategies. This period is where successful trainees distinguish themselves from their peers. This is the time to work insanely hard at learning the business by coming early and staying late, reading everything, watching the market, and asking as many questions as possible of more experienced traders. By Month 6 trainees should be starting to formulate trading strategies on their own. In a firm that provides a positive learning environment, they will be encouraged to bring ideas to more senior staff for evaluation, critique, and almost certainly ridicule. Early-stage trading ideas, even from gifted larval-stage Masters of the Universe, tend to be fairly misshapen things. Having them mercilessly torn apart and constructively digesting the feedback is a key differentiator between those that will succeed and those that will not.

The trainee graduates from this phase when she has earned responsibility for a trading book. Most commonly the new trader will start with a reduced set of limits and a modest initial goal and operate under the close supervision of a more senior risk-taker.

Early Career Problems – Surviving the First Really Bad Trade

As discussed in Chapter 14 – Managing Positions, sooner or later every trader will have to deal with a significant losing position. Young traders are particularly vulnerable, due to their relative lack of experience anticipating dangerous market conditions, aptitude at handling them, and absence of built-up credibility with the desk and senior management.

The first disastrous trade is frequently a career-defining moment for a young trader. If he manages the problematic position efficiently and acquits himself in a professional manner, he will earn respect and a continued ability to do business. Making a bad situation worse and exhibiting poor behavior will likely ensure that the trader's first bad trade will be his last.

Phase 3 – Productivity
1-3 Years. The trader has his own book and set of performance expectations and must demonstrate early and continuous success, coupled with a well-organized thought process and a disciplined approach. The first year of having a trading book is, in reality, a continued audition for the job. Management will be focused not just on the money that is made or lost, but also how it is made or lost. Does this trader show promise? Does he have the capacity to grow into something special? Are there any flaws in technique, or impediments to development? Does he respond to critique, handle taking a loss, and manage difficult positions in hostile markets? Do they trust this person to make money? And, the ultimate question (most commonly asked rhetorically to the ether by hedge fund managers while staring pensively into a single malt scotch) is, would I give this person my money to trade?

Phase 4 – Master of the Universe
Year 4+. The trader develops technical expertise in his market segment. A key point to remember is that, while the trader is fully in the moment and totally synchronized with the market, the sands are already shifting beneath his feet. Markets do not remain the same; they gradually evolve. One of the unexpected negative aspects of fully concentrating on the present is a lack of energy to devote to understanding or anticipating future market evolutions.

Phase 5 – Going Big or Moving Up
Year 6+. Once the trader has achieved a level of competence in the market and become a steady producer she will face a developmental fork in the road. She can choose to continue to grow the size of her business, either in her current seat or at a larger, more aggressive firm, with a goal of producing ever-increasing P&Ls and bonus payouts.

Alternatively, the trader can move into a management role and take control of a group of more junior traders, becoming responsible for the productivity of the desk and being paid based on the performance of the team. A trader who has moved into a pure management role becomes hostage to the productivity, or lack thereof, of the group. It can be extremely frustrating dealing with an underperforming group, particularly for a trader who has historically been extremely successful as an individual. The temptation will be to dive in and start micromanaging every position and/or change the decision paradigm, because if autonomy did not work, then groupthink and a firm-wide view must be the answer (or vice versa). Abruptly shifting the operational marching orders midyear can be very jarring, particularly for traders expecting and/or demanding a certain level of autonomy and saddled with a set of goals they are expected to achieve.

Mid-Career Problems – The Side Effects of the Trading Lifestyle
Becoming a professional trader involves substantial, intentional changes to cognitive processes, responses to stimuli, and emotional states not unlike the conditioning for a fighter pilot, a firefighter, or a surgeon. It is an intentional transformation that can be difficult for non-industry people to grasp, and this can prove problematic in interpersonal relationships. A scientist is allowed to be cold, analytical, and intellectually aloof. A doctor or surgeon can be imperious, pedagogical, and cocky because they have trained themselves to handle critical life or death decisions with clinical detachment. A trader just has a job, and nobody around

him will ever understand why he can't "leave it at the office, like everyone else." There is an intellectual and in some cases moral high ground occupied by scientists, doctors, and the like that a professional speculator will never achieve. They are doing it for some other reason (though that reason is usually some roundabout means to self-fulfillment); a trader is just doing it for the money.

There is no more "average" for a trader, there are only good days and bad days. Traders become so used to being bombarded with stimuli and living in a never-ending fight-or-flight response mode that any cessation thereof can lead to instant complete and total boredom. This is a gateway to all sorts of self-destructive behavior done in the name of self-amusement.

Traders think that money is always the answer to any issue, real or perceived, and will try to buy their way out of problems, bribe or tip their way to better service, and hedge life's risks with two sets of dinner reservations and movie tickets in case the concert gets rained out. Traders start to measure life in terms of dollar equivalents and time away from work in opportunity cost. Traders can become very insensitive to other people's issues that appear to be curable with money, which can be extremely offensive to normal people who don't happen to have more cash than they know what to do with.

If a trader experiences significant success, she may develop the ugly tendency to start to think that people who aren't as rich must be idiots, or else they would be rich, too. This is one of the most unfortunate aspects of the business, the creation of a linkage between money and value as a person. This also happens among peers on a trading desk who, after a long enough time in the business, will almost certainly drift apart socio-economically.

Phase 6 – Everything Dies
Trading is a hard way to make an easy living. After a decade or more of early mornings, sleepless nights, and day-to-day trench warfare it is very common for traders to find themselves staring out the window thinking "I don't have to be here." This is often followed closely by the realization that they do not, in fact, want to be there any more. There is no shame in admitting this. Those who have achieved their financial goals will frequently call in rich, getting out on top and presumably moving on to a life of leisure on a sun-drenched island. I hear it's nice.

Even for traders that still love the job, there will come a time when it asks more of them than they are willing or able to give. Traders become obsolete, which can happen for a number of reasons. They can be worn down by the stress of grinding it out day after day until they just can't take it any more. They may have become undisciplined or sloppy, not have kept pace with industry evolution, or proven unable to master some critical new skill or technique. Every dinosaur who attempts to cling to a seat will eventually realize that younger, smarter, more aggressive traders are pushing them out of the market. It is an intensely uncomfortable, disconcerting feeling. It also doesn't last long.

The trick, then, is how to move through Phases 1-3 as quickly and profitably as possible and maximize the productivity in Phases 4 and 5. There are a number of things that a trader can do to improve the quality and extend the duration of his career.

How to Become a Better Trader: Troubleshooting Trading Technique

Forensic Self-Diagnosis

It is surprising how little thought many traders put into diagnosing the potential causes of extended periods of sub-optimal performance. They will attempt to tough out a seemingly never-ending stretch of bad results, doing the same things that got them into trouble without entertaining the possibility that they may be the loss-making part of the equation. The very best traders have a keen sense of when they are out of synch with the market and have a process for forensically evaluating their performance and diagnostically examining their execution technique and view-derivation methodology.

The obvious starting point for the trader's analysis is the historical fluctuations in the daily P&L. The trader will want to be alert for any periods where their P&L flat-lines or turns south, exhibits larger than normal swings, or has sharp drawdowns relative to the year-to-date total. Once identified, the trader must then break down the problematic section of the performance history on a position-by-position, strategy-by-strategy basis. He should be principally concerned with:

- The ratio of winning to losing trades.
- The size of the winning trades relative to the losing trades.
- The distribution of P&L across all trades.

The trader should reconstruct the pre-trade rationale for each position, including the analysis that lead to the view, the key fundamental and/or technical drivers, and how the thesis played out in the market. There are a number of common problematic behavioral patterns that the trader must be alert for:

- A large number of small winning trades eclipsed by a few large losing positions could indicate an over-eagerness to book profits that is sub-optimizing the good positions, a lack of discipline that is allowing small losing positions to balloon into large problems, or both. Is the trader exhibiting poor discipline with well-placed stops, or setting stop-losses too generously for the potential profit inherent in the trade? Is the trader sub-optimizing good trades that would have been more productive if allowed to more time and latitude to work?
- An equal number of similarly-sized winning and losing positions that net to zero could speak to poor trade selection. The trader must tighten up criteria in an effort to tilt the balance to a net winning ratio.
- An obvious connection between the winning or losing trades, either strategically, thematically, or in the tools and resources used to derive the view.

Chapter 16 - Navigating the Corporate Culture

Forensic self-diagnosis is not intended to be an exercise in self-flagellation. The goal is to look for problems and behaviors that the trader was unable to diagnose in the moment, but which may be blatantly obvious after the fact. Traders fortunate enough to have a trustworthy colleague(s) with good technique may be able to avail themselves of an external critique, which may yield a fresh perspective or provide additional clarity.

Understanding the Value of the Implied Option

Every trading job with a worthwhile compensation plan has an inherent asymmetry of personal risk and potential reward called the implied option or the trader's option. In the worst-case scenario the trader will fail, losing money for the firm and being fired mid-year as a result. The economic loss to the trader will be the salary he would have collected for the duration of the year, plus all of the free soda from the vending machine. If a trader is successful, he will be paid according to the established compensation plan, which at a merchant or hedge fund can be a double-digit percentage of his booked profits. The relationship between the trader's base salary for the year relative to the potential bonus he could earn will form a personal risk/reward ratio.

A large base salary with trivial incentive compensation will lead a trader to adopt a conservative approach designed to eliminate the risk of being fired, a smaller paycheck with huge upside potential will result in aggressive positions designed to maximize the potential bonus payout. The trader's option is the primary reason that the firm must align the individual's compensation with the goals and culture of the organization, as any trader worth his seat will quickly figure out the optimal way to approach the risk/reward inherent in the proposition.

The degree to which the trader's operational environment is well or poorly defined will greatly impact his ability to evaluate the implied option and determine the optimal course of action.

Ambiguous Operating Conditions

Ambiguity is the enemy of good decision making, and can result from poorly defined objectives, unclear operational mandates, inconsistent application of standards, and a host of other factors. Managers without the benefit of a trading background often fail to comprehend why traders need to understand the operational parameters that govern their business, the targets expected of them, and the resources available to achieve those goals. If management cannot or will not define the trader's risk box then it is incumbent on the trader to attempt define it for herself, proposing a set of operational parameters (notional, V@R, products, term, monthly stop, annual stop, etc.) and formally requesting approval for their utilization to achieve a P&L target. Management may or may not approve, but at least the trader will have started what could potentially be a productive conversation about the limits and targets the firm would be comfortable with.

Calibrating Aggression

Given the compensation plan and the perception of the value of the implied option, a trader must consider the strategic issue of how to budget risk or capital across the course of a trading year.

Calibration of aggression is primarily a consideration for traders with a proprietary, discretionary component to their risk taking. A flow-based trader at a bank will do as much margin-producing business as she can, and a natural with a programmatic hedge strategy will sell when the market conditions intersect with his pre-planned execution points. Neither will worry about what else they could or should be doing.

Proprietary traders at banks and hedge funds are given a risk allocation and expected to utilize it to generate profits for the firm. The trader will be allowed to run negative for a period of time, frequently significantly so, as long as management believes in the trader and his position and is willing to take the pain to weather the storm. Failure to produce a targeted level of year-end profitability will frequently be punished just as severely as losing money.

For all traders there is a relationship between:

- Goals
- Allocated limits
- Allowable stop-loss
- Current market conditions
- Value of the implied option

A trader should start with a plan, which can be either short or long term. He can choose to be conservative and budget his resources to last the entire year, or set up a shorter-term allocation schedule that mandates some level of success to fund the remainder of the year.

If a trader's goals relative to his limits are large, with a profit target of 5-10X or more of the allocated stop-loss, then an aggressive strategy that deploys a significant portion of the available risk early in the year is most logical (and may in fact be necessary). If the goals are more modest, with a profit target of 2X or less of the allocated stop-loss, it may make sense to more evenly budget the risk across the year.

The trader's plan will have to be flexible enough to allow for the pursuit of new and interesting opportunities and respond to both risk-reducing drawdowns and risk-enhancing profits. The trader's initial plan has to live inside the limit and resource box defined by the firm (and/or the trader's management). As seen in Chapter 12, once the trading year begins, the limit and resource allocation problem becomes very path dependent. A more conservative approach that holds a relatively larger amount of resources in reserve will yield a higher probability of results clustered around zero, leading to small positive and negative years and a higher probability of keeping a somewhat lower paying job. Embracing a more volatile approach will lead to a dispersion of results and increase chances of being fired—or paid like a rock star.

The consequence of the trader's relative level of aggression and the positions she accumulates will be profits and losses. The trader will need to understand how both impact their ability to do business.

Dealing With Winning

When a trader is a winner (especially a big winner) the world instantly starts to revolve around her. Everyone wants to talk with her, and everybody laughs at her jokes, however terrible. She will be given more authority, more influence, faster promotion, and most importantly, paid lots and lots of money. Radically exceeding expectations has a tendency to earn the trader a much, much larger goal for the next year, which she may be unable to achieve for a number of reasons:

- Radical outperformance is frequently a product of good trading, extremely favorable market conditions, and a non-trivial quantity of luck, none of which are guaranteed to repeat.
- Management has a tendency to increase profit targets much more aggressively than it allocates loss limits, and a successful trader can find herself needing to take outsized risks, possibly leading to P&L swings that she cannot withstand.
- Winning all of the time can convince a trader that it is impossible for her to lose, leading to a degradation in her decision-making process and proof that it is, indeed, possible for her to lose.

It can be difficult to maintain perspective. Even if the trader does, it can be difficult for management to maintain perspective.

Dealing With Losing

The ability to lose without losing focus is a key determinant of long-term trading success. Traders with good self-diagnostic tools are generally able to handle it better than others, as are those with a strong belief in their demonstrated edge in the market and confidence in themselves and their methodology. All traders are susceptible to having their confidence shaken, which typically happens for the following reasons:

- Having a can't-miss, once-in-a-lifetime opportunity not work out.
- Taking a larger-than-normal risk and suffering larger-than-normal losses.
- Taking a painful loss on a position that immediately rebounds into what would have been a profitable trade.
- Enduring a long series of losing trades, even if they are each individually sub-critical, that erodes the trader's confidence.
- Experiencing a discipline break down that turns what should be a moderate loss into a problem.

The psychological damage of large losing positions can be devastating, but tends to be relatively short lived, even if the complaining and self-pity are not. Long stretches of never-ending losing positions are far more mentally taxing. The trader will begin to doubt his view and methodology. He may also begin to doubt himself, which is much more problematic. As seen in earlier in the chapter, a trader must have a process for self-diagnosing technique. He must also have a way to critically examine himself, running a diagnostic to determine if he is in the correct headspace to be in the market and if not, performing a system reboot via a temporary cessation of activity, taking time away from the desk, etc.

How Winning and Losing Affect the Trader's Ability to Do Business

Consider a series of six monthly P&Ls from three different traders, all of whom are up $600,000 at the end of Month 6:

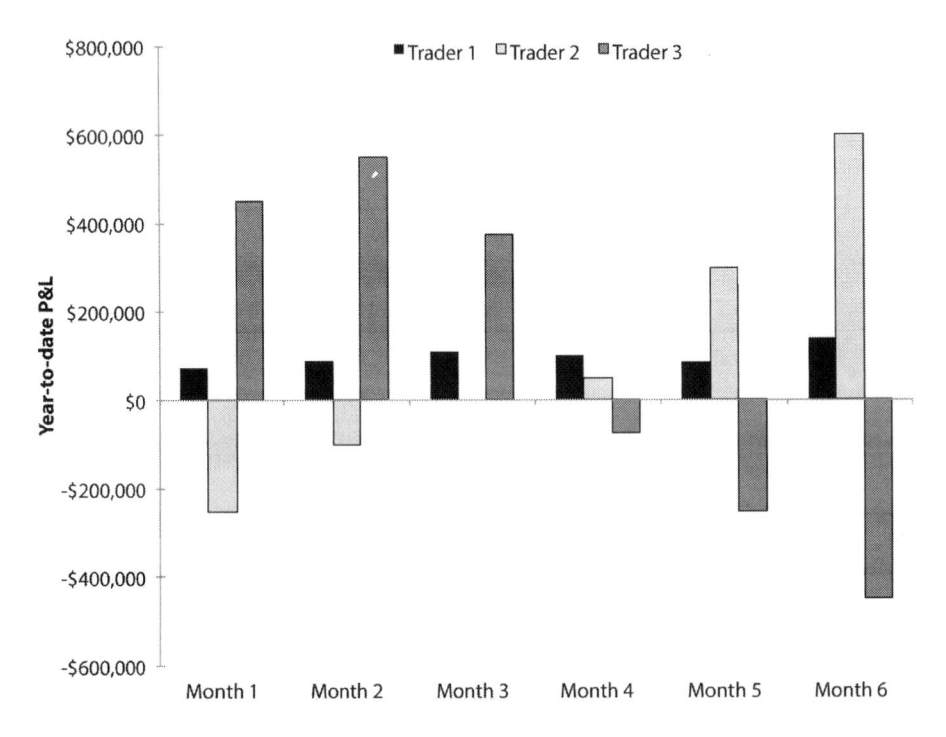

Figure 16.3 Performance figures for three traders averaging $100,000/month.

Trader 1 has been consistently grinding out small profits, earning between $75-$140k with no losing months and with the peak profit achieved in Month 6. Trader 2 started off with rough Months 1 and 2, pulled it together with a break-even Month 3 and positive Month 4, then really started performing in Months 5 and 6, finishing with a strong $600k (comprising her entire profit for the year) in the last month. Trader 3 has been going in the opposite direction, and after killing it for the first quarter posted a small loss in Month 4, a bigger one in Month 5, and finished very poorly with a $450k loss in Month 6. Depending on how their firm takes P&L to date into consideration for the Month 7 limit allocation, each could face dramatically different operational constraints going forward.

- A trading firm that only concerns itself with YTD profitability would see all three traders equally and likely maintain their current limit allocations.
- A trading firm that focuses on recent profitability would see that Trader 1 has made $325K in the last three months, Trader 2 earned $950K, and Trader 3 has lost $775K. Trader 1 would likely see limits increase, Trader 2 would receive a much larger allocation, and Trader 3 would either stay the same or have his ability to do business decreased.

- A formula-driven firm that used a 60% weighting for the most recent month, 25% for the previous month, and 15% for the month prior would derive metrics of +$120K for Trader 1, +$443K for Trader 2, and $–344K for Trader 3. Again, Trader 1 would gain more ability to do business, but on a percentage basis Trader 2 has more radically outperformed and would be rewarded accordingly. In a formula-driven firm, Trader 3 would almost certainly lose a portion of his ability to do business.

There is almost always a "recency" bias in management's interpretation of trader productivity. In a non-quantitative sense, based on their recent results management will view Trader #2 as a winner, Trader #3 as a loser, and #1 as unproductive, even though they all have the same current P&L. This is a classic example of both how perception is reality in the trading business, and that the only thing that matters is what a trader has done for the firm lately.

Working With Support Staff
The modern professional trader is almost never a lone wolf. At anything other than the smallest shops, he will rely on a variety of support functions from deal entry to risk management to analytical and operational support. The ability to productively interact with the other groups on the floor and the other traders is critical.

Working With Internal Fundamental Analysts
A strong fundamental research group with a deep understanding of the markets can make the job of any trader vastly easier. The trader's relationship with the analyst is, in many ways, analogous to that of a golfer and a caddy. Some players want a detailed reading of the conditions, an assessment of the strategic options, and a mutual decision on the plan of action. Others want the caddy to shut up, hand them the right club when they ask for it, and not make any noise in their backswing. While the latter seems dismissive, in many cases it is actually a self-defense mechanism. Many traders with highly refined methodologies carefully manage their informational inputs to get what they know they need and no more, preferring to not have too many voices in their heads when making decisions. Others are just jerks.

The interaction between researcher and trader will be, to a great extent, defined by the reporting structure. There are a number of trader-analyst constructs, ranging from directly assigned, on-desk quants to horsepower-for-hire, centrally dispatched out of a 175 IQ bullpen via a needs-based algorithm.

There is also a hierarchy of analytical services, including producing:

- Data
- Reports
- Information
- Trading strategies

The Big Bang Theory
A data-producing analyst is a fairly straightforward functionary. Traders tell them what they want (or they tell the trader what they can produce), and an analyst delivers it on schedule and

in a usable format. There can be horsepower issues with analysis that is highly numerate or only semi-automatable, as there can be significant post-production time necessary to prepare it for consumption. It is important that the trader understands any interpretive areas of the process and be able to verify that the finished product is what was requested. There is nothing worse than getting a data set that immediately yields a good, tradable thesis only to hear "I screened out all of the weird numbers. There were, like, a ton. Those are the good ones. It took forever, too, so those numbers are as of last Thursday. No, wait. Tuesday, I think."

Some analysts like to view the market they are examining like a physics problem and assume that an elegant yet elusive answer is lurking just beneath the surface like some logarithmic Loch Ness Monster. This is particularly true of hard science PhDs, who have been approaching the world this way since they went off to college at age seven for a glowing future of wedgies, swirlies, and all-night MMORPG sessions on the department mainframe. Their general tendency is to always drill down, getting deeper into the fractal until one day they realize that they're 34 million lines of code in, they've been wearing the same shirt since November, and that the trader who asked them the question was fired a long, long time ago. In addition to Perpetual Grad Student Risk, the secondary danger is that Dr. Strangelove actually reports back with an answer to seventeen decimal places, which does not matter much if the current market is bid at $1 and offered at $9.

Flying Report Monkeys

Any moderately useful data set or research report will end up getting emailed and forwarded all over the place and, sooner or later, might accidentally be seen by someone important. This is a disaster. The analyst who spent a month of nights and weekends scraping the package together will be woken from their fitful under-desk slumber, given a brisk pat on the head and informed that they are now expected to produce the entire 67-page slide deck by 8:00AM every morning for distribution to the entire firm, Board of Directors included. Perversely, the reward for innovative, original work is frequently being sentenced to an assembly-line existence of menial production of that same work. This is doubly true if the product in question requires highly specialized skills, like spell checking or changing the font size.

Deep Thinkers

An analyst that produces real, actionable Information is worth her weight in gold, and significantly more, in many cases. Traders with the latitude to do so will typically try to hire super-productive analysts to be their on-desk support, both to protect a valuable resource and to deny it to other traders. Super-studious analysts are not always as cool with this as might be expected. If they wanted to talk to people and solve real problems they wouldn't have gotten a PhD in theoretical physics.

Questions Traders Ask Analysts

In addition to the normal process-related activities that make up an analyst's day-to-day duties, she will inevitably have to field any number of research requests and information queries from the management and traders they support. Among the more likely questions any analyst should anticipate:

Chapter 16 - Navigating the Corporate Culture

- Fair value questions – What is the analyst's best point estimate (or failing that, range estimate) of the fair value of the market or expected value of a variable? Traders will typically use this to buttress an argument that the current market is too cheap or expensive.
- Scenario runs or change cases – What is the price of Product A given changes in variables X, Y, and Z? Traders will ask this as an abbreviated form of scenario analysis to get a feel for the range of potential price outcomes for a shift in the fundamentals. They may also ask to see how the internal view differs from an external forecast that has one or more key variables with a different value.
- Summary of vendor views – What is the rest of the market looking at, how does that consensus aggregate, and where is the internal view relative to that? If there are any major discrepancies, what are they and why do they exist?
- Regulatory or market rules impact – How is this impending piece of legislation going to impact the firm's position or view?

Creating a Productive Work Relationship

Good analysts tend to really buy into their work, which is great when it leads them to a timely, considered piece of research. The problem arises when the analyst becomes so deeply convicted that he cannot (or will not) acknowledge any challenges to his conclusions or changes to his fundamental case. There's nothing scarier to a commercial person than hearing an analyst shrug off a devastating counter-argument with, "I don't care. I'm sticking to my guns." The best working relationships with fundamental analysts are predicated on a clear understanding that the analyst is intellectually free to change his view instantly, completely, and with no regard to prior work, if the facts dictate. The last thing any trader wants is a piece of research that takes game-changing information and presents it as a minor incremental shift to be more consistent with previous publications (or worse, ignores it altogether). If something changed, it changed, and the trading desk needs to know about it. Now.

Some analysts also have a tendency to want to be absolutely certain before revealing their analysis in its full and complete form, and as a result sometimes sit on a crucial piece of information until they have "developed the thesis" or "finished the study." Meanwhile, the rest of the market is reacting. It is vital that the trader build a relationship where analysts feel free to bring forward anything they deem pertinent, instantly.

An Analyst Who Trades Is a Trader

Good analysts are occasionally (rarely) recognized and given a trading book of their own or a participatory share in the profits of strategies they have helped devise. In most cases they are also expected to maintain their analytical workload. It is almost impossible for this to actually work well, for two main reasons.

First, the analyst will inevitably focus her efforts on P&L generating activities to the detriment of information gathering and processing duties. Even with the most dedicated and well-intentioned worker, it is impossible that there not be some degradation of service to former clients. Given the razor-thin line that separates success and failure, no trader can afford to tolerate a reduced level of service. Second, and worse, since the analyst has by definition left a detached, unbiased job in favor of one involving committing decisions with financial outcomes, her analysis cannot be fully trusted regardless of how conscientiously prepared and well-intentioned it may be. The best analysts feel intellectually free to change their opinions as needed, and once they have a significant vested interest in a particular outcome this may no longer be possible. The trader is then forced to try to interpret whether the analyst is bullish because of the facts, or bullish because she hopes her position pays out.

Working With the Risk Group
Traders must do everything within their power to maintain a productive relationship with the risk group. Depending on the institution, the trading-risk interface can range from an atmosphere of collegial respect and cooperation to distrust and open suspicion. Whatever the prevailing dynamic, the trader must do his best to work well with risk. The rules are the rules and the enforcement policy is the enforcement policy, but if the risk group does not fully trust the trader's actions and explanations there is always latitude for the baseline level of observation, verification, and reporting to be significantly enhanced, which is not something any trader wants to deal with.

The risk group can also make a trader's life significantly easier by responding to requests for position simulations and V@R impact calculations in a timely manner, advising the trader about correlation and volatility changes that will impact his positions, and warning him of potential limit breaches based on intraday market conditions that can allow the trader time to manage the exposure before it becomes a reported violation.

Working With the Compliance Group
The need to stay current in an ever-evolving regulatory environment has led to a significant expansion in the scope and authority of the compliance function at virtually every trading firm. The compliance group is responsible for the education, surveillance and, if necessary, discipline of the firm as a whole and the transactional front-office staff in particular.

The compliance staff is charged with understanding the totality of the firm's business, from macro-level strategies to transactional minutiae, and being aware of any and all current and pending regulation that could potentially impact its operation. The compliance group will offer mandatory training courses to ensure that every trader is aware of the current regulatory environment, how it impacts their business, and cognizant of any anticipated evolution of the rules, regulations and laws.

Members of the compliance group will review, frequently with the assistance of special-purpose keyword search software, every recorded phone conversation, e-mail, instant message, and text sent or received on a trader's work computer and company-provided cell phone. Any questionable activity or suspect communication will be immediately flagged and the trader in question called into the office to explain their actions in detail.

Maintaining a culture of compliance is taken incredibly seriously at all trading firms. Traders must learn to engage the compliance staff and proactively consult with them prior to transacting any novel piece of business, negotiating a non-standard transaction, or entertaining a new market or product. A collaborative, collegial relationship is critical to ensure that the trader has the benefit of the compliance group's far broader perspective on the potential ramifications of any market activity.

Bluntly put, a poor working relationship with the risk group could potentially result in a trader inadvertently taking an action that could imperil their career. A poor working relationship with the compliance group could potentially result in a trader inadvertently taking an action that could imperil their career and expose themselves, their management, and their firm to massive fines and the very real potential for significant jail time. Not taking maximum advantage of the firm's internal resources to ensure that they are operating within the rules, regulations and laws that govern their market is all risk and no reward for the trader.

Dealing With the Trading Floor
The trading floor is a workplace unlike any other, and can vary significantly from firm to firm. The atmosphere on the floor is determined by the trading culture, and the trading culture is determined to a great degree by the head trader and his lieutenants. Some floors are hushed libraries of academic intensity, silent except for grinding teeth, mouse clicks, and the soft snap of Advil and Adderall bottles being opened and closed. In a more clubby atmosphere one might see formerly staid bankers slouching around at a hedge fund in polo shirts and deck shoes, alternating world-weary market chatter with shot-by-shot analysis of the last round of golf. At a global financial powerhouse the floor will be a football-field-sized maze of desks, screens, and over-dressed stress cases ready to out-intense the other ex-lacrosse bros for a chance at the Associate Junior Vice-President slot opening up next fiscal year. At a scrappy up-and-comer the trading room will be furnished with homemade plywood desks and lawn chairs, and the three founders will try to out-gamble their cash burn in their shorts and flip-flops while playing first-person shooters on the office Xbox.

Succeeding as a trader is dependent on being accepted on the floor, whatever its quirks and characteristics. It may feel disconcertingly like being back in high school.

The lack of privacy and the noise (if the floor is noisy) can be problems, at first. A trader needs to learn to develop "room hearing," the knack of listening to everything at once and straining out the relevant information from the audio soup. At some trading shops, dealers are encouraged to yell out any new and interesting fact for general consumption. The air will fill with customer orders, trades, news items and rumors; also profanity, jokes, insults, and more profanity. So much profanity. Sensitive souls need not apply.

Dealing With Other Traders
There is a wide spectrum of acceptable trader-to-trader conduct, ranging from cultures of collegial, collaborative respect to Battle Royale, kill-everyone-you-see fight clubs. A new trader on the desk must figure out the interpersonal dynamic and get with the program as quickly as possible, as the penalty for transgressing against the established culture is usually being distrusted and ostracized. It is hard for an axe murderer to blend in in a room full of university professors, but even harder for a university professor to survive in a room full of axe murderers.

There is a great deal of both official and unofficial hierarchy present on a trading floor. Rank confers org-chart status but profitability (particularly massive profitability) earns the trader a slightly creepy mixture of worship and fawning sycophancy from the rest of the desk. The arrival of a new analyst or trader will involve a shuffling of the established order and instigate a series of quasi-friendly, semi-confrontational exchanges as each wolf in the pack measures himself against the interloper and tries to assert dominance. While busy fending off a stream of challenges from peers, a new trader must be extremely careful not to accidentally pick a fight with one of the big hitters on the floor, who will be obliged by her status to deliver a public, humiliating, beat down. The ironic thing is that this is just as likely to happen in a hedge fund full of physics PhDs as it is in a bar full of pit traders, it will just involve more equations and less chest-to-chest yelling and (probably quite real) threats that someone is about to get KTFO.

The trader must also quickly develop an understanding for the level of integrity and trust present in the culture and learn to operate within that framework. Unfortunately, many of the worst characteristics in human nature happen to be extremely useful on a trading floor, and the path to advancement can frequently be shortcut with some judicious backstabbing and sleazy behavior. In a morality play there would be a karmic come-uppance in the final act, but in reality terrible people are generally allowed to continue being terrible as long as they are also massively profitable. This categorically does not mean that a trader must be a liar, a cheat, or a thief to succeed, but it does mean that sooner or later she will have to deal with one.

Dealing With the Boss
This is the critical relationship a trader will have at his firm. Being employed in a trading group is a proactive endeavor and the boss, typically the head trader, will be under constant pressure to justify the existence of each member of their group. The primary means of justification is, of course, profits. Profitable traders are granted all manner of latitude, which they habitually abuse in predictable fashions. Nobody fires a massively profitable trader, ever. However, a marginally profitable trader may be shuffled off into another group or a different function if he is sufficiently underperforming his peers and they can make the case that someone could do more with the chair.

Dealing With the Boss's Boss and the Need to Interact With Senior Management
The simple fact is, a trader's direct superior can do little advance her career, particularly if they are one rank apart. A trader's boss can't promote an employee to be his equal, only his boss can do that. The more senior management knows and understands a trader's uniqueness and contributions, the easier it is for it to justify paying and promoting him. Nobody writes a big check to someone he's never heard of, and nobody promotes the invisible man.

Take advantage of available opportunities to interact with senior management in semi-professional or social environments. If there is a mentoring program available, sign up. Seize all opportunities to present to risk management committees, board meetings, etc. Even tee-totaling hacks need to learn how to play golf and figure out how to tolerate being out at bars. The coterie of lieutenants around the head trader generally works like a wolf pack, every wolf has a place in the order and runs when the pack runs. If the boss is playing 18 then hitting the bar, being unwilling to participate negatively distances the trader from his peers.

Chapter Sixteen Summary

Very little is given on a trading floor, everything is earned. An aspiring trader will frequently have to make his way onto the desk via a rotation in a support function, the duration of which will depend on his ability to add value and his skill at making that capability known to management. The relative ease of attaining a junior trader seat will vary with the evolutionary state of the market, with the early-middle and middle stages of development offering the most opportunities. The reward for fighting their way onto the desk is a career spent fighting the market, fighting peers for recognition and advancement, fighting management for a fair share of the profits, and fighting to remain current and competent in an unsympathetic industry that continually evolves. A trader must learn to troubleshoot technique and find a way to deal with the emotional stress of winning and losing. The trader must also develop productive working relationships with the support staff, analysts, risk management group, compliance group, and the other members of the trading desk.

Resources

- *Liar's Poker: Rising Through the Wreckage on Wall Street* by Michael Lewis
- *Bombardiers* by Po Bronson
- *The Buy Side: A Wall Street Trader's Tale of Spectacular Excess* by Turney Duff
- *When Genius Failed: The Rise and Fall of Long-Term Capital Management* by Roger Lowenstein

00

Conclusion

The Most Important Lesson
The goal of *Trader Construction Kit* is to explain simply, methodically, and with maximum clarity how to be a professional trader. It was never supposed to be a book about my personal trading style, as that information would be all-but worthless to anyone else. A trader's style must be self-constructed to leverage their unique strengths, de-emphasize their inherent weaknesses, and designed to efficiently operate within the market they inhabit.

There is no universally "right" way to trade; there is only a most effective way for a particular individual to trade a specific market.

With the logical corollary:

Since a productive trading methodology is an outgrowth of an individual's unique personal characteristics, no one can teach someone else how to trade. They have to teach themselves.

This is the most important lesson for young traders, who will be continually bombarded with unsolicited, frequently contradictory risk-taking advice from their peers, superiors, and the guy who refills the soda machine on Tuesdays.

Trader Construction Kit provides a methodological framework, over which a trader can develop their approach to the market. Chapters on fundamental and technical analysis, volatility and risk, developing a view, evaluating implementation strategies, executing trades and managing positions, pricing and hedging structured transactions, and surviving on a trading floor provide a solid information base and a blueprint for future development. For those that are committed to the craft, this is only the beginning. To build on this foundation, a neophyte risk-taker must develop a depth of knowledge about their specific market and a breadth of knowledge about trading in general. An aspiring trader must face the market, immersing themselves as deeply as their circumstances allow to learn it's characteristics and begin to develop actionable views on the future of price. There is no shortage of theoretical textbooks, market memoirs, and other resources available to broaden a trader's knowledge base. A list of notable texts is provided in the Appendix.

The core fundamentals that underlie all trading methodologies are constant. Recall from Chapter 7:

The ability to make a rigorous, intellectually honest assessment of the probable risks and the potential reward inherent in a proposition is the single most important determinant of long-term trading success.

Discipline, toughness, competitiveness, ethics, and the other characteristics of successful traders do not go out of style. Almost everything else does change, rapidly. Rules, regulations and laws will be created and modified. Old drivers will lessen in effect and new influences will gain importance. Technological advances will lead to better, faster tools, but will make obsolete those that do not embrace and master them. The market will continually evolve, and every trader's approach to and interactions with it must evolve in tandem to enable them to remain a productive participant.

This is the end of *Trader Construction Kit*, but just the beginning of your self-assembly process.

Get to work.

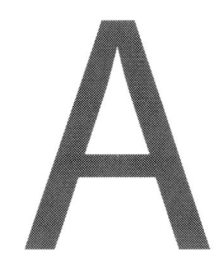

Appendix A - Resources

Financial Books and Textbooks:

- *Advances in Financial Machine Learning* by Marcos López de Prado
- *A Quantitative Primer on Investments with R* by Dale W.R. Rosenthal
- *Bollinger on Bollinger Bands* by John Bollinger
- *Bombardiers* by Po Bronson
- *Charlie D. The Story of the Legendary Bond Trader* by William D. Falloon
- *Data Science for Business* by Foster Provost and Tom Fawcett
- *Dynamic Hedging: Managing Vanilla and Exotic Options* by Nassim Nicholas Taleb
- *The Education of a Speculator* by Victor Niederhoffer
- *Elliott Wave Principle: Key to Market Behavior* by Robert R. Prechter, Jr. and A.J. Frost
- *The Smartest Guys In The Room: The Amazing Rise and Scandalous Fall of Enron* by Bethany McLean and Peter Elkind
- *Extraordinary Popular Delusions and The Madness of Crowds* by Charles Mackay
- *Fiasco: The Inside Story of a Wall Street Trader* by Frank Partnoy
- *Flash Boys: A Wall Street Revolt* by Michael Lewis
- *Hedge Hogs: The Cowboy Traders Behind Wall Street's Largest Hedge Fund Disaster* by Barbara T. Dreyfuss
- *Japanese Candlestick Charting Techniques* by Steve Nison
- *Liar's Poker: Rising Through the Wreckage on Wall Street* by Michael Lewis
- *Market Wizards: Interviews with Top Traders* by Jack D. Schwager
- *Merchants of Grain: The Power and Profits of the Five Giant Companies at the Center of the World's Food Supply* by Dan Morgan

- *Metal Men: How Marc Rich Defrauded the Country, Evaded the Law, and Became the World's Most Sought-After Corporate Criminal* by A. Craig Copetas
- *The New Market Wizards: Conversations with America's Top Traders* by Jack Schwager
- *The Complete Guide to Option Pricing Formulas* by Espen Gaarder Haug
- *Options Markets* by John C. Cox and Mark Rubinstein
- *Option Volatility & Pricing: Advanced Strategies and Techniques* by Sheldon Natenberg
- *Options, Futures, and Other Derivatives* by John C. Hull
- *Pit Bull: Lessons from Wall Street's Champion Day Trader* by Martin Schwartz
- *Python for Data Analysis, 2e* by Wes McKinney
- *Python for Finance, 2e* by Yves J. Hilpisch
- *Reminiscences of a Stock Operator* by Edwin Lefèvre
- *Rogue Trader* by Nick Leeson
- *Short* by Cortright McMeel
- *Technical Analysis of the Financial Markets: A Comprehensive Guide to Trading Methods and Applications* by John J. Murphy
- *The Black Swan: The Impact of the Highly Improbable* by Nassim Nicholas Taleb
- *The Bonfire of the Vanities* by Tom Wolfe
- *The Buy Side: A Wall Street Trader's Tale of Spectacular Excess* by Turney Duff
- *The Evaluation and Optimization of Trading Strategies, 2e* by Robert Pardo
- *The Man Who Solved the Market* by Gregory Zuckerman
- *The Money Bazaar: Inside the Trillion-Dollar World of Currency Trading* by Andrew Krieger
- *The Psychology of Technical Analysis: Profiting from Crowd Behavior and the Dynamics of Price* by Tony Plummer
- *The Vandal's Crown: How Rebel Currency Traders Overthrew The World's Central Banks* by Gregory J. Millman
- *Traders Guns and Money: Knowns and Unknowns in the Dazzling World of Derivatives* by Satyajit Das
- *Trading Natural Gas: Cash, Futures, Options and Swaps* by Fletcher J. Sturm
- *Value at Risk: The New Benchmark for Managing Financial Risk, 3rd Edition* by Philippe Jorion
- *When Genius Failed: The Rise and Fall of Long-Term Capital Management* by Roger Lowenstein

Poker Books:

- *Every Hand Revealed* by Gus Hansen
- *Doyle Brunson's Super System: A Course in Power Poker* by Doyle Brunson and Chip Reese
- *The Biggest Game in Town* by Al Alvarez
- *The Psychology of Poker* by Alan N. Schoonmaker
- *The Theory of Poker: A Professional Poker Player Teaches You How to Think Like One* by David Sklansky

Appendix B – Data Science & Programming

Introduction
The market is always changing.

In the four years since the publication of the first edition of Trader Construction Kit, the baseline requirements to be a successful trader have taken an evolutionary step function toward a more quantitative, data-driven job description.[76] There are three principal reasons:
1. The devaluation of "traditional" data, which has become so democratized across the industry that there is less value to be derived from even cutting-edge analysis. Unfortunately, there is still plenty of opportunity to underperform by limiting informational inputs and/or running a slipshod analytical process.
2. The rise of alternative data, fueled by:
    a. mobile devices equipped with data-harvesting applications, resulting in an explosion of acquirable, analyzable data from social media, e-mail, and location data.

---

[76] While a lot of people with job titles like Chief Data Scientist and AI Whisperer would like you to believe that they just invented all of this technology, much of it has been around for decades. I got my first exposure to a neural network circa 1998, when a colleague and I ordered a simplistic model from an ad in the back of a magazine and tried to force-feed it some poorly curated data. Surprisingly, it did not achieve self-awareness, realize that humans were a virus destroying the planet and try steal a bunch of launch codes, etc. It also didn't do anything remotely useful, due to a combination of garbage-in/garbage-out training data and copious amounts of operator error. If only we had had PhDs and better job descriptions...

  b. machine interpretable data sources like speech-to-text and text parsing.
  c. exhaust data as a byproduct of normal business activities and mining internal/proprietary data sets.
3. Extremely powerful analytical tools on cloud-based platforms that allow advanced high-volume data processing in seconds, anywhere, at minimal cost.

The basics of data science and programming are relevant for several types of financial professionals:

1. Those just starting a career in trading or trading-related support functions who will be immersed in a data-rich environment and expected to remain productive during a decades-long increase of informational saturation.
2. Those looking to transition to the trading desk from a non-commercial role; for them, possessing skills at deriving information from data will likely be the incremental value-add that gets them onto the desk.
3. Mid- to late-career practitioners clinging to a trader-centric, decision-making model that is, for most, already a thing of the past.[77]

The traditional analytical workflow involved the investigation of fundamental factors that the trader had determined to be (or had the potential to be) market moving. The trader would develop the theory and the technology (rudimentary though it may have been) "on-desk," keeping as much control and ownership of the intellectual property for as long as possible. Only when the trader realized that they could not fully or productively implement the analytical methodology—due to a lack of knowledge, technical skill, or bandwidth—would they delegate development and production to an on-desk analyst or the quantitative group. The entire process was trader driven and trader managed. This is no longer the case.

The primary difference is that the trader is no longer exclusively driving the development of the tools and techniques designed to be deployed in the market. The trader was formerly the sole arbitrator of utility, and every incremental piece of information was either an improvement to the trader's view of the market or worthless. A trader's conscious perception of market-moving fundamentals is a very, very narrow focus when compared with a universe of trillions of data points collected from myriad sources in real time. This river of data is harvested and curated by teams of quantitative strategists, who may exist as a parallel alpha generation channel or supplant the trader entirely, as has become possible in extremely developed markets.

---

[77] Am I implicitly saying that Trader Construction Kit is obsolete? Far from it. Though the job description "trader" is currently falling out of fashion in favor of "strategist" or "quantitative portfolio manager," I maintain that any individual taking risk in a market is a trader and must understand how markets work and how to employ a disciplined, consistent methodology. It doesn't matter if their "alpha generation engine" is a legal pad and a telephone or a quantum supercomputer running GLaDOS.

Appendix B – Data Science & Programming

Traders must develop basic data acquisition and analysis skills to remain relevant in this new quantitative age.

Even more challenging is the fact that much of the analysis that traders will be presented with in the future will literally be like nothing they have ever seen before. Much of the old-school (which for the purposes of this discussion means "done this morning") analysis was extension, scaling, and efficiency applied to processes that traders had developed, but had delegated to cheaper and more highly skilled or specialized technicians. The types of analysis that modern data science is making possible were never part of even the most sophisticated trader's arsenal, and as a result, traders may be wholly unfamiliar with these techniques and their inherent strengths and weaknesses. As the analytical techniques become ever more sophisticated, the trader must, at the bare minimum, be superficially familiar with the operational characteristics and idiosyncrasies of the information being presented.

In his 2018 masterwork *Advances in Financial Machine Learning*, Marcos López de Prado describes an in situ factory for the processing of financial data into actionable strategies that involves the work of data curators, feature analysts, strategists, a deployment team, and a portfolio oversight function that shepherds the model through embargo, paper trading, graduation to live trading, re-allocation of resources relative to performance, and finally decommission.[78] While it is difficult to argue with the logic of de Prado's research lab as an alpha generation engine, it is worth noting that it represents a luxury available to only the largest firms by virtue of the resources it would demand and the level of patience it would require. Implementation would require millions of dollars of highly specialized headcount, a significantly larger budget for technology and data, and months or even years to build out.[79]

The question is, how much of this rigorous, structured approach can be appropriated and replicated on-desk with the trader's smaller resource base?

I struggled with whether or not to present this material in the main body of the text as an expansion of Chapter 3 – Fundamental Analysis or as an appendix at the end of the book. I opted for the latter approach because, bluntly, I am not a programmer or data scientist. Despite a coding hobby that started in the fifth grade (on a green-screen, all-caps Apple II computer) and a professional career that involved working with significant nontraditional data inputs, I cannot claim anywhere near the same level of subject matter expertise that I can with trading-related topics. I feel that it is absolutely critical that early-career traders develop programming and data handling skills, so much so that I would be remiss in not providing some basic information from my ongoing self-education on the topic.

Data science and programming are very large, complex topics. In this Appendix I will be presenting an extremely condensed, entry-level overview of the material, designed to be a

---

[78] Marcos López de Prado, *Advances in Financial Machine Learning*. (Hoboken: John Wiley & Sons, Inc., 2018), 7-9.
[79] According to the website alternativedata.org as of 2019 the type of figures one would expect at a $10B hedge fund are $1.5-2.5M/year in base salary expenses and $3-4M/year for data.

jumping-off point for the reader's own explorations of the topics. The goal is to provide context for the importance of developing programming and data science skills and hopefully reduce the inevitable initial stumbles and wrong turns. As always, I will be referencing and recommending the benchmark texts in the field, several of which were just published within the last year.[80]

This appendix is designed to help the trader accomplish two primary goals:
1. develop the basic ability to acquire, manipulate, and interpret data on-desk.
2. achieve a familiarity with more advanced analytical methodologies in order to make intellectually informed decisions about the deliverables received.

To do that, we will incrementally examine three primary topics:
1. The types of data currently available.
2. The basics of data science, including cleaning data, and an overview of the types of analytical techniques that are commonly employed.
3. An overview of modern programming languages, including a data-cleaning example in Python.

Types of Data

In Chapter Three – Fundamental Analysis I asserted that there were three principal ways to achieve a material advantage analyzing data:
1. run a different, hopefully superior, process relative to the rest of the market on a standard data set to get an internal, proprietary answer to the value question.
2. run an industry-standard process with better data or more refined assumptions about the future state of the dominant price drivers to get a different answer to the value question.
3. run a better proprietary process on a superior data set with more refined assumptions.

The easiest way to gain an informational advantage is to have access to underlying data that is not publicly available or not appreciated as having analytical or predictive value. Alternative Data is the current darling of the marketplace, and huge sums of money and time have been devoted to deploying advanced analytical techniques on:
- mobile device data, including location, and data collected by applications residing on the device;
- social media, including posted content, searches, likes, etc.;
- email and web search data;

---

[80] Disclosure: As of the publication of this book, I have not received any direct or indirect compensation from any of the individuals, products, or services mentioned in this Appendix (or indeed, the book as whole). My recommendations are based on my firsthand experiences and a belief that the products/services are valuable additions to a trader's toolkit. That said, I am not familiar with every resource and the pace of innovation will only increase with time, so the reader is advised to seek out alternatives to my suggestions and make a decision based on particular circumstances.

- web scraping;
- speech-to-text translation and parsing of conference calls and television broadcasts;
- text data mining across all platforms, including traditional and social media;
- data derived from satellite images, drone cameras, and other sensor inputs;
- exhaust data, a byproduct of other information-centric processes;
- internally generated data obtained by data mining customer activities.

There are approximately 445 data vendors who in 2019 sold $1B worth of alternative data to the buy-side of the investment management industry, a market segment expected to grow to $1.7B by 2020.[81] With that many eyes on such a very large prize, the chances of a trader stumbling on a novel, untapped data resource are slim (but not zero, so keep looking). The biggest challenge for traders is figuring out what data from that vast menu of offerings can actually add incremental alpha, and then finding some way to be able to afford the data.

Data Science

Paradoxically, the more unique and valuable a potential data set is, the more likely it is that it will be a complete mess that requires a significant investment of time and effort to turn it into usable grist for the mill. It is generally accepted that cleaning and formatting can consume over 50% of the effort involved in putting a data set into production.

Traders are accustomed to operating on spreadsheets of price data, where they may perform basic calculations like deriving historical volatility, etc. By and large, price data that is obtained from an exchange will likely be highly formatted, so the only cleaning necessary will be a scan for the occasional rogue closing mark, etc. Traders sourcing data from end-of-day, broker-provided sheets will likely need to engage in a higher level of data cleaning to account for missing/unobserved prices or wide markets. Even hand-entering a stack of spotty broker sheets is still a significantly simpler proposition than cleaning a large alternative data set, which may not have any sort of consistency with regard to labeling, formatting, uniformity of format between character strings and numbers, missing data, incorrect data, non-standard formats, etc.

Cleaning Data: Worst. Thing. Ever.

What does it mean to clean a data set, in practice? Thinking back to the Product X case study, imagine a trader working for an energy merchant developing a view of the market and trying to understand the growth in Chinese demand. After doing some research, the trader discovers a vendor offering the rights to a data set composed of the shipping records of an Australian port that serves as a primary loading point for spot cargoes headed to China. By comparing this new data with current information about volumes in transit, the trader may be able to gain an increased understanding of the pace of growth in Chinese demand. The trader eagerly signs a one-year exclusive deal for the data set, which will arrive in a series of monthly files

---

[81] Source: alternativedata.org website, 2019.

that comprise the loading and shipping logs of the port. The first file from the vendor arrives like this:[82]

Vessel	Vessel Type	Departure Date	Destination	Tons Loaded	Insured	Insured Value
Yosemite	Panamax	1/3/20	China	48,132	y	$ 5,968,368
Joshua Tree	Panamax		China	45,648	y	$ 5,569,056
Pawtuckaway	Panamax	1/5/20	China	44,327	y	$ 199,472
Shawangunks	Capesize		China	144,000 Tons	y	
RMNP	VLOC	1/8/20	China	198,673		
Oliana	Neopanamax	1/9/20	China	119,373	y	$14,802,252
Joe's Valley	Capesize	1/10/20		145,505	y	$18,042,620
Horse Pens 40	Capesize	1/11/20	China	145,222	y	$17,862,306
Fontainebleau	Capesize		China	145,209	y	$18,005,916
Hueco Tanks	Capesize	1/13/20	China	141,000 Tons	y	
Castle Hill		1/16/20	China	145,081	y	$17,990,044
Bishop	Capesize	1/17/20		147,812	y	$18,328,688
Magic Wood	Neopanamax	1/18/20	China	117,411	y	$14,558,964
Rumney	Neopanamax	1/19/20	China	111,660	y	$14,069,160
Lincoln Woods		1/20/20				
Sustenpass	Handymax	1/21/20		36,292	y	$ 4,536,500
Cresciano	Handymax	1/22/20	China	37,500T	y	
Ceuse	Handymax		China	39,178	y	$ 156,712
Red Rocks	Handymax	1/25/20	China	39,107	y	$ 195,535
Squamish	Handymax	1/26/20	China	38,188	y	$ 4,888,064

Table b.1   Unformatted shipping data set.

What the trader has received is a relatively poorly formatted data set that will require a considerable amount of cleaning to be put to use. There are gaps in the data, inconsistencies in formatting, and what appear to be clear inaccuracies that will have to be removed, which will necessitate the services of an analyst who is familiar with both standard data science techniques and the physical market the data set is drawn from. Cleaning data is often about visually inspecting the rows and columns and applying specialist knowledge as to what needs to be fixed, how it can be fixed, and what is beyond repair and needs to be discarded.

Taking a close look at the data, the trader will need to take action (or at least consider doing so) on the following:
- There are one or more missing values for the Vessel Type, Departure Date, Destination, Tons Loaded, Insured, and Insured Value columns. The analyst can either live with that, determine if it is possible to fill in the missing data by making logical inferences, or delete the problematic rows.
- The data for Tons Loaded is inconsistent, some having an alphanumeric "Tons" or "T" after the numbers.

---

[82] The shipping database is obviously an extremely condensed, textbook-friendly example. A real-world data set that would merit the attention of a quant researcher would be orders of magnitude larger and substantially more complicated.

- The Insured Value column has numbers that start with a "$," which probably implies that they are alphanumeric strings and not numbers. This will be verified once the data is imported.
- Three of the vessels have radically smaller insured cargo values for similar tonnage levels, which bears investigating.
- Almost nothing is known about Lincoln Woods, which has almost no data associated with the vessel. The analyst can either assume it is a Neopanamax like Magic Wood and copy its loading data or delete the row. There isn't a right answer, and the trader/analyst will have to live with the impacts of either choice. Removing it will definitely understate volumes (if it was carrying Product X), but guessing will give a false sense of accuracy due to the manufactured data.

At all times, a trader must keep in mind the questions they want the data set to answer in order to best understand how to clean it, what to keep, and what to discard. Given the small amount of data the trader has to work with, it makes sense to do as much as possible to try to preserve rows by making logical assumptions to fill in blanks and inconsistencies, where appropriate. There almost certainly will be additional issues that arise after the data is imported and the user attempts to manipulate it in Python. As an example, the Product X Shipping Data will be cleaned using basic Python code in the following section on programming.

Once it has been cleaned and processed, the data set will have certain characteristics. It will be composed of some number of observations, n, each of which will have parameters or characteristics, p. The ratio of n to p will impact the analytical techniques that can be brought to bear, as will the composition of the data as either all-numerical or possessing fields/parameters that are non-numerical.

Common Data Science Models and Analytical Techniques
There are a wide variety of models that data scientists have developed to make sense out of different types of unruly data. Each is designed to approach the data set with a particular technique and each will have distinct strengths and weaknesses. Model training methodologies are divided into two groups, those that are said to employ *supervised* learning and those that use *unsupervised* learning.

Supervised learning occurs when a model attempts to predict the value of a target variable by analyzing a set of data. Supervised learning requires that the target is present in the data set and has been identified or "labelled." The two main types of supervised learning are *linear regression* and *classification* (regression where the target variable is non-quantitative). Traders are usually interested in how changes in a set of observed variables will impact price, which implies the use of supervised learning models where the price response is the target.

Unsupervised learning occurs when a model is given a data set and is allowed to form conclusions without intervention. Common tools include *principal components analysis* and *clustering*. Analysts and quantitative researchers are more likely to employ unsupervised learning methods to investigate how novel data sets are internally organized.

Other commonly employed models include *logistic regression, support vector machines (SVM), random forests, gradient boosting,* and *k-nearest neighbors (kNN).*[83]

Once a trader has selected the model best suited to their analytical goals and the characteristics of the data, they must develop a plan for "training" it.

Training a Model on Historical Data
There is a fundamental difference in how most traders (both systematic and non-systematic) utilize their data resources and the rigor and efficiency employed by quants and data scientists. As an example, consider a trading firm that has five years of EOD close data that it would like to use to train a model in an attempt to derive tradable patterns. In the following diagrams, data that is used for model training will be represented by a white rectangle and data used for model validation and test data will be shown as a gray rectangle.

Basic Trader Method of Training a Model
The most obvious method for deriving informational content from historical information is to run the preferred model or process on the entirety of the data set, then apply the lessons immediately via a simulated trading account or, for the brave and/or insane, directly in a live market. Visually, this approach looks like:

Training Data

| 1 | 2 | 3 | 4 | 5 |

Figure b.1 The totality of a five-year data set used to train a model.

There are two primary problems with this approach:

1. When all of the available data are used for training, there are none left to validate the training results. With no testing other than perhaps a period of paper trading, the trader will have no idea how effective the historically derived trading signals are going forward until they experience the effects directly on their P&L.
2. Using all of the data to train the model increases the chances that the model will become overfit, a condition where the model has effectively memorized the past instead of deriving productive insights. Overfitting will be explored in greater depth later in the appendix.

The error of not employing any test or validation is common for nonquantitative traders unaware of or unaccustomed to good data-handling procedures. Some traders actually view this method of testing as a benefit, as it ensures that their model is incorporating the most

---

[83] Unfortunately, an exploration of the features and the relative strengths and weaknesses of each model lies outside of the scope of this appendix (and my practical experience, to be honest). Interested readers should look to *Data Science for Business* by Foster Provost and Tom Fawcett.

Appendix B – Data Science & Programming

recent market conditions. In some cases, they may actually overweight the more recent history in their results, as it is more "relevant."

Model Training Using Out-of-Sample Data and Walk-Forward Analyses
A more refined technique employed by systematic traders is the use of out-of-sample data, where the trader reserves a portion of the available data for post-training testing of the model. An out-of-sample test applied to the same five years of data would look like:

```
          Training Data                    Test
    [ 1 ] [ 2 ] [ 3 ] [ 4 ]               [ 5 ]
```

Figure b.2   Out-of-sample test, with four years of training data and one year of test data.

The model is trained on the data from Years 1-4, then run on the Year 5 data to evaluate its performance in a controlled environment.

A more granular approach involves splitting the data into a number of subsets, each of which will be apportioned into a training and out-of-sample test set. This technique is called a Walk-Forward Analysis (WFA), and would look like:

```
       Training Data      Test
       [ 1 ] [ 2 ]      [ 3 ]
             [ 2 ] [ 3 ]      [ 4 ]
                   [ 3 ] [ 4 ]      [ 5 ]
```

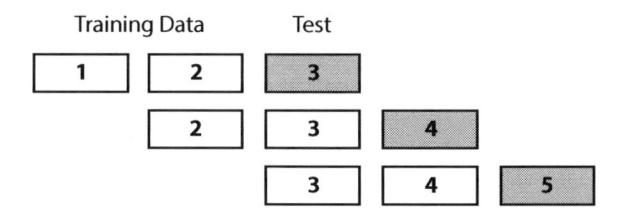

Figure b.3   A Walk-Forward Analysis using three iterations of two years of training data and one year of test data.

The trader trains the model on two years of data, then tests on one, then repeats the process. The five years of available data allow for three iterations of the cycle. As described in Robert Pardo's *The Evaluation and Optimization of Trading Strategies*: "The primary goal of the walk forward test is to determine whether the performance of a trading model under optimization is the result of a robust and repeatable process or the illusory result of overfitting. In other words, the primary purpose of a Walk-Forward Analysis is to determine whether a trading strategy's performance is real or not."[84]

Out-of-sample testing and Walk-Forward Analysis are commonly used by systematic traders who derive rules-based trading signals from price data and associated metrics. They will deploy a learning model that attempts to optimize profitability from a price history using

---

[84] Robert Pardo, *The Evaluation and Optimization of Trading Strategies*, 2nd ed. (Hoboken: John Wiley & Sons, Inc., 2008), 238.

indicators like moving averages, Bollinger Bands, Fibonacci retracement levels, relative strength, candlestick patterns, etc. as inputs. Some brokerage platforms offer the ability to run a WFA, giving even retail traders access to the technology.

More Complex Model Training Methods
A more advanced way to efficiently utilize the available training material is to perform a cross validation study, where the total data is divided into a number of tranches called "folds." Each iteration of the training holds out a different fold of data for testing, allowing the model to learn from the remainder. This may (depending on the number of folds chosen) allow for more training/test cycles than a WFA. It also offers a greater diversity of test data, since WFA training data is always from the first sequential periods with the test occurring at the end.

Using our sample data, a cross validation using a 5-fold holdout would look like this:

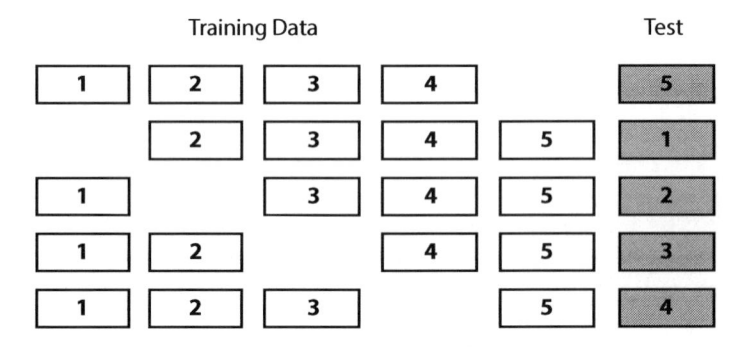

Figure b.4 Cross validation using five folds.

A further refinement involves adding an additional period of model validation between the training data and testing, a procedure called Nested Holdout Testing:

Figure b.5 Nested Holdout testing with five iterations of three years of training data, a year of validation, and a year of test data.

Appendix B – Data Science & Programming

This type of Nested Holdout Testing is beyond the capabilities of most (if not all) on-desk traders and will likely be the exclusive provenance of specialized data scientists working in the quantitative group. The water gets even deeper from there, as quantitative metrics can be calculated to score the relative learning performance of different models on the same data set to derive both the optimal model and the optimal training program.

What should be clear is that data science and model development done by experienced practitioners is a recursive, iterative process that bears little resemblance to the once-through processing done by most on-desk traders and analysts.

Common Data Science Pitfalls

There are three primary concerns facing anyone attempting to deploy advanced analytical techniques in the financial markets:
1. Relative scarcity of data
2. Overfitting past data
3. Spurious correlations/connections

Relative Scarcity of Data

One of the biggest problems inherent in training a model on financial data is the (relative) paucity of available data. Data scientists teaching an AI to correctly identify a photo as a cat or a dog will feed the model millions of labelled images. By comparison, a decade of EOD close data for an equity or commodity will only contain 2,520-ish observations. Imagine the challenge of trying to deploy sophisticated analytical techniques in a new market or on a recently developed product, where there is even less information to work with. Traders focused on shorter-term or intraday strategies can at least take advantage of the significantly higher data intensity offered by using hour or minute (or even finer for HFT traders) observations, but they must be aware from the outset that they may not be providing their model with sufficient observations to render a robust result.

Overfitting

The primary concern of experienced quantitative traders and data scientists is the potential for a model to draw too much information from a historical data set, a condition referred to as overfitting. The problem is summarized by Robert Pardo in his system trading bible, *The Evaluation and Optimization of Trading Strategies*:

> More specifically, the *overfitting* or *overoptimizing* of a trading strategy is the identification of parameters that produce good trading performance on in-sample price history but produce poor trading performance on an out-of-sample price history. It matters not if the out-of-sample data are an unseen historical sample or real-time data—the result will be the same.[85]

---

[85] Robert Pardo, *The Evaluation and Optimization of Trading Strategies*, 2nd ed. (Hoboken: John Wiley & Sons, Inc., 2008), 283.

In general, every model has a learning curve. Training a model is the process of allowing it to form useful generalizations based on historical data. There is a fine balance between extracting the maximum productive development from the training set and allowing the model to effectively memorize the features of the data. The reason for this is best summarized by Provost and Fawcett in their text *Data Science for Business*:

> Why does performance degrade? The short answer is that as a model gets more complex it is allowed to pick up harmful spurious correlations. These correlations are idiosyncrasies of the specific training set used and do not represent characteristics of the population in general. The harm occurs when these spurious correlations produce *incorrect* generalizations in the model.[86]

Clearly, the obvious question is how to manage the relationship between productive training and the potential for overfitting.

> The answer is not to use a data mining procedure that doesn't overfit because all of them do. Nor is the answer simply to use models that produce less overfitting, because there is a fundamental trade-off between model complexity and the possibility of overfitting… There is no single choice or procedure that will eliminate overfitting. The best strategy is to recognize overfitting and manage complexity in a principled way.[87]

Managing complexity effectively means allowing a model to learn only to the point where its performance on test data continues to improve. Once the out-of-sample testing on an incremental iteration meaningfully degrades, the evolution process must be brought to a halt and the model declared to be "trained," with its ultimate utility to be determined by additional testing.

Spurious Correlations
One of the first lessons in elementary statistics is that correlation does not imply causation. Just because one variable has been historically associated with another does not mean that there is necessarily any logical, rational reason for this relationship to carry forward into the future. When dealing with simpler, humanly comprehensible data sets, this was not as much of a problem. Current technology allows ML algorithms to derive nontraditional relationships from vast data sets, which is a net positive when those relationships are proved to have a basis in logic and a net negative when they are seen to be just statistical oddities.

A trader relying on an in-house quantitative team to develop and employ the more complex, sophisticated techniques like nested holdout must understand the basic fundamentals of how each technique is employed and its relative strengths and weaknesses. The trader has to be

---

[86] Foster Provost and Tom Fawcett, *Data Science for Business*. (Sebastapol: O'Reilly Media, Inc., 2013), 124.
[87] Foster Provost and Tom Fawcett, *Data Science for Business*. (Sebastapol: O'Reilly Media, Inc., 2013), 113.

aware of how the utilized techniques are susceptible to data scarcity issues, overfitting, and spurious correlations and what the quant team has done to minimize their effects.

Programming

Traders concerned about the steep learning curve for learning programming should keep in mind:
1. Programming languages have never been more powerful and simpler to use, and there have never been as many resources available to help the novice coder get up to speed.
2. The end result is the only thing that matters. Ugly but functional code written by a practitioner is often better than virtuoso code written by a non-market-facing "expert." Kludgy stuff that does exactly what the trader wants in a way they can understand is far, far more useful than something "better" that they may not trust or that does not result in as useful an output/product.
3. The trader should not worry about aspects of programming not relevant to the task at hand. For on-desk development in the finance industry, this typically means basic data input/output, data handling, analytics, and data visualization with a few critical modules.
4. A lot of the work has already been done by other, smarter people. Many of the classic problems in finance have already been solved and the code has already been real-world tested, allowing the trader to look at something known to work and build along those lines or, failing that, simply copy and paste the code. Even better, chances are that almost anything a non-elite programmer might need to do with data has already been coded, documented, and made available for free download and use by an altruistic developer.

Modern modular programming languages allow extremely powerful functionality to be imported and deployed with a handful of commands. Most look like poorly written English, which is a dramatic improvement from older coding environments.

While Most Code Is Stable, Not Everything Is Vetted

One common issue for institutional users is that while almost every problem they will typically encounter will have a pre-packaged, ready-to-use modular solution, there is no guarantee that it was created in a rigorous, stable manner by a trusted author. The standard Python packages have been widely adopted and extensively tested by a large developer and user community, which should inspire a level of confidence. A trader looking to solve a bleeding-edge problem with a piece of poorly documented code apparently authored by someone named "3rg0 Pr0xy" and downloaded from a sketchy Tor site should be extremely wary of the results, at least initially. Prudence would dictate a period of A/B testing against any comparable analytical resource and possibly code review by IT/Analytics/Quant/Risk before implementation.

The need for audit and verification will almost certainly rear its head if the trader elects to put any original code into production. Any institution will need to ensure that the trader's code does as claimed, particularly with regard to:

1. valuation: if the code produces any sort of value estimates, the assumptions and calculations will need to be verified.
2. resource load: the code must not put undue stress on any part of the IT infrastructure. Attempting to query data from a website every microsecond or up/download giant files can tax the system infrastructure to the detriment of other users and processes.
3. stability: the code must not crash the system or contain any malevolent instructions.

Traders should also note that if original code was written on a company-provided machine/system it is the property of the company, which is something many traders and quants have realized to their extreme peril after leaving to go to a competitor.

New Code Must Play Well with Legacy Systems
Another institution-specific problem is the need for any new code/systems to interface with legacy software that may have been written in another decade, in a different programming language, and with little to no commentary or documentation. Getting all of the pieces of the puzzle to play well together is critical, as poor interconnectivity can easily result in a garbage in/garbage out scenario. Even trickier, the oldest, grimiest code is often found in the mission critical functions where, once it was functioning properly, it would typically be frozen, and no updates performed for fear of breaking the goose that was laying the golden eggs.[88]

2. Popular Modern Programming Languages
There are three primary languages employed on-desk in the modern financial ecosystem, C++, R, and Python, with a new entrant called Julia starting to attract attention due to its speed and ease of use.

C++
C++ is a language created in 1985 by Danish computer scientist Bjarne Stroustrup. C++ is criticized for being overly complicated and difficult to read, but the code is very fast and there is a large amount of it in legacy systems at financial institutions. More information about C++ can be found at: https://isocpp.org.

R
R is a 1995 programming language written by Ross Ihaka and Robert Gentleman. R is primarily used for statistics and data mining applications and is the language of choice for many quantitative researchers in the financial community. To learn more about R, see: https://www.r-project.org.

Python
Python is the 1991 creation of Guido van Rossum. Python is the current gold standard for on-desk development for the same reason that the Black-Scholes model is the benchmark for

---

[88] Updating legacy code is *serious* business, particularly for systems that directly interact with a live market. The cautionary tale is Knight Trading, who inadvertently activated dormant code during an update and caused its trading algorithm to lose $400M in 30 minutes. Read more about it in Chapter 11.

option pricing models: it finds the sweet spot on the Venn diagram between being powerful enough to be useful and easy enough for low- and mid-level practitioners to understand, learn, and deploy. More information about Python can be found at the official site: https://www.python.org.

Python used to be available in two different flavors, the current 3.x release and the now-obsolete 2.x series that concluded with version 2.7. They are not exactly 100% compatible. At the time of this writing, Python 3.x has become the standard, and all of the code that one could reasonably expect to need has been ported. The reader should be careful when attempting to use any programming resources or homebrew/legacy code that is 2.7-specific, as there can be errors if used in a 3.x environment.

Julia
Julia is a 2012 language built by Jeff Bezanson, Stefan Karpinski, Viral B. Shah, and Alan Edelman at MIT. Julia offers the ease of use of Python combined with (almost) the speed of C++. It is early in the adoption cycle and competing against the heavily entrenched Python ecosystem, but Julia definitely looks like the future. More information can be found at: https://juliacomputing.com.

Given the relative strengths and weaknesses of competing languages, I feel that Python currently offers the best combination of power, flexibility, ease of use and, critically for a novice coder, a large ecosystem of support and resources. Obviously, if you are working at a firm with significant legacy infrastructure developed in another language, learn that first, but for those starting from scratch or doing their own solo development program, Python is the way to go.

Anaconda: The Best Python Platform for Beginners
Anaconda is a programming platform developed in 2012 that contains a library of the most common Python modules and a set of applications designed to facilitate coding and editing. Anaconda is available to download at: https://www.anaconda.com.

Within Anaconda, the novice programmer will do most of work within a code editing environment called the Jupyter Notebook (more information at https://jupyter.org). This somewhat spartan application is actually a versatile environment where the programmer can directly type in code, import modules and files, perform all manner of numerical analysis, and generate inline output graphics.

When a Jupyter session opens, the basic Python waiting for the user will typically need to be augmented with additional functionality to perform many of the tasks that a trader, analyst, or data scientist will require. Python is a modular programming language, and to add additional tools the coder must use the **import** function, which brings onboard the individual commands or packages of instructions the trader requires.

The standard Anaconda installation includes most of the modules employed by financial professionals; the most commonly used are matplotlib, numpy, and pandas.

Essential Python Modules:

Matplotlib

Matplotlib (website https://matplotlib.org) is an extremely useful module that allows the user to take imported data and easily transform it into visualizations ranging from simple plots to complex renderings. As a basic example, we will re-generate the simple line plot of FEB ProdX prices seen in Figure 4.24. The first step is loading the data, which requires importing a module called xlrd that allows us to import an Excel file of FEB ProdX OHLC data.

```
import matplotlib.pyplot as plt
%matplotlib inline
import xlrd

book = xlrd.open_workbook("Product_X_FEB_ProdX.xlsx")
Feb_ProdX = book.sheet_by_name("Sheet1")
Feb_Close = Feb_ProdX.col_values(4, start_rowx=1, end_rowx=253)

plt.figure(figsize=(9.5, 6))
plt.plot(Feb_Close)
plt.title('FEB ProdX Contract Closing Prices')
```

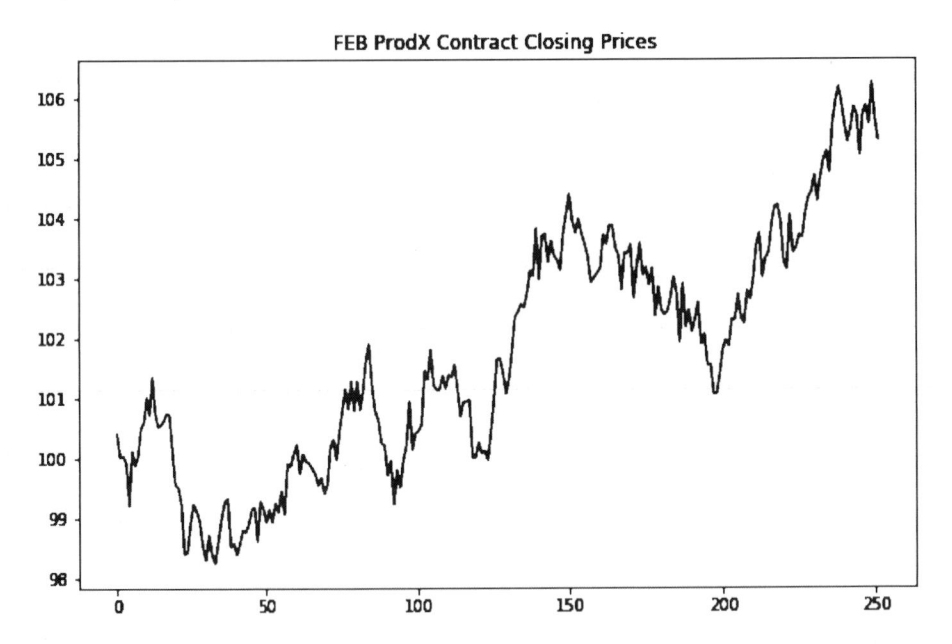

Figure b.6 Re-creation of Figure 4.24 using imported data and the Python module matplotlib.

Numpy

Numpy (website: https://numpy.org) is the standard Python module for basic mathematical and statistical operations with an emphasis on handling multidimensional arrays.

Building on the initial code and data imported in the previous section, the trader can use numpy to calculate basic metrics on the historical ProdX prices:

```
import numpy as np

# Use the var command to calcluate the variance of Feb_Close
print(np.var(Feb_Close))

# Use the std command to calculate the standard deviation of Feb_Close
print(np.std(Feb_Close))

3.690246598639456
1.9210014572195035
```

Pandas

Pandas (website https://pandas.pydata.org) is the 2008 creation of programmer Wes McKinney, and is (at the time of this writing) the Holy Grail of data wrangling Python modules.[89] Pandas has math functionality and file I/O capabilities, but where it really shines is the ability to deal with large, poorly formatted data sets using its menu of tools for slicing, dicing, and julienning DataFrames.

A DataFrame is "a rectangular table of data and contains an ordered collection of columns, each of which can be a different value type (numeric, string, Boolean, etc.)"[90] DataFrames are indexed by both column and row, and can be operated on by the array[91] of editing tools that comprise the pandas module.

Recall the Product X Shipping Dataset from earlier in the Appendix. After weighing the benefits of attempting to fill in missing data vs. the purity of deleting any problematic rows, the trader has decided to attempt to retain as much information as possible. Specifically, the trader decides to:
1. Remove the redundant Insured column, as the presence of insurance is already seen by the Insured Value column, which is significantly more interesting.
2. Remove the three ships that with the anomalously low insured value of their cargo, as they do not appear to be carrying Product X.
3. Fill in all destination fields as "China."
4. Fill in the missing insured values as "0" and change the data items to integers, so they can be arithmetically operated on.
5. Plug in the Magic Wood tonnage to the empty field in Lincoln Woods, as in the absence of loading information it makes sense emulate a mid-range vessel.
6. Copy the vessel sizes for Joe's Valley to Castle Hill and for Magic Wood to Lincoln Woods.

---

[89] True story: I first learned about this Python module in 2013, when the resident Russian Hipster Coder on the desk abruptly stood up, shucked off his giant DJ headphones and declared "I f--king love pandas!" He did this over and over again over the next few days. There was… some concern.
[90] Wes McKinney, *Python for Data Analysis*, (Sebastapol: O'Reilly Media, Inc., 2018), p128.
[91] Data structure pun!

7. Modify the non-numeric text strings "Tons" and "T" in the Tons Loaded column.
8. Interpolate departure dates for Joshua Tree, Shawangunks, and Fontainebleau from the loading dates of ships adjacent to them.
9. Add a new column called "Material Price" that calculates the price of the tonnage loaded on each vessel.

To begin cleaning the data the trader will launch Anaconda and open a Jupyter notebook. The following code imports pandas and deactivates a warning for a certain type of data editing, then uses the read_csv command, to read the comma-delimited file "Product_X_Shipping_Dataset_Python.csv" and store it in DataFrame product_x_shipping. The code below is "commented," where explanations of each section's functionality are described, starting with a "#" to tell Python that the following text is not a command to be executed.

```
import pandas as pd
pd.options.mode.chained_assignment = None   # Deactivates a flag for a
certain type of DataFrame overwriting
product_x_shipping = pd.read_csv("Product_X_Shipping_Dataset_Python.csv")
```

	Vessel	Vessel Type	Departure Date	Destination	Tons Loaded	Insured	Insured Value
0	Yosemite	Panamax	1/3/20	China	48132	y	5968368
1	Joshua Tree	Panamax	NaN	China	45648	y	5569056
2	Pawtuckaway	Panamax	1/5/20	China	44327	y	199471.5
3	Shawangunks	Capesize	NaN	China	144,000 Tons	y	NaN
4	RMNP	VLOC	1/8/20	China	198673	NaN	NaN
5	Oliana	Neopanamax	1/9/20	China	119373	y	14802252
6	Joe's Valley	Capesize	1/10/20	NaN	145505	y	18042620
7	Horse Pens 40	Capesize	1/11/20	China	145222	y	17862306
8	Fontainebleau	Capesize	NaN	China	145209	y	18005916
9	Hueco Tanks	Capesize	1/13/20	China	141,000 Tons	y	NaN
10	Castle Hill	NaN	1/16/20	China	145081	y	17990044
11	Bishop	Capesize	1/17/20	NaN	147812	y	18328688
12	Magic Wood	Neopanamax	1/18/20	China	117411	y	14558964
13	Rumney	Neopanamax	1/19/20	China	111660	y	14069160
14	Lincoln Woods	NaN	1/20/20	NaN	NaN	NaN	NaN
15	Sustenpass	Handymax	1/21/20	NaN	36292	y	4536500
16	Cresciano	Handymax	1/22/20	China	37,500T	y	NaN
17	Ceuse	Handymax	NaN	China	39178	y	156712
18	Red Rocks	Handymax	1/25/20	China	39107	y	195535
19	Squamish	Handymax	1/26/20	China	38188	y	4888064

Table b.2 The unformatted shipping data set imported into a pandas DataFrame.

Python has imported the data and is using the correct column headers, but has assigned a numeric index to the rows, starting at zero. The trader can change this using:

```
# Set the row axis to the vessel name instead of a number
product_x_shipping = product_x_shipping.set_index("Vessel")
```

Appendix B – Data Science & Programming

From there, the trader continues making the edits described above:

```
# Remove the redundant Insured column
product_x_shipping = product_x_shipping.drop("Insured", axis = 1)

# Remove the ships that do not appear to be carrying Product X
product_x_shipping = product_x_shipping.drop(["Pawtuckaway", "Ceuse", "Red 
Rocks"], axis = 0)

# Fill in all missing Destination fields as China.
product_x_shipping["Destination"] = 
product_x_shipping["Destination"].fillna("China")

# Fill Missing Insured Values as 0 and turn all numbers into integers
product_x_shipping["Insured Value"] = product_x_shipping["Insured 
Value"].fillna(0)
product_x_shipping["Insured Value"] = product_x_shipping["Insured 
Value"].astype(int)

# Change Lincoln Woods Tons Loaded to match Magic Wood
product_x_shipping.loc["Lincoln Woods", "Tons Loaded"] = 117410

# Fill in missing vessel types for Castle Hill and Lincoln Woods
product_x_shipping.loc["Castle Hill", "Vessel Type"] = "Capesize"
product_x_shipping.loc["Lincoln Woods", "Vessel Type"] = "Neopanamax"

# Remove the text strings from the Tons Loaded Column
product_x_shipping.loc["Shawangunks", "Tons Loaded"] = 144000
product_x_shipping.loc["Hueco Tanks", "Tons Loaded"] = 141000
product_x_shipping.loc["Cresciano", "Tons Loaded"] = 37500

# Don't have departure dates for three vessels, make the assumption that 
they are staggered within the
# window between known departure dates
product_x_shipping.loc["Joshua Tree", "Departure Date"] = "1/5/20"
product_x_shipping.loc["Shawangunks", "Departure Date"] = "1/7/20"
product_x_shipping.loc["Fontainebleau", "Departure Date"] = "1/12/20"

# Convert Tons Loaded into integers and calculate the average material 
price onboard
product_x_shipping["Tons Loaded"] = product_x_shipping["Tons 
Loaded"].astype(int)
product_x_shipping["Material Price"] = product_x_shipping["Insured Value"] 
/ product_x_shipping["Tons Loaded"]
material_price = product_x_shipping["Material Price"]
```

Leading to a final, cleaned Product X Shipping data set:

Vessel	Vessel Type	Departure Date	Destination	Tons Loaded	Insured Value	Material Price
Yosemite	Panamax	1/3/20	China	48132	5968368	124
Joshua Tree	Panamax	1/5/20	China	45648	5569056	122
Shawangunks	Capesize	1/7/20	China	144000	0	0
RMNP	VLOC	1/8/20	China	198673	0	0
Oliana	Neopanamax	1/9/20	China	119373	14802252	124
Joe's Valley	Capesize	1/10/20	China	145505	18042620	124
Horse Pens 40	Capesize	1/11/20	China	145222	17862306	123
Fontainebleau	Capesize	1/12/20	China	145209	18005916	124
Hueco Tanks	Capesize	1/13/20	China	141000	0	0
Castle Hill	Capesize	1/16/20	China	145081	17990044	124
Bishop	Capesize	1/17/20	China	147812	18328688	124
Magic Wood	Neopanamax	1/18/20	China	117411	14558964	124
Rumney	Neopanamax	1/19/20	China	111660	14069160	126
Lincoln Woods	Neopanamax	1/20/20	China	117410	0	0
Sustenpass	Handymax	1/21/20	China	36292	4536500	125
Cresciano	Handymax	1/22/20	China	37500	0	0
Squamish	Handymax	1/26/20	China	38188	4888064	128

Table b.3   A cleaned data set resident in a DataFrame in python.

This type of visual inspection and plug-and-replace cleaning is only possible for very small data sets, and must quickly give way to methods that involve significant sorting, applying true/false tests, and loop structures that progress through the data and make modifications based on logic-based statements such as "if X, then do Y, else do Z."

This is an example of the basic, getting-your-hands-dirty, on-desk processing that traders will be expected to be able to manage on their own going forward.

What should be obvious to the reader is that the final data set is the product of a process that involved multiple subject matter expert decisions to include/exclude or modify observations, any of which could have been made differently by an analyst or trader with a different perspective on the relative importance of each data item or the appropriate level of analytical rigor to employ. There is not yet (to my knowledge) a standardized methodology for data sanitization, and in the absence of an established process every firm, group, and individual is free to self-define their own practices as they see fit. A trader must be completely familiar with the totality of the processes employed by the analysts and quants at their firm, as the cleaning process will have a tremendous impact on the composition of the data that will form the basis for their view of the market.

For those readers new to programming in general and to Python in particular, I should point out what every experienced quant is thinking right now: "That is the most awful code I have ever seen." They are correct, it is terrible. The `pd.options.mode.chained_assignment = None` command in the Product X Shipping example exists for the sole purpose of disabling a feature that actually criticizes my code for being rubbish. I elected to show the reader the full extent of my anti-skills because:

1. I wanted to demonstrate that suboptimal, ugly code can work, and that a program that achieves the trader's objective is (in most cases) good enough.
2. Code shaming is a real thing, and beginning programmers are often discouraged and give up when their kludgy creations are taunted by Z3r0 C00l and L0rd N1k0n, the semi-pro Counterstrike players from the quant group who have been speaking a mix of Parseltongue and FORTRAN since they were 13 (or, about four years ago).
3. For most people, there is no way to learn to write good, tight code without first writing a lot of bad code, then being motivated to learn how to do it better and more efficiently.

First focus on learning how to get usable, value-added results by whatever craptastic method necessary, then worry about what the people with the CMU CS PhDs are going to think. If your ugly code earns you a $10M bonus, you can give them a ride back to Wean Hall in your Ferrari.

The previous examples barely scratch the surface of the power and flexibility of numpy, matplotlib, and pandas. I highly encourage the reader to visit each module's website (listed above as well as in the Resources section at the end of the appendix) and to study the data handling and visualization examples to get a fuller sense of what each is capable of.

Other Important Python Modules
There are a number of other modules that traders and analysts use to process and deploy financial data. Among the most popular are:

BeautifulSoup
BeautifulSoup (website https://www.crummy.com/software/BeautifulSoup/bs4/doc/) mines data from web pages.

Plotly
Plotly (website https://plot.ly/python/) allows the user to produce interactive graphics.

Xlwings
Xlwings (website https://www.xlwings.org) allows for the integration of Python code and Excel spreadsheets: a useful tool for users dealing with an Excel-centric environment or seeking to build tools for non-coders.

Scikit-Learn
Scikit-Learn (website https://scikit-learn.org) is a machine learning (ML) module that can be used for classification, regression, clustering, dimensionality reduction, and feature extraction.

Modern programming languages, environments, and resources make learning to create and deploy code simpler than it has ever been, but it is still not simple. A trader or analyst looking to push beyond the basic, Anaconda-standard Python modules will have to learn to install packages with a utility called PIP and troubleshoot problems on coding-centric sites like GitHub and StackOverflow.

Conclusion

It has never been easier to learn the basics of data science and coding. If the trader is a do-it-yourself type, I would suggest starting with Anaconda and either *Python for Finance* by Hilpisch or *Python for Data Analysis* by McKinney. For those that prefer a more structured approach, there are online programs available at whatever price point and depth of coverage a trader could desire, from low-stress, free videos all the way up to Berkeley and MIT open courseware.

Whatever the method, any trader that intends to have a place on the desk going forward must master the basics of programming and data science to stay relevant.

So, get to work.

Appendix B – Data Science & Programming

Resources for Continued Study

Reference Texts:
Python for Finance, 2e by Yves J. Hilpisch (O'Reilly Media, 2019)
Python for Data Analysis, 2e by Wes McKinney (O'Reilly Media, 2017)
Advances in Financial Machine Learning by Marcos López de Prado (John Wiley & Sons, Inc., 2018)
The Evaluation and Optimization of Trading Strategies, 2e by Robert Pardo (John Wiley & Sons, Inc., 2008)
Data Science for Business by Foster Provost and Tom Fawcett (O'Reilly Media, 2013)

Python Websites:

Anaconda	https://www.anaconda.com
BeautifulSoup	https://www.crummy.com/software/BeautifulSoup/bs4/doc/
MatPlotLib	https://matplotlib.org
Numpy	https://numpy.org
Pandas	https://pandas.pydata.org
Plotly	https://plot.ly/python/
Scikit-Learn	https://scikit-learn.org/stable/
Xlwings	https://www.xlwings.org

General Programming Resources:

GitHub	https://github.com
StackOverflow	https://stackoverflow.com

Online Self-Study Programming Courses:

DataQuest	https://www.dataquest.io
DataCamp	https://www.datacamp.com
Metis	https://www.thisismetis.com

Structured Programs/Credential Courses:

CAIA's FDP Institute	https://fdpinstitute.org
MIT Open Courseware	https://ocw.mit.edu/index.htm

Index

abridged modern history of trading, 25
Archimedean Trade Selection, 433

backwardation, 51
balance sheets, 68
   balancing item, 70
   data quality, 70
   demand, 69
   net balance, 69
   storage, 70
   supply, 69
Black-Scholes Model, 355

commonly traded instruments, 50
   call options, 58
   fixed-for-floating swaps, 53
   floating-for-floating swap, 54
   forward contracts, 50
   futures contracts, 52
   options, 57
   physical products, 50
   put options, 58
   swaps, 53
complex valuation models, 75
contango, 51
continuum of risk, 27

data, 64
   disorganized observational price data, 64
   issue with close data, 66
   non-price fundamental data, 66
   structured observational price data, 65
   systematic price data, 65
defining steps of market evolution, 49
developing a fundamental view, 63
developing a market view, 213
   alignment of fundamentals and technicals, 217
   articulating trader's view, 229
   definition of a view, 213
   determining commitment level, 220
   developing view of market, 213
   fundamental information, 214
   market risk-reward ratio, 223
   probability-adjusted market risk-reward ratio, 225
   risk-reward calculus, 223
   strategy risk-reward ratios, 227
   technical analysis, 216
   volatility and risk environment, 221

directional trading strategies, 253
   advantages of directional trades, 254
   breakout trades, 259
   common strategies, 258
   determining risk and reward, 281
   directional trading for financials, 282
   directional trading for hedgers, 281
   directional trading for merchants, 283
   directional trading for speculators, 283
   disadvantages of directional trades, 256
   identifying market turns, 270
   identifying retracements and reversals, 278
   identifying tops and bottoms, 279
   instruments, 280
   range-trading strategies, 266
   trend and momentum trades, 262

Elliott Wave Theory, 125
entry of new market participants, 49
evaluating trades, 434
   complexity, 439
   controllability, 440
   determining an entry point, 444
   determining an exit point, 445
   determining potential trade size, 442
   evaluation process, 434
   event stop, 450
   execution strategy, 451
   exposure size relative to market, 443
   factoring in real costs, 440
   five subjective performance characteristics, 439
   hard stop, 449
   hedging unwanted risks, 452
   how goal impacts risk deployment, 438
   how it will be done, generating a trading plan, 444
   how style impacts risk deployment, 437
   liquidity, 440
   pre-planned defensive hedging, 450
   profit targets, 446
   proximity, 439
   responsiveness, 439
   stop-loss levels, 447
   trailing stop, 449
   what can be done, given resources, 434
   what could be done, given P&L and stop-loss, 436
   what should be done, evaluating alternatives, 438
   what will be done, applying probability-adjusted risk-reward, 442
event path of future fundamental drivers, 80
evolution of markets, 48
   early stage, 48
   early-medium stage, 48
   late stage, 49
   medium stage, 48
   medium-late stage, 49

fair value calculations, 71
   supply stacks, 72
financial intermediaries, 31
   customer-facing traders, 35
   description of, 32
   how traders make markets, 37
   how traders run the book, 38
   location of margin and risk, 36
   organizational structure, 34
   origination process, 35
   proprietary trading, 39
flowchart
   idealized trading process, 3
   origination process, 35
fundamental analysis, 67
   analytical methodologies, 68

Greek risks, 358

hedgers or naturals, 27
   approach to trading, 31
   description of, 27
   discretionary hedging, 30
   hedging programs, 30
   organizational structure, 29
   structured/programmatic hedging, 30

implications of position expiration, 56

Index

managing positions, 483
    dealing with large losers, 498
    dealing with large winners, 499
    evolution of fundamental or technical thesis, 484
    evolution of risk environment, 485
    evolution of risk-reward calculus, 485
    finding time to trade, 497
    herd mentality, 496
    increasing position size, 486
    managing a position at a financial, 502
    managing a position at a merchant, 502
    managing a position at a natural, 501
    managing a position at a speculator, 502
    managing a single position, 484
    managing another trader's position, 495
    managing correlation, 501
    managing emotion while holding a position, 498
    managing shared positions, 496
    managing stops and tagets with gap risk, 488
    managing stress, 483
    managing thematically cohesive portfolios, 500
    managing thematically diverse portfolios, 501
    modifying position size, 486
    reducing position size, 487
    response to stimulus, 493
    trading around a trend, 491
merchants, 40
    approach to trading, 42
    description of, 40
    organization structure, 42
most important lesson, 551

navigating corporate culture, 531
    calibrating aggression, 539
    dealing with losing, 541
    dealing with other traders, 547
    dealing with the boss, 548
    dealing with the boss's boss, 548
    dealing with the trading floor, 547
    dealing with winning, 541
    evolutionary state of market influences types of jobs, 533
    getting a trading job, 532
    how winning and losing affect ability to do business, 542
    lifecycle of a trader, 535
    trading desk org chart, 531
    trading group structure, 532
    troubleshooting trading technique, 538
    understanding the trader's implied option, 539
    working with internal analysts, 543
    working with the compliance group, 546
    working with the risk group, 546

option strategies, 333
    ability to combine into structures, 335
    advantages of option trades, 335
    butterflies, iron, 351
    call/put skew, 346
    can be generally too cheap or expensive, 336
    collars, 347
    common option structures, 343
    common strategies, 337
    complex value determination, 337
    conversions, 342
    converting calls and puts into straddles, 345
    definition of derivatives, 333
    delta, 358
    disadvantages of option structures, 336
    exercise, 381
    extrinsic value, 369
    gamma, 360
    impacts of volatility on price, 365
    implied volatility, 356
    implied volatility as pricing tool, 366
    inputs to Black-Scholes, 356
    intrinsic value, 369
    known downside, 335
    lesser Greek risks, 365
    limitations of Black-Scholes, 357
    managing Greek risks, 373

managing option portfolios, 371
modeling non-linear risks, 354
must pay premium, 337
non-linear risk, 335
option and derivative pricing models, 355
option basics, 334
option trading for financials, 383
option trading for hedgers, 382
option trading for merchants, 383
option trading for speculators, 384
options as levered forwards, 341
poor liquidity, 336
put-call parity, 341
quotation and execution of structures, 353
ratio spreads, 350
single-option trades, 338
slow-developing market, 337
straddle price as volatility measurement, 345
straddles, 343
strangles, 346
theta, 363
traded instruments, 380
vega, 362
vertical spreads, 349
volatility smile, 367

physics of trading 101, 48
poker
    characterization of styles, 10
    tight/aggressive as template for trading, 12
PowerCo structured transaction example, 513
    identifying risks, 524
    local market gas vs. local market power, 518
    modifying initial valuation for economic reality, 523
    physical gas vs. physical power, 521
    PowerCo deal for a financial, 526
    PowerCo deal for a merchant, 526
    PowerCo deal for a natural, 526
    PowerCo deal for a speculator, 527
    PowerCo request for proposal, 513
    preliminary evaluation of the deal, 514
    risk mitigation plan, 525
    seller's perspective on deal, 513
    valuation challenges, 514
    valuing financial gas vs. financial power, 516
pricing & hedging structured transactions, 505
    being unable to price transaction, 510
    booking the transaction, 511
    common deal mispricing errors, 510
    deal modeling, 507
    embedded options, 509
    failure to understand nuances, 510
    getting greedy on pricing, 511
    hedging methodology, 512
    managing the deal, 512
    missing something, 511
    origination & structuring process, 506
    post-hedging value extraction, 512
    trader's responsibilities, 508
    what are structured transactions?, 505
Product X
    rationale for case study, 7
Product X directional strategies, 285
    best instruments to use, 285
    best strategies to employ, 285
    chronological location of exposure, 286
    long-term trend trade, 291
    position timing, 288
    short-term explosion trade, 289
    trade strategy #1, 289
    trade strategy #2, 291
Product X evaluating trades, 454
    characteristics of candidate strategies, 454
    evaluating performance characteristics, 457
    trading plan, 461
Product X fundamentals, 84
    balance sheet, 88
    base case, 92
    bear case, 94
    bull case, 96
    description of market, 84
    even path and drivers, 99
    fundamental summary, 100
    initial supply stack, 91

supply/demand drivers, 90
year-end supply stack, 91
Product X managing positions, 504
Product X market description, 61
Product X market view, 232
    base case, 234
    bear case, 235
    Bollinger Band study, 241
    bull case, 236
    combining fundamental and technical perspectives, 243
    event path, 237
    Fibonacci study, 241
    initial balance, 234
    market drivers, 232
    market view, 251
    measurments and objectives, 242
    pattern study, 240
    probability-adjusted risk-reward ratio, 251
    rewards, 250
    risk-reward ratio, 250
    risks, 250
    summary fundamental analysis, 238
    summary technical analysis, 242
    support and resistance study, 239
    technical analysis, 238
    trend study, 238
    volatility and risk environment, 246
Product X option strategies, 386
    best strategies to employ, 386
    characteristics of option markets, 386
    deriving implied volatility from observations, 387
    historical volatility, 386
    long calls as leveraged outrights, 389
    long straddles as volatility/directional position, 392
    option price grid, 389
    trade strategy #6, 390
    trade strategy #7, 395
    volatility smiles, 387
Product X quantitative strategies, 429
    algorithmic trading system, 430
    arbitrageur, 430
    deep thinker, 429
    executor, 430
    operator assisting, 429

    trade strategy #8, 429
    trade strategy #9, 431
Product X risks, 207
    black swan risk, 209
    clearing/margin risk, 211
    contract risk, 210
    counterparty/credit risk, 210
    liquidity risk, 209
    market risk, 209
    parametric value at risk, 207
    product risk, 209
    simulation value at risk, 207
    summary risk analysis, 211
    volatility risk, 210
Product X spread strategies, 315
    backstop illiquid spreads with transport, 323
    best strategies to employ, 315
    physical and financial basis spreads, 318
    time spreads, 324
    trade strategy #3, 328
    trade strategy #4, 330
    trade strategy #5, 331
Product X technicals, 134
    Bollinger Band study, 138
    Elliott analysis, 135
    Fibonacci study, 140
    moving average study, 136
    pattern analysis, 139
    summary technical analysis, 143
    support or resistance, 142
    trending or not, 134
Product X trading mechanics, 482
Product X volatility
    Bollinger Band study, 169
    calculating historical volatility, 169
    categorizing, 168
    summary volatility analysis, 173

quantitative strategies, 399
    advantages of quantitative strategies, 399
    algorithmic predators, 416
    arbitrageurs, 413
    arms race, 401
    bad code risk, 402
    can humans compete?, 424

data-sensitive, 401
deep thinkers, 404
disadvantages of quantitative strategies, 400
discipline can compensate for human flaws, 400
executors, 405
expandable, 400
first-mover advantage, 399
implications of machine trading, 423
infrastructure intensive, 400
measuring risk and reward, 401
operator assisting, 403
overtraining on historical data, 401
quantitative strategies for financials, 426
quantitative strategies for hedge funds, 427
quantitative strategies for hedgers, 426
quantitative strategies for merchants, 427
types of quantitative strategies, 402

risk, 175
   aggregating trader limits, 187
   bank's risks, 204
   black swan risk, 192
   clearing/margin risk, 200
   collecting position data, 176
   collecting price data, 176
   contract risk, 200
   correlation, 177
   counterparty/credit risk, 199
   enforcing risk policy, 192
   evolving risk, 203
   expected shortfall, 183
   hedger's risk, 203
   institutional risk management, 175
   liquidity risk, 194
   market risk, 194
   merchant's risks, 204
   parametric value at risk, 180
   portfolio value at risk, 182
   product risk, 199
   relationship between volatility and risk, 175
   reporting on exposures, 188
   simulation value at risk, 180
   speculator's risks, 205
   the hedger's dilemma, 203
   trader risk limits, 185
   trading risk management, 192
   value at risk, 179
   value at risk shortcomings, 183
   volatility risk, 199

scenario analysis with analogs, 74
shift in analysis consensus, 78
   boundary conditions, 79
   capitulation of resistance, 78
   consensus evolves to proprietary view, 78
   forecasting the forecasters, 79
   game theory and forecasts, 80
   solo breakaway, 78
   spheres of influence, 80
speculators, 43
   approach to trading, 47
   asset managers, 43
   description of, 43
   hedge funds, 44
   individuals and small firms, 46
   organizational structure, 47
spread strategies, 295
   basis/transportation spreads, 309
   common strategies, 299
   common structures, 306
   complexity of response, 298
   correlation breakdown, 298
   cross-commodity spreads, 309
   disadvantages of spread trading, 298
   drift trades, 303
   explosion and reversion, 299
   express variety of views, 296
   good risk-reward mechanics, 297
   limit-efficient, 297
   liquidity challenges, 299
   quantitative trades, 305
   self-hedging exposure, 297
   spread trading for financials, 312
   spread trading for hedgers, 311
   spread trading for merchants, 312
   spread trading for speculators, 312
   terminology, 295
   time spreads, 307

Index

stylistic species of traders, 19
    fundamental, 20
    quantitative, 20
    technical, 20

technical analysis, 101
    advantages, 102
    analysis time frames, 104
    chart types, 103
    congestion levels, 123
    definition of a trend, 105
    disadvantages, 103
    drawing trend lines, 107
    end of a trend, 108
    fractal nature, 117
    imperfect patterns, 129
    incorporating fundamentals, 102
    inexact trend lines, 130
    intermediate trend, 107
    macro trend, 106
    micro trend, 107
    pragmatic approach, 103
    support and resistance, 109
    trend, 105

technical measurement techniques, 118
    Bollinger Bands, 120
    Fibonacci retracements, 121
    moving averages, 119
    pattern-implied objectives, 118
    volumes as an indicator, 123

technical patterns
    bear flag continuation, 113
    bull flag continuation, 112
    flat ascending triangle continuation, 111
    flat descending triangle continuation, 112
    head and shoulders reversal, 114
    no pattern, 116
    no prediction, 116
    rectangle consolidation, 115
    rounding bottom reversal, 114
    taking out prior high or low, 113
    triangle continuation, 111
    widening triangle consolidation, 116

trading mechanics, 463
    adding or taking liquidity, 466
    available execution options, 472
    basic mechanics, 463
    being passive, 479
    common execution mistakes, 476
    contingent order, 474
    dealing direct with a counterparty, 472
    electronic exchanges, 473
    execution at a financial, 480
    execution at a hedger, 479
    execution at a merchant, 480
    execution at a speculator, 480
    execution system, 473
    factoring in intraday events, 471
    factoring in market conditions, 464
    fat-fingering, mis-clicking, and out-trading, 478
    incorrectly identifying current conditions, 477
    indecision, 478
    industrial-sized execution challenges, 467
    lack of urgency, 477
    limit order, 474
    linked order, 475
    liquidity does not equal depth, 466
    machine-friendly orders, 475
    market order, 474
    multi-product execution, 476
    not having a clear idea of what trying to accomplish, 477
    odd lots, 475
    order types, 473
    panicking, 478
    partial fills, 475
    understanding liquidity and depth, 466
    working with a broker, 473

traits of bad traders, 17
    do not admit they are wrong, 17
    do not take responsibility, 17
    ignore their limitations, 18
    make same mistakes, 17
    make simple things complicated, 18
    thrill-seeking trading, 18
    trade too much, 18

traits of successful traders, 13
    ability to suffer, 15
    disciplined, 13

    ethical, 16
    hard working, 16
    hypercompetitive, 16
    intellectually honest, 14
    learn from their mistakes, 15
    positive, 16
    prepared, 16
    rationally accepting of failure, 14
    self-analytical, 13
transforming data into information, 77
TV set question, 9
    revisted, 22
types of trading strategies, 21
    directional, 21
    option, 21
    quantitative, 21
    spread, 21
    structured transactions, 22

Vitruvian trader, 9
volatility, 145
    bid/offer depth, 148
    causes, 148
    distributions of volatility, 160
    how markets react to information, 151
    impacts for physical traders, 162
    impacts to financial traders, 162
    implied volatility, 160
    intraday vs. day-over-day, 145
    invisible volatility, 166
    liquidity holes, 161
    measuring historical volatility, 156
    observing and categorizing, 152
    volatility is not a constant, 163

Index

Printed in Great Britain
by Amazon